P9-CKT-034

REVIEW TEXT IN UNITED STATES HISTORY

SECOND EDITION—REVISED

Paul M. Roberts

AMSCO

AMSCO SCHOOL PUBLICATIONS, INC.
315 Hudson Street / New York, N.Y. 10013

To Meg: my wife, lifelong companion, and best friend

When ordering this book, please specify: *either* **R 489 P** *or*
REVIEW TEXT IN UNITED STATES HISTORY, SECOND EDITION

ISBN 0-87720-857-3

Photo Acknowledgments: The Bettmann Archive, 450;
National Aeronautics and Space Administration, 451 (bottom);
Reuters/Bettmann, 452 (bottom), 453 (both); UPI/Bettmann, 451
(top), 452 (top)

Maps by Burmar Technical Corporation

Preface

National concern with school reform has focused renewed attention on the teaching of United States history. *Review Text in United States History, Second Edition* seeks to address this concern by imparting to students a sense of the sweep and drama of our nation's story, and by providing them with an understanding of the chronological flow of events that helped shape the America we live in today. The book is designed to meet the varied needs of teachers in American history throughout the country. Its purposes are threefold: (1) to serve as a concise text, (2) to supplement a more elaborate text, and (3) to be used as a review text to prepare students for periodic and terminal examinations.

Among the many useful features of *Review Text in United States History, Second Edition* are the following:

1. The material is presented in simple language, in uncomplicated sentences, and in short and easily digested paragraphs. Care has been taken to make the content comprehensible to students of most levels of ability.

2. Emphasis is placed upon significant facts, important historical trends, and major contributors to American progress. To promote understanding, events are portrayed within a framework of causality wherever possible.

3. Numerous maps are provided to illustrate the geographic setting of historical events. Political cartoons are used to enliven the text and help encourage critical thinking and discussion.

4. Abundant question material is interspersed throughout the book to test the student's mastery of each topic. Adequate provision has been made for each level of ability. Many questions call for careful reasoning and a mature grasp of the subject matter. These should be identified as honor questions and assigned with discretion.

—P.M.R.

Contents

UNIT VIII.   MODERN AMERICA EMERGES

UNIT IX.   THE UNITED STATES BECOMES A
WORLD POWER

UNIT X.   THE UNITED STATES ASSUMES WORLDWIDE
RESPONSIBILITIES

UNIT XI.   PRESIDENTIAL ADMINISTRATIONS SINCE
WORLD WAR II

UNIT XII.   THE FEDERAL GOVERNMENT AND CIVIC
RESPONSIBILITY

APPENDIX

Maps

UNIT I. EUROPEANS EXPLORE AND COLONIZE THE AMERICAS

Part 1. Events in Europe Lead to the Age of Exploration

EUROPE BECOMES ISOLATED AFTER THE FALL OF ROME

For many centuries much of Europe was part of the Roman Empire and enjoyed a highly developed civilization. Literature and the arts flourished. A network of fine roads connected a large part of Europe with Rome. Roman ships plied the Mediterranean Sea, linking Europe with North Africa and the Middle East. People traveled widely, and an extensive trade was carried on among the far-flung Roman provinces. As the years passed, however, the empire gradually declined. It finally collapsed in the 5th century A.D., when barbarian tribes from northern Europe overran the empire and sacked the city of Rome. (476)

Following the fall of Rome, Europe entered the Early Middle Ages (sometimes called the *Dark Ages*), a period of decline that lasted for more than 500 years. During this time, memory of the flourishing Greek and Roman civilizations of ancient times faded. Travel and trade came to a halt, and Europe became isolated from the rest of the world. Most Europeans were bound to feudal estates as serfs. They lived in ignorance and poverty, and had little knowledge of anything beyond their daily routine of life.

THE CRUSADES SPARK EUROPE'S REAWAKENING

The reawakening of Europe began when Europeans tried to conquer Palestine, the birthplace of Christ. This land, the site of present-day Israel, is situated on the eastern shore of the Mediterranean Sea. In the 11th century, Muslim tribes occupied the area. They not only terrorized Christians making pilgrimages to the Holy Land, but also threatened Constantinople, center of the Eastern (or Greek) Orthodox Church.

To end the menace to Christendom, Pope Urban II in 1095 called on the people of Western Europe to march on the Holy Land and drive out the invaders. This expedition became known as the *First Crusade*. During the next 200 years numerous other such expeditions were undertaken. Although the Crusaders failed to win permanent control of Palestine, they succeeded in arousing Europe and ending its isolation.

By participating in the Crusades, thousands of Europeans had the opportunity to visit distant lands. They observed unfamiliar cultures and became acquainted with new products and luxuries. They brought home with them spices, such as pepper, cinnamon, nutmeg, and cloves. Spices preserved foods and improved their taste. The Crusaders also brought back healing drugs; dyes for coloring cloth; beautiful silks,

1

linens, rugs, and tapestries; rare perfumes; and precious stones. Soon all Europe wanted to buy these previously unknown products of the Orient. In addition, by their tales of adventure and travel and by their descriptions of great cities and strange peoples, the Crusaders aroused Europe's interest in foreign lands. Marco Polo

A BRISK TRADE DEVELOPS IN EASTERN GOODS

The goods so eagerly sought by Europeans came from such faraway places as Cathay (China), the Spice Islands (in the East Indies—now Indonesia), India, and Persia (Iran). Asiatic traders transported the products to ports on the eastern Mediterranean. Here Italian merchants purchased the goods and shipped them to Italy for distribution throughout Europe.

The coastal cities of Italy controlled this highly profitable trade because of their favorable location on the Mediterranean. The wealthiest and most powerful of the Italian trading cities were Venice and Genoa.

MARCO POLO STIMULATES INTEREST IN THE ORIENT

Marco Polo, son of a wealthy Venetian merchant, accompanied his father and his uncle on an expedition to the Far East. Young Marco won the friendship of Kublai Khan, the mighty ruler of China, and entered his service. For nearly 20 years Marco Polo traveled to various parts of the Orient on diplomatic missions for the Khan. In 1295 the Polos returned to Italy laden with treasures. Marco Polo then wrote a book about his travels, in which he vividly described the magnificent cities, great riches, and strange products of the East.

The Book of Marco Polo, which was widely read throughout Europe, further increased the demand for Eastern products. By providing information about the distant lands that produced these goods, it encouraged European merchants to consider the possibility of traveling to the Orient and buying directly from the producers.

THE OLD TRADE ROUTES PROVE UNSATISFACTORY

The trade routes bearing the flow of commerce between Europe and the East were beset with obstacles. At sea the ships were attacked by pirates. On land the caravans were set upon by robbers. In 1453 Constantinople, a main terminal of Eastern trade, was captured by the

Three Asian Trade Routes Lead to the Eastern Mediterranean

Northern Route (mostly overland)	Middle Route (sea and land)	Southern Route (mostly water)
By camel caravan across Asia to the eastern shore of the Black Sea. Then by ship to Constantinople.	By ship across the Indian Ocean and through the Persian Gulf. Then overland by caravan to a Mediterranean trading center, such as Antioch.	By ship across the Indian Ocean and through the Red Sea. Then overland, or down the Nile River, to the Mediterranean city of Alexandria.

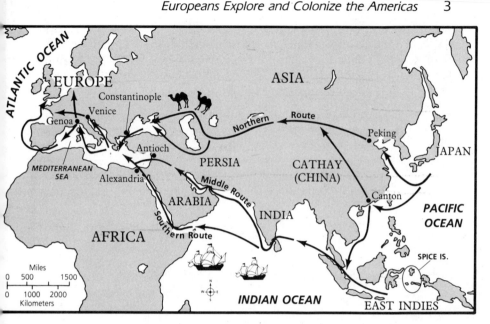

Early Trade Routes From the East to Europe

Ottoman Turks—Muslims originally from Central Asia. Their hostility toward Europeans and the heavy taxes they imposed on goods passing through the city seriously hindered trade.

Furthermore, the cost of Eastern goods was very high. Each shipment passed through many hands before reaching the marketplaces of Europe, and every trader handling the wares made a profit. An article selling for $1 in the Orient cost between $70 and $100 in Europe.

OTHER COUNTRIES HOPE TO BREAK THE ITALIAN MONOPOLY

Throughout the 1300's and 1400's, the commercial cities of Italy controlled the European trade in Eastern goods. Over this span of time, Portugal, Spain, France, and England gradually became unified nations under strong and ambitious monarchs. A spirit of national pride developed in these Atlantic-coast countries. They resented the Italian monopoly of Eastern trade and wanted a share for themselves. Unable to send their ships into the Italian-dominated Mediterranean, they dreamed of finding a new route to China and India. They reasoned that an *all-water* route would be cheaper, safer, and faster than the old routes, which were only partly over water.

SCIENTIFIC PROGRESS ENCOURAGES EXPLORATION

During this period Europe was in the midst of an intellectual reawakening called the *Renaissance*. It was a time of great cultural activity and of progress in science and invention. The following developments encouraged Europeans to undertake voyages of exploration in search of an all-water route to the Orient:

1. **Aids to Navigation.** Technical improvements made longer voyages

possible. The development of larger and sturdier vessels reduced the dangers of ocean travel. The *compass*, which had been brought to Europe from China, enabled navigators to steer a course when beyond sight of land. An improved *astrolabe* helped sailors measure latitude and thus determine their position at sea. An improved *rudder* gave mariners better control over a ship's steering.

2. Printing. The invention of movable type by *Johann Gutenberg* in the 1440's made possible the printing of books on a printing press. Earlier, books were laboriously copied by hand and were very expensive. Gutenberg's invention led to the wide distribution of maps, sea charts, and travelers' tales. These publications increased geographic knowledge and aroused curiosity about distant countries.

3. Maps. *Cartographers* (mapmakers) prepared more accurate charts of the seas, adding new geographic details as reported by sailors and other travelers.

4. Gunpowder. The introduction of gunpowder into Europe from China led to the development of cannon and muskets. Armed with these new weapons, sailors and exploring parties had little to fear from hostile natives in strange lands.

PORTUGAL FINDS A NEW ROUTE TO THE ORIENT

Portugal was the first European country to launch voyages of exploration. Chiefly responsible was *Prince Henry*, known as "the Navigator."

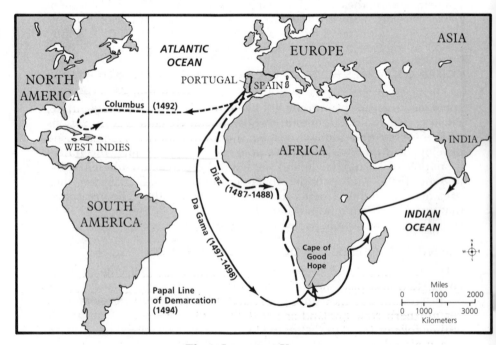

Three Important Voyages

Keenly interested in the sea, he founded a school of navigation and sent expeditions to explore the western coast of Africa. By the time of his death in 1460, Portuguese mariners had discovered the Azores, Madeira, and the Cape Verde Islands in the Atlantic, and had ventured 1,500 miles down the African coast.

After Prince Henry's death, the Portuguese continued to press southward. Finally, in 1488, *Bartholomeu Diaz* rounded the Cape of Good Hope on the southern tip of Africa. Ten years later, in 1498, *Vasco da Gama* sailed around Africa and across the Indian Ocean to India, thus opening up an all-water route to the East. As a result of his voyage, the center of Europe's commerce with the Orient shifted from the Mediterranean to the Atlantic. For a time, Portugal became the leading commercial nation of Europe. It carried on a flourishing trade in Eastern goods and established trading posts in Africa, India, and Southeast Asia.

COLUMBUS REACHES AMERICA

Christopher Columbus, an Italian navigator, believed that the earth is round and that he could reach the East by sailing westward across the Atlantic. For many years he tried to secure financial support for such a voyage. Finally, Queen Isabella and King Ferdinand of Spain, hoping to bring wealth and prestige to their country, agreed to finance him.

In August, 1492, Columbus departed from Palos, Spain, with a small crew and three ships: the *Santa Maria*, the *Pinta*, and the *Niña*. For weeks his tiny fleet sailed westward across the Atlantic. At last, on October 12, Columbus sighted land, an island in the Bahamas. He landed and took possession of the area in the name of Spain. Believing that he had reached the East Indies, he called the copper-colored natives *Indians*. While continuing his search for the Asian mainland, he discovered the Caribbean islands of Cuba and Hispaniola. (Today Hispaniola is shared by Haiti and the Dominican Republic.) In the spring of 1493 Columbus returned to Spain, where he was received with great acclaim.

Columbus made three more voyages to the Caribbean. He came upon Jamaica, Puerto Rico, Trinidad, and Honduras. He landed at the mouth of the Orinoco River on the mainland of South America. He also sailed along the Isthmus of Panama, vainly seeking a westward passage that would lead to the fabled cities and riches of the Orient. Until his death in 1506 Columbus believed that he had traveled to Asia and remained unaware that he had reached a part of the world previously unknown to Europeans.

(Columbus may not have been the first European to visit America. In the 9th and 10th centuries, Vikings from Scandinavia had planted settlements on Iceland and Greenland. Then in about 1000 A.D. *Leif Ericson*, a Viking from Greenland, explored the coast of North America and landed at a place he called *Vinland*. Historians disagree about its exact location, but they have suggested Newfoundland, Nova Scotia, and northern New England as possibilities. Since Ericson's voyage was neither followed up by further exploration nor generally known at the time, it played no part in the development of the Western Hemisphere.)

THE WORLD IS DIVIDED

To prevent disputes between Portugal and Spain over rival claims to new territory, the Pope divided the world into two parts. In 1493 he drew a *Line of Demarcation* from the North Pole to the South Pole about 300 miles to the west of the Azores in the Atlantic. The following year this line was moved 1,000 miles farther west. Portugal could claim all newly found lands east of the line; Spain, all territories west of it. Thereby, Spain was given control over all of the Western Hemisphere except Brazil, which fell on the Portuguese side. Portugal was given a free hand in Africa and the Far East. Portugal and Spain accepted the Line of Demarcation. The other European countries ignored it.

PORTUGAL TAKES POSSESSION OF BRAZIL

While sailing down the African coast on his way to India in 1500, *Pedro Cabral,* a Portuguese sea captain, veered westward and sighted the coast of Brazil. He landed and claimed the area for Portugal. The Portuguese, busy with developing their Far Eastern trade, did not attempt to colonize their new possession until 1530, when they settled Bahia in northern Brazil. This city became the region's economic and political center, serving as Brazil's capital for over 200 years. In southern Brazil the Portuguese founded the cities of São Paulo and Rio de Janeiro.

(Brazil remained in Portuguese hands until 1822, when it broke from the mother country and declared its independence. It has retained the Portuguese language, customs, and traditions to the present day.)

THE NEW WORLD IS NAMED AMERICA

Amerigo Vespucci, an Italian navigator, participated in several voyages of exploration to the Western Hemisphere. He accompanied a Spanish expedition that explored the northern coast of South America (1499), part of which had already been visited by Columbus, and joined a Portuguese expedition that sailed down the coast of Brazil (1501). In letters describing his exploits, he claimed that he had discovered an unknown continent—a New World. A geographer mistakenly credited Vespucci with the discovery of a land mass not seen by Columbus and suggested that it be called "America," in Amerigo Vespucci's honor. At first, the name was used only for South America, but it was later applied to North America as well.

Multiple-Choice Test

Select the letter preceding the word or expression that best completes each statement.

1. The period immediately following the fall of Rome is known as the (*a*) Renaissance (*b*) Age of Discovery (*c*) Early Middle Ages (*d*) High Middle Ages.
2. Leif Ericson reputedly visited North America about (*a*) 100 (*b*) 300 (*c*) 500 (*d*) 1,000 years before Columbus.
3. The first Portuguese explorer to sail around Africa and on to India was (*a*) Diaz (*b*) Vespucci (*c*) da Gama (*d*) Prince Henry.

4. An expedition undertaken by Europeans to gain control of Palestine is known as the *(a)* Siege of Constantinople *(b)* Northern Route *(c)* First Crusade *(d)* Astrolabe.
5. Eastern products sought by Europeans came from all of the following places EXCEPT *(a)* the Spice Islands *(b)* Cathay *(c)* Persia *(d)* Scandinavia.
6. An Italian who visited the Orient and wrote an account of his travels that was widely read in Europe was *(a)* Leonardo da Vinci *(b)* Marco Polo *(c)* Urban II *(d)* Kublai Khan.
7. All of the following vessels accompanied Columbus on his first voyage across the Atlantic EXCEPT the *(a)* *Pinta* *(b)* *Niña* *(c)* *Victoria* *(d)* *Santa Maria.*
8. The New World was named "America" in honor of *(a)* Columbus *(b)* Vespucci *(c)* Cabral *(d)* Queen Isabella.
9. Each of the following places has been suggested as the site of Vinland EXCEPT *(a)* Greenland *(b)* Newfoundland *(c)* Nova Scotia *(d)* New England.
10. A person who makes maps is called *(a)* a landscape artist *(b)* a physicist *(c)* an astrologer *(d)* a cartographer.

Matching Test

Match the items in Column *A* with those in Column *B*.

Column A	Column B
D 1. Line of Demarcation	*a.* Portuguese settlements in the New World
i 2. Antioch, Alexandria	*b.* First European to reach the Cape of Good Hope
J 3. Constantinople	*c.* First European to discover Brazil
h 4. Venice, Genoa	*d.* Division of world by the Pope
a 5. Bahia, Rio de Janeiro	*e.* Caribbean islands explored by Columbus
C 6. Cabral	*f.* Developer of movable type
b 7. Diaz	*g.* Islands in eastern Atlantic discovered by the Portuguese
f 8. Gutenberg	*h.* Italian trading centers
g 9. Azores, Cape Verde	*i.* Asian trade route terminals on the eastern Mediterranean Sea
e 10. Cuba, Hispaniola	*j.* Key center of the Eastern Orthodox Church

Modified True-False Test

If the statement is correct, write the word *true.* If the statement is incorrect, substitute a word or phrase for the italicized term to make the statement correct.

1. The *northern* trade route from the Orient to the Black Sea was mostly overland.
2. The coastal cities of *Spain* were the first European centers of the profitable trade that developed between Europe and the Orient.
3. *The Netherlands* was the first country to find an all-water route to the East.
4. The *Spaniards* discovered Brazil and took possession of the area.
5. Constantinople, a major terminal of Eastern trade, was captured by the *Crusaders* in 1453.

Essay Questions

If newspapers had existed in earlier times, the headlines listed below might have been written. Show how the event described in each headline contributed to the discovery of the New World.

1. LISBON SHIPYARD LAUNCHES LARGE VESSEL EQUIPPED WITH RUDDER, COMPASS, ASTROLABE, AND MUSKETS
2. EUROPEAN MERCHANTS RESENT ITALIAN MONOPOLY OF TRADE WITH ORIENT
3. POPE URBAN II RALLIES CHRISTIANS TO DRIVE MUSLIMS FROM HOLY LAND
4. COLUMBUS, A GENOESE MARINER, STATES BELIEF THAT WORLD IS ROUND

Part 2. Spain in the New World

SPAIN EXPLORES A LARGE PART OF AMERICA

After 1492 Spain took the lead in launching expeditions of exploration and colonization. Its motives were to acquire wealth, found an overseas empire, and bring the Roman Catholic religion to the Indians. In addition, Spanish adventurers were eager to seek their fortunes in the newly discovered territories.

The following explorers and *conquistadors* (conquerors) were chiefly responsible for fulfilling Spain's ambitions:

Juan Ponce de León, while searching for a legendary spring called the Fountain of Youth, came upon Florida (1513).

Vasco de Balboa crossed the Isthmus of Panama and sighted the Pacific Ocean (1513). His discovery showed that a vast ocean lay between the New World and the Orient.

Ferdinand Magellan, a Portuguese mariner in the service of Spain, led an expedition that was the first to *circumnavigate* (go completely around) the earth (1519–1522). Departing from Spain with a fleet of five ships, he crossed the Atlantic to South America, traveled southward along its coast, passed through the strait that now bears his name, and entered the Pacific. Magellan then sailed northwest across the Pacific and reached the Philippine Islands. Here he was killed by natives. Only one of his ships, the *Victoria,* eventually made its way back to Europe—returning by way of the East Indies, the Indian Ocean, and the southern tip of Africa.

This voyage (see map below) proved that the world is round.

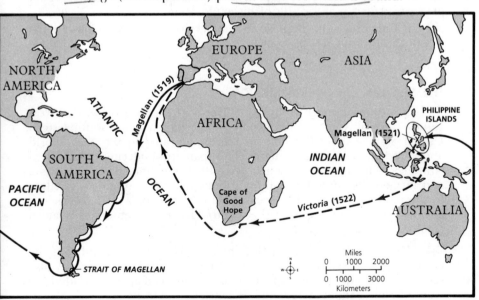

Magellan's Expedition Circles the Globe

9

Hernando Cortés led an expedition to Mexico to seek gold and claim land for Spain. Landing on the Gulf coast, he established a base at Veracruz and proceeded to march inland toward Tenochtitlán—capital city of the empire controlled by the Aztec Indians. En route, he enlisted the support of other Indian groups that resented paying tribute to the Aztecs. Upon reaching Tenochtitlán, the Spaniards were welcomed by *Montezuma*, the Aztec emperor. They later seized and imprisoned him, however, massacred many Aztec nobles, conquered the city, and took possession of its treasures of gold and silver. Cortés added Mexico to the Spanish Empire (1519–1521).

Cabeza de Vaca became the first European to explore southern Texas, New Mexico, and Arizona (1528–1536). His travels aroused the interest of the Spanish in exploring the interior of North America.

Francisco Pizarro led a small band of conquistadors to Peru, the heartland of the vast Inca empire that stretched for nearly 3,000 miles along the Pacific coast of South America. He captured the Inca ruler, *Atahualpa*, and promised to set him free upon payment of a huge ransom in gold. After the ransom was paid, Pizarro ordered Atahualpa slain. The leaderless empire soon collapsed. Pizarro occupied Cuzco, the Inca capital, seized the Inca's immense supply of gold, and added Peru to the Spanish Empire (1531–1533).

Francisco Coronado, seeking the treasures of the legendary "Seven Cities of Cíbola," explored the southwestern part of the United States (1540–1542). A member of his party traveled up the Colorado River to the Grand Canyon.

Hernando de Soto, traveling westward from Florida, explored the southern part of the United States. He was the first European to discover the Mississippi River (1541). Spain claimed the entire Gulf Coast region of North America as a result of his explorations.

Juan Cabrillo, a Portuguese in the service of Spain, explored the coast of California (1542).

THE SPANISH EMPIRE IN AMERICA

Spain acquired control of South America (except Brazil), the West Indies, Central America, Mexico, Florida, California, and southwestern United States. About 200,000 Spaniards migrated to the New World and founded some 200 settlements. The Spaniards built cities; established churches, schools, and missions; mined precious metals; raised cattle; and farmed the land. They shipped huge quantities of gold and silver to the mother country. This wealth made Spain for a time the richest and most powerful nation in the world. The major centers of Spanish colonization were:

1. The West Indies. Santo Domingo, on Hispaniola Island, was the earliest seat of Spanish rule in the New World. The Spaniards also settled the islands of Puerto Rico, Jamaica, and Cuba, and founded the cities of San Juan, Santiago, and Havana.

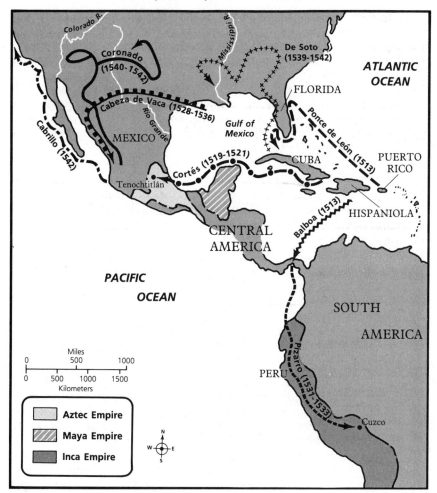

Spanish Explorations and Conquests in the New World

2. Mexico and Central America. Veracruz, founded by Cortés in 1519, and Mexico City, site of the ancient Aztec capital city of Tenochtitlán, became important Spanish centers in Mexico. The Spaniards also conquered and settled Panama, Guatemala, Honduras, Costa Rica, Nicaragua, and El Salvador in Central America.

3. South America

a. The Spanish Main. The northern coast of South America was known as the *Spanish Main*. By the middle of the 16th century, the Spaniards had established Santa Marta, Cartagena, and other cities along this coast. From these ports, large quantities of gold and silver were shipped to Spain. The Spanish Main was therefore a favorite target of English, French, and Dutch pirates.

b. Other Settlements. In 1535 Pizarro moved the capital of Peru from the Indian city of Cuzco to Lima, on the Pacific Ocean. Asunción, the present capital of Paraguay, was settled two years later. In 1538 Gonzalo de Quesada defeated the Indians of Colombia and founded Bogotá in the interior highlands of that country. Pedro de Valdivia, the conqueror of Chile, settled Santiago in 1541. Buenos Aires in Argentina was permanently established in 1580. By the end of the 16th century, Spanish settlements were located throughout all of South America except Brazil.

4. In Present-Day United States

a. Florida. St. Augustine, founded by *Pedro Menéndez* in 1565, was the first permanent settlement established by Europeans in what is now the United States. The Spaniards also built mission stations for Indians in northern Florida, as well as in Georgia and the Carolinas. In addition, a fort was erected at Pensacola to protect the Gulf Coast against invaders.

b. The Southwest. Spanish colonists occupied the region north of Mexico and named it New Mexico. They subdued the Indians and set up large cattle ranches in what is now Texas, New Mexico, and Arizona. Santa Fe, founded in 1609, became the capital. Other Spanish cities in the region included Albuquerque and El Paso. In East Texas, beginning in 1716, they planted fortified settlements and missions from Matagorda Bay on the Gulf of Mexico to San Antonio and northeastward to Nacogdoches. *(In response to LA salle)*

c. California. In 1769 the Spaniards founded San Diego, the first European settlement in California. Other Spanish settlements included Monterey (which became the capital), San Francisco, Santa Barbara, San Jose, and Los Angeles. *Father Junípero Serra,* a Franciscan priest, called the "Father of California Missions," was an outstanding contributor to Spanish settlement in California. He founded 9 of the 21 Indian missions established in the area. The economic life of California centered about these missions. Here the Indians were taught to raise crops, tend livestock, use European tools, make furniture, build roads and bridges, and construct Spanish-style dwellings and churches.

CHARACTER OF SPANISH COLONIAL RULE

1. Government. The Spanish colonies were divided into large provinces, called viceroyalties. Each was administered by a *viceroy* appointed by the king. As the king's personal representative, the viceroy exercised complete power. He carried out the laws enacted by the Council of the Indies in Spain, collected taxes, controlled the finances, and was responsible for the welfare of the Indians. The people had little voice in the government.

2. Commercial Regulations. Spain strictly supervised the commercial life of its colonies. Mining and agriculture were encouraged, but the production of goods that would compete with Spanish manufactures was prohibited. Also, the colonists were permitted to trade only with the mother country.

3. People of Spanish America. Only Spanish Catholics were permitted to emigrate to the colonies. European-born Spaniards constituted the ruling upper class in Spanish America. Below this group were the *creoles*, colonists born in Spanish America to Spanish parents. They owned or managed the plantations, ranches, and mines, and engaged in commerce and the professions. Although creoles served as local officials, they were not permitted to fill high governmental positions.

Next in importance were the *mestizos*, people of mixed Spanish and Indian parentage. They functioned as laborers, small farmers, artisans, and tradespeople. At the bottom of the social scale were the Indians and blacks. Both groups served as slaves on the plantations and in the mines. Blacks were imported from Africa after large numbers of Indians had died from smallpox and other diseases introduced by Europeans.

4. Treatment of the Indians. The king decreed that Indians should be treated in a humane manner, but this order was generally disobeyed. In practice, the Indians were ill-treated and abused by the colonists.

Catholic missionaries sought to protect and aid the Indians by gathering them into mission villages. Here the missionaries converted and educated the Indians, taught them trades and better farming methods, and attempted to guard them against abuses.

SPAIN'S LEGACY TO AMERICA

For about 300 years a large part of the Western Hemisphere was governed by Spain. During this time Spain helped shape the course of American civilization in the following ways:

1. Religion. The Spaniards introduced Christianity into the New World. They converted thousands of Indians to Roman Catholicism. They built churches in every city and village in Spanish America, including the magnificent cathedrals in Lima and Mexico City. The cathedral in Mexico City, begun in 1573, is still the largest church structure in the Americas.

2. Language. Spanish is the official language in nearly all of the countries of Latin America. In the United States, Spanish is widely spoken in Florida, Texas, New Mexico, Arizona, and California, as well as in many large, Northern cities such as New York. The language of the country has been enriched by the numerous Spanish place-names in the United States. These include Florida, Nevada, Colorado, Los Angeles, San Francisco, Sacramento, El Paso, and Rio Grande. English-speaking Americans have also adopted such Spanish words as fiesta, siesta, ranch, rodeo, corral, plaza, patio, guitar, barbecue, tornado, bronco, desperado, bonanza, canyon, mustang, and hammock.

3. Foods and Animals. The Spaniards brought over the following fruits, plants, and animals unknown in the New World: oranges, lemons, olives, sugarcane, wheat, rice, horses, cattle, donkeys, pigs, and sheep.

4. Education. The first universities in the Western Hemisphere were founded in the 1550's at Lima and Mexico City. The Spaniards also set up in Mexico City the first printing press in the Americas.

5. Architecture. Many private dwellings in Florida, California, and the Southwest reflect the Spanish influence to this day. They are one-storied and have stone or adobe (clay brick) walls, arched doorways, open courts, high ceilings, and tile roofs. Churches in these areas feature such Spanish architectural characteristics as round arches, domed roofs, and rectangular bell towers.

Multiple-Choice Test

1. The Inca Indians, a people with an advanced civilization, lived in what is now (*a*) Mexico (*b*) Honduras (*c*) Peru (*d*) Canada.
2. The conquistadors were interested mainly in (*a*) establishing colonies for refugees (*b*) finding gold and silver (*c*) setting up independent states (*d*) Europeanizing the Indians.
3. An inheritance that most Latin American countries received from Spain, and still retain, is their (*a*) democratic form of government (*b*) freedom of religion (*c*) loyalty to the Spanish crown (*d*) language.
4. The first permanent settlement established by Europeans in what is now the United States was (*a*) St. Augustine (*b*) Santa Fe (*c*) Pensacola (*d*) San Antonio.
5. Ponce de León's search for the Fountain of Youth resulted in the exploration of (*a*) California (*b*) Florida (*c*) the Mississippi River (*d*) Texas.
6. Spain founded all of the following New World settlements EXCEPT (*a*) Lima (*b*) San Diego (*c*) São Paulo (*d*) Buenos Aires.
7. The capital city of the Aztec Indians was (*a*) Cuzco (*b*) Tenochtitlán (*c*) Vera Cruz (*d*) Cartagena.
8. Each of Spain's New World provinces was governed by (*a*) an intendant (*b*) a conquistador (*c*) a mestizo (*d*) a viceroy.
9. An explorer who sought the "Seven Cities of Cibola" was (*a*) Coronado (*b*) Pizarro (*c*) Cabrillo (*d*) Balboa.
10. The northern coast of South America was called (*a*) Hispaniola (*b*) Yucatán (*c*) the Spanish Main (*d*) the Gold Coast.

Completion Test

Write the word or expression that correctly completes each statement.

1. Hernando de Soto became the first European to discover the _Miss_ River.
2. _Serra_, a Spanish priest, is known as the "Father of California Missions."
3. A Portuguese mariner in the service of Spain, _Cabrillo_, explored the coast of California in 1542.
4. _Alvarez_ was the first Spanish explorer to travel through Texas and New Mexico.
5. The Indian leader _Montezuma_ was subdued by the Spaniards when they conquered Mexico in 1519–1521.
6. Native-born Latin Americans of Spanish descent were called _Creoles_.
7. The Inca Indians, led by _Atahualpa_, unsuccessfully resisted the Spanish attack on their empire in 1531–1533.
8. The offspring of intermarriages between Spaniards and Indians were known as _mestizos_.

9. The earliest seat of Spanish rule in the New World was the city of _Santo Domingo_.
10. The first printing press to be set up in the New World was located in _mexico City_.

Essay Questions

1. Name *five* Spanish explorers who visited parts of present-day United States and list the region that each explored.
2. List *five* lasting Spanish contributions to life in the Americas.
3. Spain controlled a vast empire in the New World for more than 300 years.
   a. Describe the structure of Spanish colonial government during this period.
   b. What economic regulations did Spain impose on its colonies?

Part 3. France in the New World

MOTIVES FOR FRENCH EXPLORATION

Although France sponsored a few voyages of exploration in the early 1500's, it was too involved in domestic religious conflicts at that time to compete with Portugal and Spain for overseas possessions. Not until the next century did France take steps to establish settlements in America. Among the reasons for French interest in the New World were the following: (1) It hoped to find a passage to the East Indies through or around North America. (2) It wished to build an overseas empire in the Western Hemisphere. (3) It wanted to gain control of the fishing banks off Newfoundland. (4) French traders were attracted by opportunities to obtain furs in North America. (5) The Catholic Church in France was eager to send missionaries to convert the Indians.

FRANCE EXPLORES NORTH AMERICA

Giovanni da Verrazano, an Italian sea captain in the service of France, explored the eastern coast of North America from North Carolina to Nova Scotia (1524). He was the first European to discover New York Harbor and Narragansett Bay.

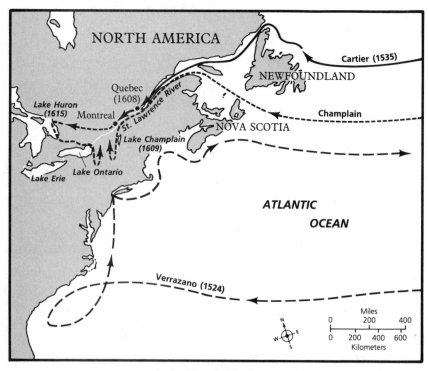

Early French Explorers

16

Jacques Cartier became the first European to find the St. Lawrence River. He sailed up that waterway to the site of Montreal (1534–1535).

Samuel de Champlain, the "father of New France," founded the first permanent French colony at Quebec (1608). He also was the first European to discover Lake Champlain (1609) and explore northern New York State.

Father Jacques Marquette, a Jesuit missionary, and **Louis Joliet**, a fur trader, explored the central portion of the Mississippi River (1673).

Robert Cavelier de la Salle sailed down the Mississippi to the Gulf of Mexico and claimed the entire territory for France (1682). He named the territory "Louisiana" in honor of King Louis XIV. Earlier he had explored western New York and the Ohio Valley, erected trading posts

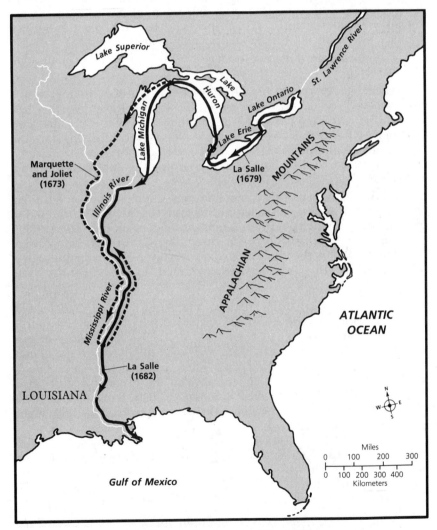

The French Explore the Mississippi

and forts in the Great Lakes region, and built the first sailing vessel to navigate the Great Lakes.

THE FRENCH EMPIRE IN AMERICA

As a result of their explorations, the French claimed Canada, the Great Lakes region, and the Mississippi Valley. (See map, page 17.) Control of the St. Lawrence River, the Great Lakes, and the Mississippi River system provided them with a natural highway to the interior of North America.

The French established few large settlements in *New France*—as their empire in North America was called. Concerned chiefly with developing a profitable fur trade with the Indians, the French built trading posts and forts at strategic points to control the waterways and to serve as centers for the Indian trade. Scattered throughout the wilderness were Indian missions set up by French priests. After 150 years of French control, New France was inhabited by only 80,000 settlers.

The following were among the major centers of French colonization in America:

1. Canada. The capital of New France was Quebec, situated atop a steep wall of rock overlooking the St. Lawrence River. Another key center was the trading post of Montreal. In the province of Acadia (later renamed "Nova Scotia" by the British) were several thriving farming and fishing communities. Also in Acadia, on Cape Breton Island, stood the powerful fortress of Louisbourg, guarding the approach to the St. Lawrence.

(The Acadians met with a sad fate during the French and Indian War. After the region was ceded to England, the inhabitants refused to give up their French loyalties, language, and traditions. As a result, thousands of Acadians were deported by the British. Some were distributed among the English colonies. Many resettled in Louisiana. The plight of the Acadians is recounted in Longfellow's poem *Evangeline.*)

2. In Present-Day United States. The French established trading posts, forts, and missions at such key locations as Niagara Falls, Pittsburgh (Fort Duquesne), Detroit, Green Bay, St. Louis, Memphis, Natchez, Mobile, and New Orleans. The largest French colony within the United States was in present-day Louisiana. The fertile soil and warm climate of the lower Mississippi Valley encouraged the French to start farms and plantations. New Orleans, founded by Jean-Baptiste Le Moyne (*Sieur de Bienville*) in 1718, became a thriving seaport and trading center.

CHARACTER OF FRENCH COLONIAL RULE

1. Government. New France was divided into two provinces: Canada and Louisiana. Each was administered by a royal governor, or *intendant,* appointed by the king of France. The king's officials exercised complete control over the colonists. The people had no voice in the government.

2. Landholding. The system of landholding in New France was similar to that used in the mother country. Large estates were granted to *seigneurs* (lords), who in turn rented small farms to *habitants* (settlers). This system tended to discourage the immigration of pioneers: colonists who wished to acquire free land and develop farms of their own in the wilderness.

3. Religious Restrictions. Only French Catholics were allowed to immigrate to New France. French Protestants (Huguenots) who wished to come to the New World generally settled in the English colonies.

4. Relations With the Indians. Unlike the English, the French did not clear the forests, drive out the wildlife, and take over Indian lands for homes and farms. Therefore, the French, on the whole, maintained better relations with the Indians than did the other Europeans in the New World. French fur traders lived among the Indians, treating them fairly and assisting them in numerous ways. Many Frenchmen married Indian women. Their offspring, called *métis*, or half-breeds, contributed to the spread of settlement by serving as scouts, guides, and explorers.

One Indian group, the Iroquois, opposed the French because Champlain had aided the Algonquins in a fight against them in the early 17th century. The powerful Iroquois Confederacy later prevented the French from settling central New York and sided with the English in the wars between England and France.

5. Missionary Activity. Missionaries and priests, called *Black Robes* by the Indians, followed the fur traders into the wilderness. They set up missions and Christianized the Indians. Among the notable French missionaries were (*a*) *Father Jacques Marquette*, the explorer of the Mississippi, (*b*) *Father Louis Hennepin*, the first European to see the Falls of St. Anthony on the upper Mississippi in present-day Minneapolis, and (*c*) *Father Isaac Jogues*, the first European to come upon Lake George, in New York. Slain by the Iroquois, this Jesuit martyr was declared a saint by the Catholic Church.

FRANCE'S LEGACY TO AMERICA

1. Religion. As a result of the work of French missionaries and priests, the Catholic Church became firmly established in the Mississippi Valley and in eastern Canada.

2. Language and Customs. Many people in Louisiana, in northern New York and New England, and in the Canadian province of Quebec speak French and observe French customs to this day. In Louisiana, counties are called "parishes" as they were in the days of French control. *Mardi Gras*, a French festival held the last day before Lent, is still celebrated in New Orleans.

Numerous words of French origin have been adopted by English-speaking Americans. These words include *butte, chowder, lacrosse, portage,* and *rapids*.

3. Place-Names. Many geographic names in the United States are of French origin. Some well-known ones are Detroit, St. Louis, Vermont, Duluth, Lake Champlain, Maine, Fond du Lac, Eau Claire, and Baton Rouge.

Completion Test

1. _____, an Italian explorer in the service of France, explored the eastern coast of North America in 1524.
2. Louis Joliet and _____, a Jesuit missionary, explored the central section of the Mississippi River in 1673.
3. _____ was the first European to discover the St. Lawrence River.
4. A French missionary, _____ was slain by the Iroquois and was later elevated to sainthood by the Roman Catholic Church.
5. _____ is often called the "father of New France."

Multiple-Choice Test

1. The earliest French explorers were (*a*) searching for places to found new cities (*b*) looking for a passage to the East Indies (*c*) seeking a haven from religious persecution (*d*) attempting to prove that the world is round.
2. In North America the French explored and claimed (*a*) the St. Lawrence and Mississippi valleys (*b*) Mexico and the Southwest (*c*) Delaware Bay and the Hudson Valley (*d*) Long Island and the Connecticut Valley.
3. The French founded (*a*) St. Augustine and Detroit (*b*) Santa Fe and Duluth (*c*) Pensacola and Louisbourg (*d*) Quebec and New Orleans.
4. The capital of New France was (*a*) Fort Duquesne (*b*) Cape Breton Island (*c*) Quebec (*d*) Montreal.
5. Royal governors of New France were called (*a*) *seigneurs* (*b*) *habitants* (*c*) *intendants* (*d*) *métis*.

Modified True-False Test

1. French Huguenots in the New World settled in the *English* colonies.
2. The Europeans who treated the Indians best were the *French*.
3. *Sieur de Bienville* headed an expedition that sailed down the Mississippi to its mouth, claimed the region for France, and named it "Louisiana."
4. The *Algonquin* Confederacy opposed the French and prevented them from gaining control of central New York.
5. Present-day Nova Scotia was originally named *Green Bay* by the French.

Essay Questions

1. Describe contributions made by the French to American life.
2. List *five* reasons for French interest in the New World.
3. What factors restricted the growth of the non-Indian population in New France?
4. (*a*) Describe the relationship of the French with the Indians. (*b*) What roles did the (*1*) missionaries and (*2*) fur traders play in this relationship?

Part 4. England in the New World

ENGLAND RISES TO POWER

When Elizabeth I became queen in the middle of the 16th century, England launched a program of commercial and naval expansion. It also began to challenge Spain's supremacy in Europe, the Far East, and the New World. Daring English "sea dogs," like *Sir John Hawkins*, enriched England's trade at the expense of Spain by smuggling slaves and English goods into the Spanish colonies in America. Others, like *Sir Francis Drake*, preyed on Spanish treasure ships and looted Spanish settlements in the New World.

In 1588 King Philip II of Spain sent a mighty fleet, or armada, to conquer England. In a decisive sea battle, the small but fast English ships outmaneuvered the clumsy Spanish warships and destroyed many of them. Soon afterwards, a storm wrecked a large part of the escaping Spanish fleet. With the defeat of the *Spanish Armada*, England gained control of the seas and began to build a worldwide empire.

REASONS FOR ENGLAND'S INTEREST IN AMERICA

At first, England, like the other nations of Europe, sent explorers to the New World to seek a passage to the East Indies. As its economy grew, however, England became more interested in founding overseas colonies. These, the English hoped, would provide an outlet for the country's expanding industries, and a market for its manufactured goods.

The New World attracted (1) landless and poverty-stricken people who sought to better their living conditions, (2) those who were deprived of their political or religious freedom at home, and (3) adventurers who hoped to acquire riches in the colonies.

ENGLAND'S EXPLORERS AND EARLY COLONIZERS

John Cabot, an Italian navigator in the service of England, made two voyages to the New World (1497–1498). He explored the eastern coast of North America from Labrador to Virginia. Cabot was the first explorer to reach the mainland of North America. (See the map on page 22.)

Sir Martin Frobisher, seeking a water passage to the Pacific above the northern coast of America, came upon Baffin Island and Frobisher Bay in northern Canada (1576).

Sir Francis Drake, retracing Magellan's path around South America, looted Spanish treasure ships and settlements on the Pacific coast of that continent. He then sailed up the west coast of North America and explored the coastline of California. He named the region *New Albion* and claimed it for England. He then headed across the Pacific and returned to England via the Indian Ocean (1577–1580). Drake thus became the first English mariner to circumnavigate the globe.

21

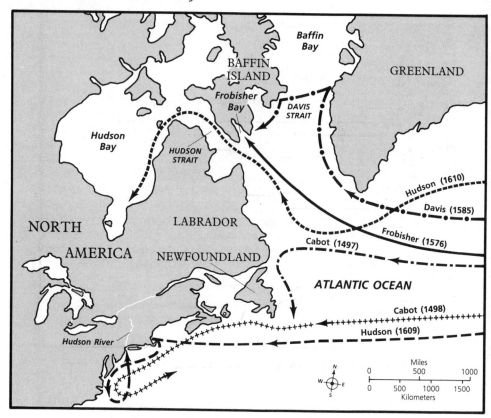

Explorers Search for a Northwest Passage

John Davis led three expeditions in a fruitless search for a northwest passage to the East Indies (1585–1587). He was the first European to enter Davis Strait and Baffin Bay in the Arctic region of North America.

Sir Humphrey Gilbert made two unsuccessful attempts to plant a colony in Newfoundland (in 1578 and 1583).

Sir Walter Raleigh founded a settlement on *Roanoke Island*, off the coast of present-day North Carolina (1587). It disappeared without a trace sometime before 1590 and became known as the *Lost Colony*. One of the lost colonists was *Virginia Dare*, the first English child born in America.

Henry Hudson, seeking a northwest passage to the Orient, sailed through Hudson Strait and became the first European to enter Hudson Bay (1610).

THE ENGLISH EMPIRE IN AMERICA

As a result of its explorations, England claimed a large part of North America. Beginning in 1607, English settlers emigrated to America in large numbers and established thriving colonies along the Atlantic

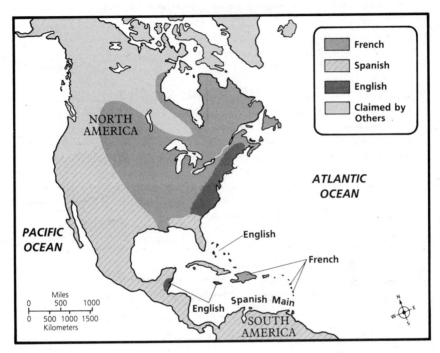

French, Spanish, and English Claims in the New World (About 1700)

seaboard. (See map above.) These colonies later broke away from their mother country and formed the United States of America. (For a full discussion of the English colonies in America see Unit II.)

Identification Test

Identify the person described in each of the following autobiographical sketches:

1. Although an English sea captain, I was working for a company of Dutch merchants when I explored the river that now bears my name. On my second trip to the New World, which was sponsored by an English group, I discovered a great bay in northern Canada.

2. Five years after Columbus's first voyage, I sailed to the New World for the king of England. I made another trip the following year. During these voyages, I explored the eastern coast of North America, and discovered the great fishing grounds off the coast of Newfoundland that are now known as the "Grand Banks." England based its claims to the North American mainland on my voyages.

3. I was the first English mariner to circumnavigate the globe. On that trip I stopped at what is now California to refit my ship. I claimed this land for England and named it "New Albion."

Modified True-False Test

1. English adventurers who attacked Spanish treasure ships and settlements in the New World were called *conquistadors*. sea dogs
2. *John Davis* was the first European to discover Baffin Bay in the Arctic region of North America.
3. The "Lost Colony" was located on *Roanoke Island*.
4. An English promoter who attempted unsuccessfully to plant a colony in Newfoundland was *Sir Walter Raleigh*.
5. *Sir Martin Frobisher* sought a northwest passage to the Orient in 1576 and discovered a bay in northern Canada that now bears his name.
6. Christianity was introduced into the New World by the *English*. Spanish
7. *Virginia Dare* was the first English child born in America.
8. An event of 1588 that made English overseas expansion possible was the decisive defeat of the *French Flotilla*. Spanish Armada
9. The English colonies were located along the *Atlantic seaboard*.
10. England embarked on a program of commercial and naval expansion during the reign of *Queen Elizabeth I*.

Part 5. The Netherlands in the New World

HUDSON EXPLORES THE COAST OF NORTH AMERICA

Long ruled by Spain, the Dutch rebelled in 1581 and declared their independence. Being great traders and seafarers, they took steps to obtain a share of the rich Far Eastern trade. A group of Dutch merchants hired *Henry Hudson*, an English navigator, to find a new water route to the Indies. In his vessel, the *Half Moon*, Hudson explored the North American coast from Maine to Carolina, becoming the first European to discover the Hudson River (1609). He sailed up the river as far north as present-day Albany.

THE DUTCH SETTLE NEW NETHERLAND

As a result of Hudson's voyage, the Dutch claimed the area from the Hudson River Valley southward to Delaware Bay. They called this region *New Netherland*. In 1614 Dutch merchants established a fur-trading post near Albany. Ten years later 30 families came to New Netherland. They were sent by the Dutch West India Company, to which the Dutch government had granted exclusive trading and colonizing rights in the New World. Most of the settlers went up the Hudson River to the area of the first Dutch trading post, where they founded *Fort Orange*. (See the map on page 26.)

Within the next two years, additional colonists arrived. Many of them settled in the vicinity of New York Bay and on the lower Delaware River. A large settlement was made on Manhattan Island. This town, named *New Amsterdam*, soon became the seat of government, chief port, and main trading center of New Netherland.

THE DUTCH ADOPT THE PATROON SYSTEM

To encourage settlement, the Dutch West India Company offered the title of *patroon* and a large estate to anyone who would bring in 50 adults and settle them as tenants on his land. The patroon would supply his tenants with homes, cattle, and tools. In return the tenants would give him part of their produce. The patroon had complete authority over his tenants.

A number of wealthy Dutch land promoters and merchants acquired patroonships in the Hudson Valley, which soon became a region of large estates. The experiment failed to attract many settlers, however, because colonists were (1) unwilling to submit to the strict economic and political controls of the patroon system, and (2) able to obtain ownership of land and greater political freedom in the other colonies.

The largest and most successful patroonship was *Rensselaerswyck*. Owned by Kiliaen Van Rensselaer, it included most of present-day Albany and Rensselaer counties. Other patroonships were controlled by the Stuyvesants, the Schuylers, and the Roosevelts.

25

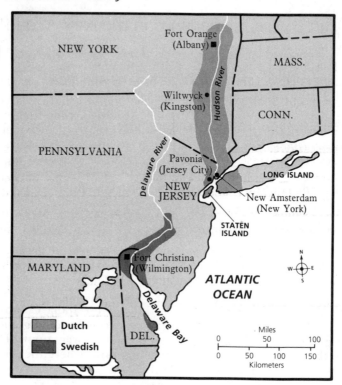

Dutch and Swedish Settlements in the New World

GOVERNMENT OF NEW NETHERLAND

The colony was governed by a director general, or governor, appointed by the Dutch West India Company. Since the main purpose of the colony was to earn profits for the company's shareholders by trading with the Indians, little interest was taken in the welfare of the settlers. The company did not give the people a voice in the government. It imposed heavy taxes and forbade the colonists from trading with the Indians. It left education, care of the sick and poor, and other services to the Dutch Reformed Church.

The first governor of New Netherland was *Peter Minuit,* who bought Manhattan Island from the Indians for $24 worth of trinkets, beads, and knives. The last and most famous governor was *Peter Stuyvesant*—an intolerant, autocratic, and bad-tempered individual. During his administration (1647–1664), new settlements were made at Wiltwyck (Kingston) and Schenectady. The population of the colony grew from 2,000 to 8,000.

THE DUTCH ANNEX NEW SWEDEN

In 1638 a group of Swedes, sponsored by a Swedish trading company, settled Fort Christina, on the site of present-day Wilmington, Delaware.

Shortly thereafter, additional settlers arrived, built forts along the Delaware River, and named the region *New Sweden.* The colonists devoted themselves to farming and fur trading with the Indians.

The Dutch were jealous of the Swedish fur trade and feared further colonization by Sweden. In 1655, therefore, Stuyvesant captured the Swedish forts and annexed New Sweden to New Netherland.

THE NETHERLANDS' LEGACY TO AMERICA

1. Architecture. Many dwellings, particularly in New York State, reflect the Dutch architectural influence to this day. The characteristic Dutch house was made of brick or stone, had a steeply pitched roof, stepped gables, entrance stoop, and a two-section door (Dutch door).

2. Place-Names. Many place-names in New York State (Catskill, Brooklyn, Yonkers, Bowery, and Tappan Zee) are derived from the Dutch.

3. Sports. Two popular sports—bowling and ice skating—were introduced into the New World by the Dutch.

4. Famous People. Three presidents of the United States—Martin Van Buren, Theodore Roosevelt, and Franklin D. Roosevelt—were descendants of early Dutch settlers.

Multiple-Choice Test

1. The Dutch settled (a) Fort Christina and Wiltwyck (b) New Amsterdam and Fort Orange (c) Veracruz and Staten Island (d) Schenectady and Wilmington.
2. The first explorers of the region that is now New York State were in the service of (a) England and Sweden (b) Italy and France (c) France and the Netherlands (d) Spain and Portugal.
3. Settlements in North America were established by all of the following countries EXCEPT (a) Spain (b) the Netherlands (c) France (d) Portugal.
4. Two countries that made the greatest effort to bring Christianity to the Indians of the New World were (a) Portugal and Sweden (b) Spain and France (c) England and the Netherlands (d) Sweden and England.
5. Fur trading was one of the main reasons why the first settlements in the New World were made by all of the following EXCEPT the (a) French (b) Swedes (c) Spaniards (d) Dutch.
6. One of the earliest settlements in the region that is now New York State was (a) Utica (b) New Amsterdam (c) Jamestown (d) Saratoga.
7. The term *patroon* generally refers to (a) a military officer (b) a land agent (c) an owner of a large estate (d) an immigrant from Europe.
8. The nation that did NOT claim territory in or send explorers to present-day New York State at one time or another was (a) England (b) France (c) the Netherlands (d) Spain.
9. A Dutch governor who purchased Manhattan Island from the Indians was

(a) Peter Minuit (b) Peter Stuyvesant (c) Kiliaen Van Rensselaer (d) Henry Hudson.

10. All of the following place-names in New York State are derived from the Dutch EXCEPT (a) Brooklyn (b) Catskill (c) Tappan Zee (d) Niagara Falls.

UNIT II. THE COLONIAL PERIOD

Part 1. Colonization by England

VIRGINIA (1607)

JAMESTOWN IS SETTLED

King James I of England issued a charter to the London Company (joint-stock) (later known as the Virginia Company) to establish a colony in the New World. In 1607 this group of merchants planted the first permanent English settlement in America, at Jamestown, Virginia. It was located near the mouth of the James River, which empties into the Atlantic. (See map, page 31.)

EARLY HARDSHIPS

At the start, everything went wrong with the venture. Interested chiefly in finding gold, the first colonists did not concern themselves with planting crops or building homes. The site chosen for the settlement was swampy and unhealthful. As a result, more than half of the settlers died of famine and disease during the first seven months. Indians added to the hardship of the colonists by their frequent attacks upon the settlement.

To *Captain John Smith,* an adventurer and soldier, goes the credit for saving the colony. He took command of the settlement and demanded that all able-bodied men perform some work, such as building homes and planting crops. He also succeeded in obtaining food from the Indians. Because of an injury, Smith returned to England in 1609. Without his leadership, the colony almost perished. That winter was known as the "starving time."

FACTORS LEADING TO THE COLONY'S SUCCESS

Although fresh supplies and additional settlers were sent to Jamestown, the colony remained on the verge of failure until several important changes took place.

1. Land Is Given to Settlers. One of the main reasons for the lack of early progress was that the colonists were merely employees of the London Company. All property, including land, belonged to it. Under the governorship of *Sir Thomas Dale,* interest in agriculture was stimulated by allowing settlers to obtain tracts of land as tenant farmers. A few years later the colony allotted settlers larger farms outright. Now that the colonists could raise their own crops and enjoy the fruits of their labor, they worked harder and the colony began to thrive.

2. Tobacco Cultivation Is Started. Planter *John Rolfe* introduced the cultivation of tobacco, a product acquired from the Indians. He also developed a method of curing the tobacco leaf to make it commercially

29

acceptable. Meanwhile, smoking was becoming fashionable in England, and the colonists began to raise tobacco on a large scale to meet the increasing demand. In 1617 Virginia exported 20,000 pounds of tobacco. Within the next 10 years the figure jumped to 500,000 pounds.

The labor needed to work the tobacco fields was first supplied by *indentured servants*. These were poor persons who were eager to settle in the New World but had no money to pay their passage. They agreed to work without wages for a period of years for anyone who paid their way to America.

In 1619 the first black Africans arrived as prisoners aboard a Dutch ship and were purchased by the settlers as indentured servants. Later, to meet the evergrowing need for labor on the expanding tobacco plantations, other Africans were brought over and sold to the colonists as slaves.

RELATIONS WITH THE INDIANS

At first, the Indian chief *Powhatan* sought to drive out the colonists. Legend has it that John Smith was captured by the Indians and was about to be slain when the chief's daughter *Pocahontas* intervened and saved him. In 1614 Pocahontas married John Rolfe, the tobacco planter. Thereafter, until Powhatan's death, there was peace between the colonists and the Indians. When the Indians broke the peace in 1622 by massacring nearly 350 people, the settlers fought back and finally drove the Indians from the area.

REPRESENTATIVE GOVERNMENT BEGINS

The colonists had little voice in the affairs of government until 1619, when the Virginia Company permitted them to form a representative assembly. Called the *House of Burgesses*, it was composed of two delegates, or burgesses, from each settlement in Virginia. The House of Burgesses was the first elective legislature in America. Only male landowners, however, could vote.

VIRGINIA BECOMES A ROYAL COLONY

In 1624 James I revoked the company's charter and made Virginia a royal colony. The king now appointed the governor and the council— as the upper house of the legislature was called. The colonists, however, continued to elect the members of the lower house—the House of Burgesses.

GROWTH OF VIRGINIA

With the arrival of farmers and craftsworkers, and women and children, Virginia grew steadily. Settlements spread from the banks of the James River to the York and Rappahannock rivers. Restless pioneers began to leave the coastal area for the inland region, pushing the frontier westward. By 1650 the population of Virginia was 15,000. In 1685 it was 60,000.

Williamsburg, a settlement north of Jamestown and the site of the College of William and Mary, became the capital of Virginia in 1699.

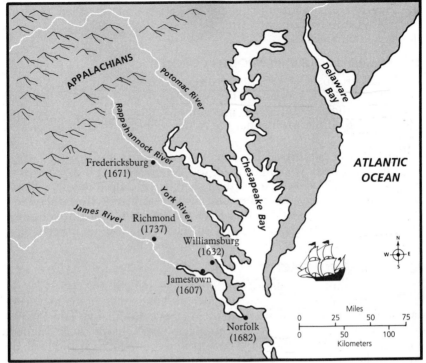

Early Virginia

It remained the political, cultural and social center of Virginia until 1780, when the capital was transferred to Richmond.

(Williamsburg is a fascinating tourist attraction today. Its streets, its homes, its shops—even the dress of the men and women employed in Williamsburg—have been restored in the spirit of colonial times. Williamsburg provides an authentic and vivid picture of life in the *Old Dominion,* as colonial Virginia was known.)

THE NEW ENGLAND COLONIES

RELIGIOUS REFORMERS CRITICIZE THE CHURCH OF ENGLAND

In the 16th century the Anglican Church was made the official Church of England. Everyone was required to support it. Persons who attended any other religious services were subject to fines and imprisonment.

Nevertheless, many English people criticized the practices and organization of the Anglican Church. One group, the *Puritans,* wished to simplify, or "purify," the church from within. Other reformers, called *Separatists,* broke away completely and set up independent churches that were more in keeping with their beliefs.

SEPARATISTS SEEK A REFUGE

To escape persecution, a number of Separatists fled to Holland, where religious freedom was permitted. But they were not happy there because the country was foreign to them, and they wished to raise their children in an English environment. After some years, they decided to seek a new home in America.

THE PILGRIMS FOUND PLYMOUTH COLONY

A small group of Separatists received permission from the Virginia Company to settle on its land in the New World. They obtained financial backing for their venture from a group of English merchants to whom they pledged all the profits that the colony would earn in its first seven years.

Thirty-five Separatists, calling themselves *Pilgrims*, and about 65 other English men and women set sail for America on the *Mayflower* in September, 1620. Blown far north of their original destination by heavy storms, they finally sighted the coast of New England. Here the weary travelers decided to settle, rather than continue southward to Virginia. In December, 1620, they landed at Plymouth, Massachusetts, and established a settlement. (See the map on page 34.)

MAYFLOWER COMPACT

Before landing, the colonists faced the need to establish a government of their own. They were now outside the limits of Virginia and were not subject to the regulations of the Virginia Company. The Pilgrim leaders drew up the *Mayflower Compact*, which 41 adult males signed, pledging to enact just and equal laws for the common good and to abide by these laws.

This agreement was one of the earliest expressions of self-government in America.

EARLY HARDSHIPS AND THE FIRST THANKSGIVING

The colonists suffered greatly during their first winter at Plymouth. Shelter was inadequate, disease was widespread, and food was scarce. Fortunately, neighboring Indians were helpful. *Massasoit*, an Indian chieftain, made a treaty of peace with the Pilgrims that was maintained for many years. Two Indians, named *Squanto* and *Samoset*, showed the Pilgrims how to grow corn and where to hunt and fish.

In the fall of 1621 the Pilgrims set aside a day of thanksgiving for the year's blessings. They invited the Indians to join them in a celebration of peace and plenty. This festival became known as the first *Thanksgiving*.

DEVELOPMENTS IN PLYMOUTH COLONY

John Carver, the first governor of the colony, died soon after the Pilgrims landed at Plymouth. He was succeeded by *William Bradford*, who governed wisely for many years. Under his leadership: (1) Each adult male acquired land of his own. Earlier in the colony's history all the land had belonged to the community and had been worked in common. (2) The Pilgrims repaid the merchants who had sponsored their undertaking, thus achieving financial independence.

Plymouth Colony, though successful, remained small. In 1691 it was merged with Massachusetts Bay Colony. Plymouth is important as the first permanent English settlement in New England.

PURITANS ESTABLISH MASSACHUSETTS BAY COLONY

In 1628 a small group of Puritans, led by John Endecott, settled at Salem. Like the Separatists at Plymouth, these Puritans came to the New World to escape religious persecution. The following year influential Puritans in England formed the Massachusetts Bay Company and acquired the rights to a large tract of land in New England. Under the company's sponsorship, over 1,000 Puritans came to the Massachusetts Bay area in 1630, settling in and around Boston. *John Winthrop*, an able and wealthy Puritan, became the first governor of the Massachusetts Bay Colony. Boston was made the capital.

A PURITAN COMMONWEALTH IS ORGANIZED

The harsh laws enforced against critics of the Anglican Church led to a "Great Migration" of Puritans from England. In the next decade about 20,000 Puritans came to New England.

The Puritan Church became the official church of the Bay Colony. All residents were compelled to support it. Those who criticized it were threatened with banishment. Only male church members were permitted to vote or hold public office. The clergy wielded great political power as governmental advisers. They also supervised the daily lives of the people and demanded that everyone live according to Puritan beliefs.

PURITANS SETTLE CONNECTICUT

Many persons were dissatisfied with conditions in the Bay Colony and sought new homes in the wilderness. A leader in this movement was *Thomas Hooker*, a Puritan pastor in New Towne (Cambridge) who disapproved of the harsh rule of the colony's leaders. In 1635 a small group of his followers migrated to the fertile Connecticut River Valley and settled Hartford. Hooker led the rest of his supporters there the following year. Other settlers from Massachusetts founded Wethersfield and Windsor. Farther south, in lower Connecticut, Puritans from England settled in and around New Haven.

FUNDAMENTAL ORDERS OF CONNECTICUT

In 1639 Hartford, Wethersfield, and Windsor joined forces and formed a unified government. They drew up a constitution with provisions for (1) electing deputies to a legislature, (2) choosing a governor, (3) limiting the terms of office of public officials, and (4) assuring fair taxation. This document, called the *Fundamental Orders of Connecticut*, was the first written constitution in America.

THE CONNECTICUT SETTLEMENTS ARE UNITED

Until the 1660's the settlements in lower Connecticut functioned independently as New Haven Colony. In 1662 King Charles II united all the towns of Connecticut into a single colony.

RHODE ISLAND IS FOUNDED

Roger Williams, a young Puritan minister in Salem, believed in freedom of religion and advocated the separation of church and state. His

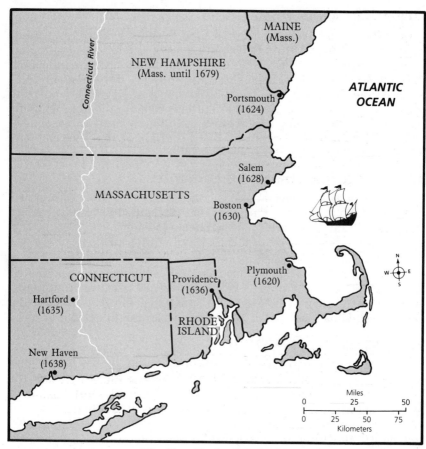

The New England Colonies

outspoken views so angered the officials of the Massachusetts Bay Colony that they brought him to trial and banished him to England. Williams fled and spent the winter among the Narragansett Indians. The following spring, other colonists from the Bay Colony joined him. He purchased land in the Narragansett Bay area from the Indians and in 1636 founded Providence.

Anne Hutchinson also came to Rhode Island after being banished from the Bay Colony for criticizing the Puritan Church. With her followers she settled at Portsmouth. Other colonists from Massachusetts founded Newport and Warwick. After receiving a charter from England authorizing them to establish their own government, the four settlements formed a unified colony known at first as *Providence Plantations* and later as Rhode Island.

RELIGIOUS FREEDOM IN RHODE ISLAND

Under Roger Williams, Rhode Island adopted the principle of complete separation of church and state. The government was prohibited from passing laws restricting religious liberty or imposing religious qualifications for voting or officeholding. As a result, people of all faiths were attracted to Rhode Island, and the colony prospered and grew.

Rhode Island was the first American colony to guarantee all its people religious freedom. This policy has since become a fundamental principle of American democracy.

NEW HAMPSHIRE IS SETTLED

In 1622 *John Mason* and *Sir Ferdinando Gorges* acquired the rights to a large area in northern New England. Several years later their holdings were divided, New Hampshire going to Mason and Maine to Gorges. Starting in 1623, both men established a number of small trading posts and fishing stations. Soon settlers from the Bay Colony began to migrate northward into these areas. Massachusetts then annexed both New Hampshire and Maine. It retained control of New Hampshire until 1679, when the king granted New Hampshire a charter that made it a separate royal colony. Massachusetts retained Maine until 1820.

MARYLAND

LORD BALTIMORE BECOMES PROPRIETOR OF MARYLAND

George Calvert, the first Lord Baltimore, was a prominent Catholic noble and a friend of King Charles I. Seeking a haven for Catholics, who were being persecuted in England, he obtained from the king a tract of land to found a colony. He died shortly thereafter, and the grant passed to his son. *Cecilius Calvert*, the second Lord Baltimore, became the first individual *proprietor*, or owner, of an American colony. As proprietor, Lord Baltimore personally owned all the land and could assign, sell, or rent it as he saw fit. He was empowered to levy taxes, establish courts, and control church matters. However, he could make laws only with the advice and consent of the freemen of the colony.

MARYLAND IS SETTLED

In 1634 a settlement was established at St. Mary's, near the mouth of the Potomac River. Leonard Calvert, brother of the second Lord Baltimore, became the first governor. The colony prospered from the start. The settlers were industrious and maintained friendly relations with Indians living in the area. Food was plentiful, and the climate and soil were well adapted to the cultivation of tobacco, which soon became an important source of income.

MARYLAND PROVIDES RELIGIOUS FREEDOM FOR CHRISTIANS

Although Maryland was established as a refuge for Catholics, Christians of all denominations were welcome there. People from Virginia and New England, as well as from England, flocked to the colony. Before long, Protestants outnumbered Catholics. To prevent religious disputes and to protect Catholics against discrimination, Lord Baltimore in 1649 successfully urged the passage of a *Toleration Act*. This law provided that all Christians should be free to worship as they pleased.

Although toleration in Maryland was limited to Christians, this act was nonetheless an important step toward religious liberty in America.

THE MASON-DIXON LINE RESOLVES A BOUNDARY DISPUTE

After the settlement of Pennsylvania, Maryland and Pennsylvania quarreled over the boundary between the two colonies. The dispute was finally settled in 1767, when two English surveyors, Charles Mason and Jeremiah Dixon, were called in to determine the actual boundary line.

The *Mason-Dixon Line* later became famous as the boundary between the free states and the slave states.

NORTH AND SOUTH CAROLINA

THE CAROLINAS ARE SETTLED

In 1663 King Charles II issued a charter to eight nobles to settle the region south of Virginia. These individuals received the same proprietary rights as Lord Baltimore enjoyed in Maryland. The area assigned to them was called "Carolina"—named in honor of a former English king, Charles I. (*Carolus* is Latin for Charles.)

Ten years earlier, in 1653, settlers from Virginia had begun to move into present-day North Carolina, establishing farms in the vicinity of Albemarle Sound. This settlement became part of the new colony. Other people were also attracted to Carolina. From Europe came French Huguenots, Germans, Scots, and Scotch-Irish. Anglicans, as well as Quakers and other dissenters, came over from England. In the northern part of Carolina, the settlers produced tobacco and *naval stores* (tar and turpentine); in the southern part, they grew rice and indigo. The main port and largest city in Carolina was Charles Town (now Charleston), founded by the proprietors in 1670 in the southern part of their grant.

NORTH AND SOUTH CAROLINA ARE SEPARATED

The Carolinians grew dissatisfied with proprietary rule, and there was constant friction between the elective assemblies and the governors. The English government became displeased with the proprietors because of the frequent disorders that broke out in Carolina and because of the proprietors' failure to maintain law and order. Opposition from both the colonists and the mother country led the proprietors to surrender their charter to the crown. In 1729 North Carolina and South Carolina became separate royal colonies.

NEW YORK AND NEW JERSEY

NEW NETHERLAND BECOMES NEW YORK

The English had long been irritated by the presence of the Dutch in New Netherland. (1) England viewed the area as part of its North American claim, which was based on Cabot's explorations. (2) New Netherland was a barrier separating New England from the English colonies to the south. (3) The Dutch, in violation of English trade laws, were carrying on extensive trade with the English colonies. (4) English merchants were envious of the profitable Dutch fur trade with the Indians. (5) England wished to gain control of New Amsterdam, which had one of the finest harbors on the east coast of North America.

When Charles II became king of England, he granted New Netherland to his brother James, the Duke of York. In 1664 an English fleet sailed to New Amsterdam and demanded the surrender of New Netherland. Governor Stuyvesant wanted to resist. But the people refused to support him, and he was forced to surrender without firing a shot.

In honor of the Duke of York, the English changed the names of the colony of New Netherland and of the town of New Amsterdam to New York. Beverwyck, the town that had grown up around Fort Orange, was renamed Albany. Wiltwyck became Kingston.

NEW YORK ACQUIRES A REPRESENTATIVE GOVERNMENT

The Duke of York administered the colony's affairs through an appointive governor and council, and he denied the people representation in the government. When the colonists protested, he appointed *Thomas Dongan* governor and authorized him to call a representative assembly. The assembly met in 1683 and drew up a *Charter of Liberties and Privileges*.

The document provided for the creation of an elective assembly, freedom of worship, and trial by jury. Dongan's charter was short-lived, however. When the Duke of York became King James II in 1685, he voided the charter and abolished the legislature. Representative government was not restored until 1691, after James II had been overthrown.

PART OF NEW NETHERLAND BECOMES NEW JERSEY

The region between the Hudson and Delaware rivers had been a part of New Netherland and was inhabited by a scattering of Dutch and Swedish settlers. When the Duke of York took possession after the Dutch surrender, he gave the area to two of his friends, *Sir George Carteret* and *Lord John Berkeley*. The new proprietors named their colony New Jersey. They encouraged colonization by promising settlers liberal grants of land, representative government, and freedom of religion. English Puritans and Quakers, as well as Scots, Scotch-Irish, and Germans, flocked to New Jersey, and the colony grew rapidly.

A group of Quakers purchased Berkeley's proprietary rights to the section known as West Jersey. Another group of Quakers and some non-Quakers acquired Carteret's province of East Jersey. In 1702, when the proprietors surrendered their governmental powers to the king, the two provinces of New Jersey were united into one royal colony.

PENNSYLVANIA AND DELAWARE

THE QUAKERS LOOK TO AMERICA FOR REFUGE

The Society of Friends was a Protestant sect that arose in England in the middle of the 17th century. Its members were called *Quakers* because their leader, George Fox, had once warned a judge to "tremble and quake at the word of the Lord."

Maintaining that an "inner light" was a person's spiritual guide, the Quakers saw no need for formal church rites or ceremonies. They believed that all people are equal in the eyes of God, and refused to remove their hats or bow down before anyone, no matter how high his or her rank. They considered slavery evil. Believing that war is sinful, they refused to fight or serve as soldiers.

Persecuted for their beliefs both in England and in many of the American colonies, the Quakers dreamed of establishing a colony of their own where they could live according to their principles.

WILLIAM PENN EMBARKS ON A "HOLY EXPERIMENT"

As a young man, *William Penn*, the son of a wealthy English admiral, became an ardent Quaker. In 1681, in payment of a large debt that Charles II owed his father, Penn obtained a grant of land in the New World. In honor of Admiral Penn, the king named this vast region *Pennsylvania* ("Penn's woods").

Penn planned to establish a proprietary colony where people of all creeds and nationalities would live together peaceably, where everyone would be equal before the law, and where all would enjoy freedom of speech and religion. He viewed his venture as a "holy experiment."

The first settlers arrived early in 1682 and founded the city of *Philadelphia* (a term meaning "brotherly love") at the junction of the Delaware and Schuylkill rivers. Before the year ended, Penn arrived to take charge of his colony, and 23 shiploads of colonists came over.

PENNSYLVANIA GROWS AND PROSPERS

Under William Penn's guidance, Pennsylvania expanded rapidly and became one of the largest and most successful of the English colonies.

1. Large Immigration.   Penn's liberal attitude toward self-government, land purchases, and religion attracted many Europeans to the colony. Among the settlers were English and Welsh Quakers, Irish Catholics, Scotch-Irish Presbyterians, and German members of several different religious groups (ancestors of the Pennsylvania Dutch of today). The colonists were industrious, skilled, and thrifty. As settlements spread northward and westward along the Delaware, Schuylkill, and Susquehanna rivers, Pennsylvania became a region of prosperous farms and villages. Philadelphia, its capital, became the largest city in the colonies.

2. The Great Law of Pennsylvania.   To guarantee a responsible and democratic government, Penn drew up a constitution that became known as the *Great Law of Pennsylvania*. It provided for (*a*) a governor to be appointed by the proprietor, (*b*) an elective legislature, (*c*) religious freedom, (*d*) protection against unfair trials, (*e*) reasonable punishment and humane treatment for wrongdoers, and (*f*) the education of children.

3. Friendly Relations With the Indians.   Penn dealt fairly and honorably with the Indians of Pennsylvania. He paid them for their lands and negotiated a treaty that bound the settlers and Indians to live in peace "as long as the sun and moon give light." He kept his promises to the Indians and maintained friendly relations with them as long as he lived.

PENNSYLVANIA ANNEXES DELAWARE

When New Netherland fell to the English, the section that had been New Sweden also became the property of the Duke of York. He renamed the area *Delaware*.

To provide Pennsylvania access to the sea, the Duke ceded Delaware to William Penn. Delaware remained a part of Pennsylvania until 1703, when it was permitted to set up its own legislature. Until the American Revolution, however, Delaware was administered by the governor of Pennsylvania.

GEORGIA

THE LAST OF THE THIRTEEN COLONIES IS FOUNDED

James Oglethorpe, an influential member of Parliament, received a charter from King George II to establish a colony between South Carolina and Florida. In honor of the king, the colony was named Georgia. It was to serve (1) as a refuge for imprisoned debtors who wished to get a fresh start in the New World, and (2) as a barrier to Spanish expansion northward from Florida.

In 1733 Oglethorpe led a small band of settlers to Georgia and founded *Savannah*. Few ex-prisoners came to Georgia, but poverty-stricken people from the British Isles, oppressed Swiss and Germans, and pioneers from Carolina did settle there, and the colony grew.

GEORGIA BECOMES A ROYAL COLONY

Georgia's governing body, a board of trustees, sought to make Georgia a colony of small, independent farmers. The trustees limited landholding and forbade the use of slaves. These policies, though well intentioned, were opposed by the colonists. They wished to expand their landholdings into plantations and to acquire slaves to work the land. In 1752 the trustees turned over their charter to the crown, and Georgia became a royal colony. Plantations and slavery soon developed into major institutions in Georgia's economy.

Identification Test

1. Because of my Quaker practices, I was dismissed from Oxford University. I asked King Charles II for a grant of land in America as payment of a large debt he owed my father. Here I granted the settlers a measure of religious freedom and treated the Indians fairly.
2. I was an English noble and a Roman Catholic. When the English government persecuted people of my faith, I founded a colony where Catholics could worship freely. Its largest city was named after me.

3. I was banished from Massachusetts Bay Colony for my views on politics and freedom of religion. I established a colony in southern New England. Because Indians aided me, I called my first settlement Providence.

4. I became the leader of the Jamestown colony and warned the colonists: "no work, no food." This policy saved the colony from failure.

5. I was born in England and felt sympathetic toward those who were sent to prison for debt. I received a grant of land in America and founded a colony as a haven for English debtors.

Timeline Test

On the timeline below, the letters *A–G* represent 25-year intervals. For each event listed, write the *letter* that indicates the time period in which the event occurred.

```
1600   1625    1650   1675    1700   1725    1750   1775
├───┬───┬───┬───┬───┬───┬───┤
   A  |  B  |   C   |  D  |  E   |  F   |  G
```

1. New Netherland surrendered to the English.
2. The settlements of Connecticut formed a single colony.
3. The first settlement was planted in Maryland.
4. The Puritans started a "Great Migration" to New England.
5. The Mason-Dixon Line was drawn to settle a boundary dispute between Maryland and Pennsylvania.
6. The first settlements were established in the Carolinas.
7. New Jersey was acquired by the English.
8. The city of "brotherly love" was founded.
9. The area originally called New Sweden was taken over by the English.
10. The first settlement was established in Georgia.
11. Jamestown was founded.
12. Delaware was granted its own legislature.
13. North and South Carolina became separate colonies.
14. Williamsburg became the capital of Virginia.
15. The Pilgrims landed at Plymouth.

Multiple-Choice Test

1. Squanto and Samoset were Indians who helped the early settlers of (*a*) Massachusetts (*b*) New York (*c*) Pennsylvania (*d*) Virginia.
2. The early colonists generally settled (*a*) in a mountainous region (*b*) in the plains region (*c*) in the piedmont region (*d*) near bodies of water.
3. The "Pennsylvania Dutch" originally came from (*a*) Germany (*b*) the Netherlands (*c*) Sweden (*d*) Belgium.
4. The House of Burgesses was (*a*) a company that sold spices (*b*) the first building erected in New Amsterdam (*c*) a lawmaking body of colonial Virginia (*d*) the home of the governor in Williamsburg.
5. The 13 original colonies did NOT include (*a*) Georgia (*b*) New Hampshire (*c*) North Carolina (*d*) Florida.
6. The name of a man who did NOT found a colony in America is (*a*) Thomas Hooker (*b*) John Mason (*c*) Peter Stuyvesant (*d*) Sir Ferdinando Gorges.

7. In 1619 the first representative colonial assembly met in (a) New Amsterdam (b) Plymouth (c) St. Augustine (d) Jamestown.
8. Which type of colony was established by William Penn? (a) proprietary (b) charter (c) indentured (d) royal.
9. The Mayflower Compact served as a basis for self-government for the (a) Dutch of New Amsterdam (b) Huguenots of South Carolina (c) Pilgrims of Plymouth Colony (d) Quakers of Pennsylvania.
10. A Charter of Liberties and Privileges was adopted by a New York assembly under the governorship of (a) Thomas Dongan (b) Peter Stuyvesant (c) Kiliaen Van Rensselaer (d) Peter Minuit.
11. The first permanent English settlement in North America was established at (a) Charleston (b) Jamestown (c) Plymouth (d) Roanoke.
12. An important reason why the Pilgrims came to America was to (a) find gold (b) trade with the Indians (c) obtain freedom of the press (d) secure religious liberty.
13. The most important crop of colonial Virginia was (a) fish (b) indigo (c) rice (d) tobacco.
14. People who agreed to work for a period of years in return for their passage to America were called (a) indentured servants (b) slaves (c) pioneers (d) migrant workers.
15. Most English settlers came to the New World to (a) obtain the right to vote (b) make a better living (c) escape from English taxation (d) escape from Queen Elizabeth's rule.

Matching Test

Column A	Column B
1. Massasoit	a. Tobacco planter
2. William Bradford	b. First governor of Massachusetts Bay Colony
3. Leonard Calvert	c. Critic of Puritan Church who was banished from Massachusetts Bay Colony
4. Sir George Carteret	d. Indian who aided the settlers at Jamestown
5. Peter Stuyvesant	e. Governor of Plymouth Colony
6. John Rolfe	f. The second Lord Baltimore
7. John Winthrop	g. Indian who aided the settlers at Plymouth
8. Anne Hutchinson	h. Proprietor of East Jersey
9. Pocahontas	i. Surrendered New Netherland to the English
10. Cecilius Calvert	j. First governor of Maryland

Essay Questions

1. During the 17th and 18th centuries many people emigrated from England. (a) Give *three* reasons why people left England. (b) Why did the Pilgrims leave Holland? (c) What was the Mayflower Compact?
2. a. Which religious group founded the first colony in Pennsylvania?
   b. Name a colony founded by a clergyman who was banished from another colony.
   c. What was the Toleration Act of 1649?
   d. Tell about the first Thanksgiving Day, explaining why it was held.

3. Select *five* of the following colonies and give *one* reason why each colony selected was founded: Georgia, Jamestown, Maryland, New Netherland, Pennsylvania, Plymouth, and Rhode Island.

4. a. Select the *letter* preceding the word or expression that best completes the statement or answers the question. Base your answers on the cartoon below and on your knowledge of the colonization of America.

(1) This ship sailed from a port in   (a) the Mediterranean area   (b) England   (c) Scandinavia   (d) northwestern France.

(2) The style of clothing worn by the passengers identifies them as the settlers of   (a) Massachusetts   (b) Virginia   (c) Delaware   (d) Maryland.

(3) The clouds in the cartoon represent   (a) dangers awaiting the settlers in the New World   (b) troubles left behind in the Old World   (c) unfavorable weather in their homeland   (d) winds that blew the ship across the ocean.

(4) The rainbow in the cartoon represents   (a) fair weather in South America   (b) smooth sailing   (c) the Fountain of Youth   (d) opportunities in America.

(5) The two Indians in the cartoon represent the idea that   (a) the passengers made the voyage to establish trade with the Indians   (b) the Indians had learned that the boat was on its way   (c) relations between the colonists and Indians were both friendly and unfriendly   (d) there were only a few Indians in this land.

b. Tell about *two* contributions to the American way of life that we have inherited from the colony founded by these passengers.

Part 2. Aspects of Colonial Life

ECONOMIC LIFE

THE GEOGRAPHY OF THE COLONIES

1. New England (New Hampshire, Massachusetts, Rhode Island, and Connecticut). Dense forests, rich in timber and fur-bearing animals, covered the hills and valleys of New England. Throughout the region there were numerous streams and waterfalls. Many harbors dotted the coastline, and the offshore waters teemed with fish.

Good farmland, however, was limited. The soil was rocky, and the terrain hilly. The growing seasons were short, and the winters long and severe. (To locate the colonies, see the map on page 44.)

2. Middle Colonies (New York, New Jersey, Pennsylvania, and Delaware). The coastal plain and river valleys of the Middle Colonies were fertile and well suited to agriculture. Rainfall was ample, and the climate moderate. Rivers provided access to the interior. Excellent harbors were found at the mouths of the Hudson and Delaware rivers. Timber and fur-bearing animals abounded in the inland forests.

3. Southern Colonies (Maryland, Virginia, North Carolina, South Carolina, and Georgia). The Southern Colonies were favored with fertile soil, a warm climate, abundant rainfall, and a long growing season. Broad, slow-flowing rivers linked the inland areas with the coastal ports. Pine forests were widespread in the Carolinas. Extensive marshes covered much of South Carolina and Georgia.

GEOGRAPHIC CONDITIONS INFLUENCE ECONOMIC LIFE

Since geographic conditions varied in the three sections of colonial America, colonists in each section earned their living in different ways. Because of the harsh climate and poor soil, many New Englanders found farming unprofitable. Utilizing the other natural resources of their area, they turned to such pursuits as fishing, lumbering, and shipbuilding. In New England and the Middle Colonies, people took advantage of their excellent harbors to develop trade and commerce. Because of the fertile soil and mild climate, Southern colonists found it most profitable to devote themselves to farming.

IMPORTANCE OF FARMING

Farming was the chief occupation in all the colonies. It engaged the efforts of nine-tenths of the colonists and supplied most of the necessities of life. Although the farms varied in size and type, the typical American colonist lived on a small, self-supporting, family-operated farm.

Because travel was slow and difficult, particularly in the backwoods areas, the colonial farm family had to rely upon itself for its many needs. There was often a division of labor. Men and boys would clear the land, raise crops and cattle, build the house and furniture, and make farm implements and tools. Women and girls cared for the vegetable garden

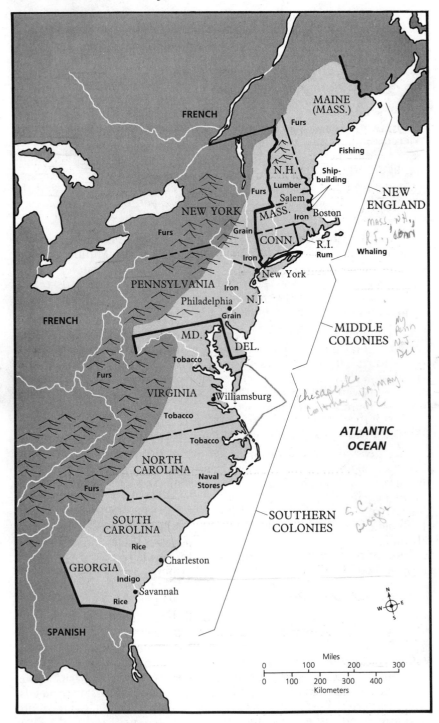

The Thirteen English Colonies (1750)

and poultry, cooked and preserved food, made candles and soap, spun wool and linen yarn, wove cloth (called *homespun*), and made the family's clothing.

The necessity for self-reliance gave colonial farmers a feeling of independence, a love of freedom, and a sense of responsibility.

COLONIAL AGRICULTURE

1. New England. The average New England farm was small. It produced food primarily for the family, with little left over for sale. The main crop was corn, or maize. Also grown were barley, rye, flax (used for making linen), and a variety of vegetables and fruits. Farmers raised chickens and pigs and owned one or two horses, a pair of oxen, some cattle, and possibly a few sheep.

2. Middle Colonies. The Middle Colonies were known as the "bread colonies" because of their abundant grain crops, particularly wheat and corn. The farmers also planted fruit orchards, grew vegetables, cultivated flax, and raised poultry, cattle, sheep, hogs, and horses. Except in the Hudson Valley, a region of large estates, the average farm in the Middle Colonies was of moderate size.

3. Southern Colonies. For their own needs, Southern farmers raised corn, wheat, vegetables, fruits, and livestock. In addition, they produced three major *cash crops*—crops grown for sale rather than for a farmer's own use.

a. Tobacco. Virginia, Maryland, and North Carolina produced millions of pounds of tobacco for export. For a long time tobacco was the most important crop of the South.

b. Rice. The coastal lowlands and marshes of South Carolina and Georgia were ideal for growing rice. This product therefore became the chief cash crop of the region and brought prosperity to planters.

c. Indigo. The leaf of this plant yields a blue dye that was in great demand by the English textile industry for coloring cloth. Indigo was second only to rice as a cash crop in South Carolina and Georgia.

Most Southern farms were small, family-operated enterprises similar to the ones that existed in the other colonies. However, commercial agriculture in the South was dominated by *plantations*, or large farms consisting of hundreds or thousands of acres. The plantation system of agriculture arose because: (1) European demand for Southern crops was heavy. (2) Tobacco, rice, and indigo could be profitably produced on a large scale with unskilled labor. (3) Large tracts of fertile land were available.

The typical plantation was a self-sufficient unit, almost independent of the outside world. It was worked by slaves and indentured servants who lived on the premises. It not only raised a cash crop but produced most of its own food and other necessities. Usually located along a riverbank, it had its own docking facilities to enable oceangoing sailing ships to load and unload cargo. Wealthy planters imported luxury goods such as expensive clothing, furniture, and housewares from England in exchange for the produce that they exported.

The Southern plantation was the big business enterprise of the colonial period.

COLONIAL INDUSTRY (manufacturing enterprises)

1. Local Industries. In every well-established community, local industries arose to serve the needs of the colonists. Blacksmiths shoed horses and produced tools and iron goods. Leatherworkers made harnesses and shoes. Cabinetmakers built furniture. Millers operated gristmills to grind grain into flour; sawmill operators cut logs into lumber. These enterprises were usually conducted on a small scale by the owner and *apprentices*—boys who were placed under the care of a master craftsworker for a certain number of years to learn a trade.

2. Fishing and Whaling. The waters off New England teemed with cod, halibut, mackerel, haddock, and herring. Enormous quantities of fish were caught. The fish were salted, dried, and shipped to Europe and the West Indies. The principal ports of the New England fishing fleets were Gloucester, Marblehead, and Salem.

Oyster fishing was a profitable occupation in Maryland, Virginia, and the Long Island region of New York.

Whaling was another important economic activity. Whaling vessels sailed from New Bedford, New London, and Nantucket Island, in New England, and from Sag Harbor on Long Island. Whale oil brought high prices, since it was widely used as fuel for lamps.

3. Shipbuilding. To meet the great demand for fishing boats and merchant vessels, New England developed a flourishing shipbuilding industry. Shipbuilders used timber from nearby forests and imported iron, canvas, and rope from England. New England vessels became world famous for speed and seaworthiness. The principal shipbuilding centers were Boston and Salem.

4. Lumbering. The great forests of New England were another important source of income for the colonists. Lumberjacks felled the trees and hauled them overland by oxen or floated them downstream to nearby sawmills. Here the lumber was prepared for such commercial uses as building ships and houses.

Other important lumbering centers in colonial America were the Hudson Valley, southeastern Pennsylvania, and North Carolina.

5. Production of Naval Stores. The forests of yellow pine that covered North Carolina yielded great quantities of pitch, tar, resin, and turpentine. These naval stores were in great demand by American and English shipbuilders for such purposes as making ships watertight.

6. Fur Trading. Furs and hides were income producers in all the colonies. In New England and the Middle Colonies, fur traders bought furs at trading posts in Fort Orange (Albany), Springfield (in central Massachusetts), and elsewhere. Here the Indians would bring their season's catch and trade it for axes, knives, beads, cloth, guns, ammunition, and rum. In the Southern Colonies, fur traders traveled to distant Indian villages far in the interior to purchase pelts and hides.

7. Distilling. Molasses imported from the West Indies was used to manufacture rum. By 1750 distilleries in the New England towns of Providence, Newport, Boston, and Medford were producing several million gallons of rum a year for domestic consumption and for use in the African slave trade.

8. Ironworking. The discovery of iron ore in southern New England, the Hudson Valley, and southeastern Pennsylvania led to the establishment of a small but thriving ironworking industry. The colonists in these areas produced pig and bar iron, as well as such finished articles as chains, anchors, barrel hoops, utensils, and tools.

COLONIAL COMMERCE (Business)

1. New England. New England merchants carried on an extensive trade with Europe, the West Indies, and the other colonies. They exported fish, whale oil, furs, lumber, ships, leather goods, and ironware. They imported cloth, glass, china, silverware, tea, and wine. Boston became a thriving port and the commercial center of New England.

Much of New England's commerce was in the form of *triangular trade.* One pattern of trade operated as follows: (*a*) Rum, manufactured in New England, was shipped to the west coast of Africa, where it was traded for black slaves. (*b*) The slaves were transported to the West Indies and sold for molasses and hard money (gold and silver). (*c*) The molasses was brought to New England, where it was distilled into rum, thus beginning another cycle of triangular trade. The money was used to pay for imports of English goods.

A second pattern of triangular trade operated as follows: (*a*) Grain, meat, lumber, and fish were brought to the West Indies and exchanged for sugar, molasses, and fruit. (*b*) These products were transported to England and traded for manufactured goods. (*c*) The manufactured goods were carried back to America and sold to the colonists.

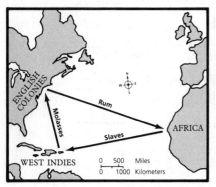 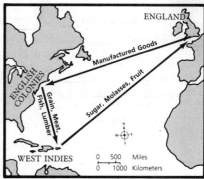

Two Triangular Trade Routes

2. Middle Colonies. Furs, iron, and lumber were exported to England in exchange for manufactured goods. Wheat, beef, lumber, and horses were shipped to the West Indies in exchange for sugar, molasses, and wine. Philadelphia and New York were the chief trading centers and ports of the Middle Colonies.

3. Southern Colonies. Although the Southern Colonies carried on some trade with the West Indies, the main commerce of the South was with England. Southerners exported tobacco, rice, indigo, naval stores, and hides to the mother country. In return, the South imported tools, furniture, clothing, china, silverware, linens, wines, and tea. Charleston was the main seaport in the South. Savannah and Baltimore also emerged as trading centers.

SOCIAL AND CULTURAL LIFE

HOW THE COLONISTS LIVED

1. Homes. The earliest homes of the new settlers were either bark-covered huts or crudely built log cabins set in small clearings in the woods. Later, when they could pay more attention to comfort and beauty, the colonists built more substantial homes.

In New England, the typical colonial house was a low wood cottage with a sloping roof. It was dignified but simple, with little outside adornment. In New York, the Dutch influence was reflected in brick homes with steeply pitched roofs. In Pennsylvania, many houses were built of stone obtained from nearby quarries.

In the Southern Colonies, wealthy planters built spacious mansions with wide porches, large halls, and graceful stairways. The main house was usually surrounded by a number of separate buildings: a kitchen, barn, carriage house, laundry, etc.

After 1720 Georgian architecture became popular among the well-to-do in all parts of British America. Houses of this type were stately in appearance. Built of brick or stone, they were two or three stories high, had sloping roofs, and several chimneys. The interior effect was one of elegance. There were many large rooms, elaborate fireplaces, graceful staircases, polished floors, and intricately carved woodwork.

2. Furnishings. In the average home, the furnishings were simple and practical. Whether made by a member of the household or a village craftsworker, the tables, chairs, cupboards, beds, and other furniture were built for long life and hard wear. Colonial furniture had a beauty and simplicity that are admired and imitated to this day.

The wealthy merchants and planters imported their furnishings from England. Upper-class homes usually contained fine mahogany furniture, expensive linens, silverware, and china.

3. Heating and Lighting. The fireplace was an important feature in the colonial dwelling. It was used not only to heat the house but also to cook the food. In the evenings, whale-oil lamps, candles, and the fireplace supplied light.

4. Food. Food was plentiful but plain. Cooking was done in iron pots hung over the fire. Meat was roasted on rotating spits. Bread was baked in ovens built into the fireplace.

There was no refrigeration. Meats had to be salted, dried, or smoked; vegetables and fruits had to be preserved or dried to assure an adequate supply of food over the winter.

5. Recreation. The colonists worked hard, but they found time for pleasure during the winter months and on holidays. Fishing, hunting, ice skating, sleighriding, cockfighting, dancing, cardplaying, and cricket were their chief forms of relaxation. People also got together at house raisings, corn huskings, elections, fairs, religious services, and weddings.

Wealthy Southern planters enjoyed such pastimes as horse racing, fox hunting, and elaborate balls. Puritans in New England, on the other hand, disapproved of idle amusements. Viewing the Sabbath as a day of rest and worship, they enacted strict "blue laws." These forbade all forms of entertainment on Sunday.

6. Travel and Communication. The earliest colonial roads were narrow Indian trails. By the middle of the 18th century, the main seacoast cities were linked by *post roads*, roads over which the mail was carried. A traveler journeying over one of these roads on horseback or by stagecoach encountered many hazards: deep ruts, countless tree stumps, unbridged streams, mud in the spring, dust in the summer, and snow in the winter.

Inland travel was even more difficult, since the country was covered by dense forests. Travelers either followed Indian trails or paddled their way along one of the many rivers.

Because of the lack of good roads, few colonists journeyed far from home.

SOCIAL CLASSES

Class distinction in colonial America was not entirely determined by birth, as it was in Europe, but also by occupation, property, and income. The population was divided into the following three broad classes:

1. The **upper class** dominated the economic, political, and social life of colonial America. It was made up of (*a*) plantation owners in the Southern Colonies and large landholders in the Middle Colonies, (*b*) wealthy merchants in the cities of New England and the Middle Colonies, (*c*) Puritan clergy in New England, and (*d*) government officials, lawyers, and doctors.

2. The **middle class** made up the bulk of the population of the colonies. It consisted of (*a*) small, independent farmers, (*b*) craftsworkers who served as shipwrights, blacksmiths, shoemakers, millers, bakers, brewers, carpenters, etc., and (*c*) shopkeepers.

3. The **lower class** consisted of (*a*) indentured servants, who were bound to their employers for a period of years to work off the cost of their passage to America, and (*b*) slaves, who were bound to their masters for life. Indentured servants and slaves were found in all the colonies.

POPULATION

1. Population Growth

Year	Population	Year	Population
1625	2,000	1755	1,500,000
1640	50,000	1763	2,000,000
1690	250,000	1775	2,750,000
1715	435,000		

2. Regional Distribution. About half of the people lived in the Southern Colonies. The remainder were divided almost equally between New England and the Middle Colonies.

3. Colonies in Order of Population (1775)

Rank	Colony	Rank	Colony
1	Virginia	8	Connecticut
2	Massachusetts	9	New Jersey
3	Pennsylvania	10	New Hampshire
4	North Carolina	11	Georgia
5	New York	12	Rhode Island
6	Maryland	13	Delaware
7	South Carolina		

4. Different Races and Nationalities. European whites constituted 80% of the population of colonial America, and African blacks 20%. Nine-tenths of the blacks were slaves.

Settlers of English origin comprised the largest group in the colonies. Germans, Scots, Scotch-Irish, Irish, and Dutch were also found in large numbers. There were smaller groups of Swiss, French Huguenots, Swedes, Welsh, Spaniards, and Belgians.

Note: All the population data above excludes the Indians. The various Indian tribes inhabiting colonial America did not view themselves as English subjects but as independent nations.

EDUCATION

Educational facilities were limited, and most children did not advance beyond the "three r's" (reading, 'riting, and 'rithmetic). Pupils learned their letters by means of a *hornbook*. This device consisted of a sheet of paper mounted on a board and covered by transparent horn to protect it against wear. The hornbook contained the alphabet, the Lord's Prayer, or verses from the Bible.

The most widely used textbook in colonial days was the *New England Primer*. This book taught the alphabet, reading, and religion by means of rhymed sayings, such as:

In *Adam's* Fall
We Sinned all.

Thy Life to Mend
This *Book* Attend.

The *Cat* doth play
And after slay.

1. New England. The Puritans established the first public school system in the colonies. In 1647 Massachusetts passed a law requiring each town of 50 or more families to have a primary school. Each town of 100 or more families was also required to establish a Latin grammar school to prepare qualified boys for college.

Harvard, the first college in the English colonies, was founded by the Puritans at Cambridge, Massachusetts, in 1636 to train young men for the ministry. Later, the Puritans founded *Yale* in Connecticut and *Dartmouth* in New Hampshire. The Baptists established the College of Rhode Island (*Brown*), also for the purpose of preparing students for the ministry.

2. Middle Colonies. In New Netherland, education was controlled by the Dutch Reformed Church, which supported schools in almost every community. The church opened the first primary school in New Amsterdam in 1638 and the first Latin school about 20 years later.

When the English took over New Netherland, they made no provision for public education. Until the Revolution, only church-sponsored schools and private academies existed in New York.

In Pennsylvania, William Penn established schools as early as 1683. The schools were supported by the parents of the attending children.

In New York, the Anglicans established King's College (*Columbia*). In New Jersey, the Presbyterians founded the College of New Jersey (*Princeton*), and the Dutch Reformed Church started Queen's College (*Rutgers*). These institutions were intended mainly to prepare young men for the ministry. In Pennsylvania, Benjamin Franklin and others founded the College and Academy of Philadelphia (*University of Pennsylvania*) for the teaching of *secular* (nonreligious) subjects. It offered a wide variety of courses designed to prepare its students for many different careers.

3. Southern Colonies. The children of the plantation owners were educated at home by private tutors, or were sent to England. However, the children of the small farmers, frontier settlers, indentured servants, and slaves received little or no education.

The *College of William and Mary*, the second oldest institution of higher learning in the English colonies, was founded in 1693 at Williamsburg, Virginia, by the Anglicans. Many of the Virginians who took a prominent part in the Revolution were educated there.

LITERATURE AND THE ARTS

1. Newspapers. The *Boston News-Letter*, started in 1704, was the first permanent colonial newspaper. By the middle of the century, weekly newspapers were being published in almost every colony. By discussing political questions, these publications helped shape public opinion and paved the way for the revolt against England.

2. Libraries. During the early part of the colonial period, living conditions were hard, and people had little leisure time for reading or studying. Books imported from abroad were expensive and were bought mainly by ministers, lawyers, and wealthy merchants. The only books to be found in most homes were the Bible and an *almanac*—a book giving general information about such subjects as astronomy, the weather, and farming.

As interest in education grew, public libraries began to appear. The first circulating library was founded in Philadelphia in 1731 through the efforts of Benjamin Franklin. It was called a *subscription library* and was supported by its members. Only they could borrow books from it. By the time of the Revolution, there was a subscription library in every large town. The result was that, as Franklin said, "Reading became fashionable, and our people became better acquainted with books, and were observed by strangers to be better instructed and more intelligent than people in the same rank generally are in other countries."

3. Literature. The writings of the colonial period were mainly religious and historical. John Cotton, Roger Williams, Thomas Hooker, Cotton Mather, and Jonathan Edwards—all Puritan clergymen of New England—wrote sermons and other religious works. Edwards' *On the Freedom of the Will* earned him great fame. A noteworthy historical work was William Bradford's *History of Plymouth Plantation*.

An outstanding contributor to the literature of the period was Benjamin Franklin. His *Poor Richard's Almanac*, which he published annually from 1732 to 1757 under the pen name Richard Saunders, presented useful information, proverbs, and rules of conduct in a witty and interesting manner. It was widely read throughout colonial America. His *Autobiography*, published after the Revolution, assured Franklin a place on the list of major contributors to American literature.

4. Painting. The colonists produced little of permanent value in the fields of music, drama, or sculpture. In painting, however, especially toward the end of the colonial period, a number of noteworthy contributors emerged.

Benjamin West, a Pennsylvanian who lived most of his life in England, is known for his historical paintings: *The Death of Wolfe* and *Penn's Treaty With the Indians*.

John Trumbull of Connecticut, another historical painter, is noted for his *Battle of Bunker Hill*, *The Signing of the Declaration of Independence*, and *The Surrender of Cornwallis*.

John Singleton Copley of Massachusetts painted portraits of prominent New Englanders, including Samuel Adams and John Hancock.

Charles Willson Peale of Maryland painted portraits of George Washington and Benjamin Franklin.

Gilbert Stuart of Rhode Island produced notable portraits of George Washington and other early American leaders.

POLITICAL LIFE

DEVELOPMENTS IN NEW ENGLAND

1. Importance of the Town. Most New Englanders settled in small, compact villages rather than on widely dispersed farms. Each town had a *common*, or village green, around which the settlement was built. Living closely together, the people were able to exchange news and opinions with their neighbors. They thus kept well informed and politically alert.

The *town* was the principal unit of local government. The center of each town's political activities was the town hall, where colonists held their *town meetings*. In open discussion all free men who belonged to the established church could vote on such matters of public concern as (*a*) the selection of local officials and representatives to the colonial legislature, (*b*) taxes for the support of their minister and schools, and (*c*) local laws.

2. New England Confederation. In 1643 Massachusetts Bay, Plymouth, Connecticut, and New Haven formed the *New England Confederation*. Its main purpose was to provide a united defense against the Indians, Dutch, and French. The government of the Confederation consisted of two representatives from each colony. Matters relating to war and relations with other colonies were to be dealt with in common. However, each colony was to remain independent in its internal affairs. Though the Confederation was dissolved in 1684, it is important as the first colonial attempt to form a union.

3. King Philip's War. The Indian chief Massasoit had been friendly to the settlers. However, his son, known as "King Philip," seeing the settlers seize more and more Indian land, rallied the Indians of New England to drive out the colonists. Through the New England Confederation, the colonists organized a military force to combat the Indians.

King Philip's War (1675–1678) was a long and costly struggle. Many lives were lost, a dozen settlements were wiped out, and half the villages of New England were damaged. The Indians were finally defeated, and their power in New England was permanently broken.

4. Dominion of New England (1686–1689). When James II became king of England in 1685, he decided to enforce English trade regulations and to strengthen English control in the colonies. He united New York, New Jersey, and the New England colonies into a single royal province called the *Dominion of New England*. He appointed *Sir Edmund Andros* as governor. The charters of the colonies were revoked, elective legislatures were abolished, and town meetings were curbed. Assisted by a council appointed by the king, Andros made the laws, levied taxes, and set up his own courts. He also halted colonial trade with countries other than England. Andros' tyrannical rule lasted for three years.

In 1689 James II was overthrown in what is called the "Glorious Revolution." When the news reached America, a Boston mob attacked Andros, forced him to surrender, and sent him back to England. The new king broke up the Dominion of New England and restored the charters to the individual colonies. Massachusetts, however, which had been largely self-governing, was made a royal colony.

DEVELOPMENTS IN THE MIDDLE COLONIES

1. Leisler's Rebellion (1689). When New York was joined to the Dominion of New England, Andros appointed Francis Nicholson his deputy governor for New York. Nicholson's autocratic rule aroused much anger.

With King James II overthrown in England and Governor Andros deposed in Boston, discontented New Yorkers revolted. *Jacob Leisler*, a German-born merchant and a captain in the militia, led the revolt and seized control of the colony. Nicholson fled to England.

Leisler was popular with the common people but was bitterly opposed by the aristocrats, whose influence he sought to curb. He administered the government for two years (1689–1691), until he was replaced by a royal governor sent over by the new English king. Leisler's enemies convinced the newly appointed governor that Leisler was guilty of treason. As a result, Leisler was arrested, sentenced to death, and hanged.

2. The Zenger Trial (1735). *John Peter Zenger*, a German immigrant, settled in New York City and became a printer and publisher. In his newspaper, the *Weekly Journal*, Zenger carried articles criticizing the royal governor, William Cosby. Angered by these attacks, Cosby ordered Zenger's arrest. At his trial in 1735, Zenger was defended by Andrew Hamilton of Philadelphia, one of the ablest lawyers of the day. Hamilton argued that as long as someone told the truth, that person had the right to expose and oppose an unjust government.

The jury brought in a verdict of "not guilty," and Zenger was freed. This case established the principle of *freedom of the press*. The decision made it possible for newspapers to criticize openly the government and its policies. The Zenger trial thus helped the growth of the movement for independence.

DEVELOPMENTS IN THE SOUTHERN COLONIES

1. Local Government. The plantation system of agriculture kept the settlers widely separated and prevented the growth of many towns. The prevailing unit of local government in the Southern Colonies was the *county*.

2. Bacon's Rebellion. In the 1670's marauding Indians began to attack frontier farms in Virginia, slaying the inhabitants and burning their homes. When the royal governor, Sir William Berkeley, refused to take action against the attackers, the farmers decided to act on their own. Led by *Nathaniel Bacon*, they organized a small force and destroyed a band of the raiders (1676). Berkeley proclaimed Bacon a traitor. Many people, however, rallied around Bacon. He marched to Jamestown, the capital, with 500 men and forced the governor to authorize a campaign against the Indians.

After Bacon and his men left the capital, Berkeley labeled them rebels and ordered their arrest. Upon hearing this, Bacon attacked Jamestown, set it afire, and seized control of the government. The governor fled. Shortly thereafter, Bacon became ill and died. Berkeley returned, suppressed the revolt, and hanged a number of Bacon's followers. King Charles II, angered by the governor's harsh measures, removed Berkeley from office.

EMERGING PATTERN OF DEMOCRACY IN THE COLONIES

OUR DEMOCRATIC HERITAGE FROM ENGLAND

The people of England, over the centuries, limited the power of their monarchs and gained a voice in the government. They also won many important civil rights. These democratic rights are contained in such documents as the *Magna Carta* (1215), the *Petition of Right* (1628), the *Habeas Corpus Act* (1679), and the English *Bill of Rights* (1689), as well as in English common (unwritten) law.

When the English settlers came to the New World, they claimed that they brought with them "the rights of Englishmen." These rights became the basis of law and government in the colonies, and the foundation upon which the American way of life later developed. The colonists cherished their democratic inheritance. They opposed every effort by the British government to destroy it, and they finally took up arms against the mother country to defend it.

"The Rights of Englishmen"

1. The people have the right to be represented in their government.
2. Only the people, through their elected representatives, have the right to levy taxes and enact laws.
3. People accused of wrongdoings have the right to be tried fairly and to be judged by a jury of their equals.
4. People have the right to a *writ of habeas corpus*, a court order entitling them to be (a) informed of the charges against them (b) given a speedy trial, and (c) released on bail while awaiting a decision in their case.
5. A person may not be arrested, and a person's home may not be entered and searched, without a written court order, or *warrant*.
6. Soldiers may not be lodged in a private home without the permission of the owner.
7. The people have the right to ask the government to correct abuses and injustices.

DEMOCRATIC ADVANCES IN COLONIAL POLITICAL LIFE

England was separated from its colonies by 3,000 miles of ocean. It was deeply involved in acquiring territory and expanding trade in all parts of the world. England therefore did not attempt to supervise its American settlements too closely during the early part of the colonial period. As a result, the colonists enjoyed a great amount of freedom. They learned to rely upon themselves and to manage their own political affairs. They gained a large measure of self-government and made notable advances toward democracy.

1. Milestones of Colonial Democracy

a. Virginia House of Burgesses. Established in 1619, this body was the *first representative assembly* in America. Male property owners, through their elected representatives, gained a voice in the government and a share in the making of laws. Similar lawmaking bodies were later introduced into all the colonies. Most colonial legislatures consisted of two houses: a *council*, or upper house, generally appointed by the governor; and an *assembly*, or lower house, elected by the voters.

b. Mayflower Compact. Drawn up by the Pilgrims in 1620, this document set forth the principle of *government by the consent of the governed.* This phrase means that a government derives its authority from the people and that it retains power only as long as the people support it.

c. Fundamental Orders of Connecticut. Drawn up in 1639 under the guidance of Thomas Hooker, the Fundamental Orders of Connecticut was the *first written constitution* in America. A constitution outlines the form of a government and defines the authority of government officials.

d. New England Town Meetings. In each New England village the people held periodic town meetings. In this way the people themselves directly managed the affairs of the community. The town meeting is an example of *direct democracy*.

e. Power of the Purse. The elected assemblies had the power to levy taxes and authorize the spending of public funds. This power is called the *power of the purse*. By threatening to withhold the money necessary to pay government salaries, an assembly could force the governor to comply with its wishes in such matters as approving legislation and appointing officials.

f. Zenger Trial. The jury in the Zenger Trial (1735) declared that a person may not be punished for making true accusations against the government. This decision helped establish the principles of *freedom of speech* and *freedom of the press*.

2. Undemocratic Features of Colonial Government

a. The right to vote was given only to male property owners. In some colonies, particularly Massachusetts, there were also religious qualifications for voting.

b. In all the colonies except Connecticut and Rhode Island, the governors were not elected. They were appointed by either the king or the proprietor.

c. In most of the colonies, the governors appointed officials without the consent of the assembly. They also chose the council, or upper house, of the legislature.

d. Laws passed by a colonial legislature could be killed, or *vetoed*, by a non-elected official—either the governor or the king.

DEVELOPMENT OF RELIGIOUS FREEDOM IN COLONIAL AMERICA

The intolerant attitude of many early colonists toward the religious beliefs of others changed as time passed. Rhode Island, Maryland, and Pennsylvania led the way toward religious toleration.

1. Roger Williams welcomed people of all faiths to Rhode Island. He established the principle of *separation of church and state*, that is, that the church and the civil government should not interfere in each other's affairs.

2. The Toleration Act of 1649 in Maryland extended protection against discrimination to Christians of all denominations.

3. In Pennsylvania, William Penn granted religious freedom to all who believed in God.

As more and more Europeans came to the New World, they brought with them a wider variety of religious beliefs and practices. The American colonists gradually became more tolerant of denominational differences and learned to accept and respect the diverse beliefs of their new neighbors.

Multiple-Choice Test

1. Which of the following industries was NOT an important economic activity of colonial times?   (*a*) fishing   (*b*) shipbuilding   (*c*) coal mining   (*d*) lumbering.

2. The Puritans can best be described as   (*a*) carefree   (*b*) warlike   (*c*) tolerant   (*d*) religious.

3. All of the following colleges were founded during the colonial period EXCEPT   (*a*) Harvard   (*b* Columbia   (*c*) William and Mary   (*d*) Cornell.

4. In 1676 a rebellion of Virginia settlers against Governor Berkeley was led by   (*a*) Nathaniel Bacon   (*b*) John Smith   (*c*) Andrew Hamilton   (*d*) Jacob Leisler.

5. In colonial days homespun material for clothing was made from linen and   (*a*) cotton   (*b*) wool   (*c*) silk   (*d*) rayon.

6. Which precedent was established in the excerpt below, from the Massachusetts School Law of 1647?

> It is therefore ordered that every township in this jurisdiction, after the Lord hath increased them to the number of 50 householders, shall then forthwith appoint one within their town to teach all such children as shall resort to him to write and read, whose wages shall be paid either by the parents or masters of such children, or by the inhabitants in general. . . .

(*a*) Parents are solely liable for the costs of their children's education.   (*b*) The primary function of education is religious.   (*c*) Providing basic education is a community responsibility.   (*d*) Private schools are entitled to public funds.

7. During colonial times the principal occupation in America was   (*a*) manufacturing   (*b*) mining   (*c*) slave trading   (*d*) farming.

8. The New England colonies included   (*a*) New York and Vermont   (*b*) New Jersey and Rhode Island   (*c*) Massachusetts and Connecticut   (*d*) Delaware and Maine.

9. John Peter Zenger's trial helped to obtain   (*a*) voting rights for women   (*b*) freedom of the press   (*c*) lower taxes   (*d*) better conditions in colonial prisons.

10. The colony most noted for town meetings was (a) Delaware (b) New York (c) Massachusetts (d) Virginia.

11. Which characteristic had become common to most colonial governments by 1770? (a) elective governorships (b) universal manhood suffrage (c) representative assemblies (d) separation of church and state.

12. All of the following were prominent Puritan clergymen EXCEPT (a) John Cotton (b) Cotton Mather (c) Jonathan Edwards (d) George Calvert.

13. The *History of Plymouth Plantation*, a primary source of information on early days in colonial New England, was written by (a) John Endecott (b) John Carver (c) Jonathan Edwards (d) William Bradford.

14. The Mayflower Compact is best described as a (a) promise of the signers to enact just laws and to abide by these laws (b) declaration of the group's independence (c) constitution describing the government that the Pilgrims proposed (d) charter from the Virginia Company.

15. Which person would most likely have had a college education during early colonial times? (a) a merchant (b) a printer (c) a farmer (d) a clergyman.

16. All of the following were noted portrait painters EXCEPT (a) John Singleton Copley (b) Roger Williams (c) Charles Willson Peale (d) Gilbert Stuart.

17. During the colonial period, the representative assemblies exercised control over the royal governors by (a) using the power of the purse (b) vetoing royal proclamations (c) refusing to hold legislative sessions (d) threatening to form alliances with the French.

18. Benjamin Franklin is noted for all of the following achievements EXCEPT: (a) He founded the first colonial circulating library. (b) He published *Poor Richard's Almanac*. (c) He was one of the founders of the University of Pennsylvania. (d) He served as the royal governor of Pennsylvania.

19. The Fundamental Orders of Connecticut was (a) a royal decree revoking the charter of Connecticut (b) the first written constitution in America (c) an order issued by Massachusetts forbidding the migration of settlers to Connecticut (d) an agreement drawn up by the colonists to establish a New England Confederation.

20. All of the following were landmarks in the growth of democracy in colonial America EXCEPT the (a) House of Burgesses (b) Mayflower Compact (c) Zenger Trial (d) Magna Carta.

21. In 1750 the main towns along the eastern seaboard were linked by (a) post roads (b) Indian trails (c) canals (d) railroads.

22. All of the following were important colonial ports EXCEPT (a) Buffalo (b) Boston (c) New York City (d) Philadelphia.

23. Blacks comprised about (a) 1% (b) 5% (c) 20% (d) 50% of the population of colonial America.

24. The colony that ranked first in population in 1775 was (a) Pennsylvania (b) New York (c) Virginia (d) Massachusetts.

25. Literary works produced by New England writers during the early colonial period stressed (a) economic problems (b) scientific findings (c) religious themes (d) political developments.

Matching Test

Column A	Column B
g 1. Pennsylvania, New York, New Jersey	*a.* Important products of New England
h 2. China, silverware, tea	*b.* Tobacco colonies
i 3. Tar, pitch, turpentine	*c.* New England fishing centers
b 4. Virginia, Maryland, North Carolina	*d.* Ironworking centers
a 5. Fish, lumber, ships	*e.* Southern trading centers
d 6. Southern New England, the Hudson Valley, southeastern Pennsylvania	*f.* Products grown on plantations
j 7. New England, Africa, the West Indies	*g.* Bread colonies
c 8. Gloucester, Marblehead, Salem	*h.* Imports from England
e 9. Charleston, Savannah, Baltimore	*i.* Naval stores
f 10. Tobacco, rice, indigo	*j.* Corners of triangular trade

Modified True-False Test

1. Laws passed by the Puritans for the observance of the Sabbath were called *Fundamental Orders.* Blue Laws
2. During the colonial period, approximately 50% of the people were farmers. 90%
3. Youngsters who worked for a master craftsworker in return for instruction in a trade were called *habitants.* apprentices
4. In the three-cornered trade that the New England colonies carried on with Africa and the West Indies, the main product shipped from the West Indies to New England was *spices.* Molasses
5. During the early colonial period, the lowest social class comprised *indentured servants and slaves.* T
6. The *Boston News-Letter,* started in 1704, was the first permanent colonial newspaper. T
7. The College of William and Mary, the second oldest institution of higher learning in the English colonies, was established in *Jamestown,* Virginia. Williamsburg
8. The textbook most widely used in colonial times was the *New England Primer.* T
9. The principal unit of local government in New England was the *county.* Town
10. The political organization formed by Massachusetts Bay Colony, Connecticut, Plymouth, and New Haven in 1643 was called the *Dominion of New England.* New England Confederation

Essay Questions

1. If you were living in colonial times, explain briefly why you would have supported *or* opposed each of *three* of the following people: Nathaniel Bacon, Thomas Dongan, Sir Edmund Andros, John Peter Zenger, Jacob Leisler, King Philip, and Anne Hutchinson.
2. Explain *three* present-day practices or institutions that we have inherited from the colonial period.
3. (*a*) Name *two* leading home industries of colonial days that are *not* usually carried on in the home today. (*b*) Describe how the industries named were

carried on in the colonial home. (c) Name *two* commodities that were exported from America during the colonial period. (d) Name *two* commodities that had to be imported.

●4. Describe the geographic conditions that influenced the early settlers to do each of the following: (a) Develop fishing, lumbering, trading, and shipbuilding in New England. (b) Develop the plantation system of agriculture in the South.

5. Explain how modern homes differ from colonial homes in regard to *five* of the following: lighting, heating, interior decoration, outside appearance, water supply, cooking utensils, and food storage.

6. Describe life in *either* colonial New England *or* colonial Virginia. Include in your answer the following: industries, religion, education, government, and amusements.

7. Compare the American schools of colonial days with the schools of today in regard to each of the following: subjects taught, number of children attending, and types of school buildings.

8. Among some of the early developments of democracy in the English colonies are the following: town meeting, written constitution, freedom of the press, Mayflower Compact, representative government, public schools, and religious freedom.

   a. Select *five* of the above and for each one chosen name a colony that is noted for that democratic practice.

   b. Select *two* of the above developments and tell why each is important in the history of our country.

UNIT III. THE COLONISTS STRUGGLE FOR FREEDOM

Part 1. England Gains Control of North America

ENGLAND AND FRANCE COMPETE FOR WORLD POWER

As Spain declined as a world power, England and France became the two great rivals for leadership in Europe, control of the seas, and possession of India and North America. Competing for dominance, the two countries fought each other in a succession of wars during the 17th and 18th centuries.

RIVALRY BETWEEN FRANCE AND ENGLAND IN NORTH AMERICA

The underlying causes of Anglo-French rivalry in North America were conflicting territorial claims and competition over the fur trade. When war broke out in Europe between France and England in 1689, the American colonists were drawn into the struggle. In the next 74 years, the French and English fought four intercolonial wars in North America. The first three originated in Europe but soon spread to the colonies, where they were known as King William's War (1689–1697), Queen Anne's War (1701–1713), and King George's War (1744–1748). In the course of these conflicts, the French and their Indian allies often raided English frontier settlements, and the English unsuccessfully tried to conquer Canada.

The fourth and conclusive struggle, the French and Indian War (1754–1763), differed from the other three in that it broke out in North America and later spread to Europe.

CAUSES OF THE FRENCH AND INDIAN WAR

The immediate cause of the French and Indian War was a dispute between France and England over possession of land west of the Appalachians. The conflict arose in the 1740's when traders from the English colonies began to extend their operations beyond the Appalachians into the Ohio Valley. (See map, page 64.) This development brought the English into competition with the French for the Indian fur trade. English colonists also looked to the fertile valley as a place to found new settlements.

Insisting that the land was theirs, the French in 1753 began to build a chain of forts from Lake Erie southward to the Ohio River. Asserting Britain's claim to the area, Governor Robert Dinwiddie of Virginia sent George Washington, a 21-year-old surveyor and fellow Virginian, into the area to demand that the French leave the Ohio Valley. The French refused.

OUTBREAK OF THE FRENCH AND INDIAN WAR (1754)

The French next built a fort, called *Fort Duquesne*, at the point where the Allegheny and Monongahela rivers join to form the Ohio River. This strategic site (the location of present-day Pittsburgh) was the key to the Ohio Valley and a gateway to the West.

Governor Dinwiddie responded to the challenge by sending a force of militia, under Washington, to seize Fort Duquesne. About 40 miles from the fort, the colonials defeated a small detachment of French soldiers and then hastily built an outpost, which they named *Fort Necessity*. The French, however, returned with reinforcements and forced the Virginians to surrender. Washington and his men were permitted to return home. This action in 1754 marked the opening of the war.

Comparison of the English and French Colonies (1754)

The English Colonies	The French Colonies
1. The settler population was 1,250,000, concentrated in 13 colonies along the Atlantic seaboard.	1. The settler population of New France was 80,000, widely scattered over an area 20 times the size of the English possessions.
2. The English colonies were firmly established and largely self-sufficient. Agriculture, the leading occupation, was the basis of permanent settlement. Other occupations included shipbuilding, lumbering, manufacturing, and commerce.	2. The French devoted themselves mainly to fur trading with the Indians. Though this activity was a source of great wealth, it did not encourage permanent settlement. French settlers depended upon imports from Europe to a larger extent than did English settlers.
3. Each of the 13 English colonies was a separate governmental unit. Authority was divided between the officials appointed by the English government and the elected representatives of the settlers. The separate colonies had great difficulty in uniting, even against a common danger.	3. The government of New France was highly centralized. The king and his officials exercised complete authority. In the French colonies, a plan of action could be put into effect swiftly.
4. Relations with the Indians were generally poor. The Indians feared the English because settlers had occupied their land and cut down their forests, thus spoiling their hunting grounds and forcing them to move. Only the Iroquois Confederacy sided with the British* against the French.	4. The French established friendly relations with many Indian groups. French fur traders and missionaries treated the Indians well and helped them in many ways. The Algonquins, Hurons, and most other tribes supported the French against the English.

*When England and Scotland merged in 1707, the combined countries adopted the name "Great Britain." Since that time, "Great Britain" (or simply "Britain") and "England" have been used interchangeably—as have the terms "British" and "English."

AN INTERCOLONIAL CONGRESS IS HELD IN ALBANY

With the threat of war overhanging the colonists, representatives of seven of the colonies met at Albany, New York, in 1754. The purposes of the *Albany Congress* were (1) to secure the allegiance of the Iroquois Confederacy, and (2) to unite the colonies in matters of defense. To accomplish these objectives, Benjamin Franklin, representing Pennsylvania, proposed the *Albany Plan of Union*. It provided for a congress of delegates representing all the colonies. This "grand council" would have the power to maintain an army, levy taxes, negotiate with the Indians, and control westward expansion of settlements.

The colonial legislatures and the British government both rejected the plan. England rejected it because it believed that a union of the colonies would make them too strong. The colonies rejected it because each was unwilling to give up any of its powers of local government to a grand council. Although defeated, the Albany Plan was an important milestone on the road to union.

THE ENGLISH SUFFER DEFEATS IN THE EARLY PART OF THE WAR

1. Braddock's Defeat (1755). Edward Braddock was sent by England to command the British forces in North America. In his first campaign, he led an army of English troops and colonial militia against Fort Duquesne. Unfamiliar with wilderness warfare, Braddock marched into a trap a few miles from the fort. A combined force of French and Indians, hidden behind trees and rocks, surprised the British. Braddock was mortally wounded and his army completely routed. Braddock's aide, Washington, rallied the survivors and led them back to safety.

2. Further English Reverses. In the next few years, the British lost such key outposts as Fort Oswego on Lake Ontario and Fort William Henry on Lake George. They also suffered heavy losses in an unsuccessful attack on Fort Ticonderoga in New York, and failed to capture Louisbourg, the strategic French naval base in Nova Scotia.

JOIN, or DIE.

This famous cartoon appeared in Benjamin Franklin's newspaper, the *Pennsylvania Gazette*, shortly before the Albany Congress convened in 1754.

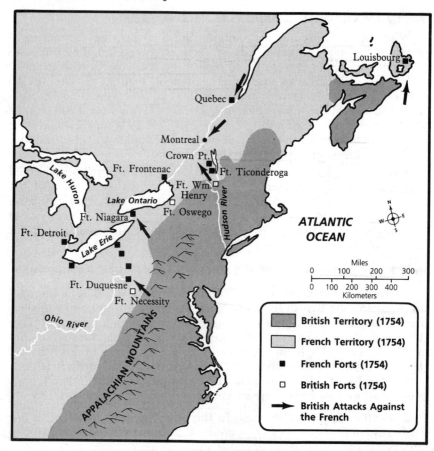

The French and Indian War

THE TIDE TURNS AFTER PITT ASSUMES LEADERSHIP IN ENGLAND

When William Pitt became Prime Minister of Great Britain in 1757, the situation immediately began to improve. Pitt sent reinforcements and supplies to America, appointed able officers to lead the troops, obtained greater support for the war effort from the colonial legislatures, and instilled new spirit into the people, both in England and in the colonies. In 1758 the British and colonials conquered Louisbourg. They drove the French from Fort Duquesne and renamed it Fort Pitt. In 1759 they captured Fort Niagara in western New York, and took over the French forts at Ticonderoga and Crown Point in northeastern New York.

THE ENGLISH CONQUER CANADA

The city of Quebec was the most powerful French stronghold in North America. It was situated on a high cliff overlooking the St. Lawrence River and seemed incapable of capture. In 1759 a British fleet, carrying 9,000 British troops under the command of James Wolfe, sailed up the river and laid siege to the city. For four months Wolfe tried unsuccessfully to crack Quebec's defenses. Finally, he risked a surprise maneuver. In the dead of night, he landed his men at the foot of a cliff near the city and climbed the steep heights, which the French had considered unscalable. The next morning, on the Plains of Abraham, a desperate battle was fought in which both Wolfe and the Marquis de Montcalm, the French commander, were killed. The British defeated the French and captured the city. The *Battle of Quebec* was the decisive battle of the war.

The following year the British took Montreal, thus completing their conquest of the French Empire in North America.

TREATY OF PARIS (1763)

Under the terms of the Treaty of Paris, France ceded Canada and all the land east of the Mississippi River (except New Orleans) to Britain. New Orleans and the region that France claimed west of the Mississippi went to Spain. Spain, an ally of France, ceded Florida to England in exchange for Cuba, which Britain had seized during the war. France retained two small islands in the Gulf of St. Lawrence for fishing stations, and several islands in the West Indies.

EFFECTS OF THE FRENCH AND INDIAN WAR

1. **Upon England.** (*a*) Great Britain emerged from the war as the strongest nation in the world and the dominant power in North America.

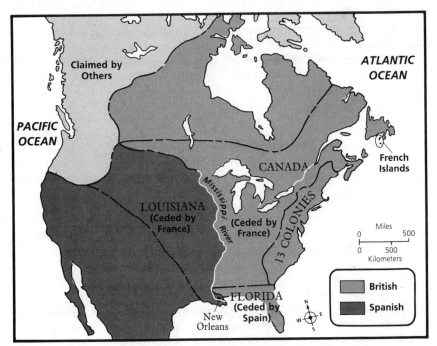

North America After the Treaty of Paris (1763)

(b) Heavily in debt as a result of the war, Britain began to look to its American colonies for additional revenue.

2. Upon the Colonies. (a) With the removal of the French menace, the colonists became less dependent on the mother country for protection. (b) The war shaped the colonists into experienced soldiers and taught them the importance of unity and cooperation. (c) The victory assured the survival of English ideas, language, and institutions in North America.

Multiple-Choice Test

1. A military outpost built by George Washington in western Pennsylvania in 1754 was (a) Fort William Henry (b) Fort Oswego (c) Fort Pitt (d) Fort Necessity.
2. The Albany Plan of Union was drawn up by (a) Samuel Adams (b) Benjamin Franklin (c) George Washington (d) Edward Braddock.
3. Which country lost all its territory on the mainland of North America in 1763? (a) England (b) Spain (c) France (d) Holland.
4. In the French and Indian War, the Iroquois Confederacy was (a) on Britain's side (b) on France's side (c) neutral (d) against both countries.
5. The French and Indian War broke out over conflicting claims by England and France to the (a) St. Lawrence Valley (b) Hudson Valley (c) Mississippi Valley (d) Ohio Valley.
6. One of the underlying causes of the French and Indian War was Anglo-French rivalry over (a) possession of Florida (b) control of the Middle Atlantic coastal regions (c) ownership of gold deposits (d) control of the fur trade.
7. The influence of the early French on American culture has been felt most in (a) Louisiana (b) California (c) Florida (d) Massachusetts.
8. The Treaty of Paris of 1763 fixed the western boundary of the 13 colonies at the (a) Missouri River (b) Appalachian Mountains (c) Mississippi River (d) Rocky Mountains.
9. An important result of the French and Indian War was that it (a) ended the Indian menace (b) caused France to cede its claims west of the Mississippi to England (c) made the colonists more dependent upon Britain for protection against European invaders (d) fostered a spirit of intercolonial cooperation.
10. The intercolonial wars fought between the French and the English in North America from 1689 to 1748 included all of the following EXCEPT (a) King George's War (b) Queen Anne's War (c) King William's War (d) King Philip's War.

Completion Test

1. The French were defeated at the Battle of Quebec by the British under the command of _____.
2. Fort Duquesne, an important outpost during the French and Indian War, is now the site of the city of _____.

3. In an attempt to capture Fort Duquesne, General _____ was badly defeated in 1755 by the French and their Indian allies.
4. During the intercolonial wars between France and England, the Algonquins and the Hurons sided with the _____.
5. The region that the British renamed "Nova Scotia" was originally called _____ by the French.
6. Before 1763, Louisbourg and New Orleans marked the extremities of the _____ Empire in North America.
7. The Allegheny and Monongahela rivers unite in western Pennsylvania to form the _____ River.
8. Governor _____ of Virginia sent George Washington to warn the French to leave the region south of Lake Erie.
9. The policies instituted in 1757 by _____, Prime Minister of Great Britain, enabled the British to defeat the French in North America.
10. The French commander who was killed on the Plains of Abraham in 1759 was _____.

Essay Questions

1. Compare the French and English colonies in North America with reference to population, occupations, government, and religion.
2. a. List *two* effects of the French and Indian War on England.
   b. List *three* effects of the war on the American colonies.
3. What were the terms of the Treaty of Paris?
4. Of all the countries that attempted to establish colonies in North America, England was the most successful. (*a*) Give *one* reason why France failed to retain control of its empire in America. (*b*) Give *two* reasons why the English were more successful than other peoples in establishing colonies in North America. (*c*) Compare the attitudes of the English and the French toward Indians.

Part 2. Growing Differences With England

ENGLAND'S ATTITUDE TOWARD ITS COLONIES

Like the other colonial powers of Europe, England believed that colonies existed for the benefit of the mother country. England viewed its American possessions as a (1) *source of food and raw materials* that were in short supply at home, and (2) *market for its finished products*. England sought to (1) curb colonial manufacturing that might compete with its own industries, and (2) keep other European countries from sharing in the colonial trade. The policy of regulating colonial commerce in the interest of the mother country was an outgrowth of the economic theory known as *mercantilism*.

ENGLAND IMPOSES TRADE AND MANUFACTURING REGULATIONS

Starting in 1650, England passed a series of trade regulations called the Navigation Acts. (1) No goods could be shipped to or from any colony except in English ships. (2) Certain articles produced in the colonies could be sold only to England. These *enumerated* (listed) articles included tobacco, indigo, sugar, rice, furs, and naval stores. (3) European goods destined for the colonies must first be sent to England (where duties could be collected) and reshipped from there on English ships. Then, in 1733, Parliament adopted the *Molasses Act*, placing heavy duties on sugar and molasses imported by the colonists from the French West Indies.

Laws were also enacted to restrict colonial manufacturing. (1) The *Woolen Act* (1699) forbade the export of woolen goods either overseas or from one colony to another. (2) The *Hat Act* (1732) banned the export of beaver hats. (3) The *Iron Act* (1750) prohibited the manufacture of iron products (tools, utensils, and hardware).

THE REGULATIONS HAVE LITTLE EFFECT AT FIRST

For many years these regulations did not seriously interfere with colonial trade. Too involved in European wars and empire building to pay much attention to its American colonies, England made little attempt to enforce the acts strictly. The colonists, in turn, generally ignored them. Smuggling became a widespread practice in all the colonies.

ENGLAND'S COLONIAL POLICY CHANGES

With the close of the French and Indian War, England's policy toward its American colonies stiffened. It felt that the colonists had benefited by the defeat of the French in North America and should help pay the cost of the war. England was faced with a large debt and heavy taxes at home. Furthermore, it had to bear the expense of maintaining an army in America to protect colonists against Indian attacks. To raise additional revenue, England decided not only to enforce the existing trade laws but to introduce new taxes as well.

Realizing that its hold on the colonies was weak, England also decided to strengthen its political control over them. During the wars with France, the English government had found it difficult to raise colonial troops and to stop colonial merchants from illegally trading with the Spanish and French.

ENGLAND'S NEW POLICY IN ACTION

1. Writs of Assistance. Even before the French and Indian War ended, the colonists showed that they would oppose any attempt by England to impose stricter controls on trade. In 1761 officials began to use *writs of assistance* to curb illegal colonial trade with foreign nations. These writs were general search warrants that permitted customs officers to enter and search any ship, home, or warehouse for smuggled goods.

Reaction. James Otis, a Boston lawyer representing a group of Massachusetts merchants, challenged the legality of the writs. He asserted that their use was an act of tyranny and that they violated a fundamental right of English people: to be free from unreasonable searches and seizures. When the courts ruled that the writs were legal, the British continued their use until the Revolution. Otis' arguments rallied public opinion against the writs, and the colonists continued to protest their use.

2. Proclamation of 1763. *Pontiac*, a chief of the Ottawa Indians, led the Western tribes in a war against the English. Before he was finally defeated, he had destroyed most of the British frontier forts and killed many settlers. To avoid further trouble with the Indians, Britain issued the *Proclamation of 1763*. This act (*a*) ordered all settlers in the Ohio Valley to move back east, (*b*) forbade the establishment of new settlements west of the Appalachians, and (*c*) prohibited traders from entering the region without government approval.

Reaction. The colonists, especially those on the frontier, resented the proclamation. They regarded it as an attempt by England to keep them from developing the new, fertile lands that they had helped win from the French. Many pioneers ignored the proclamation and migrated westward into the forbidden area.

3. Sugar Act (1764). *George Grenville*, British Prime Minister from 1763 to 1765, was largely responsible for shaping England's new colonial policy. Among other things, he persuaded Parliament to pass the *Sugar Act*. (*a*) This law raised duties on refined sugar, textiles, and other goods imported from any place other than Britain or a British colony. (*b*) To discourage smuggling, the new law lowered the duty on molasses. (*c*) The act also added more products to the list of enumerated articles that could be sold only to England.

In addition, Grenville took steps to enforce the Navigation Acts. He sent more customs officers to America and assigned royal inspectors and naval patrols to wipe out smuggling.

Reaction. The merchants of New England and the Middle Colonies complained that the higher import duties and the strict enforcement of the trade laws would ruin the colonial economy. In defiance of the law, they continued to smuggle goods into the country and to carry on trade with foreign nations.

4. Quartering Act (1765). This act of Parliament required the colonial legislatures to provide funds, living quarters, and supplies to help meet the expense of maintaining British troops in America.

Reaction. The colonists objected to England's policy of keeping a large army in America in time of peace and opposed paying for its support. When New York's assembly refused to provide all the supplies requested by the commander of the British troops, Parliament suspended the assembly's legislative powers until it complied.

5. Stamp Tax (1765). Upon Grenville's recommendation, Parliament passed the *Stamp Act.* This law placed a tax on newspapers, almanacs, pamphlets, playing cards, and legal documents (wills, licenses, deeds, etc.). The act required that stamps be purchased from the government and be affixed to these articles.

Reaction. Because it affected all the people, not just a special group as did the trade regulations, the stamp tax stirred up a "hornet's nest" in America. Patriotic societies, known as the *Sons of Liberty*, were formed to organize resistance to the tax. Stamp-tax collectors were mobbed and driven from their homes. Merchants pledged to halt the import of British goods, and people vowed to *boycott* (stop buying) English products until the tax was repealed. At the urging of *Patrick Henry*, the Virginia House of Burgesses passed a resolution asserting that it had the sole power to tax Virginians. "No taxation without representation" was the slogan of the day.

A high point in the colonial protest came in the fall of 1765 when delegates from nine colonies convened the *Stamp Act Congress* in New York City. Demanding the repeal of the stamp tax, the delegates drew up a declaration in which they stated the main arguments of the colonists: (*a*) The colonists were entitled to the "rights of Englishmen." (*b*) Taxation without the consent of the people's own elected representatives was a violation of these rights. (*c*) Since the colonists were not represented in the English Parliament, that body could not impose taxes on them.

The violent colonial opposition to the stamp tax disturbed the British. In England even some prominent leaders, such as William Pitt, spoke out against the tax. More important were the protests of those English merchants who suffered substantial losses because of the colonial boycott. Therefore, Parliament in 1766 repealed the stamp tax but, at the same time, asserted its right to tax the colonies by passing the *Declaratory Act*. It stated that Parliament had full authority over the colonies "in all cases whatsoever."

6. Townshend Acts (1767). Charles Townshend, the new English Chancellor of the Exchequer (treasury), was responsible for Parliament's

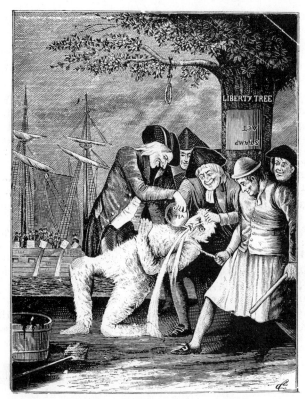

Colonists Humiliate Tax Collector

passage of a series of revenue measures known as the *Townshend Acts*. Under this legislation: (*a*) Duties were levied on colonial imports of glass, lead, paint, paper, and tea. (*b*) The revenue from these duties was to be used to pay the salaries of such colonial officials as governors and judges. (Previously, their salaries had been controlled by the colonial legislatures.) (*c*) The right to use writs of assistance to enforce the Navigation Acts was reaffirmed.

    Reaction. The Massachusetts legislature, under the leadership of *Samuel Adams*, urged the colonies to cooperate in resisting British taxation. The colonists responded with another boycott of English goods.

    The effectiveness of the boycott led to the repeal of all Townshend taxes except the one on tea (1770). This duty, though slight, was kept to show that Parliament retained its right to tax the colonies.

    Although tensions lessened somewhat after the repeal of the Townshend Acts, American Patriots took steps to organize themselves to oppose English policies whenever conditions required united colonial action. In 1772 Samuel Adams issued a call to the towns of Massachusetts to form *Committees of Correspondence* to keep each other informed of new developments. The idea soon spread, and most colonies formed committees for the purpose of maintaining contact with one another.

7. Boston Massacre (1770). In Boston, as elsewhere, there was bitter feeling between colonists and the *redcoats*, as the British troops were called. On one occasion, shortly before the repeal of the Townshend Acts, a crowd of Bostonians shouted insults and threw snowballs at a detachment of British soldiers. The redcoats fired into the crowd, killing five townspeople and wounding six others. (Among those slain was Crispus Attucks, a black man.) This incident became known as the *Boston Massacre.*

Reaction. The angry citizens of Boston, led by Samuel Adams, demanded the removal of the British troops. To prevent an uprising, the governor withdrew the soldiers from the city. News of the Boston Massacre spread throughout the colonies and aroused indignation everywhere.

8. Tea Act (1773). The British East India Company was in financial distress, partly as a result of the colonial boycott of English tea. To save the company from ruin, Parliament passed the *Tea Act*, which allowed the company to ship tea to America without paying the existing heavy duty in England. This exemption enabled the company to undersell the colonial importers of English tea as well as smugglers of foreign tea.

Reaction. Colonial merchants denounced the Tea Act because: (*a*) It gave the East India Company exclusive control of the tea trade in America and would ruin many American tea merchants. (*b*) Parliament could grant similar rights to other English firms and put all colonial merchants out of business.

In New York and Philadelphia, public clamor forced the company to send its loaded ships of tea back to England. In Charleston, the tea was locked up in a warehouse and left to rot. In Boston, the citizens refused to permit the unloading of three tea ships. During the night of December 16, 1773, the *Boston Tea Party* took place. Bostonians disguised as Indians boarded the ships and dumped 342 chests of tea (worth $75,000) into the harbor.

9. Intolerable Acts (1774). Parliament moved quickly to punish Massachusetts for the Boston Tea Party and to reassert its authority over the colonies. It passed four coercive laws that the colonists called the *Intolerable Acts.* They included the following measures:

a. The port of Boston was closed to all commerce until the colonists paid for the destroyed tea.

b. The people of Massachusetts were deprived of the right to elect officials, to select jurors, and to hold town meetings. Thomas Gage, British commander-in-chief in America, was appointed military governor of the colony.

c. British soldiers and officials accused of crimes in Massachusetts were to be tried in England, not in the colony.

d. A new Quartering Act required the people in all the colonies to feed and house British soldiers.

Parliament also passed an act extending the boundary of the Canadian province of Quebec southward to the Ohio River. Although the *Quebec Act* was not intended as a measure to punish the colonists, people in the colonies regarded it as another "intolerable act" because it (1) gave to Canada territories claimed by several of the 13 colonies, and (2) imposed upon settlers in the Ohio Valley the centralized, undemocratic governmental structure that the Canadians had inherited from the French.

Reaction. With Boston Harbor closed to commerce, the people of the city faced economic ruin. The other colonies rallied to support Boston by sending food and supplies to the stricken city. Some colonial leaders warned that the measures adopted by the British government to punish Massachusetts endangered the liberties of all the colonies. Others declared that Massachusetts was "suffering in the common cause of America." There was widespread agreement that united action was necessary, and a call went out to convene an intercolonial congress.

THE FIRST CONTINENTAL CONGRESS (1774)

Delegates from all the colonies except Georgia met in Philadelphia in September, 1774. At this *First Continental Congress*, the delegates took the following steps:

1. They issued a *Declaration of Rights and Grievances*, stating that (a) colonists were entitled to all "the rights of Englishmen," and (b) colonial legislatures had the exclusive right to levy taxes on the colonists (subject only to veto by the king).

The declaration denounced the Intolerable Acts as unjust, unconstitutional, and destructive of American rights. It also criticized the British government for (a) enacting revenue measures, (b) dissolving colonial assemblies, and (c) maintaining a standing army in the colonies in peacetime.

2. They entered into an agreement (called the *Continental Association*) not to trade with Britain or to use English goods until the offensive legislation was repealed. Committees were to be formed in each community to see that the boycott was carried out and to make the names of violators public.

3. They agreed to meet again the following spring if colonial grievances were not settled by then.

THE FIRST SHOT IS FIRED

Anticipating trouble, the citizens of Massachusetts began to expand and strengthen their local militia units. They called themselves *Minutemen*, since they stood ready for action at a minute's notice. They drilled regularly and armed themselves with ammunition and weapons. In defiance of Thomas Gage, the British military governor, the Massachusetts assembly met secretly and prepared for war. Gage sent troops to capture the "rebel" ringleaders, John Hancock and Samuel Adams, who were rumored to be in Lexington, and to seize stores of gunpowder hidden in Concord.

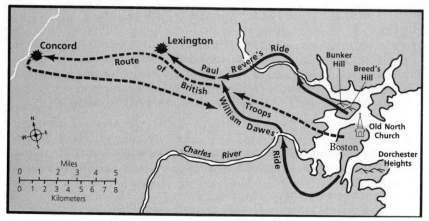

Outbreak of the Revolution

Some colonists, however, learned of Gage's plans. Two Patriots, *Paul Revere* and *William Dawes*, rode through the night and warned the countryside of the oncoming British. When the British troops arrived at Lexington the next day (April 19, 1775), they were met by the local Minutemen. In an exchange of shots, 18 colonials were killed or wounded. The British then proceeded to Concord, and another skirmish took place. As the English marched back to their base in Boston, the aroused colonials, hiding behind houses, trees, and stone walls, poured a steady fire into the redcoats. Almost 4,000 Americans participated in the action that day. The British suffered 273 casualties, the colonials suffered 93.

In March, 1775, just before the outbreak of hostilities in Massachusetts, Patrick Henry delivered a speech urging that Virginia prepare for war. He closed with "Is life so dear, or peace so sweet, as to be purchased at the price of chains and slavery? Forbid it, Almighty God! I know not what course others may take; but as for me, give me liberty, or give me death!"

"Disperse, ye rebels; lay down your arms." — British officer to Minutemen at Lexington.

"Stand your ground. Don't fire unless fired upon; but if they mean to have a war, let it begin here!" — Captain John Parker's order to the Minutemen at Lexington.

> By the rude bridge that arched the flood,
> Their flag to April's breeze unfurled,
> Here once the embattled farmers stood,
> And fired the shot heard round the world.
> —*Concord Hymn*, Ralph Waldo Emerson

Multiple-Choice Test

1. In 1774 England passed the Intolerable Acts in order to punish (a) Williamsburg for Patrick Henry's speech (b) New York City for refusing to provide quarters for British troops (c) Boston for dumping tea into the harbor (d) Philadelphia for holding the First Continental Congress.
2. Committees of Correspondence were organized in Massachusetts by (a) Paul Revere (b) Samuel Adams (c) Patrick Henry (d) James Otis.
3. General search warrants were called (a) bills of lading (b) writs of habeas corpus (c) bills of rights (d) writs of assistance.
4. According to the theory of trade that the colonial powers of Europe practiced, (a) the mother country existed for the benefit of the colonies (b) colonies were free to do as they wished (c) colonies existed for the benefit of the mother country (d) colonies were unimportant to the mother country.
5. England first restricted colonial trade by the (a) Navigation Acts (b) Stamp Act (c) Intolerable Acts (d) Declaratory Act.
6. The Boston Tea Party was a (a) colonial social custom (b) major battle (c) party given by the governor of Massachusetts (d) protest against English trade regulations.
7. England adopted a firmer policy toward its American colonies during the reign of (a) King James II (1685–1688) (b) Queen Elizabeth I (1558–1603) (c) King George III (1760–1820) (d) King Henry VIII (1509–1547).
8. The First Continental Congress was called as a result of the (a) Townshend Acts (b) Sugar Act (c) Stamp Act (d) Intolerable Acts.
9. The statement "No taxation without representation" protested taxation of the English colonies by (a) royal governors (b) the king of England (c) colonial assemblies (d) Parliament.
10. Who said "Give me liberty or give me death"? (a) Patrick Henry (b) George Washington (c) Benjamin Franklin (d) John Parker.
11. The place generally associated with the phrase "the shot heard round the world" is (a) Fort Ticonderoga (b) Concord (c) Boston (d) Fort Duquesne.
12. A young Virginian who opposed interference by England in colonial affairs was (a) William Dawes (b) William Penn (c) John Adams (d) Patrick Henry.
13. All of the following were colonial steps toward union EXCEPT the (a) Albany Congress (b) Declaratory Act (c) New England Confederation (d) Stamp Act Congress.
14. Many colonists objected to the Proclamation of 1763 because it (a) limited the issuance of paper money (b) prohibited settlement on Western lands (c) increased the tax on sugar imported from the French West Indies (d) required colonial authorities to provide housing for British troops stationed in America.
15. The colonists' main objection to the stamp tax was that it (a) discouraged foreign trade (b) hindered colonial manufacturing (c) infringed upon their rights as English people (d) favored lawyers and publishers at the expense of farmers.

16. All of the following enactments of Parliament attempted to curb colonial manufacturing EXCEPT the (*a*) Hat Act (*b*) Tea Act (*c*) Woolen Act (*d*) Iron Act.

17. The French, Spanish, and English colonies in the New World were most similar in that they all (*a*) welcomed anyone who wished to settle in their midst (*b*) were permitted representative legislative assemblies (*c*) were regulated by their mother countries in matters relating to trade and industry (*d*) enjoyed religious freedom.

18. Actions taken by all of the following English leaders aroused the anger of the colonists in the years between 1763 and 1775 EXCEPT (*a*) William Pitt (*b*) Charles Townshend (*c*) George Grenville (*d*) Thomas Gage.

19. Citizens of Massachusetts who banded into militia groups and secretly prepared for war were called (*a*) Associators (*b*) Redcoats (*c*) Minutemen (*d*) Bluecoats.

20. Which of the following events occurred LAST? (*a*) The Albany Congress convened. (*b*) The port of Boston was closed to commerce. (*c*) The Navigation Acts were passed. (*d*) The Stamp Act Congress met.

Modified True-False Test

1. Patriotic societies, called the *Sons of Liberty*, were formed to resist the Stamp Tax.

2. In the years preceding the Revolution, the colonists formed *Societies of Cooperation* to maintain contact with one another. Committees of Correspondence

3. *Andrew Hamilton*, a Boston lawyer, rallied public opinion against the use of writs of assistance. James Otis

4. William Dawes and *John Hancock* rode through the night to warn the populace that the British were coming. Paul Revere

5. The practice of secretly bringing goods into a country to avoid payment of import duties is called *mercantilism*. Smuggling

6. The name of the Indian chief whose actions led to the Proclamation of 1763 was *Squanto*. Pontiac

7. Prime Minister *William Pitt* launched Britain's new colonial policy in 1763. Grenville

8. The law passed by Parliament that required colonists to house and feed British troops was the *Quartering Act*.

9. In 1765 the colonists convened the *First Continental* Congress to discuss united action against the tax imposed by Parliament that year. Stamp Act Congress

10. Duties were levied on glass, paper, paint, and tea by the *Townshend* Acts.

11. The practice of refusing to buy products made by a particular manufacturer or imported from a particular country is called a *lockout*. boycott

12. In 1770 British soldiers fired into a mob of New England townspeople in an incident that became known as the *shot heard round the world*. Boston Massacre

13. The British *South Seas* Company was granted a virtual monopoly of the tea trade in the American colonies. East India

14. The colonists considered the *Declaratory* Act intolerable because it gave to Canada territories claimed by Virginia and several other colonies. Quebec

15. In 1774 the colonies made an agreement, called the *Continental Association*, to halt trade with Britain and to stop using English goods.

Essay Questions

1. (*a*) What is meant by "taxation without representation"? (*b*) Name *three* taxes to which the colonists objected. (*c*) Explain how the colonists tried to have each of these taxes abolished.
2. a. Rearrange the following events by placing them in the order in which they occurred:

   > Formation of the first Committees of Correspondence
   > First Continental Congress
   > New England Confederation
   > Albany Congress
   > Stamp Act Congress

   b. Explain how *two* of the above promoted union among the colonies.
3. (*a*) Why did some colonists convene an intercolonial conference in 1774? (*b*) Name and describe the provisions of the document issued by the delegates at this conference. (*c*) Upon what other decision did the delegates agree?

Part 3. The War for Independence

THE SECOND CONTINENTAL CONGRESS

In May, 1775, at the State House (later called Independence Hall) in Philadelphia, the *Second Continental Congress* assembled. John Hancock of Massachusetts was elected president. The delegates were faced with the choice of giving in to the mother country or of continuing to resist until colonial grievances were satisfied. They decided to resist, by force if necessary.

To provide for the defense of the colonies, Congress (1) established a *Continental Army*, which included the Minutemen around Boston, (2) appointed George Washington commander-in-chief of this army, and (3) issued a call to the colonies to raise troops and help pay for the war effort.

(4) At the same time, however, the delegates reaffirmed their loyalty to the British crown. They appealed to King George III to prevent further hostile action by Great Britain, so that peaceful relations might be reestablished.

FIGHTING BETWEEN COLONIES AND MOTHER COUNTRY EXPANDS

1. Ticonderoga and Crown Point. In Vermont, Ethan Allen organized a group of Patriots called the *Green Mountain Boys*. They secretly crossed Lake Champlain into northeastern New York and captured the British forts at Ticonderoga and Crown Point (May, 1775). Badly needed cannon and ammunition were seized and sent to the aid of the Americans in the Boston area.

> "Surrender in the name of the great Jehovah and the Continental Congress."— Ethan Allen at Fort Ticonderoga.

2. Battle of Bunker Hill. After the fighting at Lexington and Concord, about 10,000 militiamen set up camps around Boston. As more and more colonials came to their aid, they decided to drive the British from the city. In order to obtain a commanding position over the city and the harbor, the American forces secretly occupied Breed's Hill (near Bunker Hill) and began to fortify it (June, 1775). The next day, the British tried to seize the hill but were repulsed with heavy losses in their first two attempts. When the British made their third charge, the colonials' supply of ammunition ran out, and the redcoats captured the position. In this Battle of Bunker Hill (actually fought on Breed's Hill), the Americans inflicted far more casualties than they suffered, and proved their courage and fighting ability.

78

The war in the Boston area ended in March 1776, after Lexington, Concord, Bunker Hill. Washington seized Dorchester Heights (overlooks Boston) and British were at the mercy of the cannon mounted on these heights. Howe withdrew his troops freeing the city of occupation.

"Don't fire until you see the whites of their eyes."—William Prescott's instructions to the Continental soldiers during the Battle of Bunker Hill.

(March 1776)

3. Freeing of Boston. Two weeks after the Battle of Bunker Hill, *(Actually fought on Breed Hill)* George Washington arrived in the Boston area to assume command of the Continental Army. His first tasks were to organize his forces, drill his troops, and plan his strategy. The following spring (March, 1776), the Americans seized Dorchester Heights, a position overlooking Boston Harbor, and fortified it with the artillery captured at Fort Ticonderoga. The British were now at the mercy of the cannon mounted on these heights. William Howe, who had succeeded Gage as commander-in-chief, was forced to withdraw his troops from Boston, and the city was freed from British occupation.

4. Invasion of Canada. Hoping to gain the support of the French colonists in the province of Quebec, the Americans daringly launched a two-pronged invasion of Canada in the fall of 1775. One column, led by Richard Montgomery, pushed up along Lake Champlain, captured Montreal, and proceeded to the city of Quebec. Here it was joined by another force, under Benedict Arnold, which had made a very difficult march across the interior of Maine. The combined attack on Quebec ended in failure. Montgomery was killed, Arnold was wounded, and many Americans were taken prisoner. The colonials then attempted to besiege Quebec but finally retreated to Ticonderoga in the spring of 1776 when British reinforcements drove them off.

5. Fighting in the South. In North Carolina an army of 1,500 Loyalists (colonists who sided with the mother country) was severely defeated by the Patriots at Moore's Creek Bridge early in 1776. Later that year, the British attempted to attack Charleston, South Carolina, but were driven off by the Americans.

THE COLONISTS MOVE CLOSER TOWARD INDEPENDENCE *(Paine's Common Sense)*

Even while bitter fighting was going on, many colonists still hoped for reconciliation with the mother country. Such an outcome, however, grew less probable as the months passed. King George III was stubbornly determined to force the colonials to bow to England's authority. He proclaimed them to be in a state of rebellion and approved an act of Parliament closing the colonies to all trade and commerce. He also hired *Hessians* (soldiers from Hesse, in Germany) to help put down the uprising.

These moves infuriated the colonists. People began to talk of complete separation from England. *Thomas Paine*, a recent immigrant from England, greatly spurred the movement for independence by his pamphlet, *Common Sense*. In it he ridiculed the British monarchy, argued that it was absurd for a whole continent to be controlled by a small island 3,000 miles away, and called upon America to sever its ties with Britain. Thousands of people were swayed by Paine's arguments.

Meanwhile the Second Continental Congress began to exercise the functions of a central government as it (1) established an intercolonial post office with Benjamin Franklin as postmaster general, (2) sent emissaries abroad to seek foreign aid, (3) organized a navy and authorized American vessels to attack English ships, and (4) proclaimed the opening of colonial ports to trade with all countries except Great Britain.

Comparison of American and British Strengths and Weaknesses

American Strengths	American Weaknesses
1. A great leader—George Washington. 2. Fighting for homes and freedom. 3. Conditioned by pioneer life to hardship. 4. Received military and financial aid from foreign countries. 5. Accustomed to the use of firearms. 6. Military experience gained in the struggles against both the Indians and the French. 7. Fighting on familiar ground.	1. One-third of the people, known as *Tories* or *Loyalists,* opposed the rebellion and remained loyal to the mother country. 2. Inadequate financial resources; paper money (called *Continentals*), issued in great quantity, soon lost its value. 3. Virtually no manufacturing facilities; had to rely on foreign purchases for military supplies. 4. Shortage of supplies and ammunition. 5. Short-term enlistments; continuous turnover of men in army. 6. Unaccustomed to military discipline. 7. Lacked a strong navy.

British Strengths	British Weaknesses
1. Well-equipped and well-trained forces. 2. Professional military leadership. 3. Powerful navy capable of transporting troops to the fighting fronts and blockading the American coastline. 4. Able to hire foreign soldiers to supplement its own troops. 5. Possessed the financial means and manufacturing facilities to supply its armies adequately with materials of war. 6. Received the support of American Loyalists.	1. Unaccustomed to wilderness warfare. 2. Leaders underestimated American military ability. 3. Separated from the battlefronts by 3,000 miles of ocean; reinforcements and war orders took months to reach America. 4. Hired soldiers had no interest at stake except their pay. 5. Unable to devote complete effort to the fighting in America because England was also at war with France, Spain, and the Netherlands. 6. Some politicians in England opposed the war; Lord Chatham (William Pitt) and Edmund Burke, leaders of the *Whig* party, sympathized with the American cause.

INDEPENDENCE IS PROCLAIMED (JULY 4, 1776)

In June, 1776, Richard Henry Lee of Virginia introduced a resolution in Congress which stated: "These United Colonies are, and of right ought to be, free and independent states. All political connection between them and Great Britain is, and ought to be, totally dissolved."

Acting upon Lee's resolution, Congress chose a committee to draw up a *Declaration of Independence* (see pages 545–548). This document, most of which was written by Thomas Jefferson, is one of the great cornerstones of democracy. It opens with a statement of the natural rights to which all people are entitled, as follows:

"We hold these truths to be self-evident:

- that all men [people] are created equal;
- that they are endowed by their Creator with certain unalienable rights;
- that among these are life, liberty, and the pursuit of happiness;
- that to secure these rights, governments are instituted among men [people] deriving their just powers from the consent of the governed;
- that whenever any form of government becomes destructive of these ends, it is the right of the people to alter or to abolish it, and to institute new government, laying its foundations on such principles, and organizing its powers in such form, as to them shall seem most likely to effect their safety and happiness."

The document then listed 27 "injuries and usurpations," or acts that King George III and Parliament had committed against the colonists. It pointed out that the colonists had repeatedly petitioned the king to correct these injustices but that their appeals had been ignored. For these reasons, the Declaration concluded, the 13 colonies were dissolving their connection with England and establishing themselves as free and independent states.

The Declaration of Independence was adopted by Congress on July 4, 1776. All ties with Great Britain were now severed, and a new nation, the *United States of America*, was born. The rebellion that had started as an attempt by the colonists to protect their rights as English citizens became a struggle for independence.

> Benjamin Franklin is said to have declared at the signing of the Declaration of Independence: "We must all hang together, or most assuredly we shall all hang separately."

THE BRITISH OCCUPY NEW YORK CITY

After the British abandoned Boston, the war shifted from New England to the Middle Colonies. Recognizing the strategic value of New York City, Washington brought his army to defend the area, while Howe made plans to capture it. In July, 1776, supported by a strong fleet, the British occupied Staten Island. In the next four months they drove the Continental Army from Brooklyn Heights in Long Island, Harlem Heights in Manhattan, and White Plains in Westchester County. Washington's skillful handling of his army prevented its complete destruction by the more powerful enemy. He finally managed to withdraw across the Hudson River to New Jersey, leaving New York City in the hands of the English.

Nathan Hale, a young schoolteacher from Connecticut who became an officer in the Continental Army, volunteered for spy duty behind the British lines to obtain information for Washington. He was captured and sentenced to death by hanging. His last words were: "I only regret that I have but one life to lose for my country."

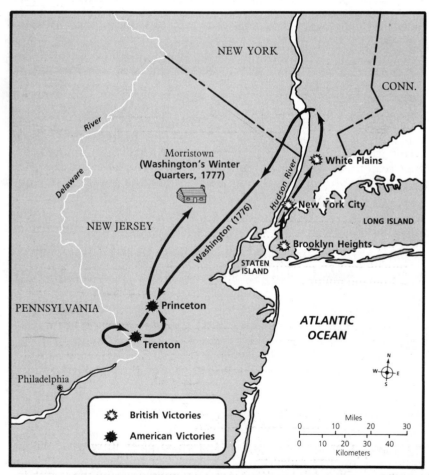

Washington's Campaigns (July, 1776–January, 1777)

BATTLES ARE FOUGHT AT TRENTON AND PRINCETON

Pursued by the British, the battered Continental Army retreated across New Jersey. As the Americans crossed the Delaware River into Pennsylvania, they seized all the boats on the river, thereby preventing the British from following. On Christmas night in 1776, in a blinding storm, Washington led his men across the ice-choked Delaware. He surprised the Hessians encamped in Trenton and completely routed them, capturing nearly 1,000 prisoners and a large quantity of supplies. Thereupon, Howe dispatched a force under Charles Cornwallis to bag "the old fox," as Washington was called. Outmaneuvering the redcoats, Washington defeated two British regiments at Princeton. He then established winter quarters for his troops in the hills around Morristown, New Jersey. The bold strokes at Trenton and Princeton put new hope into the Continentals.

THE BRITISH PLAN TO DIVIDE THE COLONIES

To isolate New England from the other colonies, the British in 1777 planned to conquer New York State by a three-pronged drive, as follows: (1) John Burgoyne was to lead an army southward from Canada along Lake Champlain. (2) Barry St. Leger was to bring another force from Canada to Oswego, on Lake Ontario, and then march eastward through the Mohawk River Valley. (3) William Howe was to lead a third army northward up the Hudson River Valley from New York City. The three were to meet at Albany. (See the map on page 84.)

The British strategy failed. (1) St. Leger encountered fierce resistance in the Mohawk Valley and was forced to retreat to Canada. (2) Howe, for reasons of his own, sent his army to attack Philadelphia, thus failing to carry out his part of the plan. (3) Burgoyne was defeated at Saratoga.

THE AMERICANS WIN A DECISIVE VICTORY AT SARATOGA

According to plan, Burgoyne marched southward from Canada and captured Fort Ticonderoga. From that point on, he ran into trouble. His soldiers became exhausted, supplies ran short, and the aroused settlers fought him every step of the way. To capture American supplies, Burgoyne sent an expedition to Bennington, Vermont. But a force of New England militia met the expedition and routed it. Finally, Burgoyne and his men were surrounded near Saratoga, New York, by a colonial army commanded by Horatio Gates. Two fierce battles followed. Decisively defeated, Burgoyne surrendered his entire army on October 17, 1777.

The American victory in the *Battle of Saratoga* proved to be the turning point of the war. It wrecked the British plan to divide the colonies and boosted Continental morale. It also convinced France to aid the American cause openly.

THE BRITISH CAPTURE PHILADELPHIA

Instead of proceeding up the Hudson to meet Burgoyne, William Howe and his army sailed from New York City to Chesapeake Bay and marched on Philadelphia. Washington attempted to stop the British but

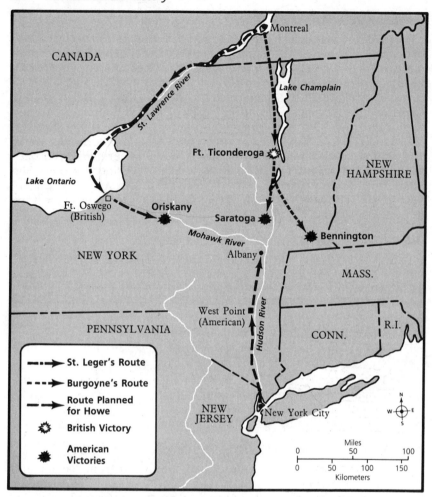

The British Attempt to Divide the Colonies (1777)

was beaten at Brandywine. Howe occupied Philadelphia, the American capital, in September, 1777. When the Americans tried to drive the British from Philadelphia, they were beaten back at nearby Germantown.

Washington then withdrew and set up winter quarters at Valley Forge. That winter (1777–1778) was a bitter experience for the American army. Shelter was inadequate, warm clothing was unobtainable, food was scarce, and pay was irregular. The disheartened troops endured almost unbearable hardships. It is a great tribute to Washington that he was able to keep his army together and have a fighting force ready for the following year's campaigns.

FOREIGN COUNTRIES AID THE AMERICAN CAUSE

Hoping to weaken England, other European powers (such as France, Spain, and Holland) extended help to the American colonists in the form of supplies, credit, and munitions. But they did so secretly. Early

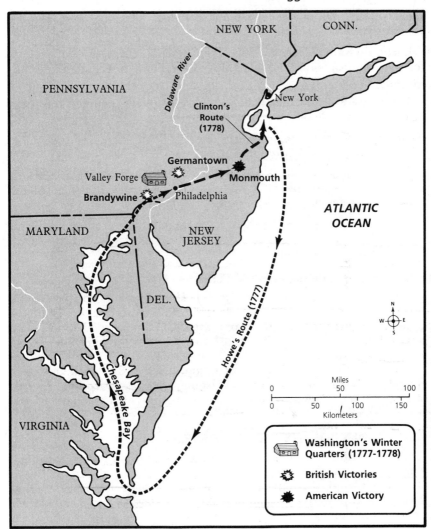

The British Capture, Then Abandon, Philadelphia

in 1778, after the British defeat at Saratoga had shown that an American victory was possible, France entered into an open alliance with the United States. Benjamin Franklin, one of the three commissioners that Congress had sent to France to secure aid and to arrange a treaty, played a key role in the successful negotiations. The two countries signed a military and trade agreement under which France sent money, supplies, a small army, and a fleet of ships to aid the Americans. This assistance played an important role in America's final victory.

FOREIGN VOLUNTEERS HELP THE AMERICANS

In addition to the help provided by foreign governments, America benefited from the efforts of a number of liberty-loving Europeans who came to the aid of the rebellious colonists. Among these foreign volunteers were:

Baron de Kalb, a German-born French army officer, fought valiantly for the Americans until he was killed at the Battle of Camden in South Carolina (1780).

Thaddeus Kosciusko, a Polish military engineer, planned the fortifications at West Point.

Marquis de Lafayette, a wealthy French noble, rendered invaluable service as an aide to Washington.

Casimir Pulaski, a Polish army officer and noble, led a corps of cavalry in the Continental Army. He lost his life at the siege of Savannah, Georgia (1779).

Baron Friedrich von Steuben, a Prussian officer, reorganized and trained the Continentals at Valley Forge. He is often called the "drillmaster of the Revolution."

THE BRITISH ABANDON PHILADELPHIA

Henry Clinton replaced Howe as British commander-in-chief in the spring of 1778. Fearing an attack by the French navy and wishing to concentrate British strength in one area, Clinton decided to evacuate Philadelphia and return to New York City. Washington left Valley Forge and followed the British into New Jersey. In a battle at Monmouth, the Continentals nearly succeeded in routing the English, but the redcoats escaped and reached New York. Washington took up a position north of the city and contained the British within the area for most of the remainder of the war.

CLARK CONQUERS THE OLD NORTHWEST

On the frontier, the British were inciting the Indians to attack American settlements. To end these raids, *George Rogers Clark,* in 1778–1779, led a band of frontier settlers into the region north of the Ohio River. He captured the British forts at Kaskaskia and Cahokia (in present-day Illinois) and at Vincennes (in present-day Indiana). When a British force from Detroit retook Vincennes, Clark and his troops marched nearly 250 miles through the wilderness in the dead of winter, surprised the garrison at Vincennes, and forced its surrender. Thus, the Americans gained control of the Old Northwest.

THE WAR IS ALSO FOUGHT AT SEA

Before the French fleet came to the aid of the Continentals, American seapower consisted of only a few small warships and a number of *privateers* (privately owned merchant vessels and fishing boats that were fitted with guns and authorized to attack enemy ships). These naval units brought supplies and munitions over from Europe. They also seized military equipment en route to the British forces in America, attacked English ships on the high seas, and raided English coastal towns. By the end of the war, they had captured or destroyed nearly 800 British vessels.

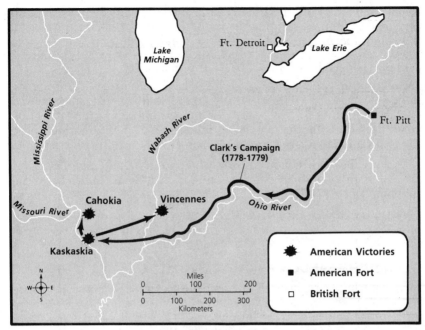

Clark Conquers the Old Northwest

Two of the outstanding naval heroes of the war were *John Paul Jones* and *John Barry.* (1) Jones, a sailor of Scottish descent, seized many English merchant ships and raided the coast of Britain. Commanding the *Bonhomme Richard*, he fought and captured the English warship *Serapis* in the most dramatic naval battle of the Revolution (1779). (2) Barry, a native of Ireland, won fame for his brilliant exploits in capturing British men-of-war.

> During the early part of the naval battle between the *Serapis* and the *Bonhomme Richard*, the American warship suffered severe damage. When the British commander requested his surrender, John Paul Jones replied, "I have not yet begun to fight."

ARNOLD PLANS TO SURRENDER WEST POINT

Benedict Arnold had fought valiantly for the American cause in the early part of the war and had played an important role in the Continental victory at Saratoga. Later, in 1780, he was given command of West Point, a fortress controlling the Hudson River. Soon thereafter, he entered into a plot to surrender this key fort to the British.

Arnold's scheme was discovered when John André, an English officer with whom he was negotiating, was captured with plans of the fort in his possession. Learning of André's capture, Arnold escaped to a British warship in the Hudson River. He was made an officer in the British army and fought against the Patriots for the rest of the war. In America, the name Benedict Arnold has come to mean "traitor."

THE BRITISH ATTEMPT TO CONQUER THE SOUTH

Failing to make headway in New England and the Middle Colonies, the British transferred their activities to the South. At first they enjoyed considerable success. They captured the seaports of Savannah (1778) and Charleston (1780). They next defeated an American army under Gates at Camden, South Carolina (1780). However, a British attempt to

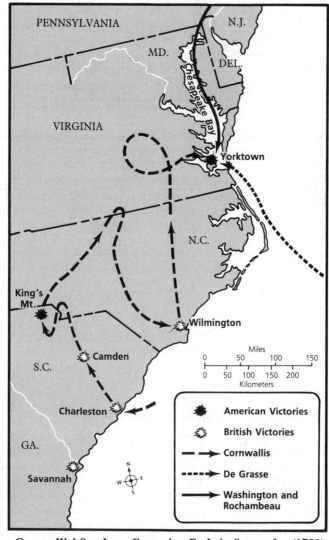

Cornwallis' Southern Campaign Ends in Surrender (1781)

invade North Carolina was beaten back at King's Mountain, in the fall of 1780, by a force of frontier sharpshooters.

Washington sent *Nathanael Greene*, one of his ablest generals, to take charge of the Continental troops in the South. Greene skillfully lured the British army under Cornwallis into the interior of North Carolina, far from its bases of supply on the coast. Though Greene lost nearly every battle, he so weakened the English that they were forced to withdraw to the coast—to Wilmington, North Carolina. Greene then turned south and recaptured most of the inland positions held by the English in South Carolina and Georgia. By the summer of 1781 the British area of occupation in the South had been reduced to the seacoast cities of Savannah, Charleston, and Wilmington.

CORNWALLIS SURRENDERS AT YORKTOWN (Oct. 19, 1781)

Cornwallis brought his army northward from Wilmington and invaded Virginia. He made several attempts to destroy the American forces defending the area, but the outnumbered Continentals, led by Lafayette, succeeded in eluding him. Returning to the Virginia coast, he established a base at Yorktown, near the mouth of Chesapeake Bay (August, 1781). Here he hoped to obtain supplies and reinforcements by sea and to prepare for a more successful campaign the following spring. But he never got the chance.

Washington, who had been keeping watch on Clinton's army in New York, now decided to strike a surprise blow at the British in the South. Together with the French, he devised a plan for trapping the British. Accordingly, a French fleet under François de Grasse sailed to the Yorktown area from the West Indies and sealed off the entrance of Chesapeake Bay. Cornwallis was thus prevented from receiving help by sea. Washington, reinforced by 5,000 French troops under Jean Baptiste Rochambeau, marched his army from New York to Virginia and laid siege to Yorktown.

Cornwallis was now trapped by the combined American and French troops on land and by de Grasse's fleet offshore. After several weeks of desperate fighting, Cornwallis realized that his position was hopeless. On October 19, 1781, he surrendered his entire army of 8,000 soldiers. This was the last major battle of the war.

BRITAIN RECOGNIZES AMERICAN INDEPENDENCE

Although the British still occupied New York City and the Southern seaports, their hopes for victory were shattered. The English people were weary of the war and wanted peace. Early in 1782 Parliament voted to end hostilities and to start peace negotiations. By the *Treaty of Paris*, signed in September, 1783, Britain acknowledged the independence of the 13 colonies. It agreed that the boundaries of the new nation were to be the Atlantic Ocean on the east, the Mississippi River on the west, Canada on the north, and Florida on the south. It also granted Americans full fishing privileges in the Newfoundland area. In addition, England returned Florida to Spain.

Two colonists who performed outstanding service in financing the War for Independence were *Robert Morris*, a Philadelphia banker, and *Haym Salomon*, a Polish Jew who emigrated to America in 1772, settling in New York City and becoming a wealthy merchant. They raised funds to purchase supplies for Washington's armies, obtained loans from abroad, and pledged their own fortunes to support the war effort. Morris has been called the "financier of the Revolution."

The United States (1783)

Multiple-Choice Test

✳ 1. The last major battle of the American Revolution was fought at (a) Bunker Hill (b) Valley Forge (c) Trenton (d) Yorktown.

✳ 2. The first skirmish of the Revolution occurred at (a) Boston (b) Breed's Hill (c) Lexington (d) Ticonderoga.

✳ 3. The Declaration of Independence resulted in (a) the Boston Massacre (b) a change in the purpose of the Revolutionary War (c) the immediate ending of the Revolutionary War (d) the passage of the Intolerable Acts.

✳ 4. The turning point of the American Revolution occurred on New York soil at the battle of (a) Oriskany (b) White Plains (c) Crown Point (d) Saratoga.

✳ 5. At the close of the American Revolution, the western boundary of the United States extended to (a) the Ohio River (b) the Appalachians (c) the Mississippi River (d) Lake Erie.

6. Two foreign military leaders who came to this country to help the colonists fight for independence were (a) de Kalb and Burgoyne (b) Howe and Cornwallis (c) Pulaski and von Steuben (d) Kosciusko and Burke.

✳ 7. The words "all men are created equal" are found in the (a) Fundamental Orders of Connecticut (b) Declaration of Rights and Grievances of 1774 (c) Declaration of Independence of 1776 (d) Maryland Act of Toleration.

8. An outstanding American general in the Revolution was (a) Patrick Henry (b) Nathanael Greene (c) Thomas Jefferson (d) Robert Morris.

✳ 9. The Fourth of July is an important holiday for Americans because on that day (a) the Battle of Lexington was fought (b) the First Continental Congress convened (c) Cornwallis surrendered to Washington (d) the Declaration of Independence was adopted.

✳ 10. Who was the chief author of the Declaration of Independence? (a) Benjamin Franklin (b) Thomas Paine (c) James Madison (d) Thomas Jefferson.

11. Which American general defeated the British at the Battle of Saratoga? (a) Nathanael Greene (b) Richard H. Lee (c) Horatio Gates (d) George Rogers Clark.

12. In the Revolutionary War, aid for the colonies was secured from France largely through the efforts of (a) George Washington (b) Benjamin Franklin (c) Edmund Burke (d) John Hancock.

✳ 13. Which is a fundamental principle of government expressed in the Declaration of Independence? (a) free education as a responsibility of government (b) division of powers between federal and state governments (c) direct election of public officials (d) a government based on the consent of the governed.

14. In which pair is the second event a direct result of the first? (a) British surrender at Saratoga—signing of a treaty of alliance with France (b) Intolerable Acts—Boston Massacre (c) Treaty of 1783—signing of the Declaration of Independence (d) George Washington's assumption of command of the Continental Army—battles at Lexington and Concord.

✳ 15. In 1775–1776 one factor that tended to delay the separation of the colonies from Great Britain was the (a) publication of anti-British pamphlets (b) willingness of King George III to compromise (c) feeling of loyalty to England of many of the colonists (d) military aid supplied to the colonies by France.

16. Important battles of the Revolutionary War occurred at all of the following

places EXCEPT (*a*) Moore's Creek Bridge (*b*) King's Mountain (*c*) New Orleans (*d*) Trenton.

17. New York State was of great importance to the Patriots during the American Revolution for all of the following reasons EXCEPT its (*a*) nearness to Canada (*b*) outlet to the ocean (*c*) location in relation to the other colonies (*d*) great deposits of coal and oil.

18. John Hancock, Robert Morris, and Haym Salomon were alike in that they all (*a*) were immigrants from England (*b*) performed valuable nonmilitary services during the American Revolution (*c*) served as delegates to the Continental Congress (*d*) signed the Declaration of Independence.

19. Thomas Paine wrote a political pamphlet entitled (*a*) *The Impending Crisis* (*b*) *Sense and Sensibility* (*c*) *Common Sense* (*d*) *On to Revolution*.

20. All of the following were English military leaders who fought against the colonists in America EXCEPT (*a*) William Howe (*b*) Barry St. Leger (*c*) Henry Clinton (*d*) Lord Chatham.

Identification Test

1. During a heavy battle that lasted for hours, the captain of the British ship asked me if I had lowered my flag. I shouted in reply, "I have not yet begun to fight."

2. Before I was hanged by the British for spying behind their lines, my last words were, "I only regret that I have but one life to lose for my country."

3. On the night of May 9, I secretly led my force of 83 men across Lake Champlain. The next morning I surprised the British garrison at the fort situated on the western shore of the lake and demanded the surrender of the fort "in the name of the great Jehovah and the Continental Congress."

4. After dark on June 16, we began to erect fortifications on the hill. The next morning our work party was discovered by the British, and we were shelled by their ships in the harbor. Shortly thereafter the British sent an assault force to dislodge us. Realizing that our supply of powder was low and that we had to make every shot count, I gave my men the following order: "Don't fire until you see the whites of their eyes."

5. I worked with Thomas Jefferson and John Adams on the drafting of the Declaration of Independence. When the signing took place, I said, "We must all hang together, or most assuredly we shall all hang separately."

Modified True-False Test

1. During the Revolution, colonists who wanted England to be victorious were called *Loyalists*.

2. The English at Yorktown were led by *Thomas Gage*. Cornwallis

3. The expression "life, liberty, and the pursuit of happiness" appears in the *Declaration of Independence*.

4. The BONHOMME RICHARD, commanded by *John Barry*, defeated the British frigate SERAPIS in a famous naval battle. J. P. Jones

5. *George Washington* was the commander-in-chief of the colonial armies.

6. Paper money issued by the American colonies was called *greenbacks*. Continentals

7. The *Tory* party in England sympathized with the American cause. whig

8. German soldiers hired by the English to fight the colonists were called *Huguenots*. Hessians

9. Cannon captured from the British at *Concord* helped drive the British from the Boston area.   Ft. Ticonderoga

10. The winter of 1777–1778, when Washington encamped at *White Plains*, has been called "the darkest hour of the Revolution."   Valley Forge

Matching Test

Column A	*Column B*
e 1. John Hancock	*a.* General who was defeated at Saratoga
h 2. Ethan Allen	*b.* Aide to Washington
j 3. Richard Montgomery	*c.* American who conquered the Old Northwest
a 4. John Burgoyne	*d.* Naval hero who captured many British war-
b 5. Marquis de Lafayette	ships
i 6. Thaddeus Kosciusko	*e.* First president of the Second Continental
c 7. George Rogers Clark	Congress
d 8. John Barry	*f.* American who attempted to betray West Point
f 9. Benedict Arnold	to the British
g 10. François de Grasse	*g.* Foreign admiral who commanded the fleet at
	Yorktown
	h. Leader of the Green Mountain Boys
	i. Engineer who planned the fortification of
	West Point
	j. General who was killed in an unsuccessful
	attack on Quebec

Essay Questions

1. Explain how *each* of the following contributed to the American Revolution:
   a. mercantilism
   b. "the rights of Englishmen"
   c. the French and Indian War

2. Mention an important historical event relating to the American Revolution connected with each of *five* of the following places: New York City, Philadelphia, Yorktown, Breed's Hill, Valley Forge, Trenton.

3. a. Describe the British plan to conquer New York State.
   b. Give *two* reasons why the battle fought at Saratoga was the major turning point of the American Revolution.

4. Foreign aid played an important role in the American victory over England. (*a*) Why did France come to the aid of the colonists? (*b*) Name *three* Europeans who enlisted in the American cause and describe a contribution made by each.

5. Compare American and British strengths and weaknesses during the Revolutionary War.

UNIT IV. FORMATION OF THE NEW NATION

Part 1. The Constitution Becomes the Supreme Law of the Land

THE NATION UNDER THE ARTICLES OF CONFEDERATION

THE ARTICLES OF CONFEDERATION (1781)

To provide a central government for the new nation, the Continental Congress drew up a written constitution, the *Articles of Confederation*, and in 1777 sent it to the states for *ratification*, or approval. Ratification was delayed until 1781 because of a dispute among the states over conflicting Western land claims.

The Confederation government lacked power and was unable to function efficiently because of certain fundamental weaknesses:

Weakness	Result
1. No provision was made for an executive or judicial branch of government. (Only a legislative branch—Congress—was created.)	1. There was no president to enforce the laws passed by Congress, and there were no federal courts to settle disputes between states or between residents of different states.
2. Congress did not have the power to tax; it could only request funds from the states.	2. Since its requests were either ignored or met only partially, Congress never had enough money to run the government or to meet its financial obligations.
3. The right to regulate currency and to issue money was given to both Congress and the states.	3. So much paper money was issued by Congress and the individual states that such currency lost its value. By the end of the war, "not worth a Continental" became a synonym for worthlessness.
4. Congress lacked the power to regulate trade among the states or with foreign countries.	4. States taxed each other's products, quarreled over navigation rights on rivers that served as boundaries between them, and set up their own systems of tariffs on foreign imports. Foreign nations refused to negotiate commercial agreements with the United States because Congress was unable to enforce them.
5. Each state, regardless of population, had only one vote in Congress.	5. Heavily populated states, such as Virginia and Massachusetts, felt that they were inadequately represented in Congress.

Weakness	Result
6. At least 9 of the 13 states had to approve a measure before it could be passed by Congress; all 13 had to approve an amendment to the Articles.	6. It was difficult to obtain passage of legislation and virtually impossible to amend the Articles.

THE CRITICAL PERIOD (1781–1789)

This period in the life of the new nation is aptly called *critical*. It was a time of such great difficulty for the country that many people feared the United States would collapse. Congress was beset with financial problems, and was unable to maintain law and order or to exercise any real authority. The government lost the respect of foreign nations. The states quarreled among themselves and nearly came to blows over boundary disputes.

Financial distress was widespread. In the summer of 1786, debt-ridden farmers from western Massachusetts, fearing the loss of their farms through mortgage foreclosure, rose in rebellion. They were led by Daniel Shays, a former captain in the Continental Army. The rebels forced the closing of a number of state courts that were prosecuting debtors, and they threatened to seize the federal arsenal in Springfield. To cope with this crisis, Massachusetts raised a large force of militia and finally put down *Shays' Rebellion* (February, 1787).

ACCOMPLISHMENTS OF THE CONFEDERATION

Despite its limitations and weaknesses, the Confederation government succeeded in achieving the following:

1. It led the American people through the last phase of the Revolution and negotiated the Treaty of Paris, which ended the war.

2. It kept the 13 states together until they were ready to accept a stronger plan of union.

3. It laid the foundation for America's later expansion westward by (a) providing for the sale of public land to settlers (see "Ordinance of 1785," page 140), and (b) evolving a plan of government for the Northwest Territory (see "Ordinance of 1787," pages 140–141).

FRAMING THE CONSTITUTION

A CONSTITUTIONAL CONVENTION IS CALLED (1787)

Delegates from Maryland and Virginia met at Washington's home in Mount Vernon, Virginia, in 1785 and succeeded in settling some troublesome problems concerning shipping on the Potomac River. The success of the *Mount Vernon Conference* prompted the Virginia legislature to invite all the states to attend a meeting in 1786 at Annapolis, Maryland, to discuss common problems of commerce and river navigation rights. Only five states were represented at the *Annapolis Convention*.

At the urging of Alexander Hamilton of New York, the conference adopted a resolution calling upon Congress to summon another convention the following year, not only to discuss commercial problems but also to consider ways and means of improving the national government. Although it was reluctant at first, Congress finally endorsed the idea and called a conference. All the states except Rhode Island agreed to attend. This conference eventually became known as the *Constitutional Convention*. It convened at Independence Hall in Philadelphia in May, 1787.

THE DELEGATES

Present at the Constitutional Convention were many of the nation's ablest and best-known leaders. They were politically experienced, conservative, realistic, and well qualified for the task ahead. About half of the 55 delegates were lawyers; most of the others were either planters or merchants.

Among the delegates who distinguished themselves at the Convention were *George Washington* of Virginia, who was elected president of the Convention; *Benjamin Franklin* of Pennsylvania, the popular 81-year-old diplomat and philosopher, whose sound advice and good humor helped settle many disagreements; *James Madison* of Virginia, the "father of the Constitution," whose detailed record of the proceedings is our main source of information on what took place during the conference; *Alexander Hamilton* of New York, who vigorously advocated that the powers of the national government be strengthened; and *Gouverneur Morris* of Pennsylvania, who prepared the final draft of the Constitution. Other noted participants included *James Wilson*, a brilliant lawyer from Pennsylvania, *Roger Sherman* of Connecticut, and *William Paterson* of New Jersey.

Absent from the Convention were many outstanding Revolutionary Patriots. Samuel Adams and John Hancock were not chosen as delegates. Patrick Henry refused to attend because he disapproved of the conference. John Adams and Thomas Jefferson were busy representing the United States abroad—the former, in Britain, and the latter, in France.

CONSTITUTIONAL COMPROMISES

Though the Convention had been called for the purpose of revising the Articles of Confederation, this idea was soon scrapped. The members turned instead to the task of framing a new constitution. During the discussions that ensued, serious differences arose that threatened the success of the Convention. It is to the everlasting credit of the "Founding Fathers" (or "Founders") that a spirit of compromise prevailed and a workable instrument of government was created. The following were the important problems and their solutions:

Problem 1. The large states favored the *Virginia Plan*. This called for representation in Congress to be based on population. The small states, fearful of being outvoted in Congress because of their limited population, supported the *New Jersey Plan*. This proposed that each state have equal representation.

Solution: The Great Compromise (Connecticut Compromise). The problem was solved by creating a Congress consisting of two houses. In the upper house, the *Senate,* each state was to be represented equally by two senators. In the lower house, the *House of Representatives,* each state was to be represented on the basis of population.

Problem 2. To obtain maximum representation but minimum taxation, the Southern states proposed that (*a*) slaves be counted as part of the population in determining representation in the House of Representatives, and (*b*) slaves not be counted for the purpose of direct taxation by the federal government. The Northern states vehemently opposed this plan.

Solution: The Three-Fifths Compromise. The problem was solved by providing that five slaves be counted as three persons for both representation and direct taxation.

Problem 3. The manufacturing and shipping interests of the North wanted Congress to have the power to regulate interstate and foreign commerce. The farming interests of the South feared that Congress might use this power to tax agricultural exports. The South also feared that Congress might prohibit the importation of slaves.

Solution: The Commerce Compromise. The problem was solved by granting Congress the power to regulate interstate and foreign commerce and to levy tariffs on imports. But Congress could not tax exports. Nor could Congress restrict the importation of slaves for a period of 20 years—that is, until 1808.

FEATURES OF THE CONSTITUTION

THE PREAMBLE

In an introduction called the *Preamble,* the delegates stated the general purposes and intentions of the Constitution, as follows:

"We the people of the United States, in order to form a more perfect Union, establish justice, insure domestic tranquility, provide for the common defense, promote the general welfare, and secure the blessings of liberty to ourselves and our posterity, do ordain and establish this Constitution for the United States of America."

SEPARATION OF POWERS: THREE BRANCHES OF GOVERNMENT

The Founders provided that the powers and duties of the federal government be divided among three separate branches: legislative, executive, and judicial.

1. Legislative Branch of Government

   Duty: To make the laws.
   Structure: A *Congress* of two houses.
               a. *Senate*—two members from each state. (The present membership is 100.)

        b. House of Representatives—members from each state on the basis of population. (The present membership is 435.)

2. Executive Branch of Government

    Duty: To enforce the laws.

    Structure: A *President* to serve as the Chief Executive; a *Vice President;* and numerous executive assistants appointed by the President. (At present there are 14 executive departments and many administrative agencies to assist the President in carrying out the laws. The heads of the executive departments serve on the President's advisory board, or *Cabinet.*)

3. Judicial Branch of Government

    Duty: To interpret the laws.

    Structure: A *Supreme Court* and lower federal courts. (At present the Supreme Court is made up of nine justices, one of whom serves as Chief Justice. The lower courts consist of 13 *courts of appeals,* 94 *district courts,* and several special courts.)

CHECKS AND BALANCES

The framers of the Constitution set up a system of *checks and balances.* This system gives each branch of government enough power to prevent another branch from becoming too powerful.

1. Legislative Checks. Congress can check the President by refusing to appropriate money for an executive department. It can also refuse to authorize the creation of new administrative agencies and can abolish existing ones. The Senate can reject a treaty made by the President. (A two-thirds vote of the Senate is required to ratify a treaty.) It can reject presidential appointments by a majority vote. The House of Representatives has the power to *impeach* the President, that is, to charge that official with wrongdoing. The Senate has the power to try the President on such charges.

Congress can check the judiciary by its power to create or abolish lower federal courts. Congress can also impeach federal judges.

The Senate and House can check each other, since a bill must be passed by both houses before it becomes law.

2. Executive Checks. Presidents can check Congress with their power to veto bills. (Congress may override presidential vetoes by a two-thirds vote of both houses.) Presidents can check the courts with their power to appoint federal judges (with the approval of the Senate). They may also pardon persons convicted by the courts.

3. Judicial Checks. The judiciary can check the other two branches by declaring acts of Congress and actions of the President *unconstitutional* (contrary to the Constitution). This power is called *judicial review.*

THE PEOPLE, TOO, ARE SUBJECT TO CHECKS

The people's power over the government is also subject to checks. To prevent voters from upsetting the entire machinery of government at any one election, the terms of officeholders vary. Representatives serve two-year terms; Presidents, four-year terms; and senators, six-year terms.

Many delegates at the Constitutional Convention distrusted the people's ability to choose officials wisely. Hence, it was provided that the President be elected indirectly by an electoral college (see pages 524–525) and that judges be appointed instead of elected. Until the passage of the Seventeenth Amendment, the Constitution also provided that senators be chosen by the state legislatures.

DIVISION OF POWERS BETWEEN THE NATIONAL AND STATE GOVERNMENTS

Although those who wrote the Constitution aimed to create a strong central government, they were equally determined to provide adequate authority to the states. The states gave up certain specific powers to the national government. These are called *enumerated,* or *delegated, powers.* But the states retained other powers for themselves. These are called *residual,* or *reserved, powers.* In general, the national government was to be responsible for matters affecting the nation as a whole, and the states were to concern themselves with local affairs. Such a system, which divides powers between the national government and the state governments, is called a *federal system of government.*

POWERS DELEGATED TO THE FEDERAL GOVERNMENT

1. To levy and collect taxes uniformly throughout the country.
2. To borrow money.
3. To coin money and regulate its value.
4. To establish post offices and post roads.
5. To regulate interstate and foreign commerce.
6. To control the seat of the national government and protect federal property.
7. To declare war.
8. To make treaties with foreign nations.
9. To raise and support armies; to provide and maintain a navy.
10. To establish rules for the naturalization of aliens.
11. To make all laws that are "necessary and proper" for carrying out the foregoing powers. This general statement has enabled the federal government to stretch its powers beyond those specifically given to it. It is therefore known as the *elastic clause.* Powers derived from the elastic clause are called *implied powers,* since they are not specifically mentioned in the Constitution but are implied from those that have been enumerated.

POWERS RESERVED TO THE STATES

Many people feared that the federal government would take on powers that had not been given to it by the Constitution. To prevent this, the *Tenth Amendment* was adopted in 1791 (as part of the Bill of Rights). This amendment made clear that the powers not delegated to the federal government were reserved to the states.

The following are some of the powers exercised by the states:

1. To provide for a system of education.
2. To make laws on marriage and divorce.
3. To establish voting qualifications. (Today, however, suffrage cannot be denied because of race, color, or sex to citizens 18 years old or older.)
4. To provide for local government.
5. To pass local laws for the health, safety, and welfare of the people.
6. To punish crimes within the state.
7. To regulate business within state borders.
8. To construct roads, bridges, parks, and other public works within the state.

CONCURRENT POWERS

Some powers, called *concurrent powers,* may be exercised by both the federal and the state governments. For example, both may (1) collect taxes, (2) borrow money, and (3) establish courts.

POWERS DENIED TO THE FEDERAL GOVERNMENT

1. To levy taxes on exports.
2. To favor one state over another.
3. To suspend the right to the *writ of habeas corpus* except in cases of rebellion or invasion. (A writ of habeas corpus is a court order that a prisoner has the right to obtain. The writ orders the detaining officers to state their reasons for holding him or her. If they cannot show a legal cause for their action, the court will order the prisoner released. Thus, the writ of habeas corpus protects a person against arbitrary arrest and unlawful imprisonment.)

POWERS DENIED TO THE STATES

1. To levy taxes on imports or exports.
2. To coin money.
3. To make treaties with foreign countries.
4. To engage in war unless invaded.
5. To maintain an army or navy in time of peace (except that a state may raise a militia to keep order).

POWERS DENIED TO BOTH FEDERAL AND STATE GOVERNMENTS

1. To grant titles of nobility.
2. To pass an *ex post facto law*—a law that punishes a person for a past action that was not unlawful at the time it was committed.
3. To pass a *bill of attainder*—a law that deprives a person of his or her civil rights without a trial.

AMENDING THE CONSTITUTION

One of the basic weaknesses of the Articles of Confederation was the extreme difficulty of changing, or *amending*, it. Such a procedure required the unanimous consent of all the states. The Founders overcame this weakness and made the Constitution a flexible document, capable of changing with changing times. The Constitution can be amended in four ways. The method most frequently used is to have an amendment proposed by a two-thirds vote of both houses of Congress and then to have it ratified by the legislatures of three-fourths of the states. (Twenty-seven amendments have been added to the Constitution, and all but the Twenty-first were ratified by this procedure.)

THE STRUGGLE FOR ADOPTION

THE CONSTITUTION IS SUBMITTED TO THE STATES

In September, 1787, the Constitution was completed and sent to the states for ratification. The approval of nine states was necessary before the new plan of government could be put into effect.

The issue of ratification touched off a great debate among the people and divided the nation into two factions. The *Federalists* supported the Constitution, and the *Anti-Federalists* opposed it.

Merchants, manufacturers, large landholders, professionals, and government bondholders were generally Federalists. They stood to benefit from the establishment of a strong central government capable of regulating commerce, maintaining law and order, and stabilizing the nation's finances. Anti-Federalists included small farmers, frontier settlers, city laborers, debtors, and others who believed that the states should retain maximum power and independence. The Anti-Federalists argued that the Constitution granted the federal government too much power and that it made no provision for safeguarding the fundamental rights of the people. The promise that a bill of rights would be added to the Constitution after its adoption helped to quiet this opposition.

THE CONSTITUTION IS ADOPTED (1788)

Delaware was the first state to ratify, followed in short order by Pennsylvania, New Jersey, Georgia, and Connecticut. After a sharp political struggle, Massachusetts approved the Constitution by a close vote. Maryland and South Carolina then fell into line. In June, 1788, New Hampshire became the ninth state to ratify, thereby assuring the adoption of the Constitution. Soon afterward, the important state of Virginia sent in its acceptance.

In New York, ratification met with difficulty. Alexander Hamilton, James Madison, and John Jay wrote letters to newspapers in which they analyzed the Constitution, answered criticisms, and urged the people to support ratification. These letters were later published in a book called *The Federalist*. The essays played a large part in winning support for the Constitution. New York ratified in July, 1788. North Carolina and Rhode

Island were the last states to ratify, doing so after the new government had been established and had gone into operation.

A BILL OF RIGHTS IS ADDED TO THE CONSTITUTION

The first 10 amendments, together known as the *Bill of Rights,* were added to the Constitution in 1791. These amendments guarantee people the following:

1. Guarantees of Basic Personal Rights: freedom of speech, press, and religion; the right to assemble peaceably and to request the government to correct abuses.

2. Military Guarantees: freedom to form a militia; protection against the lodging of soldiers in private homes in time of peace.

3. Legal Guarantees: assurance of the right of trial by jury in both criminal and civil cases; protection against excessive bail, excessive fines, and cruel punishment; protection against loss of life, liberty, or property without due process of law; security against unreasonable searches and seizures of persons and property; fair compensation for property seized by the government.

Multiple-Choice Test I

1. Which act was passed by Congress while the Articles of Confederation was in force? (*a*) the Boston Port Bill (*b*) the Ordinance of 1787 (*c*) the Proclamation of 1763 (*d*) the Toleration Act.
2. The federal Constitution gives the power to declare war to (*a*) the states only (*b*) both the federal government and the states (*c*) the people only (*d*) the federal government only.
3. The first ten amendments to the Constitution are called the (*a*) Preamble (*b*) Great Compromise (*c*) Bill of Rights (*d*) Fundamental Orders.
4. All states of the United States have equal representation (*a*) in the Cabinet (*b*) on the Supreme Court (*c*) in the Senate (*d*) in the House of Representatives.
5. The framers of the Constitution provided for a system of checks and balances in order to prevent (*a*) any one branch of the government from becoming too strong (*b*) the federal government from obtaining too much power over the states (*c*) the states from seceding (*d*) the United States from joining foreign alliances.
6. *The Federalist* was a (*a*) newspaper in colonial New York (*b*) series of articles explaining and urging adoption of the Constitution (*c*) famous ship used in the Revolution (*d*) pamphlet written by Thomas Paine promoting the idea of independence.
7. The original purpose of the Constitutional Convention was to (*a*) write a new Declaration of Independence (*b*) revise the Articles of Confederation (*c*) provide a government for the Northwest Territory (*d*) draw up a Bill of Rights.
8. The number of members in the House of Representatives from each state is based upon (*a*) wealth (*b*) size (*c*) influence (*d*) population.

9. Federal laws are passed by (a) the President (b) Congress (c) the Cabinet (d) the Supreme Court.

10. The Preamble of the Constitution states the (a) term of office of the President (b) provisions of the Bill of Rights (c) methods of amending the Constitution (d) reasons for framing the Constitution.

11. Presidential appointments of ambassadors and Cabinet members must be approved by (a) the Senate only (b) the House of Representatives only (c) both houses of Congress (d) the Supreme Court.

12. Freedom of speech, press, and religion are guaranteed in the (a) Declaration of Independence (b) original Constitution (c) Bill of Rights (d) Articles of Confederation.

13. The Constitution became effective as soon as it was ratified by (a) the Constitutional Convention (b) a majority of the states (c) nine states (d) all of the states.

14. The Great Compromise of the Constitutional Convention of 1787 dealt with (a) control of the slave trade (b) the election of the President (c) regulation of commerce (d) representation in Congress.

15. The Constitution established the Supreme Court as (a) part of the legislative branch (b) part of the executive branch (c) part of the judicial branch (d) an independent agency.

16. Which quotation is taken from the Constitution? (a) "We hold these truths to be self-evident ..." (b) "... that government of the people, by the people, for the people, shall not perish from the earth." (c) "These are the times that try men's souls." (d) "We the people of the United States, in order to form a more perfect Union ..."

17. One step in the procedure by which amendments to the Constitution may be adopted is (a) a one-third vote in each house of Congress (b) ratification by two-thirds of the state legislatures (c) ratification by three-fourths of the state legislatures (d) a majority vote of both houses of Congress.

18. Most of the opposition to the federal Constitution in 1788 came from (a) bankers (b) small farmers (c) lawyers (d) merchants.

19. The Bill of Rights was added to the Constitution chiefly because of the people's distrust of (a) a strong central government (b) political parties (c) banks and corporations (d) strong state governments.

20. Our federal Constitution did NOT make provision for (a) coinage of money (b) separation of powers (c) political parties (d) a system of checks and balances.

Multiple-Choice Test II

1. An important reason for the delay in the ratification of the Articles of Confederation was that (a) some states laid claims to Western lands (b) the Articles did not provide a Bill of Rights (c) there was no provision for an executive branch (d) each state delegation could cast only one vote.

2. The Articles of Confederation and the Constitution were alike in that both provided for (a) the separation of powers (b) a strong executive (c) a judicial branch (d) a federal form of government.

3. All of the following are enumerated powers of Congress EXCEPT the power to (a) establish post offices and post roads (b) build canals and

improve harbors (c) coin money and regulate its value (d) establish rules for the naturalization of aliens.

4. According to the original Constitution, who was to be elected by a direct popular vote? (a) the Vice President (b) ambassadors (c) representatives (d) senators.

5. When Congress makes laws "necessary and proper for carrying into execution the foregoing powers," it is using (a) the power of judicial review (b) the elastic clause (c) a concurrent power (d) a reserved power.

6. The President's veto of a bill passed by Congress is an example of (a) a reserved power (b) habeas corpus (c) a bill of attainder (d) checks and balances.

7. Dissatisfaction with economic conditions under the Articles of Confederation was forcefully illustrated by (a) Shays' Rebellion (b) Leisler's Rebellion (c) the Ordinance of 1785 (d) Bacon's Rebellion.

8. Which reinforced the principle established in the John Peter Zenger case? (a) the Declaration of Independence (b) the Preamble to the Constitution (c) the First Amendment to the Constitution (d) the Articles of Confederation.

9. The Constitution prohibits the national government from (a) taxing imports (b) taxing exports (c) setting up federal district courts (d) regulating interstate commerce.

10. All of the following are concurrent powers EXCEPT the power to (a) levy taxes (b) borrow money (c) establish courts (d) make treaties with foreign nations.

11. Which is required for both houses of Congress to pass a bill over the President's veto? (a) a simple majority vote (b) a two-thirds vote (c) a three-fourths vote (d) a unanimous vote.

12. James Madison's "Journal" was a (a) biography of Madison (b) record of money spent by Congress (c) newspaper supporting the Constitution (d) record of happenings at the Constitutional Convention.

13. The delegates who helped draw up the Constitution included (a) Samuel Adams and Thomas Jefferson (b) Patrick Henry and John Hancock (c) Benjamin Franklin and Gouverneur Morris (d) William Penn and Roger Williams.

14. A famous New Yorker who helped write the Constitution and then worked hard to have it ratified by New York State was (a) Alexander Hamilton (b) Benjamin Franklin (c) James Wilson (d) William Paterson.

15. The delegate chosen to serve as president of the Constitutional Convention was (a) James Madison (b) George Washington (c) Benjamin Franklin (d) Roger Sherman.

16. The members of the Constitutional Convention were mostly (a) frontier settlers (b) small farmers (c) people of wealth and position (d) clergy.

17. The United States is NOT a (a) republic (b) monarchy (c) nation (d) democracy.

18. Presidents can check the judiciary by their power to (a) pardon convicted persons (b) veto judicial decisions (c) impeach judges (d) declare judicial acts unconstitutional.

19. The Bill of Rights guarantees to American citizens all of the following rights EXCEPT (a) freedom of religion (b) protection against unreasonable

searches and seizures of persons and property (*c*) the right to overthrow the government by force (*d*) trial by jury.
20. A democracy is a form of government in which the supreme power is retained by the (*a*) President (*b*) Supreme Court (*c*) army (*d*) people.

Modified True-False Test

1. The United States was governed under the Articles of Confederation from *1775* to 1789.
2. The term of office of a member of the Senate is *six* years.
3. The Connecticut Compromise was a compromise between the *commercial and agricultural interests* at the Constitutional Convention.
4. *George Washington* is known as the "father of the Constitution."
5. Shays' Rebellion took place during the *Revolutionary War*.
6. Under the *Articles of Confederation*, each state had only one vote in Congress.
7. The Constitutional Convention convened in *1781*.
8. The Constitution provides that treaties with foreign nations must be ratified by a two-thirds vote of the *House of Representatives*.
9. Under the Constitution, states *may* levy tariffs on imports.
10. The Articles of Confederation did not grant Congress the power *to levy taxes*.
11. At Independence Hall in *Boston*, delegates met to improve the Articles of Confederation.
12. The *Virginia Plan* was supported by the large states at the Constitutional Convention.
13. A *federal system of government* is a system that divides powers between a national government and state governments.
14. The *First* Amendment to the Constitution provided that the powers not delegated to the federal government were reserved to the states.
15. According to the Constitution, neither the federal government nor the state governments may pass an *ex post facto law*.

Essay Questions

1. Classify each of *five* of the following powers as legislative, executive, or judicial: passing a tax bill, convicting a person of a crime, determining the constitutionality of a law, impeaching the Vice President, appointing ambassadors, and making a treaty with a foreign power.
2. Explain or define the underlined expressions in the following paragraph:

   The Constitution of the United States provides for a federal republic through a system of delegated powers, reserved powers, and concurrent powers. The principle of checks and balances and the protection of civil liberties are additional safeguards against despotic government.

3. The Constitution is one of the greatest documents ever written. Tell briefly why each of *five* of the following provisions was included in the Constitution:
   a. Only a natural-born citizen of the United States may be President.
   b. Only Congress may coin money.

c. Each state may have only two members in the Senate.

d. A state may not make a treaty with a foreign country.

e. Congress may not grant titles of nobility.

f. Only Congress may declare war.

g. Congress may pass a bill over the President's veto.

h. The Supreme Court may interpret a law passed by Congress.

4. The Constitution divides the powers of government between the states on the one hand and the national government on the other. (*a*) List *two* powers possessed by the national government but not by the states. (*b*) List *one* power which belongs largely to the states rather than to the national government. (*c*) List *two* powers possessed by both the state and national governments.

5. The Constitution of the United States has been amended only 27 times since its adoption. (*a*) Why were the first 10 amendments added to the Constitution? (*b*) List *three* rights that they guarantee and tell why you think each right is important.

Part 2. The New Government Begins to Function

BACKGROUND AND CHARACTER OF GEORGE WASHINGTON

EARLY LIFE

George Washington was born on February 22, 1732, in Westmoreland County, Virginia. Raised on a farm, he received little schooling during his early years. He spent his time outdoors learning to ride, hunt, swim, and sail. After his father's death, young George went to live with his older half brother, Lawrence, who owned a plantation called Mount Vernon. On this large estate on the banks of the Potomac River, George received private tutoring, acquired the manners of a Virginia gentleman, and became an expert surveyor. His surveying trips acquainted him with frontier life, the ways of the Indians, and wilderness lore. When Lawrence died in 1752, George became the master of Mount Vernon.

FRENCH AND INDIAN WAR PERIOD

In 1753 the governor of Virginia sent the 21-year-old Washington on a dangerous 500-mile journey through the wilderness to warn the French to leave the Ohio Valley. Later, Washington led a small band of militia against the French there, but his outnumbered Virginians were defeated and driven back. In 1755 Washington accompanied an ill-fated British expedition against Fort Duquesne as an aide to General Braddock. Washington won fame for his bravery during the battle and for his skill in organizing the British retreat. Put in command of Virginia's militia, he defended the frontier against enemy attacks during the next three years.

BETWEEN WARS

In 1759 Washington married Martha Custis, a wealthy and socially prominent widow, and settled down to the work he enjoyed most: farming and managing his Mount Vernon plantation. He also engaged in public affairs as a member of the Virginia House of Burgesses.

When Britain began to impose stricter controls upon the colonies, Washington became one of the leaders of colonial opposition to British policies in America. Upon hearing that English troops had occupied Boston after the Boston Tea Party, he declared to the Virginia legislature, "I will gladly enlist at my own expense 1,000 men and march to the relief of Boston." Later, he served in the First and Second Continental Congresses.

REVOLUTIONARY WAR

Appointed commander-in-chief of the Continental Army in June, 1775, Washington devoted the next eight years to the struggle for independence. He overcame all obstacles and led the Americans to victory over the British. Independence having been won, he resigned his commission and retired to his Mount Vernon estate.

CRITICAL PERIOD

In the difficult years after the war, Washington advocated strengthening the national government. Chosen to preside over the Constitutional Convention, he used his great influence to keep the conference from breaking up during the bitter debates. Afterwards his support of the Constitution helped sway public opinion in favor of ratification.

When the time came to choose a President to head the new government, all eyes turned to George Washington. Admired as a national hero, he would bring to the presidency the proven qualities of sound judgment, courage, determination, and leadership that had distinguished him during the Revolution. His wide experience in public affairs and his lofty sense of patriotism made him an admirable choice for President. Although he would have preferred to remain a private citizen, Washington agreed to serve his country.

> George Washington is frequently called the "father of our country." He has been described as "first in war, first in peace, and first in the hearts of his countrymen."

ORGANIZING THE GOVERNMENT

THE FIRST PRESIDENTIAL ELECTION

George Washington was unanimously elected to serve as the first President under the Constitution. Leaving Mount Vernon, he journeyed to New York City, the first capital of the new government, and took the oath of office on the balcony of Federal Hall on April 30, 1789.

John Adams was elected Vice President.

BEGINNING OF THE CABINET SYSTEM

To help the President carry out his duties, the first Congress created three executive departments: State, Treasury, and War. To head these departments, Washington appointed able people whose judgment and opinions he valued. For the position of Secretary of the Treasury, the most important post at the time, he selected a brilliant young lawyer, *Alexander Hamilton. Thomas Jefferson,* an experienced diplomat, became Secretary of State. *Henry Knox,* a general during the Revolution, was appointed Secretary of War.

Washington made it a practice to meet with his department heads to discuss problems of government and to seek advice on vital issues. Together with *Edmund Randolph,* the Attorney General, they became the President's advisory board: the first Cabinet.

A FEDERAL COURT SYSTEM IS ESTABLISHED

The Judiciary Act of 1789 provided that the Supreme Court be composed of six judges: a Chief Justice and five associate justices. To complete the first federal court system, Congress established 13 district courts and 3 circuit courts.

To serve as the first Chief Justice of the United States, Washington appointed John Jay, an experienced lawyer, diplomat, and politician from New York who had actively supported the ratification of the Constitution.

DOMESTIC DEVELOPMENTS

HAMILTON'S FINANCIAL PROGRAM

The most serious domestic problem facing the government was the nation's finances. Money borrowed from foreign sources and from American citizens by the Second Continental Congress and the Confederation government had not been repaid. The individual states, too, were saddled with large debts. In addition, the federal treasury was empty, and money was needed to operate the government.

To Alexander Hamilton, the Secretary of the Treasury, fell the task of placing the nation's finances on a sound foundation. To achieve this goal, Hamilton offered the following recommendations to Congress:

1. Payment of the Foreign Debt. The nation owed about $12 million to foreign creditors. To restore our credit abroad, Hamilton proposed that the entire debt be paid in full. This measure was approved with little objection.

2. Payment of the Domestic Debt. The nation owed about $40 million to Americans. During the Revolution the government had borrowed money by selling *bonds* to private individuals. A bond is a written promise (in the form of a certificate or document) to pay back a loan with interest. These bonds had not been redeemed, or paid back. Also, the government, instead of paying cash to soldiers, had given them *pay certificates*. These IOU's, or promises to pay at a later date, had not been settled.

After the war many of the original holders sold their bonds and pay certificates to speculators for as little as ten cents on the dollar. People were not sure that the new government would pay the debts that had been incurred before it came into existence. However, Hamilton proposed that the government redeem the bonds and IOU's at their full value. Only in this way, he argued, could the government's financial credit at home be restored. Over the opposition of those who claimed that full payment would serve only to enrich the speculators, Congress accepted Hamilton's recommendation.

3. Assumption of State Debts. The individual states had incurred debts of about $22 million during the Revolution. Hamilton proposed that the federal government take over, or *assume,* these debts. He argued that, since the states had borrowed chiefly to finance the war, the debts were a national obligation.

The Northern states, having large unpaid debts, favored the assumption of debts by the federal government. Many of the Southern states opposed it because they had already paid off a large part of their indebtedness. Hamilton won the support of Southern members of Congress by meeting their demand that the nation's permanent capital be located in the South. As a result of this bargaining, Congress approved (*a*) the federal assumption of state debts, and (*b*) the location of the national capital along the Potomac River. (Philadelphia was made the temporary capital.)

4. Funding the Debt. The government was unable to pay off its foreign and domestic debts immediately. Hamilton therefore proposed that the old bonds and pay certificates be exchanged for new, interest-bearing bonds. These would be paid back in full after 15 or 20 years. This part of Hamilton's program, called *funding the debt,* was also passed by Congress.

5. Establishment of a National Bank. Hamilton proposed that a national bank be organized to (*a*) provide a safe depository for federal funds received as taxes, (*b*) make it easier for the government and private individuals to borrow money, and (*c*) create a uniform and stable currency throughout the country through the issuance of sound paper money. The bank would be chartered for 20 years. It would have its headquarters in Philadelphia with branches in various parts of the country. It would be privately owned and managed, though the government would own one-fifth of its stock.

Hamilton's bank proposal stirred up much controversy. Many people feared that the bank would have too much power and would monopolize the banking business. Jefferson and his followers maintained that the measure was unconstitutional because the Constitution did not specifically grant Congress the power to charter banks. (This point of view is called *strict construction,* or *strict interpretation,* of the Constitution.) Hamilton contended that the measure was constitutional because Congress had the right to coin money and regulate its value, to regulate trade, to collect taxes, and to borrow money. He claimed that his bank proposal was "necessary and proper" for carrying out these powers. (This point of view is called *loose construction,* or *broad interpretation,* of the Constitution.) Hamilton prevailed, and in 1791 Congress established the first *Bank of the United States.*

6. Creating an American Coinage System. To replace the many different foreign coins then in circulation, Hamilton proposed that an American coinage system be adopted. Congress approved the recommendation and established a United States Mint in Philadelphia in 1792. The following year, the first American gold, silver, and copper coins were put into circulation.

7. Levying an Excise Tax. Congress passed a tariff act in 1789 placing duties on certain imports, but revenues from this source proved insufficient to meet the expenses of government. To provide additional income, Congress approved Hamilton's recommendation that an excise tax be placed on the manufacture of distilled liquor, or whisky. (An *excise tax* is a tax on goods produced or services performed within the country.)

Western farmers keenly resented this tax since whisky was an important source of their income. Instead of transporting bulky crops to Eastern markets, they distilled their surplus grain into whisky. Whisky was not only easier to transport, but also brought a higher price than the grain itself.

Opposition to the whisky tax was especially strong in western Pennsylvania. In defiance of the government, the farmers refused to pay the tax and threatened federal tax collectors with violence. Washington raised a force of 13,000 troops and sent them to quell the *Whisky Rebellion* (1794). Several of the ringleaders were arrested, and order was quickly and bloodlessly restored. By taking vigorous action, the government demonstrated its ability to enforce the laws.

8. Levying a Protective Tariff. Hamilton urged the adoption of a protective tariff to discourage the importation of foreign goods and to stimulate the growth of American industry. This was the only important recommendation by Hamilton that was rejected by Congress.

EFFECTS OF HAMILTON'S POLICIES

Hamilton's financial program produced the following favorable results: (1) The nation's credit was firmly established. (2) The government's revenue needs were met. (3) Commerce and industry were stimulated. (4) The government won the support of influential business leaders and the respect of the people.

RISE OF POLITICAL PARTIES

As stated before, Hamilton's plans aroused opposition as well as support. The division of opinion over his program led to the emergence of two political parties during Washington's administration. Supporters of Hamilton's policies formed the *Federalist party*. Opponents, led by Thomas Jefferson, organized the *Democratic-Republican*, or *Republican*, *party*. This party was the forerunner of the present-day Democratic party. (The present-day Republican party was not formed until 1854.)

The Federalists were backed by the well-to-do merchants, bankers, and manufacturers. The party was especially strong in New England. The Democratic-Republicans were supported by the small farmers, frontier settlers, small shopkeepers, and laborers. The party's chief strength was in the South and West. The two parties reflected the opposing views of their leaders, Jefferson and Hamilton.

Washington is usually considered to be a Federalist, but he did not officially side with either party. In fact, he even warned against the "spirit of party," pointing out that political parties would lead to jealousy, hatred, and "riot and insurrection." The Federalists controlled the government during the presidencies of Washington and his successor, John Adams. Their administrations are therefore generally known as the Federalist period.

Jefferson (Democratic-Republican)	Hamilton (Federalist)
1. Was a strong advocate of the rights of the people and a firm believer in democracy; had faith in the ability of the people to govern themselves wisely.	1. Was fearful of placing too much power in the hands of the people; believed that men of wealth, position, and property were best able to govern.
2. Believed that the states and the people should retain as many rights and powers as possible; stood for strict construction of the Constitution to limit the powers of the federal government.	2. Favored a strong national government; advocated loose construction of the Constitution to broaden the powers of the federal government.
3. Contended that the small, independent farmer was the backbone of a democratic America; feared that the growth of industry and the rise of cities would threaten republican principles; favored the encouragement of farming; opposed Hamilton's financial program.	3. Believed that America's future depended upon the development of a balanced and diversified economy; urged the encouragement of industry and commerce by the adoption of his financial program.

FOREIGN PROBLEMS

WASHINGTON'S PROCLAMATION OF NEUTRALITY

In 1793 France was at war with Great Britain, Spain, and other European powers. France expected the United States to come to its aid in return for the assistance it had provided the colonies during the Revolution. Believing that involvement in the conflict would seriously hurt the young nation, Washington issued a proclamation of neutrality. In it he declared that the United States would remain at peace with both sides, and warned American citizens to avoid unfriendly acts against any of the warring nations.

THE GENÊT AFFAIR

The French government sent a diplomatic agent, "Citizen" Edmond Genêt, to obtain help from the United States. Upon arrival in 1793 he (1) began to organize, on American soil, military expeditions against Spanish-held Florida and Louisiana, (2) issued French army commissions to Americans, and (3) fitted out armed ships that would sail from American ports to prey on British merchant ships.

When Genêt ignored several warnings to halt these activities, Washington requested the French government to recall its minister. Though recalled, Genêt never returned home. Fearing arrest and execution, he requested, and was granted, permission to remain here and later became a U.S. citizen.

DISPUTES WITH GREAT BRITAIN

1. Over Frontier Posts. In violation of the Treaty of Paris of 1783, the British continued to retain many forts and trading posts in the Northwest Territory. From these bases, they carried on an extensive fur trade, sold firearms to Indians, and incited Indian attacks on American frontier settlements in the Ohio Valley. The British justified their occupation of American territory by claiming that the United States had not honored the provisions of the peace treaty regarding the payment of debts owed to English merchants by Americans.

2. Over Freedom of the Seas. American foreign trade increased sharply after the outbreak of war in Europe. As a neutral nation, the United States traded with both sides. To halt the flow of supplies to France, the British navy in 1793 began seizing neutral ships bound for France or the French colonies and taking their cargoes. In less than a year, 250 U.S. vessels were seized. On many occasions American sailors were removed from their ships and *impressed* (forced) into service in the British navy. The United States complained bitterly over these violations of freedom of the seas, but England ignored the protests.

THE JAY TREATY WITH ENGLAND

To avert war, Washington sent John Jay to England to arrange a settlement of these troublesome issues. Jay negotiated a treaty in 1794 that provided for (1) withdrawal of British troops from the Northwest Territory, (2) payment of debts owed to English creditors by Americans, and (3) compensation to American shippers for vessels and cargoes seized by the British.

The *Jay Treaty* was widely criticized, however, because (1) England refused to stop seizing American ships bound for French territory, and (2) no provision was made for halting the impressment of American sailors. But after much urging by Washington, the Senate ratified the treaty. Washington hoped that the treaty would help to preserve peace at a time when the nation was ill-prepared to fight a major war. (The treaty succeeded in postponing a showdown with England until the War of 1812.)

THE PINCKNEY TREATY WITH SPAIN

To settle problems arising from Spanish control of Louisiana and Florida, Washington sent Thomas Pinckney to negotiate a treaty with Spain. Concluded in 1795, the *Pinckney Treaty* granted U.S. citizens navigation rights on the lower Mississippi River and the right to use New Orleans as a transfer point. Thus, American produce could be floated down the Mississippi on river boats, deposited in New Orleans, and then transferred to ocean-going vessels without the payment of duties to Spain. This *right of deposit* was important to Western farmers because New Orleans, at the mouth of the Mississippi, was their only outlet to markets in the eastern United States and in Europe. The treaty also settled the disputed U.S.-West Florida boundary.

WASHINGTON IS SUCCEEDED BY ADAMS

WASHINGTON'S FAREWELL ADDRESS

Washington was reelected for a second term in 1792. Four years later, weary of the responsibilities of office and worn out by the strife and turmoil of politics, he refused to run for a third term and announced his intention to retire. In the fall of 1796 he issued his *Farewell Address* to the American people. This famous document greatly influenced U.S. domestic and foreign policies for many years thereafter. In it Washington (1) cautioned people against the dangers of sectional jealousy and excess party spirit, (2) stressed the importance of maintaining a firm union and a strong central government, (3) advised the nation to steer clear of permanent alliances with foreign nations, and (4) suggested that America's best course was to avoid involvement in European affairs.

At the expiration of his second term in March, 1797, Washington retired to his home at Mount Vernon. Here, in December, 1799, America's great leader died.

THE FEDERALISTS ELECT JOHN ADAMS PRESIDENT

John Adams of Massachusetts was a member of the First and Second Continental Congresses, was a signer of the Declaration of Independence, helped negotiate the treaty of peace with England in 1783, and served as the nation's first Vice President. Chosen by the Federalists as their presidential candidate in the election of 1796, Adams won by a narrow margin over his Democratic-Republican opponent, Thomas Jefferson. Having received the second highest number of electoral votes, Jefferson became Vice President. (This method of electing the President and the Vice President was later changed. See page 116.)

by the 12ᵗʰ amendment

THE XYZ AFFAIR (1797)

Relations with France, already strained, worsened after the United States signed the Jay Treaty with Great Britain. The French felt that the United States had allied itself with the British against them. Armed French vessels began to seize American merchant ships bound for English ports, and the French government refused to receive the U.S. minister, Charles Pinckney.

Adams sent a delegation to France to seek a settlement of differences between France and the United States. Three French agents, officially identified only by the letters X, Y, and Z, refused to start negotiations unless they received a large sum of money as a bribe for certain French officials. They also insisted that the United States grant France a large loan. The U.S. envoys indignantly rejected these demands.

The *XYZ Affair* aroused a storm of protest in this country. Anti-French sentiment mounted sharply. The slogan "Millions for defense, but not one cent for tribute" was heard everywhere. In preparation for war, Congress enacted a number of defense measures and created a Department of the Navy (1798) to build up U.S. sea power.

AN UNDECLARED WAR IS FOUGHT WITH FRANCE (1798–1800)

Although war was not officially declared, a number of naval battles were fought in the next two years between American and French vessels. The tiny U.S. Navy gave a good account of itself, capturing more than 80 French ships against the loss of only one American vessel. Faced with the prospect of a full-scale war with the United States, the French government let it be known that it was ready to receive the U.S. minister and negotiate a settlement. President Adams then sent another group of envoys to France. A satisfactory agreement was reached, thus bringing the undeclared war to an end.

ALIEN AND SEDITION ACTS (1798)

While the French crisis was at its height, the Federalist-dominated Congress passed a series of harsh laws known as the *Alien and Sedition Acts.* (An alien is a resident who is not a citizen; sedition means treason.) These acts (1) raised the residence requirement for citizenship from 5 to 14 years, (2) empowered the President to imprison or deport any alien considered dangerous to the nation's peace and safety, and (3) made it a crime for any person to publicly criticize the government or its officials.

The Alien and Sedition Acts aroused a storm of protest. Recent immigrants (many of them pro-Democratic-Republican in outlook) feared the threat of deportation and resented their inability to acquire citizenship for 14 years. Citizens everywhere objected to the restrictions on freedom of speech and press. Ten Democratic-Republican editors and printers were fined and imprisoned for publishing articles critical of the government.

Although the Federalists defended the Alien and Sedition Acts as necessary war measures, the acts' apparent aims were to (1) strengthen Federalist control of the government, (2) weaken the power and influence of the Democratic-Republican party, and (3) curb political opposition.

KENTUCKY AND VIRGINIA RESOLUTIONS

The legislatures of Kentucky and Virginia passed resolutions (1798–1799) declaring the Alien and Sedition Acts unconstitutional and void. The *Kentucky* and *Virginia Resolutions,* written by Thomas Jefferson and James Madison respectively, stated: (1) The states created the national government. (2) The powers of the national government are strictly limited to those expressed in the Constitution. (3) Each state has the right to judge for itself whether Congress has exceeded its constitutional powers. (4) A state need not obey an act that it considers unconstitutional.

These principles formed the basis of *states' rights,* a doctrine that the South later used to oppose high tariffs and defend slavery.

END OF THE FEDERALIST PERIOD

THE FEDERALISTS LOSE CONTROL OF THE GOVERNMENT

In the presidential election of 1800 the Federalists nominated John Adams for a second term. Opposing him was the Democratic-Republican candidate, Thomas Jefferson. The Democratic-Republicans won a sweeping victory at the polls, gaining control of both the executive and legislative branches of the government.

The defeat of the Federalists marked their complete downfall from power. They were unable to regain their former supremacy in later elections, and finally disappeared from the political scene some 15 years later. Several reasons explain their decline. (1) Their policies served the interests of commercial and manufacturing groups, rather than those of farmers and laborers, who made up the majority of the population. (2) The common people resented the Federalists' aim to keep the government in the hands of the few and well-to-do. (3) The passage of the Alien and Sedition Acts aroused the fears of the people that the Federalists would destroy their civil liberties.

THE HOUSE SELECTS JEFFERSON OVER BURR

An unusual problem arose in the presidential election of 1800. According to the Constitution, members of the electoral college were to vote for two candidates without indicating which office each was to fill. The person receiving the highest number of votes was to become President; the next highest, Vice President.

In this election, the Democratic-Republican party had nominated Thomas Jefferson for President and Aaron Burr for Vice President. Since each Democratic-Republican elector cast two votes for that party's candidates, the vote in the electoral college resulted in a tie between Jefferson and Burr.

The Constitution provides that when two candidates are tied in the electoral college, the House of Representatives must choose between them. Although Jefferson was his party's choice for President, Federalist members of the House attempted to swing the election to Burr. They preferred Burr because his political views were closer to those of the Federalists than were Jefferson's. The deadlock was finally broken when Hamilton, an influential Federalist who distrusted Burr, declared himself in favor of Jefferson. Hamilton's support swayed the House to choose Jefferson.

(To prevent a recurrence of such a situation, the *Twelfth Amendment* was adopted in 1804. It provided that electors cast separate ballots for President and Vice President.)

"MIDNIGHT JUDGES"

Shortly before the Federalists left office, Congress passed an act increasing the number of judges and other federal court officials. By filling these positions with their supporters, the Federalists hoped to maintain control of the judicial branch of the government. In his last hours as President, Adams worked far into the night signing appointments to the new positions. Hence, these officials became known as "midnight judges," or "midnight appointees."

When the Democratic-Republicans came into office, they quickly repealed this act and removed most of the midnight appointees.

ACHIEVEMENTS OF THE FEDERALISTS

During their 12 years in office (1789–1801), the Federalists (1) put the Constitution into operation, (2) firmly established the powers of the federal government, (3) solved the nation's financial problems, (4) helped develop commerce and industry, and (5) kept the country out of war with England and France.

MARSHALL STRENGTHENS THE SUPREME COURT

In 1801, several weeks before the expiration of his term, President Adams appointed a staunch Federalist, John Marshall of Virginia, as Chief Justice. For the next 34 years, until 1835, Marshall dominated the U.S. Supreme Court. His decisions increased the influence and authority of the nation's highest tribunal, and established its power of *judicial review*, that is, the Court's right to rule on the constitutionality of acts of Congress, executive actions, and state laws. A supporter of the doctrine of broad interpretation of the Constitution, Marshall also helped to expand the powers of the federal government.

Among his noteworthy decisions were the following:

1. *Marbury* v. *Madison* (1803). William Marbury was a Federalist "midnight judge" who had been appointed as a justice of the peace by Adams. Before he could take office, however, Marbury would have to obtain an official authorization, or commission, from the new administration's Secretary of State, James Madison. When this document was withheld, Marbury asked the U.S. Supreme Court to issue an order compelling Madison to deliver it. He brought his case directly to the Supreme Court, rather than to a lower federal court, because a provision of the Judiciary Act of 1789 permitted such a procedure.

Speaking for the Supreme Court, Marshall ruled that the Court lacked jurisdiction in the matter, and dismissed Marbury's suit. He declared further that the section of the Judiciary Act of 1789 that empowered the Court to handle such cases was unconstitutional because it granted the Supreme Court powers that had not been assigned by the Constitution.

This case is considered a landmark because (*a*) it was the first time that the Supreme Court declared an act of Congress null and void, and (*b*) it introduced the principle of judicial review.

2. *Fletcher* v. *Peck* (1810). The Georgia legislature, influenced by members who were in the pay of land speculators, granted huge tracts in the Yazoo River country (now part of Mississippi) to some private land companies. The following year, a new legislature canceled the transaction, claiming that it had been based on fraud and corruption.

Marshall and the U.S. Supreme Court ruled that, despite the motives of the legislators, the original grant was a contract and must be honored. It also invalidated the legislation revoking the grant, observing that the Constitution denied states the power to pass laws "impairing the obligation of contracts."

This decision was the first to affirm the Court's right to invalidate a state law that conflicted with the Constitution.

3. *Dartmouth College* v. *Woodward* (1819). The Court took a similar stand in a case involving Dartmouth. That college had received a royal charter from King George III in 1769, and had been operating as a private institution governed by its own board of trustees for many years. In 1816 the legislature of New Hampshire revamped the school's charter and placed Dartmouth under state control. When a state court upheld the action of the legislature, the school's former trustees appealed the case to the U.S. Supreme Court.

Marshall and the Court held that a charter to a private corporation (whether a school or business) constituted a contract, and thus was protected by the Constitution. The tribunal therefore declared New Hampshire's action unconstitutional.

4. *McCulloch* v. *Maryland* (1819). A law enacted by Maryland imposed a burdensome tax on the operations of the Baltimore branch of the federally sponsored Bank of the United States. James McCulloch, the branch's cashier, ignored the law, arguing that it was unconstitutional. When Maryland brought suit against McCulloch and won favorable rulings in the state's courts, the case was appealed to the U.S. Supreme Court.

At issue were two important questions: (*a*) Did Congress have the power to establish a national bank? (*b*) Can a state tax a federal agency? Marshall, speaking for a unanimous Court, held that the act creating the bank was constitutional because Congress had the power to regulate the value of money, and that establishing a bank was "necessary and proper" for carrying out this responsibility. He also denied Maryland the right to tax the bank, asserting that "the power to tax involves the power to destroy."

5. *Gibbons* v. *Ogden* (1824). Aaron Ogden headed a private company that had been granted exclusive rights by the New York legislature to operate steamboats on state waters. After some years of providing passenger and freight service to ports along the Hudson River, the company extended its operations across the lower Hudson to New Jersey. Thomas Gibbons, holder of a federal license, also ran a steamboat service between the two states. Ogden contended that Gibbons was violating his monopoly rights, and the New York courts ruled in his favor.

The U.S. Supreme Court, however, disallowed Ogden's claim and invalidated the New York grant. Marshall observed that only the federal government has the power to regulate *interstate commerce* (trade between two states).

Multiple-Choice Test

1. The first Chief Justice of the United States was a New Yorker named (a) John Marshall (b) George Clinton (c) John Jay (d) Gouverneur Morris.
2. The President of the United States seeks advice most often from the (a) Cabinet (b) Conference of Governors (c) Congress (d) Supreme Court.
3. In his Farewell Address, George Washington advised the American people to (a) maintain a large army and navy (b) avoid permanent alliances with foreign nations (c) support the two-term tradition for the presidency (d) seek westward expansion.
4. An important result of Hamilton's financial policies was the (a) expansion of states' rights (b) weakening of the federal government (c) strengthening of the federal government (d) support of small farmers for the federal government.
5. In which pair was the first item a cause of the second? (a) Washington's Proclamation of Neutrality—American Revolution (b) XYZ Affair—increase in resentment toward France (c) Genêt Affair—French and Indian War (d) Jay Treaty—increase in resentment toward Spain.
6. A problem common to the administrations of both George Washington and John Adams was (a) navigation on the Potomac River (b) the extension of slavery (c) the lack of a stable currency (d) strained relations with France.
7. The Pinckney Treaty settled a dispute between the United States and Spain concerning (a) access to the Rio Grande (b) trade with the West Indies (c) use of the Grand Banks (d) navigation on the Mississippi River.
8. The Virginia and Kentucky Resolutions were protests against the (a) excise tax on whisky (b) creation of the first Bank of the United States (c) Alien and Sedition Acts (d) adoption of the federal Constitution.
9. Washington's Proclamation of Neutrality was issued chiefly to meet problems raised by (a) Canada (b) France (c) Holland (d) Spain.
10. Which provision of the treaty ending the American Revolution was NOT carried out by Great Britain until after the Jay Treaty went into effect? (a) evacuation of British troops from United States soil (b) British acceptance of the Mississippi River as the western boundary of the United States (c) formal recognition of the United States (d) granting Americans fishing rights in Newfoundland's coastal waters.
11. On which issue were Alexander Hamilton and Thomas Jefferson in closest agreement? (a) establishing a national bank (b) locating the national capital in the South (c) favoring manufacturing over farming interests (d) supporting strict interpretation of the Constitution.
12. Which was one of the greatest contributions of the Federalist party to the United States? (a) U.S. aid to France (b) the theory of states' rights (c) a decentralized banking system (d) strengthening of the central government.
13. Which event was viewed as an attempt by the Federalist party to weaken the Democratic-Republican party? (a) ratification of the Jay Treaty (b) creation of the Bank of the United States (c) passage of the Alien and Sedition Acts (d) publication of the XYZ dispatches.
14. The right of judicial review of acts of Congress by the Supreme Court was established by (a) John Marshall (b) John Jay (c) Alexander Hamilton (d) Thomas Jefferson.

15. On Hamilton's recommendation, the war debts of the individual states were (a) taken over by the federal government (b) repaid by the states themselves (c) canceled by the creditors (d) absorbed by the British government.
16. Jefferson believed in (a) government by the people (b) government by the upper classes (c) a strong central government (d) strong ties with England.
17. In *Marbury* v. *Madison* the U.S. Supreme Court (a) voided the Alien and Sedition Acts (b) disallowed a land grant made by the Georgia state legislature (c) declared a section of the Judiciary Act of 1789 unconstitutional (d) ruled that Jefferson should be chosen President over Burr.
18. The requirement that presidential electors must vote separately for President and Vice President was provided in the (a) original federal Constitution (b) Fifth Amendment (c) Twelfth Amendment (d) Judicial Act of 1789.
19. Federal judges appointed by President Adams on the eve of his departure from office became known as (a) moonlighters (b) circuit riders (c) midnight judges (d) featherbedders.
20. All of the following financial proposals of Alexander Hamilton were accepted by Congress EXCEPT (a) assumption of state debts (b) funding of foreign and domestic debts (c) levying an excise tax (d) levying a protective tariff.

Modified True-False Test

1. Washington took the oath of office as President of the United States on the balcony of Federal Hall in the city of *Baltimore*.
2. *Aaron Burr* was the first Vice President of the United States.
3. *Henry Knox* was the nation's first Secretary of State.
4. An excise tax passed by Congress on Hamilton's recommendation stirred up discontent among frontier farmers and brought on *Shays' Rebellion*.
5. The creation of the first Bank of the United States is an example of *loose* construction of the Constitution.
6. The first United States Mint was established in the city of *Philadelphia*.
7. Most merchants, bankers, and manufacturers supported the *Democratic-Republican* party in the 1790's.
8. The U.S. government under the Constitution began in the year *1783*.
9. Western farmers received the *right of deposit* at New Orleans as a result of the Pinckney Treaty.
10. The election of *John Adams* as President was decided in the House of Representatives.

Essay Questions

1. "First in war, first in peace, and first in the hearts of his countrymen" describes George Washington, the "father of our country." (a) What were George Washington's wartime services to the nation? (b) What were his peacetime contributions before he became President? (c) Describe his contributions as President of the United States.
2. Alexander Hamilton, the nation's first Secretary of the Treasury, played a key role in the administration of President Washington. Describe Hamilton's program for solving the nation's financial problems.
3. Compare the political views of Hamilton and Jefferson.

UNIT V. FIRST HALF OF THE NINETEENTH CENTURY

Part 1. Era of Jefferson, Madison, and Monroe

BACKGROUND AND ACCOMPLISHMENTS OF JEFFERSON

EARLY YEARS

Born in 1743 on the Virginia frontier, in Albemarle County, Thomas Jefferson was raised on his family's plantation. At 17 he entered William and Mary College, and after graduating took up the study of law. A brilliant student, he became one of the best educated people in colonial America, acquiring a profound grasp of history, law, and philosophy, and a broad knowledge of mathematics, science, architecture, and scientific farming. He married Martha Skelton in 1772 and settled at *Monticello* (near Charlottesville, Virginia). Here he built a magnificent house, a showplace to this day. He devoted himself to farming, law, and scientific and literary pursuits.

POLITICAL LIFE

A member of the House of Burgesses from 1769 to 1775, Jefferson took an active part in the colonial cause. In 1775 he became a delegate to the Second Continental Congress, and in the following year he drafted the immortal Declaration of Independence. From 1776 to 1781 he served once more in the Virginia legislature and then as governor of that state. During this period he drafted and submitted to the legislature a proposal to enact a law that would separate church and state, and assure religious toleration in Virginia. It failed to pass in 1779, but was adopted in 1786. Jefferson considered this *Virginia Statute for Religious Freedom* one of his three most important accomplishments. The other two were the Declaration of Independence and the founding of the University of Virginia.

Elected to the Confederation Congress in 1783, he formulated a plan of government for new territories that became the basis for the Northwest Ordinance. From 1785 to 1789 he represented the United States abroad, helping to negotiate commercial treaties with France and England, and serving as minister to France.

In 1789 Washington appointed Jefferson the nation's first Secretary of State. Four years later he resigned his post because of political disagreements with Hamilton. To build an organized opposition to Hamilton's policies, he helped found the Democratic-Republican party. Jefferson was elected Vice President in 1796 and President in 1800. At the end of his second term in 1809, he retired to his home at Monticello. Until his death in 1826, the "Sage of Monticello" worked energetically at his many interests: experimenting with new farming methods; corresponding with the great people of his time; advising his successors in the White House; and planning the design, construction, and curriculum of the University of Virginia.

JEFFERSON AS PRESIDENT

Jefferson's inauguration was the first to be held in Washington, D.C., then a village of unpaved streets and unfinished public buildings. An advocate of simplicity, Jefferson did away with much of the formality and pomp introduced by the Federalists. He put an end to the weekly receptions and stately balls held by his predecessors.

The following were some of the significant events of Jefferson's two terms in office: (1) The Alien and Sedition Acts were either repealed or allowed to expire, and those who had been imprisoned under these laws were pardoned. (2) The residence requirement for citizenship was lowered to five years. (3) All excise taxes, including the one on whisky, were repealed. (4) Under the expert financial guidance of *Albert Gallatin,* Jefferson's Secretary of the Treasury, federal expenses were cut and the federal debt substantially reduced. (5) The United States Military Academy at West Point was established (1802). (6) The importation of slaves was prohibited (1808).

The most significant event of Jefferson's administration was the acquisition of Louisiana.

THE LOUISIANA PURCHASE (1803)

BACKGROUND

Louisiana, the enormous territory lying between the Mississippi River and the Rockies, was ceded to Spain by France after the French and Indian War. New Orleans, at the mouth of the Mississippi, dominated the river route that was a natural highway for frontier farmers of Kentucky, Tennessee, and the Ohio Valley. It was comparatively easy for the Westerners to float their produce down the Ohio River into the Mississippi to New Orleans, and from there to transship goods to markets in the East and in Europe. To haul their crops overland through the wilderness and across the mountains was virtually impossible. Therefore, in 1795, the United States obtained from Spain, by the Pinckney Treaty, the right to navigate the lower Mississippi and to deposit goods in New Orleans.

AMERICA PURCHASES THE TERRITORY FROM FRANCE

Hoping to restore the French Empire in North America, Napoleon forced Spain to return Louisiana to France in 1800. Two years later the American right of deposit in New Orleans was withdrawn. Faced with the loss of their outlet to Eastern markets, Westerners appealed to President Jefferson for help. Fearing Napoleon's presence at the nation's back door and aiming to help the frontier farmers, Jefferson authorized Robert Livingston and James Monroe to negotiate the purchase of New Orleans from France.

On the verge of war with England and in need of money, Napoleon abandoned his dream of an empire in North America. He was therefore very willing to do business with the Americans, and astonished the U.S. representatives by offering to sell not just New Orleans but the entire Louisiana Territory for $15 million. Seizing the opportunity to acquire this vast domain so cheaply, Livingston and Monroe accepted the offer.

Although Jefferson was pleased with the amazing bargain, he was also troubled over the constitutional problem that it raised. He believed in strict construction, and the Constitution did not specifically state that the government had the right to purchase foreign territories. Nevertheless, convinced that Louisiana was essential to the future development of the United States, Jefferson urged the Senate to ratify the treaty. In this instance he supported a broad interpretation of the Constitution.

IMPORTANCE OF THE LOUISIANA PURCHASE

(1) By giving the United States control of the entire Mississippi River, the Louisiana Purchase assured an outlet to the sea for Western goods. (2) It doubled the area of the United States. (3) Because of the fertility and resources of the region, the purchase added immeasurably to the wealth of the country. (4) From the Louisiana Territory, 13 states have been carved in whole or part: Louisiana, Arkansas, Missouri, Iowa,

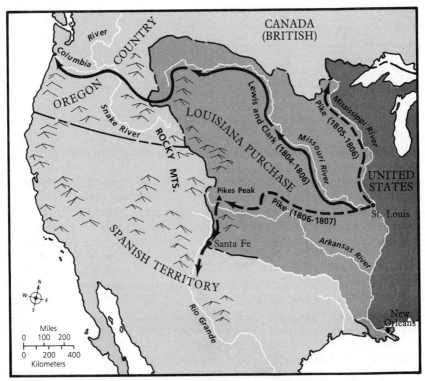

The Louisiana Purchase Is Explored

Minnesota, North and South Dakota, Nebraska, Kansas, Oklahoma, Colorado, Wyoming, and Montana.

THE LEWIS AND CLARK EXPEDITION (1804–1806)

In 1804 Jefferson sent *Meriwether Lewis* and *William Clark* to explore the northern part of the Louisiana Purchase. The expedition started from St. Louis, followed the Missouri River to its source, crossed the Rocky Mountains into the Oregon Country, and followed the Columbia River to the Pacific Ocean. The explorers were aided greatly by a Shoshone Indian woman, *Sacajawea,* who served as a guide and interpreter. The reports of Lewis and Clark acquainted the nation with the climate, fertility, physical features, animals, and Indian tribes of this great region. Furthermore, their exploration of the Oregon Country laid the basis for a later U.S. claim to that area.

THE EXPLORATIONS OF PIKE

Seeking the source of the Mississippi River, Zebulon Pike in 1805–1806 explored the northern part of the Louisiana Purchase. Then in 1806–1807 he led another expedition—this one to explore the southwestern part of the region. He headed westward across the plains to the upper Arkansas River and followed it to the Rockies, where he discovered Pikes Peak in Colorado. Turning south, Pike reached the Rio Grande in Spanish territory. Imprisoned by the Spaniards in Santa Fe and then released, he returned home via Texas (then owned by Spain).

THE BARBARY PIRATES MOLEST AMERICAN SHIPPING

WAR WITH TRIPOLI

Morocco, Algiers, Tunis, and Tripoli, all located on the coast of North Africa, were called the *Barbary States.* They made it a practice to attack foreign ships passing through the Mediterranean, seize their cargoes, and hold their crews for ransom. For many years the United States, as well as the maritime nations of Europe, paid large sums of money to the Barbary States to keep their ships from being attacked.

During Jefferson's administration, the ruler of Tripoli demanded a higher tribute from the United States. When the President refused, Tripoli declared war (1801). Jefferson thereupon sent a small squadron of ships to blockade that country's coastline. *Stephen Decatur,* then a young naval lieutenant, performed the most daring exploit of the war. One night he sneaked into the harbor of Tripoli and destroyed a U.S. vessel that the Tripolitans had captured and converted into a warship.

The American blockade finally forced Tripoli to sue for peace and to promise to leave American ships alone (1805).

DECATUR'S EXPEDITION AGAINST ALGIERS

The United States continued to pay tribute to the other Barbary States, and American shipping was not interrupted. During the War of

1812, however, Algiers began to attack and seize American vessels passing its coast and to imprison U.S. citizens. In 1815 President James Madison sent Stephen Decatur with a fleet of ships to stop the raids. When Decatur captured two Algerian warships and brought his fleet into the harbor of Algiers, the ruler of Algiers agreed to stop interfering with American commerce. Decatur also forced the remaining Barbary States to guarantee the safety of U.S. ships, thus ending America's troubles with the Barbary pirates.

EVENTS LEADING TO THE WAR OF 1812

INTERFERENCE WITH AMERICAN SHIPPING

When England and France renewed their war in 1803, American neutrality was again endangered. Each warring nation refused to recognize the right of neutral countries to trade with its enemy. Both interfered with U.S. shipping, but Britain's superior seapower made it the worse offender. The British seized hundreds of American ships and confiscated the cargoes. They impressed thousands of U.S. sailors into the British navy.

Anti-British sentiment mounted sharply in 1807 when the *Leopard*, a British man-of-war, demanded to search the American warship *Chesapeake*. England claimed that English deserters were aboard. When the American commander denied the claim and refused to permit the search, the British opened fire, killing or wounding 21 sailors. The English then boarded the vessel and removed four of the men.

THE UNITED STATES ATTEMPTS ECONOMIC PRESSURE

Jefferson believed that the two warring nations needed American produce and that the United States could force them to come to terms by withholding its goods. He therefore asked Congress to pass an *Embargo Act*. Enacted in 1807, it aimed to stop all American trade with foreign ports.

The embargo failed to change French and English policies. In addition, it had a disastrous effect on the American economy. Merchants and shippers were faced with ruin; many, in desperation, turned to smuggling. Shipbuilding came to a halt. Unemployment spread throughout the Northeast as sailors, dockworkers, clerks, and carpenters were idled. Farmers, too, were hurt by the loss of foreign markets for their crops.

Opposition to the measure was so great that it was repealed. A new law, the *Non-Intercourse Act* (1809), reopened trade with all nations except England and France. This measure, too, failed to curb French and British attacks on U.S. ships, and it was allowed to lapse after a year.

THE "WAR HAWKS" AGITATE FOR WAR

The so-called "War Hawks" were a group of young Republican politicians from the West and South who were strongly nationalistic and keenly desired American expansion. Their leaders included Henry Clay of Kentucky and John C. Calhoun of South Carolina, both of whom had been elected to Congress in 1810. The War Hawks clamored for war with England, hoping to conquer British-held Canada and Spanish-held Florida. (Spain was England's ally at the time.) The War Hawks became influential in Congress and played an important role in stirring up the nation's war spirit.

THE UNITED STATES DECLARES WAR ON ENGLAND (1812)

James Madison of Virginia, nominated by the Democratic-Republicans to succeed Jefferson, became the nation's fourth President in 1809. For the next three years he made every effort to keep the country out of war. But the interference with American shipping continued, and the demand for war became more insistent. Finally, in June, 1812, Madison requested and Congress approved a declaration of war against Great Britain.

Although there was deep resentment against France as well as England, American hostility toward Britain was greater. (1) Many people still remembered England as the enemy in the Revolution. (2) The powerful British navy was doing greater damage to U.S. shipping than was France's smaller fleet. (3) The British, unlike the French, were impressing American sailors. (4) Westerners believed that the English, based in Canada, were arming Indians and inciting them to attack frontier settlements. (5) The War Hawks wanted to drive the British from Canada, both to end the Indian threat and to annex Canada to the United States.

HIGHLIGHTS OF THE WAR OF 1812

AMERICAN HANDICAPS

1. The United States Was Not Militarily Prepared for War. The regular army was small, badly equipped, and without competent leadership. For its fighting force on land, the country had to rely on hastily recruited and untrained militia. At sea, the United States had a navy of 16 warships. Although it performed many heroic feats, this tiny fleet was hardly a match for Britain's mighty navy, the largest in the world.

2. The Nation Lacked Money to Carry on the War. After hostilities began, foreign trade came to a virtual standstill. This situation caused a sharp decline in tariff revenues, a major source of income for the government. Also, the government found it difficult to borrow money because: (*a*) Many wealthy people in the Northeast opposed the war. (*b*) The Bank of the United States was no longer available for floating loans. (Its charter had expired in 1811, and the Democratic-Republicans had refused to renew it.)

3. The Nation Was Not United in Support of the War. There was much opposition to the war in the commercial Northeast, especially in New England. Although they were hurt by England's seizure of their ships, American merchants and shipowners made so much profit from their successful voyages that they were willing to risk a few losses. They considered the outbreak of war a calamity because it meant the end of all trade with their most important customer, England. Calling it "Mr. Madison's War," the New England States refused to support the government's efforts to finance the war through the sale of bonds.

In 1814 politicians in New England called a meeting at Hartford, Connecticut. The *Hartford Convention* passed resolutions condemning the war and recommending constitutional amendments to protect the interests of New England. Some extremists even talked of *seceding* (leaving the Union) and concluding a separate peace with England. Before any action could be taken, however, the War of 1812 ended.

The Hartford Convention discredited the Federalists, who were then predominant in New England, and helped to drive their party out of existence.

THE WAR AT SEA

During the first year of the war, the Americans proved their ability at sea by scoring a number of outstanding victories against the British. The warship *Constitution,* commanded by Isaac Hull, destroyed the British frigate *Guerrière* in a furious battle off Nova Scotia and later, under William Bainbridge, defeated the *Java* off Brazil. These victories earned the *Constitution* the nickname "Old Ironsides." The *United States,* commanded by Stephen Decatur, captured the *Macedonian;* and the *Wasp* defeated the *Frolic.*

American naval vessels and privateers preyed on British shipping, seizing or destroying about 1,500 ships during the course of the war. Eventually, however, the numerically superior British navy drove the Americans from the sea, established a blockade of the U.S. coast, and brought U.S. foreign commerce to a standstill.

In a fierce duel between the British frigate *Shannon* and the American warship *Chesapeake* in 1813, the British were winning the battle. The last order given by the dying American captain, James Lawrence, was "Don't give up the ship!"

These words became the rallying cry of the United States Navy.

THE CANADIAN CAMPAIGN FAILS

For three years the Americans vainly tried to conquer Canada. In 1812 they attacked from three separate points: Lake Champlain, the Niagara River, and Detroit. Each attack failed. The next year a force of raiders invaded and burned York (Toronto) and then withdrew. Later, an unsuccessful attempt was made to take Montreal.

In 1814 an army under Jacob Brown and Winfield Scott crossed the Niagara River into Canada. The Americans seized Fort Erie, inflicted a severe defeat on the British near the Chippewa River, and fought the British to a draw at Lundy's Lane. They then pulled back to Fort Erie,

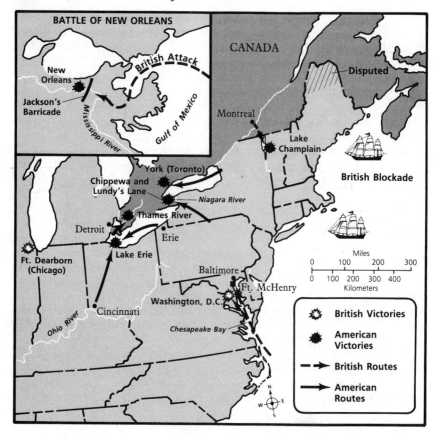

The War of 1812

successfully withstood a British siege, but finally withdrew across the
border, thus abandoning their plans to capture Canada.

THE AMERICANS LOSE AND REGAIN THE NORTHWEST

Early in the war the British captured Detroit, and their Indian allies
destroyed Fort Dearborn (Chicago). These defeats left the British in
control of Lake Erie and the upper part of the Northwest Territory.
The United States, however, regained possession of the region as
follows:

1. Battle of Lake Erie. Using timber from nearby forests, the Americans laboriously constructed a small fleet of vessels at Erie, Pennsylvania,
on Lake Erie. The tiny squadron, commanded by *Oliver Hazard Perry*,
engaged the British in 1813 and decisively defeated them in one of the
fiercest naval battles of the war. In reporting his victory, Perry sent the
famous message, "We have met the enemy and they are ours."

2. Battle of the Thames. Perry's victory gave the United States control
of Lake Erie and forced the British to abandon Detroit and withdraw
to Canada. William Henry Harrison led a force of American frontier

militia across Lake Erie into Canada in pursuit of the British and their Indian allies. He overtook them at the Thames River and decisively defeated them (1813). *Tecumseh,* a Shawnee Indian chief who wielded great influence over the Northwest tribes, was killed during the fighting. His death caused most Indians to desert the British. As a result of this battle, the British hold on the Northwest Territory was broken.

THE BRITISH TAKE THE OFFENSIVE

After Napoleon's downfall in Europe in 1814, the British turned their full attention to winning the war in North America. They sent a large force of veteran troops across the Atlantic and planned to crush the Americans with attacks at three strategic points: Lake Champlain, Chesapeake Bay, and New Orleans.

1. Battle of Lake Champlain. About 11,000 British troops descended from Canada and invaded New York along the western shore of Lake Champlain. Before proceeding southward, however, they had to gain control of the lake. The British had a fleet on the lake, as did the Americans. The British confidently expected that their more heavily armed warships would destroy the American vessels in short order. When the Battle of Lake Champlain took place, however, the American fleet, commanded by *Thomas Macdonough,* skillfully outmaneuvered the British and defeated them completely (1814). As a result, the British army was forced to retreat to Canada, and the invasion of New York was abandoned.

2. Burning of Washington. Also in 1814, a squadron of British ships entered Chesapeake Bay and landed troops in Maryland, south of Washington. Marching on the poorly defended U.S. capital, the English routed a force of militia at Bladensburg and entered Washington almost unopposed. In retaliation for the destruction of government offices at Toronto by American raiders the year before, the British set fire to many government buildings in Washington, including the Capitol and the White House. They then withdrew from the city.

3. Attack on Baltimore. The British fleet in Chesapeake Bay next sailed northward to attack Baltimore, but found the city prepared to resist invasion. The English landing party met strong opposition from American troops and was stopped at the outskirts of the city. The fleet tried to destroy Fort McHenry, which guarded the entrance to the city's harbor, but failed despite an all-night bombardment. Unable to crack Baltimore's defenses, the British gave up the attack and soon after left Chesapeake Bay.

On September 13, 1814, an American, *Francis Scott Key,* went aboard a British ship to seek the release of an American prisoner. While detained on the ship for the night, he witnessed the English bombardment of Fort McHenry. Next morning he saw the American flag still flying over the fort. This sight inspired him to write the verses of *The Star-Spangled Banner,* which later became the U.S. national anthem.

4. Battle of New Orleans. Thwarted at Chesapeake Bay and Lake

Champlain, the British tried to carry out the third part of their plan. They transported 7,500 troops through the Gulf of Mexico and landed them near New Orleans. The American soldiers defending the area, led by Indian fighter *Andrew Jackson*, erected a barricade and awaited the enemy. Early in January, 1815, the English launched their attack. In the battle that followed, the British were decisively defeated, suffering more than 2,000 casualties at the hands of the sharpshooting Westerners. American losses were 71 killed or wounded.

This great victory at New Orleans, after many defeats on land, restored the nation's pride. It also made a national hero of Andrew Jackson. However, it did not influence the outcome of the war. A treaty of peace had been signed in Europe two weeks earlier (December 24, 1814), but the news had not yet reached America. *Also it had not been ratified)*

TREATY OF GHENT — *British + Americans agree to: Status quo Ante Bellum*

By the end of 1814 both sides were eager for peace. Meeting in Ghent, Belgium, representatives of England and the United States concluded a treaty of peace. It ended the state of war and restored the boundaries existing before hostilities began. No reference was made to the impressment of sailors or the violation of America's rights at sea. Although this *Second War for Independence* against England did not end in victory for either side, it had important effects on the United States.

RESULTS OF THE WAR OF 1812

1. The war inspired a spirit of *nationalism* (national unity and patriotism) among the people. America turned away from Europe and began to concentrate on developing its resources and building a great nation.

2. The United States showed the world that it was prepared and able to defend its rights. It thus earned the respect of England and other foreign nations.

Relations with Britain improved greatly after the war, and several problems were solved by friendly discussion and negotiation. The *Rush-Bagot Agreement,* signed in 1817, provided that neither nation would maintain warships on the Great Lakes. The *Treaty of 1818* (*a*) fixed the disputed boundary between Canada and the United States from Minnesota to the Rockies along the 49th parallel, (*b*) reaffirmed American fishing rights off the coasts of Labrador and Newfoundland, and (*c*) opened the Oregon Country to settlers from both countries.

3. The war encouraged the growth of American industry. Unable to obtain manufactured goods from abroad during the war, the United States was forced to develop and expand its own production facilities.

4. The war stimulated westward expansion by removing armed opposition by Indians in the region between the Appalachian Mountains and the Mississippi River. In the Northwest Territory the Indian confederacy collapsed with the death of Tecumseh. In the Old Southwest the power of the Creeks was broken by Jackson's campaigns against them in 1813-1814.

ACQUISITION OF FLORIDA (1819)

AMERICANS OCCUPY WEST FLORIDA

Spanish Florida consisted of the long peninsula jutting into the Atlantic (East Florida) and a narrow stretch of land along the Gulf of Mexico extending westward to the Mississippi (West Florida). America claimed a large part of the Gulf Coast strip as part of the Louisiana Purchase. When American colonists north of New Orleans revolted against Spanish rule, the United States annexed the area in 1810. Three years later, during the War of 1812, American troops captured the Spanish fort at Mobile and occupied this part of West Florida, despite Spain's protests.

SPAIN CEDES FLORIDA

Spanish control of the rest of Florida created many problems for the United States. Runaway slaves fled to Florida. Some Indians living there raided settlements in Georgia and Alabama and returned to the safety of Spanish territory. Pirates and smugglers also used Florida as a base of operations.

In 1818 Andrew Jackson invaded Florida in pursuit of Seminole Indians who had been raiding American settlements across the border. He thoroughly punished the Indians and captured several Spanish forts. James Monroe, who had succeeded Madison as President in 1817, warned Spain that it must either police its territory adequately or cede it to the United States.

But Spain was unable to send more troops to the area because it was busy trying to put down revolts in its Latin American colonies. Fearing that it would lose Florida to America by conquest, Spain in 1819 agreed

The United States Acquires Florida

to give the territory to the United States. In turn, the United States agreed to (1) assume Spain's $5 million debt to U.S. citizens and (2) give up its claim to Texas—a region that it had previously contended was part of the Louisiana Purchase.

THE MONROE DOCTRINE (1823)

SPAIN'S COLONIES WIN INDEPENDENCE

The same spirit of freedom that had led the North American colonies to revolt against England inspired the Spanish colonists south of the United States to revolt against their mother country. Taking advantage of Spain's involvement in the Napoleonic Wars in Europe, the Spanish colonists started a revolt in Venezuela in 1810. The revolt soon spread throughout Latin America. One country after another declared its independence. Finally, in 1824, a Spanish army was decisively beaten in the *Battle of Ayacucho* in Peru. Shortly thereafter, Spain's control of Latin America, except in Cuba and Puerto Rico, came to an end.

Among the patriots who led the fight for independence in Spanish America were the following:

Francisco Miranda, an early revolutionary in Venezuela, touched off the first revolt against Spain.

Simón Bolívar, called "the Liberator" and the "George Washington of South America," helped free the northern part of South America from Spanish domination. Venezuela, his native country, as well as Colombia, Ecuador, Peru, and Bolivia, owe their independence to his leadership. *Bolivia* was named in his honor.

José de San Martín led the struggle for independence in the southern part of South America. He liberated Argentina and Chile and helped wrest Peru from Spanish control.

Miguel Hidalgo y Costilla was a parish priest in the Mexican town of Dolores. He rallied the Indians of Mexico in an unsuccessful attempt to overthrow the Spaniards. Though he was captured and executed, his heroic efforts earned him the title, "father of Mexican independence."

Agustín de Iturbide, a native-born Mexican of Spanish descent, was an officer in the Spanish army. He joined the Mexican rebels, defeated the Spaniards, and in 1821 proclaimed the independence of Mexico.

ATTITUDES OF OTHER NATIONS TOWARD THE NEW REPUBLICS

Most rulers on the continent of Europe disliked democracy. They became especially fearful of democratic uprisings when Napoleon's troops carried the ideas of the French Revolution (liberty, equality, fraternity) throughout Europe. Therefore, after Napoleon's defeat, Russia, France, Prussia, and Austria joined in an alliance to crush revolution wherever it might arise. The king of Spain sought the help of this alliance to regain control of Latin America.

England did not want Spain to reacquire its former colonies in Latin America. England was developing a profitable trade of its own with the newly created countries.

The Americas (1825)

The United States sympathized with the aims of the Latin American patriots and supported their cause by extending recognition to the new republics. The United States was alarmed at the possibility of further European intervention in the Western Hemisphere.

RUSSIA SEEKS TO EXPAND IN NORTH AMERICA

At this time, too, a new threat arose on the Pacific coast of North America. Starting from its base in Alaska, Russia began to expand southward. In 1821 Czar Alexander I extended Russia's claim as far south as the 51st parallel. This line was within the Oregon Country.

AMERICA PROCLAIMS THE MONROE DOCTRINE

When it seemed that the European powers would try to win back Latin America for Spain, President Monroe acted. In 1823 he issued a strong warning to Europe to keep out of the Western Hemisphere. This proclamation, known as the *Monroe Doctrine*, became a cornerstone of American foreign policy. It made the following points:

1. The American continents are not open to further colonization by European powers.

2. Any attempt on the part of European powers to interfere with the existing governments in the Americas will be regarded by the United States as an unfriendly act.

3. The United States will not interfere in European affairs or with the existing European colonies in the Western Hemisphere.

THE MONROE DOCTRINE PROTECTS THE WESTERN HEMISPHERE

Russia withdrew from its outposts in Oregon and, by a treaty with the United States in 1824, fixed the boundary between the Oregon Country and Alaska at 54°40' north latitude.

England supported the Monroe Doctrine in order to maintain its markets in Latin America. The other powers, faced with the hostility of both Britain and the United States, dropped their plans to reconquer Spain's former colonies. The Monroe Doctrine thus achieved its purpose of protecting the Western Hemisphere from further European interference.

Multiple-Choice Test

1. During the War of 1812, Thomas Macdonough won a naval victory on (a) Lake George (b) Lake Champlain (c) the Hudson River (d) Long Island Sound.

2. The United States acquired Florida from (a) England (b) France (c) Spain (d) Portugal.

3. An important result of the Embargo Act of 1807 was that it (a) injured New England's shipping (b) forced England and France to respect American rights (c) influenced Jefferson to purchase Louisiana (d) involved the United States in a war with France.

4. Which states are in the area included in the Louisiana Purchase? (a)

Louisiana and Alabama (*b*) Ohio and Colorado (*c*) Missouri and Kansas
(*d*) Indiana and Wisconsin.

5. The Louisiana Territory was explored by (*a*) Mason and Dixon (*b*)
Jefferson and Gallatin (*c*) Clay and Calhoun (*d*) Lewis and Clark.

✗ 6. One purpose of the Monroe Doctrine was to (*a*) take all the land in South
America from European countries (*b*) make the United States a great
world power (*c*) prevent Spain from regaining control of Latin America
(*d*) drive Great Britain from Canada.

7. In the struggle for independence in the countries of Latin America, all of
the following were leaders EXCEPT (*a*) San Martín (*b*) Cabeza de Vaca
(*c*) Miranda (*d*) Bolívar.

8. Latin American countries that obtained their freedom from Spain during
the early decades of the 19th century include all of the following EXCEPT
(*a*) Argentina (*b*) Puerto Rico (*c*) Chile (*d*) Bolivia.

✗ 9. All of the following were Presidents of the United States in its early years
EXCEPT (*a*) Hamilton (*b*) Madison (*c*) Adams (*d*) Monroe.

✗ 10. The document that warned Europeans that the Americas were closed to
future colonization by European countries was (*a*) Washington's Proclamation of Neutrality (*b*) the Embargo Act (*c*) Washington's Farewell
Address (*d*) the Monroe Doctrine.

✗ 11. During the War of 1812, American forces invaded (*a*) Cuba (*b*) California
(*c*) Mexico (*d*) Canada.

✗ 12. The defense of Baltimore in September, 1814, inspired Francis Scott Key
to write (*a*) *America the Beautiful* (*b*) *The Star-Spangled Banner* (*c*) *The Battle
Hymn of the Republic* (*d*) *Yankee Doodle*.

✗ 13. Which section of the United States was most strongly opposed to the War
of 1812? (*a*) the Middle Atlantic states (*b*) the New England states (*c*) the
Southern states (*d*) the Western states.

14. Which was a direct result of the purchase of the Louisiana Territory? (*a*)
an amendment to the Constitution permitting the federal government to
purchase land (*b*) the elimination of Spain from the North American
continent (*c*) the opening of a vast region for fur trading and land
development (*d*) the extension of America's boundary westward to the
Pacific Ocean.

✗ 15. A result of the War of 1812 was the following: (*a*) The Federalist party
gained in popularity. (*b*) American industrialization was postponed for 50
years. (*c*) A spirit of nationalism took hold in America. (*d*) Britain lost its
position as the world's leading power.

✗ 16. Removal of warships from the Great Lakes—waterways that serve as part
of the border between Canada and the United States—dates back to the
(*a*) Treaty of Paris of 1763 (*b*) Treaty of Paris of 1783 (*c*) Treaty of Ghent
of 1814 (*d*) Rush-Bagot Agreement of 1817.

17. Which was an important reason for the success of the Monroe Doctrine in
the early 19th century? (*a*) economic aid by the United States to Latin
America (*b*) United States control of the Atlantic and Pacific oceans (*c*)
British support of United States policy (*d*) United States influence in world
affairs.

✗ 18. The War of 1812 is sometimes called the (*a*) War of the Roses (*b*) Second
Napoleonic War (*c*) Second War for Independence (*d*) War Between the
States.

✻19. As a result of the War of 1812, the United States (*a*) gained territory west of the Mississippi (*b*) acquired colonies in the Caribbean area (*c*) replaced Britain as the leading naval power (*d*) won the respect of foreign nations.

20. All of the following occurred during Jefferson's administration EXCEPT the (*a*) negotiations with France for the purchase of New Orleans (*b*) war with Tripoli (*c*) impressment of American sailors by the British (*d*) outbreak of war with England.

Matching Test

Column A	*Column B*
1. Sacajawea	*a.* Hero of the war against the Barbary pirates
2. Stephen Decatur	
3. Oliver Hazard Perry	*b.* A leader of the War Hawks
4. Tecumseh	*c.* "Father of Mexican independence"
5. James Monroe	*d.* Winner of the Battle of the Thames
6. James Madison	*e.* Indian ally of the British in the Northwest Territory
7. Henry Clay	
8. James Lawrence	*f.* President during the War of 1812
9. Miguel Hidalgo y Costilla	*g.* Guide of Lewis and Clark
10. William Henry Harrison	*h.* President when the U.S. acquired Florida
	i. Naval commander who said "Don't give up the ship!"
	j. Naval commander who said "We have met the enemy and they are ours."

Completion Test

1. A group of young American politicians who agitated for war with England in the early 1800's were known as the _____.
2. In 1814 New Englanders opposed to "Mr. Madison's War" convened the _____.
3. _____ was an explorer of the Louisiana Territory whose name is given to one of the peaks of the Rocky Mountains.
4. _____ is called the "George Washington of South America."
5. The eastern boundary of the Louisiana Territory was the _____ River.
6. _____ became a national hero by defeating the British in the Battle of New Orleans in 1815.
7. The War of 1812 was ended by the Treaty of _____.
8. The boundary between Canada and the United States from Minnesota to the Rockies was fixed at the _____ parallel by the Treaty of 1818.
9. _____ was James Madison's successor as President.
10. The warship *Constitution* earned the nickname "_____" during the War of 1812.

Essay Questions

1. Below are listed famous war leaders. Cite a battle in which each fought and tell why each of these battles proved to be important in American history.
   - *a.* James Wolfe
   - *b.* Horatio Gates
   - *c.* Oliver Hazard Perry

2. Thomas Jefferson is recognized as one of the greatest leaders our nation has had. Write a brief biographical account of this great leader. Include in your answer *one* important contribution he made in each of ~~five~~ *six* of the following areas: (Do not repeat in one part of your answer information given in another part.)
   - *a.* government service
   - *b.* human rights
   - *c.* territorial expansion of the United States
   - *d.* architecture
   - *e.* science
   - *f.* education

3. Explain *one* way in which geography has influenced each of the following: the growth of New Orleans, the purchase of the Louisiana Territory, American interest in West Florida, and the acquisition of East Florida.

4. The Monroe Doctrine has become a cornerstone of American foreign policy. (*a*) What circumstances led to the proclamation of the Monroe Doctrine? (*b*) What did the Monroe Doctrine state? (*c*) What were the effects of the Monroe Doctrine?

Part 2. Westward Expansion and Early Industrial Progress

AMERICA FACES WESTWARD

THE STATES CEDE THEIR WESTERN LAND CLAIMS

The charters issued to seven of the original colonies contained grants of land extending from the Atlantic indefinitely westward. As the East became settled, pioneers and fur traders began to penetrate the area west of the Appalachian Mountains. The Western lands now assumed great importance.

Claims to Western lands overlapped, and bitter disputes arose among the states over ownership. States with fixed boundaries, like Maryland, argued that the Western territory should be national property, controlled and governed by Congress for the benefit of all the states. Maryland refused to ratify the Articles of Confederation until the Western claims were relinquished. To break the deadlock that threatened the Confederation, New York agreed to yield its claims, and the other states followed suit.

As a result, the national government under the Articles of Confederation acquired possession of the nation's Western lands: the territory between the Appalachian Mountains and the Mississippi River. The area south of the Ohio River became known as the *Old Southwest;* the region north of the Ohio, the *Old Northwest.*

SETTLEMENT OF THE OLD SOUTHWEST

1. Kentucky and Tennessee. Some years before the Revolution, pioneers from North Carolina and Virginia established settlements in the vicinity of the Watauga River in northeastern Tennessee. Attracted by the fertility of the land and the abundance of game, other pioneers soon followed. They settled in the rich valleys of the Cumberland, Tennessee, and Kentucky rivers and their tributaries. They came in such numbers that the first Western states to be settled and admitted into the Union were Kentucky in 1792 and Tennessee in 1796.

Among the people who pioneered the settlement of these states were:

Daniel Boone, a famous hunter and Indian fighter, was chiefly responsible for opening the upper part of the Old Southwest to large-scale settlement. One of the first to explore the region that is now Kentucky, he found a path across the Appalachians through the Cumberland Gap. The *Wilderness Road,* which he blazed through the gap, became a main highway for migration into the territory. Boone led a group of settlers into Kentucky and in 1775 founded Boonesborough. (See map, page 143.)

James Harrod established the first settlement in Kentucky at Harrodsburg in 1774.

James Robertson was one of the early settlers of the Watauga Valley in northeastern Tennessee. He led a band of pioneers far inland in 1779 and planted a settlement at Nashville on the Cumberland River.

John Sevier, a leader in the settlement of Tennessee, became its first governor when it achieved statehood in 1796. He had won fame during the Revolution when he led a force of frontier militia across the Great Smoky Mountains into the Carolinas and helped defeat the British at the Battle of King's Mountain.

2. Mississippi and Alabama. The lower part of the Old Southwest was organized as the Mississippi Territory and opened to settlement in 1798. Southern planters moved into the area with their slaves and

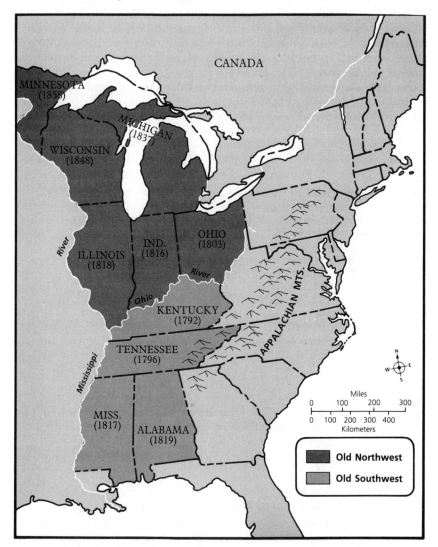

New States Are Formed From the Old Northwest and the Old Southwest

established large cotton plantations in the fertile lowlands. Settlement was hindered by the opposition of the Creek Indians until Andrew Jackson defeated them at the Battle of Horseshoe Bend in 1814. Thousands of Southerners now felt safe to leave their worn-out farms in the Carolinas and Georgia and migrate westward. Their main route was through Georgia, around the southern end of the Appalachians.

Mississippi became a state in 1817, and Alabama in 1819.

THE OLD NORTHWEST IS OPENED TO SETTLEMENT

The Confederation Congress passed several important laws to regulate the settlement and development of the Old Northwest.

1. The **Ordinance of 1785** provided that the land be surveyed and divided into six-mile-square *townships*. A township was to be subdivided into 36 *sections,* each containing one square mile (640 acres) of land. One section in each township was to be set aside for the support of public schools. The land was then to be offered for sale at public auction at a minimum price of $1 per acre.

(Each purchaser was required to buy a full section of land. Since most settlers could not afford to do so, land companies bought up much of the land, subdivided it, and sold the smaller lots to settlers at a profit.)

Property boundaries in the original 13 states were often irregular and uncertain, causing confusion and legal disputes. The Ordinance of 1785 established a uniform, orderly system for surveying and dividing land to avoid similar problems in the Old Northwest—and in later additions to the public domain as well.

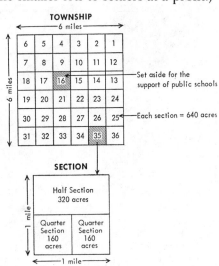

2. The **Ordinance of 1787 (Northwest Ordinance)** organized the Old Northwest into the *Northwest Territory* and provided a plan for its government as follows:

a. Congress would provide a temporary government by appointing a governor and three judges to administer the territory.

b. When the territory had 5,000 adult male settlers, a representative legislature was to be established.

c. When a part of the territory attained a population of 60,000, it would be eligible for admission into the Union as a state equal to the original states "in all respects whatever."

d. No less than three and no more than five states were to be created from the territory.

e. Personal rights, such as freedom of religion, freedom of speech, and trial by jury, were guaranteed.

f. Slavery was prohibited.

g. Public schools were encouraged.

The Northwest Ordinance is generally considered the outstanding achievement of Congress under the Articles of Confederation. (1) It established the pattern for the administration of America's public lands from the Appalachians to the Pacific. (2) It assured the development of new states on a basis of equality with the original 13. (3) It guaranteed that civil liberties, democratic government, and public education would accompany the pioneers into the wilderness.

> "I doubt whether one single law of any lawgiver, ancient or modern, has produced effects of more distinct, marked, and lasting character than the Ordinance of 1787."
>
> —*Daniel Webster*

SETTLERS FLOCK TO THE NORTHWEST TERRITORY

1. Ohio. Many New Englanders deserted their rocky, hillside farms for the rich, level lands of the Ohio Valley. Pioneers from New York and Pennsylvania, as well as newly arrived immigrants from Europe, also headed west. In 1788 the first permanent American settlement in Ohio was made at Marietta, at the junction of the Muskingum and Ohio rivers. Cincinnati, farther west on the Ohio, was founded in the same year. In 1796, on the shores of Lake Erie, Moses Cleaveland laid out the city that bears his name (with a slightly different spelling).

As the number of settlers in Ohio increased, so did Indian resistance to the spread of settlement. An attempt to end the Indian threat failed in 1791, when an army detachment under Arthur St. Clair was defeated by a combined force of Chippewas, Miamis, Shawnees, and Ottawas led by Chief Little Turtle. President Washington then appointed "Mad Anthony" Wayne, a Revolutionary War hero, to take charge of the campaign against the Indians. In 1794, at the Battle of Fallen Timbers in northwest Ohio, Wayne won a decisive victory over Little Turtle's warriors. By the Treaty of Greenville, signed by 12 tribes the following year, the Indians ceded much of Ohio and part of Indiana to the United States, and agreed to leave that area.

In 1803 Ohio became a state and was admitted into the Union.

2. Indiana, Illinois, Michigan, and Wisconsin. To resist the influx of settlers into the remaining portions of the Northwest Territory, Indians in the area, led by the Shawnee chief Tecumseh, formed a defensive tribal confederacy. In 1811 frontier forces under *William*

Henry Harrison launched an attack against the confederacy's main center in western Indiana, defeating the Indians in the Battle of Tippecanoe. Then, during the War of 1812, Harrison routed Tecumseh's Indian confederacy along with the British in the Battle of the Thames. After the war a tremendous wave of pioneers surged into the territory. Indiana became a state in 1816, and Illinois in 1818.

Settlement of the northern sections of the Northwest Territory proceeded more slowly. Michigan attained statehood in 1837, and Wisconsin in 1848.

ROUTES TO THE WEST

In their trek westward, the pioneers used the following land and water routes:

1. Ohio River Route. Thousands of settlers brought their families and possessions overland to Pittsburgh. Here they boarded flatboats and floated down the Ohio River to points in Ohio, Indiana, Illinois, northern Kentucky, and western Tennessee. This route was the great natural gateway to the West.

2. Mohawk Route. New Englanders and New Yorkers followed the Mohawk River and the Genesee Turnpike westward to Lake Erie. In 1825 the Erie Canal opened an all-water route from Albany to Buffalo. The canal became a principal pathway to the West.

3. National Road. The federal government built a road from Cumberland, Maryland, to Wheeling, Virginia (now West Virginia), on the Ohio River. It was opened to traffic in 1818. This *National Road, or Cumberland Road,* was later extended across Ohio and Indiana into Illinois.

DISTRIBUTION OF POPULATION

When the first national census was taken in 1790, the population of the United States was 3,929,000. Of this total, only 109,000, or about 3%, lived west of the Appalachian Mountains. In 1830 the fifth census showed that about 30% of the total population of 12,866,000 was located in the West.

WHY PEOPLE WENT WEST

From the founding of Jamestown until the 1890's, the frontier played a major role in the development of the country. Throughout this 300-year period, as people moved farther and farther west, new frontiers were constantly being opened. These undeveloped areas attracted many different kinds of people: (1) restless, adventurous, and dissatisfied Americans seeking a fresh start in life, (2) farmers whose lands were poor, (3) laborers who had lost their jobs in times of depression or who wished to acquire land of their own, and (4) immigrants who had just arrived from Europe.

OUTLOOK OF THE PIONEERS

On the frontier, people were respected more for their courage, skills, and industriousness than for their nationality, social position, or pock-

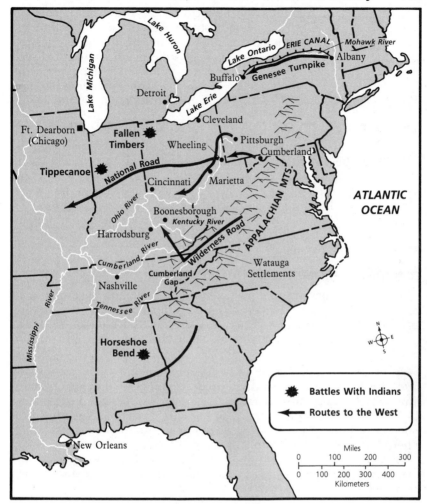

Routes to the West

etbook. People tended to accept one another as social and political equals. Common problems and dangers drew pioneering families together and helped create a spirit of neighborliness and cooperation. Living in a land of opportunity, pioneers were optimistic, filled with hope for the future. They had a strong sense of loyalty toward the national government, because it had sold them land on easy terms and protected them against Indians. They vigorously advocated the extension of political democracy.

BEGINNINGS OF INDUSTRIALIZATION IN THE NORTHEAST

THE INDUSTRIAL REVOLUTION STARTS IN ENGLAND

The term *Industrial Revolution* means (1) the change from hand methods of production to machine methods, and (2) the shift of manufacture from the home to the factory. The Industrial Revolution began in England in the textile industry during the second half of the 18th century. The invention of spinning and weaving machines operated by water power made possible the large-scale manufacture of thread and cloth. Steam began to replace water as a source of power in the late 1760's with the development of a practical steam engine by *James Watt*. England became the leading manufacturing nation in the world.

THE INDUSTRIAL REVOLUTION COMES TO THE UNITED STATES

Great Britain attempted to guard the secrets of its new machinery by forbidding the emigration of skilled workers and by prohibiting the exportation of any machine, model, or sketch. However, *Samuel Slater,* a skilled English textile worker, succeeded in emigrating to the United States, and from memory constructed the machinery necessary to spin cotton yarn. He built the country's first successful cotton mill in Pawtucket, Rhode Island, in 1790. Slater is called the "father of the American factory system."

CONDITIONS PROMOTING INDUSTRIALIZATION

Industrialization progressed slowly at first because manufactured goods could be imported cheaply from England. However, when imports were halted by the Embargo Act of 1807, the Non-Intercourse Act of 1809, and the War of 1812, domestic manufacturing began to expand rapidly.

In the North, especially in New England, conditions were unusually favorable for the spread of the factory system. (1) The interruption of trade with Europe left merchants and shippers with idle capital to invest in manufacturing facilities. (2) The numerous rivers and streams provided an abundant source of water power to run the new factories. (3) There was an adequate supply of labor, drawn from nearby farms and from among newly arrived immigrants. (4) Finally, New England had a tradition of craftsmanship and had many ingenious mechanics among its people.

THE TEXTILE INDUSTRY DEVELOPS

Francis C. Lowell was one of the first wealthy New England merchants to invest his fortune in the manufacture of cotton. He constructed spinning machinery and a new type of power loom, and established a factory at Waltham, Massachusetts (1813). Here, for the first time, the spinning and weaving processes, from the raw cotton to the woven cloth, were conducted under one roof.

Similar factories sprang up throughout New England, and by 1840 there were 1,350 cotton mills in operation. They employed 75,000 people and produced $46 million worth of cotton goods annually. Power weaving was also adapted to the manufacture of woolen products. By 1840 the woolen industry was turning out $20 million worth of goods annually.

The importance of the factory system and machine production is graphically demonstrated by the declining cost of cotton cloth. As production became more efficient, the price fell from 40¢ a yard in 1815 to 4½¢ in 1830 and 2¢ in 1860.

CONTRIBUTORS

Eli Whitney invented the *cotton gin* (1793), a machine that made possible the separation of cotton seeds from cotton fiber 50 times faster than by hand labor. This mechanical method of cleaning cotton encouraged the South to increase its cotton production tremendously—from 100,000 bales in 1800 to 730,000 in 1830, and to 5,400,000 in 1860. The cotton gin assured an adequate supply of raw cotton to the booming textile industry in the North.

Elias Howe invented the *sewing machine* (1846). This invention revolutionized the making of clothing, increased the demand for cotton and woolen cloth, and shifted the manufacture of clothing from the home to the factory.

THE GOVERNMENT AIDS AMERICAN INDUSTRY

After the War of 1812 English manufacturers attempted to regain their lost American markets by shipping large quantities of goods to this country and selling them at prices lower than American-made articles. To prevent the destruction of the nation's infant industries, Congress in 1816 passed America's first protective tariff. Duties on imports were raised so that American manufacturers could undersell their foreign competitors. The tariff thus encouraged the growth of domestic industry.

That same year Congress chartered the second Bank of the United States. By enlarging the banking system, establishing a uniform and stable currency, and providing better credit facilities, this move also helped American manufacturers.

THE SYSTEM OF INTERCHANGEABLE PARTS IS INTRODUCED

In 1798 Eli Whitney conceived the idea of using interchangeable parts in the manufacture of muskets. Instead of producing one gun at a time by hand and fashioning each part to fit just that weapon, he planned to manufacture, by machine, large quantities of identical parts: triggers, barrels, stocks, etc. These standard parts would then be assembled into finished products. In this way muskets could be produced quickly and cheaply, and defective or broken parts could be replaced easily.

Although Whitney did not fully succeed in setting up such an operation, other inventors did. Among them was *John Hall*, a skilled armorer employed at the Harpers Ferry Armory. Hall devised a complete system of interchangeable parts in the manufacture of rifles.

The system of interchangeable parts was soon applied to the production of pistols, clocks, and watches. It was later extended to farm machinery, sewing machines, stoves, and innumerable other products. It became a basic principle of American industry and later spread throughout the world.

THE GROWTH OF CITIES

Before the Industrial Revolution came to America, the vast majority of the population lived in rural areas. With the spread of the factory system and the demand for workers to operate the new machinery, many people turned from farming to industry as a means of earning a living. In order to provide homes for the workers, new villages, towns, and cities sprang up in the vicinity of the factories.

Between 1800 and 1860 the number of cities with a population of 8,000 or more rose from 6 to 141. The percentage of the population living in urban (city) areas rose from 3% to 16%.

The crowding of thousands of people into cities created many difficult problems relating to housing, control of diseases, food and water supply, garbage disposal, police and fire protection, transportation, recreation, and education.

WORKING CONDITIONS IN THE EARLY FACTORIES

Working conditions in the early factories were quite different from those today. The average workweek was from 12 to 14 hours a day, 6 days a week. Many workers toiled from sunrise to sunset in poorly lighted, badly ventilated, unsanitary factories. Child labor was common. Children and women received little pay for their labor. These unsatisfactory conditions caused much discontent among the workers and in later years gave rise to labor unions.

RISE OF THE IRON, COAL, AND STEEL INDUSTRIES

During the colonial period, charcoal (charred wood) was the fuel used to smelt iron. Later, charcoal was replaced by bituminous (soft) coal. Then in 1830 a method was developed for using anthracite (hard) coal as a fuel in iron-making. The demand for iron (and later for steel) was great. These metals were needed for machinery, stoves (which were replacing fireplaces), farm implements, and rails. With the discovery of deposits of iron ore and coal in western Pennsylvania, Pittsburgh became the country's iron and steel center.

IMPROVEMENTS IN AGRICULTURE

At the beginning of the 19th century, farming methods were crude and unscientific. Farmers were still using the wooden plow, the sickle (for cutting), and the flail (for separating grain from the stalk). Every step in the growing process, from plowing to threshing, was done by hand. Farmers did little to improve the soil, using neither drainage nor crop rotation nor fertilizers.

In the first half of the century, new farm machinery and many improved implements were introduced. Metal plows began to replace wooden ones. The cradle and then the reaper replaced the sickle. The thresher was substituted for the flail. Mowing and haying machines, seed drills, and cultivators were developed. These inventions enabled farmers to increase their productivity and meet the nation's rising demand for foodstuffs.

CONTRIBUTORS

Charles Newbold built the first iron plow to be cast in a single piece (1797).

Jethro Wood devised a three-piece cast-iron plow with interchangeable parts (1819).

Cyrus McCormick developed the reaper (1834). This machine made possible the harvesting of grain quickly, cheaply, and efficiently.

John Deere built the first steel plow (1837). Its success in turning tough sod helped speed the settlement of the prairie.

PROGRESS IN TRANSPORTATION

TURNPIKES

Turnpikes—hard-surfaced roads built of macadam, stones, earth, or planks—were constructed with private capital for profit. Tolls were charged for their use. The turnpike was the first improvement made in land transportation after the Revolutionary War.

The era of turnpike construction began in 1794 with the completion of the Philadelphia-Lancaster Turnpike in Pennsylvania. Thousands of miles of toll road were built during the next quarter century, especially in New England and the Middle Atlantic states. A notable example was the *Genesee Turnpike* between Albany and Buffalo in New York State.

This network of turnpikes helped link the East with frontier settlements, enabled farmers to bring their produce to market, and stimulated the flow of manufactured goods to the West. Toll charges, however, made the cost of travel and freight transportation quite high. Many people therefore began to demand that the federal government build free roads.

THE NATIONAL ROAD

In 1811 the federal government started the construction of a great *National Road* (also called the *Cumberland Road*) to link the East with the Northwest Territory. The first section, opened in 1818, led from Cumberland, Maryland, on the Potomac River, to Wheeling, Virginia (now West Virginia), on the Ohio River. The National Road was later extended to Columbus, Ohio, and finally to Vandalia, Illinois.

The National Road became one of the chief arteries of Western migration and East-West commerce. It eventually became part of U.S. Route 40, a modern automobile highway.

LAND VEHICLES

To transport freight by land, Americans developed the *Conestoga wagon,* or *covered wagon.* This canvas-covered vehicle was large and sturdy, and had a high body and broad-rimmed wheels. It was drawn by four or six horses or oxen. Its bottom was often watertight to enable the wagon to ford streams and float in deep water. The Conestoga wagon was also used by settlers to carry their families and possessions to new homes in the West.

Stagecoaches were the chief means of carrying passengers and mail overland. These four-wheeled, oval-shaped carriages seated about eight people and traveled at a rate of from two to six miles an hour, depending upon road conditions. Stagecoach lines maintained regular routes on turnpikes and public roads. Inns along the highways served as stations where passengers dined and spent the night, and where tired horses were exchanged for fresh teams.

THE STEAMBOAT

Though John Fitch and other American inventors had succeeded in propelling boats by means of a steam engine in the late 18th century, the credit for building the first commercially successful steamboat goes to *Robert Fulton*. In 1807 his *Clermont* steamed up the Hudson River from New York to Albany, a distance of 150 miles, in 32 hours. Before long, steamboats were carrying passengers and freight on almost every navigable waterway in the United States.

EFFECT OF THE STEAMBOAT ON THE WEST

Steamboats provided Westerners with much-needed improvements in water transportation. Not only could produce be shipped downstream to New Orleans more cheaply and quickly, but boats could now return upstream, against the current, bringing back supplies and manufactured goods.

The first steamboat to sail Western waters was the *New Orleans,* built at Pittsburgh in 1811. By 1820 there were 60 steamboats in service on the Mississippi River and its tributaries. The number rose to nearly 300 in 1837 and to more than 1,000 in 1860. Travel time on Western rivers was cut by two-thirds, and transportation costs were reduced by one-half. Thriving river ports sprang up: Pittsburgh, Cincinnati, and Louisville on the Ohio; St. Louis, Vicksburg, and Natchez on the Mississippi.

FASTER SAILING SHIPS ARE BUILT

Although steamboats succeeded in crossing the Atlantic as early as 1819, they did not replace sailing vessels on the high seas until much later. Beginning in 1818, American shipbuilders put swift and sturdy *packets* (sailing ships carrying passengers, mail, and cargo on a regular schedule) into transatlantic service. In the 1840's they introduced a new type of sailing craft capable of outdistancing anything afloat. This was the American *clipper ship.* These long, graceful, high-masted vessels, with a great spread of sails, set many speed records. They dominated the world's sea lanes for 20 years. Among the famous clippers were the *Flying Cloud* and the *Great Republic,* both built by America's leading naval designer, *Donald McKay.*

After 1860 the development of steamships with iron hulls ended the supremacy of the clippers. The new steamships were equipped with powerful engines and screw propellers, invented in 1837 by *John Ericsson*.

THE ERIE CANAL

Under the leadership of Governor *De Witt Clinton* of New York, the Erie Canal was started in 1817. When completed in 1825, this 363-mile waterway linked the Hudson River near Albany with Lake Erie at Buffalo. Its artificial channel, 42 feet wide at the top, 28 feet wide at the bottom, and 4 feet deep, was dug by manual labor. It took eight years to complete and cost over $7 million. Stone aqueducts led the canal over streams. A series of locks raised or lowered the boats from one level to another as they progressed through the canal. It was the greatest engineering project undertaken up to that time in America.

EFFECTS OF THE CANAL

By providing an all-water route from the Atlantic Ocean to the Great Lakes, the Erie Canal (1) gave the settlers in the upper Northwest Territory an easy route to the East, (2) reduced freight costs between the East and West to one-tenth their former level, (3) stimulated the settlement and economic development of upstate New York, (4) made New York City the greatest shipping and trading center in the country, and (5) became the main artery of westward migration from New York and New England.

Its success began an era of canal building throughout the nation. By 1837 about 3,000 miles of canal had been built. In the Middle West, canals linked the Great Lakes with tributaries of the Mississippi River. The Pennsylvania Canal connected Philadelphia and Pittsburgh. Since the Allegheny Mountains are situated between these two cities, a continuous waterway could not be dug. To cross the 35-mile stretch of mountains, a portage railway was devised. The loaded canal boats were placed on rails and hauled across the mountains by engines and ropes.

RAILROADS

In England *George Stephenson* developed a practical steam locomotive in 1814 and built the first railway for public use. Interest in railroads spread to the United States. In 1828 construction was begun on the first passenger railroad in this country, the *Baltimore and Ohio*. Its first section, extending from Baltimore westward for 13 miles, was opened to traffic in 1830. Horse-drawn cars were used at the start, but the animals were soon replaced by iron horses—locomotives. The first of these was the *Tom Thumb*, designed and built by Peter Cooper. The following year, the *Mohawk and Hudson Railroad* began operating between Albany and Schenectady, using another American-built locomotive, the *De Witt Clinton*. A third line was completed in 1833 between Charleston and Hamburg, South Carolina, a distance of 136 miles. Several short lines were built during the 1830's to connect major cities. By 1840 nearly 3,000 miles of track were in use.

REASONS FOR THE GROWTH OF RAILROADS

Between 1840 and 1860 railroads replaced highways and canals in importance and became the chief carriers of the nation's commerce. By 1860, 30,000 miles of track crisscrossed the land east of the Mississippi, and rail connections linked the important Middle Western cities with the Atlantic seaboard. Among the reasons for the growth of railroads were the following: (1) They cost less to build than canals and provided faster transportation. (2) They could reach inland regions inaccessible by water. (3) They were dependable throughout the year, even in winter when canals and rivers were frozen. (4) They were capable of hauling far larger quantities of freight than horse-drawn wagons and transporting many more passengers than stagecoaches.

PROGRESS IN COMMUNICATION

IMPORTANCE OF RAPID COMMUNICATION

In a country as large as the United States, efficient and rapid communication is essential. Speedy communication enables the government to function effectively. It serves to bring all parts of the country closer together and thus to cement national unity. Businesses and the news media are dependent upon it. In time of national crisis, instant communication is imperative.

INVENTION OF THE TELEGRAPH

Samuel F. B. Morse developed an electrical instrument by means of which messages could be tapped out in the form of "dots and dashes" (Morse code) and transmitted over a wire. This device was the telegraph. Aided by a money grant from Congress, Morse strung a telegraph line between Washington, D.C., and Baltimore in 1844 and transmitted messages between the two cities. By 1860, a network of telegraph lines extended through all areas east of the Mississippi.

> "What hath God wrought!" was the first message transmitted by telegraph— May 24, 1844.

OTHER EARLY CONTRIBUTIONS TO SCIENCE AND INVENTION

Joseph Henry experimented with electricity and invented an improved electromagnet (1829), a device that made possible the development of the telegraph.

Samuel Colt invented the revolver (1835).

Charles Goodyear perfected a process for vulcanizing (hardening) rubber (1844). This made possible the use of rubber in industry, in the home, and in wearing apparel.

Richard M. Hoe invented the rotary printing press (1846). By speeding up the printing process, Hoe's invention led to a tremendous increase in newspaper production and circulation.

William T. G. Morton, a dentist, introduced the use of ether as an anesthetic (1846). This discovery was a great boon to surgery.

Multiple-Choice Test

1. An important reason why the earliest factories in the United States were located in New England was the region's (*a*) nearness to coal mines (*b*) abundance of iron deposits (*c*) abundance of water power (*d*) well-developed system of canals.
2. A highway built from Cumberland, Maryland, to Vandalia, Illinois, was called the (*a*) Genesee Turnpike (*b*) Lincoln Highway (*c*) National Road (*d*) Wilderness Road.
3. At the time construction on the original Erie Canal was begun, the governor of New York State was (*a*) George Clinton (*b*) De Witt Clinton (*c*) Thomas Dongan (*d*) Francis Nicholson.
4. The first cotton mill in the United States was built by (*a*) Samuel Slater (*b*) Elias Howe (*c*) Robert Fulton (*d*) Francis Lowell.
5. Which river valley once served as the main highway from eastern New York to the Great Lakes? (*a*) Genesee (*b*) Hudson (*c*) Champlain (*d*) Mohawk.
6. The basic plan for governing new territories acquired by the United States was set forth in the (*a*) federal Constitution (*b*) Monroe Doctrine (*c*) Northwest Ordinance (*d*) Declaration of Independence.
7. All of the following states were created from the Old Northwest EXCEPT (*a*) Illinois (*b*) Indiana (*c*) Montana (*d*) Ohio.
8. Important products carried on the Erie Canal when it was first opened included all of the following EXCEPT (*a*) lumber (*b*) petroleum (*c*) potatoes (*d*) wheat.
9. The Ordinance of 1787 included provisions in regard to all of the following EXCEPT (*a*) the way in which states could be created (*b*) slavery in the Northwest Territory (*c*) the election of U.S. senators by the people (*d*) education.
10. Which man is NOT paired with the field in which he was most prominent? (*a*) Francis Lowell—textile industry (*b*) Robert Fulton—literature (*c*) Donald McKay—ship designing (*d*) George Stephenson—railroads.
11. Westward expansion before 1830 was promoted by the (*a*) Mohawk and Hudson Railroad and the Delaware River (*b*) Cumberland Road and the Erie Canal (*c*) Baltimore and Ohio Railroad and the Santa Fe Trail (*d*) Philadelphia-Lancaster Turnpike and the Missouri River.
12. The Western frontier contributed to American democracy by (*a*) establishing the first public elementary school system (*b*) supporting the Federalist party after it declined in the East (*c*) serving as a symbol of economic opportunity and political equality (*d*) opposing the construction of public works by the federal government.
13. The land conveyance most widely used by the early pioneers to transport their families and possessions westward was the (*a*) stagecoach (*b*) barge (*c*) flatcar (*d*) Conestoga wagon.

14. The first two Western states to be admitted into the Union after the establishment of the United States were (*a*) Ohio and Indiana (*b*) Louisiana and Mississippi (*c*) Kentucky and Tennessee (*d*) Florida and Alabama.

15. The factory system of manufacturing was first used in the United States in making (*a*) steel plows (*b*) cotton cloth (*c*) shoes and clothing (*d*) railroad equipment.

16. The term *Industrial Revolution* means (*a*) a revolt against the government by workers in factories (*b*) disorder caused by strikes (*c*) the seizure of factories by workers (*d*) the change from hand methods to machine methods of production.

17. One invention that greatly speeded the settlement and cultivation of the prairie region of the United States was the (*a*) cotton gin (*b*) sewing machine (*c*) steel plow (*d*) power loom.

18. An Indian chief who led tribal resistance to the spread of settlement in the Northwest Territory was (*a*) Powhatan (*b*) Tecumseh (*c*) Massasoit (*d*) Sacajawea.

19. James Robertson was a pioneer in the settlement of (*a*) Kentucky (*b*) Tennessee (*c*) Illinois (*d*) Ohio.

20. What is the best definition for the term *American frontier?* (*a*) a fixed boundary line (*b*) a coastline (*c*) a shifting area marking the farthest extent of pioneer settlement (*d*) the dividing line between American and Spanish settlements.

Identification Test

1. On May 24, 1844, as I sat tensely at the key of my instrument in Washington, I wondered whether my message "What hath God wrought!" would be received in Baltimore.

2. I loved frontier life. Before the Revolution I blazed the Wilderness Road to the West and led many settlers to Kentucky.

3. I was among the first to make a paying business of the steamboat. In 1807 my first steamboat, the *Clermont,* sailed up the Hudson River.

4. As a young shop employee I heard a visitor suggest that clothes could be made more cheaply if there were a machine to do the sewing in less time. I worked hard at this suggestion, and in 1846 I patented a machine which greatly changed the clothing industry.

5. I performed many experiments mixing chemicals with rubber. One day I accidentally dropped a sulfur-and-rubber mixture on a hot stove, and thus discovered the process of vulcanizing. This led to a new industry, which today makes hundreds of products.

6. As a boy I was interested in mechanical things such as watches. During a visit to Georgia in 1792, I· saw the need for a machine to clean cotton by separating the fiber from the seeds. My invention led to a great increase in the production of cotton.

7. In 1834 I patented the first machine to cut grain. In Chicago I established a factory which later became the International Harvester Corporation.

8. I was born in Virginia and emigrated to eastern Tennessee in the 1770's. During the Revolution I led a force of frontier militia across the Great Smoky Mountains and defeated the British at King's Mountain in North

Carolina. Later I became the first governor of the newly created state of Tennessee.

9. During the Revolution I earned the nickname "Mad Anthony" for my daring military tactics. In the 1790's President Washington sent me to the Northwest Territory to end the Indian threat. In western Ohio I decisively defeated the Indians at Fallen Timbers and negotiated a treaty with them that opened the area to settlement.

10. While practicing dentistry in Boston in the 1840's, I learned about a new substance, called ether, that might serve as a painkiller. I experimented with it on myself and tested it successfully on a patient. My process of using ether as an anesthetic proved a great boon to surgery.

Modified True-False Test

1. The first passenger railroad built in the United States was the *Pennsylvania* Railroad.
2. The Northwest Territory included the region north of the *Tennessee* River and east of the Mississippi River.
3. The first practical steam locomotive was developed by *Samuel Slater,* an Englishman.
4. The TOM THUMB was designed and built by *De Witt Clinton.*
5. The FLYING CLOUD was a well-known *clipper ship.*
6. The first steamboat on the Mississippi River system was called the *New Orleans.*
7. The era of turnpike construction was ushered in with the completion of the *Philadelphia-Lancaster Turnpike* in 1794.
8. The system of interchangeable parts in manufacturing was conceived by *Francis C. Lowell.*
9. The first protective tariff was enacted by Congress in *1816.*
10. To encourage American industrialization after the War of 1812, Congress chartered the second *Bank of the United States.*
11. The first practical steam engine was developed by *James Watt,* an English inventor.
12. The first permanent settlement in Ohio was made at *Marietta* in 1788.
13. Provision for the survey, division, and sale of public lands was made by the enactment of the *Northwest Ordinance.*
14. The defeat of the Creek Indians by Andrew Jackson at the Battle of *Fallen Timbers* opened the lower part of the Old Southwest to settlement.
15. The Cumberland Gap provided a route for the *National* Road in the 1770's.

Essay Questions

1. Explain how *each* of the following persons contributed to the westward expansion of the United States: Daniel Boone, Sacajawea, Cyrus McCormick, William Henry Harrison, and De Witt Clinton.
2. Read the following section. Then, for *each* statement or question below, select the number of the item that best completes the statement or answers the question. Base your answer on the information contained in the selection.

   If George Washington could have visited the United States in the 1840's, his thoughts might have run somewhat like this:

"I find it hard to believe that over 20,000,000 people now live in the United States, and that towns have been built beyond the Mississippi River. When I became President in 1789, there were only 4,000,000 people, and most of these lived along the Atlantic coast. Can this great city be New York, where I took the oath of office as President? The city I knew had 60,000 inhabitants; today, they tell me, it is the largest city in the New World and has a population of 500,000. What is this engine belching smoke and sparks that carries people across the countryside? When I traveled from Mount Vernon to New York in 1789, I depended on horses. I see factories where machines spin thread to weave it into cloth. Who ever heard in my day of a machine that could spin 80 threads at one time? Here is a boat run by steam. It travels against the current of a river! In my time we depended on the wind to drive our boats. Who would have believed that this country could change so greatly in 50 years!"

a. How much greater was the population of the United States in 1840 than in 1789? (1) twice as great (2) five times as great (3) twelve times as great (4) twenty times as great.

b. George Washington was inaugurated in (1) Boston (2) Mount Vernon (3) New York (4) Baltimore.

c. A method of transportation used in the 1840's but not in Washington's time was the (1) airplane (2) automobile (3) sailboat (4) railroad.

d. The changes described in the paragraph took place within a period of about (1) 10 years (2) 20 years (3) 50 years (4) 70 years.

e. In Washington's time most of the people in the United States lived (1) west of the Mississippi (2) along the eastern seaboard (3) in the deep South (4) in the Northwest.

3. a. Describe some of the road conditions that made land travel in the United States disagreeable during the late 1700's.

b. (1) Name *one* of the kinds of wagons in which Americans traveled before the building of railroads.
(2) Give a general description of the wagon named.

c. State *two* reasons why Americans preferred to travel by water when it was possible.

4. Explain briefly how the Industrial Revolution in America affected each of the following: method of producing goods, amount of goods produced, development of transportation, wealth of the country, and manner in which people lived.

5. The Ordinance of 1787 was an outstanding achievement of Congress under the Articles of Confederation. List the important provisions of the ordinance and briefly explain the importance of each.

6. a. List *five* early American inventors and name an invention of each.
b. Show *one* way in which each invention changed American life.

7. Since the Revolutionary War, science and invention have greatly changed methods of transportation and communication. Explain how each of *five* of the following would have been accomplished most efficiently at the time indicated:

a. Sending a message from New York City to Boston in 1825.

b. Traveling from New York City to London in 1845.

c. Transporting goods from Albany to Buffalo in 1830.

d. Sending freight from Philadelphia to Lancaster in 1795.

e. Traveling from Cleveland to Chicago in 1860.

f. Shipping freight from New Orleans to Pittsburgh in 1820.

g. Sending a message from Washington, D.C., to Atlanta in 1850.

h. Carrying the mail from Cumberland to Wheeling in 1820.

8. Write a paragraph telling how the pioneers settled the region west of the Alleghenies. Include the following: *three* routes they used, *two* reasons for their moving westward, and *three* dangers they faced.

9. a. Why did the colonists use so much "homespun" in the early years of our history?

   b. Why was New England the center of manufacturing for so many years?

   c. Give either *two* advantages or *two* disadvantages of factory-made goods of today compared with the handmade goods of the colonial period.

Part 3. Age of Jackson

ANDREW JACKSON BECOMES PRESIDENT

ELECTION OF 1824

President Monroe's administration is often called the "Era of Good Feelings" because it was marked by political harmony. Toward the end of Monroe's second term, however, national unity began to give way to sectional rivalry. Dissimilar economic interests caused the North, South, and West to take opposing stands on the important issues of the day.

In the presidential campaign of 1824, the West was represented by two candidates: Henry Clay of Kentucky and Andrew Jackson of Tennessee. New England supported John Quincy Adams of Massachusetts; the South favored William H. Crawford of Georgia. When the electoral votes were counted after the election, it was found that none of the four candidates had won a majority. Jackson, however, received the most votes. The selection of a President was now up to the House of Representatives. Clay threw his support to Adams, and the House chose Adams as President.

THE DEMOCRATIC-REPUBLICAN PARTY SPLITS

The election of 1824 aroused much controversy. Jackson's supporters claimed that their candidate should have been chosen President because he had received more votes than Adams. They accused Clay of having made a "deal" to back Adams in return for the promise of an appointment as Secretary of State. The bitterness arising from this dispute led to a split in the Democratic-Republican party. The group supporting Adams and Clay took the name *National Republicans.* Jackson's followers continued to call themselves *Democratic-Republicans,* or simply *Democrats.*

JACKSON IS ELECTED IN 1828

In the election of 1828, the National Republicans nominated Adams for a second term, and the Democrats chose Jackson as their candidate. Backed almost solidly by the West and South, and supported by the small farmers and factory workers in the Middle Atlantic states, Jackson was elected President by a large majority.

BACKGROUND AND ACHIEVEMENTS OF JACKSON

EARLY LIFE

Born of Scotch-Irish parents in Waxham, South Carolina, in 1767, Andrew Jackson was raised on a nearby farm owned by his uncle. At the age of 13 he joined the militia and fought in the Revolution. Captured by a British raiding party, he was ordered to shine an officer's boots. When he refused, young Andrew received a saber blow which cut his arm to the bone and inflicted scars that remained throughout his life. He hated the British from that time on.

156

POLITICAL AND MILITARY CAREER

After the war Jackson studied law, moved westward, and became a lawyer in the frontier community of Nashville. He helped draft the constitution for the new state of Tennessee. He served in Congress as a representative and a senator, and then returned to Tennessee to become a judge of that state's supreme court. Retiring in 1804, he devoted himself to farming, breeding racehorses, running a general store, and carrying on a trade in land, horses, and slaves.

When the War of 1812 broke out, Jackson volunteered his services to the nation. He defeated the Creeks in the Battle of Horseshoe Bend in Alabama and routed the British at New Orleans. He earned the nickname "Old Hickory" for his toughness and endurance and emerged from the war as a national hero and the idol of the West. Jackson later added to his reputation by campaigning successfully against the Seminole Indians in Florida and serving as military governor of the territory after it was acquired from Spain. Elected to the Senate in 1823, he resigned two years later to campaign for the presidency.

CHARACTER AND OUTLOOK

Andrew Jackson's election is often referred to as the "Revolution of 1828." Unlike his predecessors in the White House, who had been men of wealth, culture, and high social position, Jackson had risen from poverty. He was considered a man of the people. Moreover, "Old Hickory" was the first Westerner to become President. A man of strong character, colorful personality, and firm beliefs, he provided the nation with vigorous leadership during his two terms in office. His influence was so great that this period in U.S. history is often called the *Age of Jackson,* or the *Jacksonian Era.*

Jackson's slogan was "Let the people rule!" He considered himself the representative of the common people and believed it his duty as President to carry out their demands. His courage, honesty, and independence of character were admired by many, but his quick temper and strong will made many enemies. His opponents called him "King Andrew I."

THE SPOILS SYSTEM

Jackson believed that: (1) Every citizen had an equal right to hold public office. (2) Appointive officeholders should serve for only a short time to enable more people to have a chance at government jobs. Rotation of jobholders would prevent the growth of a bureaucracy—a class of permanent officials. (3) Federal offices should be in the hands of friends and supporters of the victorious candidate. He dismissed hundreds of federal employees and replaced them with his own appointees.

The practice of appointing people to government jobs as a reward for party loyalty was given the name *spoils system,* from the expression "to the victors belong the spoils." Although introduced by Jackson on the national level as a democratic reform, it was nevertheless a poor practice. Efficient and experienced civil servants faced the loss of their jobs whenever a new party came into power. Party loyalty rather than competence became the basis for federal appointments.

JACKSON OPPOSES NULLIFICATION

In 1828, while Adams was President, Congress passed a tariff act that imposed very high duties on imports. Southerners protested vigorously because a high tariff increased the cost of manufactured goods that they had to buy. They argued that the Tariff Act of 1828 was passed not to raise revenue but to protect the interests of Northern manufacturers at the expense of Southern farmers. Southerners called it a "tariff of abominations."

In 1832 a tariff act was passed lowering some of the duties levied in 1828 but continuing the principle of "protection." Denouncing both tariff laws as oppressive and unjust, the South Carolina legislature adopted an *Ordinance of Nullification*. By this act, South Carolina (1) declared the tariff laws null and void and not binding on the people of South Carolina, (2) prohibited federal officials from collecting the duties in South Carolina, and (3) threatened to withdraw from the Union if the government attempted to collect the duties by force.

Jackson sent a message to the people of South Carolina asserting that no state can refuse to obey the laws of the land or leave the Union. He made preparations to enforce the tariff by military means if necessary.

To avoid armed conflict, Congress, under the leadership of Henry Clay (the "Great Compromiser"), passed the *Compromise Tariff of 1833*. It provided for a gradual reduction in import duties over the next 10 years. Accepting the compromise, South Carolina repealed its nullification ordinance.

JACKSON DESTROYS THE NATIONAL BANK

Jackson believed that the second Bank of the United States (1) aided merchants, manufacturers, and bankers at the expense of the common people, (2) concentrated power in the hands of a few and was therefore undemocratic, and (3) exercised too much influence economically and politically. In 1832, four years before the charter of the Bank was due to expire, Congress voted to renew it. Jackson vetoed the bill. The Bank became the main issue in the election of 1832. Jackson, continuing to speak out against the Bank during the campaign, won by a landslide. He thereupon proceeded to destroy the Bank by withdrawing government funds from it. He deposited the money in several dozen state banks. These depositories were popularly called "pet banks" or "Jackson's pets." His enemies charged that they were selected because of their officers' pro-Jackson sympathies.

JACKSON'S INDIAN POLICY

Jackson sympathized with frontier dwellers who said that Indians east of the Mississippi should give up their lands to settlers. He convinced Congress to set aside large tracts west of the Mississippi as Indian territory, and then proceeded to transfer Eastern tribes to these areas. The largest removal occurred in the Old Southwest, home of the Creeks,

Choctaws, Cherokees, Chickasaws, and Seminoles (the *Five Civilized Tribes*). So many Indians died on the long, overland march to their new homelands that the journey became known as the "Trail of Tears."

By the time that Jackson left office, relatively few Indians remained east of the Mississippi, although some tribes did fight to retain their lands. Notable among these were the Sauk and Fox Indians, led by Black Hawk, in the upper part of the Northwest Territory, and the Seminole Indians, under Osceola, in Florida.

END OF THE JACKSONIAN ERA

FORMATION OF THE WHIG PARTY

In the early 1830's the National Republicans merged with other groups opposing Jackson and formed the Whig party. Led by Henry Clay and Daniel Webster, the Whigs were backed by commercial and manufacturing people in the Northeast. The party favored (1) rechartering the national bank, (2) high protective tariffs, and (3) a strong central government. Some elements in the party did not support this program but joined the Whigs because they disliked Jackson.

VAN BUREN SUCCEEDS JACKSON AS PRESIDENT

As Jackson's second term came to a close, his popularity among the common people was greater than ever. Before leaving office and retiring to the *Hermitage,* his Tennessee home, he persuaded the Democrats to nominate his Vice President and long-time adviser, Martin Van Buren of New York, for the presidency. Van Buren easily won the election of 1836 and became the nation's eighth President.

THE PANIC OF 1837

No sooner had Van Buren assumed office than the nation entered a period of severe depression, called the *Panic of 1837.* State-chartered "pet banks" and Western "wildcat banks" had engaged in unsound practices. They issued paper money that was not backed by gold or silver, and gave loans too freely. People used the borrowed money to speculate in public lands.

President Jackson had become alarmed over the excessive land speculation and the oversupply of paper money. He had therefore issued the *Specie Circular* in 1836 ordering the government to accept only specie (gold and silver), and not paper money, in payment of public lands.

The Specie Circular had a disastrous effect upon the economy. Land prices fell because money was harder to borrow and because land could be purchased only with gold or silver. Speculators were ruined. Many banks failed because they could not meet the demands of depositors who wanted to exchange their paper money for gold or silver.

Prices of manufactured goods and farm products declined sharply. Factories and mills closed down, canal and railroad building stopped, and unemployment spread. Wage earners in the Northeast were especially hard hit by the panic. The depression lasted for several years, and the nation did not fully recover from its effects until 1844.

ESTABLISHMENT OF AN INDEPENDENT TREASURY

In 1840 Van Buren recommended and Congress passed the *Independent Treasury Act.* This law provided for the establishment of subtreasuries in the nation's principal cities where federal funds were to be deposited and safeguarded. Thereby the government was made independent of the nation's privately owned banks and was given exclusive control over its funds. The act was repealed in 1841 but was repassed in 1846. The subtreasury system lasted until the early 1900's, when it was merged with the Federal Reserve System.

THE WHIGS ELECT HARRISON AND TYLER

To oppose Van Buren in the election of 1840, the Whigs nominated William Henry Harrison of Ohio, the renowned Indian fighter who had defeated Tecumseh's forces in the Battle of Tippecanoe. Their candidate for Vice President was John Tyler of Virginia, a former Democrat who had broken with Jackson over the nullification issue. The Whig campaign slogan was "Tippecanoe and Tyler too." Suffering a decline in popularity because of the Panic of 1837, the Democrats lost the election.

TYLER BECOMES PRESIDENT

The Whig victory was short-lived. One month after assuming the presidency, Harrison died of pneumonia, becoming the first President to die while in office. Vice President Tyler succeeded him. A believer in states' rights and a weak central government, which were the principles of the Democratic party, he opposed the policies of the party that had elected him. He vetoed many bills passed by the Whig-controlled Congress and finally broke with the Whigs completely.

WEBSTER-ASHBURTON TREATY

An important achievement of Tyler's administration was the settlement of a dispute with England over the boundary between Maine and Canada. Daniel Webster, then Secretary of State, negotiated a treaty in 1842 by which the United States received a large part of the disputed area, including the fertile Aroostook Valley.

The British also agreed to adjust the U.S.-Canadian boundary between Lake Superior and Lake of the Woods. Thereby, the United States obtained what is now northeastern Minnesota—an area that includes the rich iron deposits of the Mesabi Range.

DEMOCRATIC ADVANCES AND SOCIAL REFORMS

GROWTH OF POLITICAL DEMOCRACY

The spirit of democracy that had swept Jackson into office gave rise to many political reforms, including the following:

1. **Expansion of Democracy in the States.** (*a*) Following the example of the newly admitted Western states, the older states in the East began to abolish religious and property qualifications for voting. Suffrage was gradually extended to all adult white males. (*b*) Property qualifications for officeholding were lowered or removed. Thus, more people became eligible for government positions. (*c*) A number of high state positions were made elective. (*d*) Terms of elected officials were shortened to enable the people to vote them out of office more quickly. (*e*) The selection of presidential electors was taken out of the hands of the state legislatures and given to the people.

2. **Nominating Conventions.** Before the Jacksonian Era, each party's leaders in Congress held a conference, or *caucus*, and chose their party's candidates for President and Vice President. In the late 1820's the party caucus was replaced by the more democratic *nominating convention*. This is a national conference held by each party at which delegates representing the entire membership select the party's nominees.

REFORM MOVEMENTS ARISE

The democratic spirit of the Age of Jackson stimulated movements to correct unjust and evil conditions. Reformers supported the following causes:

1. **Abolition of Slavery.** Some opponents of slavery, called *abolitionists,* demanded that slavery be abolished. *William Lloyd Garrison,* a leading abolitionist, published a newspaper, *The Liberator,* in which he denounced slavery as a national sin and advocated the immediate freeing of all slaves.

2. **Care of the Mentally Ill and Physically Handicapped.** In the early 19th century, insane persons were treated as criminals rather than as sick people. The prevailing practice was to keep them chained or caged. Largely through the efforts of *Dorothea Dix,* state-supported institutions were established for the proper treatment and sympathetic care of the mentally ill.

Samuel G. Howe and other humanitarians made the nation aware of the conditions of the sightless, hearing impaired, and disabled. Schools were founded to educate the physically handicapped and to teach them trades so that they could lead productive lives.

3. **Prison Reform.** Dorothea Dix and others exposed the miserable conditions in the nation's prisons. As a result of their work, imprisonment for debt was abolished, living conditions in prisons were improved, and efforts were made to prepare offenders for useful lives after their release from jail.

4. **Temperance.** Reformers led a crusade against the evils of alcoholic beverages, condemning heavy drinking because it resulted in drunkenness, crime, and poverty. At first, they urged moderation, or *temperance,* but later campaigned for *prohibition*—a total halt to the sale of intoxicating beverages. The temperance movement gained widespread acceptance.

By 1856, 13 states either prohibited or restricted the sale of alcoholic drinks. (For later developments, see page 298.)

5. Women's Rights. Women began to agitate for equal rights to property, employment, education, and participation in government. Under the leadership of *Lucretia Mott* and *Elizabeth Cady Stanton,* a women's rights convention was held at Seneca Falls, New York, in 1848. The convention adopted a declaration demanding that women "have immediate admission to all the rights and privileges which belong to them as citizens of the United States."

Despite hostility and ridicule, the feminist movement made some headway, particularly in the second half of the 19th century. Women gained increased opportunities for higher education and acquired the vote in some Western states. However, it was not until the 20th century that the feminist movement succeeded in achieving most of its goals (see pages 298–300).

WORKERS SEEK TO BETTER THEIR CONDITION

The spirit of democracy that prevailed during the Age of Jackson encouraged workers to form labor unions and agitate for a variety of reforms and improvements. Supported by humanitarians, workers in the 1830's achieved many gains. These included equal suffrage for all white men, free public schools, recognition by some courts of labor's right to organize and strike, abolishment of imprisonment for debt, a 10-hour workday, and some restrictions on child labor.

The labor movement suffered a severe setback during the Panic of 1837, when thousands of people lost their jobs. Trade unionism revived in the 1850's but again declined because of high unemployment during the Panic of 1857. After the Civil War the labor movement came to life again and gradually became a major force in the American economy (see pages 265–273).

PUBLIC EDUCATION SPREADS

Before the 1830's opportunities for schooling were extremely limited, and most children received little formal education. With the expansion of suffrage during the Jacksonian Era, thoughtful people realized that citizens needed to be educated if they were to vote intelligently and participate wisely in the affairs of government. This touched off the demand that all children receive an education at public expense.

The movement for free public schools made rapid headway. Before long there emerged statewide systems of elementary schools (particularly in the Northern states), training schools for teachers, new teaching methods, improved textbooks, and better school buildings. By the middle of the century nearly all the states offered some form of free elementary education.

Secondary schools developed more slowly. The first public high school was founded in Boston in 1821. Yet, as late as 1860, Massachusetts had only 78 public high schools, Ohio 48, and New York 41. These schools were intended primarily for boys.

Secondary and higher education for females were provided at (1) private high schools, known as academies or female seminaries, (2) a few colleges, such as Oberlin and Antioch, that admitted both men and women, and (3) several women's institutions of higher learning, including Wesleyan College in Georgia and Mt. Holyoke College in Massachusetts.

Among noteworthy contributors to education were the following:

Henry Barnard reformed the public school systems of Connecticut and Rhode Island. He published the *American Journal of Education,* which helped to inform teachers of new educational methods. He served as the first U.S. Commissioner of Education.

De Witt Clinton, governor of New York, pioneered the establishment of a public school system in his state. He encouraged new subjects, more school libraries, and better textbooks. He persuaded the state legislature to provide more money for schools.

Mary Lyon, a pioneer in higher education for women, founded Mt. Holyoke Female Seminary, later called Mt. Holyoke College, in Massachusetts.

Horace Mann, the best-known educational reformer of his time, served as secretary of the Massachusetts Board of Education. He supervised the expansion of the state system of public elementary schools, helped establish many new high schools, improved and broadened courses of study, organized a state teachers' association, and founded the nation's first school for the training of teachers.

Noah Webster wrote a series of spellers, grammars, and readers that helped to standardize spelling, pronunciation, and English usage throughout the country, and influenced the education of millions of schoolchildren. His two-volume reference work, *An American Dictionary of the English Language,* published in 1828, also met with great acclaim.

Emma Willard advocated educational equality for women. In 1821 she founded a female seminary, now called the Emma Willard School, at Troy, New York. Students were instructed in philosophy, mathematics, and other subjects until then considered "too difficult" for women.

CULTURAL ADVANCES BEFORE 1860

AN AMERICAN LITERATURE DEVELOPS

With the exception of Benjamin Franklin's works, little of literary worth was produced by American writers before the War of 1812. After 1815, however, a distinctive American literature began to appear. The first important writers were Washington Irving, James Fenimore Cooper, and William Cullen Bryant. The public was delighted with the stream of stories, poems, essays, and novels that flowed from the pens of these talented authors. As time passed, more and more people acquired a taste for reading, and writers were assured of an ever-growing audience for their literary efforts.

There were several reasons for the increasing interest in books. (1) With the spread of the free public school movement, more young people obtained an education. (2) People enjoyed more leisure time, especially in the urban areas of the East. (3) The development of better lighting, such as whale-oil lamps, made it easier for people to read in the evening.

Among the noteworthy writers of the period before 1860 were the following:

George Bancroft produced a 10-volume *History of the United States,* which traced the progress of America from the time of its discovery to the establishment of the national government.

William Cullen Bryant, poet and editor of the *New York Evening Post,* wrote *Thanatopsis,* the first widely read poem by an American.

James Fenimore Cooper was the first important American novelist. *Leatherstocking Tales* is a series of five novels of frontier life, including *The Last of the Mohicans* and *The Deerslayer.*

Ralph Waldo Emerson, an outstanding American essayist, advised readers to be self-reliant, to lead noble lives, and to seek truth and beauty.

Nathaniel Hawthorne, short-story writer and novelist, portrayed the stern Puritanism of earlier days in New England. His outstanding novels are *The Scarlet Letter* and *The House of the Seven Gables.*

Oliver Wendell Holmes wrote the poems *Old Ironsides* and *The Wonderful One-Hoss Shay,* which are still known to millions today. One of his widely read prose works is *The Autocrat of the Breakfast Table.*

Washington Irving wrote about the early Dutch settlers of New York. *Diedrich Knickerbocker's History of New York* pokes good-natured fun at Dutch manners and customs. *Rip Van Winkle* and *The Legend of Sleepy Hollow* are short stories based on legends of the Hudson River Valley.

Henry Wadsworth Longfellow brought to life early American history and legends in such poems as *The Song of Hiawatha, Evangeline, The Courtship of Miles Standish,* and *Paul Revere's Ride.*

James Russell Lowell, poet and literary critic, wrote *The Biglow Papers,* in which he opposed the Mexican War and denounced slavery.

Herman Melville won fame for his book *Moby Dick,* the story of Captain Ahab's pursuit of a whale. This novel is America's greatest sea story.

Francis Parkman was a famous historical writer. His great work (written mostly after 1860), *France and England in the New World,* is a series of volumes describing the struggle between these two powers for control of North America. His earlier works, *The California and Oregon Trail* and *History of the Conspiracy of Pontiac,* are also well known.

Edgar Allan Poe won acclaim throughout the world as a poet, short-story writer, and critic. *The Pit and the Pendulum* and *The Cask of Amontillado* are short stories filled with horror and suspense. *The Gold Bug* and *The Murders in the Rue Morgue* are first-rate mystery stories. *The Raven* and *Annabel Lee* are well-known poems.

William H. Prescott, a famous historian, popularized the reading of history by his dramatic narratives of the Spanish Empire in America: *History of the Conquest of Mexico* and *History of the Conquest of Peru.*

William Gilmore Simms, a popular Southern writer, wrote the widely read romantic novels *Guy Rivers* and *The Yemassee.*

Harriet Beecher Stowe wrote the immensely popular novel of slave life in the South, *Uncle Tom's Cabin.* This book helped arouse considerable sentiment against slavery.

Henry David Thoreau, a student of nature, believed in simple living and self-reliance. His famous book, *Walden,* describes his experiences and observations while living in the woods.

John Greenleaf Whittier was a poet and abolitionist. His *Barbara Frietchie* and *Ichabod* are antislavery poems. *Maud Muller, The Barefoot Boy,* and *Snow-Bound* are poems describing life in rural New England.

NEWSPAPERS AND MAGAZINES ATTAIN WIDE CIRCULATION

The 1830's witnessed the rise of a new trend in newspaper publishing: "the penny press." To attract more readers, newspapers reported the happenings of the day in an interesting and simple style and offered copies for sale at the nominal price of a penny. The first successful penny daily was the New York *Sun,* founded in 1833 by Benjamin H. Day. Two years later James Gordon Bennett started the *New York Morning Herald.* His paper was the first to print financial news, report crimes and social affairs, and discuss the theater. In 1841 Horace Greeley founded the New York *Tribune,* which helped to stir up antislavery sentiment and campaigned for temperance and women's rights. (Greeley popularized the phrase "Go west, young man.") Ten years later, *The New York Times,* one of America's most influential papers, appeared under the editorship of Henry J. Raymond.

Other city dailies were the Philadelphia *Public Ledger,* the Boston *Daily Times,* the Baltimore *Sun,* the Detroit *Free Press,* the New Orleans *Picayune,* the Cleveland *Plain Dealer,* and the Chicago *Daily Tribune.*

Aided by such inventions as the telegraph, which made possible the instantaneous transmission of news, and the rotary press, which sped up the printing process, newspapers increased their circulation immensely. By 1860 penny dailies were being published in every major city, and Americans in all parts of the country were able to keep abreast of the news.

Magazines, too, grew in popularity. Among the important periodicals that flourished before 1860 were *Godey's Lady's Book,* the most popular women's magazine; the *North American Review;* the *Southern Literary Messenger; Harper's New Monthly Magazine* (later called *Harper's Magazine*); and the *Atlantic Monthly.*

Multiple-Choice Test

1. The term *Era of Good Feelings* is associated with the administration of (*a*) Andrew Jackson (*b*) Martin Van Buren (*c*) John Tyler (*d*) James Monroe.
2. One immediate effect of President Jackson's Specie Circular was to increase the (*a*) sales of public land (*b*) demand for hard money (*c*) value of paper currency (*d*) general prosperity of the country.

3. An important cause of the Panic of 1837 was the (*a*) end of the frontier (*b*) shortage of paper money (*c*) building of the Baltimore and Ohio Railroad (*d*) speculation in Western lands.

4. The West was influential in bringing about the election of (*a*) John Quincy Adams (*b*) James Madison (*c*) Andrew Jackson (*d*) James Monroe.

5. In a United States presidential election, the electoral vote was distributed in this manner:

CANDIDATE	A	B	C	D
% OF ELECTORAL VOTE	38	38	16	8

Based on this information, which is a valid statement about the outcome of the election? (*a*) Candidate *A* was declared the winner immediately after the election. (*b*) Candidate *A* became President and Candidate *B* became Vice President. (*c*) Another presidential election was held in order to determine a winner. (*d*) The President was chosen by the members of the House of Representatives.

6. Which two events occurred during the administration of the same President? (*a*) destruction of the second Bank of the United States—passage of the Compromise Tariff of 1833 (*b*) enactment of the "tariff of abominations"— Panic of 1837 (*c*) Rush-Bagot Agreement of 1817—Louisiana Purchase (*d*) passage of the Independent Treasury Act—acquisition of Florida from Spain.

7. In which respect was the presidency of Martin Van Buren like that of John Quincy Adams? (*a*) Each faced a financial crisis. (*b*) Each served only one term. (*c*) Each acquired new territory for the United States. (*d*) Each was from New York State.

8. The practice of replacing many federal jobholders with political appointees whenever a new administration assumes office is known as the (*a*) merit system (*b*) lottery (*c*) Washington merry-go-round (*d*) spoils system.

9. The Independent Treasury Act provided for the establishment of (*a*) wildcat banks (*b*) pet banks (*c*) federal subtreasuries for the deposit of government funds (*d*) a federal deposit insurance corporation.

10. The term *Trail of Tears* is associated with the (*a*) Ordinance of Nullification (*b*) Battle of Tippecanoe (*c*) "Five Civilized Tribes" (*d*) election of 1824.

11. All of the following advances in political democracy were made in the Jacksonian Era EXCEPT (*a*) the abolition of property qualifications for voting and officeholding (*b*) the selection of presidential electors by the voters rather than by the state legislatures (*c*) the introduction of the national nominating convention (*d*) the direct election of U.S. senators.

12. The Seneca Falls Declaration and Resolutions (1848) concerned (*a*) temperance (*b*) prison reform (*c*) women's rights (*d*) care of the mentally ill.

13. An outstanding humanitarian, responsible for reforms in prisons and mental institutions, was (*a*) Dorothea Dix (*b*) Lucretia Mott (*c*) Henry David Thoreau (*d*) Nathaniel Hawthorne.

14. Which author is NOT paired with one of his works? (*a*) William Cullen Bryant—*Thanatopsis* (*b*) James Fenimore Cooper—*Moby Dick* (*c*) Henry Wadsworth Longfellow—*The Song of Hiawatha* (*d*) Edgar Allan Poe—*The Raven*.

15. All of the following were leaders in the movement for the establishment of public schools EXCEPT (*a*) Henry Barnard (*b*) De Witt Clinton (*c*) William Prescott (*d*) Horace Mann.
16. Two women noted for their work in founding schools were (*a*) Harriet Beecher Stowe and Elizabeth Cady Stanton (*b*) Lucretia Mott and Dorothea Dix (*c*) Mary Lyon and Martha Washington (*d*) Emma Willard and Mary Lyon.
17. Which statement is true for both Washington Irving and James Fenimore Cooper? (*a*) They wrote stories about life in early America. (*b*) They founded successful newspapers. (*c*) They won fame for their poems. (*d*) They were leaders in the temperance movement.
18. One of the pioneers in the campaign for women's suffrage was (*a*) Noah Webster (*b*) Emily Dickinson (*c*) Clara Barton (*d*) Elizabeth Cady Stanton.
19. All of the following writers expressed strong antislavery sentiment EXCEPT (*a*) William Lloyd Garrison (*b*) Harriet Beecher Stowe (*c*) William Gilmore Simms (*d*) John Greenleaf Whittier.
20. The phrase "Go west, young man" was popularized by (*a*) Benjamin Day (*b*) Horace Greeley (*c*) Ralph Waldo Emerson (*d*) Henry David Thoreau.

Modified True-False Test

1. The *Webster-Ashburton* Treaty, negotiated between Britain and the United States, settled a boundary dispute between Maine and Canada.
2. "Tippecanoe and Tyler too" was a campaign slogan in the election of *John Quincy Adams* and John Tyler.
3. The name of President Jackson's home in Tennessee was the *Hermitage*.
4. The *Shawnee* Indians, led by Osceola, resisted the government's efforts to remove them from their tribal lands in Florida.
5. Groups opposing Jackson formed the *Federalist* party in the 1830's.
6. South Carolina's Ordinance of Nullification grew out of its opposition to the "*tariff of abominations.*"
7. State banks selected by the Jackson administration for the deposit of federal funds were popularly called *subtreasuries.*
8. A conference held by a party's congressional leaders for the purpose of selecting a presidential candidate was known as a *nominating convention.*
9. The *temperance movement* advocated limiting or prohibiting the sale of alcoholic beverages.
10. A term used to describe the rise of low-cost newspapers in the 1830's is "the *free* press."

Essay Questions

1. Read the selection below carefully and then answer the questions that follow:

"With the election of Andrew Jackson, there came a new era in American politics. The control of government had for some time been passing from the hands of the rich and aristocratic into those of the common people. Andrew Jackson, who was elected President largely because of his record in the War of 1812, was himself a man of the common people. He was set in his ways and was inclined to hate those who opposed him; yet he was a great figure. Other great political leaders of this time were John Quincy Adams, Henry Clay, Daniel Webster, and John C. Calhoun."

   a. What change had been gradually taking place in the control of government previous to Jackson's administration?

   b. What fact contributed to the election of Jackson?

   c. Mention *two* characteristics of Jackson.

   d. Name *three* great political leaders of this period other than Jackson.

2. Discuss *each* of the following with respect to Andrew Jackson:

   a. *two* battles that made him prominent and that led to his nomination as a presidential candidate

   b. *one* important domestic issue that arose during his administration

   c. *one* lasting influence that he has had on the history of our nation

Part 4. The United States Expands to the Pacific

ANNEXATION OF TEXAS

SETTLEMENT BY AMERICANS

After winning independence from Spain in 1821, Mexico encouraged American immigration by offering liberal grants of land to settlers. Thousands of Americans migrated to Texas, then part of the Mexican state of Coahuila. The region, well adapted to large-scale cotton growing, attracted many Southern planters, who brought along their slaves. By 1835 more than 20,000 Americans had settled there.

The American settlers soon became dissatisfied with Mexican rule. Differences in languages and customs, repeated changes in government, and quarrels over taxation and political representation proved to be constant sources of friction. When the Mexican government took steps to abolish slavery and halt further immigration, the Americans rebelled.

THE LONE STAR REPUBLIC (1836)

The Texans drove out the Mexican garrisons and proclaimed their independence. Determined to put down the rebellion, the Mexican president, Antonio López de Santa Anna, led a large force of Mexican troops into Texas. He surrounded a small band of Texans stationed in the *Alamo,* an old Spanish mission in San Antonio. When the garrison, commanded by William B. Travis, refused to surrender, Santa Anna stormed the fortress and captured it after every occupant had been killed or wounded. Then he murdered all of the wounded. "Remember the Alamo!" became the rallying cry of the aroused settlers. At the *Battle of San Jacinto,* in 1836, Texans under Sam Houston decisively defeated the Mexican army and forced it to withdraw from Texas.

With independence won, the settlers established the Republic of Texas. (It was also known as the *Lone Star Republic* because its flag had a single white star set in a blue field.)

TEXAN HEROES

Stephen F. Austin founded the first American colony in Texas (1821). Austin, the capital, was built on the land granted by the Spanish government to Moses Austin, Stephen's father.

Davy Crockett, a frontier fighter and hunter from Tennessee, joined the Texans in their revolt against Mexico. He was killed during the siege of the Alamo.

Sam Houston was the outstanding hero of the Texas rebellion. He defeated the Mexicans and captured Santa Anna at the Battle of San Jacinto. In 1836 he was elected the first president of the Republic of Texas.

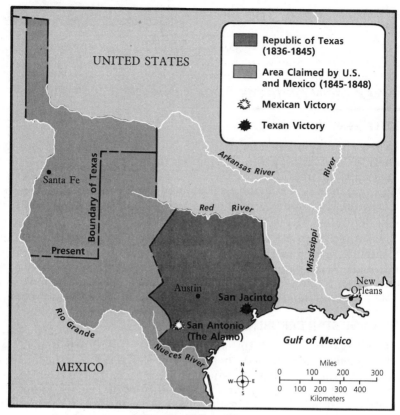

The Republic of Texas

TEXAS REQUESTS ADMISSION TO THE UNION

Texas asked the United States government for admission to the Union. This request was rejected at first because: (1) Many Northerners were opposed to the extension of slavery and to the increase of Southern strength in Congress. (2) Many Americans feared that the annexation would involve the United States in a war with Mexico.

As time passed, sentiment changed in favor of admitting Texas, mainly because: (1) The new republic might fall under the domination of a foreign power. (2) The annexation of Texas would increase the size of the United States and help fulfill the nation's "manifest destiny" to expand to the Pacific.

(The phrase *manifest destiny* first appeared in a magazine editorial that supported the annexation of Texas. The author of the editorial declared that it was "the fulfillment of our manifest destiny to overspread the continent allotted by Providence for the free development of our yearly multiplying millions." The term soon gained widespread acceptance as justification for American expansionism.)

EXPANSION IS THE MAIN ISSUE IN 1844

In the election of 1844 the Democratic party came out for a program of expansion. The Democrats demanded the "reoccupation of Oregon" (a territory held jointly by England and the United States) and the "reannexation of Texas" (claiming that the area already belonged to the United States as part of the Louisiana Purchase). Campaigning on this issue, the Democratic candidate, James K. Polk of Tennessee, defeated his Whig opponent, Henry Clay, and became the 11th President of the United States.

TEXAS ENTERS THE UNION

Accepting the election results as an indication that the nation favored the annexation of Texas, Congress acted quickly. In 1845 it passed a resolution admitting Texas into the Union as the 28th state.

ACQUISITION OF OREGON

LOCATION OF THE OREGON COUNTRY

The Oregon Country consisted of an area bounded by the Rocky Mountains on the east, the Pacific Ocean on the west, Mexican California on the south, and Russian Alaska on the north. Originally Russia, Spain, England, and the United States all claimed the region. Spain withdrew its claim by the Florida Treaty of 1819. Russia gave up its claim in 1824, when the southern boundary of Alaska was fixed at latitude 54°40′.

AMERICA'S CLAIM TO THE TERRITORY

The United States based its claim to Oregon on the following: (1) Captain *Robert Gray,* a New England sea captain, discovered the Columbia River in 1792. (2) Lewis and Clark explored the area in 1804–1806. (3) *John Jacob Astor* founded a fur trading and trapping station in 1811 at Astoria, at the mouth of the Columbia River.

ENGLAND'S CLAIM TO THE TERRITORY

England's claim to Oregon was based on the following: (1) James Cook sailed to the Oregon coast in 1778. (2) George Vancouver explored the region in 1792. (3) The Hudson's Bay Company in 1824 established a fur trading station at Fort Vancouver (near present-day Portland) on the lower Columbia River.

AMERICANS SETTLE THE OREGON COUNTRY

In 1818 a temporary agreement was reached between England and the United States providing for the joint occupation of the Oregon region. Settlement was begun in the 1830's by American missionaries who went to the Oregon Country to convert the Indians. Noteworthy were *Jason Lee,* who explored the Willamette Valley and founded in 1834 the first Indian mission (Methodist) and farming settlement in the Oregon Country (near present-day Salem, Oregon); *Marcus Whitman* and his wife *Narcissa,* who led a group of settlers to Oregon and set up a Presbyterian mission at Walla Walla (in the present-day state of Washington); and *Father Pierre Jean De Smet,* who established Catholic missions in the Oregon Country and on the Great Plains.

Glowing reports soon reached the East and Middle West of the fertile lands and pleasant climate beyond the Rockies, and started a "Great Migration" in 1843. Caravans of Conestoga wagons, or "prairie schooners," left from Independence, Missouri; crossed the Great Plains; went through the Rockies at South Pass (the Cumberland Gap of the West); and followed the winding Snake River to the Columbia River. This 2,000-mile-long route was known as the *Oregon Trail.* By 1845 about 5,000 Americans had migrated to the region. The pioneers founded settlements and introduced self-government. As more and more Americans settled in the Oregon Country, the demand grew for the United States to take over the entire territory.

SETTLEMENT OF THE OREGON DISPUTE

The Democrats won the election of 1844 partly on the promise of "fifty-four forty or fight." This slogan called for the acquisition of the entire Oregon Country, even if the action led to a war with England. After the election, however, the two nations negotiated a peaceful settlement. In the Treaty of 1846, England obtained the northern part

The Bettmann Archive
**In this British cartoon, Brother Jonathan (the United States)
prepares to do battle with Great Britain over Oregon.**

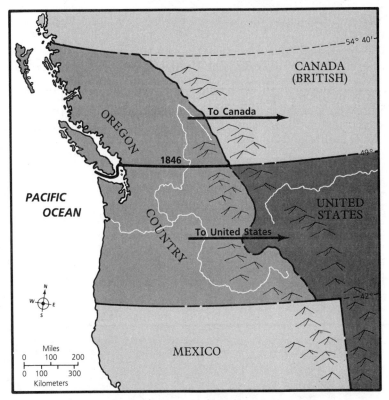

Settlement of the Oregon Dispute

of the Oregon Country, and the United States acquired the southern part.

By this agreement, the Treaty Line of 1818, which formed the boundary between Canada and the United States from Minnesota to the Rockies, was extended westward to the Pacific Ocean. The boundary follows the 49th parallel.

In 1848 a territorial government was set up in the Oregon Territory, and 11 years later the southwestern section was admitted into the Union as the state of Oregon. Also formed from this territory were the states of Washington and Idaho, and parts of Montana and Wyoming.

THE MEXICAN WAR (1846–1848)

CAUSES

Relations between the United States and Mexico had been strained almost from the beginning of Mexico's independence from Spain. There were two major causes of friction: (1) Property of U.S. citizens living in Mexico had been damaged during uprisings and other disturbances. The Mexican government held back payment of damage claims. (2)

Mexico still claimed Texas and resented American annexation of the territory.

The immediate cause of the Mexican War was a dispute over the southern boundary of Texas. The United States claimed the Rio Grande as the boundary, while Mexico considered the boundary to be the Nueces River, some 150 miles to the north. In early 1846 President Polk sent a U.S. force under Zachary Taylor to the disputed area to protect Texas from a threatened Mexican invasion. When Mexico sent troops across the Rio Grande and fought several skirmishes with the Americans, the President asked Congress for a declaration of war (declared on May 13, 1846).

HIGHLIGHTS OF THE WAR

1. Zachary Taylor, called "Old Rough and Ready," invaded northern Mexico. After a series of battles, he captured the fortified city of Monterrey. Continuing his advance into Mexico, he defeated a numerically superior Mexican army under Santa Anna in the *Battle of Buena Vista* (February, 1847).

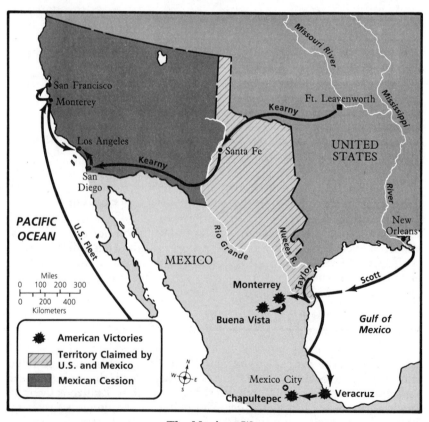

The Mexican War

2. Stephen Kearny, marching from Fort Leavenworth on the Missouri River, invaded the Mexican province of New Mexico and occupied its capital, Santa Fe. He then continued on to California, which was already in revolt. American settlers in that area, led by the explorer *John C. Frémont,* had risen up against the Mexicans in 1846 and proclaimed the independent Republic of California. They were assisted by an American naval force, commanded by *John Sloat* and later by *Robert Stockton,* which took possession of the ports of Monterey, Los Angeles, and San Francisco. This uprising is known as the *Bear Flag Revolt* because the rebel flag bore the figure of a grizzly bear.

Upon reaching California, Kearny helped to end Mexican resistance and to complete American occupation of the region (1847).

3. Winfield Scott landed near the powerful Mexican fortress of Veracruz and captured it after a short siege. He then started a march to the capital, Mexico City, 250 miles away. He defeated Santa Anna in a series of battles along the way, stormed the fortified hill of Chapultepec (the last barrier to the capital), and occupied Mexico City (September, 1847). This U.S. victory brought the war to an end.

TREATY OF GUADALUPE HIDALGO (1848)

By this treaty Mexico recognized the Rio Grande as the southern boundary of Texas. Furthermore, Mexico ceded the territories of New Mexico and Upper California (the *Mexican Cession*) to the United States. In exchange, Mexico received $15 million in cash, and the United States assumed all claims of American citizens against Mexico.

From the Mexican Cession were formed the states of California, Nevada, and Utah, most of Arizona, and parts of New Mexico, Colorado, and Wyoming.

ZACHARY TAYLOR, MEXICAN WAR HERO, BECOMES PRESIDENT

Zachary Taylor of Louisiana, the Whig party candidate, won election as the nation's 12th president in 1848. An army officer for 40 years, he had seen service in the War of 1812 and had fought against Indians in the Northwest Territory and in Florida. His victories at Monterrey and Buena Vista during the Mexican War made him a national hero and helped him gain the presidency. He died in the summer of 1850, after serving as President for only 16 months, and was succeeded by Vice President *Millard Fillmore* of New York.

SETTLEMENT OF CALIFORNIA

CALIFORNIA UNDER SPANISH AND MEXICAN RULE

The first Europeans to settle California were Spaniards. They established some large ranches in the valleys, a few settlements along the coastline, and a chain of Indian missions. Contact with the outside world was limited to infrequent visits of ships from New England carrying articles of trade. Not until the 1840's did American pioneers show any interest in settling in California. As late as 1846 the non-Indian population of the area included about 8,000 Mexicans of Spanish descent and 500 Americans.

TRAIL BLAZERS OF THE FAR WEST

Among the early American pioneers who blazed a trail to the Far West were the following:

Jedediah Smith, a hunter and fur trapper, traveled from Great Salt Lake to California in 1826. He was the first American to cross the deserts of Utah and Nevada and the Sierra Nevada Mountains.

Ewing Young, led a party of fur trappers from Santa Fe to California in 1829. He later explored a large part of California and pioneered in the settlement of Oregon.

John C. Frémont, known as "the Pathfinder," led three trips of exploration to the Far West (1842–1846). He mapped the Oregon Trail, explored the Great Basin region of western Utah and Nevada, and crossed the mountains to California and the Pacific coast. His reports aroused great interest in the Far West.

Kit Carson, a famous trapper and mountain guide, hunted in the region west of the Rockies and served as a guide to Frémont on his expeditions to the Far West.

DISCOVERY OF GOLD IN CALIFORNIA (1848)

Shortly before California became part of the United States by the Treaty of Guadalupe Hidalgo, gold was discovered in the Sacramento Valley. The find was made by James Marshall, a construction worker building a sawmill for John Sutter. Sutter, a Swiss-American settler, had established a ranch at the junction of the Sacramento and American rivers. Word spread quickly, first locally, then throughout the nation, and finally to all the world. Visions of sudden wealth dazzled the country, and "gold fever" spread like wildfire. Miners, soldiers, laborers, farmers, clerks, and professional people raced toward the gold fields.

ROUTES USED BY THE FORTY-NINERS

The Forty-Niners, so named after the year of the great gold rush, used every available means of transportation in their trek to California. Many came by land, using packhorse, stagecoach, pushcart, and covered wagon. The trip from the Atlantic coast to California took five months. The Forty-Niners had to cross mountains, deserts, and treacherous streams. They faced thirst, hunger, and hostile Indians. Many died along the way.

Thousands of Forty-Niners went by sea. Some sailed down the Atlantic coast and around Cape Horn. Others sailed to the Isthmus of Panama, hiked overland through jungle and swamp to the Pacific coast, and then completed their journey to California by boat.

GROWTH OF CALIFORNIA

An estimated 100,000 people flocked to California in 1849. During the next few years many more arrived. The output of gold rose from

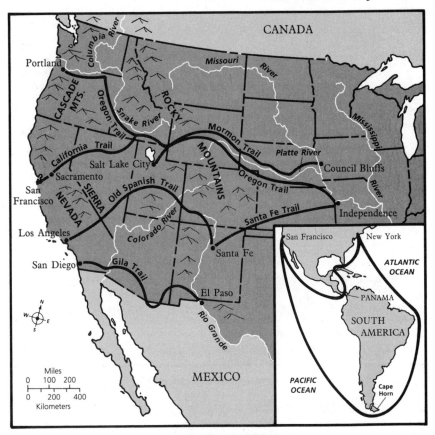

Routes to the Far West

$5 million in 1848 to $40 million in 1849 and $55 million in 1851. A few Forty-Niners struck it rich in the gold fields and made their fortunes overnight. Some grew wealthy by providing the miners with food, supplies, and services at fantastically high prices. Others, failing to achieve wealth quickly, turned to cattle raising, fruit growing, and other pursuits.

Life in the mining camps was rough and lawless. Gambling, drinking, brawling, and gunfighting were everyday occurrences. The miners were the prey of desperadoes who came to the camps to obtain gold the easy way—by theft or murder. In order to protect themselves, law-abiding people organized *vigilance committees*. The vigilantes preserved law and order, and administered quick "frontier justice" to criminals.

The Californians adopted a constitution, organized a government, and applied to Congress for statehood. In 1850 California was admitted as the 31st state of the Union.

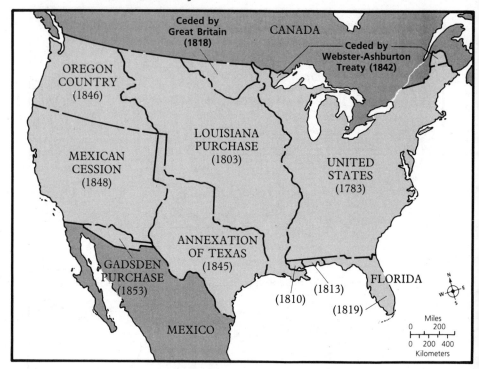

Territorial Growth Before 1860

SETTLEMENT OF UTAH

FOUNDING OF THE MORMON SECT

Joseph Smith founded the Church of Jesus Christ of Latter-Day Saints (Mormon Church) in 1830 at Fayette, New York. This religious sect gained many converts. Led by Smith, the Mormons migrated in succession to Ohio, Missouri, and Illinois. In each instance, attempts at settlement failed because of the hostility of non-Mormon neighbors.

THE MORMONS SETTLE IN UTAH

When Joseph Smith was killed by a mob in Illinois in 1844, *Brigham Young* assumed the leadership. The Mormons then embarked on a migration to the Far West in search of a haven where they would be free from persecution. In 1847 Brigham Young and a pioneer band of Mormons reached the Great Salt Lake Valley in Utah and founded Salt Lake City. Other Mormons soon followed. With cooperative effort and religious zeal, the settlers changed the barren wasteland to a land of plenty.

In 1850 Utah was organized as a territory with Young as its governor. Statehood, however, was delayed for many years because the Mormons believed in *polygamy*, the practice of having more then one wife at the same time. Some years after they finally abolished the practice, Utah was admitted as the 45th state (1896).

THE GADSDEN PURCHASE (1853)

Franklin Pierce of New Hampshire, a Democrat, won the election of 1852 and became the nation's 14th President. The following year he authorized the U.S. minister to Mexico, James Gadsden, to negotiate the purchase of a strip of land along the southern boundary of New Mexico and Arizona. The United States wanted this land for a proposed railroad to the Pacific. The Gadsden Purchase, which cost $10 million, completed the present boundary between the United States and Mexico.

Multiple-Choice Test

1. The claims of the United States to the Oregon Country were settled in 1846 by (*a*) an agreement with Spain (*b*) an agreement with Great Britain (*c*) war with Great Britain (*d*) purchasing the territory from Mexico.

2. A famous battle cry of the Texans in the war against the Mexicans in 1836 was (*a*) "Remember the Alamo!" (*b*) "O, Susanna!" (*c*) "Fifty-four forty or fight!" (*d*) "Remember the *Maine!*"

3. The Mormons founded what is now the state of (*a*) Arizona (*b*) California (*c*) New Mexico (*d*) Utah.

4. As a result of the Mexican War, the United States acquired (*a*) Alaska (*b*) Puerto Rico (*c*) California (*d*) Louisiana.

5. Which of these areas was the LAST acquired by the United States? (*a*) Florida (*b*) Texas (*c*) Gadsden Purchase (*d*) Mexican Cession.

6. Which of these religious groups had its beginning in New York State? (*a*) Methodists (*b*) Quakers (*c*) Presbyterians (*d*) Mormons.

7. Marcus Whitman, a Presbyterian missionary, encouraged settlers to come to (*a*) Oregon (*b*) Maine (*c*) Texas (*d*) Florida.

8. A person associated with the early history of California was (*a*) Davy Crockett (*b*) John Jacob Astor (*c*) John C. Frémont (*d*) Daniel Boone.

9. Of the following titles, the one that would be most appropriate for a book covering the history of the United States from 1800 to 1850 is (*a*) *The Conquest of a Continent* (*b*) *The Expansion of the United States From the Mississippi to the Pacific* (*c*) *The Exploration and Colonization of America* (*d*) *The Struggle for Independence.*

10. A state that was known as the Lone Star Republic before it joined the Union was (*a*) Texas (*b*) Florida (*c*) California (*d*) Nevada.

11. Which of the following events most immediately preceded the Mexican War? (*a*) establishment of Texan independence (*b*) occupation by U.S. soldiers of disputed territory north of the Rio Grande (*c*) the Gadsden Purchase (*d*) the election of James K. Polk.

12. "Fifty-four forty or fight" was a campaign slogan in the presidential campaign of (*a*) James K. Polk (*b*) Andrew Jackson (*c*) Zachary Taylor (*d*) Millard Fillmore.

13. Which was an argument used by the United States in the 1840's to support its claim to the Oregon Country? (*a*) A provision of the Jay Treaty had ceded the territory to the United States. (*b*) France had ceded its claim to the territory to the United States. (*c*) Zebulon Pike's explorations had

established American claims to the territory. (*d*) American missionaries and fur traders had settled in the territory.

14. Which was a direct result of the Mexican War? (*a*) The United States annexed Texas. (*b*) Congress appropriated funds for the Lewis and Clark expedition. (*c*) Mexico accepted the Rio Grande as the southern boundary of Texas. (*d*) Many of the sectional differences between the North and the South were resolved by the acquisition of new territory.

15. The Mexican War was ended by the (*a*) Treaty of Ghent (*b*) Webster-Ashburton Treaty (*c*) Treaty of Guadalupe Hidalgo (*d*) Treaty of Paris.

16. The Bear Flag Revolt occurred in (*a*) Oregon (*b*) Utah (*c*) California (*d*) New Mexico.

17. All of the following were American military leaders in the Mexican War EXCEPT (*a*) Stephen Kearny (*b*) Joseph Smith (*c*) Winfield Scott (*d*) Zachary Taylor.

18. All of the following Americans were involved in the struggle for Texan independence from Mexico EXCEPT (*a*) Robert Gray (*b*) Davy Crockett (*c*) William B. Travis (*d*) Sam Houston.

19. All of the following were trailblazers to the region west of the Rockies EXCEPT (*a*) Jedediah Smith (*b*) Kit Carson (*c*) John Sevier (*d*) Ewing Young.

20. The Mormons founded Salt Lake City under the leadership of (*a*) Joseph Smith (*b*) Brigham Young (*c*) John Sutter (*d*) John Jacob Astor.

Modified True-False Test

1. The slogan "Fifty-four forty or fight" refers to the dispute over the possession of the *Louisiana Purchase.*
2. "Old Rough and Ready" was the nickname given to *Brigham Young.*
3. The Mexican president who fought Texans in 1836 was *Agustín de Iturbide.*
4. *John Jacob Astor* was a fur trader who established a trading station at the mouth of the Columbia River.
5. Gold was first discovered in the Sacramento Valley of California on the property of *Ewing Young.*
6. Those who participated in the great migration to the gold fields of California were called *Mormons.*
7. *Jedediah Smith,* an explorer of the Far West, became known as "the Pathfinder."
8. People who formed groups to preserve law and order in the mining camps were known as *vigilantes.*
9. An important natural boundary between the United States and Mexico is the *Missouri River.*
10. The term used by American expansionists to justify the acquisition of new territory was "*manifest destiny.*"

Essay Questions

1. The expanding frontier has influenced the nation in several ways. Select *two* of the following statements and show how each applies to the history of the nation: (*a*) The expanding frontier has helped the growth of democracy.

(*b*) The expanding frontier has led to conflicts. (*c*) The expanding frontier has helped the nation to achieve greater economic self-sufficiency.

2. Study carefully the following outline on the territorial expansion of the United States. You will note that *five* items are omitted. For *each* blank space in the outline, select the proper item chosen from the list below the outline.

Territorial Expansion Within the United States (1803–1853)

I. Louisiana Purchase, 1803
    A. . . . .
    B. Doubled the area of the United States

II. . . . .
    A. Ceded by Spain in 1819
    B. Removed the danger of Indian attacks

III. Annexation of Texas, 1845
    A. Favored by Polk in his campaign for the presidency
    B. . . . .

IV. . . . .
    A. Claim partly based on activities of fur trappers
    B. Established boundary at 49th parallel

V. The Mexican Cession, 1848
    A. Included New Mexico and Upper California
    B. Partially settled by the Forty-Niners

VI. The Gadsden Purchase, 1853
    A. Acquired during President Pierce's administration
    B. . . . .

List of items:

Bought from France for $15,000,000
Acquisition of Florida
Bought from Russia for $7,200,000
Helped to cause the Mexican War
Wanted chiefly to provide a railroad route to the West Coast
Settlement of Oregon Dispute, 1846

3. One of the most important developments in American history was the great westward migration which resulted in the settlement of the territory between the Appalachians and the Pacific. (*a*) Give *three* reasons why Americans left the farms, towns, and cities in the East to settle in the West. (*b*) Give the name of an important leader in the settlement of *each* of the following: California, Texas, Oregon, and Utah. (*c*) Describe a contribution of *each* person named.

4. (*a*) Describe some of the difficulties Easterners experienced in going to California in the days of the gold rush. (*b*) Describe the route taken by most pioneers who migrated to Oregon in the 1840's.

UNIT VI. DIVISION AND REUNION

Part 1. Sectionalism and Slavery Lead to Disunion

FACTORS GIVING RISE TO SECTIONALISM

Geography plays an important role in shaping history. The climate, natural resources, and physical features of an area determine the ways people make their living. These economic activities, in turn, influence the political and social outlook of the area.

In the North, the livelihood of many people depended on shipping, trade, and manufacturing. Central to the economy of the South was the plantation system of agriculture and the use of slave labor. And in the West, most people lived on medium-sized farms, which were operated by pioneering families without the use of hired help.

As the economic interests of the three sections grew more dissimilar in the early 1800's, Americans began to look at political issues from a *sectional* (regional), rather than a *national,* point of view.

SECTIONAL VIEWS DIFFER ON KEY POLITICAL ISSUES

1. Tariff. The North favored a protective tariff to safeguard its manufacturers from foreign competition. The South, having little industry to protect, opposed the enactment of such a tariff because it increased the cost of goods that Southerners had to buy. The West supported the North's position on this issue.

2. National Bank. The North demanded a federally backed national bank, because a strong banking system helped to stabilize currency and credit. The South and West argued that a national bank tended to tighten money and credit and placed too much power in the hands of a few bankers. These two regions came out for cheap money and locally controlled state banks—both of which would make borrowing easier.

3. Internal Improvements. The West insisted that roads and canals be built at the federal government's expense to speed transportation and facilitate the shipment of surplus products to market. This demand was supported by the North because better transportation helped to expand its trade. The South, whose trade with the West was limited, resented paying for projects that provided little benefit to its people. It also claimed that federally funded internal improvements were unconstitutional.

4. Cheap Western Land. To encourage settlement, the West asked the federal government to make land available in the territories at low cost and on easy terms. The South, seeking to expand the plantation system and to extend slavery into the newly acquired territories, also favored cheap land. The North, however, opposed the idea because westward migration reduced the supply of labor for its mills and factories.

CONFLICTING VIEWS ON THE NATURE OF THE UNION

THE NATURE OF THE UNION

The United States was formed out of 13 separate colonies. By adopting the Constitution, the states created a national government but also kept their own state governments. Disputes later arose as to which rights and powers had been retained by the states and which had been transferred to the federal government.

CALHOUN SPEAKS OUT FOR STATES' RIGHTS AND NULLIFICATION

The chief spokesperson for states' rights was John C. Calhoun. He was the author of the *South Carolina Exposition and Protest,* which, in 1828, declared the "tariff of abominations" unconstitutional.

Calhoun expressed the states' rights view on the nature of the Union as follows: (1) The Union was a *compact,* or agreement, among sovereign states. (2) Each state had the right to decide for itself whether a federal law was constitutional. (3) If a state judged an act unconstitutional, it had the power of nullification, that is, to declare the law null and void within its own borders.

(Many Southern leaders supported these ideas. South Carolina attempted to implement the doctrine of states' rights when it adopted its Ordinance of Nullification in 1832. See page 158.)

WEBSTER DEFENDS THE UNION IN A DEBATE WITH HAYNE

In the Senate in 1830, Robert Hayne of South Carolina and Daniel Webster of Massachusetts engaged in a historic debate on the nature of the Union. Hayne presented the case for states' rights and nullification. Webster, in defending the Union, declared that: (1) The nation was a union of people rather than of states. (2) The federal government was supreme over state governments. (3) Only the Supreme Court, not the states, had the power to judge a law unconstitutional. He concluded with the ringing words, "Liberty and Union, now and forever, one and inseparable."

THE SLAVERY ISSUE SPLITS THE NATION

SLAVERY BECOMES A SECTIONAL INTEREST

Slavery was introduced into colonial America in the 1600's when thousands of African blacks were forcibly brought to the New World and sold to settlers. Slavery became most deeply rooted in the South because of the need for cheap labor on the plantations. By 1760 there were about 300,000 slaves in the Southern colonies and 100,000 in the Middle Colonies and New England.

After the Revolution, slavery declined in the North. Not only did the Declaration of Independence (which declared the equality of man) exercise an important influence, but most Northerners found slavery unprofitable. A number of Northern states enacted legislation in the 1780's to abolish slavery, and the Ordinance of 1787 prohibited slavery in the newly organized Northwest Territory.

In the South, on the other hand, slavery increased in importance with the invention of the cotton gin and the expansion of the plantation system. The region's slave population grew from 650,000 in 1790 to 3.2 million in 1850.

Slave ownership in the South was distributed rather unevenly. Three-fourths of the free population consisted of small farmers and city dwellers who owned no slaves. Of the remaining fourth, more than half owned 5 or fewer slaves and nearly all the others held less than 20. The large planters, with 50 or more slaves, represented about 2% of the region's landowners. But they wielded so much power that they dominated the South economically, politically, and socially.

Non-slaveholding whites in the South generally supported the planter class in its defense of slavery. Some hoped to acquire slaves of their own and become plantation owners. Others believed that slave labor was essential to the South's development and prosperity. And nearly all held the view that blacks were racially inferior and were therefore destined to occupy a lower social position than whites.

In the first half of the 19th century, slavery became a sectional issue that divided the nation into two opposing camps: North and South. In this instance, the designation "North" meant all the non-slaveholding, or *free,* states and territories; and "South" referred to those areas that permitted the practice of slavery.

BLACKS DEMONSTRATE THEIR OPPOSITION TO SLAVERY

Uprooted from their ancestral homes, deprived of their culture, and forced to live in a strange and foreign environment, slaves demonstrated their anger and resentment in numerous ways. In the spirituals they sang, they communicated to each other a longing for freedom and messages of rebellion. By feigning illness and laziness, they sought to deprive owners of their labor. Many ran away. Some also resorted to uprisings, as follows:

1. In the early 1700's a series of slave outbreaks occurred in South Carolina. One of the most serious was the so-called *Cato Conspiracy* at Stono, near Charleston, South Carolina, in 1739. A group of slaves killed two guards at a warehouse, seized a supply of arms, and attempted to escape to Spanish Florida. In the pursuit that followed, all but 10 were captured or slain. Thirty whites and 44 blacks lost their lives in this incident.

2. In 1800 a slave named Gabriel Prosser organized a rebellion that became known as the *Gabriel Plot.* After months of planning, he assembled over a thousand slaves on the outskirts of Richmond, Virginia. and proceeded to march on the city. The authorities, warned of the plot by informers, sent in troops to disperse the insurgents. Scores were arrested and 35 were executed, including Prosser.

3. *Denmark Vesey*, a free black working as a carpenter in Charleston, planned an uprising of city-dwelling slave artisans in 1822. When word of the plot leaked out, nearly 150 blacks were arrested and about 40, including Vesey, were hanged.

4. One of the most violent slave eruptions took place in Southampton County, Virginia, in 1831. Nat Turner, a mystical and rebellious preacher and slave, led an uprising that started with the slaying of his master's family and quickly spread throughout the area. Before the *Nat Turner Insurrection* was finally put down by federal and state troops, about 60 whites and 100 blacks had been killed. Turner and about 20 other black participants were tried and put to death.

FREE AND SLAVE STATES

Of the original thirteen states, six were slaveholding and seven were free. Between 1791 and 1819, when nine new states were admitted to the Union, five were slave and four were free, thus balancing the number of free and slave states at eleven each.

	FREE STATES	SLAVE STATES
ORIGINAL STATES	New Hampshire Massachusetts Rhode Island Connecticut New York New Jersey Pennsylvania	Delaware Maryland Virginia North Carolina South Carolina Georgia
NEW STATES (1791–1819)	Vermont Ohio Indiana Illinois	Kentucky Tennessee Louisiana Mississippi Alabama

MISSOURI COMPROMISE (1820)

Missouri, a slaveholding area, applied for statehood in 1819. The application was opposed by Northern members of Congress because Missouri's admission as a slave state would (1) upset the balance between the free and slave states, giving the South control of the Senate, and (2) set a dangerous precedent by extending slavery into the northern part of the Louisiana Purchase.

After Maine requested admission as a free state, Congress enacted the *Missouri Compromise* (1820). It provided that (1) Maine be admitted as a free state, (2) Missouri be admitted as a slave state, and (3) slavery be prohibited in the rest of the Louisiana Purchase north of latitude 36°30′ (the southern boundary of Missouri). (See map, page 186.)

ABOLITIONISTS ATTACK SLAVERY

Beginning in the 1830's, Northern reformers, called abolitionists, formed antislavery societies and agitated for the freeing of all slaves.

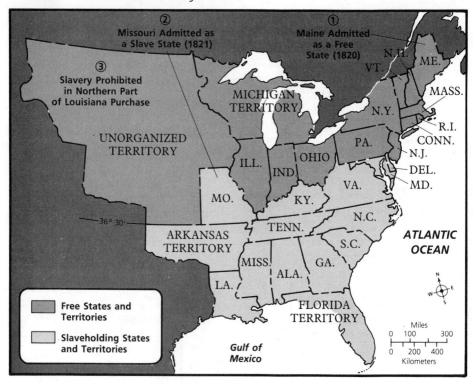

The Missouri Compromise (1820)

Abolitionist leaders included William Lloyd Garrison, whose publication, *The Liberator,* was the most influential antislavery newspaper in the country; *Theodore Weld* and his wife, the former *Angelina Grimké,* prominent writers, lecturers, and organizers of abolitionist societies; and *Frederick Douglass, Harriet Tubman,* and *Sojourner Truth,* former slaves who spoke out against slavery and helped other blacks escape to freedom.

Also contributing to the growth of antislavery sentiment in the North were (1) the writings of John Greenleaf Whittier and James Russell Lowell, (2) the speeches of *Wendell Phillips* and *Theodore Parker,* and (3) the novel *Uncle Tom's Cabin* by Harriet Beecher Stowe (1852).

Some abolitionists helped runaway slaves gain their freedom by organizing the "underground railroad." Slaves escaping from their Southern masters were secretly led northward from one hiding place, or "station," to another until they were safely out of reach of their pursuers.

REACTION TO THE ABOLITIONISTS

Many Southerners strongly resented the attempts of abolitionists to overturn the established basis of their economic and social life. They claimed that the picture of slavery drawn by abolitionists was unfair and exaggerated. They also pointed out that, by helping slaves to escape, abolitionists were violating federal law, which provided for the return of runaway slaves.

Many Northerners, particularly those who did business with the South, also severely criticized abolitionists. Politicians, too, deplored the sectional bitterness aroused by abolitionists. But despite this opposition, the abolitionist movement spread. By 1840 there were 2,000 abolition societies in the Northern states, with a total membership of 175,000.

The Free-Soil Party. In the election campaign of 1848, antislavery Democrats and Whigs banded together to form the Free-Soil party. They nominated Martin Van Buren of New York for President; declared their opposition to the extension of slavery into the territories; and adopted the slogan, "Free soil, free speech, free labor, and free men." Although they failed to carry a single state, the Free-Soilers influenced the outcome of the election. Van Buren split the Democratic vote in New York, enabling Zachary Taylor, the Whig candidate, to win that state's 36 electoral votes and assuring his election as President. (If Lewis Cass, the Democratic candidate, had carried New York, he would have won the presidency.)

COMPROMISE OF 1850

Between 1836 and 1848 six more states were added to the Union: Arkansas, Michigan, Florida, Texas, Iowa, and Wisconsin. Since three were free states and three were slaveholding, the balance between North and South was maintained, now at 15 states each.

With the acquisition of the Mexican Cession in 1848, the problem of the extension of slavery to the territories flared up again. The South demanded that slavery be permitted in the new region; the North insisted that slavery be prohibited. The issue came to a head in 1850 when California, a part of the Mexican Cession, sought admission as a free state. The debate on this question aroused so much bitterness that many observers thought the nation would split apart.

After much discussion, Congress accepted five separate proposals submitted by Henry Clay that, as a group, became known as the *Compromise of 1850*. They provided that (1) California be admitted as a free state, (2) the territories of Utah and New Mexico, which formed the rest of the Mexican Cession, be organized on the principle of *popular sovereignty* (also called *squatter sovereignty*)—that is, the people of the region should decide for themselves whether or not they wished to permit slavery, (3) the slave trade, but not slave ownership, be prohibited in the District of Columbia, the nation's capital, (4) Texas give up its claim to part of New Mexico in return for $10 million, and (5) a new law be passed to help slaveowners regain their runaway slaves.

FUGITIVE SLAVE LAW (1850)

The *Fugitive Slave Law*, enacted as part of the Compromise of 1850, amended and strengthened an earlier law that had been in effect since 1793. It (1) placed fugitive slave cases under the jurisdiction of the federal government; (2) empowered special U.S. commissioners to issue warrants for the arrest and return of fugitives to their masters; (3)

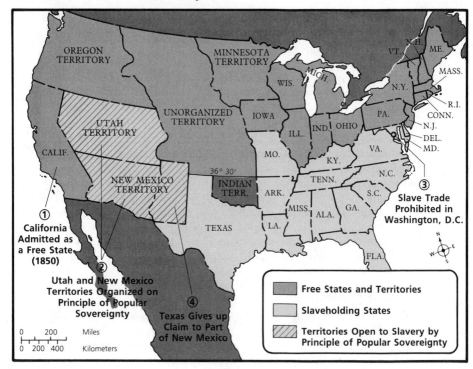

The Compromise of 1850

authorized the commissioners to deputize citizens to assist them in enforcing the law; and (4) imposed stiff fines or jail sentences upon those who refused to cooperate or who aided escaping slaves. Many Northerners refused to obey the law, however, and continued to assist fugitive slaves. The "underground railroad" became more active than ever.

KANSAS-NEBRASKA ACT (1854)

Senator Stephen A. Douglas of Illinois proposed a bill to establish territorial governments in the unorganized northern portion of the Louisiana Purchase. Passed by Congress in 1854, the Kansas-Nebraska Act provided for the creation of the territories of Kansas and Nebraska. The question of slavery was to be resolved on the basis of popular sovereignty, thus repealing the Missouri Compromise, which had prohibited slavery in the northern part of the Louisiana Purchase.

Resolution of the slavery issue by popular sovereignty made Kansas a bloody battleground. As settlers from both the North and the South poured into the new territory, pro- and antislavery elements competed for control. Antagonism between the two groups erupted into open warfare. So many lives were lost that the territory became known as "Bleeding Kansas."

FORMATION OF THE REPUBLICAN PARTY

Dissatisfied with the stand of the existing parties on the question of extending slavery into the territories, a group of Northern Whigs, Free-Soilers, and Democrats in 1854 formed the *Republican party*. They called for the repeal of the Kansas-Nebraska Act and the Fugitive Slave Law, and for the abolition of slavery in the District of Columbia. As this platform proved popular in the North, the new party gained many adherents there.

ELECTION OF 1856

In 1856 the Republicans nominated John C. Frémont of California to oppose both the Democratic candidate, James Buchanan of Pennsylvania, and the Whig candidate, former President Millard Fillmore of New York. Buchanan won the election and became the nation's 15th President. The Republicans, however, showed surprising strength. Frémont received a large popular vote and won the electoral votes of about two-thirds of the free states. The Whigs received little support and, following this defeat, ceased to be a factor in national politics.

DRED SCOTT DECISION (1857)

In 1834 Dred Scott, a slave, was taken by his master from the slave state of Missouri into free territory. After a few years he was taken back to Missouri. Scott then sued for his freedom, contending that his stay in a territory where slavery was prohibited had made him free. His case eventually reached the U.S. Supreme Court. In 1857 a majority of the justices ruled that Scott was a slave, not a citizen, and thus was not entitled to bring suit in a federal court. They declared further that since slaves were property and Congress had no right to deprive citizens of their property, owners could take their slaves into any U.S. territory. The Missouri Compromise, which had prohibited slavery in certain territories, therefore violated the Constitution and was void, said the Court.

The Dred Scott decision enraged many Northerners because it made possible the extension of slavery into all territories.

LINCOLN-DOUGLAS DEBATES

In the Illinois senatorial campaign of 1858, the Democratic candidate, Stephen A. Douglas (the "Little Giant"), was opposed by Abraham Lincoln, the Republican nominee. Douglas was an eloquent orator and one of the leading political figures in the country. Lincoln challenged Douglas to a series of debates on the vital issues of the day.

In the course of these discussions, which attracted national attention, every aspect of the slavery issue was debated. In one debate, held in Freeport, Illinois, Lincoln presented Douglas with a problem. The principle of popular sovereignty permitted a territory to exclude slavery. The Dred Scott decision said that slavery could not be excluded from a territory. Which of these two, Lincoln asked, did Douglas favor? Douglas answered that the people could exclude slavery from a territory in spite of the Dred Scott decision. His answer (called the "Freeport Doctrine") so offended Southern Democrats that they refused to back him for the presidency in 1860.

Although Lincoln lost the 1858 senatorial election, the debates made him nationally famous and helped him gain the Republican nomination for President in 1860.

JOHN BROWN'S RAID (1859)

John Brown was a fanatical abolitionist who favored freeing slaves by force. After participating in the bloody fighting between proslavery and antislavery factions in Kansas, he returned to the East and conceived a plan to stir up a slave uprising in the South. With a group of 18 men, he attacked and seized the government arsenal at Harpers Ferry, Virginia. His purpose was to obtain a supply of weapons to arm slaves and lead them in revolt. Captured by federal troops after most of his men had been killed or wounded, he was tried for treason, found guilty, and hanged.

Abolitionists regarded Brown as a martyr to the antislavery cause and commemorated his deed in a marching song entitled *John Brown's Body*. Southerners viewed the raid as further proof that the abolitionists and "Black Republicans" (people who advocated racial equality) of the North were plotting to destroy the Southern way of life.

PRELUDE TO WAR

ELECTION OF LINCOLN (1860)

When the Democratic party held its national nominating convention in the spring of 1860, it was unable to agree upon a presidential candidate and a platform that would be acceptable to all factions in the party. It split into two groups, the Northern delegates choosing Stephen A. Douglas of Illinois as their candidate, and the Southern delegates selecting John C. Breckinridge of Kentucky.

The Republicans nominated Abraham Lincoln of Illinois for President. The party declared its opposition to the extension of slavery and to "nativist" demands that the naturalization laws be changed to abridge the rights of immigrants. It came out for federally sponsored internal improvements, a protective tariff, a railroad to the Far West, and free land for Western settlers.

Aided by the split in the Democratic party and the appeal of the Republican platform to both Northern and Western voters, Lincoln won the election. The sectional nature of his victory is demonstrated by the fact that Lincoln won all the electoral votes in all the free states except New Jersey (where he won four and Douglas three), but he failed to carry a single slave state.

SOUTH CAROLINA SECEDES FROM THE UNION

Earlier that year Southern leaders had warned that the election of a Republican President would cause the South to leave the Union. With

A Job for the New Cabinet Maker

Lincoln's victory, South Carolina took steps to carry out this threat. A state convention on December 20, 1860, declared that "the Union now subsisting between South Carolina and the other states . . . is hereby dissolved."

FORMATION OF THE CONFEDERACY

By February, 1861, Alabama, Florida, Georgia, Louisiana, Mississippi, and Texas—in addition to South Carolina—had withdrawn from the Union. Delegates from the seceding states met at Montgomery, Alabama, and formed the *Confederate States of America.* They drew up a constitution which resembled the Constitution of the United States except that it (1) emphasized the sovereign and independent character of each state, (2) recognized and protected slavery, and (3) forbade the levying of protective tariffs and the use of government funds for internal improvements.

Jefferson Davis of Mississippi was chosen President of the Confederacy and Alexander H. Stephens of Georgia, Vice President.

BUCHANAN TAKES NO ACTION TO STOP THE SECESSIONISTS

While these events were taking place, President Buchanan stood by helplessly. (Lincoln had not yet been inaugurated.) Although Buchanan hoped to see the Union preserved, he stated that neither he nor Congress had the power to prevent a state from seceding. During the last months of his administration, the secessionists took over nearly all federal property in their states. This included forts and arsenals, with their large supplies of weapons; customhouses and post offices; and the New Orleans Mint, with its stock of gold and silver coins. Anxious to preserve the peace until his term expired, Buchanan made no attempt to interfere with the seizure of federal property.

INAUGURATION OF LINCOLN

On March 4, 1861, Lincoln took the oath of office as the 16th President of the United States. In his Inaugural Address, he announced to the nation that (1) he did not intend to interfere with slavery in the states where it existed, (2) no state could lawfully withdraw from the Union, and (3) he would (*a*) carry out the laws in all the states, (*b*) "hold, occupy, and possess the property and places belonging to the government," and (*c*) "collect the duties and imposts" to which the government was entitled. He closed with a strong appeal to the South to preserve the Union. (For quotations from this speech, see page 197.)

Multiple-Choice Test

1. The most important reason for the increase in the number of slaves in the United States after 1793 was that (*a*) the Constitution protected slavery (*b*) the invention of the cotton gin made cotton-growing highly profitable (*c*) many immigrant families brought slaves with them (*d*) the annexation of Florida and Texas added to the slave population.

2. During the period from 1820 to 1860, the chief question raised in Congress when a territory applied for statehood was whether it (*a*) favored a high tariff (*b*) had rich natural resources (*c*) would attract immigrants from Northern Europe (*d*) would allow slavery.

3. During the period from 1800 to 1850, which section or sections favored protective tariffs and internal improvements? (*a*) South and West (*b*) North and West (*c*) North only (*d*) South only.

4. Which political leader was most closely identified with the doctrine of states' rights? (*a*) John C. Calhoun (*b*) Henry Clay (*c*) Abraham Lincoln (*d*) Daniel Webster.

5. The Compromise of 1850 provided for the (*a*) admission of Maine into the Union (*b*) admission of California into the Union (*c*) repeal of the Missouri Compromise (*d*) abolition of slavery in Kansas.

6. *Uncle Tom's Cabin*, a story that influenced many men and women to join the abolitionists, was written by (*a*) Wendell Phillips (*b*) William Lloyd Garrison (*c*) John Greenleaf Whittier (*d*) Harriet Beecher Stowe.

7. The name of a political leader who opposed the doctrine of states' rights was (*a*) Robert Hayne (*b*) Jefferson Davis (*c*) Alexander Stephens (*d*) Daniel Webster.

8. Abolitionists believed that (*a*) all slaves were well cared for (*b*) slavery should be encouraged in the Northern states (*c*) slaves should be set free (*d*) the slave trade with Africa should be increased.

9. In the election of 1860, the Republican party (*a*) favored freeing the slaves (*b*) favored popular sovereignty (*c*) opposed internal improvements at federal expense (*d*) opposed the extension of slavery.

10. The event that most immediately preceded the Civil War was (*a*) the publication of *Uncle Tom's Cabin* (*b*) the secession of South Carolina (*c*) John Brown's Raid (*d*) the passage of the Kansas-Nebraska Act.

11. From 1820 to 1850, conflicts between the North and the South concerned chiefly (*a*) tariffs and slavery (*b*) treatment of Indians and immigration policy (*c*) cheap money versus sound money (*d*) isolationism versus cooperation with foreign nations.

12. Which principle concerning slavery was established by the Dred Scott decision? (*a*) Congress had the power to abolish slavery. (*b*) Congress could not exclude slavery from the territories. (*c*) Slavery was illegal north of latitude 36°30′. (*d*) The issue of slavery should be decided by popular sovereignty.

13. Southern Democrats refused to support the Democratic candidate, Stephen A. Douglas, in the election of 1860 because he (*a*) was a Northerner (*b*) had taken a stand against slavery (*c*) had introduced the Kansas-Nebraska Bill (*d*) had formulated the Freeport Doctrine during his debates with Lincoln.

14. In the 1830's slavery was permitted within the United States in (*a*) the Northwest Territory (*b*) the lands of the Mexican Cession (*c*) Missouri (*d*) Pennsylvania.

15. The political leader whose proposals became known as the Compromise of 1850 was (*a*) John C. Calhoun (*b*) Henry Clay (*c*) Zachary Taylor (*d*) Abraham Lincoln.

16. One direct result of the passage of the Kansas-Nebraska Act was the (*a*) formation of the Republican party (*b*) rise of the abolition movement (*c*) migration of settlers from the Kansas-Nebraska region (*d*) John Brown's raid on Harpers Ferry.

17. Before the Civil War, the South objected to high tariffs because they (*a*) kept the price of cotton low (*b*) increased the cost of slaves (*c*) increased prices of manufactured goods (*d*) helped Western farmers at the planters' expense.

18. Which would be the most appropriate title for a book about the people who helped slaves escape to the North in the period before the Civil War? (*a*) *Go West, Young Man* (*b*) *The Blockade Runners* (*c*) *The Underground Railroad* (*d*) *The Triangular Traders.*

19. All of the following men were presidential candidates in the election of 1860 EXCEPT (*a*) Abraham Lincoln (*b*) John C. Breckinridge (*c*) Jefferson Davis (*d*) Stephen A. Douglas.

20. The secession of the first seven Southern states took place during the administration of President (*a*) Franklin Pierce (*b*) James Buchanan (*c*) Abraham Lincoln (*d*) Millard Fillmore.

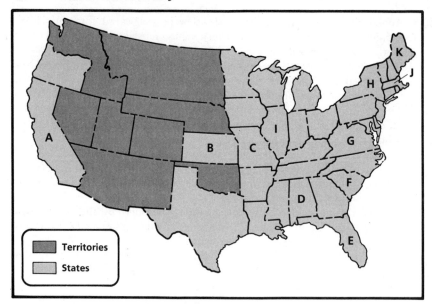

Map Test

The statements below identify states and territories that are located on a map of the United States in the period just prior to the Civil War. For *each* statement write the *letter* that indicates the location of that area on the map. (A letter may be used more than once.)

1. As a result of the Compromise of 1820, this state was admitted to the Union as a slave state.
2. This state was the first to secede from the Union.
3. According to the Compromise of 1850, this state entered the Union as a free state.
4. In this state the Nat Turner Insurrection occurred.
5. Part of a territory granted popular sovereignty by a law sponsored by Stephen A. Douglas in 1854, this area was the site of bloody battles between pro- and antislavery forces.
6. In this state delegates from the seceding states organized the Confederacy and established the first Confederate capital.
7. This state was admitted as a free state as a result of the Compromise of 1820.
8. This state was the scene of the Lincoln-Douglas debates and the home of the Union's wartime President.
9. This state was the home of the U.S. senator who was the chief spokesperson for states' rights and the author of the famous Exposition and Protest of 1828.
10. This state was the home of the U.S. senator who, in the course of a historic debate on states' rights, said: "Liberty and Union, now and forever, one and inseparable."

Essay Questions

1. While the United States for 50 years before the Civil War was outwardly strong and healthy, there were within it conditions or factors that finally caused the Civil War in 1861. Describe fully how each of *two* of the following widened the difference between the North and South: protective tariffs, slavery, the Fugitive Slave Law, and geographic factors.

2. (*a*) What is meant by the term *states' rights?* (*b*) Describe *one* instance when states' rights became a problem of national importance and tell how the problem was solved.

3. (*a*) What was the Compromise of 1850 and how did it, for a time, prevent war? (*b*) What was the Dred Scott decision and what effect did it have on Northern opponents of slavery?

4. Compare the views of the North, South, and West on *each* of the following issues: a national bank, internal improvements at federal government expense, and cheap Western land.

5. Explain each of the following terms used in connection with the Civil War period: "bleeding Kansas," "underground railroad," nullification, abolitionists, and squatter sovereignty.

Part 2. The Civil War

THE WARTIME PRESIDENT, ABRAHAM LINCOLN

EARLY LIFE

Abraham Lincoln was born on February 12, 1809, on a farm in central Kentucky near present-day Hodgenville. When he was seven years old, the Lincoln family moved to Indiana. In this wilderness area young Abe spent his boyhood. A tall and strong lad, he worked hard at the many tasks required on a frontier farm: helping to build a log cabin, felling trees, splitting rails, plowing, hoeing, and harvesting. He had little opportunity to attend school, but he learned to "read, write, and cipher (do arithmetic)." Though books were scarce, he managed to borrow a number of good books and spent his spare time reading and studying. In this way he acquired an education.

AS A YOUNG MAN

In 1830 the Lincolns moved westward to a farm in Illinois. Lincoln, now a young man of 21, helped his family get settled and then struck out on his own. After working for a while on a Mississippi flatboat, he went to live in the frontier settlement of New Salem, Illinois. For six years he clerked in a store, served as village postmaster, and practiced surveying. In his spare time he studied law, often walking 40 miles to borrow law books from a friend in Springfield.

He was very popular among his neighbors, who liked him for his friendliness, humor, and storytelling ability. They also admired him for his honesty (he earned the nickname "Honest Abe"), for his strength (he was a champion railsplitter), and for his sportsmanship.

CAREER

Urged by his friends, Lincoln ran for the Illinois legislature and in 1834 was elected on his second try. He served as a state legislator for four two-year terms. During this time he was admitted to the bar and began to practice law in Springfield, the state capital. Elected to Congress as a Whig, he served in the House of Representatives for one term (1847–1849). He then returned to his law practice and rose to prominence as one of the leading lawyers in downstate Illinois.

Lincoln opposed the extension of slavery into the territories. After the passage of the Kansas-Nebraska Act, Lincoln helped organize the Republican party in Illinois. At the party's first national convention, in 1856, he was proposed as the Republican candidate for Vice President but failed to secure the nomination. Two years later he was chosen to run against Stephen Douglas for the U.S. Senate. During the campaign, which aroused the interest of the nation, Republicans everywhere were impressed with Lincoln's forthright stand against the extension of slavery, as well as with his keenness of mind and his ability to present his views clearly and simply. Although he lost the election, he gained a national reputation.

WARTIME PRESIDENT

At the party's next national convention, held at Chicago in 1860, "Honest Abe, the Railsplitter," received the Republican nomination for President. Winning the election over a divided opposition, he took over the reins of government at a time of disunion and conflict. With perseverance, faith, and dignity, Lincoln led the nation through the tragic period of the War Between the States, or Civil War. Reelected for a second term in 1864, he helped bring the war to an end. In April, 1865, while witnessing a performance at Ford's Theater in Washington, D.C., Lincoln was assassinated by a half-crazed Southern actor, John Wilkes Booth. The great leader's untimely death was a severe blow to the nation.

IMPORTANT SPEECHES

Lincoln's outlook and character are revealed by his eloquent speeches, statements, and proclamations, some of which follow:

1. "A House Divided." On accepting the Republican nomination for senator in 1858, Lincoln expressed his views on the status of slavery in the United States.

> "A house divided against itself cannot stand. I believe this government cannot endure half slave and half free. I do not expect the Union to be dissolved—I do not expect the house to fall—but I do expect it will cease to be divided. It will become all one thing, or all the other."

2. First Inaugural Address. When Lincoln took the oath of office as President in March, 1861, seven Southern states had seceded and formed the Confederacy. At the conclusion of his First Inaugural Address, he appealed to the people of the South to preserve the Union and prevent the outbreak of war.

> "In *your* hands, my dissatisfied fellow-countrymen, and not in *mine*, is the momentous issue of civil war. The government will not assail *you*. You can have no conflict without being yourselves the aggressors. *You* have no oath registered in heaven to destroy the government, while I have the most solemn one to 'preserve, protect, and defend it.'
>
> "We must not be enemies. Though passion may have strained, it must not break our bonds of affection. The mystic chords of memory, stretching from every battlefield and patriot grave to every living heart and hearthstone all over this broad land, will yet swell the chorus of the Union, when again touched, as surely they will be, by the better angels of our nature."

3. Emancipation Proclamation. Despite his personal view that slavery violated basic human rights and was essentially evil, Lincoln believed that his primary duty as President was to save the Union rather than to free the slaves. In 1862, in a letter to Horace Greeley, editor of the New York *Tribune*, Lincoln wrote:

"My paramount object in this struggle *is* to save the Union, and is *not* either to save or destroy Slavery. If I could save the Union without freeing *any* slave, I would do it; if I could save it by freeing *all* the slaves, I would do it; and if I could do it by freeing some and leaving others alone, I would also do that."

Becoming convinced that a "radical and extreme measure" was necessary to upset the Southern war effort and to keep England from recognizing the Confederacy, Lincoln announced in the fall of 1862 that he would declare free all slaves residing in states and districts still in rebellion against the United States on January 1, 1863. The Emancipation Proclamation freed no slaves immediately, since it applied only to Confederate areas over which the federal government had no control. But it did serve notice that slavery would be abolished in these areas after the Union regained possession. Undertaken as a war measure, the proclamation marked the beginning of the end of the institution of human slavery in the United States.

4. Gettysburg Address. In his speech dedicating the national cemetery at Gettysburg, Pennsylvania, in 1863, Lincoln said,

"Fourscore and seven years ago our fathers brought forth on this continent a new nation, conceived in liberty, and dedicated to the proposition that all men are created equal."

He called upon the nation to continue "the unfinished work which they who fought here have thus far so nobly advanced." He concluded as follows:

". . . we here highly resolve that these dead shall not have died in vain; that this nation, under God, shall have a new birth of freedom; and that government of the people, by the people, for the people, shall not perish from the earth."

5. Second Inaugural Address. In March, 1865, the war was nearing its end. At his second inauguration, Lincoln appealed to the people to forget their bitterness, to avoid a spirit of vengeance, and to reunite.

"With malice toward none; with charity for all; with firmness in the right as God gives us to see the right, let us strive on to finish the work we are in; to bind up the nation's wounds; to care for him who shall have borne the battle, and for his widow and his orphan; to do all which may achieve and cherish a just and lasting peace among ourselves, and with all nations."

OUTBREAK OF WAR

CAUSES OF THE WAR

Since the economic interests of the industrial North and the agricultural South differed, the two sections held opposing views on such issues as (1) the protective tariff, (2) a national bank, (3) internal improvements at federal government expense, and (4) the extension of slavery into new territories in the West.

The two sections also held opposing views on the nature of the Union. The North contended that the Union was "one nation, indivisible" and could not be dissolved. The South maintained that the Constitution was a compact, or agreement, among independent states and that a state had the right to terminate the compact if it so desired.

In addition to sectionalism, slavery, and states' rights, other causes of the Civil War were abolitionist activity, mutual distrust, and lack of understanding between the North and the South.

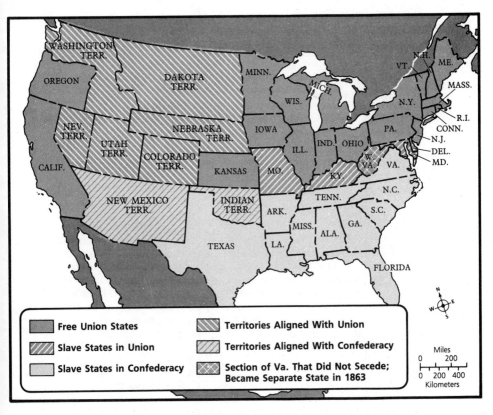

Alignment of States and Territories (1861)

Comparison of the North and South

	Federal Union	Confederacy
States	*Twenty-three states.* Oregon had joined the Union in 1859, Kansas in 1861. West Virginia was admitted in 1863.	*Eleven states.* In addition, the South had the support of many proslavery people in the four slaveholding border states that remained in the Union.
Population	*Twenty-two million.* A large flow of new immigrants during the war years provided additional people for the armed forces, agriculture, and industry.	*Nine million.* Of these, 3½ million were slaves. The enslaved blacks worked the farms, freeing the white men for military service.
Industry	*Ample industrial facilities.* Possessing 85% of the nation's factories and 90% of its skilled workers, the North was able to produce all the supplies and weapons it needed.	*Limited industrial facilities.* The agriculture South had to rely on imports for its materials of war. The superior Northern navy blockaded Southern ports and prevented goods from coming in or going out.
Transportation	*Extensive railroad system; large merchant marine; naval supremacy.* A network of railroads linked the Northeast to the Ohio and Mississippi valleys, thereby facilitating movement of troops and supplies.	*Inadequate railroad system; few merchant ships and naval vessels.* The South had less than 30% of the nation's railroad mileage at the start of the conflict. Its rail facilities suffered widespread destruction in the course of the war because most of the fighting took place on Southern soil.
Finances	*Enough money to finance the war.* The North was able to raise much money because it had strong banking institutions and controlled 70% of the nation's wealth. It levied high excise taxes on goods and services; raised tariff rates on imports; introduced an income tax; issued paper money, or *greenbacks*, that was not backed by gold but by the government's credit; and sold government bonds to individuals and banks.	The Confederate government was hampered financially by the loss of customs duties on imports (because of the Northern blockade), by the unwillingness of foreign bankers to provide substantial loans, and by opposition at home to direct taxation by the central government. Revenue raised through excise taxes and the sale of Confederate bonds proved insufficient for the government's needs. The Confederacy therefore issued huge quantities of paper money, which declined in value as the war progressed. By 1865 a Confederate paper dollar was worth less than 2 cents.

Comparison of the North and South

	Federal Union	Confederacy
Military Forces	*Few experienced officers; troops in need of much training.* Many of the nation's military leaders joined the Confederate army when their native states seceded. The city dwellers and factory workers who joined the Union army were unprepared for the rugged life of a soldier. When voluntary enlistments proved inadequate, Congress passed a Conscription Act requiring all men age 20–45 to register for military service. The first draft took place in 1863.	*Superior military leadership; good soldier material.* The best army officers in the country at the onset of the war were Southerners. Southern troops were accustomed to outdoor life and the use of firearms and horses. They also had the advantage of fighting on their own soil. Starting in 1862 the Confederacy drafted into military service every able-bodied white male between the ages of 18 and 35.

FORT SUMTER (APRIL, 1861)

Fort Sumter, in the harbor of Charleston, South Carolina, was one of the few forts in the South still controlled by the federal government at the time of Lincoln's inaugural. When the new President sent a ship to deliver supplies to the fort's garrison, Confederate batteries opened fire on Fort Sumter and compelled its surrender.

This event, touching off the war, united the entire North in support of the Union. Lincoln issued a call for volunteers, and thousands flocked to join the army. Four more Southern states—Virginia, North Carolina, Tennessee, and Arkansas—seceded and joined the Confederacy. Richmond, Virginia, became the Confederate capital. The border slave states of Maryland, Kentucky, Missouri, and Delaware were persuaded by the North to remain in the Union. They were assured that the war was being fought, not to destroy slavery but to preserve the Union and bring back the seceding states.

MAIN EVENTS OF THE WAR (1861–1865)

THE UNION'S FIRST CAMPAIGN IN THE EAST FAILS (1861)

The North hoped to crush the rebellion quickly by invading Virginia and capturing Richmond, the Confederate capital. In July, 1861, Lincoln ordered Irvin McDowell, commander of the Union army stationed along the Potomac River, to attack a Confederate force that was guarding a key rail center at Manassas Junction, Virginia—about 25 miles from Washington. The Southerners, led by Pierre Beauregard, were encamped on the south bank of a stream called Bull Run.

Northerners were so confident of victory that on the day of the battle (July 21), sightseers from the nation's capital drove down in carriages to witness the defeat of the *Rebels* (a popular nickname for the seces-

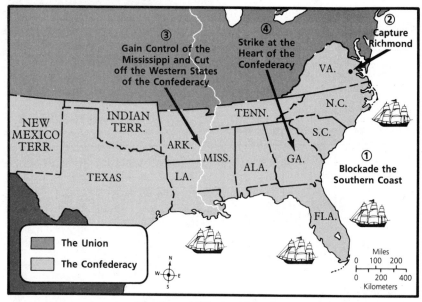

Northern Military Objectives

sionists). McDowell launched his attack before dawn and by midafternoon his forces appeared to be winning. But the arrival of fresh Confederate reinforcements under Joseph Johnston and the heroic stand of the Virginian Thomas J. Jackson (thereafter called "Stonewall") turned the tide in favor of the Southerners. As the Rebels counterattacked, the exhausted Union troops slowly gave way, then panicked, beating a hasty retreat back to Washington.

> During the early fighting at Bull Run, Union forces began to drive back the Confederates. Seeking to halt the retreat of his demoralized troops, a Confederate general shouted: "Look! There is Jackson standing like a stone wall! Rally behind the Virginians!" And rally they did.
>
> Thus did Thomas J. Jackson earn the nickname "Stonewall."

The Union defeat in the *First Battle of Bull Run* made the North aware that the war would not be won easily. It also convinced Lincoln that the army needed better leadership and more thorough training. Demoting McDowell, he appointed George B. McClellan commander of the Union forces in the capital region.

The capture of Richmond continued to be the Union's main military objective in the East for the next four years. Many fierce battles took place and both sides suffered heavy losses. Lincoln kept replacing generals, but at first none could match the brilliant Southern commander in northern Virginia, Robert E. Lee (later general-in-chief of all Confederate forces), or his daring associate, "Stonewall" Jackson. It was not until Ulysses S. Grant was brought in from the West to assume command of all the Union armies (March, 1864), that the North had a military leader the equal of Lee and Jackson.

THE UNION NAVY BLOCKADES THE SOUTH

Shortly after the fall of Fort Sumter, Lincoln ordered the navy to set up a blockade of the Southern coast from Virginia to Texas. At the outset its effect on Southern commerce was limited because fewer than 50 ships were available to police the 3,500-mile Confederate coastline. But as the Union expanded its fleet by converting civilian craft into warships and constructing new vessels, the blockade grew ever tighter. The Confederates countered by building a number of swift blockade-runners to bring in needed supplies from abroad. Some managed to get through, but many others were captured.

The blockade was so effective that the export of Southern cotton fell by more than 90%. With its main source of income cut off, the South found it difficult to purchase war materials and meet its financial obligations.

A HISTORIC NAVAL BATTLE IS FOUGHT

In an attempt to break the Northern blockade, the Confederates converted a wooden naval vessel, the *Merrimac*, into an armored warship by covering its sides with metal plates. On March 8, 1862, the Confederate ironclad (renamed the *Virginia*) destroyed several Northern naval vessels made of wood. The next day, however, it met its match in the *Monitor*, a strange warship designed by John Ericsson. The *Monitor*, described as "a cheese box on a raft," had a flat iron hull with a revolving turret, from which powerful guns could be fired in any direction. The *Monitor* engaged the Southern warship in a fierce sea battle and compelled it to withdraw. This historic naval battle, the first between ironclad vessels, not only saved the Northern blockade but also transformed naval warfare by making wooden warships obsolete.

THE NORTH GAINS CONTROL OF THE MISSISSIPPI (1862–1863)

A key aim of the Union armies in the West was to gain possession of the Mississippi River and thus divide the Confederacy. The following military events highlight the Union's struggle for this strategic waterway:

1. Fort Henry and Fort Donelson. With the aid of a flotilla of river gunboats commanded by Andrew Foote, Union troops under Ulysses S. Grant captured Fort Henry on the Tennessee River and Fort Donelson on the Cumberland River (February, 1862). Control of the Cumberland

Grant, a relatively unknown army officer before the Union victory at Fort Donelson, earned instant fame by his reply to the Confederate general who requested the terms of surrender: "No terms except an unconditional and immediate surrender can be accepted."

From that time on, *Ulysses Simpson* Grant became known as *Unconditional Surrender* Grant.

River by the Union navy forced the Confederate army to abandon Nashville, the capital of Tennessee, and to withdraw to Corinth—a rail junction in northern Mississippi.

2. Shiloh. Grant brought his army to southern Tennessee, set up camp about 20 miles north of Corinth, and made plans to attack. He was joined by several divisions of inexperienced troops, including a division commanded by William Tecumseh Sherman, and awaited the arrival of additional reinforcements from Nashville.

Seeking to regain the initiative, the Confederates decided to strike at Grant before he was ready to attack them. On the morning of April 6, 1862, the Rebels began their assault. The action took place near a small country church called Shiloh. After a long day of confused fighting, marked by heavy losses on both sides and the death of the Confederate commander, Albert S. Johnston, the Union forces were on the verge of defeat. During the night, Grant's strength was augmented by the arrival of fresh troops.

When the battle resumed the next day, the reinforced Union army began to drive the Rebels back. The Confederates finally broke off the fighting and retreated to Corinth. This victory gave the North control of western Tennessee. (See the map on page 207.)

The *Battle of Shiloh* was the bloodiest in American history up to that time. Nearly one-fourth of the Union and Confederate soldiers who participated in the fighting were either killed or wounded.

3. Capture of New Orleans. David G. Farragut led a fleet of Union warships from the Gulf of Mexico into the mouth of the Mississippi. The fleet fought its way past the Confederate forts on the river, defeated the gunboats and rams that were sent to stop it, moved up to the city of New Orleans, and captured it (April 25, 1862). A Union land force then occupied the South's largest city and chief port.

Continuing upstream, Farragut captured Baton Rouge, the capital of Louisiana, and forced the surrender of Natchez, Mississippi. But Vicksburg, situated on a high bluff that gave the Confederate artillery command of the Mississippi, proved too powerful to take and Farragut withdrew southward. A second attempt by Farragut several months later also failed.

Meanwhile, the Northerners were also active on the upper Mississippi. On a stretch of river near the Kentucky-Tennessee border the Confederates had fortified Island No. 10. A combined Union attack by land forces under John Pope and gunboats of the U.S. Navy overcame the island's defenses and forced the garrison to surrender (April, 1862). Two months later, the Northern fleet fought its way down to Memphis, Tennessee, destroyed or captured the Confederate boats guarding the city, and took possession of the Southern river port.

4. Fall of Vicksburg. Except for a 200-mile stretch between Vicksburg and Port Hudson, all of the Mississippi River was in Union hands by the middle of 1862. That winter Grant attempted to reach Vicksburg by an overland advance through northern Mississippi but was forced back by Confederate cavalry raids against his supply lines.

In the spring of 1863 Grant tried again. Starting from his base in Memphis, he crossed the Mississippi above Vicksburg, marched down along the river's west bank to a point below the city, and met a Union fleet that had run past Vicksburg despite a fierce bombardment from that stronghold's artillery. The Union ships ferried Grant's troops across the river, landing them about 35 miles south of Vicksburg. Grant advanced northeastward toward Jackson, the capital of Mississippi, defeated a Confederate army under Joseph Johnston, and destroyed the city's railroad and industrial facilities. Turning westward, he fought and won a series of battles against enemy forces trying to stop him, and forced the Rebels under John C. Pemberton to pull back to Vicksburg. Unable to break through Vicksburg's defenses by direct attack, Grant laid siege to the fortress there for six weeks. Faced with starvation, the Confederate garrison finally surrendered on July 4, 1863. Port Hudson, also besieged by Union forces, fell a few days later.

These victories gave the North complete control of the Mississippi and cut off the Rebel states west of the river from the rest of the Confederacy.

BLOW AT THE CONFEDERATE CENTER (1863–1864)

The following campaigns further split the Confederacy:

1. Murfreesboro. Seeking to drive the Rebels from central Tennessee, William S. Rosecrans left Nashville in late December, 1862, and headed for Murfreesboro. As he neared that town, he encountered a Confederate force under Braxton Bragg at a stream called Stone's River. The fierce, four-day battle that took place was very costly, both sides suffering the highest casualty rates of the entire war. On the night of January 3–4, 1863, the defeated Confederates withdrew. For the next six months the two armies maneuvered around each other in the area south of Murfreesboro.

2. Campaign for Chattanooga. In June, 1863, Rosecrans began a new drive against Bragg, forcing him to pull back to Chattanooga, in southeastern Tennessee. This city, strategically located on the Tennessee River, was an important rail center and a gateway to the East. Rosecrans followed Bragg eastward, crossed the Tennessee River north and south of Chattanooga, and began to encircle the city. Fearing entrapment, Bragg evacuated Chattanooga (September 9) and withdrew southeastward into Georgia. Rosecrans occupied Chattanooga and set out in pursuit of the Rebels. Instead of retreating, Bragg consolidated his forces and awaited the arrival of the Northerners. Contributing to his strength were several divisions of reinforcements from Mississippi, as well as troops under James Longstreet that had been rushed to him from the East.

On September 19, 1863, the Confederates attacked Rosecrans at Chickamauga, a creek located 12 miles south of Chattanooga. In a two-day battle they routed their pursuers, forcing them to pull back to Chattanooga. The Northerners were saved from total defeat by the heroic stand of George H. Thomas, who earned the title "The Rock of Chickamauga" for his leadership and valor. Bragg followed up his victory by besieging Chattanooga, thus threatening its Union garrison with starvation.

In October Grant was appointed commander of all the Union armies in the West. Taking charge of operations around Chattanooga, his first move was to replace Rosecrans with Thomas. He then established a supply route to the Union forces trapped in the city by seizing a section of the Tennessee River that was beyond the range of Confederate artillery and building a bridge across the waterway. Finally he made plans to dislodge the Rebels who were surrounding the city.

Reinforced by troops under Joseph Hooker and Sherman, Grant launched an attack against two strategic heights occupied by the Confederates on the outskirts of Chattanooga. Hooker's division drove the Rebels off Lookout Mountain on November 24. The next day the combined Union forces, with Thomas' men in the lead, drove the Rebels from Mississippi Ridge. These victories lifted the siege of Chattanooga. Shortly thereafter, the Confederates gave up their attempt to retake Knoxville, which had been seized by a Union army in September. Thus, by the end of 1863, all of Tennessee was in Northern hands.

3. Fall of Atlanta. With Tennessee cleared of the Rebels and Chattanooga firmly secured, Union forces were now in position to move into Georgia. Grant put Sherman in charge of this operation. In May, 1864, Sherman invaded Georgia with 100,000 men. In the weeks that followed, he relentlessly fought his way toward Atlanta. The Confederates, skillfully led by Joseph Johnston, sought repeatedly to stop his advance— at Resaca, New Hope Church, and Kenesaw Mountain—but were forced to pull back each time. In July Sherman crossed the Chattahoochee River, eight miles from Atlanta. John B. Hood, chosen by the Confederates to replace Johnston, launched three fierce attacks against Sherman's forces in the last two weeks of July, but suffered heavy losses and withdrew behind Atlanta's defenses. Unable to prevent the Northerners from encircling the city and severing its rail connections with the outside world, Hood evacuated Atlanta on September 1, 1864. The following day Sherman took possession of the city.

4. Sherman's March to the Sea. In November, after burning everything of military value in Atlanta (the spreading fire destroyed one-third of the city), Sherman began a drive to the Atlantic coast city of Savannah, Georgia—300 miles away. His army swept through central Georgia, leaving a 60-mile-wide path of destruction. Crops were burned, cattle slaughtered, railroads wrecked, and farms destroyed. Moving through the heart of the Confederacy at the rate of 10 miles a day, the Northerners reached the coast early in December, 1864. They captured Fort McAllister, south of Savannah, thereby providing the Union navy access to the area, and then proceeded to close in on the city itelf. On December 21 the Confederate garrison abandoned Savannah.

The Confederacy, divided vertically in 1863 by its loss of the Mississippi, was now also split horizontally as a result of Sherman's campaign.

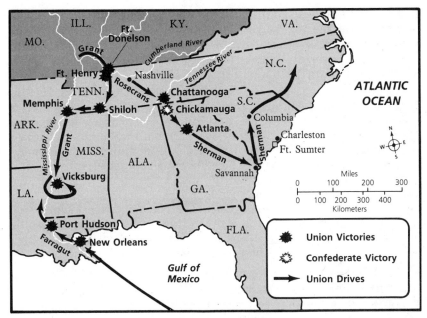

Union Forces Divide the South

THE WAR IN THE EAST (1862–1864)

For a period of eight months after the Northern defeat in 1861 at Bull Run, little action took place on the eastern front. In the spring of 1862 McClellan finally responded to Lincoln's persistent demand that the Union armies take the offensive against the Rebels. His campaign was the first of a long series of attacks and counterattacks by both sides that caused the fighting to spread from Virginia into Maryland and Pennsylvania.

1. The Peninsula Campaign (1862). A fleet of Union ships ferried McClellan's army to the peninsula formed by the York and James rivers. Although his forces outnumbered the Confederates defending the area by a margin of four to one, McClellan chose to besiege their main defense position at Yorktown rather than order a frontal attack. This one-month delay enabled the Southern general, Joseph Johnston, to shift the bulk of his army to the peninsula. In May, 1862, the Rebels evacuated Yorktown, pulled back toward Richmond, and set up a defense line on the outskirts of the capital. McClellan followed, established a base of operations nearby, and awaited the arrival of reinforcements before proceeding farther. (See the map on page 209.)

A second Union army, under McDowell, was encamped at Fredericksburg in northern Virginia. It was in position to defend Washington, if necessary, or to march southward to link up with McClellan. Two other Northern armies were also stationed in Virginia—one in the Shenandoah Valley and another in the section now known as West Virginia. To prevent these forces from joining McClellan, Stonewall

Jackson conducted a skillful hit-and-run campaign against them from late March to the middle of June. His forces marched hundreds of miles, fought numerous skirmishes against the three armies (at Kernstown, Front Royal, Winchester, Port Republic, and other places), and kept the Northerners from participating in the attack on Richmond.

While Jackson was pinning down the other Union armies with his *Valley Campaign*, the Confederates defending Richmond launched a major attack against McClellan. Both sides suffered heavy losses in the *Battle of Seven Pines* (May 31–June 1, 1862), but the conflict ended in a draw. Johnston, who had been severely wounded during the fighting, was then replaced by Robert E. Lee. Planning another offensive against McClellan, Lee ordered Jackson to move his army to Richmond. On June 26 the combined Confederate forces attacked McClellan once again. In a series of bitter engagements (at Mechanicsville, Gaines' Mill, Savage's Station, Glendale, and Malvern Hill)—collectively known as the *Seven Days' Battles*—Lee forced McClellan to retreat to Harrison's Landing on the James River. In August the Union army withdrew from the peninsula.

2. Other Campaigns of 1862. Several weeks later, John Pope led a Union army on an overland march on Richmond from Alexandria. Moving quickly to intercept him, Lee and Jackson met the Northerners in the vicinity of Manassas Junction and severely defeated them in the *Second Battle of Bull Run* (August 29–30). Continuing northward, the Confederates crossed the Potomac River and invaded western Maryland. With this bold stroke, Lee hoped to win Maryland for the South, isolate Washington, convince Britain and France to recognize the Confederacy, and force the Union to sue for peace.

Lee's advance was stopped in Maryland at Antietam Creek (near Sharpsburg) by a large Union force commanded by McClellan. Although the *Battle of Antietam* that took place on September 17—the bloodiest day of the war—ended in a draw, it proved to be a victory for the Union because Lee then decided to withdraw his exhausted and battered army to Virginia. Lincoln seized upon the failure of Lee's invasion as an opportune moment to issue the Emancipation Proclamation (see page 198).

The final Union campaign of 1862 was an overland march on Richmond in December by a large army under Ambrose Burnside. At Fredericksburg, on the Rappahannock River, Lee and Jackson met the Northerners and drove them back with heavy losses.

3. Gettysburg (1863). In May, 1863, Lee defeated a Union army under "Fighting Joe" Hooker at Chancellorsville in northern Virginia. The Southern victory, however, was offset by the loss of Stonewall Jackson, who was accidentally shot by his own men. He died shortly thereafter.

Undertaking a second invasion of the North in June, Lee led his army across Maryland into southern Pennsylvania. The Confederates seized all the food and supplies they could find; captured many free blacks and sent them south into slavery.

George G. Meade, the newly appointed Union commander, met the Southerners at Gettysburg, Pennsylvania. In a terrible three-day battle (July 1–3), climaxed by a desperate, but unsuccessful Confederate attempt (led by George Pickett) to occupy Cemetery Ridge in the face of devastating Union fire, the Southern forces were severely defeated. Lee retreated into Maryland and then escaped across the Potomac into Virginia.

The *Battle of Gettysburg* proved to be the turning point of the war. It marked the last major Confederate effort to shift the war northward onto Union soil. It also convinced Britain and France that the North would win the war, thus deterring them from extending recognition to the Confederacy.

4. Grant's Richmond Campaign (1864). In the spring of 1864 Grant took charge of Union operations on the Virginia front. Assembling a large force, he set out to destroy Lee's army and capture the Confederate capital. Early in May he crossed the Rapidan River and began to move

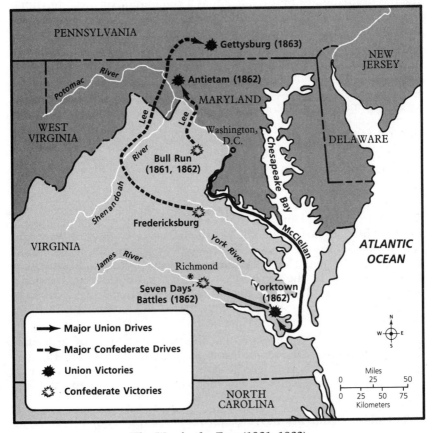

The War in the East (1861–1863)

southward. Lee opposed him every step of the way. Violent battles took place in the wooded region of *The Wilderness* (May 5–6), at *Spotsylvania Courthouse* (May 8–12), and at *Cold Harbor* (June 1–3). Despite staggering Union losses, Grant pressed on. "I propose to fight it out on this line if it takes all summer," he declared.

With Grant's army encamped at Cold Harbor, less than 10 miles northeast of Richmond, the Southerners expected him to attack their capital from that direction. But he surprised the Rebels by moving southward across the James River and advancing on Petersburg, a key stronghold that guarded the southern approach to Richmond. If Petersburg fell, the Confederates would be forced to abandon their capital, and Lee's army would be cut off. To forestall such an outcome, Lee shifted his forces to the threatened area. After repeated, costly attacks failed to crack Petersburg's defenses, Grant besieged the city for nine months.

To divert Grant, Lee sent Jubal Early to attack Washington (July, 1864). Near the outskirts of the capital, Early was stopped and driven back to Virginia. Philip H. Sheridan, while pursuing the retreating Rebels, destroyed the fertile Shenandoah Valley to make it impossible for the Confederates to use it again as a route into Northern territory. The valley was so devastated that Sheridan said, "A crow flying over the country would need to carry his rations."

END OF THE WAR (1865)

By the start of 1865, the Confederacy was on the verge of collapse. Contributing to the decline of Southern morale were the (*a*) loss of large sections of Confederate territory to the Union; (*b*) almost complete breakdown of the region's transportation system; (*c*) severe shortages of food, clothing, and other necessities; (*d*) exhaustion of Confederate forces; and (*e*) failure to obtain foreign recognition.

During the early months of 1865, the Confederacy's situation became more and more hopeless.

1. Sherman in the Carolinas. In February Sherman led his army into South Carolina and launched a new campaign of destruction similar to the one he had carried out in Georgia. Despite swampy terrain and rain-flooded rivers, he moved steadily northward and destroyed all war resources in his path. More than a dozen towns were set ablaze (either by his troops or by the retreating Confederates), including Columbia, the state's capital. The port city of Charleston, its rail connections to the interior cut off by Sherman, surrendered to Union forces that had been besieging it from the sea for nearly two years.

Advancing into North Carolina, Sherman met and drove back a Confederate force under Johnston at Bentonville (March 19) and proceeded to Goldsboro. Here he stopped to rest his troops after their 425-mile, seven-week march. He then moved on to occupy Raleigh, North Carolina.

2. Fall of Richmond. In April, 1865, after several earlier attempts to break Grant's siege had failed, Lee concluded that his outnumbered army could no longer hold Petersburg. Withdrawing his troops, he hoped to join forces with Johnston in North Carolina. Richmond was now unprotected. The Confederates evacuated their capital after blowing up its bridges, factories, and arsenals and burning all government property that could not be removed.

3. Surrender. The Union army set out in pursuit of Lee. Eighty miles from Richmond, Grant and Sheridan surrounded the Confederates. Realizing that further resistance was useless, Lee surrendered his army to Grant at *Appomattox Courthouse* (April 9, 1865). A few weeks later Johnston surrendered to Sherman in North Carolina. In May all

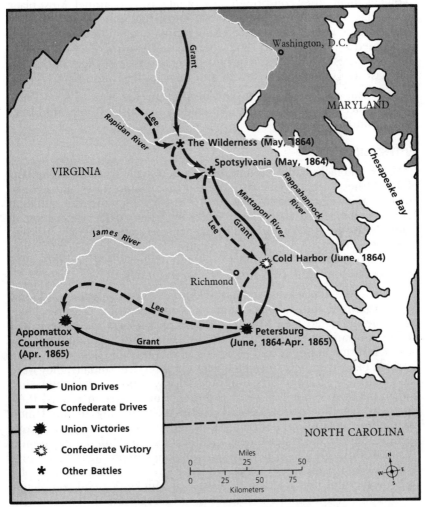

The Last Major Campaign of the War (1864–1865)

remaining Confederate forces east and west of the Mississippi also capitulated, thus bringing the war to an end.

Both sides suffered heavily in the four-year struggle. Combined casualties totaled more than 600,000 dead and nearly 400,000 wounded.

THE ROLE OF BLACKS IN THE WAR

IN THE NAVY

From the start of the war, the Union navy allowed blacks to enlist. About 20,000 blacks served in the U.S. Navy during the war. According to one estimate, they constituted 25% of all naval personnel. Most black sailors had maintenance jobs aboard ships, but some participated in combat as members of gun crews. Robert Smalls, a South Carolina slave, performed a notable feat in 1862 when he took control of a Confederate ship in Charleston harbor and turned it over to the Union fleet blockading the coast. He subsequently served as a pilot in the Union navy.

Black sailors played an important part in the war at sea. Their performance encouraged Northern leaders to consider enlisting blacks to fight on land.

IN THE ARMY

Although blacks had fought in the Revolutionary War and in the War of 1812, they had never been permitted to enroll in state militias or to enlist in the regular army. Not until the Civil War did this situation begin to change. At first, slaves freed by Union troops operating in Confederate areas were enrolled by the army as laborers. Then, in 1862, Congress authorized the President to enlist blacks for any military service "for which they may be found competent." The War Department set up a special bureau to coordinate black recruitment.

About 180,000 blacks served in the Union army during the war. They were organized into all-black regiments led by white officers. Their personnel included free Northern blacks and former slaves recruited in Union-occupied sections of the South. Despite the fact that they were issued inferior supplies and weapons and were paid less than white soldiers, black troops performed outstanding service. Initially, they were used mainly to garrison forts, to protect supply depots and wagon trains, and to perform other non-combat duties. But they soon proved their worth as frontline soldiers. Black troops participating in the Union assault on Port Hudson, Louisiana, won high praise for their courageous fighting. Several days later they helped beat back a Confederate attempt to smash through Union defenses at Milliken's Bend, near Vicksburg. The Assistant Secretary of War, who was present at the battle wrote: "The bravery of the blacks in the battle of Milliken's Bend completely revolutionized the sentiment of the army with regard to the employment of Negro troops."

RELATIONS WITH EUROPE DURING THE WAR

SENTIMENT IN ENGLAND

The ruling class in England favored the South because the British textile industry depended upon Southern cotton. However, the working class, strongly antislavery in sentiment, favored the North. Great Britain aided the South at the beginning of the war, but withdrew its support after Lincoln issued the Emancipation Proclamation and the Union won at Gettysburg and Vicksburg. These Union victories convinced England that the Confederacy would lose the war.

THE *TRENT* AFFAIR

During the war, an incident occurred that led to much ill feeling between England and the Union. In 1861 the English ship *Trent,* sailing from Cuba to Europe with two Confederate representatives as passengers, was halted on the high seas by a Union warship. The Union commander, Charles Wilkes, boarded the *Trent* and seized the two Southerners, James M. Mason and John Slidell. The British government strongly protested this interference with an English ship, demanded that Mason and Slidell be freed, and prepared to send reinforcements to Canada (still a British colony). To avert war with England, Lincoln ordered the release of Mason and Slidell.

THE *ALABAMA* CLAIMS

Though England had issued a proclamation of neutrality at the beginning of the war, it permitted its shipyards to build warships destined for the Confederate navy. One of these vessels, the *Alabama,* did great damage to Northern shipping. The United States declared England responsible for the damages and demanded *reparations* (repayment). In 1872 a court of arbitration awarded the United States $15.5 million in settlement of these claims.

THE MAXIMILIAN AFFAIR

The French government, too, favored the South because it thought that a divided United States would be unable to prevent the expansion of French influence in the Western Hemisphere. France extended loans to the Confederacy and permitted French shipyards to build ships for the Southerners.

During the war, when the United States was too involved to stop him, Napoleon III of France attacked Mexico, occupied Mexico City, and made Archduke Maximilian of Austria the emperor of Mexico. When the Civil War ended, the United States tooks steps to enforce the Monroe Doctrine. It sent an army to the Mexican border and compelled France to remove its troops from Mexico. Thereupon, the Mexicans overthrew the now unprotected Maximilian, executed him, and regained control of their country.

THE NATION EMERGES FROM THE WAR

ISSUES SETTLED BY THE WAR

The Union victory (1) established the supremacy of the federal government over the individual states, and (2) led to the abolition of slavery. Slaves were set free in 1865 by the Thirteenth Amendment.

CONDITION OF THE COUNTRY AT THE CLOSE OF THE WAR

1. The North. The war brought great prosperity to Northern agriculture and industry. The introduction of new machinery led to the expansion of the factory system and to the growth of cities. The Morrill Tariff Act of 1861, and later upward revisions, provided domestic manufacturers protection against foreign competition. The National Bank Act of 1863 created a network of national banks for the first time since Jackson destroyed the Bank of the United States. This act assured the nation a sound, uniform paper currency. European immigration during the war added 800,000 to the population. The Homestead Act (see page 229) greatly stimulated Western development. Opportunities existed for everyone, and the people looked to the future with hope.

2. The South. The war left the South in ruins. Since it had been the scene of most of the fighting, its homes, farms, and cities were devastated. Its economy was crippled; its currency and bonds were worthless. Local governments had broken down. With the freeing of the slaves, most of the large Southern planters were reduced to poverty. Many of the former slaves were homeless, jobless, bewildered by their new status, and unprepared for the responsibilities of citizenship. The South would not recover from its chaotic condition for many years.

Multiple-Choice Test

1. Which two events directly concerned relations between the United States and England? (*a*) *Alabama* claims—Maximilian Affair (*b*) Oregon boundary dispute—annexation of Texas (*c*) *Chesapeake* Affair—XYZ Affair (*d*) Rush-Bagot Agreement—*Trent* Affair.
2. The immediate cause of the Civil War was the (*a*) Dred Scott decision (*b*) attack on Fort Sumter (*c*) passage of the Thirteenth Amendment (*d*) First Battle of Bull Run.
3. The Emancipation Proclamation was (*a*) a law passed by Congress (*b*) an amendment to the Constitution (*c*) a presidential measure taken to upset the Southern war effort (*d*) a joint resolution of Congress.
4. The American demand that the French remove their forces from Mexico after the Civil War is an example of U.S. enforcement of the (*a*) federal Constitution (*b*) Monroe Doctrine (*c*) Proclamation of Neutrality (*d*) Treaty of Paris of 1783.
5. All of the following were major objectives in the Union plan for conquest of the South EXCEPT the (*a*) capture of New Orleans (*b*) capture of Gettysburg (*c*) blockade of Southern ports (*d*) capture of Richmond.
6. During the Civil War, manufacturers of cotton textiles in England tried to influence their government to (*a*) remain neutral (*b*) help the North (*c*)

increase the tariff on raw cotton imported from the United States (*d*) aid the Confederacy.

7. Lee's invasion of the North in 1863 was stopped at (*a*) Bull Run (*b*) Gettysburg (*c*) Harpers Ferry (*d*) Vicksburg.

8. During the Civil War, Lincoln's chief objective was to (*a*) punish the South (*b*) abolish slavery (*c*) preserve the Union (*d*) prevent the South from trading with England.

9. During the Civil War, the farthest north the armies of the South penetrated was (*a*) Massachusetts (*b*) New York (*c*) Pennsylvania (*d*) Virginia.

10. Lincoln's Gettysburg Address was an appeal to (*a*) the army to win the battle (*b*) Congress to grant more money (*c*) the South to free the slaves (*d*) the people to preserve a democratic nation.

11. The North gained control of the Mississippi River by capturing (*a*) Atlanta (*b*) Vicksburg (*c*) Fort Donelson (*d*) Chattanooga.

12. All of the following were Confederate military leaders EXCEPT (*a*) Thomas J. Jackson (*b*) Robert E. Lee (*c*) Jubal Early (*d*) Philip H. Sheridan.

13. The "cheese box on a raft" describes the (*a*) *Monitor* (*b*) *Merrimac* (*c*) *Alabama* (*d*) *Trent.*

14. The commanding general of the Union armies in the final stages of the Civil War was (*a*) Irvin McDowell (*b*) George B. McClellan (*c*) George H. Thomas (*d*) Ulysses S. Grant.

15. All of the following Civil War battles were fought in Maryland or Virginia EXCEPT the Battle of (*a*) Bull Run (*b*) Antietam (*c*) Chickamauga (*d*) Fredericksburg.

Modified True-False Test

1. The name of the man who assassinated Abraham Lincoln was *John Brown.*

2. Mason and Slidell, seized aboard the TRENT, were agents of the *Confederate* government.

3. Sherman marched to the sea through the state of *Virginia.*

4. In the face of criticism concerning heavy casualties, *George B. McClellan* declared: "I propose to fight it out on this line if it takes all summer."

5. The battle that marked the major turning point of the Civil War was the Battle of *Shiloh.*

6. *David G. Farragut* commanded the Union fleet that captured New Orleans.

7. The general-in-chief of the Confederate forces was *Joseph E. Johnston.*

8. The Confederate surrender took place on April 9, 1865, at *Petersburg,* Virginia.

9. "A crow flying over the country would need to carry his rations" describes the condition of the *Shenandoah* Valley after Sheridan's campaign.

10. The main military objective of the Union campaign in the East was the capture of the city of *Charleston.*

11. The "Rock of Chickamauga" describes *George H. Thomas,* whose heroic stand saved the Union forces from complete defeat during the Chattanooga campaign.

12. Thomas J. Jackson, the Confederate general, earned the title *"Old Rough and Ready"* for his bravery at Bull Run.

13. The *Fourteenth* Amendment abolished the institution of human slavery in the United States.

14. Most of the battles of the Civil War were fought south of the *Mason-Dixon* Line.
15. Ulysses Simpson Grant earned the nickname *Uncle Sam* Grant.

Matching Test

Column A

1. "In *your* hands, my dissatisfied fellow-countrymen, and not in *mine,* is the momentous issue of civil war."
2. "With malice toward none; with charity for all. . . ."
3. "My paramount object in this struggle *is* to save the Union, and is *not* either to save or destroy Slavery."
4. "All slaves in those states and parts of states in rebellion on or after January 1, 1863, are permanently free."
5. ". . . that government of the people, by the people, for the people, shall not perish from the earth."

Column B

a. Lincoln's letter to Horace Greeley
b. Lincoln's Emancipation Proclamation
c. Lincoln's Gettysburg Address
d. Lincoln's First Inaugural Address
e. Lincoln's Second Inaugural Address

Essay Questions

1. Discuss briefly *two* of the following statements, giving reasons for your agreement or disagreement with *each* statement selected. (*a*) The campaign to win the senatorship in the state of Illinois made Abraham Lincoln a national figure. (*b*) Lincoln's Gettysburg Address deserves the praise it has received. (*c*) Lincoln's views on slavery were moderate in comparison with those of other leaders of the period.
2. The Civil War was particularly tragic because Americans fought on both sides. (*a*) State *two* causes of the outbreak of the war. (*b*) State *one* advantage possessed by the South and *one* possessed by the North as the fighting started. (*c*) Give the name of a political leader in the North and of one in the South, and also the name of a military leader in each section.
3. State why each of the following incidents in the Civil War was important: the *Merrimac* and the *Monitor,* Fort Sumter, Sherman's march to the sea, the *Trent* Affair, and the meeting at Appomattox Courthouse.
4. Write a brief account of the life of Abraham Lincoln, basing your account on the outline given below:
   I. Lincoln's Boyhood
   II. Lincoln's Life in Illinois
   III. Lincoln as President
5. Compare the North and the South at the start of the Civil War, including *each* of the following: population, industrial development, transportation, financial resources, and military advantages.
6. a. What issues were settled by the Civil War?
   b. Describe the condition of the North in 1865.
   c. Describe the condition of the South in 1865.

Part 3. Reconstruction

PROBLEMS OF RECONSTRUCTION

The years immediately following the Civil War (1865–1877) are known as the *Reconstruction Period*. "Reconstruction" meant the restoration of the seceded states to the Union. The major questions facing the federal government at the time were: (1) On what basis should the Confederate states be brought back into the Union? (2) How should the Southern whites be treated? (3) What should be done for the freed slaves?

LINCOLN'S PLAN OF RECONSTRUCTION

Lincoln held the view that the Southern states had not left the Union; they had only been in a state of rebellion. While the war was still going on, Lincoln put a plan of reconstruction into effect in areas occupied by Union troops. His plan provided for (1) pardons to all Southerners (with certain exceptions) who had participated in the war, provided they took an oath of allegiance to the United States, and (2) restoration of a seceded state to the Union after 10% of the whites who had voted in the 1860 election took an oath of allegiance and formed a state government guaranteeing the abolition of slavery.

Congress opposed this plan, but Lincoln argued that his presidential powers permitted him to go ahead with it. When Andrew Johnson took over as President in 1865, he adopted Lincoln's plan.

JOHNSON BECOMES PRESIDENT

A man of humble background, Andrew Johnson was born and raised in North Carolina. He became a tailor and migrated to Tennessee to practice his trade. Entering politics as a Democrat, he held a number of local offices, and was elected to the U.S. House of Representatives and to the governorship of Tennessee. Serving in the U.S. Senate at the outbreak of the war, he remained loyal to the Union when his state seceded. He was later appointed military governor of occupied Tennessee.

Seeking to gain the support of Democrats for Lincoln's reelection in 1864, the Republicans nominated Johnson as his running mate. Assuming office as Vice President, he became the nation's 17th President after Lincoln was assassinated in 1865.

JOHNSON ATTEMPTS TO RECONSTRUCT THE SOUTH

Implementing Lincoln's reconstruction plan, Johnson (1) pardoned all Southerners who took the oath of allegiance (except for a few important ex-Confederates who had to request special pardons), (2) recognized the four state governments already established by Lincoln, and (3) appointed temporary governors in the other seven states, empowering them to hold elections and form state governments.

By the end of 1865, all but one of the Southern states had set up new state governments, abolished slavery by ratifying the Thirteenth Amendment, and elected representatives and senators to the U.S. Congress. Thereupon, Johnson announced that these states were restored to the Union.

CONGRESS REJECTS JOHNSON'S PROGRAM

When Congress convened in December, 1865, it rejected Johnson's actions. It refused to seat the newly elected Southern members of Congress, and declared invalid the newly formed state governments in the South. Among the reasons why Congress condemned Johnson's program were the following:

1. Congress was dominated by a group of *Radical Republicans*, led by Representative Thaddeus Stevens and Senator Charles Sumner. They held the view that the former Confederate states were "conquered provinces" and should be punished for their disloyalty.

2. Congress wished to curb the powers of the President—powers that had expanded greatly during the war years. Congressional leaders claimed that only the legislative branch had the authority to readmit the seceded states.

3. State legislatures in the South had begun to enact "Black Codes" to regulate the status of the *freedmen* (as the former slaves—male and female—were now called). These laws did extend certain rights to blacks, such as the right to own property, make contracts, sue in court, and undertake legal marriages. But the codes also excluded blacks from jury service, denied them the right to testify against whites in court, and required them to obtain special licenses for any occupation other than farming. A few states allowed local authorities to arrest unemployed blacks for vagrancy, impose fines, and hire them out to work for white landowners to pay off the fines. Some states also stipulated that young blacks lacking "adequate" parental support could be bound out as "apprentices" to their former masters.

Congress viewed the Black Codes as proof that Southern whites were seeking to reenslave the freedmen.

4. Under Johnson's plan, most Southern white males had the right to vote, but no provision had been made to *enfranchise* (give the vote to) freedmen. Southern whites, blaming the Republican party for their defeat, were overwhelmingly Democratic. Blacks, on the other hand, were pro-Republican because that party had helped them gain their freedom. Thus, Southern Democrats did not want to give freedmen the vote. Republicans feared that without the black vote they would lose the South to the Democrats, who then might be strong enough to gain control of Congress.

CONGRESS ASSUMES CONTROL OF RECONSTRUCTION

Starting in 1866 Congress proceeded to put its own plan of reconstruction into effect.

1. Freedmen's Bureau. This federal agency had been set up in 1865 on a temporary basis to care for the newly freed slaves. In 1866 Congress passed a *Freedmen's Bureau Bill* (over Johnson's veto) extending the life of the agency and enlarging its scope. Bureau agents helped freedmen find jobs; furnished them with food, clothing, and shelter; supervised their education; and attempted to protect their civil rights.

2. Civil Rights Act of 1866. This law (also passed over Johnson's veto) aimed to protect freedmen from such discriminatory legislation as the Black Codes. It bestowed citizenship on the blacks and affirmed their right to enjoy "equal and full benefit of all laws and proceedings for the security of person and property as is enjoyed by white citizens."

3. Fourteenth Amendment. To forestall any attempt by future legislators to nullify the Civil Rights Act, Congress took steps to guarantee rights of blacks constitutionally by proposing the Fourteenth Amendment in 1866. (It was ratified in 1868.) The amendment defined all native-born and naturalized persons, including blacks, as citizens and provided that no state shall (*a*) "make or enforce any law which shall abridge the privileges and immunities of citizens"; (*b*) "deprive any person of life, liberty, or property, without due process of law"; or (*c*) "deny to any person within its jurisdiction the equal protection of the laws."

The amendment also barred Confederates who had held either local, state, or federal government positions before the war from again holding public office; voided the Confederate war debt; and forbade payments to slaveholders for losses arising from emancipation.

Tennessee ratified the Fourteenth Amendment in 1866 and was restored to the Union. The other 10 former Confederate states rejected the amendment.

4. Reconstruction Acts. The *First Reconstruction Act*, passed in March, 1867, over Johnson's veto (and several follow-up measures enacted later), spelled out terms of the congressional plan to reconstruct the South.

a. The ten unreconstructed states were divided into five military districts, each policed by federal troops under the command of a military governor.

b. To qualify for readmission, a state had to hold a convention and frame a new constitution guaranteeing black suffrage.

c. Convention delegates were to be elected by all citizens eligible to vote, including former slaves. Ex-Confederates disqualified from holding office by the proposed Fourteenth Amendment were barred from voting.

d. When a state had organized a new government acceptable to Congress and had ratified the Fourteenth Amendment, it would be restored to the Union.

THE SOUTHERN STATES ARE READMITTED

Seven Southern states met the requirements laid down by Congress and were readmitted to the Union in 1868. The following year Congress proposed the Fifteenth Amendment, prohibiting any state from denying the right of a citizen to vote "on account of race, color, or previous condition of servitude." The three remaining states were required to ratify this amendment as an additional condition for readmission. (So too did Georgia, whose earlier readmission had been revoked when it expelled elected black members from its state legislature.) Upon meeting all the requirements for readmission, these states were restored to the Union in 1870.

CONGRESS IMPEACHES THE PRESIDENT

Relations between President Johnson and Congress were very strained. Republican members of Congress disliked Johnson because: (1) He opposed their plans for reconstructing the South. (2) He vetoed many of their bills. (3) He was tactless in his dealings with them. (4) He had been a Southern Democrat before the war and was therefore distrusted.

To prevent the President from dismissing officeholders who supported the congressional reconstruction plan, Congress enacted the *Tenure of Office Act* in 1867. It required the approval of the U.S. Senate for the discharge of any federal official whose appointment had been made with the advice and consent of the Senate. Johnson defied the act, which he claimed was unconstitutional, by dismissing his Secretary of War, Edwin M. Stanton—a Radical Republican. Thereupon, in February, 1868, the House of Representatives *impeached* the President; that is, it charged him with wrongdoing.

The Senate, sitting as a court, tried Johnson on the impeachment charges. Lacking one vote, the Radical Republicans failed to muster the two-thirds vote necessary for his removal. Johnson was therefore acquitted and remained in office until the end of his term.

GRANT IS ELECTED PRESIDENT

Ulysses S. Grant of Ohio, the Civil War hero, was nominated by the Republicans for the presidency in 1868 and was elected as the 18th U.S. President. During his two terms in office (1869–1877), Grant supported the congressional plan for reconstructing the South. Lacking political experience, Grant chose his advisers and appointees unwisely, with the result that his administration was marred by political and financial scandals. It was also beset by economic problems arising from the Panic of 1873.

RECONSTRUCTION GOVERNMENTS RULE THE SOUTH

The state governments organized under congressional reconstruction were controlled by the Republicans. The party's membership in the South comprised the following groups:

1. Blacks. About 80% of the Republican voters in the South were black males. Nearly all were poor and illiterate ex-slaves. Many of the black leaders and officeholders, however, could read and write and were either clergy, land-owning farmers, skilled craftsworkers, or owners of small businesses. Between 1869 and 1880, 14 Southern blacks served in the House of Representatives and two—Hiram R. Revels and Blanche K. Bruce—served in the Senate. Blacks held seats in every Southern state legislature, but only in the South Carolina assembly did they constitute a majority.

2. Carpetbaggers. Although white migrants from the North made up about 3% of the Republican voters, they dominated the party's leadership in the South. They included (*a*) Union army officers who had stayed on after the war because they liked the climate or were attracted by economic opportunities in the post-war South; (*b*) agents of the Freedmen's Bureau, many of them working as teachers or supervisors of the schools established for blacks; (*c*) businesspeople seeking to invest their capital in the Southern economy; and (*d*) self-serving politicians who sought to gain power with the aid of the black vote. Southerners called them all "carpetbaggers" (because some carried their possessions in bags made of carpet material).

3. Scalawags. Southern whites who cooperated with carpetbaggers and blacks were known as "scalawags" (a derogatory term meaning "animals of little value"). Among them were (*a*) people who had been Unionist in sympathy at the outbreak of the war; (*b*) small farmers who had always resented the pre-war, slaveholding planter class; (*c*) those who shared the carpetbaggers' vision of a new South; and (*d*) some who hoped to profit by allying themselves with the party in power.

During their tenure in office, the reconstruction governments accomplished much that was worthwhile. They (*a*) established free, statewide public school systems for both races; (*b*) rebuilt the bridges, roads, public buildings, and other community facilities that had been destroyed by the war; (*c*) provided state aid for the restoration and expansion of the region's railroads; (*d*) set up industrial commissions to attract investment in Southern enterprises; (*e*) expanded state involvement in social welfare; (*f*) reformed and modernized the judicial system; and (*g*) enacted civil rights and antidiscrimination laws.

Since many of these undertakings were costly, state and local expenditures, taxes, and debts rose sharply. Property owners, forced to pay higher taxes than ever before, criticized the "carpetbag governments" for fiscal irresponsibility and mismanagement. Southern Democrats accused government officials of dishonesty, bribery, and graft. Examples cited were (*a*) legislators and governors who accepted bribes from railroad promoters seeking favored treatment; (*b*) officials who awarded government contracts to friends in return for "kickbacks"; (*c*) administrators who pocketed funds appropriated for schools and public services; and (*d*) legislators who voted for the inclusion of items for personal use in state budgets.

Although many of these charges were valid, similar practices were common at the time in other parts of the country. Corruption was widespread in the post-war era and was not a unique phenomenon of the reconstruction governments in the South.

SOUTHERN WHITES REGAIN CONTROL

Unable to vote or hold office, some Southern whites resorted to violence to help restore themselves to power. Through such secret societies as the *Ku Klux Klan*, they carried out a reign of terror against freedmen and their white supporters. They beat up or lynched blacks who acted in an "insolent" manner toward whites; whipped teachers of freedmen's schools and burned down their schoolhouses; and terrorized or murdered Republican leaders and voters.

Southern whites gradually regained control of their local and state governments as: (1) Fear of violence kept many of the freedmen from the polls. (2) More young males who had not participated in the war (and therefore had the right to vote) reached voting age each year. (3) In 1872 Congress restored the rights of suffrage and officeholding to all but about 500 former Confederates.

PRESIDENT HAYES ENDS MILITARY OCCUPATION OF THE SOUTH

The two opposing candidates for President in 1876 were Rutherford B. Hayes of Ohio, Republican, and Samuel J. Tilden of New York, Democrat. Tilden polled a larger popular vote than Hayes and also led in electoral votes, but he was one electoral vote short of the total necessary for victory. But there were 20 electoral votes from four states still uncounted because of election disputes. Both parties claimed these votes. Congress appointed an Electoral Commission of seven Democrats and eight Republicans to settle the issue. This group assigned every disputed vote to Hayes, the Republican, thereby giving him the election and making him the 19th President.

The Democratic members of Congress agreed to support the decision of the Electoral Commission in return for a Republican promise to withdraw the last of the federal troops from the South. Shortly after his inauguration, in 1877, Hayes recalled the soldiers, thereby ending military occupation of the South and bringing the Reconstruction Period to an end. With the termination of military rule, the remaining Republican-controlled governments were swept out of office. However, the South remained resentful of the Republican party, and for the next 75 years the former Confederate states (the *Solid South*) voted almost unanimously for the Democratic party.

A NEW SOUTH ARISES

The New South that emerged from the ruins of the old was different in many ways. Though cotton was still the main crop, agriculture became more diversified. Corn, wheat, vegetables, fruits, and peanuts were raised along with the old staples: cotton, tobacco, and rice. The great plantations were broken up and rented to tenant farmers. Most of these renters became known as *sharecroppers*. They received animals, tools, seeds, homes, and barns from the owners and repaid their debts with a share of their produce.

The New South became an important industrial section. The raw materials, cheap labor, low taxes, and abundant waterpower of the South attracted the cotton mills previously located in New England.

The discovery of deposits of coal, iron ore, and limestone led to the building of a great iron and steel industry centered about Birmingham,

Alabama, called the "Pittsburgh of the South." Petroleum, natural gas, sulfur, lumber, zinc, and granite provided the raw materials for the development of other thriving industries. Cottonseed mills, tobacco factories, paper mills, and furniture factories also sprang up.

SOUTHERN BLACKS LOSE MANY OF THEIR CIVIL RIGHTS

For nearly a century after the Reconstruction Period, most Southern blacks were prevented from exercising their right to vote by such devices as (*a*) *poll taxes* (taxes imposed as a prerequisite for voting); (*b*) *literacy tests* (tests given to prospective voters to disqualify those who failed to meet a literacy standard set by the state); and (*c*) *grandfather clauses* (laws waiving other restrictive voting requirements for those who could prove that they or their ancestors had voted before 1867—the year that blacks were enfranchised). Through the enactment of *Jim Crow laws*, they were also kept apart, or *segregated*, from whites in housing, transportation facilities, public accommodations, and schools. In 1896 the U.S. Supreme Court in *Plessy* v. *Ferguson* upheld the legality of segregation by ruling that "separate but equal" access to public facilities did not constitute discrimination. Not until 1954, when the Court reversed its previous stand by ruling that segregation in public schools was unconstitutional, did the federal government begin to take new steps to protect the civil rights of Southern blacks (see pages 301–306).

Hesse in The St. Louis Globe-Democrat

It Takes Two to Lay the Cornerstone

Multiple-Choice Test

1. The purpose of the "Black Codes" in the Southern states during the Reconstruction Period was to (*a*) aid the carpetbaggers (*b*) grant suffrage to blacks (*c*) prevent the exploitation of freedmen (*d*) restrict the civil rights of blacks.

2. The Fourteenth Amendment to the federal Constitution forbids states to (*a*) levy income taxes (*b*) pass bankruptcy laws (*c*) deprive any citizen of equal rights (*d*) regulate interstate commerce.

3. The Radical Republicans in Congress after the Civil War were those who (*a*) regarded the Southern states as conquered territory (*b*) passed the "Black Codes" (*c*) favored Lincoln's ideas on Southern reconstruction (*d*) introduced pro-labor legislation.

4. President Lincoln's plan for reconstruction was based on the theory that the Confederate states (*a*) were to be treated as territories (*b*) could be readmitted to the Union only by Congress (*c*) had never actually left the Union (*d*) were to be occupied by Union forces for a period of 20 years.

5. During the Reconstruction Period, which branch of the national government attempted to achieve supremacy over another? (*a*) the judicial over the legislative (*b*) the executive over the judicial (*c*) the legislative over the executive (*d*) the legislative over the judicial.

6. The impeachment case against President Andrew Johnson was tried in the U.S. (*a*) House of Representatives (*b*) Court of Appeals of the District of Columbia (*c*) Supreme Court (*d*) Senate.

7. Which was an effect of slavery on the South? (*a*) It encouraged the establishment of small, family-operated farms. (*b*) It retarded industrial development. (*c*) It caused the South to favor high protective tariffs. (*d*) It brought about friendly relations between the South and the West.

8. Sharecropping emerged in the post-Civil War South as a means by which (*a*) Southern planters exchanged crops for Northern manufactured goods (*b*) more than one crop shared the available land on the plantation (*c*) former slaves formed cooperative associations to share costs of entering farming (*d*) impoverished planters and former slaves supplied each other's need for labor and land.

9. In 1876 Rutherford B. Hayes was elected President over Samuel J. Tilden by a majority vote of (*a*) the Senate (*b*) an Electoral Commission (*c*) the House of Representatives (*d*) the people.

10. During the Reconstruction Period an important objective of congressional action was to (*a*) destroy the economy of the South (*b*) restore pre-Civil War conditions in the South (*c*) retain Republican domination of the national government (*d*) pardon Southern leaders for Civil War activities.

Modified True-False Test

1. After the Civil War, the city of *Richmond* became known as the "Pittsburgh of the South."

2. The right of suffrage was given to newly freed male slaves by the *Fifteenth* Amendment.

3. A secret society organized by Southern whites to terrorize blacks was the *Midnight Judges.*

4. Northern politicians who rose to power in the South during the Reconstruction Period were referred to as *lame ducks.*
5. Southerners who cooperated with Northerners who dominated the state governments of the South were derisively called *war hawks.*
6. For more than 75 years after the Reconstruction Period, the tendency of the South to support the Democratic party gave rise to the term *Solid South.*
7. *Daniel Webster* was the leader of the Radical Republicans in the House of Representatives during reconstruction.
8. An agency established by Congress in 1865 to help the former slaves was the *Bureau of Social Welfare.*
9. The *Tenure of Office Act,* passed in 1867, made it illegal for the President to dismiss key appointive officials without the consent of the Senate.
10. The military occupation of the South came to an end during the administration of President *Grant.*

Essay Questions

1. (*a*) Show *two* differences between the presidential plan of reconstruction and the congressional plan of reconstruction following the Civil War. (*b*) Discuss *two* results of the reconstruction policy of Congress.
2. Explain how *each* of the following helped to make the Reconstruction Period a troubled era in American history: the death of Abraham Lincoln, the scalawags and carpetbaggers, and the Ku Klux Klan.
3. (*a*) Show the effect of the congressional reconstruction policy upon the status of Southern blacks. (*b*) How did their status change after 1877?

UNIT VII. THE ECONOMY TRANSFORMED

Part 1. Settlement of the Western Frontier

THE FAR WEST IS LINKED WITH THE EAST

Between the populated areas of the Middle West and the rapidly expanding settlements of the Far West stretched some 1,500 miles of unsettled territory. Beginning in 1858 stagecoach lines carried passengers and mail from the Missouri River, which was the western terminus of the railroads, to California. These stagecoaches, carrying about 10 passengers, their baggage, and several bulky sacks of mail, took three weeks to make the hazardous journey across the plains, deserts, and mountains. Heavy freight was hauled westward by long trains of Conestoga wagons drawn by oxen or mules. To speed the delivery of important mail, the Pony Express was inaugurated in 1860. Mounted on swift horses and riding day and night, relays of express riders carried the mail from St. Joseph, Missouri, to San Francisco, California, in 10 days. (See map, page 227.)

The first telegraph to the Far West was completed in the fall of 1861. Messages could now be sent from coast to coast in seconds. The transcontinental telegraph outmoded the Pony Express, which soon discontinued operations.

THE TRANSCONTINENTAL RAILROAD

During the Civil War, plans were drawn to link the Pacific coast with the East by rail. Congress authorized two railroad companies to handle the project. It voted to provide them a free right-of-way across public land, financial assistance in the form of loans, and additional large grants of land for every mile of completed road.

The *Union Pacific* began at Omaha, Nebraska, and was built westward across the prairie into Wyoming and Utah. The *Central Pacific* started at Sacramento, California, and pushed eastward across the mountains into Nevada and Utah. Each company raced to outbuild the other in order to receive a greater share of the loans and land grants. In May, 1869, the two lines met at Promontory Point, near Ogden, Utah. A person could now travel by rail from the Atlantic coast to Omaha, from there to Sacramento, and then to San Francisco.

The completion of the first transcontinental railroad was an important milestone in the history of the country. Finished goods could now be shipped by rail to Western markets. Likewise, Western raw materials and farm products could be sent to the East. The mineral and forest resources of the West were opened to development. Immigration to the West was facilitated.

During the next 25 years the *Northern Pacific*, the *Southern Pacific*, the *Atchison, Topeka and Santa Fe*, and the *Great Northern* also completed

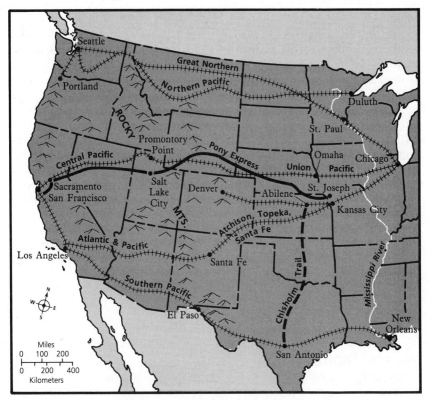

The Far West Is Linked With the East

railroad lines to the Pacific coast. The government granted more than $60 million in loans and over 125 million acres of public land to the railroads to encourage the building of these transcontinental links.

GOLD AND SILVER LURE AMERICANS TO THE ROCKIES

The discovery of gold near Pikes Peak, Colorado, and of gold and silver in Nevada brought a rush of miners and prospectors to these areas in 1858–1859. In the 1860's gold was found in Idaho, Montana, and Wyoming. These discoveries touched off a mining boom in the Rocky Mountain region similar to the one in California in 1849. In hundreds of remote places, mining towns of tents and shanties sprang up overnight, and eager fortune hunters staked out their claims and dug for the precious metals. Many of the ore deposits were exceedingly rich. At Virginia City, Nevada, the Comstock Lode alone yielded $300 million in gold and silver in 20 years. By 1890 nearly $2 billion worth of gold and silver had been taken from the mines in the Rocky Mountain area.

Other sections of the West also experienced mining booms. The discovery of gold in the Black Hills of South Dakota touched off a gold rush to that area in 1875. Later, rich strikes were made in Arizona.

DEVELOPMENT OF THE ROCKY MOUNTAIN REGION

Life in the "diggings" was rough and lawless at first, as it had been in the early days of the California gold rush. For self-protection, law-abiding citizens formed local governments and organized vigilance committees to track down and punish desperadoes.

Some of the prospectors who failed to "strike it rich" settled down to ranching and farming. Others drifted away after the easily mined surface deposits of gold and silver were exhausted. Still others took jobs with the mining companies that were being formed. These companies came into existence because mining below the surface required large sums of money for sinking shafts, erecting tunnels, and purchasing expensive machinery. In addition to gold and silver, copper, lead, zinc, and other mineral resources were also found, and mining became a permanent industry.

The timber resources and grazing lands of the Rocky Mountain region also contributed to the economic development of the area. Lumbering became an important industry in the northern part of the mountains; cattle and sheep were raised in the valleys and foothills.

SETTLING THE GREAT PLAINS

THE LAST FRONTIER

From the Missouri River westward to the Rockies existed a vast unsettled area called the *Great Plains*. Treeless and semiarid, this grass-covered prairie, thought to be unsuited for agriculture, was ignored by the earlier pioneers. Until the 1860's the area was inhabited mainly by Indians.

THE CATTLE INDUSTRY STARTS IN TEXAS

When Americans settled in Texas, they found great herds of half-wild, longhorned cattle roaming the plains. These hardy beasts were descendants of the cattle originally brought to the New World by the Spaniards. The Texans rounded up the longhorns, established ranches, and raised the animals for beef, hides, and tallow. For many years the industry was a local one because of the difficulty of transporting the cattle to Eastern markets.

THE LONG DRIVE

With the extension of the railroad into Kansas and Nebraska in the 1860's, Texas ranchers found it profitable to drive their livestock northward across the Great Plains to the rail centers, load them onto cattle cars, and ship them eastward. Each spring huge herds of cattle were rounded up, branded with the distinctive marks of their owners, and started on the *long drive* from Texas to the *cow towns* along the railroad route. Cowboys on horseback guided and guarded the cattle, prevented them from stampeding, and fought off *rustlers* (cattle thieves) and Indians. The rich prairie grass fed and fattened the herds on their long journey.

One of the most widely used routes of the long drive was the *Chisholm Trail*, which led from San Antonio, Texas, to Abilene, Kansas.

SPREAD OF CATTLE RAISING

To meet the rising demand from the heavily populated Eastern cities for beef, cattle ranches sprang up throughout the Great Plains. This expanse of unfenced, unpopulated, and government-owned grassland, known as the *open range*, became a vast pasturage for cattle. Cattle ranchers allowed their herds to graze freely over the prairie until the cattle were ready for marketing. The cattle would then be rounded up, separated by brands, and driven to the nearest railroad.

The introduction of the railroad refrigerator car in the 1870's stimulated the growth of the cattle industry. It was now possible to slaughter the steers at nearby meat-packing centers, such as Kansas City and Chicago, and ship the cleaned, or dressed, beef to the East without fear of spoilage.

COMING OF THE HOMESTEADERS

In 1862 Congress passed the Homestead Act. It granted ownership of 160 acres of public land to settlers if they paid a small registration fee, established a residence, and worked the land for five years. The offer of homesteads drew large numbers of farmers, factory workers, Civil War veterans, and immigrants to the Great Plains.

The early homesteaders encountered strong opposition from the ranchers who saw their "cattle kingdom" threatened by the farmers. Violent clashes broke out between the two groups. Nevertheless, more and more settlers arrived, established farms, and fenced in their acreage. After a time, the wild grasslands of the open range became enclosed fields of corn and wheat. By 1890 nearly all of the good farmland was privately owned, and cattle raising was restricted to fenced ranches in dry areas unsuited to crops.

FARM LIFE ON THE GREAT PLAINS

Since there were almost no trees on the prairie, a settler's first home was either a house built of sod or a *dugout*, a one-room shelter dug in the side of a hill. Lumber and coal had to be brought in by rail, and most farmers could not afford to buy them at first. Dried cornstalks, corncobs, and animal wastes were burned for fuel. To obtain water, it was often necessary to dig wells to a depth of 200 feet. Windmills were used to pump water to the surface.

Protecting crops from straying range cattle was a major problem because stones and wood for fencing were extremely scarce. This obstacle was overcome in the 1870's by the introduction of barbed wire (invented by *Joseph F. Glidden*), which made possible the construction of inexpensive but effective fences.

Despite bitterly cold winters, extremely hot summers, dust storms, droughts, grasshopper plagues, and prairie fires, the sturdy pioneers succeeded in taming the land and making the Great Plains a great wheat- and corn-producing region.

CONFLICTING INTERESTS OF INDIANS AND SETTLERS

WESTERN INDIANS

Many Indian tribes inhabited the region west of the Mississippi. Some were Eastern Indians who had resettled west of the river by agreement with the government in the 1830's. Others, like the Sioux, Comanches, Pawnees, Blackfeet, and Crows, were native to the Plains. These Indians depended upon the vast buffalo herds of the prairie for their necessities of life. Buffalo meat was their main source of food. From buffalo hides they made clothing, blankets, tepees, bridles, and bow strings. And from buffalo bones they fashioned tools and implements. In the Southwest dwelt the Pueblo Indians, who lived in multistory adobe houses and engaged in farming; the Apaches, who were nomadic hunters; and the Navajos, who were farmers and sheepherders.

THE INDIANS RESIST THE SPREAD OF SETTLEMENT

As the miners, ranchers, and farmers advanced into the area west of the Mississippi—slaughtering buffalo, occupying the land, and reducing the hunting grounds of the Indians—the Native Americans made a desperate attempt to save their homes and their way of life. For 25 years after the Civil War, one tribe or another carried on constant warfare against the settlers. They attacked wagon trains, burned and looted farms and settlements, and waged battles with federal troops.

RESERVATIONS ARE SET ASIDE FOR INDIANS

In an attempt to solve the "Indian problem," the government assigned specific areas, called *reservations,* to the various tribes. The government also agreed to furnish them with food and allow them money for their other needs. This solution did not work out well at first because: (1) Many tribes refused to give up their hunting grounds. (2) Many Indians resented being confined to restricted areas. (3) Some found life on the reservations dull and degrading. (4) Land-hungry settlers seized reservation land for farms. (5) Dishonest government agents cheated Indians of their food and allowances.

As a result, Indians frequently rose in rebellion, only to be driven back to their reservations by the U.S. Army. On one occasion a bloody Indian war was brought on by a mining rush into the Sioux reservation in the Dakotas, after gold was discovered in the Black Hills. Seeing their territory overrun by prospectors, the Sioux, led by Chiefs Sitting Bull and Crazy Horse decided to resist. Before the uprising was put down, they had ambushed and annihilated a force of 264 cavalrymen under George A. Custer in the Battle of the Little Bighorn in Montana (1876). This battle has become known as "Custer's Last Stand."

RESERVATION LIFE

By the late 1880's the Indian wars had subsided, and all the tribes had been forced onto reservations. The government established schools to educate Indian children and teach trades to the adults. In 1887 Congress passed the *Dawes Act,* granting citizenship and 160 acres of land to every Indian family that gave up its tribal way of life and took up farming. Many Indians accepted the offer, but others continued to live as tribes on reservations.

All Indians were granted citizenship in 1924. Their present population is about 1.9 million. Half of them live on reservations, where their lands comprise about 56 million acres. Some of the tribes became wealthy when oil and other minerals were discovered on their property. A few also profited by setting up gambling casinos to attract tourists to their lands. But most Indians live in poverty. In recent years, efforts have been made to provide more self-government to Indians and to encourage them to preserve their tribal cultures and skills.

END OF THE FRONTIER

ADMISSION OF NEW STATES

As the population of the West increased, the area was divided into *territories*—units of government modeled after the former Northwest Territory. From these territories, states were created and admitted into the Union. Nevada became a state in 1864, Nebraska in 1867, and Colorado in 1876. Montana, North Dakota, South Dakota, and Washington were admitted in 1889; Idaho and Wyoming in 1890. In that last year the Census Bureau announced that a frontier line no longer existed in the United States. Shortly thereafter, Utah became the country's 45th state. (See the map on page 232.)

OKLAHOMA IS OPENED TO SETTLEMENT

In the 1830's Oklahoma was set aside by Congress as Indian Territory. It remained closed to non-Indians for the next 50 years. With the spread of settlement on the Great Plains, some homesteaders (called "Sooners") attempted to settle in Oklahoma but were turned back by federal troops. Responding to demands that the Indian lands be made available to homesteaders, Congress purchased a large part of the area from the Indians and opened it for settlement.

Thousands of eager homesteaders (called "Boomers") raced into Oklahoma when the signal to enter was given on April 22, 1889. By the end of the first day's rush, 12,000 homesteads had been staked out on 1,920,000 acres of land, and a tent city with 10,000 inhabitants had sprung up on the site of Oklahoma City. Other sections of the former Indian domain were opened to settlement in the next several years. Oklahoma was organized as a territory in 1890 and became the 46th state in 1907.

ROUNDING OUT THE UNION

In 1912 New Mexico and Arizona were admitted as the 47th and 48th states. A solid block of states now extended from the Atlantic to

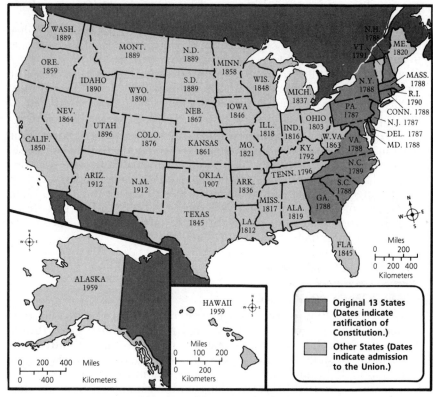

Admission of States to the Union

the Pacific and from Canada to Mexico. The 48-state Union remained unchanged for the next 47 years. It was enlarged in 1959 when Alaska and Hawaii were added to the Union as the 49th and 50th states (see pages 332–334). These are the only states that do not share a common border with any other state.

Multiple-Choice Test

1. Of the following, the LAST state to be admitted to the Union was (*a*) Florida (*b*) Oregon (*c*) New Mexico (*d*) Texas.
2. In 1860 the fastest mail service from the Missouri River to the Pacific coast was by (*a*) boat (*b*) pony express (*c*) railroad (*d*) stagecoach.
3. A major reason for the continuous warfare between the Plains Indians and the settlers was that the Indians (*a*) wanted the horses of the settlers (*b*) resented the destruction of the buffalo herds by the settlers (*c*) wanted the guns and powder of the fur traders (*d*) were determined to save their extensive farmlands.
4. The main policy of the federal government toward Indians in the period immediately following the Civil War was to (*a*) move them to reservations

(*b*) drive them from the country (*c*) require those under 16 years of age to attend public school (*d*) grant them full citizenship.

5. The major purpose of the Homestead Act of 1862 was to (*a*) raise revenue for the federal government (*b*) provide land companies with new lands to sell (*c*) create expansion opportunities for Southern plantation owners (*d*) encourage settlement of public lands for farming.

6. Which state lies in that part of the United States which was last to be settled and developed? (*a*) Kentucky (*b*) Ohio (*c*) South Dakota (*d*) Oregon.

7. A railroad company that participated in building the first transcontinental railroad was the (*a*) Great Northern (*b*) Northern Pacific (*c*) Southern Pacific (*d*) Union Pacific.

8. All of the following became important economic activities in the Rocky Mountain region EXCEPT (*a*) cotton growing (*b*) silver mining (*c*) lumbering (*d*) cattle raising.

9. A popular route of the "long drive" was the (*a*) Oregon Trail (*b*) Wilderness Road (*c*) Chisholm Trail (*d*) National Road.

10. All of the following Indians were native to the Great Plains EXCEPT the (*a*) Iroquois (*b*) Sioux (*c*) Comanches (*d*) Pawnees.

Modified True-False Test

1. An area of land set aside by the federal government for an Indian tribe to live on is called a *happy hunting ground.*

2. The first home of a pioneer on the Great Plains was usually a house built of *sod.*

3. Beginning in the 1870's fences put up by farmers of the Great Plains to protect their crops from stray cattle were made of *barbed wire.*

4. The *Apache* Indians of the Southwest engaged in farming and lived in adobe dwellings similar to apartment houses.

5. A force of cavalrymen led by *Wild Bill Hickok* was massacred by the Sioux Indians in the Battle of the Little Bighorn.

6. The law that granted citizenship and free land to Indian families that gave up their tribal way of life and took up farming was the *Dawes* Act.

7. The pioneers who settled the present state of Oklahoma were called *"Forty-Niners."*

8. The Plains animals that provided Indians with their food, clothing, and other necessities were the *reindeer.*

9. The *Morrill* Act, passed by Congress in 1862, made available 160 acres of public land to settlers who met the requirements of that law.

10. The eastern and western sections of the first transcontinental railroad were joined in 1869 at *Promontory Point* in Utah.

Essay Questions

1. (*a*) What companies built the first transcontinental railroad connecting the East with the Pacific coast? (*b*) How and why did the federal government aid the companies building this railroad? (*c*) What benefits did such a railroad bring to the East and the West?

2. In the 1850's Horace Greeley, a famous journalist, said, "Go west, young man." (*a*) Give *three* reasons why a young person might have wished to go west at that time. (*b*) Give *two* advantages that person would have had in staying in the East at that time.

3. Explain *five* of the following terms associated with the development of the West in such a way that a visitor from a foreign country would clearly understand what each term chosen means; homesteader, "long drive," open range, vigilantes, Conestoga wagon, "strike it rich," "around the Horn," and Comstock Lode.

Part 2. Progress and Problems of the Farmer

AN AGRICULTURAL REVOLUTION TRANSFORMS FARMING

AGRICULTURE BECOMES MECHANIZED

After the Civil War numerous improvements were made in farm implements and machines. In 1868 *James Oliver* introduced a superior plow with a chilled steel moldboard. (*Chilling* is a process of surface-hardening a metal by sudden cooling.) Later, the gangplow, capable of turning two or more furrows at a time, came into use. A twine binder was invented to tie sheaves of grain automatically. The reaper and thresher were united into one large machine called the *combine*, which reaped, threshed, and bagged grain mechanically in one continuous operation. There followed seed planters, corn shellers, cream separators, and a host of other laborsaving devices.

After 1900 steam tractors and then gasoline and diesel tractors began to replace horses for pulling farm machines. Motor trucks provided farmers with a new means of transporting produce to market. The extension of electric lines to rural areas gave farmers a new source of power and led to the introduction of automatic milking machines, refrigerated storage facilities, and electrically driven pumps for drawing water from wells.

The increased use of machinery not only lightened the farmers' toil, but also enabled them to (1) produce enough food to feed the nation's rapidly expanding population, (2) ship large quantities of surplus products abroad, and (3) operate larger farms with less help.

Between 1860 and 1900 the number of farms in the United States increased from about 2 million to 5.5 million, and the acreage under cultivation nearly doubled. Nevertheless the percentage of the working population engaged in farming declined by one-third (from 60% to 40%).

Even more dramatic changes took place after 1900. Although total farm output continued to rise sharply, the number of operating farms dropped from a peak of 6.5 million during the period 1915–1930 to 4 million in 1960, and to 2.1 million in the late 1990's. The percentage of the labor force employed in agriculture also declined—to 20% in the 1940's, to 10% in the 1960's, and to about 2.5% at the present time.

SCIENCE AIDS THE FARMER

Scientists helped farmers increase production, improve the quality of their produce, and find new markets. Some of the new developments were (1) better seeds and hardier plants, (2) superior breeds of livestock, (3) effective methods of combatting plant and animal diseases and insect pests, and (4) industrial uses for farm products. Scientists discovered how to maintain soil fertility and halt erosion by crop rotation, contour plowing, and low-cost inorganic fertilizers. They also taught farmers how to grow crops in regions of limited rainfall by using dry farming techniques and irrigation.

235

Two outstanding agricultural scientists were:

Luther Burbank. He established a famous experimental laboratory in California where he developed the Burbank potato, the spineless cactus, and new and improved varieties of fruits, vegetables, and flowers.

George Washington Carver. A slave during his early childhood, he became an agricultural chemist and served as director of agricultural research at Tuskegee Institute for more than 40 years. He discovered many new uses for the peanut, soybean, and sweet potato, thereby increasing demand for these crops and enabling Southern farmers to become less dependent upon cotton growing.

THE GOVERNMENT PROMOTES SCIENTIFIC AGRICULTURE

1. **Department of Agriculture.** This federal department was founded in 1862, and its head, the Secretary of Agriculture, became a member of the President's Cabinet in 1889. The department has aided the farmer by conducting research on animal and plant diseases, fighting destructive insects, discovering new crops and plant varieties suitable to American soil, operating experimental farms, analyzing soil composition, and publishing pamphlets and bulletins on all phases of farming.

2. **State Agricultural Colleges.** The *Morrill Act*, passed by Congress in 1862, granted large tracts of public land to the states. Funds from the sale of the lands were to be used to establish colleges for teaching agriculture and the mechanical arts. At these *land-grant colleges,* young farmers have received formal instruction in the science of agriculture. (These schools became the foundation of today's system of state universities.)

3. **Facilities for Experimentation.** The *Hatch Act* of 1887 provided federal funds to the states to establish agricultural experiment stations.

4. **County Agents.** The *Smith-Lever Act* (1914) authorized the Department of Agriculture to organize an Extension Service to advise farmers and keep them informed of new developments. A representative of this service, called the *county agent,* is located in each farming county.

5. **Agricultural Courses in High Schools.** The *Smith-Hughes Act* (1917) provided federal funds to high schools for the teaching of agriculture, home economics, and other vocational subjects.

6. **4-H Clubs.** These clubs were organized by the Department of Agriculture for young people in rural areas. Members learn new agricultural techniques, carry on worthwhile farming projects, and compete for prizes. The name of the clubs is derived from the pledge taken by their members: "I pledge—My *Head* to clear thinking, My *Heart* to great loyalty, My *Hands* to larger service, My *Health* to better living."

CHANGES IN RURAL LIVING

Science and invention, and the extension of government services, brought great changes in rural living in the 20th century. The introduction of *rural free delivery* (RFD) and parcel post made possible the daily delivery of letters, periodicals, and packages to rural areas. Electricity provided new benefits in the form of better lighting and appliances that eased housekeeping chores. The development of low-priced automobiles and improved roads made towns, schools, places of worship, doctors, and neighbors more accessible. The telephone, radio, and television helped relieve the loneliness of farm life. These innovations broadened the social and cultural opportunities of rural Americans and enabled farm families to live more comfortably.

FARMERS ATTEMPT TO SOLVE PROBLEMS BY GROUP ACTION

PLIGHT OF THE FARMER

Although farm production increased after 1865, farmers experienced hard times instead of prosperity. The prices they received for their produce dropped sharply after the Civil War and continued to fall until the late 1890's. But the cost of manufactured goods and machinery that they needed remained high. In addition, farmers had to pay steep freight rates to the railroads to ship their produce; heavy storage fees for the use of grain elevators, warehouses, and stockyards; and large service charges to the dealers and wholesalers who helped market their crops.

Lacking cash for expensive machinery and other improvments, farmers borrowed heavily and mortgaged their farms, frequently paying excessive rates of interest on their loans. Unable to meet their payments, many lost their farms through mortgage foreclosure. That is, the people who had loaned money to the farmers took possession of the farms. Whereas in 1865 almost all farmers owned the land that they cultivated, by 1900 over one-third of the nation's farms were worked by tenant-farmers.

FARMERS JOIN THE GRANGE

In 1867 Oliver H. Kelley founded a national association of farmers called the Patrons of Husbandry, or the *Grange*. The society spread rapidly, and by 1875 there were 20,000 local Grange lodges with a total membership of 800,000 men and women. The purpose of the organization was to bring farm families together for social and cultural activities. Since such get-togethers provided farmers an opportunity to discuss common problems and to air grievances, the Granges soon became centers of political agitation.

WORK OF THE GRANGE

In Illinois and several other Middle Western states, the Granges influenced the passage of legislation that (1) fixed maximum rates for grain storage in elevators and warehouses, and (2) regulated railroad freight rates.

When the constitutionality of the "Granger laws" was questioned, the U.S. Supreme Court ruled that: (1) A grain storage facility is subject to state regulation because it is a public utility. (A *public utility* is a business that provides a community with a vital service used by all the people.) (2) A railroad can *not* be regulated by a state because it is an interstate carrier.

Farm groups thereupon turned to the federal government for assistance against railroad abuses. Congress responded in 1887 by passing the *Interstate Commerce Act* (see page 259).

The Grange also attempted to reduce the costs and increase the incomes of farmers by organizing cooperatives. (A *cooperative*, or *co-op*, is an enterprise operated for the benefit of all its members, each of whom receives a share of the profits.) The Grange cooperatives marketed produce, stored grain, bought supplies and equipment, and manufactured machinery. These ventures proved unsuccessful, however, because of the opposition of big business and because of the farmers' lack of management experience and adequate capital.

Partly as a result of the failure of the co-ops, the Grange declined in political and economic importance. However, it continues to function to this day as a social organization.

FARMERS ADVOCATE CHEAP MONEY

Farmers wanted the government to put more money in circulation. As the supply of money increases, the value of the dollar declines and prices go up. Farmers would be helped because: (1) Rising farm prices would increase their income. (2) Cheaper money would make it easier for them to pay off the debts they had incurred earlier, when the dollar was worth more.

In the 1870's many farmers supported the *Greenback Labor party*, which advocated, among other things, that the government not only maintain but increase the amount of paper money (*greenbacks*) in circulation. (Greenbacks had been issued to help the Union finance the Civil War, but after the war the government had started to withdraw them.) The party polled over a million votes in the election of 1878 and sent 14 members to Congress. Although the Greenbackers failed to influence the government to increase the supply of paper money, they did succeed in persuading Congress to halt the withdrawal of the greenbacks still in circulation.

Farmers also joined the *free-silver movement*, which called for unlimited coinage of silver. As a result of this movement, Congress passed the *Bland-Allison Act* (1878) and the *Sherman Silver Purchase Act* (1890). These laws required the government to purchase and coin a limited amount of silver each month. Free silver advocates complained, however, that these laws did not increase the supply of money sufficiently to bring prosperity to farmers.

RISE OF POPULISM

In the 1880's farmers organized several large regional groups called *Farmers' Alliances*. In addition to providing social and educational programs for farmers, these associations came out for a broad program of political and economic reform. In 1890 the Alliances succeeded in electing a number of their supporters to state legislatures and to Congress. Heartened by this success, they decided to merge their strength with various labor groups and form the *People's party*, more commonly known as the *Populist party*. Its platform called for (1) free coinage of silver, (2) an increase in the amount of paper money in circulation, (3) a graduated income tax (a tax that imposes progressively higher rates on larger incomes), (4) postal savings banks, (5) public ownership and operation of transportation and communication facilities, (6) popular election of senators, (7) a limit of one term of office for a President, (8) adoption of such political reforms as initiative, referendum, and secret ballot (see page 292), (9) restrictions on immigration, and (10) a shorter working day for labor.

In the election of 1892 the Populist candidate for President received 1 million popular votes and 22 electoral votes. The following year a severe business decline, the Panic of 1893, swept the nation, bringing with it widespread unemployment, wage cuts, and a wave of strikes. At that time, too, Congress repealed the Sherman Silver Purchase Act. These events increased the discontent of the people and strengthened the Populist movement.

THE POPULISTS SUPPORT BRYAN IN 1896

In the election campaign of 1896, the Republicans favored keeping the *gold standard* (a monetary system using gold alone as the standard of value and as backing for paper currency). The Democrats came out for the unlimited coinage of silver (free silver). As their candidate for President, the Democrats chose *William Jennings Bryan* of Nebraska. He made an eloquent speech, known as the "Cross of Gold" speech, attacking the monetary policy of the Republicans.

Bryan's stand for free silver and his sympathetic attitude toward the problems of the farmer and the worker won him the support of the Populists. Rather than enter their own candidate in the presidential race, the Populists decided to back Bryan. They believed that such a move would prevent a split in the farm and labor vote, assure Bryan's victory, and place in the White House a person dedicated to free silver and reform. Their hopes were dashed, however, when the Republican nominee, William McKinley, won the election after a hard-fought campaign.

Shortly thereafter, the Populist party faded from the political scene. However, many of its proposals, taken up by reformers in the early 1900's, were gradually enacted into law.

FARMERS ABANDON POLITICS

As the 19th century neared its end, the condition of farmers began to improve. Increased demand for American farm produce from abroad and from the nation's own expanding urban population led to a rise in farm prices. Also, the discovery of gold deposits in Alaska and elsewhere eased the "tight money" situation by bringing about an increase in the amount of currency in circulation. With the return of prosperity, most farmers lost interest in the silver question and became less concerned with political movements.

AGRICULTURAL TRENDS IN THE 20TH CENTURY

LOW PRICES AND SURPLUSES AGAIN PLAGUE THE FARMER

With the outbreak of war in Europe in 1914, foreign demand for American agricultural produce increased, causing farm prices to rise sharply. Some American farmers expanded their production by purchasing additional land and expensive machinery. In the process, they saddled themselves with large mortgages and other debts. When the war ended in 1918, foreign demand slackened and prices fell. In the 1920's, while the rest of the nation enjoyed considerable prosperity, many farmers suffered hard times. Their condition worsened in the 1930's, when the entire economy was hit by a serious depression. During these two decades, farmers were plagued with unmarketable surpluses, low incomes, mortgage foreclosures, and bankruptcies.

THE GOVERNMENT TAKES STEPS TO AID FARMERS

The farmers' cause was taken up by such new groups as the *National Farmers Union* and the *American Farm Bureau Federation*, as well as by the *farm bloc* (members of Congress, both Democratic and Republican, from the farm states). Congress passed a variety of laws designed to help the farmer.

1. Easing Credit. As early as 1916 the *Farm Loan Act* provided for the establishment of federal land banks from which farmers could secure long-term mortgage loans at reasonable rates of interest. The *Intermediate Credit Act* (1923) provided short-term loans for crop financing. Additional credit facilities were made available in the 1930's by such measures as the *Farm Credit Act*. To consolidate the activities of all federal agencies making loans to farmers, the federal government in 1933 set up the *Farm Credit Administration (FCA)*.

2. Encouraging Cooperatives. The *Capper-Volstead Act* (1922) exempted agricultural associations from the monopoly provisions of the antitrust laws. This exemption encouraged farmers to join together into cooperatives to process and market their crops without the aid of packers, wholesalers, and other middlemen. By eliminating middlemen, farmers receive a greater share of the price paid by the consumer.

3. Limiting Production. The *Agricultural Adjustment Act of 1933* sought to raise farm prices by cutting production. Farmers were paid by the government for withdrawing from cultivation acreage used for growing corn, wheat, cotton, and other staples. After the Supreme Court declared important sections of the act unconstitutional, Congress in 1936 passed the *Soil Conservation and Domestic Allotment Act*. This law aimed to achieve the purpose of the Agricultural Adjustment Act by offering benefit payments to farmers who reduced their acreage of soil-depleting staple crops and instead planted soil-enriching grasses and plants such as clover, alfalfa, and soybeans.

As a result of this and similar legislation, farmers withdrew millions of acres from the cultivation of grain, cotton, and tobacco. But farm surpluses continued to mount. Despite the reduction in acreage, farmers expanded their output by using more fertilizer, improved seed, more mechanized equipment, enriched feed for livestock, and other modern techniques that increased productivity.

4. Storing Surpluses and Maintaining Price Levels. The *Agricultural Adjustment Act of 1938* authorized the Secretary of Agriculture to (*a*) estimate the amount of each major crop that would be needed to satisfy domestic and foreign demand, (*b*) limit the number of acres each grower could use to raise these crops, and (*c*) restrict the quantity offered for sale if large surpluses resulted despite the acreage controls. *Commodity loans* would be extended to farmers on their surplus crops through the *Commodity Credit Corporation*. These surplus crops would be stored in government warehouses until they could be sold at better prices during years of poor harvest. If, in spite of these measures, farm prices did not provide farmers the purchasing power they had before World War I, the government would make up the difference through subsidies called *parity* payments. In addition, the act continued payments to farmers for planting soil-building crops on land withdrawn from the cultivation of staples.

5. Promoting Farm Ownership. The *Farm Tenant Act* of 1937 (presently administered by the *Farmers Home Administration*) provided (*a*) low-cost, long-term loans to farm tenants, farm laborers, and sharecroppers for the purchase of land, and (*b*) financial aid to help these new farm owners buy needed supplies and machinery. This program enabled thousands of landless Americans to acquire farms of their own.

FARM CONDITIONS IMPROVE IN THE 1940's

Government price supports, loans, and payments to farmers helped double farm income between 1932 and 1940. With the outbreak of World War II, farmers again entered a period of prosperity. Domestic and foreign demand for agricultural produce was so great that farmers were able to sell at high prices all that they raised. After the war America's massive programs of relief and economic aid to the war-torn countries of Europe and Asia kept agricultural exports at a high level.

THE GOVERNMENT CONTINUES TO ASSIST FARMERS

With the return to normalcy, surpluses and falling prices began to worry the farmer once again. Legislation enacted in the post-war years extended the farm programs that had begun with the Agricultural Adjustment Act of 1938. The government continued to (1) support farm prices, (2) acquire and store surplus commodities, and (3) pay farmers for limiting acreage devoted to major crops.

Price-support operations have cost the government many billions of dollars. Billions more have been spent on surplus agricultural commodities that the government owns and stores. Opponents of the federal farm support program have argued that it is (1) costly to the government, (2) unfair to the consumer and taxpayer, and (3) unsuccessful in eliminating or even reducing surpluses. Critics have also contended that the program is a disservice to farmers in the long run because it keeps them from switching their production to crops that are in greater demand, and makes them dependent on government subsidies. Fearful of upsetting the economy, each succeeding administration from the 1950's to the 1990's approved the continuation of farm supports.

In 1996, however, Congress took steps to end government controls by passing the *Freedom to Farm Act*. It allowed farmers to decide for themselves which crops to plant and how much land to leave idle. It also replaced farm subsidies with "transition payments" that would be phased out within seven years.

POLICY CHANGES AFFECT THE FARMER

Demand for U.S. farm produce rose sharply in the 1970's as a result of (1) serious crop failures in the Soviet Union and other parts of the world, (2) the inability of underdeveloped countries in Asia, Africa, and Latin America to adequately feed their rapidly expanding populations, (3) population growth in our own country, and (4) the adoption of a federal *Food Stamp Program* to enable millions of low-income Americans to buy more food. As the government-held agricultural stockpile dwindled, federal officials began to urge farmers to expand production.

Thus encouraged, farmers took steps to increase their output by (1) investing in new equipment and machinery, (2) expanding the acreage under cultivation, and (3) buying more land. Since this expansion took place during a time of soaring inflation, farmers paid top prices for their purchases and borrowed large sums of money at high rates of interest to meet their obligations. As a result, farm debt rose sharply.

When world markets proved unable to absorb the increased yield of U.S. farms, unsold surpluses began to accumulate once again and crop prices fell below farmers' production costs. Many small farmers could not meet their debt payments and lost their holdings through foreclosure. Others abandoned farming and sought work in the cities. Still others supplemented their farm income by taking part-time jobs.

FARMING TODAY

Although the number of operating farms has declined by nearly two-thirds since 1930, total acreage under cultivation remains about the same (972 million acres). The size of the average farm, however, is considerably larger now than it was then (469 acres vs. 151 acres). Agricultural productivity has also risen sharply. In 1916 one farmer produced enough food to feed seven Americans. Today each farm worker can supply nearly 10 times that number of people.

OLD MacDONALD HAD A FARM... I.O.; I.O.U.

FORECLOSURE
Sale
TODAY

© *Kirk—The Scranton Times/Rothco*

While many small and middle-sized family farms continue to exist, an ever-increasing percentage of major crops comes from huge farming enterprises that comprise thousands of acres and raise millions of dollars worth of produce. Often organized as corporations, such farms (or *agribusinesses*) are well financed and are managed by skilled technicians. These experts utilize the most advanced scientific equipment and biochemical products available to obtain the maximum yield from each acre under cultivation.

Multiple-Choice Test

1. During the 20th century, agriculture in the United States has experienced a DECREASE in (*a*) total production (*b*) percentage of the labor force employed on farms (*c*) size of farms (*d*) production per farm laborer.
2. In the last third of the 19th century, the most controversial issue involving American farmers was (*a*) internal improvements (*b*) labor unions (*c*) cheap money (*d*) treatment of the Indians.
3. In the late 19th century, American farmers supported (*a*) the Granger movement against the railroads (*b*) the Whig party against William Jennings Bryan (*c*) the Republican party against the Greenback Labor party (*d*) protective tariffs against a policy of free trade.
4. During the period 1900–1918, farmers experienced (*a*) sharply falling prices (*b*) a decrease in the value of farmland (*c*) relative prosperity (*d*) increased opportunities for westward migration.
5. During World War I, some U.S. farmers contributed to the creation of later farm problems by (*a*) borrowing money to expand production (*b*) limiting

production to raise prices (c) forming cooperatives to market their products (d) urging the defeat of the Agricultural Adjustment Act.

6. During the period 1860–1900, the number of farms in the United States increased from about 2 million to 5.5 million. A basic reason for this increase was the (a) irrigation of desert areas in the West (b) liberal federal land policy (c) establishment of agricultural colleges (d) overcrowded conditions in the cities of the East.

7. In 1886 a Granger law then in effect was declared unconstitutional by the U.S. Supreme Court. This decision led to the (a) passage of the Sherman Silver Purchase Act (b) acceptance of acreage controls by the farmers (c) ratification of the Fifteenth Amendment (d) passage of the Interstate Commerce Act.

8. Which was an outstanding issue in the presidential campaign of 1896? (a) government ownership of railroads (b) the government's money policy (c) removal of troops from the South (d) states' rights.

9. The Morrill Act of 1862 aided education by giving (a) to each state the right to control its own schools (b) to colleges funds for research (c) to each state public land, the income from which was to be used for agricultural colleges (d) to the national government a grant of money to set up a federal office of education.

10. All of the following agricultural machines came into use after the Civil War EXCEPT the (a) combine (b) gang plow (c) tractor (d) reaper.

11. A law that provided federal funds for the establishment of agricultural experiment stations was the (a) Homestead Act (b) Smith-Lever Act (c) Hatch Act (d) Capper-Volstead Act.

12. Economic demands of farmers during the 19th century included all of the following EXCEPT (a) free homesteads (b) parity payments (c) silver currency (d) government control of railroads.

13. A political party that championed the interests of the farmers during the late 19th century was the (a) Whig party (b) Federalist party (c) Populist party (d) Bull Moose party.

14. The mechanization of agriculture in the 20th century resulted in (a) a decrease in the number of farms (b) a decrease in the amount of capital needed to start a farm (c) an increase in the number of workers needed to operate a farm (d) smaller crop surpluses.

15. All of the following laws were passed to relieve the problem of farm surpluses EXCEPT the (a) Soil Conservation and Domestic Allotment Act (b) Bland-Allison Act (c) Agricultural Adjustment Act of 1933 (d) Agricultural Adjustment Act of 1938.

Modified True-False Test

1. "I pledge . . . My Hands to larger service" is part of the pledge taken by members of the *Boy Scouts of America*.

2. *Joseph Henry* was an agricultural scientist who developed many new varieties of vegetables and fruits.

3. Members of Congress of both parties who combine forces to support legislation favorable to agriculture are called the *farm bloc*.

4. The *Hatch* Act provided federal funds to high schools for the teaching of agriculture and home economics.

5. Representatives of the Department of Agriculture who are located in farming areas to advise farmers and to keep them informed of new developments are called *county agents*.
6. *Booker T. Washington* was a scientist who discovered new uses for such agricultural products as the peanut, soybean, and sweet potato.
7. RFD, a federal service to farmers, stands for *remortgaging farm debts*.
8. The Grange, a national association of farmers, was founded in 1867 by *Patron Hus Bandry*.
9. Enterprises organized by farmers to process and market their crops without the participation of middlemen are known as *cooperatives*.
10. "Cross of Gold" was a famous speech made by *William McKinley*.

Essay Questions

1. Discuss briefly *two* reasons for agreeing or *two* reasons for disagreeing with the following statement: "The problems of farmers in the United States have remained almost the same since the coming of the Agricultural Revolution."
2. "When the farmer prospers, the nation prospers." (*a*) Explain whether you agree or disagree with this statement. (*b*) Discuss briefly why farmers did not prosper during the 1920's. (*c*) Describe *two* methods used by the federal government since 1933 to help farmers.
3. Explain the point of view of *each* of the following American farmers to the development with which the farmer is paired:
   a. Frontier farmer of Pennsylvania in the 1790's—federal excise tax on whisky.
   b. Western farmer in the 1830's—internal improvements at government expense.
   c. Middle Western farmer in the 1880's—freight rates charged by railroads.
4. (*a*) Show why farm groups have usually supported programs for cheap money. (*b*) Name *two* laws passed by Congress in the 19th century to promote cheap money.
5. William Jennings Bryan said: "Burn down your cities and leave our farms, and your cities will spring up again as if by magic; but destroy our farms and the grass will grow in the streets of every city in the country."
   a. Explain the meaning of Bryan's statement.
   b. Write a paragraph telling why you agree or disagree with Bryan's statement.
6. Giving specific facts, discuss the following statement: "The Industrial and Agricultural Revolutions have greatly influenced the life of the farmer."
7. (*a*) Discuss briefly *two* major problems that farmers face because of the nature of their business. (*b*) Describe *two* attempts that were made by farmers before 1900 to solve their problems.

Part 3. The United States Becomes a Leading Industrial Nation

AMERICAN INDUSTRY IN 1850

In 1850 America was still predominantly a land of farms, villages, and small businesses. Fewer than 1 million persons were employed in mills and factories, and the nation's annual output of manufactured goods amounted to only 1 billion dollars. Most of the country's manufacturing was centered in the Northeast. The typical manufacturing enterprise consisted of a small plant owned and operated by a single proprietor or a group of partners, producing a limited amount of goods mostly for the local market.

INDUSTRIAL GROWTH (1850–1900)

The second half of the 19th century was a period of great industrial growth for the United States. The Civil War stimulated expansion by creating a huge demand for weapons, war supplies, farm equipment, and machinery of all kinds. After the war, the extension of railway networks and the development of the nation's coal, iron, lumber, and petroleum resources brought industrialization to the Middle West and then to the Far West and the South. As a result of technical improvements and inventions, new products came into use, old industries were transformed, and new industries rose in importance.

The following factors contributed to the nation's rapid industrial growth: (1) Wealthy Europeans and Americans eagerly invested in American industrial enterprises. (2) The government maintained high tariffs to protect U.S. industries against foreign competition. (3) A network of railroads opened up national markets to manufacturers. (4) Abundant natural resources supplied industry with raw materials. (5) A continuous flow of new immigrants provided industry with an ample labor force. (6) An ever-increasing population offered an expanding market for manufactured products.

In 1890, for the first time, industrial output surpassed agricultural production in value. Ten years later, at the turn of the century, the value of manufactured goods was twice that of the country's farm products. The United States was now the leading industrial nation in the world. The chief manufacturing states in 1900 were New York, Pennsylvania, Illinois, and Massachusetts.

INDUSTRIAL TRENDS SINCE 1900

American industry continued to expand in the 20th century. Technological advances and improved machinery increased productivity and enabled manufacturers to offer the public an ever-growing variety of reasonably priced, mass-produced goods. Large sums were spent to (1) build better and larger production facilities, (2) improve existing products and develop new ones, and (3) stimulate buying through the use of advertising.

Value added by manufacture means the value of goods produced less the cost of raw materials, supplies, fuel, and power used in their production. The value added by manufacture rose from $5 billion in 1900 to more than $1.3 trillion annually in the early 1990's. The number of workers employed in manufacturing industries increased from 5 million to 18 million. The leading manufacturing states at the present time are California, New York, Ohio, Illinois, Michigan, Pennsylvania, and Texas.

RISE OF CORPORATIONS

Small, privately owned enterprises lacked the financial resources to build huge factories, purchase expensive machinery, or extend their markets nationally and internationally. To enable companies to raise large amounts of working capital, the corporate form of business came into use in the 19th century.

A *corporation* is a company usually owned by many people, each of whom becomes a part owner by purchasing shares of stock. The *stockholders* elect a *board of directors* to manage the enterprise. When money is needed for expansion, additional shares may be offered for sale to the general public. Stockholders may terminate their investment in the business by selling their stock to others. Although its individual stockholders may change, the corporation itself has perpetual life.

The corporation has replaced the single proprietorship and the partnership as the prevailing form of business organization.

CORPORATIONS COMBINE TO FORM LARGER UNITS

As corporations grew in size and wealth, a trend toward business consolidation developed. Seeking higher profits, business leaders took steps to reduce or eliminate competition by arranging agreements with competitors. They also sought to acquire complete control, or a *monopoly*, of a particular industry by linking their companies with others to form "supercorporations." In the late 1800's, the following forms of business combination emerged:

1. Pool. A *pool* was an informal agreement by competing companies to fix prices, share profits, or divide the market for their products. The first pooling arrangement was made in 1870 by rival railroads in the Middle West. It soon became a common practice among other competing railroads and then spread to other industries. Because pooling agreements were not legally binding and were frequently broken, the pool was supplanted by the trust.

2. Trust. A *trust* was a giant business combination consisting of a number of corporations engaged in the same field or in related fields. A *board of trustees* managed the combined enterprise. The stockholders in the individual companies assigned their stock to the trustees and received, in exchange, trust certificates entitling each to a proportionate share of the trust's profits.

In 1882, 40 companies, representing 90% of the country's oil refining business, established the Standard Oil Trust. Within the next decade trusts were also formed in many other industries including sugar, lead, whisky, cottonseed oil, and linseed oil.

3. Holding Company. Starting in 1887 the courts began to rule that trust agreements were illegal. As a replacement, the *holding company* was devised. Such a company did not itself engage in the production and distribution of goods or services. Rather, it held a controlling stock interest in a number of related enterprises, called *subsidiaries*, and devoted itself to directing their operations.

By 1900 there were 185 holding companies, representing one-third of all the capital invested in manufacturing activities in the country.

BUSINESS CONSOLIDATION CONTINUES IN THE 20TH CENTURY

As a result of public agitation and government intervention, efforts by big business to attain a monopoly subsided in the early decades of the 20th century. Thereafter, businesspeople placed greater stress on (1) achieving economies through large-scale, efficient operation, (2) strengthening their competitive position within the industry, (3) expanding into new geographic areas, and (4) entering new fields by acquiring additional products or services. To achieve these objectives, many companies resorted to a form of business consolidation called the *merger*. In a merger, one company absorbs another, or several combine to form a new company. Thousands of corporate mergers have taken place in the 20th century. The holding company, too, has retained its popularity as a form of business organization, particularly in the public utility industries.

Business consolidations are now subject to federal scrutiny. Mergers and holding companies that violate the antitrust laws by reducing competition are judged to be contrary to the public interest and are ordered dissolved by the courts.

ADVANTAGES OF BIG BUSINESS

Big business is able to provide the consumer with new and improved products and services at reduced prices. It can do so because it has the financial resources to (1) build modern, efficient plants, (2) acquire up-to-date, specialized machinery, (3) purchase raw materials in large quantities, (4) conduct scientific research, (5) establish a nationwide or worldwide distribution network, (6) convert industrial waste materials into useful by-products, and (7) increase sales through advertising.

DISADVANTAGES OF BIG BUSINESS

However, big business also has effects that are harmful to the economy and the consumer. It tends to (1) become monopolistic, (2) destroy competition, (3) drive out small businesses, (4) concentrate enormous wealth and power in the hands of a few, and (5) wield excessive power over government officials.

MASS PRODUCTION

To make possible the manufacture of large quantities of goods at low prices, American industry devised the techniques of mass production.

1. Standardization of Parts. The parts that make up a finished product are all of a standard size, shape, weight, etc. Machines make each part separately, and the parts are then assembled into the finished article. The idea of standardized, interchangeable parts was put forward by Eli Whitney as early as 1798.

2. Assembly Line. Manufactured goods are assembled on a conveyor belt. As the belt moves along, each worker on the assembly line attaches another part to the article being produced. When the product reaches the end of the line, it is complete and ready for use. The principle of the assembly line was popularized in the early 1900's by *Henry Ford* in the production of the Model-T automobile.

3. Labor-Saving Machinery. Machines were perfected as a substitute for or as an aid to human labor. One machine operator can do a job that previously required the work of many workers.

4. Division of Labor. In the manufacturing process, each worker performs only one operation. Previously, a skilled technician, working independently, produced the entire article.

NEW INDUSTRIES ARISE IN THE LATE 19th CENTURY

STEEL

William Kelly, a Kentucky blacksmith, discovered a new method of converting iron into steel (1851). Working independently, *Henry Bessemer*, an Englishman, developed a similar process (1856). In the Kelly-Bessemer process, or the *Bessemer process* as it is commonly known, cold air is forced through molten iron to remove its impurities. Then some carbon is added to create a tough and elastic steel. The first Bessemer converter was put into operation in the United States in 1864. A few years later a second method of steelmaking, the *open-hearth process*, was introduced.

These processes, as well as the later-developed oxygen furnace and the electric furnace, made possible the production of huge quantities of steel at low cost. Steel soon became the basic material of the economy— used for rails, trains, machinery, wire, pipe, bridges, frameworks for buildings, ships, automobiles, and innumerable consumer products.

Centered originally in the Pittsburgh area, the steel industry spread to Birmingham, Alabama; the Great Lakes region (Buffalo, Cleveland, Gary, Chicago); the Delaware River area; and Colorado, Utah, and California. Minnesota, the location of the Mesabi Range, became the main source of iron ore for the steel industry, followed by Michigan and Alabama.

PETROLEUM

Edwin L. Drake in 1859 drilled the world's first successful oil well near Titusville in northwestern Pennsylvania. Oil prospectors rushed to the area, and other producing wells were soon drilled. Railroad tank cars and pipelines were built to transport the oil to refineries. Here the thick black liquid was processed into (1) kerosene, which replaced whale oil and candles for home lighting, and (2) oil and grease, which proved superior to animal fat as lubricants for machinery. These were the main uses of petroleum until the development of the gasoline engine, the rise of the automobile, airplane, and petrochemical industries, and the use of fuel oil for heating.

Large petroleum deposits were discovered in other parts of the country. Texas, Louisiana, California, Oklahoma, Wyoming, and Alaska became the nation's leading oil-producing states. While drilling for new wells, prospectors uncovered huge pockets of natural gas. Long pipelines were laid to bring the gas to urban areas, where it was used as a fuel for cooking, heating, and the production of electricity.

ALUMINUM

Charles M. Hall in 1886 perfected a practical method, called the *Hall process*, for producing aluminum cheaply and in commercial quantities. At first used mainly for kitchen utensils, this light, flexible metal later played an important part in the development of airplanes. Additional uses were found for aluminum in construction, electrical equipment, wrappings (aluminum foil), furniture, and numerous other consumer products.

ELECTRICITY

Although electricity had been known to scientists for many years, it was not until the 1870's that this form of energy was harnessed for practical use. At that time *Charles F. Brush* developed a *dynamo* (generator) capable of producing a sustained flow of electric current, *Thomas A. Edison* invented the electric light bulb, and the electric motor came into use. Before long, power plants were built to generate electricity in commercial quantities. The first such plant was opened in New York City in 1882. Electrically driven streetcars began to operate in the large cities, electric lights replaced kerosene and gas lamps, factories started to switch over from steam power to electric power, and electrically operated home appliances came into use.

Electricity soon became one of humankind's most valued servants. Produced in abundance, transmitted by a vast network of power lines to every corner of the country, and sold cheaply to consumers— electricity raised the American standard of living substantially. The manufacture of electrical equipment, appliances, and machinery became one of the nation's most important industries.

LEADING INDUSTRIALISTS OF THE LATE 1800's

STEEL

Andrew Carnegie, called the "Steel King," dominated the iron and steel industry in the late 19th century. Operating in the Pittsburgh area, he organized a vast enterprise that produced one-fourth of the nation's steel. The *Carnegie Steel Company* owned not only the production facilities (blast furnaces and coke ovens), but also the sources of supply (coal fields, limestone deposits, and iron mines) and the means of transportation (railroads and ore ships) necessary for manufacturing and marketing steel.

OIL

John D. Rockefeller entered the oil refining business in the 1860's and soon became one of the nation's industrial giants. His *Standard Oil Company* bought out competitors or drove them out of business. He secured a monopoly, gaining almost complete control of the refining, transportation, and distribution of oil. His company, which became the nation's first trust, was dissolved by order of the courts and was broken up into a number of smaller, independent units. To this day, the various Standard Oil companies produce, refine, and distribute a large part of the petroleum products used in the United States.

MEAT-PACKING

Philip D. Armour, Nelson Morris, and **Gustavus F. Swift** were pioneers in the development of the meat-packing industry, which was located in Chicago and other Middle Western cities close to the cattle raising areas. Here great numbers of hogs and steers were slaughtered and dressed. The waste parts of the animals were converted into by-products such as glue, soap, and fertilizer. Refrigerated railroad cars transported the meat to all parts of the country.

RAILROADS

Cornelius Vanderbilt, in 1869, consolidated a number of short lines between New York City and Buffalo to form the country's first great railroad system, the *New York Central.* It was later extended westward to the Great Lakes region and northeastward to Boston. Vanderbilt pioneered the use of steel rails, steel railroad bridges, and double tracks.

James J. Hill built the *Great Northern Railway System* (1878–1893). He aided the development of the Northwest by encouraging immigrants to settle there, teaching them scientific farming, supporting schools and churches, and operating banks. Because of this work he became known as the "Empire Builder."

Edward H. Harriman reorganized the *Union Pacific Railroad,* which had become bankrupt in the Panic of 1893. He converted it into an efficient and prosperous enterprise.

FINANCE

J. Pierpont Morgan, head of the largest private banking and securities house in America, reorganized many bankrupt railroads during the late 19th century. In 1901 Morgan and his associates purchased the Carnegie Steel Company and merged it with other steel producers to form the huge *United States Steel Corporation.* This was the nation's first billion-dollar company.

TOBACCO

James B. Duke and his brother Benjamin formed the *American Tobacco Company.* They absorbed their competitors by threatening to ruin them through price wars. The huge tobacco trust that they built was ordered dissolved by the U.S. Supreme Court in 1911.

CHEMICALS

The **du Pont** family started manufacturing gunpowder in Delaware in 1801. E. I. Du Pont de Nemours became one of the world's leading companies in the development and manufacture of chemicals, dyes, plastics, and synthetic fibers.

IMPORTANT INVENTORS (1852–1911)

Elisha Otis developed a practical passenger elevator (1852). This device made possible the construction of tall buildings, or skyscrapers.

Lyman R. Blake patented a machine for sewing the soles of shoes to the uppers (1858). Four years later **Gordon McKay** developed an improved shoe-stitching machine and began mass-producing shoes in a factory.

Richard Gatling perfected the rapid-fire, revolving machine gun (1862).

Christopher Sholes developed the first practical typewriter (1868).

Thomas Alva Edison, the "wizard of electricity," invented the incandescent electric light bulb (1879), and improved the electric motor and the dynamo. He also patented over 1,000 other inventions, including the phonograph (1877) and the motion picture machine (1893).

Lewis Waterman perfected the fountain pen (1884).

Ottmar Mergenthaler invented the linotype machine (1884), which greatly sped up the setting of type.

George Eastman invented the simplified Kodak camera (1888).

Arthur D. Little developed rayon (a synthetic fabric) and artificial silk (1902).

Elmer A. Sperry patented the gyrocompass (1911) and perfected the gyroscope—an instrument used to stabilize ships and aircraft.

NEW MERCHANDISING METHODS

RETAILING TECHNIQUES CHANGE

Before the rise of big business, people purchased their everyday supplies from either (1) a small shop, where a particular kind of product was both manufactured and sold, or (2) a general store, which sold groceries, utensils, tools, fabrics, and other goods. Foodstuffs were generally sold in bulk, rather than in packages. The wants of isolated farm families were met by peddlers who drove through rural areas, their wagons stocked with wares.

When mass-produced products began to appear in large quantities, merchants developed new types of stores and new methods of merchandising.

1. Specialty Shops. To offer the public a better selection of goods, stores began to specialize in a single type of product, such as groceries or hardware. Storekeepers obtained merchandise from many different suppliers.

2. Chain Stores. Enterprising merchants opened a chain of similar stores at different locations. Savings effected through large-scale purchasing and efficient management were passed on to consumers in the form of lower prices. The first grocery store chain, which later became known as the *Great Atlantic and Pacific Tea Company (A & P)*, was founded in 1859. *Frank W. Woolworth* started his five-and-ten-cent variety store chain in 1879.

3. Department Stores. Here, goods of every description were sold under one roof. Each product category (such as women's clothing or home appliances) was featured in a separate department. Pioneers in the development of department stores included *Alexander T. Stewart* in New York City (1862), *Marshall Field* in Chicago (1865), and *John Wanamaker* in Philadelphia (1876). These merchants developed successful enterprises by buying goods in large quantities, selling for cash, creating demand through advertisements, and offering quality merchandise at fair prices.

4. Selling by Mail. Mail order selling was pioneered by two companies: *Montgomery Ward* (1872) and *Sears, Roebuck* (1895). Illustrated catalogs listing a wide variety of merchandise at reasonable prices were mailed to rural dwellers. Prospective customers studied the catalogs, chose what they wanted, and sent back their orders by mail.

5. Advertising. Advertising in newspapers and magazines became an important means of bringing products and services to the attention of the public. In the 20th century, radio and television began to serve as advertising media, especially for large companies.

6. Packaging. Manufacturers packaged their products in compact, distinctive containers, thus eliminating the need to cut, measure, or weigh articles being sold. Packaging also helped create public awareness of brands.

RECENT DEVELOPMENTS

As the economy expanded during the 20th century, merchants devised new marketing techniques and new kinds of stores to attract shoppers.

1. Supermarkets. In the 1930's grocery chains began to establish *supermarkets*—large, self-service stores stocked with a great variety of foods and everyday household goods. Customers equipped with wheeled carts selected the items they wanted from competing brands arranged on open shelves and displays throughout the store. Because they offered a wide selection of products at comparatively low prices, supermarkets soon became the dominant factor in food retailing. Their popularity posed a serious threat to the survival of small neighborhood shops operated by local merchants.

2. Shopping Centers and Malls. During the 1950's *shopping centers* began to spring up in suburban areas. Department stores, supermarkets, specialty shops, and parking lots were grouped together, enabling suburban families to buy almost everything they needed at a location near home, thus making shopping trips to the city virtually unnecessary.

In the 1970's the enclosed, temperature-controlled *shopping mall* made its appearance. Sheltered from the weather, mall visitors could stroll comfortably from store to store, dine at one of a variety of restaurants, and enjoy recreational facilities located within the complex.

3. Credit Sales. Merchants permitted customers to buy merchandise on credit, allowing them to make partial payments over a long period of time. This practice encouraged people to buy goods they needed even if they could not afford to pay for these items at the time of purchase.

4. Discount Stores. By keeping their expenses low and taking small profits on each sale, discount stores provided consumers goods of all kinds at reduced prices. The stores gave customers little service but offered them worthwhile bargains.

PROGRESS IN TRANSPORTATION

RAIL SERVICE IMPROVES

The earliest trains were drawn by small wood-burning locomotives. Seated uncomfortably in unheated, half-open coaches, passengers were often showered with sparks and burning cinders thrown off by the engine. Starts and stops were bumpy. There were no safety devices, and accidents were frequent.

As time passed, improvements were made. Firmer roadbeds were laid. Steel rails and bridges were installed. More powerful coal-burning locomotives were designed. Passenger coaches were enclosed and made more comfortable. *George Pullman* developed the sleeping car (1864) and the dining car (1868), which added to the comfort of long-distance travel. Safety devices such as air brakes (invented by *George Westinghouse* in 1869), automatic couplers, and block signals were introduced. A standard gauge (width between rails) was adopted. In the 20th century, oil-burning diesel engines replaced steam locomotives.

After the Civil War, railroad construction and operation became the country's biggest business and remained such for the next 50 years. The rail network expanded until it connected all parts of the country. Short independent lines were merged into large systems, thus making possible uninterrupted coast-to-coast passenger trips and freight shipments.

COMPETITION THREATENS THE RAILROADS

In the 1900's buses, automobiles, and airplanes diverted considerable passenger traffic from the railroads; trucks, cargo planes, and pipelines took over much of their freight business. Unable to operate profitably, some railroads went into bankruptcy or merged with stronger roads. Others cut costs by abandoning unprofitable branch lines and eliminating passenger service. "To get people back on trains," Congress established a government corporation, *Amtrak,* to run a national rail passenger system (1970). It also set up a federally sponsored company, *Conrail,* to create a new system out of six bankrupt Northeast railroads (1975).

THE AUTOMOBILE

The invention of the gasoline engine encouraged inventors to develop a practical "horseless carriage." Among the early pioneers were *Charles E.* and *J. Frank Duryea, George B. Selden,* and *Henry Ford.* Applying mass-production techniques to the manufacture of automobiles, Ford began to produce the famous Model-T car in 1909. It sold at a price within the reach of the average American. To meet the ever-growing demand for automobiles, other manufacturers soon entered the field. The number of motor vehicles (passenger cars, trucks, and buses) produced in the United States rose from 4,000 in 1900 to 187,000 in 1910, to 2.2 million in 1920, and to 3.4 million in 1930. Annual production today is about 12 million. (Many thousands of imported vehicles, manufactured in Japan, Germany, France, and elsewhere, also find a ready market in the United States each year.)

At the present time the number of registered motor vehicles in the country is more than 190 million.

IMPORTANCE OF THE AUTOMOBILE INDUSTRY

The automobile industry ranks first in the United States in the value of its finished product. It provides employment for hundreds of thousands of workers. It has stimulated the growth of such industries as oil, rubber, glass, steel, plastics, and others whose products are required for the building and operation of motor vehicles. Garages and filling stations have sprung up all over the country to serve motorists. Billions of dollars have been spent to build new roads and improve existing ones.

EFFECTS OF THE AUTOMOBILE

The automobile has helped to unify the country by breaking down isolation and stimulating travel. It has provided new uses for leisure time. It has resulted in the growth of suburban areas around large cities. It has brought the city within easy reach of the farmer. It has made available another means of transporting passengers and freight.

However, the automobile has had these harmful effects: It has caused property damage and many deaths through accidents (about 44,000 persons are killed each year in motor vehicle mishaps). It has created a serious traffic problem in urban areas. It has contributed greatly to air pollution. It has brought bankruptcy to some railroads and threatens the existence of others.

THE AIRPLANE: EARLY HISTORY

The practicability of the airplane was first demonstrated in 1896 by *Samuel P. Langley*. In 1903 *Orville* and *Wilbur Wright* made the first successful flight in a heavier-than-air flying machine at Kitty Hawk, on the coast of North Carolina. After several years of testing and improving the machine, they began to manufacture it commercially (1909). *Glenn Curtiss* designed the seaplane in 1911. During World War I, the airplane proved its worth as a weapon in warfare.

In the 1920's and 1930's spectacular flights aroused the nation's interest in aviation. *Richard E. Byrd* flew over the North Pole (1926). *Charles A. Lindbergh*, the "Lone Eagle," made a solo, nonstop flight from New York to Paris (1927). *Wiley Post* circled the globe in less than eight days (1933). *Howard Hughes* flew around the world in 91 hours (1938).

IMPORTANCE OF THE AIRPLANE

In peacetime, aircraft have become an important part of the country's transportation system. Large commercial planes carry passengers, mail, and freight to all parts of the country, across every ocean, and to every continent. With the introduction of regular jet airliner service in 1959, flight time from California to New York was cut to 4.5 hours. Transatlantic flights from New York to London or Paris now take from six to eight hours. Planes powered by jet engines and rocket motors can hurtle through the air faster than the speed of sound. (One such plane, the Concorde, provides service between New York or Washington, D.C., and Paris or London in 3.5 hours.) As an instrument serving humanity, the airplane can help to break down national isolation and make the countries of the world next-door neighbors.

In time of war the airplane can be a fearful weapon of destruction. During World War II, bombers sank warships, destroyed cities, and wrecked industrial plants and transportation facilities. U.S. planes dropping atomic bombs on the cities of Hiroshima and Nagasaki compelled the surrender of Japan.

PROGRESS IN COMMUNICATION

TRANSOCEANIC COMMUNICATION

Cyrus Field laid the first permanently successful transatlantic cable in 1866, making possible telegraphic communication between America and Europe. (An earlier cable, installed by Field in 1858, broke down after a few weeks of operation.) Cables were later laid across the other oceans, and soon all the continents were linked by telegraph wires.

THE TELEPHONE

Alexander Graham Bell invented the telephone. In 1876 it was publicly exhibited for the first time at the Philadelphia Centennial Exposition, which was held to celebrate the completion of America's first century as an independent nation. The telephone met with great acclaim. A visiting celebrity, Emperor Dom Pedro II of Brazil, listened to it and exclaimed in awe, "It talks!"

The first commercial telephone system was established at New Haven, Connecticut, in 1878. Two years later 148 telephone companies were in operation. By 1895 long-distance lines connected New York and Chicago. Twenty years after this, telephone wires spanned the continent.

Worldwide telephone service became a reality in the second half of the 20th century with the development of wireless telephones, the installation of transoceanic telephone cables, and the placement of earth-orbiting communication satellites in space. Sending and receiving phone calls while traveling in motor vehicles became possible with the introduction of cellular telephones in the 1980's. More recently, computers linked via telephone lines have sparked the formation of communication networks (such as Internet) that have millions of users.

THE WIRELESS TELEGRAPH AND RADIO

In 1896 *Guglielmo Marconi,* an Italian scientist, perfected the wireless telegraph, an instrument for sending and receiving code signals through space by means of electromagnetic (or radio) waves. This accomplishment made possible ship-to-ship, ship-to-shore, and transoceanic communication without the use of cables. Six years later *Reginald A. Fessenden,* an American physicist, demonstrated that voice messages could also be broadcast via radio waves.

In 1906 *Lee De Forest,* an American engineer (often called the "father of radio"), invented the three-element vacuum tube, or *triode.* This device enabled broadcast signals, such as voice or music, to be detected and amplified by a radio receiver. Another pioneer in the development of radio was the electrical engineer and inventor, *Edwin H. Armstrong.* He devised the basic circuitry used in radio receivers and later introduced the frequency modulation, or FM, system of static-free radio.

The first regular radio broadcasting stations, WWJ in Detroit and KDKA in Pittsburgh, were established in 1920. The industry expanded rapidly. Now there are more than 10,000 radio stations in the United States broadcasting regularly scheduled programs, and there is a radio in nearly every U.S. home. Most automobiles are also equipped with radios. Specialized vehicles, such as police cars, taxicabs, ambulances, and trucks, frequently have two-way radios, which enable their operators to send, as well as to receive, messages.

Scientists have discovered other uses for radio waves:

1. Radar (a term derived from the phrase "radio detecting and ranging") is a device that locates an object and determines its distance and direction by means of radio waves. Introduced in the 1930's, it was brought to a high state of development during World War II. Then it performed a vital service by detecting and locating enemy planes and submarines and directing artillery fire. Today radar equipment installed in commercial and military aircraft and ships warns pilots of obstacles in their path and helps guide them in bad weather. Radar is also used to track hurricanes and tornadoes. Radar stations set up along America's borders detect the approach of all ships, aircraft, or missiles, thus preventing a surprise attack from an unfriendly nation.

2. Television is the transmission of pictures as well as sounds by radio waves. A pioneer in its development was *Vladimir Zworykin,* a Russian-born American engineer who invented the iconoscope (1925)—the basis of the electronic television camera. Using an iconoscope and a cathode-ray tube, he made a successful demonstration of television in 1933. Regularly scheduled TV broadcasts were introduced by NBC in 1939, but the outbreak of World War II delayed the growth of television until 1946.

Since that time TV has expanded greatly. Today nearly every American home is equipped with a TV set. Cable television systems (CATV) and community antennae provide people living in areas of poor reception access to TV. The opening of the UHF (ultra-high frequency) band to broadcasters in 1952 increased the number of TV channels that viewers could watch. Earth-orbiting communication satellites make live, intercontinental telecasts possible and bring world events to the immediate attention of the public. Furthermore, the introduction of the videotape cassette recorder (VCR) enables Americans to tape and play back TV programs on home sets.

EFFECTS OF RADIO AND TELEVISION

Radio and television bring entertainment, education, music, drama, sports, and news into the home. They make it possible for public officials to speak directly to the people and to speed urgent messages to the nation in time of emergency. By presenting their programs to a nationwide audience, radio and television set national standards for speech, dress, and attitudes. Thereby, they help to reduce regional differences and tend to unify the country. By presenting programs about people in other lands, they also give the nation a better understanding of the world.

GOVERNMENT REGULATES BUSINESS IN THE PUBLIC INTEREST

RAILROADS

In the late 19th century, railroads engaged in many abuses that caused great hardship to Western farmers and to small shippers of freight. Among these practices were (1) charging excessive rates, (2) charging more for carrying freight over short distances, where there were no competing railroads, than for long hauls in competitive territory, (3) granting rebates, or refunds, to large shippers, and (4) obtaining legislation favorable to their interests by political activity, bribery, and corruption.

Farm organizations, labor groups, and owners of small businesses urged the government to regulate railroad transportation in the public interest. Heeding their pleas, Congress passed the following laws:

The Interstate Commerce Act (1887) provided that (1) railroad rates be reasonable, (2) special rates and rebates be discontinued, and (3) charging more for a short haul than for a long haul be done away with. To carry out the provisions of this law, Congress created the *Interstate Commerce Commission (ICC)*.

The *Hepburn Act* (1906) and the *Esch-Cummins Act* (1920) increased the ICC's power and government control over interstate railroads.

OTHER TRANSPORTATION AND COMMUNICATION FACILITIES

All forms of interstate transportation (except airlines, and gas and water pipelines) were later placed under ICC control. It was empowered to approve rates and routes, rule on mergers, and supervise the financial practices of interstate carriers. (In 1996 Congress disbanded the ICC and transferred its functions to the U.S. Department of Transportation.)

The Federal Communications Commission (FCC), established in 1934, regulates communication by telegraph, telephone, radio, and television.

The *Civil Aeronautics Board (CAB)*, created in 1940 and abolished in 1985, supervised commercial airlines. It assigned routes, regulated rates and ruled on mergers.

BIG BUSINESS

To curb the power of trusts, to eliminate abuses in business, and to protect the interests of the public, Congress enacted legislation and set up regulatory agencies as follows:

The *Sherman Antitrust Act* (1890) declared illegal any business combination that sought to restrain trade or commerce. Because its wording was vague, the act was difficult to enforce. It did not effectively halt the growth of trusts.

The *Clayton Antitrust Act* (1914) strengthened the power of the government in dealing with monopolies. It forbade agreements between companies to fix or control prices for the purpose of lessening competition. It also prohibited individuals from serving as directors of competing corporations.

The *Federal Trade Commission* (1914) was created to report on the activities of corporations subject to the antitrust laws. The FTC was empowered to issue orders prohibiting unfair business practices.

The *Federal Power Commission* (1920) was established to license hydroelectric power plant construction on public lands and to supervise the companies operating these facilities. In 1935 the agency was given the right to regulate the operations and wholesale rates of all gas and electric companies carrying on business in more than one state. Renamed the

Federal Energy Regulatory Commission (FERC), it became part of the Department of Energy in 1977.

The *Securities and Exchange Commission* (1934) was formed to protect investors by regulating stock exchanges and establishing fair trading practices in stocks and bonds. The SEC was later given the power to regulate the financial practices of public utility holding companies.

PUBLIC HEALTH

The following laws were enacted by Congress to safeguard the nation's health:

The *Meat Inspection Act* (1906) provided for (1) the enforcement of sanitary regulations in meat-packing plants, and (2) the inspection of meat by federal inspectors before being offered for sale to the public. The law was passed largely as a result of Upton Sinclair's book, *The Jungle*, which presented a shocking report of the conditions under which the nation's meat was being prepared. Federal inspection standards were later extended to meat and poultry processors operating intrastate (within the borders of a single state).

The *Pure Food and Drug Act* (1906) (1) forbade the sale of harmful and impure foods and medicines, and (2) required that foods and drugs be labeled truthfully. Federal regulation in this area was later strengthened by the *Food, Drug, and Cosmetic Act* (1938). This law not only prohibited the misbranding of foods, drugs, and cosmetics, but also (1) required manufacturers to list ingredients used in their processing, and (2) forbade the use of false and misleading advertising claims for their products.

Multiple-Choice Test

1. The "Lone Eagle," who made a solo, nonstop airplane flight from New York to Paris in 1927, was (*a*) Orville Wright (*b*) Glenn Curtiss (*c*) Howard Hughes (*d*) Charles Lindbergh.
2. One purpose of the Interstate Commerce Act of 1887 was to (*a*) regulate the freight rates of railroads (*b*) raise tariff rates on imports (*c*) prohibit the sale of impure foods (*d*) provide for irrigation projects.
3. The Pure Food and Drug Act of 1906 contained an important provision concerning goods carried in interstate commerce. This provision dealt with (*a*) federal inspection of meat (*b*) proper labeling of certain products (*c*) freedom to sell all foods and drugs produced in the United States (*d*) prohibition of the sale of patent medicines.
4. Which one of the following inventions had the greatest influence on American industrial development during the 19th century? (*a*) airplane (*b*) automobile (*c*) motion picture (*d*) steam engine.
5. Of the following, the first major step in federal regulation of business was the (*a*) Securities and Exchange Act (*b*) Sherman Antitrust Act (*c*) Interstate Commerce Act (*d*) Gold Standard Act.
6. The person whose best-known invention was in use before the Civil War was (*a*) Samuel F. B. Morse (*b*) George Westinghouse (*c*) Thomas A. Edison (*d*) Alexander Graham Bell.

7. The trend most characteristic of American business since 1900 has been the (*a*) complete disappearance of small businesses (*b*) increase in the size of many business organizations (*c*) decrease in government regulation (*d*) decline in technological development.

8. The beginning of the "Age of Big Business" in the United States is associated with (*a*) the War of 1812 (*b*) the Mexican War (*c*) the Civil War (*d*) World War I.

9. An important reason for the formation of trusts in the latter part of the 19th century was a desire to (*a*) escape federal regulation (*b*) eliminate competition (*c*) reduce prices to the consumer (*d*) outlaw the use of rebates.

10. In 1906 Congress passed the Meat Inspection Act partly as a result of a book written by (*a*) Upton Sinclair (*b*) Sinclair Lewis (*c*) Lincoln Steffens (*d*) James Russell Lowell.

11. All of the following people were important in the development of aviation EXCEPT (*a*) Glenn Curtiss (*b*) Orville Wright (*c*) Lyman R. Blake (*d*) Howard Hughes.

12. One of the first persons to start a modern department store was (*a*) John Jacob Astor (*b*) Gordon McKay (*c*) James J. Hill (*d*) John Wanamaker.

13. Which one of these events occurred LAST? (*a*) Henry Bessemer developed a new process for making steel. (*b*) Robert Fulton built the *Clermont*. (*c*) George Eastman developed the Kodak camera. (*d*) Elias Howe invented the sewing machine.

14. Which group is responsible for establishing the policies of a corporation? (*a*) board of directors (*b*) bondholders (*c*) stockholders (*d*) federal government.

15. In the years 1887–1890, Congress passed major legislation to eliminate abuses in (*a*) local government (*b*) business practices (*c*) farm credit (*d*) civil rights.

16. Which convenience was first made generally available to Americans during the period 1900–1930? (*a*) railroad transportation (*b*) telegrams (*c*) television sets (*d*) automobiles.

17. A well-known inventor whose work was NOT in the field of communication was (*a*) Cyrus Field (*b*) Guglielmo Marconi (*c*) Elisha Otis (*d*) Lee De Forest.

18. An important industry that began in the United States after 1920 was (*a*) the construction of steel plows (*b*) the manufacture of steel (*c*) petroleum refining (*d*) the manufacture of radios.

19. The most common form of business organization today is the (*a*) cooperative (*b*) trust (*c*) corporation (*d*) pool.

20. All of the following retailing developments occurred in the 20th century EXCEPT (*a*) supermarkets (*b*) shopping centers (*c*) discount stores (*d*) department stores.

Modified True-False Test

1. In the type of business consolidation called the *pool*, one company absorbs another, or several enterprises combine to form a new company.

2. The first law passed by the federal government to halt the spread of trusts was the *National Banking* Act.

3. A business organization that acquires complete control of a particular field of endeavor is said to have a *monopoly*.
4. The nation's biggest business in the period 1865–1900 was *railroading*.
5. The *printing* industry ranks first in the country today in the value of its finished product.
6. The seaplane was developed by *Charles A. Lindbergh*.
7. The government agency that currently regulates the operations of telegraph, telephone, radio, and television facilities is the *Energy Regulatory Commission*.
8. The *Smith-Lever* Act was passed in 1914 to strengthen the power of the government over big business.
9. The *Federal Trade Commission* is a government agency that is empowered to issue orders prohibiting unfair business practices.
10. The Hepburn Act and the Esch-Cummins Act increased the power of the *Interstate Commerce* Commission.

Matching Test I

Column A	*Column B*
1. Frank W. Woolworth	*a.* Invented the air brake
2. Marshall Field	*b.* Designed machinery to mass-produce shoes
3. William Kelly	*c.* Helped pioneer the development of the meat-packing industry
4. Edwin L. Drake	
5. Charles M. Hall	*d.* Developed the first practical typewriter
6. Charles F. Brush	*e.* Invented the linotype machine
7. Gustavus F. Swift	*f.* Invented the iconoscope
8. Gordon McKay	*g.* Developed a process for the commercial production of aluminum
9. Ottmar Mergenthaler	
10. George Westinghouse	*h.* Developed the railroad sleeping car
11. George Pullman	*i.* Founded the first chain of variety stores
12. Charles E. Duryea	*j.* Discovered a method of converting iron into steel
13. Lee De Forest	
14. Vladimir Zworykin	*k.* Improved the electric dynamo
15. Christopher Sholes	*l.* Drilled the first commercial oil well
	m. Helped pioneer the development of the department store
	n. Helped pioneer the development of the automobile
	o. Invented the triode

Identification Test

1. I realized that good transportation was necessary for the growth of the Pacific Northwest. I built the Great Northern Railroad and am often called the "Empire Builder."
2. I came to the United States from Scotland and became well-known for my efforts to help the deaf. I invented the telephone in 1876.
3. I organized the Standard Oil Company of Ohio and later the Standard Oil Trust. My son donated the site for the headquarters of the United Nations.

4. We were two brothers who flew an airplane powered by a gasoline engine in 1903. It was the first flight of a heavier-than-air machine in history.
5. When I was a boy, I sold newspapers on a train, and, in the baggage car, tried experiments in chemistry. In later years I invented the electric light bulb and the phonograph. I became known as the "wizard of electricity."
6. Often called the "Steel King," I won both fame and fortune in the United States. My immense fortune was made in the giant steel industry; my fame was achieved largely from my gifts of money to libraries and peace movements.
7. I pioneered in the manufacture of low-priced automobiles by specializing in only one model produced on the assembly line.
8. I joined many short railroad lines into one main trunk line, known as the New York Central System. I earned my title of "Commodore" as a steamboat owner on the Hudson River.
9. Following in my father's footsteps, I became a banker and financier. I am best known for my reorganization of bankrupt railroads and for the formation of the nation's first billion-dollar corporation.
10. After amassing a fortune in the paper business, I became interested in establishing a telegraphic link between America and Europe. I completed the laying of my first transatlantic cable in 1858, but it soon broke down. I started again and achieved complete success eight years later.

Matching Test II

Column A	Column B
1. Titusville, Pennsylvania	*a.* First center of the iron and steel indus-
2. Kitty Hawk, North Carolina	try
3. Detroit, Michigan	*b.* Leading oil-producing states today
4. Pittsburgh, Pennsylvania	*c.* A main center of the meat-packing in-
5. Minnesota	dustry
6. Texas, Louisiana, and	*d.* Site of the exposition where the tele-
California	phone was first exhibited publicly
7. Chicago, Illinois	*e.* A steel center below the Mason-Dixon
8. Birmingham, Alabama	Line
9. California, New York,	*f.* Site of the first successful oil well
and Ohio	*g.* Leading manufacturing states today
10. Philadelphia, Pennsylvania	*h.* Center of the automobile industry
	i. Location of the Mesabi Range
	j. Place where the Wright brothers ex-
	perimented with a heavier-than-air flying
	machine

Essay Questions

1. Americans now have the highest standard of living in the world. Explain and illustrate how each of the following helped to bring about this high standard of living: labor supply, inventiveness and ingenuity, and natural resources.
2. (*a*) Discuss briefly *two* reasons for the growth of "big business" in the United States. (*b*) Mention *one* federal law that was adopted for the regulation of big

business and discuss *one* reason why the regulation of big business became the concern of the federal government.

3. Some of our greatest national industries are the automobile, petroleum, meat-packing, and steel industries. Write about *one* of these industries, including in your discussion *all* of the following points:
   a. Why the industry is important.
   b. In what part (or parts) of the country most of the industry is carried on.
   c. Why it developed in that location (or those locations).
   d. What raw materials it requires.
   e. One person who was prominent in its development.

4. Listed below are four important events in the technological development of the United States. Show specifically how each of *two* of these brought about changes in the American way of life.
   a. 1903—first story portrayed in motion pictures
   b. 1903—first powered heavier-than-air flight at Kitty Hawk
   c. 1909—manufacture of the Model-T Ford
   d. 1920—start of commercial broadcasting at radio statio KDKA

5. Congress has created many special independent agencies to regulate business. (*a*) Name *three* such agencies or commissions. (*b*) For each of the agencies or commissions named in answer to *a*, explain *one* condition that led to its creation.

6. Modern factories employ mass-production techniques to turn out large quantities of goods.
   a. Describe briefly how an assembly line works.
   b. What is meant by (1) standardized parts, and (2) division of labor?
   c. Why do modern factories need a smaller proportion of highly skilled workers than did factories in the past?
   d. It is claimed that assembly line production lowers the price at which articles can be sold. Can you justify this claim?

7. The railroads have been an important means of transportation for nearly 150 years. (*a*) State *one* effect of railroads on the development of America. (*b*) When was the first transcontinental railroad built? (*c*) Compare travel by railroad before 1850 with travel by railroad today. (*d*) Name *three* other forms of transportation that exist today and state how *each* has affected railroads.

Part 4. Labor Organizes to Improve Its Position

ORIGIN OF LABOR UNIONS

The rise of the factory system resulted in the creation of a laboring class, living in cities and towns and dependent upon wages for its livelihood. Low pay; long working hours; unsanitary, dangerous, and uncomfortable working conditions; and periodic unemployment caused much dissatisfaction among workers. To improve their lot, they began to organize into unions.

A labor *union* is an association of workers formed for mutual benefit and protection. It seeks recognition by the employer as the official representative of the employees; and it tries to win higher wages, shorter hours, and better working conditions for its members.

KNIGHTS OF LABOR

Although various groups of craftsworkers in the large cities had banded together into unions in the early 19th century, their organizations were generally small and short-lived. The first important national union was organized in 1869 by *Uriah S. Stephens* in Philadelphia. Known as the *Knights of Labor*, it aimed to unite all workers—male and female, black and white, skilled and unskilled—into one large union. Every member in a given geographic area, regardless of craft, industry, or position, belonged to the same local group, or assembly.

The Knights came out for (*a*) an eight-hour workday, (*b*) equal pay for men and women performing similar work, (*c*) abolition of child labor, (*d*) consumer cooperatives and worker-owned and -operated manufacturing enterprises (producer cooperatives), (*e*) government regulation of trusts, (*f*) a graduated income tax, and (*g*) government ownership of railroads and telegraph lines. The organization's leaders did not favor the use of strikes as a labor weapon. They preferred to exert economic pressure on employers by means of boycotts, and to settle labor disputes by arbitration.

Under the leadership of *Terence V. Powderly*, its head from 1879 to 1893, the Knights attained a membership in excess of 700,000 by the mid-1880's. Starting in 1886, however, it began to lose strength; after 1893 it disappeared from view. Among the reasons for the Knights' decline were the following:

1. A series of unauthorized strikes initiated by its members proved unsuccessful and discredited the organization.

2. The conflicting interests of skilled and unskilled workers caused dissension within the union.

3. The Knights set up more than 125 cooperative ventures (including a shoe manufacturing plant and a coal mine), but most were unable to operate profitably and many failed.

4. It lost public support as a result of the *Haymarket Massacre*. This bloody incident occurred at a rally held by striking workers in Chicago's Haymarket Square in May, 1886. They had gathered to protest the

slaying of several strikers by police at the McCormick Harvester plant a short time earlier. As the meeting was nearing its end, police arrived on the scene. A bomb was thrown, killing seven police officers and wounding dozens of bystanders. Additional people were hurt in the panic that ensued. Although no one knew who actually threw the bomb, eight radical agitators were arrested for the crime, tried, and found guilty. Four were executed, one committed suicide, and the others received life sentences. (In 1893 the governor of Illinois, John Peter Altgeld, freed the three surviving prisoners, claiming that they had not received a fair trial.)

Despite the fact that the Knights of Labor had not sponsored the Haymarket rally and had condemned the bombing, the public and the press blamed the union for the incident.

AMERICAN FEDERATION OF LABOR

Founded in 1881 under a different name and reorganized in 1886 as the *American Federation of Labor* (*AFL*), this union soon became the leading organization of workers in the United States. Unlike the Knights of Labor, the AFL did not advocate sweeping political and economic reforms. Rather, it concerned itself with such down-to-earth issues as higher wages, shorter hours, and better working conditions for its members. Also unlike the Knights, it organized skilled workers by trades, or crafts. Each craft formed its own national union, consisting of many locals scattered throughout the country. The AFL served as the parent body of these self-governing national unions. Thus, it became a union of unions rather than a union of individual workers. *Samuel Gompers,* a cigarmaker by trade and one of the founders of the AFL, became its first president in 1886. He held that position for most of the next 38 years. (His successor, *William Green,* headed the AFL from 1924 to 1952. Upon Green's death, *George Meany* became the Federation's third president.)

Under Gompers' able leadership, unionized workers won important gains, and the AFL grew steadily. Its membership increased to 550,000 in 1900, 2 million in 1910, and 4 million in 1920.

The prosperity of the 1920's, opposition by employers' associations, unfavorable court decisions, and the Great Depression weakened organized labor. Membership in the AFL declined, reaching a low point of 2 million in 1933. But with the passage of favorable labor legislation during the New Deal administration of President Franklin D. Roosevelt, union membership began to rise again. By 1952 the AFL consisted of 100 national unions with a membership of 8 million.

CONGRESS OF INDUSTRIAL ORGANIZATIONS

Some leaders of the AFL opposed the Federation's ideas of (1) organizing only skilled workers, and (2) maintaining many separate craft unions within one industry. They believed that the best way to unionize the large, mass-production industries was to organize all the workers in an industry—skilled, semiskilled, and unskilled—regardless of craft, into a single industrial union.

Led by *John L. Lewis,* head of the United Mine Workers, these unionists in 1935 formed a committee for industrial organization within the AFL. Meeting opposition from craft union advocates, they broke away from the Federation and in 1938 established the *Congress of Industrial Organizations* (CIO). Lewis became the first president of the new labor group. In 1940 Lewis withdrew from office and was replaced by *Philip Murray.* Upon Murray's death in 1952, *Walter P. Reuther* assumed the presidency.

The CIO succeeded in unionizing the automobile, steel, rubber, oil-refining, textile, shipbuilding, and communications industries. By 1950 it comprised over 30 industrial unions with a membership of 6 million workers.

THE AFL AND THE CIO MERGE

In 1955 the leaders of the AFL and the CIO negotiated a merger of the two labor organizations. They hoped that unification would (1) increase labor's political influence, (2) strengthen their ability to organize non-union companies and industries, (3) eliminate competition for new members, and (4) curtail jurisdictional strikes between rival units of the two labor groups. The combined organization became known as the *American Federation of Labor and Congress of Industrial Organizations (AFL-CIO).* Its current president is John J. Sweeney.

At the present time, the AFL-CIO comprises more than 65 craft and industrial unions with a combined membership of some 13.1 million. The 12 largest affiliates of the AFL-CIO are the following:

Union	Membership
Brotherhood of Teamsters	1,400,000
United Food and Commercial Workers	1,400,000
Federation of State, County, and Municipal Employees	1,300,000
United Automobile, Aerospace, and Agricultural Implement Workers	1,300,000
Service Employees International Union	1,100,000
American Federation of Teachers	900,000
Brotherhood of Electrical Workers	800,000
Laborers' International Union of North America	750,000
Association of Machinists and Aerospace Workers	730,000
Communications Workers of America	600,000
United Steelworkers of America	550,000
United Brotherhood of Carpenters and Joiners	500,000

OTHER LABOR GROUPS

About 3.3 million working people belong to unions and associations that are not affiliated with the AFL-CIO. Independent unions include:

1. The *National Education Association,* through its 13,500 local chapters, seeks to protect the interests of its 2 million teacher-members.

2. The *United Mine Workers,* an AFL affiliate that broke away to help found the CIO and later rejoined its former parent, withdrew once again to pursue an independent course. Its present membership is 240,000.

3. There are several independent unions that represent such federal government personnel as clerical staffs of executive agencies, Treasury Department employees, and rural letter carriers. University professors have an association of their own, police are organized into a fraternal order, and locomotive engineers are bonded together as a brotherhood.

Unionized workers in 1996 comprised about 14.5% of the U.S. labor force, compared to 22% in 1980 and 36% in 1945—the peak year of the labor movement.

BITTER LABOR STRUGGLES TAKE PLACE

Employers today generally recognize the value of labor organizations and aim to settle disputes with their workers by negotiation and discussion. In the late 1800's and early 1900's, however, labor's efforts to organize and better its condition met with violent opposition from big business. Corporations refused to recognize unions, discharged employees who tried to organize workers, and hired strikebreakers to replace workers who went out on strike. The bitter labor disputes that took place during this period caused much bloodshed and destruction of property.

1. Railroad Strike of 1877. The nation's first major strike took place in 1877 when workers on the Baltimore and Ohio and other Eastern railroads walked off the job to protest a wage cut. When the railroads hired other workers to replace them, the angry strikers tried to keep the trains from running. Riots broke out, and pitched battles were fought between strikers and militia. Much property was destroyed in several railroad centers, especially Pittsburgh. Order was finally restored when President Hayes sent in federal troops. Unable to prevent the trains from running, and afraid of losing their jobs, the strikers reluctantly accepted the wage reduction.

2. Homestead Steel Strike. Refusing to take a cut in wages, workers of the Carnegie Steel Company in Homestead, Pennsylvania, struck in 1892. The company attempted to bring in 300 armed guards from a private detective agency to protect its property and break the strike. In a battle between the strikers and the guards, 10 of the detectives were killed and the rest were driven off. Under the protection of the state militia, strikebreakers were hired to resume steel production. After five months, the strike collapsed and the striking workers accepted the company's terms.

3. Pullman Strike. Threatened with a wage cut, workers at the Pullman Company's sleeping-car manufacturing plant near Chicago went out on strike in 1894. Railroad employees across the country supported the strikers by refusing to handle any train hauling Pullman cars. This support brought nearly all trains to a halt. Violence flared up when the railroads tried to keep the trains running. President Grover Cleveland dispatched federal troops to restore order and keep mail service from being disrupted. The railroads meanwhile obtained a court order, or *injunction*, that forbade the strikers from interfering with mail transportation and interstate commerce. When the strike leaders refused to call off the walkout, they were arrested for violating the injunction. With the strike leaders in jail and train service restored under the protection of federal troops, the strike was broken.

4. Anthracite Coal Strike The United Mine Workers struck in 1902 after mineowners in Pennsylvania refused to recognize the union or to discuss a wage increase. With winter approaching, President Theodore Roosevelt threatened to seize and operate the mines with federal troops to avert a fuel shortage. Thereupon, the owners agreed to allow an impartial commission to arbitrate the dispute, and the miners called off their strike. The commission awarded the miners an increase in wages but rejected their demand for union recognition.

5. General Motors Sit-Down Strike. In its attempt to unionize the automobile industry, the CIO introduced a new labor weapon—the *sit-down strike*. Late in 1936 employees of General Motors struck for union recognition and better working conditions. For six weeks the strikers refused to leave the plants, defying all efforts to oust them. This technique halted production and prevented the use of strikebreakers. The company was finally forced to agree to the demands of the strikers and to recognize the United Automobile Workers as the bargaining agent of the workers.

As the use of the sit-down strike spread, other employers were forced to meet the demands of their workers. In 1939, however, the U.S. Supreme Court declared this labor weapon illegal.

THE GOVERNMENT PASSES LABOR LEGISLATION

1. Department of Labor (1913). Congress created a separate executive department to deal with the problems of workers. According to the act creating it, the duty of the Department of Labor is to "foster, promote, and develop the welfare of the wage earners of the United States; to improve their working conditions; and to advance their opportunities for profitable employment."

2. Adamson Act (1916). It granted employees of interstate railroads an eight-hour workday with time-and-a-half pay for overtime.

3. Esch-Cummins Act (1920). In addition to strengthening government control over interstate railroads, this law created a Railroad Labor Board to settle wage disputes in the industry.

4. Norris-La Guardia Anti-Injunction Act (1932). It limited the power of federal courts to issue injunctions forbidding strikes and picketing. It also prohibited injunctions against workers who refused to honor their "yellow-dog" employment contracts (see page 273).

5. National Labor Relations Act (1935). It is also called the *Wagner Act* after its sponsor, Senator Robert F. Wagner of New York. A *National*

Labor Relations Board (NLRB) was set up to (*a*) safeguard labor's right to organize unions and bargain collectively, (*b*) protect labor against unfair practices of employers, and (*c*) investigate and mediate labor disputes.

6. Social Security Act (1935). One of the most far-reaching laws ever enacted, it marked the beginning of a sweeping new effort by the federal government to protect the welfare of its citizens. The act (*a*) established a federal pension system for retired workers, (*b*) set up a federal-state program of unemployment compensation, and (*c*) extended federal aid to the states for public assistance to the needy aged, needy children, the blind, and the disabled.

   a. Pension System. Nearly all wage earners and self-employed persons are covered by old-age, survivors, and disability insurance. The system is financed by a federal payroll tax shared equally by wage earners and their employers. (A self-employed person is taxed at a higher rate than a wage earner.)

   Insured workers become eligible for monthly pension payments when they reach the retirement age of 65. Persons may elect to retire at 62, but with lower pensions. If an insured worker dies before reaching retirement age, that person's family is entitled to benefits. Totally disabled workers may start collecting payments at any age. Social Security benefits are increased periodically if the Consumer Price Index (CPI) rises.

   b. Unemployment Compensation. Most wage earners are also covered by unemployment insurance. This federal-state program is financed by a payroll tax levied on employers.

   If workers are laid off temporarily or lose their jobs, they are entitled to weekly benefit payments for a limited period of time. The partial replacement of their lost wages provides them financial support while they seek other employment.

   c. Medicare. In 1965 Congress made a significant addition to Social Security by approving a program of health insurance for the aged. Known as *Medicare,* its purpose is to enable persons aged 65 and over to cope with high hospital costs and to assure them better medical care. It is divided into two parts:

   (1) *Hospital insurance,* financed by Social Security taxes, pays a large part of the cost of hospital and nursing-home care for the elderly.

   (2) *Voluntary medical insurance,* paid for equally by the federal government and the elderly people who sign up for the program, covers part of the cost of doctors' bills and home health services. (For Social Security updates, see pages 493 and 506.)

   7. Fair Labor Standards Act (1938). This act, known as the *Wages and Hours Act,* established a minimum wage of $.40 an hour and provided for a workweek of 40 hours with time-and-a-half pay for overtime. It applied to all businesses involved in interstate commerce. Over the years, the minimum wage was raised many times and the scope of the law was broadened to cover more workers. (See page 509 for the current rate.)

8. Taft-Hartley Act (1947). Passed by Congress over President Harry Truman's veto, this act aimed to remove certain labor abuses and to curb the power of unions. It prohibited (*a*) the closed shop, (*b*) jurisdictional strikes, (*c*) strikes by federal employees, (*d*) featherbedding, (*e*) contributions by either unions or employers to any candidate campaigning for federal office, and (*f*) high initiation fees as a requirement for union membership.

The act also required unions to release annual financial statements and union officials to take an oath that they are not members of the Communist party.

Under the act, a strike can take place only after the union gives 60 days' notice, thus providing for a "cooling-off" period. If a strike threatens the nation's health and safety, the President can obtain a court injunction postponing the strike for an additional 80 days.

9. Landrum-Griffin Act (1959). After a Senate investigating committee revealed the existence of racketeering, extortion, and misuse of funds by certain unions, Congress passed the *Landrum-Griffin Act*. It (*a*) required unions to file periodic financial reports, (*b*) barred ex-convicts from holding union office for five years after their release from prison, (*c*) barred ex-Communists from holding union office for five years after leaving the Communist party, (*d*) guaranteed union members freedom of speech at union meetings, use of the secret ballot in union elections, and protection against increases in dues without their consent, (*e*) outlawed picketing in jurisdictional disputes, (*f*) forbade secondary boycotts, and (*g*) prohibited "shakedowns"—the practice of soliciting money from employers by threatening that labor services would be halted if they refused to pay.

10. Employee Retirement Income Security Act (1974). To protect the retirement benefits of workers enrolled in private pension plans, ERISA (*a*) set standards for the operation of such plans, (*b*) forbade employers to strip long-term employees of their accrued pension rights, (*c*) required public disclosure of a plan's operations, (*d*) limited the manipulation of pension assets by trustees, and (*e*) provided more favorable tax treatment for the self-employed who set up retirement plans. It also created a governmental agency, the *Pension Benefit Guarantee Corporation,* to provide federal insurance for the assets of these plans to make sure that workers entitled to retirement benefits receive them even if their company goes bankrupt or if its pension plan collapses.

11. Mandatory Retirement Elimination Act (1986). To provide workers the opportunity to extend their working careers beyond the traditional age of retirement, if they so choose, Congress passed a law in 1978 raising the mandatory (compulsory) retirement age for most employees from 65 to 70. In 1986 Congress voted to do away with the requirement for mandatory retirement at age 70, thus allowing people to retain their jobs as long as they wished to continue working. (Until 1994, however, the age-70 mandatory retirement policy remained in effect for law enforcement personnel, fire fighters, and tenured college faculty members.)

STATE LABOR LEGISLATION

Many states also took steps to protect workers. Provisions were made for the installation of safety devices on dangerous machinery, and for proper lighting, sanitation, ventilation, and fire prevention in offices and factories. Laws were passed limiting the hours of labor for women and children, and for workers engaged in dangerous or strenuous work.

Almost all the states have *workers' compensation laws,* which require employers to carry insurance for the protection of employees. These laws assure payments to workers or their families in case of injury, permanent disability, or death resulting from the performance of their jobs. A number of states have also passed laws prohibiting discrimination in employment because of race, color, creed, sex, or national origin.

IMPORTANT TERMS RELATING TO LABOR

Arbitration. A process used to resolve a labor dispute in which both sides agree to submit the dispute to an impartial outsider and to accept that person's decision.

Blacklist. A weapon used by employers to keep union organizers from obtaining employment. The names of these people are listed and circulated so that employers will refuse to hire them.

Boycott. An organized effort by labor to discourage the purchase of goods or services from a company involved in a labor dispute.

Checkoff. The deduction by the employer of union dues from the wages of union members. The employer turns the funds over to the union.

Closed Shop. A plant where only union members may be hired.

Collective Bargaining. Discussions between representatives of labor and management for the purpose of negotiating an agreement on wages, hours, and working conditions.

Company Union. An organization of workers that is dominated by the employer.

Featherbedding. The practice of forcing an employer to use more workers than are needed.

Fringe Benefits. Gains for labor other than wage increases and improved working conditions. Such benefits include employer-supported pension plans, medical care for workers and their families, and paid vacations.

Injunction. A court order requiring a party to do, or to refrain from doing, a certain act. It may be issued, under certain conditions, to prohibit the calling of a strike or to order strikers back to work. The court can enforce an injunction by imposing fines and jail sentences on those who refuse to obey its order.

Jurisdictional Strike. A strike arising from a dispute between two unions over which one has the right to represent a group of workers.

Lockout. The shutting of a plant by an employer for the purpose of forcing workers to meet the employer's terms. An employer may also use the lockout as a protest against union demands.

Mediation. An attempt to settle a labor dispute through the efforts of an impartial person or agency. The mediator may recommend a settlement, but the parties to the dispute are not bound to accept the recommendation.

Open Shop. A plant that employs both union and nonunion workers.

Picketing. Parading by union members near a place of employment. The union seeks to inform the public of a labor dispute and to discourage persons from entering the building.

Scab. A nonunion worker hired to replace a striking employee.

Secondary Boycott. A boycott of the products of a company not directly involved in a labor dispute.

Seniority. Rights attained by a worker through length of service with a company.

Shop Steward. A person chosen by the workers of a particular shop or department to represent them in the handling of grievances.

Strike. An organized work stoppage by employees to compel an employer to meet their demands.

Union Shop. A plant that may hire both union and nonunion workers but that may retain nonunion workers only if they agree to join the union within a given time.

"Yellow-Dog" Contract. An employment agreement signed by employees in which they promise not to join a union.

Multiple-Choice Test

1. Which one of these laws deals with the relations between labor and management? (*a*) Homestead Act (*b*) Taft-Hartley Act (*c*) Clayton Act (*d*) Smith-Hughes Act.
2. A basic purpose of the Social Security Act of 1935 was to (*a*) provide income in old age (*b*) guarantee jobs for the unemployed (*c*) provide free life insurance (*d*) encourage workers to change jobs frequently.
3. The method whereby representatives of labor and management negotiate the terms and conditions of work is called (*a*) a boycott (*b*) an injunction (*c*) an open shop (*d*) collective bargaining.
4. Which person was prominently connected with the organization of labor unions? (*a*) James J. Hill (*b*) John L. Lewis (*c*) Edward H. Harriman (*d*) J. Edgar Hoover.
5. A founder and the first president of the American Federation of Labor was (*a*) William Green (*b*) Samuel Gompers (*c*) George Meany (*d*) Walter Reuther.
6. Disputes between employers and employees may be settled with the help of an outside party by (*a*) mediation (*b*) blacklisting (*c*) picketing (*d*) sabotage.
7. Unions expanded most rapidly in the decade (*a*) 1830–1840 (*b*) 1900–1910 (*c*) 1910–1920 (*d*) 1930–1940.

8. Which of the following demands of labor is of most recent origin? (a) higher wages (b) improved working conditions (c) shorter working hours (d) fringe benefits.

9. Legislation passed by Congress in 1986 (a) required all workers to retire at age 65 (b) raised the eligibility requirement for Social Security to age 70 (c) forbade the practice of compelling workers to retire because of age (d) made all citizens eligible for Medicare at age 62.

10. Which statement best describes a feature of the economic history of the United States during the period 1865–1900? (a) Business was strictly regulated by federal laws. (b) Organized labor won many important strikes. (c) Relations between business and labor were generally friendly. (d) Labor-management disputes were often marked by violence.

11. Haymarket Square is associated with (a) the first flight of the Wright brothers (b) a violent confrontation between workers and police (c) a sit-down strike at General Motors (d) a national convention of the AFL.

12. A method used to end the Pullman strike of 1894 was (a) arbitration (b) collective bargaining (c) the closed shop (d) federal troops.

13. Which was an important reason for the growth of labor unions in the latter half of the 19th century? (a) passage of the Sherman Antitrust Act (b) indifference of employers to the welfare of employees (c) increase in the number of women employed in industry (d) support of organized labor by the federal government.

14. A development that has strengthened labor unions since 1955 has been the (a) use of the sit-down strike (b) abolition of the closed shop (c) establishment of the National Labor Relations Board (d) merger of the two major national labor organizations.

15. An important reason for the decline of the Knights of Labor was the (a) influence of the Granger movement (b) high cost of membership (c) conflict between skilled and unskilled workers (d) passage of anti-labor laws by the federal government.

16. The Landrum-Griffin Act of 1959 aimed to protect the rank and file of organized labor against (a) violations of the Fair Labor Standards Act (b) exploitation by corrupt labor leaders (c) unfair state labor laws (d) unfair foreign competition.

17. An action against a company that uses or sells products from an establishment where the workers are on strike is called a (a) lockout (b) general strike (c) jurisdictional strike (d) secondary boycott.

18. Which issue caused a split within the AFL in 1935? (a) sit-down strikes (b) the Norris-La Guardia Anti-Injunction Act (c) industrial versus craft unionism (d) the National Labor Relations Act.

19. When a strike threatens the nation's health and safety, the President of the United States may (a) forbid the calling of such a strike (b) provide for government operation of plants threatened by such a strike (c) obtain an injunction to postpone such a strike (d) imprison the labor leaders who plan such a strike.

20. Labor uses all of the following in its struggle to better its working conditions EXCEPT (a) picketing (b) collective bargaining (c) the lockout (d) the closed shop.

Modified True-False Test

1. The *Norris-La Guardia* Act of 1935 guaranteed workers the right to organize and bargain collectively with employers.
2. State laws that require employers to carry insurance for the protection of their employees in the event of injury are called *fringe benefit* laws.
3. A strike arising from a dispute between two unions over the right to represent the same workers is called *a jurisdictional strike.*
4. An establishment that employs both union and nonunion labor is called *a specialty shop.*
5. Status secured by an employee through length of service with a company is called *expendability.*
6. A *shop steward* is a person chosen by the workers of a particular firm or department to represent them in the handling of grievances.
7. A technique used by labor in the 1930's to unionize the automobile industry was the *sit-down strike.*
8. The *Landrum-Griffin* Act established a minimum wage for workers producing goods for interstate distribution and sale.
9. The practice of forcing an employer to use more workers than a task actually requires is called *featherbedding.*
10. An addition to Social Security that provides health insurance for the aged is known as *Red Cross.*

Matching Test

Column A	*Column B*
1. checkoff	*a.* An association of workers formed for mutual benefit
2. blacklist	and protection
3. injunction	*b.* An establishment that hires only union members
4. lockout	*c.* The closing of a factory by an employer in order to
5. labor union	force employees to accept the company's terms
6. arbitration	*d.* The process of settling a dispute through an impartial
7. closed shop	person or agency
8. strike	*e.* Refusal of employees to work until their demands are
9. fringe benefits	granted
10. scab	*f.* An employer's record of active union workers that is
	kept for the purpose of denying them work
	g. Deduction by an employer of union dues from the
	wages of union members
	h. A nonunion worker hired to replace a striking employee
	i. A court order prohibiting a certain act, such as striking or picketing
	j. Gains for labor other than wage increases and improved working conditions

Essay Questions

1. (*a*) Discuss the following statement, giving reasons for your agreement or disagreement: "Both workers and their employers are harmed when a factory

closes down during a labor dispute." (*b*) Give *two* suggestions for improving relations between workers and employers.

2. (a) Compare the Knights of Labor and the American Federation of Labor as to organization, membership, and aims. (*b*) Discuss the reasons for the formation of the Congress of Industrial Organizations.

3. Between 1865 and 1965 working hours in manufacturing plants generally declined from over 65 hours a week to 40 hours a week. Explain how each of the following helped to cause this decline: legislation, collective bargaining, and changes in manufacturing methods.

4. a. State a specific provision of the Taft-Hartley Act with respect to each of *two* of the following: the closed shop, membership in the Communist party, and "cooling-off" periods.

   b. Show why you consider one of the provisions you have chosen to be either beneficial or harmful to labor union members.

5. (a) Discuss whether the steady march of the Industrial Revolution led to the rise of national labor organizations. (*b*) Explain why the federal government began to regulate organized labor.

6. Explain *two* ways in which federal legislation has aided labor since 1930.

7. Discuss *two* of the following statements, giving specific facts to support or reject each one selected:

   a. During the 19th century, labor experienced difficulties in organizing.

   b. Changed conditions contributed to the rapid rise in union membership after 1933.

   c. The Taft-Hartley Act marked a change in the government's policy toward labor organizations.

   d. Good labor-management relations are essential to the welfare of the United States.

8. a. In what *three* ways do labor unions aim to benefit workers?

   b. In what *two* ways does the Department of Labor seek to help workers?

9. The Social Security Act of 1935 was a "first" in its field of legislation. (*a*) What were the provisions of the original act? (*b*) Show *two* ways in which later enactments changed or added to the original law.

UNIT VIII. MODERN AMERICA EMERGES

Part 1. Immigrants Contribute to the Nation's Growth and Greatness

AMERICA, A NATION OF IMMIGRANTS

Except for Native Americans (Indians, Eskimos, and Aleuts), every person in America today is either an immigrant or the descendant of an immigrant. From the arrival of the first English settlers at Jamestown in 1607 to the landing of uprooted and homeless refugees from Europe and Asia in the years after World War II, America has been a land of refuge and opportunity.

The earliest settlers came to the New World chiefly to flee religious persecution or to seek their fortunes. Later immigrants came to escape famine, poverty, and religious and political oppression; to work on railroads and canals and in mines and factories; and to farm the Western lands. But whoever they were, wherever they came from, each brought something to contribute to America's diversity and greatness. Today, the United States is the sum of all these different parts.

Note: Unlike other immigrants, most African blacks came to this country involuntarily—as slaves. For more than 250 years, black slaves were deprived of the benefits and opportunities that other Americans enjoyed. After emancipation and a period of painful readjustment, they entered the mainstream of American society.

"OLD" IMMIGRATION

Until the 1880's most immigrants to the United States came from Northern and Western Europe. This "old" immigration consisted mainly of people from England, Scotland, Wales, Ireland, Germany, and the Scandinavian countries. The potato famine in Ireland (1845–1847) brought hundreds of thousands of Irish to America. The unsuccessful revolution of 1848 in Germany started a great migration of Germans to America's shores. After the Civil War, large numbers of Scandinavians came to settle the Western farmlands. Between 1820 and 1890 more than 12.5 million people from Western and Northern Europe migrated to this country.

"NEW" IMMIGRATION

Beginning in the 1880's, large numbers of immigrants from Southern, Central, and Eastern Europe came to America. This "new" immigration consisted mainly of people from Austria-Hungary, the Balkan states, Italy, and Russia (including Poland). They came to the United States to improve their living conditions, to secure better-paying jobs, and to escape religious persecution. They settled mostly in the large cities.

277

Immigration Since 1820 by Decades*

Years	Immigrants	Years	Immigrants
1820–1829	128,452	1910–1919	6,347,380
1830–1839	538,381	1920–1929	4,295,510
1840–1849	1,427,337	1930–1939	699,375
1850–1859	2,814,554	1940–1949	856,608
1860–1869	2,081,261	1950–1959	2,499,268
1870–1879	2,742,287	1960–1969	3,266,027
1880–1889	5,248,568	1970–1979	3,937,389
1890–1899	3,694,294	1980–1989	5,854,000
1900–1909	8,202,388		

* Immigration from the end of the Revolutionary War to 1820 is estimated at 250,000.

THE UNITED STATES BEGINS TO RESTRICT IMMIGRATION

Before 1882, America opened its gates to all who wished to come. The country was underpopulated. People were needed to dig canals; build railroads; populate the West; and work in mills, mines, and factories. While the country was expanding, it easily absorbed a great number of immigrants. As time passed, however, many Americans believed that immigration should be restricted because:

1. There was no more free land in the West.

2. Immigrants were willing to work for low wages, thereby threatening the jobs and the wage scale of American workers.

3. Illiterate immigrants became easy prey for corrupt politicians.

4. It was difficult for many of the newcomers to become Americanized. They continued to speak their own language and lived apart in communities of their own.

Starting in the 1880's, steps were taken to limit the flow of people from abroad. Laws were passed to keep out criminals, paupers, and insane and diseased persons (1882). Immigrants were required to pass a literacy test (1917). Migration from the Orient was curtailed by (1) the *Chinese Exclusion Act* (1882), which prohibited the entry of immigrants from China, (2) the *Gentlemen's Agreement* by which Japan agreed to keep its laborers from migrating here (1907), and (3) a ban on all Japanese immigration (1924).

NATIONAL ORIGINS QUOTA LAWS

After World War I, Congress passed the *Emergency Quota Act of 1921.* This was a temporary measure designed to stem the tide of immigrants who began to pour into the country from the war-scarred countries of Europe. It set a maximum quota of immigrants to be admitted each year, and it limited the number of people permitted from each country.

Limiting immigration and selecting immigrants on the basis of national origin became permanent policies with the enactment of the *Immigration Quota Law of 1924* and the *National Origins Act of 1929.* The latter provided that immigration into the United States from outside the Western Hemisphere be limited to 150,000 persons a year. A formula was worked out that fixed a quota of immigrants from each country in proportion to the number of people of that national origin living in the United States in 1920. No limits were placed upon immigration from Canada or the independent countries of Latin America.

The *McCarran-Walter Act* (1952) continued the national origins quota system but removed the ban against the immigration of Chinese, Japanese, and other Asians. (The act also set up procedures to prevent the admission of radicals seeking to overthrow the U.S. Government. In addition, it empowered the government to deport immigrants who joined a totalitarian group after their arrival here. This provision, held to be unconstitutional, was later repealed by Congress.)

DISPLACED PERSONS AND REFUGEES ARE ADMITTED

1. The Displaced Persons Act (1948). This law and several later extensions authorized the admission to the United States of more than 400,000 Europeans outside the regular immigration quotas. These people, displaced as a result of World War II, included survivors of German concentration camps, war orphans, and Eastern Europeans who had fled from their homelands when Communists took control.

2. The Refugee Relief Act (1953). This law and later extensions allowed escapees from Communist persecution in Hungary, Cuba, and Indochina, as well as refugees fleeing from political oppression in other countries, to enter the United States in numbers above the established quotas. These special programs have enabled more than 600,000 people to make new homes for themselves in America.

Main Sources of Immigration to the United States (1820–1990)
(in round figures)

Europe

Germany	7,100,000	Sweden	1,250,000	Denmark	375,000
Italy	5,400,000	France	800,000	Netherlands	375,000
Great Britain*	5,100,000	Norway	750,000	Switzerland	350,000
Ireland	4,700,000	Greece	700,000	Spain	275,000
Austria-Hungary†	4,300,000	Poland‡	600,000	Belgium	200,000
Soviet Union‡	3,450,000	Portugal	500,000		

Western Hemisphere

Canada	4,275,000	Dominican		El Salvador	225,000
Mexico	3,200,000	Republic	475,000	Ecuador	150,000
West Indies	1,175,000	Colombia	275,000	Argentina	125,000
Cuba	750,000	Haiti	225,000		

Asia

Philippines	950,000	Japan	450,000	Turkey	400,000
China	875,000	Vietnam	450,000	Hong Kong	300,000
Korea	600,000	India	425,000		

*From Great Britain came such national groups as the English, Scots, and Welsh.
†Immigrants from the Austro-Hungarian Empire included Austrians, Croatians, Czechs, Hungarians, Jews, Rumanians, and Slovaks.
‡Large numbers of Polish and Russian Jews emigrated to escape religious persecution and racial discrimination.

3. Refugee Act of 1980. Congress approved a systematic plan for the admission and settlement of refugees who are of humanitarian concern to the U.S. The number of refugees to be admitted each year would be determined by the President, after consultation with Congress.

NATIONAL ORIGINS QUOTAS ARE ABOLISHED

Many Americans thought that limiting immigration on a basis of nationality was unfair because it discriminated against many national groups. At the urging of President Lyndon B. Johnson, Congress passed the *Immigration Act of 1965,* which (1) abolished the national origins quota system, (2) limited immigration from countries in the Western Hemisphere to 120,000 a year, starting in 1968, (3) raised the annual limit on immigration from other countries to 170,000, with no more than 20,000 to be admitted each year from any one country, and (4) granted admission priority to immigrants who have close relatives in the United States, or who are refugees from communism, or whose skills and talents are needed in this country. (The *Immigration Act of 1990* raised the number of immigrants admitted each year to 700,000 in 1992–1994, and to 675,000 thereafter.)

HOW AN ALIEN BECOMES A U.S CITIZEN

To become a naturalized citizen, an applicant must be:

1. At least 18 years of age.

2. A lawful U.S. resident for five continuous years. (Short periods of absence from the country are permitted.) For husbands or wives of citizens, the period of residence is usually reduced to three years.

In order to acquire citizenship, an applicant must:

1. File a petition for naturalization.

2. Demonstrate the ability to read, write, and speak everyday English. (Exceptions: persons physically unable to do so, and persons over 50 years of age who have resided in the country for 20 years or more.)

3. Demonstrate a knowledge and understanding of the fundamentals of United States history and government.

4. Present two reliable U.S. citizens to serve as witnesses to the applicant's character, residence, and loyalty.

5. Renounce allegiance to one's former country and take an oath of allegiance to the United States.

Naturalized citizens have the same rights as native-born citizens and may hold any public office except that of President and Vice President. Children born to foreign parents living in the United States are considered native-born citizens. Foreign-born children under 16 become citizens when both parents are naturalized.

TERMS RELATING TO IMMIGRATION

Alien. A person living in a foreign country and not having rights of citizenship.

Americanization. The process of acquainting immigrants with American democratic ideals, customs, and traditions; teaching them the English language; and helping them adjust to the American way of life.

Citizen. A person either born or naturalized in the United States. An American citizen owes allegiance to the United States, receives protection from it, and enjoys all the political rights granted by the Constitution.

Emigrant. A person who leaves a country to settle elsewhere permanently. As seen from the country of departure, that individual is an emigrant.

Immigrant. A person who comes to one country from another to settle permanently. As seen from the country of arrival, the newcomer is an immigrant.

Immigration Quota. The number of persons from each foreign country permitted entry into the United States each year.

Literacy Test. When applied to immigration, this is a test given to determine whether aliens can read and write their own language. When applied to citizenship, it is a test given to determine whether they can read and write English.

Melting Pot. A term applied to a society in which many nationalities and cultures have been fused into a common product, as in the United States.

Naturalization. The process by which an alien becomes a citizen.

A SAMPLING OF IMMIGRANTS WHO CONTRIBUTED TO AMERICA

CANADIAN

James J. Hill—built the Great Northern Railroad from Lake Superior to Puget Sound (1890); earned the title "Empire Builder" for his role in the development of the Northwest.

CHINESE

I. M. Pei—architect who designed many important buildings in the United States and abroad, including the East Building of the National Gallery of Art in Washington, D.C.

An Wang—physicist who in the 1950's formed an electronics firm in the United States that soon was known worldwide for its word processors for offices.

Chien-shiung Wu—physicist who in 1957 helped disprove the widely held law of the conservation of parity.

DUTCH

Edward Bok—editor-in-chief of *The Ladies Home Journal* (1889–1919); wrote *The Americanization of Edward Bok* (1920).

Hans Kindler—founder and conductor of the National Symphony Orchestra of Washington, D.C. (1931).

Hendrik Van Loon—journalist, lecturer, and writer; author of *The Story of Mankind* (1921).

ENGLISH

Benjamin H. Latrobe—architect and civil engineer; built water supply systems for Philadelphia and New Orleans; modified plans for the national Capitol; designed many of the nation's foremost churches and public buildings in the early 1800's.

William W. Mayo—pioneer surgeon in the upper Middle West (see page 314).

Robert Morris—appointed superintendent of finance by Continental Congress, he served as financier of the American Revolution.

Thomas Paine—author of *Common Sense* (1776), a widely read pamphlet that influenced many colonists to support the cause of independence.

Joseph Priestley—an established chemist, his main research on oxygen and other chemical elements, and on the nature of electricity, was performed before he emigrated from England; his arrival in the United States in 1794 stimulated Americans' interest in the study of chemistry.

Anna Howard Shaw—physician and suffragist (see page 300).

Samuel Slater—"father of the American factory system" (see page 144).

FLEMISH

Leo H. Baekeland (born in Belgium)—chemist and inventor; a pioneer in the development of plastics, he discovered and produced the synthetic resin "Bakelite" (1909).

FRENCH

John James Audubon (born in Haiti)—artist, naturalist, and pioneer American ornithologist; his monumental work, *The Birds of America* (1827–1838), contains more than 1,000 life-size figures of some 500 species of birds.

Éleuthère Irénée du Pont—established a gunpowder manufacturing plant near Wilmington, Delaware, in 1802; became chief supplier of powder for federal government; firm developed into the giant chemical company known today as E. I. Du Pont de Nemours & Co.

Pierre Charles L'Enfant—served in the Continental Army as an engineering officer; drew up plans for the national capital on the Potomac River.

GERMAN

John Jacob Astor—fur trader and merchant; founded Astoria, at mouth of Columbia River (1811); dominated fur trading in upper Missouri Territory, Great Lakes region, and Mississippi Valley; invested in real estate in New York City; active in trade with the Far East; at time of death (1848) was richest person in America.

Albert Bierstadt—landscape painter; noted for scenic paintings of the Western wilderness; among his distinctive works is *Thunderstorm in the Rocky Mountains* (1859).

Franz Boas—anthropologist; published numerous studies of Eskimo life, Kwakiutl Indians of the Northwest, and primitive peoples in other parts of the world; his noteworthy writings include *Baffin Land*

(1885), *The Central Eskimos* (1888), and *The Mind of Primitive Man* (1911).

Fritz A. Lipmann—biochemist; won Nobel prize in medicine and physiology for work on enzymes (1953).

Ottmar Mergenthaler—inventor of the linotype machine (patented in 1884), which revolutionized typesetting and newspaper production.

Albert A. Michelson—physicist (see page 314).

Thomas Nast—political cartoonist whose dramatic cartoons helped expose the Tweed Ring in New York City (1869–1872); introduced the elephant as the symbol of the Republican party and popularized the donkey as the Democratic party symbol.

John A. Roebling—engineer; bridge builder; manufacturer; produced first wire rope in America; designed the Brooklyn Bridge to link Brooklyn and Manhattan across the East River; upon his death in 1869, bridge construction was supervised by his son, Washington A. Roebling.

Carl Schurz—helped organize the Republican party in Wisconsin; Union general in Civil War; pioneer in civil service reform; Secretary of the Interior under President Hayes (1877–1881).

Charles Steinmetz—electrical engineer (see page 314).

John Peter Zenger—journalist; laid the foundation for the American tradition of freedom of the press (see page 54).

HUNGARIAN

John von Neumann—mathematician; devised theory of games; made important contributions to quantum theory; participated in A-bomb and H-bomb projects (in the 1940's); pioneered development of high-speed computers.

©*Roger/Rothco Original*

"None of this would be here if we'd had stricter immigration laws."

Joseph Pulitzer—journalist; publisher of St. Louis *Post-Dispatch* and New York *World*; set up trust funds for establishment of a school of journalism at Columbia University and for award of Pulitzer prizes "for the encouragement of public service, public morals, American literature, and the advancement of education."

Leo Szilard—physicist; in collaboration with Enrico Fermi devised and patented a nuclear reactor (1942).

IRISH

John Barry—U.S. naval officer in Revolutionary War; performed daring exploits in command of American war vessels.

Edwin L. Godkin—founder and first editor of the weekly *Nation*; editor-in-chief of New York *Evening Post*; elevated standards of American political journalism; foe of spoils system and strong supporter of civil service in late 1800's.

Victor Herbert—composer and conductor (see page 312).

Augustus Saint-Gaudens—sculptor (see page 311).

ITALIAN

Mother Frances Xavier Cabrini—first U.S. citizen to be elevated to sainthood by Roman Catholic Church (1946); founded orphanages, hospitals, and schools; performed social work among Italian immigrants.

Enrico Fermi—physicist (see page 313).

Gian-Carlo Menotti—opera composer (see page 312).

Arturo Toscanini—world-famous operatic and symphonic conductor.

JAPANESE

Yasuo Kuniyoshi—painter, art teacher, and graphic artist; created war posters for Office of War Information during World War II; notable paintings include *Mother and Daughter* (1945) and *Amazing Juggler* (1952); first living artist honored by one-person show at the Whitney Museum of American Art.

JEWISH

Mary Antin (born in Russia)—author of *The Promised Land* (1912) and *They Who Knock at Our Gates* (1914).

Irving Berlin (born in Russia)—songwriter and composer (see page 312).

Albert Einstein (born in Germany)—physicist and mathematician (see page 313).

Felix Frankfurter (born in Austria)—influential jurist and adviser to President F. D. Roosevelt; Supreme Court justice (1939–1962) who wrote numerous works in the field of constitutional and administrative law.

Samuel Gompers (born in England)—labor leader; founder of AFL and its president for nearly 40 years (see page 266).

Sidney Hillman (born in Lithuania)—labor leader; co-founder of CIO; advocate of industrial unionism; adviser to President F. D. Roosevelt.

Simon S. Kuznets (born in Russia)—economist; his work on national income accounting became the basis for the concept of Gross National Product (GNP); awarded Nobel prize in 1971.

Isidor I. Rabi (born in Austria)—physicist; awarded Nobel prize for work in nuclear physics; conducted radar research during World War II and participated in the A-bomb project.

Haym Salomon (born in Poland)—merchant and financier; patriot who helped finance the Revolutionary War.

Isaac Bashevis Singer (born in Poland)—writer; awarded Nobel prize in literature for his short stories, children's books, and novels; his noteworthy works include *Gimpel the Fool* (1957) and *A Day of Pleasure* (1969).

Edward Teller (born in Hungary)—physicist (see page 314).

Selman A. Waksman (born in Russia)—microbiologist (see page 314).

Kurt Weill (born in Germany)—composer; created such well-known musicals as *Threepenny Opera* (1928), *Lady in the Dark* (1941), and *One Touch of Venus* (1943).

RUSSIAN

George Balanchine—choreographer and ballet master; exerted a profound influence on the development of classical ballet by his dramatic and inventive choreography; his founding of the School of American Ballet (1934) helped make New York City a major ballet center.

Wassily Leontief—economist; awarded a Nobel prize in economics (1973) for developing a method ("input-output") of analyzing a nation's economy that makes possible the prediction of future economic trends.

Vladimir Nabokov—author; an influential lecturer and professor of literature, he also wrote plays, poems, short stories, and the best-selling novels, *Lolita* (1955), *Pale Fire* (1962), and *Ada* (1969).

Louise Nevelson—sculptor; noted for her assemblages of bits of wood put together in abstract form; *Sky Cathedral* (1958) is one of her well-known constructions.

Alexander de Seversky—aeronautical engineer and aviator; invented a bombsight and other airplane devices; headed a company in the 1930's that manufactured fighter planes.

Igor Sikorsky—aeronautical engineer; built and flew first multimotor plane (1913); contributed to the design and development of the helicopter.

Igor Stravinsky—composer; achieved lasting fame for his musical scores of such ballets as *The Firebird* (1910), *Petrouchka* (1911), and *The Rite of Spring* (1913).

Vladimir Zworykin—electronics engineer, pioneered the development of television (see page 258).

SCANDINAVIAN

Ernst F. W. Alexanderson (born in Sweden)—electrical engineer and inventor; patented more than 300 inventions, many of which helped revolutionize the field of radar communications.

John Ericsson (born in Sweden)—inventor and engineer; developed the screw propeller, which transformed marine navigation; designed and built the ironclad *Monitor* for the Union Navy during the Civil War.

Jacob A. Riis (born in Denmark)—journalist, author, and urban reformer; sought to improve conditions in schools and tenements and to introduce parks and playgrounds in congested districts of New York City; wrote *How the Other Half Lives* (1890), *The Making of an American* (1901), and *Children of the Tenements* (1903).

Knute Rockne (born in Norway)—football coach at Notre Dame (1914–1931); helped popularize the game and established a reputation as a dynamic sportsman that has persisted to this day.

Ole E. Rölvaag (born in Norway)—educator and author; noted for his novels of Norwegian settlers in South Dakota in the 1870's, particularly *Giants in the Earth* (1927).

SCOTTISH

Alexander Graham Bell—inventor of the telephone; educator of deaf; founder of Bell Telephone Co. (1877).

James Gordon Bennett—editor and newspaper publisher; founded the New York *Herald*, one of the nation's most influential dailies in the mid-1800's.

Andrew Carnegie—industrialist and philanthropist; dominated American steel production in late 1800's; after retirement in 1901, devoted himself to distribution of his fortune for benefit of society; made large contributions for public libraries, public education, and international peace.

John Paul Jones—officer in Continental Navy; carried out raids against British shipping; attacked and captured British warship *Serapis* in most dramatic naval engagement of the Revolutionary War.

SPANISH

Severo Ochoa—biochemist; awarded Nobel prize in medicine and physiology for research on substances that control heredity (1959).

George Santayana—poet, essayist, and philosopher; wrote *The Sense of Beauty* (1896), *The Last Puritan* (1935), *The Realm of Truth* (1937), and *The Realm of Spirit* (1940).

SWISS

Louis Agassiz—zoologist, geologist, and educator; conducted extensive field trips to study the national history and geology of the Western Hemisphere; founded the Harvard Museum of Comparative Zoology (1859).

Albert Gallatin—politician, diplomat, and financier; as member of Congress (1795–1801), he served as leader of the Democratic-Republicans in the House and was a sharp critic of Federalist policies; as Secretary of the Treasury under Jefferson and Madison, he carried out a program of financial reform; he later helped negotiate the Treaty of Ghent (1814) and represented the United States abroad, as minister to France and England.

YUGOSLAVIAN

Louis Adamic—writer; author of *The Native's Return* (1934), *My America* (1938), and *From Many Lands* (1940).

Michael Pupin—physicist and inventor; pioneered X-ray research and development; invented numerous electrical devices to improve long-distance communication by telephone; wrote a Pulitzer prizewinning autobiography, *From Immigrant to Inventor* (1923).

Nikola Tesla—inventor; applied principle of rotating magnetic field, which he discovered in 1881, to invention of alternating current motor and to Tesla coil (transformer); developed an arc lighting system and an alternating-current power transmission system.

Multiple-Choice Test

1. The process by which an alien becomes a U.S. citizen is called   (*a*) conscription   (*b*) immigration   (*c*) naturalization   (*d*) registration.

2. Which statement is true of the immigration policy of the United States toward the end of the 19th century?   (*a*) Restrictions were placed on Mexican agricultural workers.   (*b*) Quotas were assigned to European countries.   (*c*) Criminals, paupers, and diseased and insane persons were excluded.   (*d*) Japanese immigration was limited.

3. An important reason why the United States did little to restrict immigration during most of the 19th century was that   (*a*) immigration from Europe was relatively small   (*b*) Congress lacked the power to pass restrictive laws   (*c*) labor unions favored immigration   (*d*) there was a continuing need to expand the labor force.

4. Which was a basic reason why few immigrants settled in the South during the period 1800–1860?   (*a*) fear of carpetbaggers   (*b*) unfamiliarity with farming   (*c*) competition with slave labor   (*d*) restrictions imposed by the federal government.

5. Which event occurred FIRST?   (*a*) negotiation of the "Gentlemen's Agreement"   (*b*) passage of the National Origins Act   (*c*) passage of the Chinese Exclusion Act   (*d*) passage of the Displaced Persons Act.

6. In the early 20th century, immigrants from Southern Europe to the United States settled chiefly   (*a*) in small towns along the Gulf of Mexico   (*b*) in the cities along the east coast   (*c*) on the farmlands in the North and Northwest   (*d*) on the farmlands of the Far West.

7. Which law permitted Asians to enter the United States under the quota plan?   (*a*) Immigration Quota Law of 1924   (*b*) National Origins Act of 1929   (*c*) Displaced Persons Act of 1948   (*d*) McCarran-Walter Act of 1952.

8. The Immigration Act of 1965   (*a*) excluded immigrants on the basis of racial background   (*b*) abolished the national origins quota system   (*c*) permitted unlimited immigration from countries in the Western Hemisphere   (*d*) forbade further immigration into the United States.

9. The largest number of immigrants came to the United States   (*a*) before 1870   (*b*) between 1870 and 1889   (*c*) between 1890 and 1919   (*d*) since 1920.

10. Naturalized citizens may hold any of the following public offices EXCEPT

that of   (*a*) U.S. senator   (*b*) U.S. representative   (*c*) justice of the Supreme Court   (*d*) President.

11. During the period 1840–1860, the largest number of immigrants to the United States came from   (*a*) Norway and Greece   (*b*) Scotland and France   (*c*) Ireland and Germany   (*d*) Italy and Russia.

12. A foreign-born person who resides in the United States but is NOT naturalized is   (*a*) a hyphenated American   (*b*) an alien   (*c*) a foreign agent   (*d*) a United States citizen.

13. Immigrants often encountered opposition in America because they   (*a*) made no useful contributions to American life and culture   (*b*) came from such places as Scandinavia and the British Isles   (*c*) learned quickly to speak English and to adopt American customs   (*d*) competed with Americans for jobs.

14. A person may become a United States citizen in any of the following ways EXCEPT   (*a*) by birth   (*b*) by having a friend or relative living in the United States   (*c*) by being born of American parents in a foreign country   (*d*) by the process of naturalization.

15. During the period 1880–1920, large numbers of immigrants came to the United States from all of the following countries EXCEPT   (*a*) Russia   (*b*) Italy   (*c*) Austria   (*d*) France.

Essay Questions

1. The immigration policy of the United States government has reflected trends in both the development and the problems of the country.
    a. State the government's policy in relation to immigration during each of *two* of the following periods:
        (1) 1789–1870   (2) 1880–1910   (3) 1920–1964   (4) 1965–present
    b. Explain what influenced the government's policy in *each* period selected.

2. a. Explain the attitude of *each* of the following groups toward immigration: early colonists; promoters engaged in the construction of railroads in the 1860's; and members of labor unions in the 1880's.
    b. Discuss *two* of the principal features of the Immigration Act of 1965.

3. Many immigrants have entered the United States and have contributed to its culture in many ways.   (*a*) Name *five* different national groups that have immigrated to the United States.   (*b*) Name *one* immigrant from each national group chosen who became a distinguished American and tell briefly what contribution that person made.

4. "The United States is a nation of immigrants."   (*a*) Write a paragraph explaining the meaning of this statement.   (*b*) Write a definition of each of the following: literacy test; America, the melting pot; Americanization; and American citizen.

5. Write a paragraph describing the necessary steps to be taken by an alien who wishes to become an American citizen.

6. a. Give *three* main reasons why immigrants have come to the United States.
    b. Describe the problems that new immigrants have faced upon arrival.

Part 2. Political, Social, and Cultural Progress From 1865 to the Present

IMPROVEMENTS IN GOVERNMENT

CIVIL SERVICE REFORM

The practice of appointing persons to government jobs as a reward for political loyalty was introduced on a large scale by Jackson in the 1830's. And succeeding Presidents continued the practice. The resulting evils led reformers (notably *Carl Schurz*) to agitate for the abolition of the spoils system. But not until President Garfield was assassinated by a disappointed office seeker in 1881 did the nation awaken to the need for changing the method of selecting federal employees.

With the passage of the *Pendleton Act* in 1883, a start was made in replacing the spoils system with the *merit system*. The act (1) provided for the selection of certain government employees by competitive examination, (2) prohibited their dismissal for political reasons, and (3) created a *Civil Service Commission* (now called the *Office of Personnel Management*) to supervise the operation of the federal civil service.

At first only a limited number of positions were filled by competitive examination. Under Cleveland, Theodore Roosevelt, Taft, and later Presidents, the merit system was extended. Today over 90% of the nonmilitary employees of the federal government are selected through civil service.

CONSTITUTIONAL AMENDMENTS EXPAND DEMOCRACY

1. Emancipation, Citizenship, and Voting Rights for Blacks. The *Thirteenth Amendment*, ratified in 1865, abolished slavery within the United States. The *Fourteenth Amendment*, ratified in 1868, granted citizenship to blacks and prohibited states from (*a*) enacting laws to limit the privileges of citizens, (*b*) depriving them of "life, liberty, or property, without due process of law," and (*c*) denying them "equal protection of the laws." The *Fifteenth Amendment*, ratified in 1870, declared that the right of citizens to vote shall not be denied "on account of race, color, or previous condition of servitude."

2. Popular Election of Senators. The *Seventeenth Amendment*, ratified in 1913, provided for the direct election of United States senators. Prior to that time, senators had been chosen by state legislatures.

3. Women's Suffrage. The *Nineteenth Amendment*, ratified in 1920, granted women the right to vote.

4. Eliminating "Lame Duck" Sessions of Congress. The *Twentieth Amendment* ("Lame Duck" Amendment), ratified in 1933, (*a*) ended the terms of senators and representatives on January 3 following the November election, instead of on March 4; (*b*) ended the terms of Presidents and Vice Presidents on January 20, instead of on March 4; and (*c*) fixed January 3 as the date Congress should convene each year.

This amendment abolished the short session of Congress that had run from December to March. In this session, "lame ducks" (senators and representatives who had not been reelected) continued to serve although their constituents had voted to replace them. The amendment also enabled a newly elected Congress to begin functioning almost immediately after the November elections, instead of 13 months later, as had been the practice.

5. Limiting a President's Stay in Office. The *Twenty-second Amendment*, ratified in 1951, limited a President to two elected terms. It also stated that no person may be elected more than once if he has served more than two years of another President's term.

The original Constitution set no limit to the number of terms that a President might serve. George Washington established a two-term tradition by declining to run for a third term. This practice was continued until 1940, when Franklin D. Roosevelt won a third term. He was elected to a fourth term four years later. The aim of the Twenty-second Amendment was to prevent future Presidents from holding office for unlimited periods.

6. Granting D.C. Residents the Vote. The *Twenty-third Amendment*, ratified in 1961, granted residents of the District of Columbia the right to vote for President. They had previously been excluded from national elections because the Constitution provided that presidential electors were to be chosen by the states, and the nation's capital is not a state.

7. Banning Poll Taxes. The *Twenty-fourth Amendment*, ratified in 1964, provided that a citizen could not be kept from voting in any federal election for failure to pay a poll tax.

In the past, many states had levied poll taxes as a condition of voting. This practice had been widely used in the South after the Civil War to keep blacks from voting. Over the years, most states had discontinued the practice. Only five Southern states still levied poll taxes at the time the amendment was passed.

8. Lowering the Voting Age. The *Twenty-sixth Amendment*, ratified in 1971, granted 18-year-olds the right to vote in state and local (as well as federal) elections.

Earlier, in 1970, Congress had authorized the lowering of the voting age to 18 in *all* elections. The Supreme Court upheld the right of Congress to grant the vote to 18-year-olds in federal elections. But it ruled that Congress had acted unconstitutionally when it lowered the voting age requirement for state and local elections. To prevent widespread confusion at the polls in future elections (separate registration books and special ballots or voting booths for young voters), Congress proposed the Twenty-sixth Amendment.

PRESIDENTIAL SUCCESSION

The Presidential Succession Act of 1947 placed the Speaker of the House and the President pro tempore of the Senate first and second in line of succession when there is no President or Vice President. Next in the line of succession are members of the Cabinet, starting with the Secretary of State. This law replaced the Presidential Succession Act of 1886 (see page 319). It was enacted to place elective officials ahead of appointive Cabinet officers in the order of presidential succession.

PRESIDENTIAL DISABILITY; VICE PRESIDENTIAL VACANCY

The original Constitution made no provision for a substitute Chief Executive in the event that a President became disabled and could not carry out the duties of the office. Nor did it provide for selecting a new Vice President if that office became vacant. To meet these eventualities, Congress approved the *Twenty-fifth Amendment* in 1965. Ratified by the states in 1967, the amendment provided that:

1. Whenever the President declares, or whenever the Vice President and a majority of the Cabinet declare, that the President is unable to perform the duties of the office, the Vice President shall take over as *Acting President* for the period of the President's disability.

2. Whenever the office of Vice President is vacant, the President shall appoint a new Vice President with the consent of both houses of Congress.

In 1973 the Twenty-fifth Amendment was used for the first time to fill a vice presidential vacancy when Spiro Agnew, charged with extortion, bribery, and income tax evasion, resigned that office. President Nixon nominated Representative Gerald Ford of Michigan to replace Agnew, and Congress approved his choice. The amendment was put to use a second time in 1974. Nixon, facing impeachment as a result of the Watergate scandal, resigned the presidency and was succeeded by Ford. The new President thereupon recommended Nelson Rockefeller, the former governor of New York, to fill the vice presidential vacancy. Congress confirmed the nomination.

FINANCING POLITICAL CAMPAIGNS

In 1972 Congress passed a law setting limits on the amounts presidential and congressional candidates may spend on political advertising, and requiring public disclosure of all election campaign contributions and expenditures. The following year, a Senate committee investigating the 1972 presidential campaign uncovered evidence of large illegal political contributions. This discovery led to the enactment of the *Campaign Finance Act* of 1974. It (*a*) set new limits on candidate contributions and expenditures, (*b*) provided public financing of presidential campaigns, (*c*) required candidates to submit full reports of their campaign receipts and expenses, and (*d*) created a *Federal Election Commission* to enforce the law.

OTHER POLITICAL REFORMS

1. Australian Ballot. This is a printed ballot listing all the candidates seeking election. Because it is marked by the voters in secret, it is also called a *secret ballot*. Originating in Australia, it was introduced into the United States in 1888. It gradually replaced such earlier electoral procedures as requiring people to call out their votes in public, or offering them a choice of preprinted ballots, each of which listed the candidates of only one political party. Today voting machines have largely replaced paper ballots, but elections have retained the two basic principles of the Australian ballot: a list of candidates and secrecy in voting.

2. City-Manager Plan. The voters of a municipality elect a board of commissioners or a council. That group then selects a manager to take over the operations of the government. The manager, a highly trained executive, assumes complete responsibility for the city's administration. This alternate form of city government was first adopted in 1908 by Staunton, Virginia, and has since spread to hundreds of other cities.

3. Commission Plan. The voters of a municipality elect a small group of nonpartisan commissioners. Each serves as the head of one department of the government. Jointly they act as a commission to carry out the executive and legislative duties usually performed by a mayor and a city council. First adopted in 1901 by Galveston, Texas, this form of government is now used by many other cities.

4. Direct Primary. The candidates of a political party are chosen by secret ballot at a primary election, rather than by a party convention. Popularized by Wisconsin in 1903, the practice spread to all the other states. Today almost every candidate for federal, state, or local elective office must win a primary election in order to run in the general election.

5. Initiative. A certain percentage of voters in a state or city, by signing a petition, can compel the legislature to consider a proposed bill. The initiative may also be used to place a proposed measure or constitutional amendment on the ballot. If approved by the voters, the proposal becomes law.

6. Recall. This reform permits a certain percentage of voters in a state or city to petition for the removal of an elected official before the expiration of that person's term. A special election is then held to decide whether to retain the official.

7. Referendum. If a certain percentage of voters in a state or city object to a new law, they can petition to have it submitted to the people for a vote. If it fails to receive the voters' approval, the law becomes invalid. In a number of states, constitutional amendments as well as certain bills that have been passed by the legislature are required to be submitted to the voters for approval before going into effect.

The initiative, recall, and referendum were reforms that grew out of the Progressive movement of the early 20th century. They were first employed on a statewide scale in Oregon, and later spread to other states.

8. Short Ballot. In state and municipal elections, the voter often has to vote for a lengthy list of officials, many of them minor ones. In most cases it is difficult to determine the qualifications of each candidate and to decide who is best suited for the job. The short ballot provides for

Sanders in The Kansas City Star

"Great Scott! We've lost our vote!"

the election of only a few major officials. All other offices are filled by appointment or by civil service examination.

"ONE MAN, ONE VOTE"

After 1900 there was a substantial shift in population from rural to urban areas. Nevertheless, most states failed to redraw the lines of congressional and state legislative districts to reflect this change. Therefore, according to the 1960 census, congressional districts in some densely populated urban centers contained as many as 900,000 residents, while congressional districts in some rural sections of the same state contained only 200,000 inhabitants. In such situations, a certain number of rural dwellers sent two or three representatives to Congress, while the same number of people in the city sent only one. Likewise, state legislative election districts had such population imbalances that in many instances about 30% of a state's inhabitants could elect a majority of the legislature.

In several decisions handed down in 1964, the U.S. Supreme Court ruled that (1) congressional districts within a state must be roughly equal in population, and (2) election districts of each house of a state legislature must also be apportioned according to population. The *one man, one vote* rule laid down by the Court means that one person's vote in an election is to be worth as much as another's. Its implementation has increased the representation of city and suburban dwellers and reduced the influence of rural voters.

EDUCATIONAL PROGRESS

EXPANSION OF EDUCATION

After 1865 the nation became increasingly aware of the importance of education. States passed laws making school attendance compulsory, the first such law having been enacted by Massachusetts in 1854. The number of public high schools increased rapidly. New colleges were founded. Vocational training programs were introduced. The following are some of the highlights of this growth of education:

1. The number of pupils between the ages of 5 and 17 receiving instruction in public schools rose from 7 million in 1870 to 15.5 million in 1900, 25.5 million in 1930, and 45 million in 1970. The present enrollment is about 43.5 million. Total annual expenditures for public education increased from $215 million in 1900 to $283 billion in the late 1990's.

2. In 1865 there were slightly more than 200 public high schools in the United States. In 1900 there were 6,000. Today there are some 20,500. Public high school enrollments rose from half a million in 1900 to a peak of 19 million in the late 1970's. Enrollment fell to about 12 million in the late 1990's.

3. College attendance rose from 225,000 in 1900 to about 15.5 million in the late 1990's. Today the United States has more than 3,500 public and private institutions of higher learning.

4. Parochial and private school facilities also expanded. The largest non-public system of education today is maintained by the Roman Catholic Church.

ADULT EDUCATION THRIVES

The *Chautauqua Institution*, organized in 1874 by John H. Vincent, a Methodist clergyman, stimulated the movement for adult education in the United States. Each summer thousands of people flocked to Chautauqua, in southwestern New York, to attend concerts, operas, literary readings, and educational lectures presented by famous persons. The idea spread, and "Chautauquas" were organized in other parts of the country. In the 20th century, schools and colleges established evening sessions for adults interested in furthering their education. Today millions of Americans devote part of their leisure time to learning.

FEDERAL AID TO EDUCATION

In the 1950's the school-age population began to expand at a faster rate than ever before in U.S. history. A rising tide of students engulfed the nation's schools and colleges. The cost of education rose sharply. Poorer communities in particular found themselves hard pressed to provide adequate educational facilities. Also, many able high school students could not afford to go on to college. At the same time, the nation was faced with a severe shortage of scientists, engineers, technicians, and teachers.

To meet the growing educational needs of the country, Congress in 1958 passed the *National Defense Education Act* (*NDEA*). It (*a*) authorized federal loans to college students needing financial help to continue their education, (*b*) extended fellowships to graduate students interested in college teaching careers, and (*c*) granted money to the states for the purchase of laboratory equipment, textbooks, and other materials

Fischetti, Reprinted by permission of NEA

"First we fill the hole with money—then push 'em together."

needed to improve teaching standards in science, mathematics, and foreign languages.

In the 1960's and 1970's the federal government appropriated additional billions of dollars to aid higher education. Federal funds were provided to expand existing colleges, establish new institutions of higher learning, and build teaching facilities for the training of doctors, dentists, nurses, and pharmacists. Federal assistance to needy and deserving students was also made available in the form of loans and scholarships. In 1972 Congress enlarged the government's student aid program by making every college student eligible for an annual Basic Educational Opportunity Grant of $1,400. (This sum would be reduced by the amount that the student's family could afford to contribute to his or her education.)

With the passage of the *Elementary and Secondary Education Act (ESEA)* in 1965, the government initiated a broad, multi-billion-dollar program of federal aid to the nation's public schools. In addition, the act also allotted money for textbooks and other instructional materials to students attending nonpublic schools; and provided for the creation of *supplementary education centers* to be shared by public, parochial, and private schools. These centers offered specialized subjects, such as music, art, science, foreign languages, and technical training.

A SEPARATE DEPARTMENT OF EDUCATION IS CREATED (1979)

Responsibility for administering the numerous educational programs of the federal government was scattered among many agencies and departments. At the recommendation of President Carter, Congress approved the creation of a separate, Cabinet-level Department of Education.

The new executive department assumed control of the following educational functions, programs, and agencies: (*a*) the Office of Education, previously housed in the Department of Health, Education, and Welfare; (*b*) the Defense Department's schools for overseas dependents; (*c*) the Labor Department's migrant education program; (*d*) some science education programs formerly run by the National Science Foundation; (*e*) college housing loans previously administered by the Department of Housing and Urban Development; and (*f*) the Agriculture Department's graduate school.

SLUMS AND POVERTY

SLUMS DEVELOP IN LARGE CITIES

With the spread of industrialization, more and more people moved from rural areas to cities and towns where factories offered work. Urban areas also expanded because of the increasing number of immigrants who came to America after 1880 and settled mainly in the larger cities. The number of urban centers with a population of 8,000 or more increased from 141 in 1860 to about 3,000 today. Cities with a population exceeding 100,000 rose from 19 in 1880 to 192 in 1990.

One of the most serious problems to arise from the growth of large cities has been the spread of *slums*. These are city areas where thousands of poor American and immigrant families live in overcrowded, multi-storied, poorly constructed houses called *tenements*. The buildings are often close together, one next to another, on narrow, treeless streets and alleys. Frequently they lack fresh air, sunlight, and proper sanitation facilities. They afford their tenants little privacy. They are subject to fires and other hazards. Children have no place to play except on littered streets, teeming with people and vehicles. Many of the people are too poor to feed or clothe their families properly or to obtain adequate medical care. Slum conditions lead to the spread of disease and encourage drunkenness, drug addiction, and crime.

STEPS ARE TAKEN TO AID THE SLUM DWELLER

Stirred by the wretched living conditions of the slum dweller, religious groups and public-spirited citizens formed societies to assist the needy with food, clothing, and shelter. Social workers devoted themselves to helping the poor and rendering vital community services. Two outstanding humanitarians were *Jane Addams*, founder of Hull House in Chicago (1889), and *Lillian Wald*, founder of the Henry Street Settlement in New York City (1893). The centers that they set up offered cultural, educational, and recreational facilities for recent immigrants and other urban needy.

Writers and social reformers such as Jacob A. Riis awoke the nation to the problems of the slums and agitated for civic improvements. In response, some municipalities (a) passed laws requiring landlords to provide facilities to improve sanitation, ventilation, and safety; (b) set up boards of health to safeguard the health of the people; (c) installed improved sewerage systems; (d) established sanitation departments to collect refuse and keep the streets clean; (e) set aside areas for parks and playgrounds; (f) built public hospitals and free clinics; and (g) adopted building codes and zoning ordinances to halt the spread of slum housing.

With the advent of the New Deal in the 1930's, the federal government began to cooperate with the states and cities in slum-clearance programs. Many old tenements were replaced by modern apartment buildings surrounded by lawns and play areas. Here low-income families could enjoy the advantages of good living at rentals within their means.

THE SLUM PROBLEM PERSISTS

Over the next 50 years, governmental agencies continued to conduct a vigorous campaign to rid the nation of its slums and the evils they breed. Despite the enactment of many low-cost housing and urban renewal programs and the expenditure of billions of dollars, the problem has not disappeared.

The European immigrants who made up a large part of the earlier slum population have long since elevated their economic status and moved away to better neighborhoods. They have been replaced, however, by new groups of urban poor: blacks who migrated to the cities from rural areas of the South; Hispanics from Mexico, the Caribbean region, and Central and South America; Asians from Korea, China, Vietnam, India, and Pakistan; and numerous others from distant lands.

Today's slums are often called *inner cities* because they are usually located in the oldest, most central section of a metropolis. Many of their occupants, lacking education and technical skills, either hold low-paying jobs or are unemployed. Some encounter discrimination because of their color or race. A large percentage of the slum residents depend for their survival upon financial assistance from the government (in the form of welfare, food stamps, medicaid, etc.). Contributing to the slum problem is an ever-growing number of broken families, where over-burdened mothers struggle to earn a living and raise their children without the presence and support of husbands and fathers.

WAR ON POVERTY

In 1964 Congress took a major step to correct the conditions that cause slums by passing the *Economic Opportunity Act*. This measure had been requested by President Lyndon Johnson as part of his *War on Poverty*. One of his objectives was to provide underprivileged young people the education and training needed to secure good jobs. The act, administered by the *Office of Economic Opportunity*, allotted federal funds for (a) the creation of special centers where school dropouts and unemployed youths could obtain remedial education and job training; (b) part-time jobs for needy students to enable them to continue their education; (*c*) community work projects; and (*d*) *VISTA (Volunteers in Service to America)*—a corps of volunteers who went into underprivileged neighborhoods to work with the poor.

After the Office of Economic Opportunity was disbanded in the 1970's, many of its activities were either transferred to other federal agencies or turned over to the localities and states. Starting in the 1980's, federal support for poverty programs was sharply reduced because of budget cuts, and much of the responsibility for providing help to the disadvantaged was shifted to the states.

A PROHIBITION AMENDMENT IS ADOPTED

The temperance movement had made much headway before the Civil War in bringing about the passage of antiliquor laws. After the war, the movement continued to press for the outlawing of liquor. The fight for prohibition was led by such groups as the Woman's Christian Temperance Union (WCTU), the Prohibition party, and the Anti-Saloon League. Many states passed laws curbing the manufacture and sale of intoxicating liquor, and by 1917 nearly half of the states had gone "dry." In 1919 the United States adopted the *Eighteenth Amendment*, which prohibited the manufacture and sale of liquor throughout the nation.

THE LIQUOR BAN IS LIFTED

The enforcement of prohibition became a major problem. "Moonshiners" distilled liquor illegally. "Bootleggers" sold the moonshiners' liquor and also smuggled liquor from abroad. Unlawful drinking places, called "speakeasies," sprang up everywhere. Liquor traffic fell into the hands of gangsters, who bribed officials and fought each other in gang wars. The violence and bloodshed, along with the general disrespect for the law, caused public opinion to turn against prohibition. In 1933 the Eighteenth Amendment was repealed by the adoption of the *Twenty-first Amendment*.

WOMEN'S RIGHTS

WOMEN ATTAIN GREATER FREEDOM AND EQUALITY

The machine age helped release women from the burden of household drudgery and opened many new opportunities to them for employment outside the home. Women became machine operators in mills and factories, clerical workers in offices, salesclerks in stores, and managers and proprietors of business establishments. They also entered the professions—such as law, medicine, and teaching. The number of working women rose from 2 million in 1870 to more than 7 million in 1910. About 63 million women today work or seek a paying job. This represents nearly 60% of the female population 16 years of age and over.

As women gained a greater measure of financial independence, they agitated more strongly for social and political equality. In the late 1800's and early 1900's, the movement for women's rights made much progress. More colleges opened their doors to women students. A number of states passed laws liberalizing the property rights of women and granting them the right to vote. In 1920 suffragists achieved their major political aim when the *Nineteenth Amendment* extended the vote to women throughout the country. As a result, women began to assume an increasingly important role in the nation's political life—not only as voters, but as candidates for elective public office and as appointive public officials. Among the notable "firsts" were:

Nellie Tayloe Ross—elected governor of Wyoming (1924); first woman governor; first woman director of U.S. Mint (1933).

Frances Perkins—appointed Secretary of Labor by President F. D. Roosevelt (1933); first woman Cabinet member.

Sandra Day O'Connor—appointed to the U.S. Supreme Court by President Reagan (1981); first woman Supreme Court justice.

Geraldine Ferraro—first woman nominee of a major party for Vice President; nominated by the Democratic party in 1984.

Madeleine K. Albright—appointed Secretary of State by President Bill Clinton (1997); first woman to head the Department of State.

OTHER OUTSTANDING WOMEN (A Sampling)

Susan B. Anthony—leader in the fight for women's suffrage; founded the National Woman Suffrage Association (1869). The Nineteenth Amendment is sometimes called the *Susan B. Anthony Amendment.*

Clara Barton—founder of the *American Red Cross* (1881), an organization that performs relief work in times of war and peacetime disaster. During the Civil War she organized supply and nursing services for sick and wounded soldiers and served as a nurse on the battlefield.

Ruth Benedict—anthropologist; studied Indian tribes of the Southwest and Northwest. Among her works is *Patterns of Culture* (1934).

Amelia Jenks Bloomer—19th-century social reformer; wrote and lectured on education, unjust marriage laws, and women's suffrage.

Pearl S. Buck—the only American woman to win a Nobel prize in literature (1938). She is best known for her novel *The Good Earth* (1931), a story of peasant life in China.

Amelia Earhart—pioneer aviator; first woman to make solo flight across the Atlantic (1932). She lost her life when her plane went down during a Pacific flight (1937).

Julia Ward Howe—supporter of women's suffrage and international peace; wrote the words to the *Battle Hymn of the Republic* (1862).

Helen Keller—blind and deaf since childhood, she acquired a well-rounded education and wrote many books, including *The Story of My Life* (1902) and *Out of the Dark* (1913); lectured widely on behalf of better treatment for the handicapped.

Margaret Mead—world-famous anthropologist; studied primitive societies in Southeast Asia; wrote *Coming of Age in Samoa* (1928).

Sally K. Ride—first American woman astronaut; journeyed into space as a crew member of the space shuttle *Challenger* (1983).

Eleanor Roosevelt—wife of President Franklin D. Roosevelt; humanitarian, newspaper columnist, and radio commentator. She was a delegate to the United Nations and headed its Human Rights Commission.

Anna Howard Shaw—prominent physician and lecturer on political rights for women; president of the National Woman Suffrage Association (1904).

Elizabeth Cady Stanton—pioneer in the women's suffrage movement; helped organize the first women's rights convention in Seneca Falls, New York (1848); first president of the National Woman Suffrage Association.

Sojourner Truth—despite lack of schooling, this former slave became a persuasive and well-known speaker in the cause of abolition. During the Civil War she raised funds for the Union; after the war she crusaded for black educational opportunities.

Harriet Tubman—called the "Moses" of the underground railroad, this former slave led more than 300 enslaved blacks to freedom in the years before the Civil War. During the war she served first as a nurse and then as a commander of scouts in the Union Army.

Frances Willard—educator and advocate of political rights for women; also headed the Woman's Christian Temperance Union and helped organize the Prohibition party (1882).

A PROPOSED EQUAL RIGHTS AMENDMENT IS REJECTED

Since 1923 feminists have been agitating for an end to all remaining forms of sex-based discrimination—in employment, property rights, and other areas sanctioned by law or custom. To meet their demand, Congress proposed an *Equal Rights Amendment (ERA)* in 1972. It declared that "Equality of rights under the law shall not be denied or abridged by the United States or by any state on account of sex."

The proposed amendment touched off much controversy. Supporters insisted that the ERA was needed to establish the legal equality of women as a fundamental principle of American democracy. Opponents argued that the ERA would (*a*) subject women to the draft on an equal basis with men, (*b*) deny women preferential rights to the custody of children in divorce proceedings, and (*c*) make many women liable for alimony payments to their former husbands in marital disputes.

Adoption of the ERA required the approval of 38 states, but only 35 voted for ratification within the allotted time. Although Congress extended the deadline for ratification, no additional support was forthcoming. In fact, five of the states that had approved the amendment voted to rescind their ratification. In June, 1982, the second deadline expired, and the Equal Rights Amendment was defeated.

CIVIL AND POLITICAL RIGHTS FOR BLACKS

BLACKS SEEK EDUCATIONAL EQUALITY

1. Segregation in the South. As noted in a previous unit, slaves in the South had few educational opportunities until their emancipation. After 1865 the Freedmen's Bureau and philanthropic organizations set up free schools for black children. Later the states provided schooling for all children. However, whites and blacks were placed in separate schools. (Separating one group from another on the basis of race, color, or ethnic origin is called *segregation*.)

In 1896 the Supreme Court, in *Plessy* v. *Ferguson*, held that segregation laws were legal as long as blacks and whites were provided with equal facilities.

2. The Supreme Court Declares Segregated Schools Unconstitutional. In 1954 the Supreme Court unanimously ruled in a landmark decision (*Brown* v. *Board of Education of Topeka*) that the doctrine of "separate but equal" was unconstitutional. It pointed out that:

a. "To separate them [black children] from others of similar age and qualifications solely because of their race generates a feeling of inferiority as to their status in the community that may affect their hearts and minds in a way unlikely ever to be undone."

b. "A sense of inferiority affects the motivation of a child to learn. Segregation with the sanction of law, therefore has a tendency to [retard] the educational and mental development of [black] children and to deprive them of some of the benefits they would receive in a racial[ly] integrated school system."

3. The South Desegregates Slowly. The Supreme Court ruling directly affected 17 Southern and border states and the District of Columbia. More than 3 million black students in this area were attending segregated schools. The border states and Washington, D.C., soon took steps to desegregate their educational facilities. In the region of the former Confederacy, however, opposition to the Court's decision was widespread. Many Southerners contended that integration would upset their entire social structure. They further argued that the ruling violated states' rights. Some Southern states flatly refused to desegregate their schools at all. Others made only token efforts to do so.

Over the years, however, considerable progress toward school integration has been made as a result of (*a*) desegregation orders by federal courts, (*b*) protests by civil rights groups, (*c*) threats by the federal government to withdraw aid from schools that failed to follow its desegregation guidelines, and (*d*) extensive busing of children to schools outside their immediate neighborhoods.

In 1964 about 98% of the region's black children were still enrolled in all-black schools. By 1968 this figure had dropped to 68%, and by the mid-1980's to less than 10%. In many communities, however, newly integrated public schools were soon populated largely by black students

Alexander in The Philadelphia Evening Bulletin

"Hold it!"

because many white parents had withdrawn their children and enrolled them in private academies.

4. The Problem in the North. Although Northern states have no laws providing for segregated schools, integration has also been a problem in that section of the country. Since youngsters generally attend the school nearest their home, schools in black neighborhoods are attended mostly by blacks. Civil rights groups (*a*) protested that these schools were, in fact, segregated schools, and (*b*) demanded that boards of education work for integration by sending white and black children to the same schools regardless of their neighborhood. To hasten school integration, they resorted to boycotts, demonstrations, "sit-ins," and picketing. Many white parents, opposed to the idea of having their children attend distant schools, organized counterdemonstrations and boycotts of their own. Nevertheless, Northern cities took steps to integrate their schools.

More recently, black groups have been agitating for (*a*) the decentralization of large city school systems, (*b*) community control of schools by the residents of each neighborhood, (*c*) more black teachers and administrators in schools attended by black children, (*d*) the admission of more black students to colleges, and (*e*) the introduction of Afro-American studies and other courses that would instill in black children a sense of pride in the cultural and historical contributions of their race.

To prepare culturally deprived children for successful achievement in elementary school, many communities have launched "head start" programs. These projects aim to upgrade the cultural and educational levels of pre-school children in slum neighborhoods.

BLACKS SEEK EQUAL VOTING RIGHTS

1. The Federal Government Moves to End Political Discrimination. *In theory*, the right of a Southern black to vote was no different from that of any other citizen of the United States. *In practice*, the Southern black was deprived of the right to vote, by one means or another, ever since the end of the Reconstruction Period. In 1957, for the first time in 80 years, Congress began to take steps to correct the situation.

• **The Civil Rights Act of 1957** (*a*) created a commission to investigate any denial of voting rights and of equal protection of the laws because of race, color, creed, or national origin, (*b*) established a special division in the Justice Department to handle civil rights cases, and (*c*) empowered federal courts to issue injunctions to prevent violations of voting rights and to bring to trial those who disobeyed such injunctions.

• **The Civil Rights Act of 1960** empowered the Justice Department to examine state voting records for evidence of racial discrimination. If, through a legal suit, such discrimination is proved, federal courts may appoint voting referees. The referees are authorized to issue voting certificates to people who have been prevented from exercising their right to vote.

• **The Voting Rights Act of 1965** (*a*) suspended literacy and character tests for voters in states and localities where less than 50% of the voting-age population was registered for, or had voted in, the presidential election of 1964, and (*b*) authorized the Attorney General to station federal examiners in such areas to register voters and prevent election abuses.

These enactments paved the way for the mass registration of black voters in the South. As their voting strength grew, blacks not only succeeded in electing many members of their race to public office, they also became a significant factor in state and national politics. White candidates running for office increasingly concerned themselves with issues important to blacks and conducted vigorous campaigns to win the black vote.

2. Voting Rights Protection Is Broadened. The Voting Rights Act of 1965 was renewed and expanded in later years. In 1970 Congress (*a*) extended the application of the law to Northern cities and counties where literacy tests were required and less than half the voting-age population had voted in 1968; (*b*) prohibited the use of literacy tests as a voting qualification throughout the country for the next five years; and (*c*) abolished residency requirements of longer than 30 days for presidential elections. And in 1975 Congress (*a*) broadened the act's coverage to include Hispanics, Asian-Americans, American Indians, and Alaskan natives; (*b*) required election officials to use bilingual ballots and other election materials in areas populated by voters who spoke languages other than English; and (*c*) imposed a permanent nationwide ban on literacy tests.

3. Black Participation in Government Expands. Thirty years ago there were virtually no black elected officials in the South and only a handful in the North. Today more than 10,000 blacks hold elective office

Herblock in The Washington Post

Literacy Test

in the United States—their number equally divided between North and South. Blacks have been elected mayor of such major cities as Atlanta, Chicago, Cleveland, Gary, Los Angeles, Newark, New Orleans, New York, and Washington, D.C. On the national scene, black representation in Congress rose almost 200% between 1971 and 1997—from 13 to 38 (37 in the House and one in the Senate). To strengthen their influence, black members of the House of Representatives have formed a *Congressional Black Caucus.* This group meets periodically to discuss policies that will protect the interests of the black community. Many blacks have also attained high positions in the executive and judicial branches of the federal government. Among the elective and appointive "firsts" were:

Andrew Brimmer—first black member of the Federal Reserve Board (1966).

Edward Brooke—first black elected to the U.S. Senate (1967) since reconstruction.

Shirley Chisholm—first black woman to be elected to the House of Representatives (1968).

Samuel L. Gravely, Jr.—U.S. Third Fleet; first black admiral (1971).

Daniel James, Jr.—Commander, North American Air Defense Command; first black four-star general.

Thurgood Marshall—first black justice of the U.S. Supreme Court (1967).

Colin L. Powell—first black Chairman of the Joint Chiefs of Staff, the highest military post in the U.S. (1989). ·

Robert C. Weaver—Secretary of Housing and Urban Development (1966); first black Cabinet member.

L. Douglas Wilder—Governor of Virginia (elected 1989); first elected black governor in U.S. history.

BLACKS SEEK EQUAL ACCESS TO PUBLIC ACCOMMODATIONS

The **Civil Rights Act of 1964**, enacted after more than a year of bitter debate, was the most sweeping of the laws passed by Congress to assure equal rights for blacks. It granted the federal government additional authority to speed school desegregation, curb violations of the voting rights of blacks, and end racial discrimination by employers and unions.

The law also outlawed segregation in public accommodations, such as hotels, restaurants, stores, and theaters.

Segregation in public accommodations was a practice that Southern blacks had deeply resented for many years. Their earlier efforts to gain equal access to these facilities, by the use of boycotts, demonstrations, and "sit-in" tactics, had met with some success. But these tactics had also aroused bitterness among many Southern whites and had resulted in outbursts of racial violence in many Southern cities. With the passage of the Civil Rights Act of 1964, desegregation of public facilities proceeded in a more peaceful and orderly fashion.

BLACKS SEEK EQUAL ACCESS TO HOUSING

For a number of years, efforts to obtain passage of a law to ban discrimination in housing were unsuccessful. Opposition to such a measure was finally overcome in 1968 as a result of (1) the active support of a coalition of Democratic and Republican liberals in Congress, (2) growing concern over civil unrest in the black ghettoes of the nation's cities, (3) the recommendations of the President's National Advisory Commission on Civil Disorders—including a recommendation for an enforceable federal open housing law, and (4) horror over the assassination of the black civil rights leader Martin Luther King, Jr.

The **Civil Rights Act of 1968** prohibited discrimination in the sale or rental of most houses and apartments and set up legal machinery for enforcing the law. About 80% of the nation's housing units were covered by the act. Exempted were apartment dwellings with four units or less, one of which is occupied by the owner, and single-family homes sold privately (not through a real estate agent). Also in 1968 the Supreme

© *Hy Rosen—Albany Times-Union/Rothco*

"Mountains Still to Be Climbed"

Court, in a far-reaching decision (*Jones* v. *Mayer*) that went beyond the newly enacted law, prohibited racial discrimination in *all* sales and rentals of property.

CULTURAL PROGRESS

LITERARY TRENDS AFTER 1865

In the post-Civil War period, authors devoted themselves to themes of America: the hardship of the pioneers, adventure in the Far West, and life in the various regions of the country. They also attacked existing social, economic, and political evils and recommended solutions to America's problems. As free public libraries were established, first in the large cities and then in the smaller towns, good books became available to more people, and reading became an increasingly popular pastime. Andrew Carnegie helped encourage reading throughout the country by donating large sums of money for public libraries.

Literary trends in the 20th century mirrored the ebb and flow of American life, as well as its richness and diversity. Writers of the early 1900's, preoccupied with the effect of economic, social, and biological forces on character and personality, stressed naturalism in their works. World War I produced a "lost generation" of cynical and disillusioned writers. The economic depression of the 1930's resulted in an upsurge of social problem novels. The 1940's witnessed an outpouring of books about World War II.

In the decades that followed, the nation's literary output reflected a mixture of diverse trends. A group of talented Southern authors wrote about life in that section of the country. Works by black writers attracted a large national audience. Also widely read were novels describing Jewish life in America. Some authors experimented with new techniques to dramatize their material—such as writing about serious subjects with a comical touch ("black humor"), and using a fictionalized approach to the presentation of factual matter.

Despite the competition of television, movies, and other mass media, books continue to retain their position as a major source of entertainment and instruction in America.

CONTRIBUTORS TO LITERATURE

Saul Bellow—awarded a Nobel prize in literature (1976), he is the author of *The Victim* and *The Adventures of Augie March.*

Stephen Vincent Benét—his great narrative poem, *John Brown's Body* (1928), deals with the struggle between the North and South during the Civil War.

Gwendolyn Brooks—first black poet to win a Pulitzer prize (1950), her noteworthy works include *Annie Allen* and *In the Mecca.*

George W. Cable—his short stories and novels describe life in old Louisiana. Among his works are *Old Creole Days* (1879) and *The Flower of the Chapdelaines* (1918).

Willa Cather—she realistically portrayed pioneer life in *O Pioneers!* (1913), *My Antonia* (1918), and other novels.

Stephen Crane—a novelist and short-story writer, he is best known for *The Red Badge of Courage* (1895), a powerful and moving novel about the Civil War.

Ralph Ellison—stressing the theme of racial identity, this black writer's 1952 work, *Invisible Man*, set a high standard of excellence for writing and was cited as "the most distinguished single work" published in the past 20 years.

William Faulkner—his short stories and novels, set in northern Mississippi, earned him a Nobel prize in literature. Among his many famous novels are *Intruder in the Dust* (1948), *A Fable* (1954), and *The Reivers* (1962).

F. Scott Fitzgerald—his novels reflect the disillusioned attitude of many writers during the 1920's. *This Side of Paradise* expresses jazz-age cynicism, and *The Great Gatsby* portrays the glamour, materialism, and shallowness of life among the newly rich in the post-World War I era.

Robert Frost—four-time Pulitzer prizewinner (1924, 1931, 1937, and 1943) and poet of the New England countryside, he won both popular and critical praise for such poems as *Birches*, *Mending Wall*, and *The Death of the Hired Man.*

Hamlin Garland—he described the ruggedness of pioneer life on the prairies in *Main-Travelled Roads* (1891) and *A Son of the Middle Border* (1917).

Joel Chandler Harris—his widely read Uncle Remus stories—appearing in such collections as *Uncle Remus, His Songs and His Sayings*

(1880), *The Tar Baby* (1904), and *Uncle Remus and Brer Rabbit* (1906)—are humorous animal legends that were derived from black folk tales in Georgia.

Bret Harte—a short-story writer who described frontier life in California during the gold rush, he is best known for *The Luck of Roaring Camp* (1868) and *The Outcasts of Poker Flat* (1869).

Ernest Hemingway—a novelist and short-story writer, he developed a prose style that influenced an entire generation of authors. Among his popular works, for which he won a Nobel prize, are *A Farewell to Arms* (1929), *For Whom the Bell Tolls* (1940), and *The Old Man and the Sea* (1952).

O. Henry (William Sydney Porter)—his short stories deal with life in New York City. Some of his best works were collected in *The Four Million* (1906).

Langston Hughes—part of the Harlem Renaissance movement of the 1920's, his poetry was characterized by racial pride, interest in African culture, and protest against discrimination. One of his best-known works is *Weary Blues* (1926).

Sidney Lanier—an outstanding Southern poet of the late 19th century, he is remembered for such poems as *The Song of the Chattahoochee* and *The Marshes of Glynn*.

Sinclair Lewis—he was the first American to win a Nobel prize in literature. His novel *Main Street* (1920) describes the narrowness of small-town life. *Babbitt* (1922) is the story of a typical businessman. *Arrowsmith* (1925) deals with the medical profession.

Jack London—among his adventure stories of the Arctic and the Klondike gold rush is *The Call of the Wild* (1903).

Edgar Lee Masters—his outstanding work is a book of short poems entitled *Spoon River Anthology* (1915).

Edna St. Vincent Millay—one of America's best-known poets of the 20th century, she received wide acclaim for *Renascence* and *The Ballad of the Harp-Weaver*.

Eugene O'Neill—a noted dramatist, he received a Nobel prize in literature (1936). Among his famous plays are *Anna Christie* and *Strange Interlude*.

James Whitcomb Riley—called the "Hoosier poet," he wrote humorous verses in dialect dealing with scenes of everyday life. Two of his well-known poems are *The Old Swimmin' Hole* (1883) and *When the Frost Is on the Punkin* (1911).

Edwin Arlington Robinson—three-time winner of the Pulitzer prize in poetry, he is noted for his long poem *Tristram* (1927).

Carl Sandburg—*Chicago Poems* (1915) interprets the vigor, noise, and confusion of the city. He also wrote poems of the prairie and of the common people, as well as a biography of Abraham Lincoln.

Upton Sinclair—in his novels he exposed existing social evils. *The Jungle* (1906) described the unsanitary conditions in the Chicago meat-packing industry. *Oil!* (1927) dealt with corrupt practices in the petroleum industry.

John Steinbeck—a Nobel prizewinner, he is best known for the novel *Of Mice and Men* (1937) and the Pulitzer prizewinning novel *The Grapes of Wrath* (1939).

Booth Tarkington—a novelist of American life, his widely read works include *Penrod* (1914) and other books dealing with the life and adventures of a young man. Also noteworthy are his Pulitzer prizewinning novels *The Magnificent Ambersons* (1918) and *Alice Adams* (1921).

Mark Twain (Samuel L. Clemens)—America's first important Western author, he gained a worldwide reputation for his story-telling ability and humor. *The Adventures of Tom Sawyer* (1876) and *The Adventures of Huckleberry Finn* (1885) are probably the best books ever written about boys. *Roughing It* (1872) and *Life on the Mississippi* (1883) picture life in the West.

Robert Penn Warren—a novelist and poet, he was awarded a Pulitzer prize in literature for his novel about a Southern governor, *All the King's Men* (1946); named the nation's first official Poet Laureate (1986).

Walt Whitman—known as the "poet of Democracy," his subjects were America and the American way of life. His most famous collection of poems is *Leaves of Grass* (1855). Among his other works are *Drum Taps* (1865), *Democratic Vistas* (1871), *November Boughs* (1888), and *Good-Bye, My Fancy* (1891).

Tennessee Williams—a popular playwright, he wrote such successful plays as *The Glass Menagerie* (1945), *A Streetcar Named Desire* (1947), and *The Rose Tattoo* (1951).

Richard Wright—the major works of this outstanding black novelist include *Native Son* (1940) and *Black Boy* (1945).

NEWSPAPERS AND MAGAZINES APPEAL TO A WIDER AUDIENCE

After 1865 newspapers played an increasingly important role in keeping people informed and influencing the opinions and outlook of the nation. Coverage of local and national news was expanded, and correspondents were sent abroad to report on foreign affairs. The Associated Press and the United Press (later the United Press International) gathered news for newspapers that contracted for their services. Columnists and political cartoonists helped mold public opinion. *Thomas Nast,* whose cartoons in *Harper's Weekly* helped expose the notorious Tweed Ring in New York City, was the first famous political cartoonist in the country. (Some influential editorial cartoonists of the 20th century are *Rollin Kirby, Bill Mauldin,* and *Herbert L. Block—Herblock.*)

To attract readers, newspapers added such features as comic strips, sports columns, women's pages, and crossword puzzles. Some papers sought to increase circulation by "yellow journalism" (playing up stories of crime and scandal, and overdramatizing news events with "scare" headlines and shocking photographs). This technique, first introduced by *Joseph Pulitzer,* publisher of the New York *World,* was taken up by

William Randolph Hearst, who built a powerful coast-to-coast chain of newspapers in the early 1900's. A new type of newspaper, called the *tabloid*, made its first appearance in the 1920's. Small in size, it presented the news in brief form, used many photographs, and featured crime stories and other sensational news items.

Today about 1,550 daily newspapers are published in the United States, with a combined circulation of about 58 million copies. The four largest dailies, each having a circulation of more than 1 million copies, are *The Wall Street Journal, USA Today, The New York Times*, and the *Los Angeles Times*. Three other influential papers, whose circulation exceeds 1 million only on Sundays, are the *Chicago Tribune*, the *Washington Post*, and the *Philadelphia Inquirer*.

Since nearly every family reads at least one newspaper each day, the press wields tremendous power over the opinions and attitudes of the American people.

The number and circulation of magazines also increased greatly. Today hundreds of different magazines cater to the diversified interests of the public. The leading magazines, each having a circulation in excess of 5 million, are *Odyssey, Modern Maturity, Reader's Digest, TV Guide, National Geographic, Better Homes and Gardens, Good Housekeeping, Ladies' Home Journal*, and *Family Circle*.

CONTRIBUTORS TO ART AND ARCHITECTURE

Edwin Abbey—a painter of historical subjects, his work includes a famous mural in the Boston Public Library, *Quest of the Holy Grail* (1890).

George Bellows—a popular painter of sporting events and urban scenes, his works include *Stag at Sharkey's* (1909) and *Dempsey and Firpo* (1924).

Thomas Hart Benton—a member of the regional school of painters that flourished during the 1930's and 1940's, he portrayed the lives and occupations of ordinary people of the Middle West in such paintings as *First Crop* and *Cotton Pickers*, and in his murals *History of Missouri* and *Arts of the West*.

Gutzon Borglum—a sculptor, he achieved fame for his figures of four great U.S. Presidents (Washington, Jefferson, Lincoln, and Theodore Roosevelt) carved on Mount Rushmore in the Black Hills of South Dakota (1939).

Alexander Calder—a sculptor, he popularized *mobiles* (moving sculptures made of colored spheres, disks, and wire) and *stabiles* (stationary sculptures made of such materials as wire and sheet metal). Among his well-known creations are the mobiles *The Mercury Fountain* (1937) and *The Whirling Ear* (1958) and the stabiles *Ticket Window* (1965) and *Man* (1967).

Mary Cassatt—an American impressionist who did most of her work abroad, she is noted for her use of color, for the simplicity and originality of her paintings, and for her affectionate portrayals of women and children. Examples include *Little Girl in a Blue Armchair* (1878) and *Caresse Maternelle* (1902).

Nathaniel Currier and **J. Merritt Ives**—these lithographers produced a series of prints that provided a vivid picture of American life in the 1800's. The Currier and Ives prints are still well known today.

John Steuart Curry—a 20th-century regional painter, he is known for such Middle Western scenes as *The Tornado* and *Kansas Wheat Ranch*.

Thomas Eakins—a master artist and teacher who stressed realism in his work, he is noted for such paintings as *The Surgical Clinic of Professor Gross* (1875) and *The Chess Players* (1876).

Daniel Chester French—his famous sculptures include *The Minute Man* (1873) at Concord, Massachusetts, and *Lincoln* (1922) in the Lincoln Memorial in Washington, D.C.

Robert Henri—a founder in the early 1900's of the "Ash Can School"— a group of painters who stressed the dramatic quality of everyday urban life and people—he is known for *Laughing Girl* and *Boy With a Piccolo*.

Winslow Homer—an outstanding watercolorist of the late 19th century, he is noted for his paintings of the sea and the people of Maine.

George Inness—this landscape painter is famous for his work *Peace and Plenty* (1865).

John La Farge—a 19th-century painter of landscapes and religious scenes, he is noted for his murals and his work with stained glass.

Georgia O'Keeffe—one of the most influential painters of the 20th century, she helped shape the course of modern art in America by her choice of subjects, interpretation and manipulation of natural forms, and use of color. Noteworthy are her landscapes of New Mexico and her cityscapes of New York.

Jackson Pollock—employing a distinctive abstract style of his own, he dripped color onto canvas to create such effects as mazes and rhythmic labyrinths. His works, which include *Portrait With a Dream* and *Autumn Rhythm*, stirred the art world during the 1940's and 1950's.

Norman Rockwell—a popular illustrator of books and magazines, his covers for the *Saturday Evening Post* portrayed American life with warmth and humor.

Augustus Saint-Gaudens—generally considered the greatest American sculptor, his famous statues include *Admiral Farragut* (1881), *The Puritan* (1885), *Lincoln* (1887), and the *Shaw Memorial* (1897).

John Singer Sargent—this painter is best known for his murals and many portraits of distinguished people of the late 19th and early 20th centuries.

Louis H. Sullivan—beginning in 1881, this architect designed many of the earliest tall buildings found in the large cities of the nation. He is known as the "father of the modern skyscraper."

James A. McNeill Whistler—his work, formally entitled *Arrangement in Gray and Black, No. 1: The Artist's Mother* (1872), but more commonly called *Portrait of the Artist's Mother*, is perhaps the best known painting by an American.

Grant Wood—his paintings, such as *American Gothic* (1930), depict the land and the people of the Middle West.

Frank Lloyd Wright—he enjoyed a long, successful career as an architect (1893–1959). His extremely modern designs for private homes and commercial buildings still exert a great influence on architecture around the world.

CONTRIBUTORS TO MUSIC

Samuel Barber—he is known for his orchestral compositions, such as *Adagio for Strings* (1936), and his Pulitzer prizewinning opera *Vanessa* (1958).

Irving Berlin—this composer of musical revues, musical comedies, and popular songs wrote *Alexander's Ragtime Band* (1911) and the often-sung *God Bless America* (1938). Among his stage successes are *This Is the Army* (1942), *Annie Get Your Gun* (1946), and *Call Me Madam* (1950).

Leonard Bernstein—a composer, conductor, and pianist, he is known for the symphonic composition *Jeremiah* (1942), the ballet *Fancy Free* (1944), and the musicals *On the Town* (1944), *Wonderful Town* (1953), and *West Side Story* (1957).

George M. Cohan—frequently heard works of this popular songwriter include *Give My Regards to Broadway* (1904), *You're a Grand Old Flag* (1906), and *Over There* (during World War I).

Aaron Copland—his orchestral compositions include *El Salón Mexico* (1937), *Billy the Kid* (1938), and the Pulitzer prizewinning *Appalachian Spring* (1944).

Daniel D. Emmett—a minstrel and songwriter, he composed *Dixie*, which became the war song of the South in the Civil War. He also wrote *Old Dan Tucker* and *Blue-Tail Fly*.

Stephen Collins Foster—he wrote many of America's best-loved songs, including some derived from black folk melodies. Among his popular songs are *O Susanna* (1848), *My Old Kentucky Home* (1853), and *Old Black Joe* (1860).

George Gershwin—he is considered the leading composer of symphonic jazz. His *Rhapsody in Blue* (1924) for piano and orchestra is performed frequently. His opera *Porgy and Bess* (1935) has won acclaim throughout the world.

Howard Hanson—among his compositions are the *Nordic Symphony* (1923), the opera *Merry Mount* (1934), and the Pulitzer prizewinning *Symphony No. 4* (1943).

Victor Herbert—he composed popular operettas, including *Babes in Toyland* (1903) and *Naughty Marietta* (1910).

Scott Joplin—the originator of ragtime—music featuring catchy melodies and syncopated rhythm—he is known for his compositions *Maple Leaf Rag* (1899) and *Treemonisher* (1911).

Jerome Kern—he composed musical comedies, such as *Show Boat* (1927) and *Roberta* (1933).

Frederick Loewe—a composer of musical comedies, he wrote the music for such well-known Broadway productions as *Brigadoon* (1947) and *My Fair Lady* (1956).

Edward MacDowell—one of America's foremost composers of classical music, he is known for his *Indian Suite* (1892) and *Woodland Sketches* (1896).

Gian-Carlo Menotti—an opera composer, he was awarded Pulitzer prizes for his operas *The Consul* (1950) and *The Saint of Bleecker Street* (1954). His *Amahl and the Night Visitors* (1951) is often performed on television.

Cole Porter—the popular musical comedies of this composer and lyricist include *Anything Goes* (1934), *Panama Hattie* (1940), and *Kiss Me Kate* (1948).

Richard Rodgers—he composed such well-known musical comedies of the 1940's and 1950's as *Oklahoma, Carousel, South Pacific, The King and I,* and *The Sound of Music.*

Sigmund Romberg—a composer of light operas, he wrote *The Student Prince* (1924) and *The Desert Song* (1926).

John Philip Sousa—he was a famous bandleader and composer of marches. His *Stars and Stripes Forever* (1897) is the most frequently played of all American marches.

Virgil Thomson—among his compositions is the opera *Four Saints in Three Acts* (1928) and the Pulitzer prizewinning musical score for the motion picture *Louisiana Story* (1948).

CONTRIBUTORS TO SCIENCE AND MEDICINE

Arthur H. Compton—a physicist, he won a Nobel prize for his discoveries in the field of X-rays and the nature of light (1927).

Carl F. and **Gerty T. Cori**—this husband and wife team of physicians and biochemists, co-winners of the Nobel prize in medicine/physiology (1947), investigated carbohydrate metabolism and isolated the enzyme that begins the body's conversion of starch into sugar.

Max Delbrück—a pioneer in modern molecular genetics, he was awarded a Nobel prize for his work in the "replication mechanism and genetic structure of virus" (1969).

Charles Richard Drew—an outstanding black physician and medical researcher, he pioneered the development of blood banks in the 1940's.

Albert Einstein—a physicist and mathematician, he was awarded a Nobel prize (1921) for his *theory of relativity* (explaining the complex relationships of space and time) and for his work on the photoelectric effect of light. He evolved the formula for determining the amount of energy that can be released from a given quantity of matter, and formulated a *unified field theory* (which attempts to include in a single mathematical formula all the laws of gravitation and electromagnetism).

Enrico Fermi—a Nobel prizewinning (1938) atomic physicist, he participated in the development of the A-bomb. He also discovered *neptunium* (a chemical element) and the existence of the *neutrino* (an atomic particle).

Robert H. Goddard—his pioneer work in the field of rocketry (starting in 1912) earned him the title "father of the modern rocket."

Irving Langmuir—this Nobel prizewinning (1932) research chemist developed the gas-filled tungsten electric lamp and the atomic hydrogen torch used to improve the process of welding.

Ernest O. Lawrence—winner of a Nobel prize in physics (1939), he invented the *cyclotron,* a device that produces the high-speed particles necessary for smashing atoms.

Joshua Lederberg—a biochemist, he received a Nobel prize in medicine/physiology (1958) for his "discoveries concerning genetic recombination and the organization of the genetic material of bacteria." His work opened up a new branch of biological research known as bacterial genetics.

Maria G. Mayer—a physicist, she was awarded a Nobel prize (1963) for her investigations into the structure of the atomic nucleus.

Charles H. and **William J. Mayo**—the sons of a well-known physician, these surgeons and medical researchers (together with their father, William Worrall Mayo) founded the Mayo Clinic in Rochester, Minnesota, in 1889. Here patients from the entire world come to be treated for their ailments by an outstanding staff of specialists.

Albert A. Michelson—a Nobel prizewinner in physics for his experiments and discoveries in the field of optics and optical measurement (1907), he accurately measured the speed of light.

Robert A. Millikan—for his work in contributing to our knowledge of electrons, cosmic rays, and X-rays, he was awarded a Nobel prize in physics in 1923.

Thomas Hunt Morgan—his Nobel prizewinning experiments and studies on heredity and mutations in the fruit fly (1933) laid the basis for the development of the science of genetics.

Linus C. Pauling—winner of a Nobel prize in chemistry (1954), he made important contributions to the understanding of the structure of molecules and of the forces that hold atoms together.

Walter Reed—an army surgeon and bacteriologist, he contributed to the conquest of yellow fever by discovering in 1900 that this dreaded disease is transmitted by a mosquito.

Jonas E. Salk—a specialist in virus research, he developed a vaccine to combat paralytic polio (1953). Congress awarded him the Medal for Distinguished Civilian Achievement for his work.

Glenn T. Seaborg—a Nobel prizewinning chemist (1951), he discovered such new elements as plutonium, americium, and curium.

Charles P. Steinmetz—a mathematician and electrical engineer, his pioneering work during the 1890's on the theory of alternating current and its application to generators and motors contributed greatly to the commercial development of electrical power.

Leo Szilard—a physicist, he helped create the first sustained nuclear reaction (1942).

Edward Teller—an atomic scientist, his work in nuclear physics led to the development of the hydrogen bomb (H-bomb) in the 1950's.

Harold C. Urey—this Nobel prizewinning chemist discovered a form of hydrogen called heavy hydrogen (1934).

Selman Waksman—he discovered streptomycin, terramycin, and other antibiotics, which have proved highly effective in combatting many diseases. He was awarded a Nobel prize in medicine/physiology in 1952.

James D. Watson—a geneticist, he shared a Nobel prize in medicine/physiology (1962) with two British biophysicists for the discovery of the molecular structure of DNA—the substance that transmits genetic information from one generation to the next.

Rosalyn S. Yalow—a medical physicist, she received the Nobel prize in medicine/physiology (1977) for the discovery of radioimmunoassay—

a method of measuring the concentrations of hundreds of biologically active substances, many of which are present in the body in such minute quantities that they are undetectable by any other means.

Matching Test

Column A	Column B
1. Andrew Carnegie	*a.* Painted scenes of the sea
2. Thomas Nast	*b.* Introduced the technique of "yellow jour-
3. Carl Sandburg	nalism" in newspaper publishing
4. Winslow Homer	*c.* Developed a polio vaccine
5. Joseph Pulitzer	*d.* Composed songs based on black folk melodies
6. Carl Schurz	*e.* Wrote an outstanding biography of Abraham
7. Jonas Salk	Lincoln
8. Bret Harte	*f.* Donated money to establish libraries
9. Stephen Collins Foster	*g.* Wrote about frontier life in the West
10. John H. Vincent	*h.* Agitated for civil service reform
	i. Pioneered in the field of political cartooning
	j. Pioneered the movement for adult education

Identification Test

1. I was an untiring advocate of votes for women. An amendment to the Constitution of the United States is sometimes called by my name.
2. Several years of my life were spent as a teacher and government clerk. During the Civil War, I organized supply and nursing services for sick and wounded soldiers, and served as a volunteer nurse on the battlefields. After the war, I founded the American Red Cross.
3. As wife of a President of the United States, I lived in the White House for about 12 years. Later I represented our country in the United Nations General Assembly and was chairman of the UN commission that wrote the Universal Declaration of Human Rights.
4. I was a doctor who conducted experiments in Cuba which proved that yellow fever was carried by a mosquito. My discovery helped to conquer this dreaded disease. A famous military hospital in Washington, D.C., is named in my honor.
5. Born in Denmark, I emigrated to the United States and became a newspaper reporter in New York City. Sympathizing with the plight of the city's poor, I worked to improve conditions in the schools and tenements and to introduce parks and playgrounds in congested districts. The books I wrote, including *How the Other Half Lives* and *Children of the Tenements*, aroused public interest in the problems of slum dwellers.

Multiple-Choice Test I

1. The Twenty-first Amendment to the federal Constitution repealed an amendment dealing with (*a*) the income tax (*b*) suffrage (*c*) prohibition (*d*) the election of senators.
2. The Pendleton Act helped to correct the evils of (*a*) the short ballot (*b*) the spoils system (*c*) low wages in factories (*d*) high railroad rates.

3. If the Vice President of the United States should die while in office, (a) the President would appoint a new Vice President with the consent of Congress (b) the office would remain vacant until the next election (c) the Speaker of the House would serve as the Acting Vice President (d) a special election would be held to select a replacement.

4. The appointment to office of government employees on the basis of competitive examinations is called the (a) patroon system (b) spoils system (c) merit system (d) selective service system.

5. All of the following amendments to the federal Constitution helped expand political democracy EXCEPT the (a) Fifteenth Amendment (b) Eighteenth Amendment (c) Nineteenth Amendment (d) Twenty-fourth Amendment.

6. The "initiative" provides a method of (a) submitting a law to voters for their approval after it has passed the legislature (b) removing inefficient public officials (c) proposing legislation by the voters (d) requiring the Supreme Court to decide the constitutionality of a law.

7. The *Chautauqua Institution* is (a) a biological research center (b) an Ivy League college in New England (c) a cultural center for adults (d) a federal penitentiary.

8. Which democratic idea was LAST to develop in the United States? (a) separation of church and state (b) universal suffrage (c) representative government (d) freedom of speech and press.

9. A referendum is required as the final step in (a) admitting a state to the Union (b) selecting a federal judge (c) amending many state constitutions (d) approving presidential appointments.

10. In 1954 the Supreme Court ruled against (a) segregation in public schools (b) federal buying of farm surpluses (c) the use of federal funds for low-cost housing (d) federal aid to education.

11. A person may not be elected President of the United States more than twice, according to (a) a provision of the original Constitution (b) an amendment to the Constitution (c) a law of Congress (d) custom.

12. A famous writer, known as "the poet of democracy," was (a) Edgar Allan Poe (b) Sidney Lanier (c) Walt Whitman (d) Booth Tarkington.

13. Which clause of the U.S. Constitution, as adopted in 1787, has been changed by the amending process? (a) "The House of Representatives shall have the sole power of impeachment." (b) "The Senate of the United States shall be composed of two senators from each state, chosen by the legislature thereof." (c) "The Congress shall assemble at least once in every year." (d) "All bills for raising revenue shall originate in the House of Representatives."

14. Since the adoption of the Twentieth Amendment to the Constitution, Congress convenes each year on (a) December 10 (b) January 3 (c) January 20 (d) March 4.

15. The direct primary makes possible the selection of party candidates for public office by (a) enrolled voters (b) legislative leaders (c) party convention (d) political bosses.

Multiple-Choice Test II

1. Which two men drew upon the South as background for much of their work? (a) Bret Harte and Grant Wood (b) William Faulkner and Joel

Chandler Harris (*c*) Sinclair Lewis and Thomas Hart Benton (*d*) Hamlin Garland and George Inness.

2. The U.S. Supreme Court ruled in 1964 that the distribution of seats in state legislatures must reflect the "one man, one vote" principle. As a result of this ruling, (*a*) urban districts lost control of state legislatures (*b*) the political influence of rural districts was reduced (*c*) the legal voting age was lowered (*d*) people who abstained from voting lost the right of suffrage.

3. An objective of the Civil Rights Act of 1957 was to (*a*) make lynching a federal crime (*b*) outlaw poll taxes (*c*) strengthen the provisions of the Fair Labor Standards Act (*d*) protect the voting rights of citizens.

4. In which pair is the first item an immediate cause of the second? (*a*) election of John Quincy Adams—Twelfth Amendment (*b*) assassination of President Lincoln—election of Ulysses S. Grant (*c*) assassination of President Garfield—the Pendleton Act (*d*) election of Rutherford B. Hayes—start of reconstruction.

5. The theory of states' rights, under which some Southern states resisted desegregation in the 1950's and 1960's, can be traced as far back in United States history as the (*a*) Hartford Convention (*b*) Whisky Rebellion (*c*) South Carolina Ordinance of Nullification (*d*) Kentucky and Virginia Resolutions.

6. All of the following are associated with well-known patriotic music EXCEPT (*a*) Irving Berlin (*b*) John Philip Sousa (*c*) Francis Scott Key (*d*) Norman Rockwell.

7. All of the following writers are correctly paired with their works EXCEPT (*a*) Stephen Vincent Benét—*John Brown's Body* (*b*) Sinclair Lewis—*The Jungle* (*c*) Jack London—*The Call of the Wild* (*d*) Pearl S. Buck—*The Good Earth*.

8. All of the following terms were in common use during the Prohibition Era EXCEPT (*a*) moonshiner (*b*) scalawag (*c*) bootlegger (*d*) speakeasy.

9. All of the following were noted American poets EXCEPT (*a*) Robert Frost (*b*) Edgar Lee Masters (*c*) Grant Wood (*d*) Edwin Arlington Robinson.

10. All of the following were outstanding American sculptors EXCEPT (*a*) Augustus Saint-Gaudens (*b*) Daniel Chester French (*c*) Edward MacDowell (*d*) Gutzon Borglum.

11. A political device that permits voters to petition for the removal of an elected official before his or her term expires is (*a*) the short ballot (*b*) lobbying (*c*) the recall (*d*) the commission plan.

12. Residents of Washington, D.C., were granted the right to vote in presidential elections by (*a*) an act of Congress (*b*) a referendum of the voters in the nation's capital (*c*) the adoption of the Twenty-third Amendment (*d*) a proclamation of the President.

13. Until their terms expire, members of Congress who have not been reelected are known as (*a*) ugly ducklings (*b*) sitting bulls (*c*) lame ducks (*d*) dogs in the manger.

14. Direct federal aid to public schools was initiated by the federal government in 1965 with the enactment of the (*a*) NDEA (*b*) TVA (*c*) ESEA (*d*) WCTU.

15. Segregation in hotels, restaurants, and other public accommodations was outlawed by Congress with the passage of the (*a*) Higher Education Act

of 1965 (*b*) Voting Rights Act of 1965 (*c*) Civil Rights Act of 1957 (*d*) Civil Rights Act of 1964.

Essay Questions

1. Explain important changes that have occurred in the United States since the end of the Civil War in each of *two* of the following fields: education, women's rights, and social welfare.

2. a. Describe the changes that occurred in newspaper publishing after 1865.
   b. Explain how a free press helps to safeguard democratic principles.

3. "The past 100 years have brought the U.S. Constitution and the laws of the federal government nearer to the ideals expressed in the Declaration of Independence."

   Discuss this statement, supporting your position with specific examples from *both* of the following: (*a*) the Constitution (*b*) the laws of the federal government.

4. a. State an important accomplishment of each of *five* of the following women: Julia Ward Howe, Frances Perkins, Lillian Wald, Jane Addams, Amelia Earhart, Helen Keller, and Harriet Tubman.
   b. Discuss briefly *two* reasons why new opportunities have opened to women during the 20th century.

5. a. Select the name that does NOT belong in *each* of the groups.
      (1) *Writers:* Willa Cather, Mary Cassatt, Ernest Hemingway, Hamlin Garland
      (2) *Painters:* Eugene O'Neill, John Steuart Curry, George Inness, John Singer Sargent
      (3) *Composers:* Aaron Copland, George Gershwin, John Steinbeck, Cole Porter
      (4) *Scientists:* Gerty T. Cori, Frank Lloyd Wright, Maria G. Mayer, Rosalyn S. Yalow
   b. Choose *two* of the persons above who are NOT in their correct group and explain for what *each* of these persons is famous.

6. Classify each of *ten* of the following as a scientist, writer, musician, painter, or sculptor.

Tennessee Williams	Victor Herbert
Ernest O. Lawrence	James McNeill Whistler
Richard Rodgers	Alexander Calder
Jerome Kern	Edwin Abbey
Charles Richard Drew	George W. Cable
Samuel L. Clemens	Jackson Pollock

7. a. Choose *three* of the following terms and give the meaning of each: direct election of senators, universal suffrage, merit system, city-manager plan, direct primary, and short ballot.
   b. Explain how *two* of the terms you have chosen have helped to obtain and maintain good government.

Part 3. A Chronology of Presidents (1881–1921)

GARFIELD IS ASSASSINATED; ARTHUR SUCCEEDS HIM

At the Republican National Convention in 1880, two rival factions of the party—the "Stalwarts" and the "Half Breeds"—were unable to agree on a candidate. On the 36th ballot, James A. Garfield of Ohio, a "dark horse" acceptable to both sides, secured the nomination. He defeated his Democratic opponent and succeeded Hayes as President. Four months later, in 1881, Garfield was fatally shot by a mentally deranged and disappointed office seeker. Chester A. Arthur of New York, the Vice President, thereupon became the nation's Chief Executive. Aided by public reaction to Garfield's assassination, the Arthur administration initiated civil service reform by obtaining passage of the *Pendleton Act* (1883). It also took the first steps toward strengthening and modernizing the U.S. Navy by authorizing the replacement of the fleet's antiquated, wooden vessels with steel ships.

THE FIRST POST-WAR DEMOCRATIC PRESIDENT

In 1884 the Democrats chose Grover Cleveland as their candidate for the presidency and the Republicans nominated James G. Blaine. Some Republican leaders opposed Blaine's selection because they viewed him as a foe of civil service reform. These "Mugwumps" (as they were nicknamed) switched their support to Cleveland.

The election campaign was marked by charges and countercharges of corruption and misconduct. A week before the election, a Republican spokesperson for a group of Protestant ministers described the Democrats as the party of "Rum, Romanism, and Rebellion." Blaine neither condemned this prejudicial statement nor criticized the person who had made it. His failure to do so may have cost him the election. He lost New York, a key state with a large Catholic population, by 1,150 votes, and the country as a whole by 63,000 votes. Thus, for the first time since 1856, the Democrats succeeded in winning a presidential election.

Cleveland, a native of New Jersey, had studied law in Buffalo, New York; had been an assistant district attorney and sheriff of Erie County; and had served as mayor of Buffalo and as governor of New York before assuming the presidency. An independent, honest administrator, Cleveland hated corruption. His guiding principle was "a public office is a public trust." He fought against the spoils system, extended the civil service, strengthened the power of the executive branch of the government, advocated conservation of natural resources, and favored lower tariffs.

The following were some of the accomplishments of Cleveland's first administration (1885–1889): (1) The *Interstate Commerce Act* outlawed unfair practices by railroads. (2) The *Hatch Act* encouraged scientific research in agriculture. (3) The *Dawes Act* distributed reservation land to individual Indian families. (4) The *Presidential Succession Act of 1886* provided that Cabinet members, in the order of the creation of their

319

departments, succeed to the presidency if both the President and Vice President died, resigned, or were removed from office.

HARRISON DEFEATS CLEVELAND IN 1888

In 1888 the Democrats nominated Cleveland to run for a second term and the Republicans chose Benjamin Harrison, a grandson of former President William H. Harrison, as their candidate. The main issue of the campaign was the tariff. The Republicans came out for a high protective tariff, claiming that it was needed to protect the nation's prosperity. Cleveland continued to advocate lower tariffs. In the election Harrison polled fewer popular votes than Cleveland, but he carried the key industrial states by small margins. As a result he won a majority of the electoral votes and became the 23rd President.

During Harrison's term of office: (1) Six Western states were admitted to the Union. (2) Western settlement progressed to the point where the Census Director was able to report (in 1890) that a frontier line no longer existed. (3) The *Sherman Antitrust Act* was passed. (4) The *McKinley Tariff Act* raised tariffs on imports to the highest level up to that time.

CLEVELAND IS ELECTED FOR ANOTHER TERM IN 1892

Public disapproval of the McKinley Tariff Act, bitter labor disputes, discontent among Western farmers and silver miners, and the emergence of the Populist party reduced the strength of the Republican party. In the election of 1892, with Cleveland and Harrison the major contenders once again, the Democrats won a sweeping victory. They elected Cleveland to the presidency and gained control of both houses of Congress. Although Cleveland was the 22nd person to serve as President, he is known as both the 22nd and 24th President because his two terms were not consecutive.

1. Domestic Affairs. Cleveland's second term was troubled by a serious business decline, the *Panic of 1893*. Banks failed, railroads went bankrupt, factories and mills closed down, and unemployment soared. "Coxey's Army," a band of unemployed led by Jacob S. Coxey of Ohio, marched on Washington to demand that the government provide work programs for the jobless. In addition, serious strikes broke out as still-employed workers resisted attempts to cut their wages.

Cleveland felt that to end the depression he had to maintain the gold standard and keep the nation's gold reserve from shrinking. He therefore (a) called a special session of Congress and forced the repeal of the Sherman Silver Purchase Act, and (b) purchased a large supply of gold from a group of bankers headed by J. Pierpont Morgan. These moves antagonized the advocates of free silver, thereby causing a split in the Democratic party. Cleveland also lost the support of organized labor when he sent troops to keep the mails moving during the Pullman strike, a move that helped break the strike.

2. Foreign Affairs. In a boundary dispute between Venezuela and British Guiana in South America, Cleveland invoked the Monroe

Doctrine (1895). He insisted that the United States would resist any attempt by Great Britain to extend its territory at the expense of Venezuela. As a result of his strong stand, England agreed to submit the problem to a board of arbitration, and the issue was settled peaceably. Also during Cleveland's second administration, the United States recognized the Republic of Hawaii (1894), and the Cubans tried to overthrow their Spanish rulers (1895).

THE REPUBLICANS RETURN TO POWER WITH McKINLEY

The Republicans anticipated an easy victory in 1896 because (1) the Democrats were divided on the issue of the gold standard versus free silver, (2) Cleveland's domestic policies had aroused much criticism, and (3) the Democrats had failed to restore prosperity. The Republicans nominated William McKinley of Ohio for the presidency on a platform supporting the gold standard and a high protective tariff.

The Democrats, controlled by the advocates of easy money and currency reform, came out for free and unlimited coinage of silver. They selected William Jennings Bryan of Nebraska as their standard-bearer. The Populist party joined forces with the Democrats in supporting Bryan. In the hectic campaign that followed, Bryan set himself up as the champion of the common people and pictured his opponent as the representative of big business. The Republicans, in turn, denounced Bryan as a "revolutionist" and predicted that economic chaos would result if the Democrats won. Bryan was strong in the West and South, but McKinley carried the large industrial states in the Middle West and East, and won the election.

Prosperity returned to the nation while McKinley was in office. During his administration: (1) Congress raised tariffs on imports to a new high by enacting the *Dingley Tariff Act.* (2) Congress made gold the standard of monetary value by passing the *Gold Standard Act.* (3) The Klondike gold rush began when gold was discovered in the Yukon River region of Canada and Alaska. (4) The United States fought the Spanish-American War; acquired the Philippines, Guam, and Puerto Rico; took over Hawaii and American Samoa; and established the Open Door Policy in China. (5) The Boxer Rebellion broke out in China.

McKINLEY IS ASSASSINATED

McKinley was reelected President in 1900, and his running mate, Theodore Roosevelt, became Vice President. In the fall of 1901, while attending the Pan-American Exposition at Buffalo, New York, McKinley was fatally wounded by an assassin. Upon his death, Theodore Roosevelt became the 26th President.

ADMINISTRATION OF THEODORE ROOSEVELT

EARLY LIFE

Theodore Roosevelt was born in 1858 of wealthy parents in New York City. Young Theodore, later called "Teddy" and "T.R." by millions of Americans, was a frail boy who was frequently ill during his youth. Despite his poor health, he did well at school, read widely, and spent much time on his favorite hobby, nature study. As he grew older his health improved, and he developed a sturdy body by means of exercise and sports, especially boxing.

Upon graduation from Harvard, he took up the study of law but dropped it in favor of politics. In 1881, at the age of 23, he won election to the New York State Assembly.

CAREER

During his three years in the state legislature, Roosevelt developed an interest in reform, learned to dislike political bosses, and revealed many of the traits for which he later became famous: cheerfulness, courage, and boundless energy. After the untimely death of his wife in 1884, he gave up politics and became a cattle rancher in North Dakota. For the next two years he lived a strenuous outdoor life, raising cattle, riding the range, and hunting buffalo. He then returned to New York City, where he ran unsuccessfully for mayor. He next turned to writing. The best known of his books is *The Winning of the West.*

In 1889 Roosevelt was appointed to the U.S. Civil Service Commission, where he worked hard and effectively to improve the merit system. Feeling restless at any one job, in 1895 he accepted an appointment as police commissioner of New York City. Two years later he went back to Washington to become Assistant Secretary of the Navy. In this capacity he helped prepare U.S. naval forces for a war with Spain.

When war broke out in 1898, Roosevelt resigned his position to raise and command a volunteer cavalry regiment made up largely of hard-riding polo players and cowboys. Known as the *Rough Riders,* this regiment distinguished itself in the famous charge against the Spaniards in Cuba at San Juan Hill. The exploits of the Rough Riders captured the imagination of the public and made Roosevelt a national hero.

Returning from the war, Roosevelt was elected governor of New York. Two years later the Republicans selected him as their nominee for Vice President. Roosevelt campaigned vigorously, and the Republican ticket won a landslide victory. Ten months later McKinley was assassinated, and Roosevelt succeeded to the presidency. In 1904 he ran for a full term and won an easy victory. A strong and popular Chief Executive, Roosevelt brought about many changes during his term of office.

ROOSEVELT'S "SQUARE DEAL"

Roosevelt believed that every American was entitled to a "square deal." His administration ushered in a period of reform known as the *Progressive Era,* which continued for nearly two decades, through the administrations of Taft and Wilson.

The following were some of the highlights of Roosevelt's Square Deal:

1. "Trust Busting." In the years prior to the Square Deal, trusts and holding companies had exercised increasingly greater control of industry, trade, and transportation. Big business seemed to have become more powerful than the government, and little effort had been made to enforce the Sherman Antitrust Act. Upon taking office, Roosevelt pledged to carry out the antitrust laws and to weed out evil business practices. Under his direction the Department of Justice succeeded in dissolving the Northern Securities Company, a powerful railroad holding company, and in breaking up the "beef trust." Suits were also brought against oil, chemical, and tobacco trusts. Roosevelt's antitrust activity earned him the nickname "trust buster."

2. Conservation. One of Roosevelt's most important and lasting contributions was in the field of conservation. He secured passage of the *Newlands Act* (1902) to reclaim arid lands through irrigation. He set aside nearly 150 million acres of public land as national forest reserves, and withdrew from public sale about 80 million acres of mineral land and 1.5 million acres of potential waterpower sites. He also called the state governors to a national conservation conference to discuss the problem of preserving and developing natural resources. As a result of this meeting in 1908, Roosevelt appointed a *National Conservation Commission,* headed by Gifford Pinchot. This commission conducted the first scientific study of the country's water, forest, soil, and mineral resources.

3. Other Measures. At Roosevelt's urging, Congress enacted legislation for stricter government regulation of the railroads. The *Elkins Act* made it a crime to give or receive rebates of freight charges. The *Hepburn Act* increased the power of the Interstate Commerce Commission, giving that body the power to fix railroad rates.

To protect the health of the public, Roosevelt requested legislation to prevent the sale of spoiled food, diseased meat, and foods and patent medicines containing harmful ingredients. Congress responded by passing the *Meat Inspection Act* and the *Pure Food and Drug Act.*

FOREIGN AFFAIRS

Roosevelt's outstanding achievement in foreign affairs was to start the monumental task of building the Panama Canal. He also made a major contribution to world peace in 1905 by getting Russia and Japan to end the Russo-Japanese War and then helping to negotiate a peace treaty between them. For this accomplishment Roosevelt was awarded a Nobel peace prize.

His handling of the many foreign problems that arose during his presidency is best described by one of his favorite slogans: "Speak softly and carry a big stick." By "big stick" he meant a powerful military force. Roosevelt used "big stick" diplomacy in the following situations:

1. Acquisition of the Canal Zone. Roosevelt was vitally interested in having the United States build a canal to connect the Atlantic and Pacific oceans. He therefore began to negotiate with Colombia for the acquistion of a strip of land across the Isthmus of Panama. (See map, page 328.) By 1903 the negotiations had come to a standstill. In that year the province of Panama revolted and broke away from Colombia. Roosevelt

"Big Stick" Diplomacy

thereupon ordered U.S. warships to the area to prevent Colombian troops from subduing the rebels and retaking Panama. He recognized the Republic of Panama, guaranteed its independence, and acquired control of the Canal Zone for a price that Colombia had refused.

2. The Roosevelt Corollary. Santo Domingo, today called the Dominican Republic, was in financial difficulty, and its European creditors threatened to collect their debts by force. To prevent such European intervention in Latin America, Roosevelt enlarged the scope of the Monroe Doctrine by adding the *Roosevelt Corollary.* In 1904 he stated that the United States would intervene in the internal affairs of a Latin American nation if mismanagement or wrongdoing made it impossible for that country to maintain order or pay its debts. In 1905 the United States took over the management of Santo Domingo's finances and arranged for the settlement of its foreign debts.

3. Display of Naval Strength. Disturbed by mounting anti-Americanism in Japan, Roosevelt in 1907 sent the U.S. fleet on a world cruise to demonstrate American naval might. Impressed by America's seapower, Japan entered into negotiations to settle the differences between the two countries.

ADMINISTRATION OF WILLIAM HOWARD TAFT

TAFT IS ELECTED IN 1908

Having served almost two full terms, Roosevelt decided against running again in 1908. He threw his support to his Secretary of War,

William Howard Taft of Ohio. Taft easily won the Republican nomination and then the election.

DOMESTIC POLICIES

Taft took up the fight against monopoly and initiated many antitrust suits. During his term the Supreme Court ordered the dissolution of the Standard Oil Trust and the reorganization of the American Tobacco Company, which was found to constitute a "tobacco trust."

Among the reforms enacted under Taft were (1) adoption of a postal savings bank system, (2) the inauguration of parcel post service, (3) creation of the Department of Labor, (4) expansion of civil service, (5) the *Publicity Act*, which required that contributions to campaigns for federal election be made public, (6) the *Mann-Elkins Act*, which placed telephone, cable, and wireless companies under the supervision of the ICC (this function was later given to the Federal Communications Commission), and (7) the *Sixteenth Amendment*, ratified in 1913, which authorized Congress to impose an income tax.

INTERVENTION IN NICARAGUA

During Taft's administration, a revolution took place in the Central American country of Nicaragua. The United States viewed the situation with alarm because Nicaragua is close to the Panama Canal and contains the best route for a second canal. American bankers extended a loan to Nicaragua to stabilize its finances. To assure repayment, they took over the management of the country's customs and its banking and railroad systems. When an internal uprising in 1912 threatened to upset these arrangements, Taft sent in a detachment of U.S. marines to maintain order. American occupation forces remained in Nicaragua almost continuously until 1933.

ROOSEVELT REENTERS THE POLITICAL ARENA

Although Taft frequently supported progressive legislation, he was generally considered a conservative. He signed the high-duty *Payne-Aldrich Tariff Act*, and he dismissed the ardent conservationist, Gifford Pinchot, as chief of the U.S. Forest Service. Critical of Taft's conservatism, Roosevelt in 1912 opposed Taft's bid for a second term and decided to seek the Republican presidential nomination for himself. When the Republicans, dominated by the conservative faction, renominated Taft, Roosevelt's supporters broke away, formed the Progressive party, and chose "T.R." as their candidate. Because of Roosevelt's often-repeated statement that he felt "as strong as a bull moose," the new party was popularly called the *Bull Moose party*. Its platform called for a lower tariff; a broad program of conservation; strict government regulation of big business; women's suffrage; and such social welfare proposals as minimum wage laws, an eight-hour workday, an end to child labor, and laws to protect working women.

THE REPUBLICAN SPLIT RESULTS IN WILSON'S ELECTION

At the Democratic party convention, liberals and conservatives also fought for control. On the 46th ballot the liberal group, led by William

Jennings Bryan, succeeded in nominating Woodrow Wilson, a reform governor of New Jersey, for the presidency. The 1912 election campaign was a spirited one. Wilson polled 6.25 million popular votes, Roosevelt 4 million, and Taft 3.5 million. The split in the Republican vote enabled Wilson to carry 40 states. He won 435 electoral votes to Roosevelt's 88 and Taft's 8, and became the nation's 28th President.

ADMINISTRATION OF WOODROW WILSON

BACKGROUND

Born in 1856 in Staunton, Virginia, Woodrow Wilson attended Princeton University, studied law at the University of Virginia, and did graduate work in history at Johns Hopkins University. He wrote a scholarly study of American politics entitled *Congressional Government*, became a college professor, and earned recognition as a brilliant lecturer and authority in the fields of law, government, politics, and history.

Wilson became president of Princeton in 1902, a position he held for eight years. In 1910 he was elected governor of New Jersey. During his term he fought political bossism and pushed through such reform legislation as a primary election law, a workers' compensation law, and state regulation of public utilities. His reputation as an outstanding liberal and efficient administrator won him the presidency in 1912. Four years later he was reelected for a second term.

WILSON'S "NEW FREEDOM"

President Wilson stated that the time had come to provide the American people with a "new freedom" of opportunity. He proposed, and Congress enacted, a broad program of progressive legislation.

1. Lower Tariffs. The *Underwood Tariff Act* (1913) reduced import duties to the lowest level since 1860. To make up for the expected loss of revenue, Congress levied an income tax. Such a tax was made possible by the ratification of the Sixteenth Amendment early in 1913. Although income taxes were low at first, they were later gradually increased until they became the chief source of federal revenue.

2. Banking Reform. To regulate credit and improve banking services, Congress passed the *Federal Reserve Act* in 1913. The country was divided into 12 Federal Reserve Districts, each with its own Federal Reserve Bank. Supervision over the entire system was placed in the hands of the Federal Reserve Board. The Reserve Banks were made the depositories for the excess funds of local banks within their districts. The act empowered the Board to control credit by increasing or decreasing the amount of money in circulation and by changing the interest rate on loans.

3. Regulating Big Business. Congress acted to control big business and curb unfair business practices. The *Clayton Antitrust Act* (1914) clearly defined certain unfair practices and strengthened the power of the federal government to deal with them. Congress set up the Federal Trade Commission to investigate and stop these practices.

4. Aiding the Farmer and the Worker. The *Smith-Lever Act* (1914) and the *Farm Loan Act* (1916) were passed to help the farmer. Two laws were enacted to end child labor, but the Supreme Court declared both acts unconstitutional. The *La Follette Seamen's Act* (1915) was passed to regulate the working conditions of sailors on American ships. The *Adamson Act* (1916) established a shorter workday for railroad employees. In addition, the Clayton Act exempted labor organizations from its antitrust provisions and thus encouraged unionization.

5. Constitutional Amendments. The *Seventeenth Amendment* (1913) provided for the direct election of U.S. senators; the *Eighteenth Amendment* (1919) established national prohibition; the *Nineteenth Amendment* (1920) granted women the right to vote.

FOREIGN AFFAIRS

Relations with foreign countries occupied much of Wilson's time while he was in office. The following were highlights of Wilson's diplomacy, especially in Latin America:

1. Trouble with Mexico

a. The Huerta Regime. Early in 1913, just before the end of Taft's administration, a revolution in Mexico by Victoriano Huerta overthrew the reform government of President Francisco Madero. When Wilson became President, he refused to recognize the new regime. In addition, he clamped an embargo on American arms shipments to Mexico and stationed U.S. naval units off Veracruz to prevent European war supplies from reaching Huerta. Relations worsened after Huerta's troops arrested an unarmed party of U.S. sailors at the seaport of Tampico. In 1914, when a German ship laden with arms approached the harbor of Veracruz, Wilson ordered the U.S. Navy to bombard and capture the city. War between Mexico and the United States was narrowly averted by the mediation efforts of Argentina, Brazil, and Chile. Huerta resigned, and the United States withdraw its troops.

b. Pancho Villa. Two years later, Pancho Villa, a Mexican revolutionary, raided several border towns in Arizona and New Mexico, killing a number of American citizens. Thereupon, Wilson sent an expedition under John J. Pershing into Mexico to punish Villa. The pursuit was unsuccessful, and in 1917 the troops were recalled.

2. Troops Are Sent to the Caribbean. Trouble also broke out in Haiti and in the Dominican Republic. To maintain order, prevent European intervention, and protect American interests, Wilson ordered troops into these countries and took over management of their finances. U.S. Marines remained in the Dominican Republic until 1924 and in Haiti until 1934.

3. Bryan-Chamorro Treaty. Ratified in 1916, this treaty with Nicaragua granted the United States, in return for a payment of $3 million, (*a*) a canal route across Nicaragua, and (*b*) long-term leases to a naval base on the Gulf of Fonseca on Nicaragua's Pacific coast, and to the Corn Islands off Nicaragua's Caribbean coast.

4. Other Foreign Developments. (*a*) The Panama Canal was completed and opened to commerce in 1914. (*b*) The Jones Act of 1916 declared the intention of the United States to free the Philippines at

United States Expansion and Intervention in the Caribbean

1. United States acquires Puerto Rico from Spain, 1898.
2. United States frees Cuba from Spain and occupies the island, 1898–1902; maintains law and order under the Platt Amendment, 1902–1934.
3. United States leases Guantánamo Bay from Cuba, 1902.
4. United States acquires Canal Zone from Panama, 1904.
5. United States takes over financial management of Dominican Republic and sends in troops, 1905–1924.
6. United States takes over financial management of Nicaragua, 1911, and sends in troops, 1912–1933.
7. United States occupies Veracruz, Mexico, 1914.
8. United States takes over financial management of Haiti and sends in troops, 1915–1934.
9. United States acquires rights to canal route and leases Corn Islands from Nicaragua, 1916.
10. United States acquires Virgin Islands from Denmark, 1917.

some future time, after a stable government had been established. (*c*) The Jones Act of 1917 gave Puerto Rico greater self-government and granted its inhabitants U.S. citizenship. (*d*) The Virgin Islands were acquired from Denmark in 1917.

WILSON AND WORLD WAR I

When World War I broke out in Europe in 1914, Wilson strove to remain neutral and to protect America's rights on the high seas. The slogan of his reelection campaign in 1916 was "He kept us out of war." Despite his efforts, however, the United States was finally drawn into the conflict in 1917 on the side of the Allies. During the next year and a half, Wilson devoted all his energies to the war effort. The Central Powers were finally defeated, and Germany accepted the peace program outlined in Wilson's "Fourteen Points." Wilson then went to Paris to help negotiate the Treaty of Versailles and to lay plans for a League of Nations.

Returning home, Wilson sought to win popular support for the League. While on a speaking tour in 1919, he suffered a stroke that made him a helpless invalid for the remainder of his life. His hopes for U.S. participation in an international organization to prevent future wars were shattered when the Senate rejected U.S. membership in the League of Nations.

Multiple-Choice Test I

1. The establishment of the Federal Reserve System and the creation of the Federal Trade Commission occurred during the administration of   (*a*) Grover Cleveland   (*b*) Theodore Roosevelt   (*c*) William McKinley   (*d*) Woodrow Wilson.
2. An important purpose of the Federal Reserve Act was to   (*a*) guarantee the safety of a depositor's money   (*b*) regulate credit by increasing or decreasing the amount of money in circulation   (*c*) make state banks illegal   (*d*) make private operation of banks unprofitable.
3. Which third party played a prominent role in the election of 1912?   (*a*) Farmer-Labor   (*b*) Populist   (*c*) Greenback Labor   (*d*) Bull Moose.
4. Which is the generally accepted date for the disappearance of the Western frontier?   (*a*) 1860   (*b*) 1890   (*c*) 1920   (*d*) 1950.
5. Which one of these is associated with the first decade of the 20th century? (*a*) Square Deal   (*b*) Era of Good Feelings   (*c*) New Deal   (*d*) Great Society.
6. Two Presidents who extended the merit system in the civil service were   (*a*) Ulysses S. Grant and Benjamin Harrison   (*b*) Grover Cleveland and Theodore Roosevelt   (*c*) James Polk and Martin Van Buren   (*d*) Andrew Johnson and William McKinley.
7. Which President made conservation of natural resources an important policy of the federal government?   (*a*) James A. Garfield   (*b*) Ulysses S. Grant   (*c*) Theodore Roosevelt   (*d*) Chester A. Arthur.
8. Which federal law was passed during Theodore Roosevelt's administration? (*a*) Clayton Antitrust Act   (*b*) Interstate Commerce Act   (*c*) Sherman Antitrust Act   (*d*) Pure Food and Drug Act.

9. The term *New Freedom* is used to describe the domestic program of (*a*) Grover Cleveland (*b*) Woodrow Wilson (*c*) William McKinley (*d*) William Howard Taft.

10. Who is generally recognized as a pioneer of forest conservation in the United States? (*a*) Daniel Boone (*b*) Brigham Young (*c*) Gifford Pinchot (*d*) James G. Blaine.

Multiple-Choice Test II

1. A characteristic of national politics during the period 1860–1900 was that (*a*) the Democratic party was in power most of the time (*b*) the Republican party was in power most of the time (*c*) all Presidents were Republican (*d*) third parties were inactive.

2. The Progressives of 1900–1915 advocated (*a*) reforms extending democracy in government (*b*) an increase in the supply of money (*c*) government ownership of the steel and textile industries (*d*) a "hands off" policy by government toward big business.

3. The first tariff act with a considerable reduction in rates after the Civil War was enacted during the administration of (*a*) Ulysses S. Grant (*b*) James A. Garfield (*c*) William McKinley (*d*) Woodrow Wilson.

4. Andrew Jackson and Theodore Roosevelt were similar in that both (*a*) had difficulty in carrying through most of their legislative programs (*b*) were elected by a small popular vote (*c*) felt that the President should be strictly an executive officer (*d*) were able to exercise great influence because of their personal popularity.

5. Which act attempted to free labor unions from prosecution under the antitrust laws? (*a*) Sherman Antitrust Act (*b*) Clayton Antitrust Act (*c*) Wagner Labor Relations Act (*d*) Taft-Hartley Act.

6. How a third party can affect the outcome of a presidential election was shown in the election of (*a*) 1876 (*b*) 1888 (*c*) 1904 (*d*) 1912.

7. The Panic of 1893 occurred during the administration of (*a*) William McKinley (*b*) Grover Cleveland (*c*) James A. Garfield (*d*) Chester A. Arthur.

8. The election of which President was most clearly a victory for big business? (*a*) William McKinley (*b*) Woodrow Wilson (*c*) Grover Cleveland (*d*) James Buchanan.

9. All of the following Presidents were New Yorkers EXCEPT (*a*) Chester A. Arthur (*b*) Woodrow Wilson (*c*) Grover Cleveland (*d*) Theodore Roosevelt.

10. The only President who served two terms that were not consecutive was (*a*) William McKinley (*b*) Benjamin Harrison (*c*) Theodore Roosevelt (*d*) Grover Cleveland.

Modified True-False Test

1. President Theodore Roosevelt's policy toward big business earned him the nickname *"muckraker."*

2. The name of the artificial waterway opened in 1914 that greatly shortened the all-water route between New York and San Francisco is the *St. Lawrence Seaway.*

3. The effort to preserve the riches of nature and use them wisely is called *conservation.*
4. The federal government launched a program to reclaim arid lands through irrigation with the passage of the *Hatch* Act of 1902.
5. With the proclamation of the *Gentlemen's Agreement*, the scope of the Monroe Doctrine was enlarged in 1904 to include intervention by the United States in the internal affairs of Latin American nations.
6. *William Jennings Bryan* ran as the presidential candidate of the Bull Moose party.
7. *Victoriano Huerta*, a Mexican revolutionist, raided border towns in the American Southwest in 1916.
8. The *Bryan-Chamorro* Treaty granted the United States a canal route across Nicaragua.
9. A group of unemployed that marched on Washington to demand federal assistance during the Panic of 1893 was known as *Coxey's Army.*
10. The discovery of precious metal in the Yukon River region touched off a gold rush to the *Red River* Valley.

Identification Test

1. I was the first Democrat elected to the presidency after the Civil War. Tariff and currency problems occupied much of my time. I supported the principle that "a public office is a public trust."
2. In describing my policies as President of the United States, people often refer to my words, "Speak softly and carry a big stick."
3. During my administration the United States was victorious in a short war and acquired an overseas empire. A gold rush occurred while I was in office.
4. I was the grandson of a famous Indian fighter and former President of the United States. Although I won fewer popular votes than my opponent, I received a majority of the electoral votes and became President. During my administration the Sherman Antitrust Act was passed.
5. I was elected Vice President but assumed the nation's highest office when the President was assassinated by Charles Guiteau, a disappointed office seeker. A highlight of my administration was the enactment of the Pendleton Civil Service Act.

Essay Questions

1. Show how a vital issue of their times was reflected in the political conflicts of the following pairs:
   a. William Jennings Bryan—William McKinley
   b. Theodore Roosevelt—William Howard Taft
2. Discuss *two* contributions to the political or economic development of this nation that might be emphasized in an article written about Woodrow Wilson.
3. Theodore Roosevelt's life was a story of outstanding achievement. In connection with the life of Theodore Roosevelt, discuss fully *two* of the following topics:
   a. Career before becoming President
   b. American relations with foreign countries while he was President
   c. Policy in relation to business during his presidency
   d. Achievements in conservation during his presidency

UNIT IX. THE UNITED STATES BECOMES A WORLD POWER

Part 1. Our Nation Expands Beyond Its Borders

PURCHASE OF ALASKA (1867)

Alaska became a Russian possession in 1741 when it was explored by Vitus Bering, a Danish navigator in the service of Russia. Although the Russians developed an extensive fur trade in Alaska, they did not attempt any large-scale colonization. Finding the territory of little value and fearing that England would seize it in the event of war, the Russian Czar offered to sell Alaska to the United States. Secretary of State William H. Seward negotiated its purchase in 1867 for $7.2 million. Because most Americans considered the region worthless, Alaska became known as "Seward's Folly."

More than twice the size of Texas, Alaska was sparsely populated. Most of its inhabitants were native Eskimos, Aleuts, and Indians. A few white fishermen and hunters also resided there. Its population experienced a dramatic upsurge in 1896, when gold was discovered in the Klondike region of Canada's Yukon Territory, near Alaska's eastern border. During the next three years, some 100,000 American prospectors streamed to the area. Settlements sprang up at Juneau, Anchorage, and Fairbanks. In 1912 Alaska became an organized territory.

Alaska is separated from other parts of the United States by Canada. For many years direct access to the territory from the lower 48 states was by boat (and later by airplane). To provide a land link between the two sections of the country, the United States during World War II built the 1,523-mile Alcan Highway (now called the *Alaska Highway*). The road runs from Dawson Creek, British Columbia, to Fairbanks, Alaska.

Beginning in 1916, Alaskans aspired to statehood. Their goal was finally achieved in 1959 when the territory was proclaimed the 49th state.

IMPORTANCE OF ALASKA

Alaska became an important source of gold, copper, silver, coal, lead, tin, platinum, and mercury, as well as timber, furs, and fish. The completion of the 800-mile trans-Alaska pipeline in 1977 opened the vast oil deposits in the North Slope area of Prudhoe Bay for development, thus making Alaska a major oil supplier.

Its strategic location also enables Alaska to serve as (1) a military air base for the defense of the Pacific coast, (2) part of the *North Warning System*—a series of radar stations stretching across northern Alaska and Canada that reports the flight of enemy missiles or aircraft southward

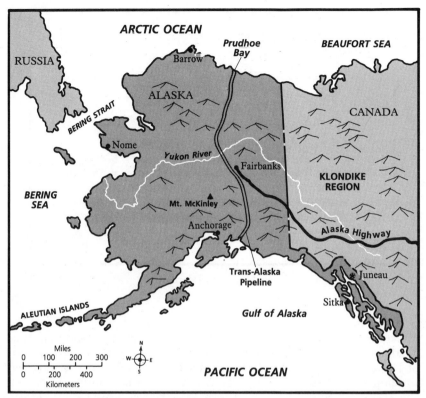

Alaska

from the polar region, and (3) a refueling base for commercial airliners flying routes from North America to other parts of the world via the North Pole.

SUPPORT FOR OVERSEAS EXPANSION GROWS

Before the Civil War, the United States depended on imports for much of its manufactured goods. With the growth of industrialization after the war, U.S. manufacturers were not only able to satisfy the needs of the domestic market, they also took steps to sell their surplus output abroad. In addition, they began to invest capital in enterprises in other countries. As U.S. commercial interests became international, Americans began to view overseas expansion more favorably. The U.S. Navy was enlarged and modernized. The United States acquired coaling stations, naval bases, defense outposts, and cable landings in the Pacific and Caribbean.

ANNEXATION OF HAWAII (1898)

The first European to discover the Hawaiian Islands, in 1778, was James Cook, an English explorer. American interest in Hawaii dates back to 1820 when missionaries went there to spread the gospel of Christianity. They established schools, introduced writing, and trained

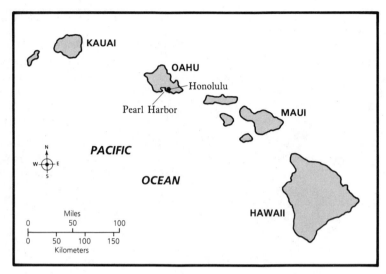

Hawaiian Islands

native teachers. Also, New England fishing vessels used the islands as headquarters for whaling operations, and Yankee merchant ships stopped at Hawaii on their way to China. Americans settled in the islands and developed large sugar plantations. Later, American planters developed the Hawaiian pineapple industry. In 1887 Hawaii leased *Pearl Harbor*, on the island of Oahu, to the United States as a naval base.

In 1893 the native ruler, Queen Liliuokalani, was overthrown in a revolution organized by American settlers led by Sanford B. Dole. The new government petitioned the United States to annex Hawaii. In 1898, after the outbreak of the Spanish-American War, Congress accepted the offer. Two years later Hawaii was organized as a territory.

Hawaii consists of eight main islands and numerous minor ones. Honolulu, on Oahu, is the capital. Situated in the central Pacific, about 2,400 miles southwest of San Francisco, Hawaii is (1) a main stopover point for commercial airliners, (2) a key naval and air base of the United States, and (3) a popular tourist center. Its chief products are sugar and pineapples.

For many years Hawaiians agitated for statehood. Their wish was finally granted in 1959, when Congress admitted Hawaii into the Union as the 50th state.

OTHER PACIFIC ACQUISITIONS

1. American Samoa. The Samoan Islands are located 2,600 miles southwest of Hawaii. In 1878 the United States obtained the right to use the harbor of Pago Pago on the island of Tutuila as a naval station. Tutuila and six other Samoan islands came under exclusive U.S. control in 1899, as the result of a treaty with Great Britain and Germany.

American Samoa today is a key U.S. naval and air base in the South Pacific. The territory is administered by the Department of the Interior. The islands' inhabitants have the status of "nationals" of the United States—a category that assures them certain basic rights (such as life, liberty, and protection of property) but not all the privileges of U.S. citizenship. Their local government consists of a popularly elected bicameral legislature and governor. They also elect a delegate to represent them (as a nonvoting member) in the U.S. House of Representatives.

2. Guam. Situated 3,700 miles west of Hawaii, Guam is the largest and southernmost of the Mariana Islands. A Spanish possession for more than 325 years, Guam was captured by a U.S. naval vessel during the Spanish-American War and was ceded by Spain to the United States when the war ended (1898). Japan seized the island in 1941; the United States retook it in 1944.

At the present time Guam is a strategic military outpost of the United States in the western Pacific. It is under the supervision of the Interior Department. The Guamanians are American citizens (but do not vote in presidential elections). Their local government consists of a popularly elected unicameral legislature and governor. The islanders also elect a nonvoting delegate to the U.S. House of Representatives. (The delegate may vote in House committees but has no vote on the House floor.)

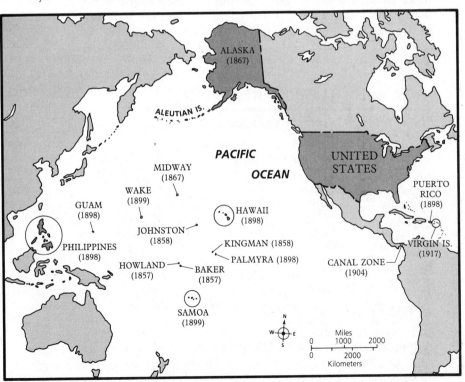

United States and Its Possessions (1918)

3. Other Island Outposts. In addition to American Samoa and Guam, the United States acquired a number of other islands during the latter part of the 19th century and later. Among them were Baker, Howland, Johnston Atoll, Kingman Reef, Midway, Palmyra, and Wake. Intended originally as coaling and cable stations, they have assumed new importance in the 20th century as commercial airfields, military air bases, and radio and radar stations.

4. Micronesia. The Carolines, Marshalls, and Marianas are three separate archipelagos, or groups of islands, that are located in the region of the western Pacific known as Micronesia. Except for Guam (a U.S. possession since 1898), all of these islands had been administered by Japan as a League of Nations mandate after World War I. After World War II the United Nations assigned Micronesia to the United States as a Trust Territory.

In 1986 the Northern Marianas (all of the Marianas except Guam, which enjoys a special status) became a commonwealth of the United States. The residents acquired the right to elect a bicameral legislature and governor and to handle their own domestic affairs. The United States retained control of the islands' foreign affairs and defense.

From the remaining trust territories, three independent nations were created: the Republic of the Marshall Islands (1986), the Federated States of Micronesia (1986), and the Republic of Palau (1994). Each negotiated a Compact of Free Association with the United States. The U.S. remains responsible for the region's defense and provides economic aid to each government. All three countries became UN members.

THE SPANISH-AMERICAN WAR (1898)

CUBA REVOLTS AGAINST SPANISH RULE

Cuba and Puerto Rico, in the West Indies, were the last remnants of Spain's former empire in the Americas. The Cubans hated Spanish rule and tried several times to win their independence. In a revolt in 1895 Cuban patriots destroyed much Spanish property. Spain retaliated by rounding up thousands of Cubans and placing them in concentration camps, where many died of hunger and disease.

American newspapers, especially those published by William Randolph Hearst and Joseph Pulitzer, dramatized incidents of Spanish cruelty. These sensational newspaper stories aroused widespread sympathy for the Cubans and touched off a demand that the United States go to the aid of Cuba. American business leaders, too, clamored for intervention in the Cuban struggle in order to safeguard their considerable investments in the Cuban sugar and tobacco industries.

AMERICA DECLARES WAR ON SPAIN

In February, 1898, the U.S. battleship *Maine*, which had been sent to Havana, Cuba, to protect American lives and property, was destroyed by an explosion of unknown origin. Public opinion placed the blame on

Spain, and all America was stirred by the slogan "Remember the *Maine!*" In April, 1898, President McKinley asked Congress for authority to intervene in Cuba. Congress adopted a joint resolution (*a*) recognizing the independence of Cuba, (*b*) demanding the withdrawal of Spanish armed forces from the island, (*c*) authorizing the President to enforce these demands, and (*d*) asserting that the United States had no intention of assuming control of Cuba. Spain responded by breaking diplomatic relations with the United States and then by declaring war. The United States in turn issued a declaration of war against Spain.

MAIN EVENTS OF THE WAR

1. The Philippines. Shortly after the outbreak of the war, *George Dewey* led a squadron of U.S. warships into Manila Bay and destroyed the Spanish fleet that was anchored there. He then blockaded the city of Manila. With the arrival of American land forces during the summer, U.S. troops under Wesley Merritt (aided by Filipino guerrillas led by Emilio Aguinaldo) attacked and occupied Manila (August, 1898). The surrender of the Spanish garrison gave the Americans control of the Philippines.

2. Cuba. In June, 1898, an American army commanded by William Shafter landed in Cuba and marched on the city of Santiago. It soon captured San Juan Hill and the village of El Caney, the outer defenses of the city. As the Americans laid siege to Santiago, the Spanish fleet guarding the city attempted to escape from Santiago Harbor, where it had been bottled up by a squadron of U.S. warships under the command of William T. Sampson. The Spanish fleet was completely destroyed, and soon afterwards Santiago surrendered (July, 1898).

3. Puerto Rico. After the fall of Santiago, U.S. troops, led by Nelson Miles, invaded Puerto Rico. Encountering little opposition, they soon occupied the island and assumed control of its management.

TREATY OF PEACE

Realizing the hopelessness of continuing the war, Spain sued for peace. With the signing of the Treaty of Paris (December, 1898), Spain granted independence to Cuba and ceded Puerto Rico, Guam, and the Philippines to the United States. For the Philippines, the United States agreed to pay Spain $20 million.

The United States emerged from the war a world power, a position that bred new problems and imposed new responsibilities.

LATER RELATIONS WITH CUBA

CUBA UNDER AMERICAN RULE

At the outbreak of the Spanish-American War, the United States declared that it had no desire to annex Cuba. Nevertheless, to maintain law and order, an American army commanded by Leonard Wood occupied Cuba for four years. During this period much progress was made. Highways were built, sanitation measures were introduced, and a modern system of education was established.

The most important accomplishment was the conquest of yellow fever. Walter Reed, an American army medical officer, proved that yellow fever was transmitted by certain mosquitoes. By eliminating breeding places for these mosquitoes, medical authorities succeeded in ridding Cuba of this deadly disease, which during the war had proved to be a more dangerous enemy than the Spanish army.

CUBAN INDEPENDENCE

In 1902 the United States withdrew its army of occupation. Cuba proclaimed itself a republic, but its independence was limited by certain provisions governing future relations with the United States that were made a part of the Cuban constitution. Known as the *Platt Amendment*, these provisions authorized the United States to (1) maintain naval bases in Cuba, and (2) intervene, if necessary, to preserve Cuban independence and to maintain law and order.

On several occasions during the next two decades, American troops were sent to Cuba to preserve order or to help put down armed rebellion against the Cuban government. In 1934, in line with President Franklin D. Roosevelt's "Good Neighbor" Policy, the United States gave up its right to intervene in Cuban affairs, thus abolishing the Platt Amendment. It did, however, retain a powerful naval base at Guantánamo Bay.

Cuba and the United States maintained close economic ties for over 50 years after the Spanish-American War. Americans invested more than $1 billion in Cuban sugar plantations, oil refineries, mines, public utilities, and retail establishments. Americans bought more than 50% of Cuba's exports, including half of its sugar crop, and supplied the island with 75% of its imports. In addition, American tourists flocked to Cuba.

When *Fidel Castro* seized power in Cuba in 1959, relations between that country and the United States became badly strained. Castro adopted a series of anti-American policies that led the United States to break off relations with Cuba in 1961 (see page 429).

LATER RELATIONS WITH THE PHILIPPINES

THE PHILIPPINES UNDER AMERICAN RULE

Unlike Cuba, the Philippine Islands were annexed and ruled directly by the United States. Many Filipinos resented American occupation, and an anti-American uprising broke out in 1899 led by Emilio Aguinaldo. It took U.S. forces three years to suppress the rebels.

Under American rule, (1) a system of public education was established, (2) public works, such as highways, bridges, and irrigation projects, were constructed, (3) a health and sanitation program was started, and (4) agriculture made rapid progress with the aid of American capital.

THE FILIPINOS MOVE TOWARD SELF-GOVERNMENT

President McKinley sent a commission headed by William Howard Taft to set up a civil government. Military rule ended in 1901, and Taft became the first civil governor. Members of the commission headed the various departments of government. In 1907 Filipinos began to share in the lawmaking process by electing an assembly of their own. Their participation in government was broadened in 1916 when the Jones Act established an elective senate to replace the appointive commission. Executive power remained in the hands of a governor general appointed by the U.S. President.

PHILIPPINE INDEPENDENCE

The Jones Act of 1916 declared the intention of the United States to set the Philippines free "as soon as a stable government could be established." The Tydings-McDuffie Act of 1934 set the date for independence as July 4, 1946. In the interim, the islands were to become a self-governing commonwealth under American protection. In 1935 Manuel Quezon was elected its first president.

In 1941, when Japan attacked the Philippines, Filipino troops fought side by side with the Americans to drive off the invaders. The Japanese were victorious, however, and occupied the islands. Until the islands were reconquered by U.S. forces under Douglas MacArthur (1944–1945), the Filipinos carried on active guerrilla warfare against the enemy. After the war, the United States kept its promise by proclaiming the Philippines an independent nation (1946). To aid the new *Republic of the Philippines,* the United States (1) gave the Philippines large sums of money to rebuild the country's war-shattered economy, (2) admitted Philippine products into the United States duty-free until 1954, and (3) signed a mutual defense agreement that permitted America to maintain military bases on Philippine soil. (The United States closed down its last military installation in the Philippines in 1992.)

COMMONWEALTH OF PUERTO RICO

PUERTO RICO WINS SELF-GOVERNMENT

The Foraker Act of 1900 (1) made Puerto Rico an unorganized territory, (2) empowered the President to appoint a governor and an executive council, or upper house of the legislature, and (3) provided for the election by the people of an assembly, or lower house. In 1917 the Puerto Ricans were granted American citizenship, and the appointive council was replaced by an elective senate. In 1947 the island was given the right to elect its own governor. Five years later, after adopting a constitution modeled after that of the United States, Puerto Rico became a self-governing commonwealth associated with the United States.

PUERTO RICAN PROGRESS UNDER AMERICAN RULE

Since 1900 there have been no tariff barriers between Puerto Rico and the United States. Because the island's exports entered the states duty-free, Puerto Rico was able to expand its output of sugar, tobacco, coffee, fruits, and livestock. Sanitation measures reduced disease and lowered the high mortality rate. Free, compulsory education reduced illiteracy. The construction of roads, hospitals, schools, buildings, and other public works provided employment and improved the country.

To raise the standard of living of the population and to keep the inhabitants from deserting the island for better jobs in the states, Puerto Rico launched an industrialization campaign in the late 1940's that became known as "Operation Bootstrap." American manufacturers opened hundreds of factories on the island to produce textiles and clothing, electrical and electronic equipment, plastics, and chemical products. Several oil refineries were built, and a large hydroelectric project was constructed to meet the increasing demand for electric power. Puerto Rico also became a popular resort area for American tourists.

In 1967 a plebiscite was held to determine if the Puerto Ricans wished to change their political status. With two-thirds of the eligible voters casting ballots, 60% supported keeping the commonwealth, 39% indicated a preference for statehood, and less than 1% voted for independence. To this day, the issue of independence, statehood, or commonwealth is a dominant theme of island politics. Proponents of all sides seek to gain control of the Puerto Rican government and to convince a majority of the people to support their views.

THE PANAMA CANAL

NEED FOR A CANAL

People long dreamed of building a canal through the narrow part of Central America to connect the Atlantic and the Pacific oceans. Such a canal would eliminate the need for sailing around South America, thus shortening the water route from New York to San Francisco by 8,000 miles. The importance of a short route became more apparent with the acquisition by the United States of new territories in the Caribbean and the Pacific. These widely dispersed holdings could be better defended if the U.S. Navy could move freely between the Atlantic and Pacific. Under President Theodore Roosevelt, the United States took steps to secure a right-of-way across the Isthmus of Panama for the construction of a canal.

ACQUIRING THE CANAL ZONE

An earlier attempt to build a canal through Panama, then a province of Colombia, had been made by a private French company under the direction of Ferdinand de Lesseps, builder of the Suez Canal. Because of financial difficulties and tropical diseases, the company abandoned the project. The French offered to sell their property and rights to the United States for $40 million. Congress authorized President Roosevelt to accept the offer provided that Colombia, which owned Panama, agreed to U.S. control of the Canal Zone. A treaty negotiated in 1903 specified that the United States would pay Colombia $10 million in cash and $250,000 in yearly rent for a strip of land six miles wide across Panama. But the Colombian senate, hoping to obtain better terms, refused to ratify the treaty. The delay aroused American anger and provoked ill feeling in Panama because Panamanians were anxious to have the canal built and feared that the United States might seek another route, in Nicaragua.

The inhabitants of Panama thereupon revolted and proclaimed their independence from Colombia. The revolution was successful largely because American warships and marines, dispatched to the area by Roosevelt, prevented the entry of Colombian military forces into Panama. The United States quickly recognized the new republic and negotiated the *Hay—Bunau-Varilla Treaty*. It granted the United States full and permanent control over a strip of land 10 miles wide for the construction of a canal. In return the United States guaranteed the independence of Panama and agreed to pay $10 million outright for the Canal Zone and an annual rental of $250,000. (Later readjustments increased the annual rental nearly tenfold.)

The French company transferred its rights and property to the United States and received $40 million. In 1921 the United States gave Colombia $25 million as compensation for the loss of its Panama province.

BUILDING THE CANAL

The canal project was placed in the hands of army engineers under *George W. Goethals*. Before construction could begin, however, the area had to be rid of malaria and yellow fever. This task was assigned to *William C. Gorgas*, an army surgeon who had worked in Cuba with Walter Reed. Sanitation measures were introduced, a sewage system was installed, swamps and ponds—breeding places for fever-carrying mosquitoes—were drained. As a result, the deadly tropical diseases were conquered.

To provide a navigable waterway across the isthmus, the engineers dammed the Chagres River to create Gatun Lake, blasted a channel through eight miles of volcanic rock at Culebra Cut (now called Gaillard Cut), and built a series of locks to raise and lower ships between the sea and Gatun Lake, which is 85 feet above sea level. The 40-mile canal, built at a cost of over $335 million, was opened to traffic in 1914.

The United States assumed control of the operation and defense of the waterway and of the civil administration of the 533-square-mile Canal Zone. Before long the Panama Canal became one of the great crossroads of the world.

THE PANAMA CANAL TODAY

As the years passed, Panamanians became increasingly resentful of U.S. control of their territory and began to agitate for its return. An outbreak of bloody anti-American rioting in 1964 led to the start of negotiations on a new treaty that would satisfy Panama's demands and also safeguard America's commercial and strategic interests. Thirteen years later, two agreements were finally concluded. The first provided for transfer of control of the waterway to Panama by the year 2000. Until that time the United States will continue to operate the canal and will retain the right to use about one-third of the former Canal Zone for military bases, canal operations, and employee housing. During this interim, Panama will receive a substantial annual payment from the United States as well as a share of canal revenues.

The second agreement dealt with the permanent neutrality of the canal. It guaranteed all nations the right to use the waterway, and granted the United States the right to defend the canal against a threat to its neutrality or operation after the year 2000.

After a bitter debate, the U.S. Senate ratified the *Panama Canal Treaties* by a margin of one vote in 1978.

THE VIRGIN ISLANDS

The United States purchased the Virgin Islands from Denmark in 1917 for $25 million. The territory consists of many islands, the most important of which are St. Croix, St. John, and St. Thomas, which has an excellent harbor. The Virgin Islands, strategically located between the Atlantic Ocean and the Caribbean Sea, guard an approach to the Panama Canal.

The territory is presently administered by the U.S. Department of the Interior. Its inhabitants are U.S. citizens. Their local government consists of a popularly elected unicameral legislature and governor. Virgin Islanders also elect a nonvoting delegate to the U.S. House of Representatives.

PAN-AMERICANISM

FRIENDSHIP WITH LATIN AMERICA

Early relations between the United States and Latin America were friendly. The people of the United States sympathized with the Latin Americans in their struggle to gain freedom from Spain at the beginning of the 19th century. The United States was the first country to recognize the independence of the new American nations. The Monroe Doctrine, with its warning to Europe to keep hands off the Americas, helped protect the newly created states.

In 1889, through the efforts of Secretary of State James G. Blaine, 17 nations of North, Central, and South America held an inter-American conference. They established a bureau for the purpose of exchanging commercial and other information of mutual interest. This bureau later became known as the *Pan-American Union*, with headquarters in Washington, D.C., in the Pan-American Building, a gift of Andrew Carnegie.

LATIN AMERICAN DISTRUST

After the Spanish-American War, America's popularity among the nations of Latin America declined. Its neighbors to the south began to fear and distrust "Yankee Imperialism" because of (1) United States annexation of Puerto Rico, (2) the Platt Amendment, which forced Cuba to accept American interference in its internal affairs, (3) the method by which the United States acquired the Canal Zone, (4) the Roosevelt Corollary to the Monroe Doctrine, which led to U.S. intervention in the Dominican Republic, Nicaragua, and Haiti, and (5) *dollar diplomacy*, the policy of using the power and prestige of the United States government to promote and protect American investments in foreign countries. (See map and accompanying text on page 328.)

THE "GOOD NEIGHBOR" POLICY

U.S. policy toward Latin America began to change during the presidency of Herbert Hoover. Shortly after his election in 1928, Hoover visited a number of countries south of the Rio Grande to assure them of U.S. interest in maintaining friendly relations. Later he refrained from intervening in the affairs of several Latin American states that were experiencing internal strife and financial problems. Finally, before leaving office in 1933, he ordered the withdrawal of U.S. troops from Nicaragua.

Picking up where Hoover left off, President Franklin D. Roosevelt in 1933 declared that the policy of the United States "from now on is opposed to armed intervention" in the affairs of Latin America. This country would no longer take upon itself alone the power to "police" the Western Hemisphere. A problem affecting the nations of the New World would become "the joint concern of a whole continent in which we are all neighbors." Roosevelt also declared his country's intention to act as a "good neighbor" and to treat the other American republics as equals.

To implement its *Good Neighbor Policy*, the United States revoked the Platt Amendment and withdrew its marines from Haiti. The United States also negotiated a peaceful settlement with Mexico, in which Mexico promised to compensate American companies for oil properties that it had taken over. These actions helped to better U.S. relations with Latin America.

Pan-American friendship was further strengthened through (1) frequent goodwill tours of Latin America by high officials of the U.S. government, (2) the adoption of a reciprocal trade program to lower tariff barriers and encourage inter-American trade, (3) the creation of the Export-Import Bank and the Inter-American Development Bank, which extended loans to Latin America for the construction of public works and the development of natural resources, and (4) Pan American conferences designed to exchange ideas, settle differences, and discuss common problems.

STRENGTHENING PAN-AMERICAN MILITARY TIES

On the eve of World War II, in 1938, the member nations of the Pan-American Union issued the *Declaration of Lima*. By this pact, each nation agreed to come to the defense of any American republic whose security was threatened by an outside power. Two years later, the Pan-American Union members set up a commission to administer the

American colonies of those European nations that had fallen or might fall to Germany and Italy.

When the United States was drawn into World War II, most of the Latin American states quickly rallied to the support of their northern neighbor. They declared war against the Axis powers, allowed the United States to establish military bases and maintain troops on their soil, and furnished much-needed raw materials for the Allied war effort.

To assure hemispheric unity in the post-war period, the American republics in 1947 drew up the *Inter-American Treaty of Reciprocal Assistance*. It provided that (1) aggression against any American nation, from within or outside the Western Hemisphere, be considered aggression against all, and (2) the signatories take collective action against the aggressor until the United Nations could intervene.

ORGANIZATION OF AMERICAN STATES (OAS)

In 1948, at the Bogotá Conference, the American republics created the *Organization of American States* (OAS). It replaced the Pan-American Union as the dominant inter-American agency. The OAS aims to (1) defend the independence and territory of the member nations (32 at present), (2) bring about the peaceful settlement of inter-American disputes, and (3) promote the economic, social, and cultural welfare of the Americas.

The OAS holds a regular Inter-American Conference every five years. If any threat to the peace of the Western Hemisphere arises, the Permanent Council of the OAS summons the foreign ministers of the member nations to a special meeting to discuss the crisis. In addition, various specialized OAS agencies seek to advance inter-American co-operation in various fields. These agencies include the (1) Economic and Social Council; (2) Council for Education, Science, and Culture; (3) Judicial (Legal) Committee; and (4) Commission on Human Rights.

ALLIANCE FOR PROGRESS

To combat economic distress and political instability in Latin America, President Kennedy in 1961 called on the people of the Western Hemisphere "to join a new Alliance for Progress—a vast effort to satisfy the basic needs of the American people for homes, work and land, health and schools." To carry out the program, Kennedy called for a minimum of $20 billion in loans and grants over the next decade. More than half was to come from the United States, the rest from the nations of Western Europe, international agencies, and private investors.

Meeting in Uruguay in the summer of 1961, delegates from the United States and all the Latin American countries except Cuba ratified the *Act of Punta del Este*, thereby launching the Alliance for Progress. This project linked Latin American measures of domestic reform and self-help with United States capital and technical skill.

A sharp increase in U.S. aid during the 1960's funded the construction of new schools, housing, water systems, power plants, and roads in many parts of Latin America. But the hoped-for inflow of new capital from private investors did not materialize. In addition, most participating countries were reluctant to adopt needed political and economic reforms. As a result, the Alliance failed to fulfill the high hopes of its founders.

CARIBBEAN BASIN INITIATIVE (CBI)

In 1982 President Ronald Reagan proposed a combined program of aid, trade, and investment to strengthen the economies of countries located in the Caribbean region. Approved by Congress the following year, the *Caribbean Basin Initiative* (CBI) provided (1) increased U.S. economic aid to ease the immediate financial problems of these countries and to stimulate their long-term economic development, (2) unlimited duty-free entry of Central American and Caribbean products into the United States for a period of 12 years (except for textiles, clothing, and sugar—which were subject to quotas), and (3) tax incentives to encourage U.S. citizens to invest in Caribbean enterprises. Congress extended the CBI indefinitely in 1990. (For the North American Free Trade Agreement, see pages 507–508.)

AMERICA BECOMES INVOLVED IN FAR EASTERN PROBLEMS

CHINA: BACKGROUND

China is a huge country in eastern Asia. Its people make up one-fourth of the world's population. The history of China goes back over 3,000 years, during which time China developed an advanced culture and a way of life that was different from that of Western nations. To preserve its culture, China tried to remain apart from the rest of the world. It made no effort to keep pace with Western industrialization or to build a modern army and navy.

In the 19th century the industrialized nations looked upon China as a source of raw materials and as a market for their finished products. Taking advantage of China's military weakness, Japan and the great powers of Europe forced the Chinese government to grant them leases to many of the country's important seaports and economic control over large sections of Chinese territory. These areas were called *spheres of influence*. It seemed that China before long would be completely dismembered by the imperialist nations.

AMERICA PROPOSES AN "OPEN DOOR" POLICY IN CHINA

Ever since the colonial period, American merchants had been carrying on a brisk trade with China. After the United States acquired Hawaii, the Philippines, and island coaling stations in the Pacific, Americans hoped to expand their commercial activities in the Far East. They found themselves at a disadvantage, however, because of the special commercial privileges wrung from China by Japan, Great Britain, Germany, Russia, and other powerful countries.

To safeguard American interests, Secretary of State John Hay in 1899 proposed that the great powers agree to an *Open Door Policy* in China. Such a policy would provide all nations equal trading rights in the country. Early in 1900 Hay announced that the Open Door Policy had been accepted by all the leading powers.

BOXER REBELLION

In 1900 an association of Chinese patriots, called the "Boxers," organized a revolt to drive out the "foreign devils" who were overrunning their homeland. They killed over 200 foreigners, destroyed foreign property, and laid siege to the foreign settlements in the capital city of Peking (now Beijing). The great powers raised an international army, including 2,500 Americans, to rescue their nationals and put down the *Boxer Rebellion*.

Secretary of State Hay feared that the other powers would use the rebellion as an excuse to seize more Chinese territory. He therefore stated that the United States opposed the further dismemberment of China and favored a continuation of the Open Door Policy. The other powers agreed but forced China to pay a large *indemnity* (fine) for the losses suffered by their nationals during the rebellion.

The United States returned a large part of its share of the indemnity to China, which used the money to further the education of Chinese students at American colleges. America's generosity, as well as its other efforts on China's behalf, earned for the United States the friendship of the Chinese people. Friendly relations were maintained between the two countries until after World War II, when China fell to the Communists.

JAPAN: BACKGROUND

Japan, like China, developed a culture that was different from that of Western nations. Fearing Western domination, Japan withdrew into isolation. Foreign ships were not permitted to stop at Japanese ports even for food and water. Shipwrecked sailors who landed on Japanese shores were refused help and were often imprisoned and tortured.

PERRY ENDS JAPAN'S ISOLATION

To end such inhumanities and to open Japan to trade, *Matthew C. Perry* brought a squadron of U.S. warships into Tokyo Bay in 1853. The following year he negotiated a treaty of friendship with Japan. The agreement opened several Japanese ports to American trade and provided for the fair treatment of shipwrecked sailors.

JAPAN BECOMES A MODERN NATION

Impressed with the modern ships, weapons, and machinery of the Western world, Japan embarked on a program of industrialization and military reorganization. It soon became a highly industrialized nation, able to compete for trade in the world's markets. It also developed a powerful army and navy.

To expand its influence and to acquire raw materials for its industries, Japan fought and won a war with China (1894–1895). It forced China to cede the island of Formosa (now called Taiwan) and to grant it a sphere of influence in Korea, which Japan later annexed. In 1905, after a war with Russia, Japan took over Russia's sphere of influence in the Chinese province of Manchuria.

U.S.-JAPANESE RELATIONS BECOME STRAINED

For 50 years after Perry's historic voyage, the United States and Japan were on friendly terms. They carried on a mutually profitable trade, and the United States encouraged Japan to westernize. In 1905, when Japan was at war with Russia, President Theodore Roosevelt brought the two sides together and arranged a peace settlement at Portsmouth, New Hampshire.

After the Russo-Japanese War, U.S. relations with Japan grew less friendly. The Japanese were dissatisfied with the peace treaty that Roosevelt had helped negotiate, claiming that they had been deprived of some of the gains they had expected from their victory. They were also angered by discrimination against Japanese residents in California and other Western states, and they resented the steps taken by the United States to bar Japanese immigration.

Americans, on the other hand, began to fear that (1) Japan aimed to win control of the entire western Pacific area and drive Americans from the Philippines, (2) Japanese commercial expansion threatened American economic interests in the Orient, and (3) Japan planned to dominate China and shut the Open Door.

Relations between the two countries grew steadily worse as the United States continued to oppose Japanese expansion in China. Japan realized that it could not hope to gain mastery of the Far East without first expelling the United States. Eventually, in 1941, the Japanese attacked the United States at Pearl Harbor and brought America into World War II.

Multiple-Choice Test I

1. Which of these did the United States acquire LAST? (*a*) Alaska (*b*) Hawaii (*c*) the Philippine Islands (*d*) the Virgin Islands.
2. Which President dedicated the United States to the Good Neighbor Policy? (*a*) Woodrow Wilson (*b*) Franklin D. Roosevelt (*c*) Theodore Roosevelt (*d*) Andrew Johnson.
3. An important reason why the United States wanted the Virgin Islands was that it wished to acquire a (*a*) regular supply of coffee (*b*) base for the defense of the Panama Canal (*c*) tourist attraction (*d*) source of rubber.
4. Which territories were acquired by the United States as a result of the Spanish-American War? (*a*) New Mexico and Oklahoma (*b*) Hawaii and Alaska (*c*) Puerto Rico and the Philippines (*d*) Florida and Texas.
5. Which President was most closely associated with the construction of the Panama Canal? (*a*) Grover Cleveland (*b*) Franklin D. Roosevelt (*c*) Theodore Roosevelt (*d*) William McKinley.
6. Since World War II, Alaska's strategic importance has increased because of (*a*) the discovery of new gold mines (*b*) the large-scale mining of uranium deposits (*c*) the air routes across the North Pole (*d*) its admission as a state.

7. A direct result of the Spanish-American War was the (a) annexation of Cuba by the United States (b) rivalry between the United States and Russia (c) purchase of the Virgin Islands by the United States (d) establishment of a colonial empire by the United States.

8. Of the following Secretaries of State, the first to formulate an American policy toward China was (a) William H. Seward (b) John Hay (c) James G. Blaine (d) Henry Clay.

9. American foreign policy in the 19th century was most influenced by (a) "Big Stick" diplomacy (b) Washington's Farewell Address (c) the Gentlemen's Agreement (d) dollar diplomacy.

10. An important cause of Latin America's hostility to the United States in the past has been the (a) application of the Roosevelt Corollary (b) original statement of the Monroe Doctrine (c) creation of the Pan-American Union (d) establishment of immigration quotas for Latin Americans.

11. Which Caribbean country accepted the Platt Amendment in 1902? (a) the Dominican Republic (b) Haiti (c) Nicaragua (d) Cuba.

12. Which Caribbean area adopted a constitution in 1952 to govern itself as a free commonwealth associated with the United States? (a) the Virgin Islands (b) the Bahama Islands (c) Puerto Rico (d) Costa Rica.

13. The event that most immediately preceded the Spanish-American War was the (a) American acquisition of Florida (b) mistreatment of Cubans by Spain (c) sinking of the *Maine* (d) occupation of Cuba by General Wood.

14. The United States would be most likely to strengthen the Good Neighbor Policy by (a) reviving dollar diplomacy (b) intervening in Guatemala (c) extending reciprocal trade agreements (d) supporting an underground movement in Argentina.

15. The United States first won recognition as a leading world naval power after the (a) War of 1812 (b) Civil War (c) Spanish-American War (d) First World War.

Multiple-Choice Test II

1. The United States decided on its Open Door Policy at a time when China (a) was in danger of being partitioned by foreign nations (b) refused to carry on trade with non-Asian powers (c) was engaged in a civil war between Communists and Nationalists (d) was undergoing rapid industrialization.

2. As Secretary of State, James G. Blaine is best remembered for his (a) weak foreign policy (b) desire to annex Mexico and Canada (c) frequent clashes with Great Britain (d) efforts to establish more friendly relations with Latin America.

3. The United States won Chinese support in the period immediately following the Boxer Rebellion by (a) encouraging Chinese expansion into Tibet (b) returning a portion of the indemnity payments (c) allowing the admission of Chinese immigrants on a quota basis (d) recognizing Chiang Kai-shek.

4. Dollar diplomacy was used by President Taft to (a) provide aid for developing nations in Africa (b) protect American investments abroad (c) promote an economic union of European nations (d) encourage adoption of an international monetary system.

5. "Seward's Folly" refers to the (a) annexation of Hawaii (b) Open Door Policy (c) purchase of Alaska (d) acquisition of Puerto Rico.

6. The purpose of the Pan-American movement was to (*a*) unite all the countries of North America (*b*) secure naval bases for the United States in South America (*c*) extend the borders of the United States westward to the Pacific (*d*) bring about friendly cooperation among the republics of the Western Hemisphere.

7. All of the following are U.S. bases in the Pacific EXCEPT (*a*) Guam (*b*) Tutuila (*c*) Wake (*d*) Guantánamo.

8. A possession of the United States that was granted complete independence in 1946 is (*a*) American Samoa (*b*) Midway (*c*) the Virgin Islands (*d*) the Philippines.

9. A former Japanese area presently administered by the United States is (*a*) Micronesia (*b*) Formosa (*c*) Korea (*d*) Manchuria.

10. A primary reason why the United States built the Panama Canal was to (*a*) increase the prosperity of Central America (*b*) improve the defense of the United States (*c*) force a reduction of railroad rates (*d*) fulfill our treaty obligations to Great Britain.

11. "Yellow journalism" was most prominent in involving the United States in (*a*) the Mexican War (*b*) the Civil War (*c*) the Spanish-American War (*d*) World War I.

12. Which pairs a period in United States history with a phase of foreign policy dominant at that time? (*a*) 1865–1890—active leadership in world affairs (*b*) 1890–1903—rejection of opportunities for overseas expansion (*c*) 1904–1910—active role in Caribbean area (*d*) 1910–1918—isolation from world struggles.

13. Which event involving United States-Latin American relations occurred LAST? (*a*) announcement of the Roosevelt Corollary (*b*) creation of the Organization of American States (*c*) opening of the Panama Canal (*d*) establishment of the Pan-American Union.

14. The Jones Act and the Tydings-McDuffie Act are associated with political developments in (*a*) Cuba (*b*) Puerto Rico (*c*) the Philippines (*d*) Hawaii.

15. The United States acquired the Virgin Islands from (*a*) Spain (*b*) Denmark (*c*) France (*d*) Great Britain.

Modified True-False Test

1. A popular slogan during the Spanish-American War was *"The Stars and Stripes Forever."*

2. In 1867 the United States purchased Alaska from *Great Britain.*

3. *Gideon Welles,* Secretary of State in Andrew Johnson's administration, negotiated the purchase of Alaska.

4. The first European to discover Hawaii, in 1778, was *Sanford B. Dole,* an English explorer.

5. *Vitus Bering,* a Danish navigator, became the first European to discover Alaska, in 1741.

6. The naval base of *Pearl Harbor* is located on the island of Oahu.

7. *George Dewey,* commander of the Pacific squadron of the U.S. Navy, destroyed the Spanish fleet in Manila Bay in 1898.

8. *Selman Waksman,* an American army medical officer, made the discovery that helped rid Cuba of yellow fever.

9. The *Caribbean Basin Initiative,* proposed in 1982, provided for duty-free

entry of products from certain Latin American countries into the United States.

10. A program to attract new industries to Puerto Rico and thereby help raise the living standards of the people has become known as *Operation Bootstrap.*

11. The Hay—Bunau-Varilla Treaty was an agreement between the United States and *Colombia.*

12. St. Thomas is an important island of the group called the *Bahama* Islands.

13. A program launched by the United States in 1961 to combat economic distress and political instability in Latin America is known as the *Declaration of Lima.*

14. Sections of China over which foreign nations exercised economic control in the late 19th and early 20th centuries were known as *spheres of influence.*

15. The American who succeeded in opening Japan to American trade in the 1850's was *David G. Farragut.*

Essay Questions

1. Show how *two* of the following have caused friction between the United States and Latin American countries: U.S. relations with Cuba, negotiations prior to building the Panama Canal, and Wilson's Mexican policy.

2. For each of the following foreign policies, discuss *one* condition that led to the formulation of this policy and *one* effect of this policy upon our foreign relations: Open Door Policy and Good Neighbor Policy.

3. Describe an action taken by the U.S. government as a result of *each* of the following developments in the Far East: Japan's isolation in the early 1800's, the emigration of Orientals from the Far East to the United States in the period 1875–1925, and the Boxer Rebellion of 1900.

4. Wars have greatly influenced political and economic developments in the United States. Discuss *one* important political and *one* important economic development that resulted from the Spanish-American War.

5. The Panama Canal is often referred to as "a crossroads of the world." (*a*) What two oceans does this canal connect? (*b*) Name *two* people who performed outstanding service during the construction of the canal and describe their contributions. (*c*) Give *two* reasons why the Panama Canal is important to the United States. (*d*) What are the main provisions of the Panama Canal Treaties of 1978?

6. Both Hawaii and Alaska were American territories that have been admitted to the Union as states. (*a*) Choose *either* area and explain how it became a U.S. possession. (*b*) Choose *either* area and tell how it is important to the United States economically and militarily.

7. Americans are proud of the record of their nation in the Philippines. (*a*) How did the Philippines become an American possession? (*b*) In what ways did the United States improve conditions among the Filipinos while the Islands were a territory? (*c*) How did the Philippines gain complete independence?

8. (*a*) How did the United States improve conditions in Cuba during the period of American occupation after the Spanish-American War? (*b*) What was the Platt Amendment? (*c*) When and why was the Platt Amendment abrogated? (*d*) What was the nature of U.S.-Cuban relations before 1960?

Part 2. World War I and Its Aftermath

WORLD WAR I (1914–1918)

CAUSES

The immediate cause of World War I was the assassination in 1914 of Archduke Francis Ferdinand, heir to the throne of Austria-Hungary, by a Serbian patriot. This act, however, was only the spark that touched off the explosion. The fundamental causes were the following:

1. Imperialism. The great European powers competed with each other for world trade and markets, for sources of raw materials, and for colonies in Africa and Asia.

2. Nationalism. Some nations sought to annex foreign areas inhabited by people of their own nationality. (For example, France wanted to regain French-inhabited Alsace and Lorraine, which Germany had seized in 1871.) Minority groups in many countries agitated for independence. (For example, Czechs and Slovaks in the Austro-Hungarian Empire hoped to establish their own nation. Poles—their country dismembered and ruled by Germany, Austria-Hungary, and Russia—wished to reclaim their partitioned homeland.)

3. Militarism. To further their imperialist and nationalist aims, the countries of Europe competed feverishly to outdo each other in building large armies and navies.

4. Opposing Alliances. Britain, France, and Russia had established the *Triple Entente*; Germany, Austria-Hungary, and Italy had formed the *Triple Alliance*. Thus, Europe was divided into two armed camps, each distrusting and fearing the other.

OUTBREAK OF THE WAR

Holding Serbia responsible for the murder of the Archduke, Austria-Hungary presented a harsh ultimatum to that country, rejected Serbia's response as unsatisfactory, and declared war. Russia, sharing a common Slavic heritage with the Serbs and opposing further Austro-Hungarian expansion in Eastern Europe, mobilized its forces to aid Serbia. Germany, rallying to Austria-Hungary's support, declared war on Russia. Expecting the French to side with the Russians, Germany also declared war on France. When the German army invaded Belgium—a nation whose neutrality had been guaranteed by the European powers ever since 1839—Britain entered the war against Germany.

By August, 1914, most of Europe had been drawn into the *Great War* (as World War I was called at the time). On one side were the *Central Powers*: Germany and Austria-Hungary—later joined by Turkey and Bulgaria. On the other side were the *Allies*: Britain, France, Russia, Serbia, and Belgium—later joined by several small European countries, as well as by Japan and Italy. (Japan supported the Allies because it hoped to acquire Germany's Pacific possessions. Italy, though a member

351

of the Triple Alliance, chose to remain neutral at the start of the war. It joined the Allies after Britain and France agreed to permit it to annex some Austrian territory after victory was won.)

STALEMATE ON THE WESTERN FRONT

Aiming for a quick victory in the West, the Germans overran Belgium, entered France, and advanced to within 20 miles of Paris. They were stopped by the French and British at the Marne River and forced to pull back. After several months of costly and desperate maneuvering, both sides dug in to maintain their respective positions. Before long, a network of trenches extended from the Swiss border northwestward through France and Belgium to the Atlantic coast. In these trenches the soldiers of both sides lived, fought, and died. Separating the opposing armies were deadly stretches of ground known as "No-Man's Land"—torn up by artillery fire and strewn with the corpses of humans and animals.

Periodically each side would mount a massive assault against the enemy's defenses in an attempt to achieve a breakthrough. Two such battles, involving millions of soldiers, took place in 1916—at Verdun and along the Somme River. Both sides suffered enormous casualties, but the strategic situation remained unchanged.

Trench warfare persisted on the Western Front until the end of the war.

RUSSIAN COLLAPSE ON THE EASTERN FRONT

The Russians undertook two invasions of eastern Germany and Austria in the early years of the war but were driven back with heavy losses. Counterattacks by the Central Powers destroyed Russia's defenses and forced the Russian army to retreat hundreds of miles inside the country's borders. By the end of 1916 Russia was in turmoil. Its army lacked weapons and supplies, thousands of soldiers were deserting, and its government had lost the support of the people. In the spring of 1917 the autocratic czarist regime was overthrown. A provisional government assumed control, and attempted to restore order and carry on the war. But conditions continued to worsen. In the fall of 1917 a radical Marxist group called the *Bolsheviks* seized power. Heeding the widespread clamor for peace, the new Soviet government agreed to accept Germany's harsh territorial and monetary demands, signed the *Treaty of Brest-Litovsk*, and in March, 1918, took Russia out of the war.

FIGHTING ON THE SOUTHERN FRONT

The Central Powers dominated Southern Europe in the early years of the war. Austrian and German armies occupied most of the Balkans (Serbia, Montenegro, Albania, and Rumania). Turkey controlled the straits connecting the Mediterranean and Black seas, thus bottling up the Russian fleet and preventing Allied aid from reaching Russia by that route. In 1915 a combined force of British, French, Australian, and New Zealand troops attempted to open the straits by storming the powerful Turkish fortifications at *Gallipoli.* After a long and costly campaign, the Allies were forced to withdraw. And in 1917 an Austro-German attack broke through the Italian defenses at *Caporetto* (on the Austro-Italian border) and sent the Italian army fleeing in disorder. Only the arrival of British and French reinforcements prevented a total Allied disaster.

ACTIVITY ON OTHER FRONTS

1. For more than four centuries much of the Middle East had been part of the Turkish Ottoman Empire. The Arabs residing within the empire had long resented Turkish rule but lacked the resources to break away. Britain, which also had interests in the Middle East, gained the support of various Arab tribes for a campaign to drive out the Turks. The British and their Arab allies carried out surprise attacks against Turkish outposts scattered throughout the area and occupied many of the empire's key centers. By 1917 Turkey's vast domain in the Middle East—extending from Mesopotamia to the Mediterranean—was largely controlled by the Allies. Crippled by the loss of its empire and by the virtual destruction of its army, Turkey withdrew from the war in October, 1918.

2. At the outbreak of the war, Britain and France seized Germany's colonial possessions on the west coast of Africa. In the following year the Union of South Africa captured German Southwest Africa for the

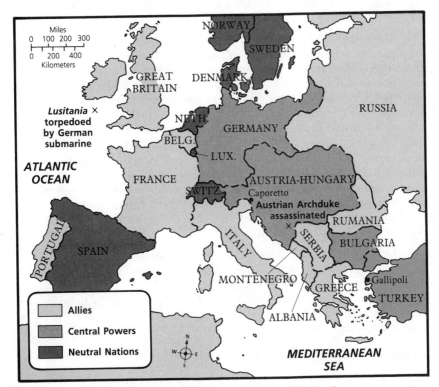

Allies and Central Powers in World War I

Allies. Britain then took possession of German East Africa. But German troops in that area refused to surrender, withdrew into the interior, and carried on guerrilla warfare against the British for the duration of the war.

3. Germany's island possessions in the Pacific—including the Carolines, Marshalls, Samoa, and New Guinea—were taken over by Japan, New Zealand, and Australia.

AMERICA ENTERS THE WAR

Soon after the war in Europe began, President Woodrow Wilson issued a proclamation of neutrality. For nearly three years the United States made every effort to stay out of the war. However, after Germany had repeatedly violated American neutrality, Wilson requested and Congress approved a declaration of war on the Central Powers (April 6, 1917). The following were some of the reasons for America's entry into the conflict on the side of the Allies:

1. Sympathy for Democratic England and France. The great majority of American citizens (*a*) sympathized with England because of common language, customs, and democratic heritage, (*b*) sympathized with France because of French aid during the Revolutionary War, and (*c*) disliked German militarism and autocracy. President Wilson, in his war message to Congress, declared that the chief reason for going to war was to "make the world safe for democracy."

2. Germany's Policy of Unrestricted Submarine Warfare. The warring powers purchased huge quantities of war materials and foodstuffs from the United States. When American ships attempted to deliver the supplies to Europe, they encountered resistance. The English navy searched U.S. ships on the high seas and seized many cargoes bound for non-Allied ports. German submarines attacked American ships bound for Allied ports and sank them without warning.

Germany's unrestricted submarine warfare resulted not only in the destruction of American property, but also in the loss of lives. The American people were therefore far more aroused against Germany than against Britain. Anti-German sentiment in the United States mounted sharply in 1915 when a German U-boat (submarine) torpedoed the English liner *Lusitania*. Almost 1,200 passengers, including over 100 Americans, died when the ship sank.

3. Other Unfriendly Acts by Germany. (*a*) German agents plotted to destroy American munitions plants, organize strikes in war industries, and sabotage shipments of supplies to the Allies. (*b*) The intercepted *Zimmermann Note* revealed that Germany was offering to help Mexico reconquer its lost territories of New Mexico, Arizona, and Texas, in case the United States entered the war.

AMERICA MOBILIZES FOR WAR

The United States raised a large army through voluntary enlistment and a compulsory draft, or *selective service*. The navy and merchant marine were enlarged. Huge sums of money were raised through increased taxes and the sale of bonds. Manufacturers curtailed the production of civilian goods to concentrate on making war supplies. Farmers expanded the acreage under cultivation to meet the increased demand for food. Labor did its part by working longer hours and avoiding strikes. To conserve vital food and fuel, Americans were asked to limit their consumption of wheat, meat, coal, gasoline, and other goods.

Contributing to the totality of the war effort was the participation of women. Entering the labor force in large numbers, they replaced men workers who had been called up for military service and helped expand the production of weapons, war supplies, and civilian goods. Many women also enlisted in the armed forces, serving as clerical personnel, ambulance drivers, and nurses.

THE UNITED STATES HELPS WIN THE WAR

The U.S. Navy, under the command of *William S. Sims*, convoyed merchant vessels and troopships across the Atlantic, blockaded German ports, laid mines, and destroyed German submarines. An American Expeditionary Force (AEF) of 2 million soldiers, under the command of *John J. Pershing*, was sent to France.

Hoping to crush the war-weary Allies before the arrival of the main body of American troops, the Germans launched an all-out offensive on the Western Front in March, 1918. The offensive continued through May. In the next two months, however, with the aid of the newly arrived American *doughboys*, who fought valiantly at Château-Thierry, Belleau Wood, and Cantigny, the German advance was stopped. The Allies then launched a counteroffensive, in which the Americans played a major role. Led by Pershing, American troops defeated the Germans at St. Mihiel, drove them from the Argonne Forest, and advanced along the Meuse River Valley toward the key German-held center of Sedan.

By the end of October, the German army was retreating all along the Western Front. In addition, the alliance of the Central Powers was crumbling. The Ottoman army had been decimated. Bulgaria had surrendered. Austria-Hungary, facing internal uprisings by its subject peoples and unable to withstand a new Allied offensive, was suing for peace. And Germany itself was threatened by mutinies in its army and navy and by a revolution at home.

Realizing that the war was lost, German leaders requested an armistice. Kaiser (Emperor) Wilhelm II of Germany abdicated his throne and fled. On November 11, 1918, an armistice was signed, and World War I came to an end.

COST OF THE WAR

Both sides suffered enormous losses during the war. Total casualties amounted to more than 37 million, including 8.5 million dead. American casualties included 116,500 dead and 204,000 wounded. The United States spent nearly $22 billion in its own war effort and loaned over $9 billion more to the Allies.

WILSON'S FOURTEEN POINTS

In an address to Congress early in 1918, President Wilson presented his program for a just and lasting peace. Known as the Fourteen Points, it called for a fair adjustment of European boundaries and colonial claims, abolition of secret treaties, recognition of the right of each national group to self-government, freedom of the seas in peace and war, reduction of armaments, and formation of a League of Nations.

TREATY OF VERSAILLES

At Versailles, France, the victorious powers in 1919 drafted a peace treaty that (*a*) forced Germany to admit its guilt in causing the war; (*b*) obligated that country to pay a huge sum as *reparations* (payments for war damages); (*c*) took away its colonial possessions in Africa and Asia; (*d*) reduced its territory in Europe; (*e*) compelled it to disarm; and (*f*) prohibited it from rebuilding a powerful military force. At President Wilson's insistence, the Treaty of Versailles also included a provision for the establishment of a League of Nations.

THE UNITED STATES REJECTS LEAGUE MEMBERSHIP

When the Treaty of Versailles—with its provision for a League of Nations—was submitted to the U.S. Senate for ratification, it encoun-

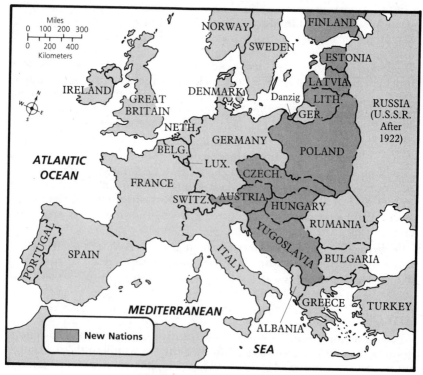

Europe After World War I

tered strong opposition. Some senators feared that, as a member of the League, the United States would become entangled in European affairs. Others felt that membership would mean a loss of independence for the country.

President Wilson appealed to the nation to support League membership. He set out on a nationwide speaking tour but, before its completion, suffered a stroke from which he never fully recovered. Senate opposition to the League was so strong that it refused to ratify the Treaty of Versailles. Later, in 1921, the United States concluded separate peace treaties with Germany, Austria, and Hungary.

LEAGUE OF NATIONS

STRUCTURE OF THE LEAGUE OF NATIONS

Though the United States did not become a member of the League, more than 50 other countries joined the organization. Its purpose was to promote international cooperation and to achieve peace and security for all nations. Its members pledged to (1) respect and preserve the territory and independence of all nations joining the League, (2) submit to arbitration all disputes that might lead to war, (3) abide by the League's decisions in such disputes, (4) apply economic sanctions (such as cutting off trade relations) and military force against member nations that resorted to war, if the League called for such measures, and (5) cooperate with the League in economic and social matters.

The member nations sent representatives to an *Assembly*, which met annually to discuss all problems with which the League was concerned. Every member country had an equal voice in the Assembly, where a unanimous vote was required to decide important matters. The League also consisted of a *Council* and a *Secretariat*. The Council, which included the great powers as well as other nations, gave special attention to international disputes. The Secretariat was the administrative organ of the League. Headquarters of the League were located in Geneva, Switzerland. Associated with the League, but not an actual part of it, was the *World Court*, to which nations could bring disputes for settlement.

USEFULNESS OF THE LEAGUE

During the quarter century of its existence, the League carried on much useful work. Through its Mandates Commission it supervised the former colonial possessions of the Central Powers. The World Court settled a number of international disputes. The League carried on relief work in war-torn countries and aided war refugees. It gathered statistics, published reports, and held international conferences to improve labor conditions, public health, education, communication, and transportation throughout the world. The United States participated in many of the League's nonpolitical activities.

THE LEAGUE IS UNABLE TO PRESERVE PEACE

Although it accomplished much that was worthwhile, the League was unable to carry out its major task: preventing aggression and war. The following were some of the reasons for this failure:

1. The League suffered a loss of prestige at the very start when the United States, one of the world's leading powers, failed to become a member.

2. It lacked effective means to punish an aggressor nation. It could only suggest that its members take action. If they refused to carry out the League's suggestions, it was powerless to do more.

3. Aggressive nations whose acts were criticized by the League simply withdrew from the organization. Germany, which became a member in 1926, resigned in 1933 after the League refused to permit it to rearm. Japan withdrew that same year when the League condemned its attack on Manchuria. Italy left in 1937 after the League condemned its invasion of Ethiopia.

4. The leading nations were unwilling to pool their strength to prevent aggression when their own interests were not directly involved.

OTHER ATTEMPTS TO REDUCE THE THREAT OF WAR

WASHINGTON CONFERENCE

At the invitation of President Warren G. Harding, the major powers met in Washington in 1921 to discuss Far Eastern problems and the reduction of naval armaments. The five leading naval powers (the United States, Britain, Japan, France, and Italy) agreed to scrap some of their large warships and to limit the number of their battleships and heavy cruisers, according to a specific formula. The powers also agreed to respect one another's interests in the Far East and to support the Open Door Policy in China.

KELLOGG-BRIAND PACT

Under the sponsorship of Secretary of State Frank Kellogg and the French Foreign Minister Aristide Briand, a pact was drawn up in 1928 and signed by most nations of the world. They agreed to outlaw war as a means of settling international disputes. The *Kellogg-Briand Pact,* however, provided no machinery for enforcement. It was hoped that public opinion would compel the signatories to live up to their pledges. Future events proved that the pact was an empty gesture. Nations bent on conquest broke their promises and continued to resort to force to gain their ends.

LONDON CONFERENCES ON NAVAL DISARMAMENT

At a conference held in London in 1930, the United States, Britain, and Japan agreed to continue restrictions on the construction of large warships. They also imposed limits on the building of smaller naval vessels. France and Italy refused to become parties to this agreement.

Five years later, as the agreement of 1930 was nearing its expiration date, a second London Conference was held. Whereas the earlier agreement had allowed Japan a navy roughly two-thirds the size of those of the United States and Great Britain, Japan now demanded naval equality. When its demand was rejected, Japan withdrew from the talks, and the race for naval superiority resumed.

DOMESTIC AFFAIRS IN THE POST-WAR YEARS

HIGHLIGHTS OF HARDING'S ADMINISTRATION

In the presidential campaign of 1920, Governor James M. Cox of Ohio, a Democrat, opposed Senator Warren G. Harding of Ohio, a Republican. Harding called for a "return to normalcy," a slogan that so appealed to war-weary Americans that they voted him into office by a landslide.

During Harding's term: (1) A separate *Veterans' Bureau* (later called the Veterans Administration) was established to supervise the various federal programs of aid to the nation's ex-soldiers. (2) A *Bureau of the Budget* (now known as the Office of Management and Budget) was created to coordinate federal expenditures and receipts, thus making government operations more businesslike. (3) The *Fordney-McCumber Tariff Act* reversed the tariff policy of the Wilson administration by raising tariffs to a new high level. (4) The *Emergency Quota Act of 1921* sharply limited immigration into the United States. (5) The Washington Conference was held.

Harding's administration was marred by a series of scandals involving several of his appointive officials. (1) Secretary of the Interior Albert Fall received large bribes from oil operators for leasing government oil reserve lands to them under particularly favorable terms. For his part in this *Teapot Dome Scandal,* Fall was fined heavily and sentenced to jail. (2) The head of the Veterans' Bureau and the Custodian of Alien Property were imprisoned for defrauding the government of huge sums of money. (3) The Attorney General was charged with receiving bribes and failing to prosecute grafters, and was forced to resign his office.

COOLIDGE SUCCEEDS TO THE PRESIDENCY

When Harding died suddenly in the summer of 1923, Vice President Calvin Coolidge of Massachusetts succeeded him. After completing Harding's term, he ran for President in his own right in 1924 and was returned to office by a huge majority.

Coolidge believed that "the business of America is business." He opposed government interference with private enterprise. He worked to reduce the public debt, to lower the cost of government, and to cut taxes. During his term, immigration was further restricted, a Soldiers' Bonus Act was passed (over his veto), and the Kellogg-Briand Pact was signed.

THE PROSPEROUS TWENTIES

During Coolidge's administration, the country enjoyed an unprecedented business boom. Industrial activity rose to a new high level, and the national wealth soared. Wages were high, and the average family enjoyed a larger income than ever before. The nation went on a buying spree. Automobiles, radios, new homes, and furniture were in great demand. Not content with purchasing from current income or savings, many people bought on the installment plan. That is, they made a small down payment and promised to pay the balance in the future. Many also used their savings to speculate wildly on the stock market in an effort to get rich quickly. Optimism ran riot, and people expected prosperity to continue forever.

American farmers, however, did not share in this prosperity. During the war they had expanded production to meet the increased demand for foodstuffs. After the war overseas demand fell off, and farm prices dropped sharply. All through the Twenties, while most other sections of the economy were enjoying a boom, farmers had to cope with surplus crops, heavy debts, and declining income.

HOOVER DEFEATS SMITH IN 1928

When Coolidge refused to run for reelection in 1928, the Republicans nominated Herbert Hoover of California. He was a mining engineer and businessperson who had earned world fame as an organizer of war relief in Europe during and after World War I. He had also served as the U.S. Food Administrator in 1917–1919 and as Secretary of Commerce under Harding and Coolidge.

The Democratic nominee was Alfred E. Smith of New York. Although "Al" Smith, the "Happy Warrior," was personally popular and had shown great executive ability as Governor of New York, he also aroused much opposition. (1) He advocated the repeal of prohibition. (2) He was a Roman Catholic. (3) He was associated with New York City's political machine, *Tammany Hall.* These factors and the so-called "Coolidge prosperity" helped the Republicans win a decisive victory. Hoover carried 40 states, including four in the traditionally Democratic "Solid South."

CRASH OF 1929

The prosperity of the Twenties came to an abrupt end in the fall of 1929 with the collapse of the stock market. Wild speculation had pushed stock prices far above their real values. When prices began to fall, frightened investors hurried to sell their stock holdings. As a result, the market declined still further. In addition, many speculators had bought on *margin.* That is, they had put up only a small part of a stock's cost and had borrowed the balance from their broker. When their broker demanded repayment and they were unable to settle their debts, they were forced to sell their stock at whatever price they could get. Panic set in. Banks and investment firms went bankrupt; depositors and investors saw their savings wiped out. Factories and mines closed down. Unemployment spread. Wages were cut sharply.

The following were some of the causes for the crash of 1929 and the depression that followed:

1. Overproduction. The prosperity of the Twenties had made business owners too hopeful. Industry had expanded too rapidly and was producing more goods than it could sell.

2. Underconsumption. The purchasing power of American consumers was not great enough to buy all the goods being produced. Farmers in particular were unable to purchase their share of America's industrial output because declining farm prices reduced their income. Foreign countries were unable to buy American goods because of war debts, reparations, and tariff barriers.

3. Unsound Financial Practices. Banks made unsound personal and business loans and did not receive full repayment. Brokers sold stock on too small a margin and thus encouraged widespread speculation. Consumers made unwise purchases on the installment plan and were later unable to complete their payments.

HOOVER TRIES TO FIGHT THE DEPRESSION

Even before the stock market crash, Hoover proposed and Congress passed the *Agricultural Marketing Act*. It was designed to stabilize farm prices by keeping surpluses from the market. A $500 million fund was set up for the purchase of surplus crops. The plan failed because the farm depression was too severe and the resources of the fund were too limited.

When the rest of the economy was hit by the depression, Hoover at first was optimistic over.the prospects of an early recovery. As the depression deepened and became worldwide, however, he took the following steps: (1) The *Reconstruction Finance Corporation (RFC)* was established to make emergency loans to financial institutions, life insurance companies, and railroads. (2) A limited program of federal public works was started. (3) States and local communities were encouraged to undertake similar projects and to obtain loans for this purpose from the RFC. (4) Payments of war debts and reparations owed to the United States by foreign governments were suspended for one year. Such a suspension of debts is called a *moratorium*. Hoover hoped that this moratorium would relieve the financial plight of European nations and enable them to buy more goods from the United States.

OTHER DEVELOPMENTS

Tariffs on imports were further increased by the *Hawley-Smoot Tariff Act*. Foreign nations retaliated by raising their tariffs, and American exports suffered a sharp decline. Also during Hoover's administration: (1) The *National Origins Act* limiting immigration went into effect. (2) The *Twentieth ("Lame Duck") Amendment* was adopted. (3) The United States participated in the London Conference on Naval Disarmament in 1930. (4) The United States issued the *Stimson Doctrine,* declaring its opposition to Japan's seizure of the Chinese province of Manchuria.

THE DEMOCRATS WIN IN 1932

In 1932 the Republicans nominated Hoover for a second term. The Democrats choose Franklin D. Roosevelt of New York as their candidate. The election took place while the nation was in the grip of the Great Depression. Business was at a virtual standstill. More than 13 million workers were jobless. Mortgages on farms and homes were being foreclosed at an alarming rate. The nation's banking system was tottering. Breadlines were a familiar sight in every large city.

Some Americans blamed the Hoover administration for causing the nation's economic distress, while others accused it of doing nothing to correct the ills of the economy. In complete rejection of Hoover, the people voted overwhelmingly for the Democrats. Roosevelt carried 42 states to Hoover's 6, and the Democrats won control of both houses of Congress.

Multiple-Choice Test

1. Which one of the following treaties was never ratified by the U.S. Senate? (*a*) the Kellogg-Briand Peace Pact (1928) (*b*) the Treaty of Versailles (1919) (*c*) the Treaty of Paris (1898) (*d*) the Washington Five-Power Pact (1922).

2. The United States joined all of the following international organizations EXCEPT the (*a*) Pan-American Union (*b*) Organization of American States (*c*) United Nations (*d*) League of Nations.

3. In which national election year was the "Solid South" broken? (*a*) 1916 (*b*) 1920 (*c*) 1928 (*d*) 1932.

4. The event that most immediately preceded U.S. participation in World War I was the (*a*) resumption of unrestricted German submarine warfare (*b*) formation of a system of European alliances (*c*) proclamation of the Fourteen Points (*d*) assassination of Archduke Francis Ferdinand of Austria-Hungary.

5. The Agricultural Marketing Act was passed during the administration of (*a*) Woodrow Wilson (*b*) Warren G. Harding (*c*) Calvin Coolidge (*d*) Herbert Hoover.

6. President Wilson's policy at the beginning of the Great War in Europe was to (*a*) send aid to nations attacked by Germany (*b*) issue a proclamation of neutrality (*c*) declare war against the Central Powers (*d*) prohibit trade with warring nations.

7. An important American contribution to world peace in the 1920's and 1930's was (*a*) support of the movement to reduce armaments (*b*) support of the League of Nations (*c*) membership in the Triple Entente (*d*) adoption of free trade.

8. The Fordney-McCumber Tariff Act and the first immigration quota law were enacted during the administration of (*a*) Franklin D. Roosevelt (*b*) Herbert Hoover (*c*) Calvin Coolidge (*d*) Warren G. Harding.

9. Japan's seizure of the Chinese province of Manchuria led to the proclamation by the United States of the (*a*) Open Door Policy (*b*) Stimson Doctrine (*c*) Good Neighbor Policy (*d*) Hoover Moratorium.

10. A cause basic to the U.S. entry into World War I was also basic to its entry

into the (*a*) Revolutionary War (*b*) War of 1812 (*c*) Mexican War (*d*) Civil War.

11. Which is most commonly associated with the administrations of Ulysses S. Grant and Warren G. Harding? (*a*) depression in business (*b*) humanitarian reforms (*c*) corruption involving public officials (*d*) territorial expansion.

12. An important factor contributing to the Great Depression in the United States was the (*a*) decline of farm prosperity during the 1920's (*b*) large military budgets of the 1920's (*c*) rapid development of the country's mineral resources (*d*) large importation of foreign goods.

13. The Kellogg-Briand Pact was an attempt to (*a*) collect war damages from Germany (*b*) reduce armaments (*c*) outlaw war (*d*) encourage the breakup of colonial empires.

14. Which phrase is associated most closely with Woodrow Wilson? (*a*) "return to normalcy" (*b*) "speak softly and carry a big stick" (*c*) "the business of America is business" (*d*) "make the world safe for democracy."

15. The main issue in the election campaign of 1932 was the (*a*) nationwide depression (*b*) tariff (*c*) Treaty of Versailles (*d*) reduction of the national debt.

Matching Test

Column A	*Column B*
1. Fourteen Points	*a.* Commander of the AEF during World War I
2. Zimmermann Note	*b.* American naval commander in World War I
3. doughboy	*c.* Term for German submarine
4. *Lusitania*	*d.* German proposal for an anti-American alliance with Mexico
5. St. Mihiel	*e.* Payments for war damages
6. William S. Sims	*f.* Compulsory enlistment of men into the armed forces
7. U-boat	
8. John J. Pershing	*g.* Wilson's peace program
9. reparations	*h.* World War I battle in which American troops distinguished themselves
10. selective service	*i.* English passenger ship torpedoed by the Germans during World War I
	j. Term for American soldier in World War I

Essay Questions

1. (*a*) List *one* immediate and *two* fundamental causes of World War I. (*b*) List *one* cause of America's entry into World War I. (*c*) Give *two* reasons for the refusal of the United States to join the League of Nations.

2. (*a*) Describe the organization of the League of Nations. (*b*) List *three* of the League's accomplishments. (*c*) Give *two* reasons why the League was unable to preserve the peace.

3. The Crash of 1929 touched off the severest economic depression in the nation's history. (*a*) Explain *two* conditions that helped to bring about the Great Depression in the United States. (*b*) Describe *two* steps that President Hoover took to cope with the depression.

Part 3. The New Deal

EARLY LIFE OF FRANKLIN D. ROOSEVELT

Franklin Delano Roosevelt, a distant cousin of Theodore Roosevelt, was born into a wealthy family in 1882 at Hyde Park, New York. He spent his boyhood on the family estate at Hyde Park, studied law at Columbia, and established a law practice in New York City. In 1905 he married Eleanor Roosevelt, a niece of President Theodore Roosevelt.

POLITICAL CAREER

In 1910 Roosevelt accepted the Democratic nomination for the New York State Senate in a predominantly Republican district and was elected. During his term he earned a statewide reputation as an opponent of political bossism and displayed an interest in the reform movements of the Progressive Era. He supported Wilson's candidacy in 1912 and was appointed Assistant Secretary of the Navy when Wilson became President. During his eight-year tenure he helped to reorganize naval shore installations and to prepare the navy for World War I. In 1920 Roosevelt was the unsuccessful Democratic candidate for Vice President.

In 1921 Roosevelt was stricken with infantile paralysis, a disability that many thought would end his public career. He fought his affliction with courage and determination. He exercised until he partially overcame the paralysis of his legs, and he learned to walk again with the aid of steel braces and a cane.

Resuming his political career, he was elected governor of New York in 1928 and again in 1930. F.D.R. attracted national attention as a vigorous administrator and as an outstanding liberal. Nominated as the Democratic standard-bearer in 1932, he was overwhelmingly chosen the nation's 32nd President. Four years later he ran again and was returned to office by a tremendous majority, carrying every state except Maine and Vermont. In 1940, with war raging in Europe, Roosevelt ran for a third term and won, thus shattering the two-term tradition that had been established by George Washington. Then in 1944 he was again reelected. He died in April, 1945, shortly after the start of his fourth term.

F.D.R. TAKES STEPS TO COMBAT THE GREAT DEPRESSION

When Roosevelt assumed the presidency in March, 1933, the nation was in the midst of the greatest peacetime crisis in its history. In his First Inaugural Address, Roosevelt asserted that "the only thing we have to fear is fear itself," and declared that the people, in their need, "have registered a mandate that they want direct, vigorous action."

Calling for a "new deal" for the "forgotten man at the bottom of the economic pyramid," he launched a program of *relief, recovery,* and *reform.* Its objectives were to (1) provide emergency assistance to the needy, (2) end the existing depression, and (3) prevent the recurrence of similar problems in the future. Roosevelt's program became known as the *New Deal.* Important New Deal measures are discussed in the pages that follow.

TO EASE THE BANKING CRISIS AND EFFECT FINANCIAL REFORMS

F.D.R.'s first official act as President in 1933 was to proclaim a national "bank holiday." All banks were closed until government examiners could investigate their financial condition. Thus, Roosevelt halted the rising tide of bank "runs." (A run occurs when depositors lose confidence in a bank, become panicky, and rush to withdraw their money.) Only sound banks were permitted to reopen. In the first of his many radio broadcasts, or *fireside chats,* to the nation, the President assured the people that the reopened banks were backed by the resources of the federal government and were "safe." This speech helped restore confidence and eased the banking crisis.

To inflate the currency and bring about a rise in prices, the government abandoned the gold standard, forbade the hoarding of gold, and devalued the dollar.

The *Federal Securities Act* (1933) required companies offering new securities (stocks and bonds) for public sale to disclose all information relating to these issues.

The *Glass-Steagall Act* (1933) prohibited banks from using depositors' money to trade in stocks and bonds. It also created the *Federal Deposit*

The Granger Collection, New York
New Deal Remedies

Insurance Corporation *(FDIC)* to protect depositors against the loss of their savings (up to a certain amount) in the event of a bank failure.

The *Securities and Exchange Commission (SEC)* was established in 1934 to supervise stock exchanges and to protect investors against dishonest practices by stockbrokers and by publicly owned corporations.

TO AID THE UNEMPLOYED

The *Federal Emergency Relief Administration (FERA)* made large sums of money available to local and state agencies for direct relief to the unemployed. Millions of families received cash to help pay for food, clothing, and shelter.

The *Public Works Administration (PWA)* and the *Works Progress Administration (WPA)* put millions of jobless to work on such projects as the construction and improvement of highways, bridges, schools, hospitals, parks, and sewers. Artists, writers, actors, musicians, and white-collar workers were employed on projects suitable to their talents and abilities.

The *Civilian Conservation Corps (CCC)* provided employment for hundreds of thousands of young men on such conservation projects as reforestation, flood control, and improvement of national parks.

The *National Youth Administration (NYA)* helped high school and college students continue their studies by providing them with part-time work.

TO AID THE RECOVERY OF INDUSTRY

The *National Industrial Recovery Act* (1933) set up the *National Recovery Administration (NRA)* for the purpose of establishing codes of fair business practice. These codes limited hours of employment, established minimum wages, and set up uniform prices for goods. This act was declared unconstitutional by the Supreme Court in 1935.

The lending power of the Hoover-created RFC was increased to extend financial aid to all struggling businesses.

The Roosevelt administration also made a strong effort to boost the economy by encouraging foreign trade: (1) The *Export-Import Bank* was created to extend loans to American manufacturers and exporters seeking to do business with nations abroad and to foreign firms wishing to import American goods. (2) The *Trade Agreements Act* (1934) authorized the President to negotiate *reciprocal trade agreements* with other nations. Roosevelt was empowered to lower tariff rates by as much as 50% on imports from countries that agreed to reduce duties on U.S. goods. Many such agreements were negotiated by Secretary of State Cordell Hull. Lowering tariff barriers helped revive international trade.

TO AID THE RECOVERY OF AGRICULTURE

The *Agricultural Adjustment Act of 1933* sought to (1) raise farm prices by curtailing production, and (2) increase farmers' incomes by paying them a bonus for acreage withdrawn from cultivation. When this act was declared unconstitutional by the Supreme Court, it was replaced by the *Soil Conservation and Domestic Allotment Act of 1936* (see page 240) and the *Agricultural Adjustment Act of 1938* (see page 241). These enactments achieved the objectives of the first law but eliminated its unconstitutional provisions.

Other measures designed to help the farmers included (1) granting loans to enable them to withhold produce from the market until prices were better, (2) refinancing farm mortgages at low interest rates to keep them from losing their land through foreclosure, (3) helping those who had lost their property to resettle on new farms or to reacquire the ones they had lost, and (4) making electric power available to isolated farm areas by a program of rural electrification.

TO HELP LABOR

The *National Labor Relations Act* (1935), or *Wagner Act*, guaranteed labor the right to organize and to bargain collectively.

The *Social Security Act* (1935) provided for the payment of pensions to aged persons and set up a cooperative federal-state program of unemployment insurance (see page 270).

The *Fair Labor Standards Act* (1938) established minimum wages and maximum hours for labor.

TO AID HOMEOWNERS AND PROVIDE LOW-COST HOUSING

The *Home Owners Loan Corporation* (*HOLC*) came to the rescue of homeowners who were in danger of losing their property because of failure to meet mortgage payments. Between 1933 and 1936 the HOLC refinanced the mortgages on more than a million homes by making low-interest, long-term loans to homeowners.

The *Federal Housing Administration* (*FHA*) was established in 1934 to encourage the construction and repair of private dwellings. The FHA insured banks and other private lending institutions against loss on residential loans.

The *United States Housing Authority* (*USHA*), created in 1937, extended loans to local communities for slum clearance and low-cost housing projects.

(In 1947 the housing activities of the federal government were placed under the supervision of the *Housing and Home Finance Agency* (*HHFA*). Responsibility for all federal housing functions and programs was transferred to the newly created *Department of Housing and Urban Development* (*HUD*) in 1965.)

TO CONSERVE AND PROTECT THE NATION'S RESOURCES

The *Tennessee Valley Authority* (*TVA*) was established in 1933 to develop the resources of the Tennessee River Valley, which includes parts of seven states. The agency erected dams and power plants along the Tennessee River and its tributaries, built transmission lines, and provided low-cost electric power to the farms, industries, and communities of the region. The TVA produced fertilizers, introduced flood-control measures, and helped halt soil erosion by a reforestation program. It also improved river navigation and otherwise advanced "the economic and social well-being of the people in the Tennessee River Basin."

(During World War II, TVA performed a vital service by supplying electricity for the manufacture of munitions, aluminum, and synthetic rubber, as well as for the operation of an atomic energy plant at Oak Ridge, Tennessee.)

Huge dams were also built in other parts of the country to generate hydroelectric power, prevent floods, improve river navigation, and irrigate arid land. Among these were *Hoover Dam,* or *Boulder Dam,* on the Colorado River (begun during Hoover's administration and completed in 1936), *Grand Coulee Dam* on the Columbia River, *Shasta Dam* on the Sacramento River, and *Fort Peck Dam* on the Missouri River.

The government also took steps to conserve the soil of the Great Plains. Farmers there were suffering from effects of a severe drought. As sources of water dried up, crops withered, cattle died, and the soil turned to powdery dust. Winds blowing across the open plains churned up the topsoil and carried it away—creating enormous dust storms and destroying the fertility of the land. With the region becoming a "Dust Bowl" and farmers abandoning their homes to seek a living elsewhere, the federal government initiated a program to curb wind erosion. The President ordered the planting of a broad belt of trees from the Dakotas to Texas, a distance of 1,000 miles. By breaking the force of the winds, anchoring the soil, and retaining ground moisture, these trees helped to make the Great Plains "green" again.

OTHER DOMESTIC ENACTMENTS

(1) The *Twenty-first Amendment,* ratified in 1933, legalized the manufacture and sale of alcoholic beverages by repealing the Eighteenth Amendment. (2) The *Federal Communications Commission (FCC)* was created to regulate interstate and foreign communications facilities. (3) The *Motor Carrier Act* placed buses and trucks engaged in interstate commerce under the supervision of the Interstate Commerce Commission. (4) The *Civil Aeronautics Act* placed air transportation under federal control. (5) The *Wheeler-Rayburn Act* strengthened government regulation of interstate electric and gas companies and ordered the breakup of many public utility holding companies. (6) The *United States Maritime Commission* was established to enlarge America's fleet of merchant ships (the merchant marine) with federal aid. (7) The *Food, Drug, and Cosmetic Act* of 1938 required manufacturers of foods, drugs, and cosmetics to list all ingredients on the labels of their products and forbade the use of false or misleading advertising.

THE NEW DEAL IS CRITICIZED AND PRAISED

At first nearly all Americans approved the measures taken by the Roosevelt administration to combat the depression and spark a business recovery. As time passed and conditions improved, however, criticism of the President and his New Deal program grew. Some Americans charged that the government was wielding too much power over business and agriculture. They argued that the nation was being led away from its traditions of free enterprise and rugged individualism, and was heading toward socialism. Others argued that the cost of the New Deal was too high (the national debt rose from \$19.5 billion in 1932 to \$49 billion in 1941). They pointed out that much money was being wasted and that the New Deal had not eliminated unemployment (8 million workers were still without jobs in 1939).

Further criticism was aroused when the President attempted, unsuccessfully, to enlarge the Supreme Court after it had ruled against a number of key New Deal measures. Enlarging the court would have permitted Roosevelt to appoint enough new judges to secure a majority favorable to the New Deal. Still further protests arose when Roosevelt broke the two-term tradition.

On the other hand, F.D.R.'s supporters enthusiastically praised the New Deal. They claimed that it had saved the nation from disaster, restored the confidence of the people, and spurred the nation's progress toward economic and social democracy.

ROOSEVELT SEEKS TO IMPROVE INTERNATIONAL RELATIONS

In foreign affairs the Roosevelt administration took steps to promote international goodwill by (1) adopting a "Good Neighbor" Policy toward the other republics of the Western Hemisphere, (2) recognizing the Soviet Union and reestablishing diplomatic relations with that country in 1933 (relations had been broken off when the Bolsheviks seized power in Russia during World War I), (3) negotiating reciprocal trade agreements with many foreign countries, and (4) setting the Philippine Islands on the road to independence by securing passage of the Tydings-McDuffie Act.

FOREIGN AFFAIRS BECOME F.D.R.'S CHIEF CONCERN

The outbreak of war in Europe in September, 1939, turned the attention of the Roosevelt administration away from domestic reform. From that time on, problems relating to the war became the President's chief concern. He devoted all his energies to preparing the country's defenses and putting the nation on a war footing. In the second half of his administration, Roosevelt assumed a new role: America's commander-in-chief in World War II.

Multiple-Choice Test

1. The Tennesseee Valley Authority was created primarily to (*a*) develop irrigation projects (*b*) improve the economic life of an entire region (*c*) make money for the government (*d*) protect wildlife.
2. On which river is the Grand Coulee Dam located? (*a*) Colorado (*b*) Columbia (*c*) Sacramento (*d*) Snake.
3. Between 1932 and 1938 the federal government spent large sums of money in (*a*) fighting a war (*b*) paying a great part of the cost of public education (*c*) providing work for the unemployed (*d*) lending money to help foreign countries.

4. In describing the New Deal Era, most historians agree that the federal government (*a*) preserved states' rights as supreme over federal powers (*b*) increased its control over the economy of the United States (*c*) restricted the activities of labor unions (*d*) retarded the establishment of social welfare programs.

5. Woodrow Wilson and Franklin D. Roosevelt were alike in that both were (*a*) members of the Republican party (*b*) elected to the presidency more than twice (*c*) members of the Democratic party (*d*) elected by the House of Representatives.

6. A criticism of the New Deal was that it (*a*) weakened the power of the President (*b*) did not deal with important issues (*c*) promoted a "hands off" policy by the government toward business (*d*) greatly increased the national debt.

7. One reason that Congress adopted reciprocal tariff legislation in the 1930's was to (*a*) discourage world trade (*b*) increase U.S. foreign markets (*c*) help make the United States a self-sufficient nation (*d*) encourage the expansionist policies of Germany, Italy, and Russia.

8. The best explanation for Franklin D. Roosevelt's election to the presidency for a third and fourth term was the (*a*) reluctance of voters to change leadership in the midst of a great crisis (*b*) popularity of his running mates (*c*) ratification of the Twentieth Amendment (*d*) split of the "Solid South."

9. The policies of Theodore Roosevelt and Franklin Roosevelt that differed MOST were those concerning (*a*) the protection of the consumer (*b*) conservation of natural resources (*c*) the power of the presidency (*d*) the countries of Latin America.

10. Which is a reason why Franklin D. Roosevelt asked Congress to increase the number of Supreme Court judges? (*a*) The Court had declared many New Deal laws unconstitutional. (*b*) There was too much work for nine justices. (*c*) More experienced justices were needed for the work. (*d*) Until 1932 there had been more than nine Supreme Court justices.

11. Which New Deal agency was invalidated because of a ruling by the U.S. Supreme Court? (*a*) Civilian Conservation Corps (*b*) Federal Deposit Insurance Corporation (*c*) Public Works Administration (*d*) National Recovery Administration.

12. Which was a significant result of the Great Depression? (*a*) the failure of the Republican party to win the presidency since that time (*b*) a sharp increase in the proportion of Americans engaged in agriculture (*c*) the establishment by the federal government of certain safeguards against depressions (*d*) the elimination of poverty in the United States.

13. Which of the following statements relating to Franklin D. Roosevelt's administration is NOT true? (*a*) F.D.R. shattered the two-term tradition. (*b*) The President declared a national banking holiday in 1933. (*c*) Fireside chats were common occurrences during the New Deal Era. (*d*) The New Deal Era was marked by the passage of the Hawley-Smoot Tariff and other high protective tariff measures.

14. All of the following legislation was enacted during the administration of Franklin D. Roosevelt EXCEPT the (*a*) Fair Labor Standards Act (*b*) National Defense Education Act (*c*) Social Security Act (*d*) National Labor Relations Act.

15. Which of the following statements relating to Franklin D. Roosevelt's life

and career is NOT true? (*a*) His home was at Hyde Park, New York. (*b*) He served in the Cabinet of President Coolidge. (*c*) He suffered from the effects of infantile paralysis. (*d*) He ran for Vice President of the United States in 1920.

Reading Selection Test

In philosophy the New Deal was democratic, in method evolutionary. Because for fifteen years legislative reforms had been dammed up, they now burst upon the country with what seemed like violence, but when the waters subsided it was clear that they ran in familiar channels. The conservation policy of the New Deal had been inaugurated by Theodore Roosevelt; railroad and trust regulation went back to the [1880's]; banking and currency reforms had been partially achieved by Wilson; the farm-relief program borrowed much from the Populists, labor legislation from the practices of such states as Wisconsin and Oregon. Even judicial reform, which caused such a mighty stir, had been anticipated by Lincoln and Theodore Roosevelt. And in the realm of international relations the policies of the New Deal were clearly continuations of the traditional policies of strengthening national security, maintaining freedom of the seas, supporting law and peace, and championing democracy in the Western world.

—Nevins and Commager, *A Pocket History of the United States*

Directions: Read the selection above. Base your answers on the information in the selection and on your knowledge of history. For *each* statement write the *letter* preceding the word or expression that best completes the statement.

1. A suitable title for the selection is (*a*) The New Deal—A Strange Phenomenon on the American Scene (*b*) Precedents for the New Deal (*c*) The New Deal—A Passing Phase in American History (*d*) The New Deal—A Return to Conservatism.
2. Many students of history do not agree with the view that legislative reforms had been "dammed up" during the 15-year period preceding the New Deal. All of the following legislative measures were passed during this 15-year period EXCEPT the (*a*) Norris-La Guardia Act (*b*) Reconstruction Finance Corporation Act (*c*) Sherman Antitrust Act (*d*) Agricultural Marketing Act.
3. This selection traces the origin of many of the policies of the New Deal to all of the following EXCEPT (*a*) former Presidents (*b*) legislation of certain Western and Middle Western states (*c*) minority parties (*d*) the Supreme Court.
4. According to the selection, legislative reforms of the New Deal are characterized by all of the following adjectives EXCEPT (*a*) democratic (*b*) evolutionary (*c*) reactionary (*d*) traditional.
5. According to the selection, some legislative precedents for the New Deal were furthered in the United States by all of the following Presidents EXCEPT (*a*) Abraham Lincoln (*b*) Theodore Roosevelt (*c*) Calvin Coolidge (*d*) Woodrow Wilson.

Essay Questions

1. America's future will be influenced by the natural resources available in the country; these resources must, therefore, be conserved. (*a*) Name *four*

natural resources located within the country that should be conserved. (*b*) Give *two* reasons why *one* of the resources named should be conserved. (*c*) How does the federal government attempt to conserve *one* of the nation's important natural resources?

2. The administration of Franklin D. Roosevelt was marked by various reform measures. Discuss briefly an important reform measure that was passed in each of *three* of the following fields: conservation, housing, labor, and agriculture.

3. The New Deal continues to shape Americans' way of life today. Show how each of *three* New Deal laws passed in the 1930's still affects Americans.

4. Assume that you are a writer on a newspaper.
   a. Write the news story describing the events indicated by the following headline:

   F.D.R. INAUGURATED; SAYS
   ONLY THING WE HAVE TO
   FEAR IS FEAR ITSELF

   b. Write an editorial evaluating the domestic program of Franklin D. Roosevelt's administration.

5. In the years 1933–1939 Congress created many special independent agencies.
   a. Name *three* such agencies or commissions that are still in existence today.
   b. Describe *one* function of each agency or commission named in answer to *a*.

6. Among the procedures developed by the federal government to help prevent or control an economic depression are the following: public works projects, minimum wage laws, parity payments to farmers, reciprocal tariff agreements, and higher margin requirements for purchases of securities. For each of *two* of these procedures, (*a*) state what cause of depression the procedure is designed to prevent or control, and (*b*) explain how that procedure is expected to work.

Part 4. World War II

CALENDAR OF EVENTS LEADING TO WORLD WAR II

1922. *Benito Mussolini,* founder of the Fascist party, staged a march on Rome with his "Black Shirt" followers and forced the Italian king to appoint him head of the government. After consolidating his power, he assumed the title *Il Duce* ("the leader") and established a fascist dictatorship. Supported by a large force of secret police, Mussolini placed all aspects of Italian life under his control. He curbed free speech and free press, abolished independent labor unions, and suppressed political parties that opposed him. He also began to rearm Italy for the purpose of creating a new Roman Empire.

1931. Japan invaded and conquered the Chinese province of Manchuria and set up the puppet state of *Manchukuo.* Both the United States and the League of Nations condemned Japan's action. Japan ignored the protests, withdrew from the League, and prepared to extend its conquests.

1933. *Adolf Hitler* became Chancellor of Germany when his *Nazi* party won the largest bloc of seats in the *Reichstag,* or parliament. Granted emergency powers to deal with the country's unrest, he transformed Germany's republican government into a dictatorship and appointed himself the nation's *Führer* ("leader"). In the *totalitarian* state that he set up, the Nazis exercised total control of everyday life and demanded that Germans subordinate their own interests to those of the party. Hitler's "storm troopers" and *Gestapo* (secret police) ruthlessly suppressed all internal opposition and began a campaign of persecution and harassment of German Jews.

1935. Mussolini's army invaded and conquered Ethiopia, an independent kingdom in Africa. Hitler, declaring that Germany was no longer bound by the Treaty of Versailles, began a massive rearmament program.

1936. Hitler sent in troops to reoccupy the Rhineland, a region along the French border. This action violated Germany's earlier agreement with the Allies to keep the area demilitarized. In the same year the *Spanish Civil War* broke out when Spanish army leaders, led by *Francisco Franco,* revolted against their republican government. Aided by troops, weapons, and planes sent by Germany and Italy, Franco's Nationalist forces (the *Falange*) defeated the Republicans (or Loyalists), took control of Spain, and established a fascist dictatorship headed by Franco. Germany and Italy formed the *Rome-Berlin Axis.* Japan later joined the two European powers to form the *Rome-Berlin-Tokyo Axis.*

1937. Japan invaded China. Its well-organized military machine overran most of the northern provinces and occupied key seaports in other parts of China. Though England and the United States

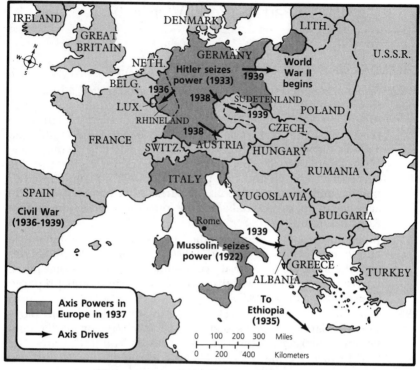

Hitler and Mussolini Bring on World War II

condemned Japan's action, they continued to sell it such vital war materials as oil, scrap iron, steel, and machinery.

1938. The United States protested against Japanese violations of the Open Door Policy in China. Japan retorted that the Open Door was now closed. Hitler's legions marched into Austria and annexed it to Germany. Turning his attention to the Sudetenland, a part of Czechoslovakia inhabited by many Germans, he demanded that it be turned over to Germany or else he would take it by force. France and England, anxious to avoid war, *appeased* Hitler by persuading Czechoslovakia to yield. *Winston Churchill* (later England's wartime Prime Minister) declared, "Britain and France had to choose between war and dishonor. They chose dishonor. They will have war."

1939. Italy invaded and conquered its tiny neighbor, Albania. Germany annexed the rest of Czechoslovakia. Germany then signed a nonaggression pact with the Soviet Union. Assured that Russia would remain neutral, Hitler invaded Poland. Realizing that their policy of appeasing Hitler had failed and that the Nazis had embarked on a plan of world domination, France and England went to the aid of Poland and declared war on Germany.

THE AXIS POWERS SCORE EARLY GAINS

Poland quickly fell to the armed might of Germany. The end came when Soviet troops entered Poland from the east and the two invaders divided the helpless country between them. In the spring of 1940 German *blitzkrieg* (lightning war) tactics crushed Denmark, Norway, Luxembourg, the Netherlands, and Belgium. France fell in June, 1940, after only 17 days of fighting. The German *Luftwaffe* (air force) then began a massive air assault against London and other British industrial centers and ports. The purpose of the bombings was to weaken Britain, demoralize its people, and pave the way for an invasion of the British Isles. The *Royal Air Force (RAF)*, however, put up so valiant a defense that the Germans were forced to abandon their invasion plans.

Stopped in England, the Axis leaders turned to the Balkans. German forces occupied Rumania, and Italy invaded Greece. When the Greeks succeeded in holding off the Italians, Germany joined the fray and conquered Greece as well as Yugoslavia. Meanwhile Axis troops in North Africa began to drive eastward toward Egypt and the Suez Canal.

With Western and Southern Europe in his control, Hitler turned his attention eastward. Tearing up his nonaggression treaty with the Soviet leader, Joseph Stalin, he invaded Russia (June, 1941). German *Panzer* (armored) divisions quickly overran the Ukraine and reached the outskirts of Moscow. Now that the Soviet Union was fighting the common foe, it became one of the Allies.

THE UNITED STATES STRIVES TO MAINTAIN NEUTRALITY

During most of the 1930's Americans viewed events in Europe and the Far East with only passing concern. The guiding principle of U.S. foreign policy was isolationism. Americans were disappointed that World War I had not resulted in a lasting peace or in making the world safe for democracy. Post-war events only seemed to prove that America would do well to stay clear of the rivalries and jealousies of the European powers.

In 1935 and in 1937 Congress passed several *Neutrality Acts* to prevent U.S. involvement in foreign wars. These acts (1) forbade the export of arms to warring nations, (2) authorized the President to require warring powers to pay cash for all purchases made in the United States and to transport the cargo in their own ships, (3) forbade loans to any nation at war, and (4) barred U.S. citizens from traveling on ships of warring nations.

AMERICAN AID TO THE ALLIES "SHORT OF WAR"

As Germany took over one country after another in Europe and Japan expanded its empire in the Far East, responsible leaders began to fear for America's safety. Public opinion gradually turned away from isolationism. Americans viewed with horror, fear, and anger the brutal pattern of Axis conquest.

In 1939 U.S. neutrality legislation was revised to permit the sale of arms and munitions on a "cash-and-carry" basis. The provisions of this law favored the Allies. In 1941 the *Lend-Lease Act* authorized the President to sell, exchange, lease, or lend arms, equipment, and supplies to any nation whose defense was considered vital to the security of the United States. Because vast quantities of war material were shipped to the Allies, America became known as the "arsenal of democracy." The lend-lease aid that the United States extended to the Allies during the war amounted to more than $50 billion.

A NATIONAL DEFENSE PROGRAM IS LAUNCHED

The United States made preparations for defense in the event of war. Congress appropriated billions of dollars to strengthen the army, navy, and air force. In 1940 it passed the *Selective Service Act*, authorizing an expansion of the nation's armed forces by means of a draft. This act established the first peacetime program of compulsory military service in U.S. history. Also in that year, the United States traded 50 over-age destroyers to Britain in return for the lease of British naval and air bases in the Western Hemisphere, from Newfoundland to British Guiana (now Guyana). These bases increased the defensive strength of the United States and helped it safeguard the Panama Canal. Later, American troops were sent to protect the Dutch West Indies, Dutch Guiana (now Suriname), Iceland, and Greenland.

THE UNITED STATES AT WAR

On December 7, 1941, squadrons of Japanese planes made a surprise attack on Pearl Harbor, the great naval base in Hawaii. Over 2,000 Americans were killed, and a large part of the U.S. fleet and air force was destroyed. This treacherous act took place while Japanese envoys were in Washington on a "peace" mission. "Remember Pearl Harbor!" became the rallying cry of a shocked and angry America. The next day President Roosevelt asked Congress to declare that a state of war existed between the United States and Japan. Stating that December 7, 1941, was "a date which will live in infamy," he asserted that "we will not only defend ourselves to the uttermost but will make it very certain that this form of treachery shall never again endanger us."

On December 11 Germany and Italy declared war on the United States. For the first time in its history, America was involved in a war for survival in both the Atlantic and the Pacific. In a message to Congress, President Roosevelt said, "The forces endeavoring to enslave the entire world now are moving towards this hemisphere. Never before has there been a greater challenge to life, liberty, and civilization."

ORGANIZING THE HOME FRONT

World War II was a *total* war. Every phase of American life was affected. The draft age was extended so that all men between the ages of 18 and 45 were subject to call for military service. By 1945 nearly 12.5 million men were serving in the nation's armed forces, most of them overseas. About 285,000 women, too, served in uniform, performing noncombat duties that released men for battle.

Industry mobilized for the production of essential war materials, especially airplanes, guns, tanks, and ships. War plants operated 24 hours a day, 7 days a week. The *War Production Board* organized and directed the war production program. The *War Manpower Commission* controlled the supply of labor. More than 20 million people worked in key war industries.

To finance the war, the nation was called upon to buy billions of dollars of war bonds. Taxes were increased, and income taxes were collected on a "pay-as-you-go" plan. That is, a part of each employed person's wages was deducted weekly in the form of *withholding taxes.* This system replaced the older method of paying income taxes only at the end of the year.

Food and other scarce items, such as shoes, gasoline, and fuel oil, were rationed to assure each person a fair share of the available supply. The *Office of Price Administration* supervised the rationing program. It also controlled prices and rents to prevent inflation. The *War Labor Board* settled labor disputes and prevented work stoppages. The *Office of War Information* was responsible for the release of war information to the public. The *Office of Civilian Defense* organized an army of volunteers to protect the civilian population in the event of air raids.

Mobilizing all its resources, the United States went all out to win the war as quickly as possible.

HIGHLIGHTS OF THE WAR IN EUROPE

When the United States entered the war in December, 1941, Britain and Russia had their backs to the wall. German forces were encamped along the west coast of Europe waiting for an opportunity to invade England. London and other English cities were being battered by heavy air raids. The sea lanes to Britain were being menaced by German U-boats, planes, and mines, which threatened to halt the flow of vitally needed supplies. A large part of the Soviet Union had been occupied by the Nazis, and many major Russian cities were under siege.

Before long, thousands of American merchant vessels convoyed by the U.S. Navy were steaming across the Atlantic carrying planes, tanks, jeeps, guns, and other supplies needed for modern warfare. And millions of G.I.'s (a popular nickname for American soldiers, derived from the abbreviation of the term "Government Issue") were arriving at camps and bases in the British Isles.

In the spring and summer of 1942 the Allies began massive bombing raids on enemy industrial centers and military installations. This action was the first step in the Allied counteroffensive. In the fall of 1942 the Allies began their march toward victory in Europe as follows:

1. Russia. The German army had driven 1,000 miles into the Soviet Union to the gates of Stalingrad. There the Red army made its stand. In the fierce three-month *Battle of Stalingrad* (1942–1943), the Russians defeated and captured a large German army corps. The Nazi offensive was halted, and the Soviets began to drive the enemy back.

2. North Africa. Led by *Bernard L. Montgomery*, the British Eighth Army defeated Erwin Rommel's *Afrika Korps* at El Alamein, Egypt, and pursued the retreating German Panzer divisions westward across Libya. Meanwhile, in November, 1942, American troops under *Dwight D. Eisenhower* landed at the ports of Casablanca, Oran, and Algiers, in enemy-occupied French North Africa. These landings constituted the greatest amphibious (sea-and-land) operation of the war up to that time. The Axis forces in Africa were caught between the Americans on the west and the British on the east. In May, 1943, they were finally trapped in Tunisia and were forced to surrender. All of North Africa was now in Allied hands.

3. Italy. In July, 1943, a combined force of Americans, British, and Canadians invaded Sicily, an island at the southern tip of Italy. Its capture brought on a political crisis in Italy, and Mussolini was forced to resign. In September the Allies invaded the Italian mainland, and Italy surrendered. Hitler, however, rushed German troops to Italy to check the Allied advance. Bloody battles were fought at Salerno, Cassino, and Anzio. Finally, in June, 1944, American forces marched into Rome and liberated the city from the Nazis.

4. Western Europe. On *D-Day*, June 6, 1944, after long and careful preparation, the combined might of the Allied forces stormed ashore on the beaches of Normandy, France. This invasion, the largest amphibious operation in history, was directed by Eisenhower. The attacking force included 4,000 ships, 11,000 planes, airborne parachute troops, and fully equipped tank divisions. After beachheads were established along the coast, reinforcements poured in and the Allies smashed ahead in several directions. One force, advancing eastward, liberated Paris in August, 1944. Another, spearheaded by mobile armored units under the command of *George S. Patton,* raced through Brittany and northern France and freed these areas from German occupation. At the same time an additional invasion force landed on the southern coast of France and proceeded northward along the Rhone Valley. Before the end of the year, all of France was in Allied hands.

In September, 1944, the Allies retook Brussels and Antwerp in Belgium, parachuted airborne troops into Holland, liberated Luxembourg, and began an invasion of Germany. More than 2 million Allied troops participated in the drive against the enemy's homeland. The Germans made a desperate effort to stop the invasion. In December they launched a massive counterattack against U.S. troops in the Ardennes Forest region of Belgium, driving the Americans back more than 50 miles and creating a large bulge in the Allied defense lines. At Bastogne the outnumbered Americans halted their retreat and dug in. Surrounded by the Germans and threatened with annihilation, they refused to surrender. They held back the enemy until rescue forces arrived and defeated the Germans in the *Battle of the Bulge.*

Resuming the offensive, the Allies pushed forward into Germany, crossed the Rhine River in the spring of 1945, and advanced eastward to the Elbe River. Here, in April, they joined forces with the Russians, who had fought their way across Poland and had occupied most of

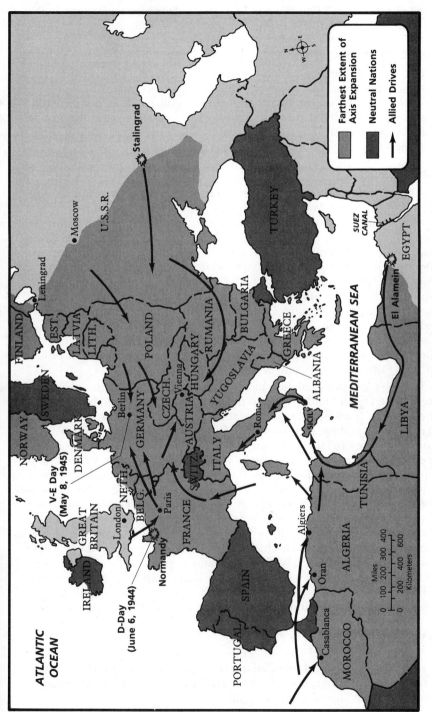

Allied Drives in Europe and North Africa

eastern Germany. (The Soviets had also driven the Nazis out of the Balkans and the rest of Eastern Europe.)

SURRENDER OF GERMANY

On May 1 German radio stations announced that Hitler had committed suicide. The following day the Russians entered Berlin. With its armies destroyed, its territory overrun, and its cities bombed out, Germany surrendered unconditionally. This action brought the war in Europe to an end. The official date of the surrender, May 8, 1945, became known as *V-E Day* (Victory-in-Europe Day).

NAZI ATROCITIES

Although sketchy reports of Nazi brutality had filtered out of Europe during the war, it was not until Allied troops entered German-occupied territory that the full extent of their criminal behavior and inhuman practices became known to the world. In country after country the Nazis had rounded up millions of young and healthy civilians and shipped them to Germany to work as slave laborers in factories and on farms. Poorly fed, penned like cattle, and forced to labor beyond human limits, countless thousands perished. The Germans had also set up *concentration camps* for political prisoners; members of resistance groups; "useless" elderly and mentally retarded people; and Gypsies, Slavs, and other Eastern Europeans whom they considered "inferior." Kept alive while they could perform useful work, the inmates were tortured, deprived of food, and ultimately murdered by their captors.

Europe's Jewish population had been singled out for the most barbaric treatment. During Hitler's rise to power in the early 1930's, he had used the German Jews as scapegoats, blaming them for Germany's defeat in World War I and for its post-war problems. After becoming the Führer, he deprived Jews of their property and rights, rescinded their citizenship, and in 1939 began a series of mass arrests—sending men, women, and children to concentration camps. Two years later he proceeded to carry out a program of extermination that he called the "Final Solution to the Jewish problem." In every city and village of German-occupied Europe squads of Nazi soldiers and police rounded up the Jewish inhabitants, herded them into boxcars, and shipped them to extermination camps, such as Auschwitz and Treblinka in Poland. At these camps, equipped with gas chambers and crematoriums, the helpless victims were killed by poison gas and their bodies burned. Some 6 million Jews were slaughtered by the Nazis in the vicious campaign of racial and religious annihilation that has become known as the *Holocaust*.

JAPAN DOMINATES THE PACIFIC

The attack on Pearl Harbor temporarily crippled U.S. naval and air power in the Pacific. Japan followed up its sneak attack by invading Thailand and Malaya, occupying Guam, Wake Island, and Hong Kong, and landing troops in the Philippines.

Japan captured Manila early in January, 1942. Led by *Douglas MacArthur*, the outnumbered American and Filipino troops withdrew to *Bataan Peninsula,* where they resisted the enemy for more than three months. MacArthur was flown out of the Philippines to assume command of the Allied forces in the Southwest Pacific. Upon arriving in Australia, he defiantly declared, "I shall return." Bataan fell soon afterwards, and Jonathan Wainwright, the new U.S. commander, made a last stand on *Corregidor,* an island in Manila Bay. He finally surrendered in May, 1942.

By the middle of 1942 Japan had won control of a vast empire rich in oil, rubber, tin, and other vital natural resources. In addition to its other conquests, it held French Indochina, Burma, the Dutch East Indies, and the powerful British naval base at Singapore. The Japanese had footholds on New Guinea and the Solomon Islands and were menacing Australia. By seizing Attu and Kiska, the westernmost of the Aleutian Islands, Japan obtained a base of operations against Alaska.

THE UNITED STATES DEFEATS JAPAN

Even while involved in the European phase of the war, the United States began to send more and more ships and planes to the Pacific. Recovering its striking power, it halted the Japanese offensive, launched a series of counterattacks, and drove the enemy back to its homeland. Among the stepping-stones to U.S. victory in the Pacific were the following:

1. Coral Sea. The Japanese sent an invasion fleet to seize Port Moresby in southern New Guinea, a base that they could use as a springboard for an attack on Australia. In the *Battle of the Coral Sea* (May, 1942) both sides suffered heavy losses, but the Japanese fleet was turned back, and the threat to Australia was removed. The battle was noteworthy as the first naval engagement in history in which surface vessels did not exchange a single shot. It was fought by planes based on aircraft carriers.

2. Midway. A large Japanese naval force attempted to seize Midway Island in preparation for an invasion of Hawaii. In the *Battle of Midway* (June, 1942) the Japanese navy suffered a major defeat. The threat to Hawaii was removed.

3. Guadalcanal. U.S. marines landed on the enemy-occupied island of Guadalcanal in the Solomons (August, 1942). A series of sea, air, and land battles followed as the Japanese attempted to drive off the U.S. troops. After six months of fierce fighting, the Americans conquered the island. This victory was the first step on the long road to Tokyo.

4. Aleutians. American troops ended the threat to Alaska by landing on Attu Island in the Aleutians and destroying the enemy forces that were entrenched there (May, 1943). They also reoccupied Kiska, which the Japanese had abandoned.

5. Central Pacific. U.S. marines landed on heavily fortified Tarawa in the Gilbert Islands (November, 1943) and captured it after a bloody battle. This landing was the start of an island-hopping offensive in the Central Pacific by the U.S. Navy under *Chester A. Nimitz.* The next leap was to Kwajalein and Eniwetok in the Marshall Islands (February, 1944)

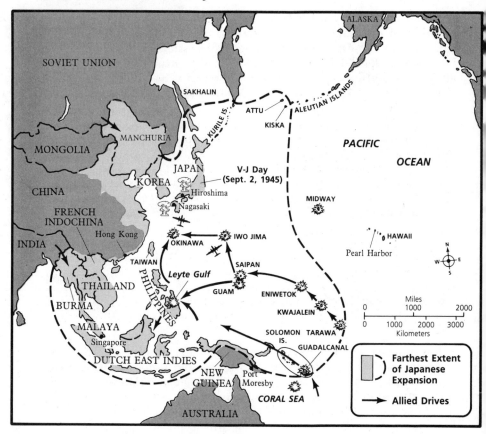

Allied Drives in the Pacific

and then to Saipan and Guam in the Mariana Islands (June, 1944). From Saipan's airfields, American long-range planes began to bomb industrial centers on Japan's home islands.

6. Philippines. MacArthur opened a drive to retake the Philippines by landing troops on Leyte, in the central part of the islands (October, 1944). The Japanese, in a desperate effort to stop the Americans, hurled their main fleet at the invasion forces. The *Battle of Leyte Gulf* was the greatest naval-air engagement in history. The Japanese were decisively defeated, and their sea power was broken. The Americans captured Manila in February, 1945, and by July had cleared the entire Philippines of the enemy.

7. Iwo Jima. U.S. marines invaded Iwo Jima, an island 750 miles from Tokyo (February, 1945), encountered fierce Japanese resistance, and suffered severe losses before completing its conquest. It was at Iwo Jima that a famous photograph was taken of the U.S. flag being raised atop Mt. Suribachi.

8. Okinawa. A combined force of U.S. infantry and marines landed on Okinawa, the principal enemy base in the Ryukyu Islands and only 360 miles from Japan (April, 1945). Air attacks by Japanese *kamikaze* (suicide) planes sank 30 American ships and damaged 300 more. After nearly three months of heavy fighting, which cost the United States 50,000 casualties, the island was conquered.

9. Atomic Bombing. Even before the United States entered the war, several distinguished scientists, among them Albert Einstein, had told President Roosevelt that it was possible to unleash the energy locked in the atom. Atomic bombs, with enormous destructive power, could be produced. The President persuaded Congress to appropriate a huge sum of money for this top-secret venture. Called the *Manhattan Project,* the undertaking drew together many of the world's greatest scientists. They completed their work in the summer of 1945, when a test bomb was secretly exploded in New Mexico.

The first atomic bomb to be used in warfare was dropped on the Japanese city of *Hiroshima* (August 6, 1945). The frightful force of this new weapon of destruction wiped out a large part of the city and brought death or injury to nearly 130,000 people. A few days later a second atomic bomb was dropped on *Nagasaki.*

SURRENDER OF JAPAN

With its navy destroyed, its empire lost, and its home islands threatened with annihilation, Japan sued for peace. On September 2, aboard the battleship *Missouri* in Tokyo Bay, the formal surrender took place. This date was proclaimed *V-J Day* (Victory-over-Japan Day).

THE ALLIES OCCUPY GERMANY AND JAPAN

1. Germany. The Allies divided Germany into four zones, separately occupied and governed by the United States, Great Britain, France, and the Soviet Union. Berlin, located within the Russian zone, was occupied by the four powers jointly. German territory east of the Oder River was turned over to Poland; and 6.5 million Germans living in Czechoslovakia, Poland, and Hungary were forcibly repatriated to Germany.

The Allies also took steps to disarm Germany, dismantle its war industries, wipe out the Nazi party, introduce democratic institutions, and bring to trial all *war criminals* (political and military leaders responsible for the war and for crimes against humanity). An International Military Tribunal, meeting in Nuremberg, Germany, tried the main Nazi leaders and sentenced 12 of them to death. Thousands of lower-ranking Nazis, tried in other courts, received lesser sentences for their crimes.

2. Japan. MacArthur, placed in charge of the occupation of Japan, disarmed that country, dismantled its war plants, and introduced a democratic form of government. (The emperor, however, was permitted to retain his throne.) An International Military Tribunal, meeting in Tokyo, tried Japan's war leaders and sentenced seven of them to death. Others received life sentences or were imprisoned for shorter terms. In addition, many high-ranking army and navy officers were tried by special courts in countries formerly occupied by the Japanese. Thousands were convicted for war offenses and more than 700 were executed.

The Allies compelled Japan to withdraw from the territories it had seized during the war and to give up all of its pre-war acquisitions. These included Formosa, Korea, Manchuria, the southern part of Sakhalin Island, the Kurile Islands north of Japan, and the Carolines, Marianas, and Marshalls in the central Pacific.

Multiple-Choice Test

1. In every war fought by the United States, the armed forces have used all of the following EXCEPT   (*a*) heavy artillery   (*b*) atomic bombs   (*c*) gunpowder   (*d*) seapower.
2. A basic characteristic of U.S. foreign policy during the years 1919-1939 was (*a*) continued refusal to recognize the Soviet Union   (*b*) leadership in forming the United Nations   (*c*) isolation with limited international cooperation   (*d*) containment of communism through alliances.
3. The immediate cause for United States entry into World War II was the (*a*) German invasion of Poland   (*b*) Italian invasion of France   (*c*) Soviet attack on Finland   (*d*) Japanese attack on Pearl Harbor.
4. In World War II the United States was called the "arsenal of democracy" because it   (*a*) welcomed war refugees   (*b*) was prepared in case of a surprise attack   (*c*) supplied the free nations with war equipment   (*d*) insisted on protecting freedom of the seas.
5. The United States obtained bases to protect its borders during World War II by   (*a*) buying them   (*b*) leasing them   (*c*) conquering them   (*d*) receiving them as gifts.
6. All of the following were U.S. military leaders in the Pacific area during World War II EXCEPT   (*a*) Douglas MacArthur   (*b*) Chester A. Nimitz (*c*) Jonathan Wainwright   (*d*) John J. Pershing.
7. It is NOT true that, in comparison with previous wars, World War II   (*a*) was less expensive   (*b*) resulted in greater loss of human life   (*c*) was fought over a larger geographical area   (*d*) involved more people.
8. The American general who directed the Allied invasion of Western Europe in World War II was   (*a*) Bernard L. Montgomery   (*b*) George S. Patton (*c*) Dwight D. Eisenhower   (*d*) Erwin Rommel.
9. Which slogan was used during World War II?   (*a*) "Make the world safe for democracy."   (*b*) "Remember Pearl Harbor!"   (*c*) "Remember the *Maine*!" (*d*) "Don't tread on me!"
10. A program of racial extermination carried out by the Nazis during World War II became known as   (*a*) blitzkrieg   (*b*) kamikaze   (*c*) the Holocaust (*d*) appeasement.
11. The Neutrality Acts of 1935 and 1937   (*a*) provided aid to the Allies "short of war"   (*b*) forbade the export of arms to nations at war   (*c*) authorized the President to lend or lease military equipment to all nations   (*d*) aimed to establish the United States as the "arsenal of democracy."

12. All of the following European countries were conquered by the Germans in the early part of World War II EXCEPT (*a*) Great Britain (*b*) France (*c*) the Netherlands (*d*) Belgium.

13. D-Day designates the day when the (*a*) Nazis surrendered (*b*) Japanese surrendered (*c*) Allies landed in North Africa (*d*) Allies invaded Normandy.

14. All of the following were important Allied victories in Europe or North Africa during World War II EXCEPT the Battle of (*a*) El Alamein (*b*) Guadalcanal (*c*) the Bulge (*d*) Stalingrad.

15. All of the following were sites of important American victories in the Pacific area during World War II EXCEPT (*a*) Casablanca (*b*) Iwo Jima (*c*) Leyte Gulf (*d*) Okinawa.

Modified True-False Test

1. *December 7, 1941*, is "a date which will live in infamy."
2. A law passed in 1940 providing for a program of compulsory military service was the *Conscription* Act.
3. *Italy*, a European country that fought against Germany in World War I, fought on the same side as Germany in World War II.
4. The term *armed resistance* describes the policy of England and France when Hitler demanded that Czechoslovakia surrender the Sudetenland in 1938.
5. World War II broke out in 1939 when Germany invaded *Poland*.
6. September 2, 1945, the date of the formal surrender of Japan, is known as *A-Day*.
7. An American general who defiantly declared "I shall return" and fulfilled this promise two years later was *George C. Marshall*.
8. American territory occupied by Japan during World War II included Attu and Kiska, two of the *Ryukyu* Islands.
9. May 8, 1945, the date that marks the end of World War II in Europe, is known as *Armistice Day*.
10. *Project X* was the code name used to designate the secret American undertaking that led to the development of the atomic bomb.

Essay Questions

1. Select *five* of the following words or expressions and briefly explain each with reference to World War II: Axis powers, lend-lease, blitzkrieg, Nazi party, convoy, withholding tax, and G.I.
2. World War II has been called a "war for survival" and a "total war." (*a*) What is meant by *each* of these terms? (*b*) How did the United States organize the home front for war? (*c*) Mention *one* important Allied victory in Europe and *one* in the Pacific.
3. The nature of warfare has changed greatly since the early days of U.S. history. Compare the Revolutionary War with World War II as to size of armies, types of weapons, communication, transportation, and countries involved.
4. At the end of World War II, the Allies were horrified to discover the nature and extent of Nazi atrocities. (*a*) Describe *three* Nazi practices during the war that the Allies condemned as "atrocities." (*b*) In your opinion did responsibility for these acts rest with the German people as well as with Germany's leaders? (*c*) Provide reasons for your answer to *b*.

UNIT X. THE UNITED STATES ASSUMES WORLDWIDE RESPONSIBILITIES

Part 1. The United Nations Is Established to Preserve the Peace

THE UNITED STATES RENOUNCES ISOLATIONISM

World War II was the costliest and mòst destructive war in history. It brought death to over 30 million soldiers and civilians, injured millions of others, cost more than a trillion dollars in direct war expenditures, and caused hundreds of billions of dollars' worth of property damage. America's armed forces suffered more than a million casualties, including 292,000 killed in battle. The nation's war costs amounted to $350 billion.

Shocked by the destructiveness of the war, the United States resolved to take whatever steps were necessary to prevent another global conflict in the future. President Roosevelt, congressional leaders, and public opinion all favored U.S. participation in an international effort to keep the post-war world at peace.

FORMATION OF THE UNITED NATIONS

FOUR FREEDOMS

In an address to Congress in 1941, President Franklin D. Roosevelt said:

"In the future days which we seek to make secure, we look forward to a world founded upon four essential human freedoms.

"The first is freedom of speech and expression—everywhere in the world.

"The second is freedom of every person to worship God in his own way—everywhere in the world.

"The third is freedom from want—which, translated into world terms, means economic understandings which will secure to every nation a healthy peacetime life for its inhabitants—everywhere in the world.

"The fourth is freedom from fear, which, translated into world terms, means a world-wide reduction of armaments to such a point and in such a thorough manner that no nation will be in a position to commit an act of physical aggression against any neighbor—anywhere in the world."

ATLANTIC CHARTER

President Roosevelt and Prime Minister Winston Churchill of England met at sea in 1941, four months before Pearl Harbor. The statement they issued, known as the *Atlantic Charter*, called for the establishment of a just peace and for an end to the use of force in the future. It suggested the "fullest collaboration between all nations in the economic field" and expressed hope for "the establishment of a wider and permanent system of general security."

MOSCOW CONFERENCE

In 1943 representatives of the United States, Great Britain, the Soviet Union, and China met in Moscow. The four powers stated that they recognized "the necessity of establishing at the earliest date a general international organization, based on the principle of the sovereign equality of all peace-loving states, and open to membership by all such states, large and small, for the maintenance of international peace and security."

DUMBARTON OAKS CONFERENCE

In 1944 representatives of the same four powers met at Dumbarton Oaks (in Washington, D.C.). They drew up plans for a post-war international organization for the maintenance of peace. The organization would be called the *United Nations* (*UN*).

YALTA CONFERENCE

Roosevelt, Churchill, and Stalin met at Yalta (in the U.S.S.R.) early in 1945. A large part of the meeting dealt with arrangements for turning over Japanese territory to the Soviets in return for Stalin's promise to enter the war against Japan, and with plans for reshuffling Poland's post-war boundaries. The three leaders also pledged to support the establishment of popularly elected governments in countries liberated from German occupation. They agreed that a conference should be held later that year to prepare a charter for the United Nations.

SAN FRANCISCO CONFERENCE

The United Nations Conference on International Organization convened in San Francisco in April, 1945, two weeks after the sudden death of President Roosevelt. After two months of work and discussion, the delegates completed and signed the *Charter of the United Nations*. In October, when the Charter had been ratified by a majority of the participating countries, the UN became a functioning organization, with 51 members. (Today nearly every country in the world is a member of the UN.)

STRUCTURE OF THE UNITED NATIONS

GENERAL ASSEMBLY

All member nations are represented in the General Assembly, each country having one vote. Decisions on "important questions" require a two-third's majority; other matters are decided by a simple majority vote.

Bastian in The San Francisco Chronicle

The General Assembly has been called the "town meeting of the world." It discusses questions of international importance. It may recommend solutions to international problems, but dangerous situations involving the use of force must first be called to the attention of the Security Council.

If the Security Council is unable to act because one of the permanent members exercises its veto power, the General Assembly may then recommend appropriate action, including the use of armed force. (This provision is called the *Uniting for Peace Resolution*. It was enacted in the 1950's, when it became apparent that excessive use of the veto in the Security Council had virtually destroyed that body's effectiveness.)

The General Assembly holds a regular session in the fall of each year. Special sessions may be called by the Secretary General at the request of the Security Council.

SECURITY COUNCIL

Fifteen member nations make up the Security Council. The United States, Great Britain, Russia, France, and China (the Big Five) are permanent members; ten nonpermanent members are elected by the General Assembly to serve on the Council for terms of two years. Each member nation of the Council is allowed one representative and one vote.

The Security Council investigates international disputes. It may (1) sever diplomatic and economic relations with a nation menacing the peace, and (2) "take such action by air, sea, or land forces as may be necessary to maintain or restore international peace and security."

Decisions of the Security Council on all important matters are made by an affirmative vote of nine members, including all of the permanent members. Thus, each of the Big Five has *veto power* over the actions of the Council.

ECONOMIC AND SOCIAL COUNCIL

This body is composed of 54 members who are elected by the General Assembly for terms of three years. It seeks to improve the living conditions of the world's inhabitants. It carries on its work by creating special commissions, conducting studies, drawing up reports, calling international conferences, and presenting its findings to the General Assembly.

TRUSTEESHIP COUNCIL

Former League of Nations mandates and colonial possessions taken from the Axis powers during World War II were assigned by the UN to several member states as trust territories. Overall supervision of the trusteeship system was placed in the hands of the *Trusteeship Council*. It aimed to protect the interests of the dependent peoples living in these areas, and to help them develop the ability to govern themselves. Over the years, one trust territory after another acquired independence. The work of the Trusteeship Council came to an end in 1994 when the U.S.-administered trust territory of Palau became a sovereign state.

SECRETARIAT

The administrative and clerical work of the UN is handled by the Secretariat. It consists of a *Secretary General,* assisted by an international staff of 2,000 people. The Secretary General is elected by the General Assembly on the recommendation of the Security Council. As the UN's chief administrative officer, this official plays an important role in the affairs of the organization.

INTERNATIONAL COURT OF JUSTICE

The Court consists of 15 judges, no two from the same country, who are elected by the Security Council and the Assembly. The Court settles disputes involving international law, interprets treaties, and rules on other legal questions that are brought before it. Its decisions are final.

If a nation refuses to abide by the Court's ruling, the Security Council may enforce obedience.

SPECIALIZED AGENCIES

A number of independent agencies, funded chiefly by contributions from the nations that make up their membership, work closely with the UN by special agreement. They are involved in various economic, social, scientific, and technical fields, as follows:

1. The **United Nations Educational, Scientific, and Cultural Organization (UNESCO)** seeks to foster better understanding among the peoples of the world through educational, scientific, and cultural exchanges and cooperation.

2. The **World Health Organization (WHO)** works to improve health standards and to combat epidemics in disease-ridden areas of the world.

3. The **Food and Agriculture Organization (FAO)** strives to combat hunger and raise nutritional levels by providing technical advice on methods of improving the production and distribution of farm products.

4. The **International Labor Organization (ILO)** aims to improve living standards and working conditions through international action.

5. The **World Bank** (International Bank for Reconstruction and Development) makes low-cost loans to its member nations for the construction of public works and other useful projects. One of its affiliates, the **International Development Association,** provides long-term, interest-free loans to the least developed countries. Another, the **International Finance Corporation,** furthers the economic development of underdeveloped countries by encouraging private investment in these areas.

6. The **International Monetary Fund (IMF)** seeks to expand international trade by promoting monetary cooperation and currency stabilization. It extends loans to financially troubled nations to ease temporary economic problems and to help them meet debt repayment obligations.

7. The **United Nations Children's Fund (UNICEF)** raises money from private sources to aid children who are victims of war and poverty.

8. The **International Atomic Energy Agency (IAEA)** seeks to promote safe, peaceful uses of atomic energy.

9. The **World Trade Organization (WTO)** provides the machinery for settling trade disputes and negotiating tariff reductions between nations.

10. Other agencies have been set up to establish international standards and regulations for civil aviation, shipping, radio, telephone, telegraph, and postal services; and to improve worldwide weather forecasting.

HOME OF THE UNITED NATIONS

The permanent headquarters of the UN is located in New York City. It comprises (1) the General Assembly Building, where the regular sessions of that body are held, (2) the Secretariat Building, which accommodates the administrative staff of the UN, (3) the Conference Building, which houses the Security Council, the Trusteeship Council, and the Economic and Social Council, and (4) the Dag Hammarskjold Library. An office building-hotel combination was added to the UN complex in the 1970's.

THE UN FLAG

In 1947 the General Assembly adopted a United Nations flag. It is light blue in color. Upon it, emblazoned in white, is a polar projection map of the world encircled by two olive branches, which are symbols of peace.

THE UN IN ACTION

SOCIAL AND POLITICAL ACHIEVEMENTS OF THE UN

1. Human Rights. A commission headed by Eleanor Roosevelt drafted a *Declaration of Human Rights*. Approved by the General Assembly, it called upon all member nations to guarantee their inhabitants freedom of thought, speech, and assembly; and the right to (*a*) life, liberty, and security of person, (*b*) equal protection under the law, (*c*) participation in government, (*d*) ownership of property, (*e*) free choice of employment, (*f*) protection against unemployment, and (*g*) a decent standard of living. The document also prohibited slavery and torture.

2. Genocide. The General Assembly outlawed the practice of *genocide* (the deliberate and systematic destruction of a racial, political, or cultural group), and agreed that perpetrators of such crimes should be brought to trial before an international court.

3. Creation of Israel. Palestine, the biblical homeland of the Jews, had been administered by Britain as a League of Nations mandate since World War I. With Hitler's rise to power, Jews seeking a haven from persecution in Europe returned to their ancestral land in large numbers. Palestinian Arabs, resenting the influx of new settlers and fearing that the newcomers would displace them, became increasingly hostile toward the Jews. Rioting and fighting between the two groups flared. Unable to cope with the situation, Britain decided to surrender its mandate and turn over the problem to the UN.

Meeting in special session, the General Assembly adopted an American-supported plan to partition Palestine into two states—one Arab and the other Jewish. The Palestinian Jews accepted the UN decision and proclaimed the independent State of Israel in May, 1948. The Palestinian Arabs, however, rejected the plan. So too did the neighboring Arab countries. Seeking to destroy the newly established Jewish state, they launched a joint attack against Israel. The Israelis fought off the invading armies. A UN mediator, the American Ralph J. Bunche, negotiated an armistice agreement between the two sides, thus bringing the first Arab-Israeli war to an end. Israel became a UN member in 1949.

4. Trust Territories. With the guidance and support of the Trusteeship Council, a number of trust territories acquired independence and self-government after 1949. These new countries include Togo, Samoa, Rwanda, Burundi, Papua New Guinea, Marshall Islands, Federated States of Micronesia, and Palau.

5. Outer Space. The UN proclaimed outer space free for all nations to explore and use on an equal basis. It helped negotiate an international agreement banning the use of weapons of mass destruction in outer space and forbidding the establishment of military bases on the moon and planets (1967).

UN EFFORTS TO SETTLE MAJOR DISPUTES

The world organization has provided a meeting place where nations can bring their problems, state their opinions, and register their complaints. It has offered disputants an opportunity to settle their quarrels by discussion rather than by force. But the UN has not been as successful in maintaining peace and ending world tensions as many had hoped. Although it has contributed to the settlement of numerous international disputes, it has also experienced its share of failures. Among its major peacekeeping involvements were the following:

1. Iran. Acting on an Iranian complaint, the Security Council influenced the Soviet Union to withdraw its troops from Iran after World War II (1946).

2. Greece. The UN sent a special commission to the Balkans to investigate Greek charges that neighboring countries were aiding Communist guerrillas who were seeking to overthrow the Greek government. The UN ordered these countries to end their interference (1946–1948).

3. Indonesia. The Security Council arranged a truce between the Dutch, who were seeking to regain possession of their colonies in the East Indies after World War II, and Indonesian nationalists who were fighting for independence. The UN also helped negotiate the formation of the independent Republic of Indonesia (1949).

4. Kashmir. The UN helped halt the warfare between India and Pakistan over the disputed province of Kashmir, and obtained their agreement to allow the inhabitants to decide by a plebiscite which nation they wished to join (1948). Despite the agreement, and without a plebiscite, India later annexed about two-thirds of the territory—an action condemned by the UN. The Kashmir issue remained a source of conflict between the two countries and touched off another round of fighting in 1965. Once again the UN intervened to end the hostilities.

5. Korea. Responding to the request of the Security Council, 17 member nations went to the aid of South Korea when it was invaded by North Korea. The UN forces drove out the aggressors and negotiated an armistice (1950–1953).

6. Egypt. Denouncing England, France, and Israel for invading Egypt, the UN demanded that they withdraw their forces. (England

and France had sent in troops to protect their interests in the Suez Canal, which Egypt had seized; Israel was retaliating for Egyptian raids on its territory.) The three nations bowed to the will of the UN. A UN emergency force supervised a truce and policed the border between Egypt and Israel (1956–1957).

7. Hungary. In 1956 popular demonstrations against the Communist-controlled government of Hungary developed into an open revolt. The Soviet Union sent in a massive invasion force to crush the uprising. Thousands of Hungarians were killed, and many more either fled or were deported. Disregarding a UN order to withdraw its troops, the Soviet Union not only helped restore the local Communists to power, it also kept a large force in Hungary to prevent a repetition of anti-Communist agitation.

8. The Congo. At the request of the Congolese government, the Security Council dispatched an emergency force to restore order in the Democratic Republic of the Congo (now called the Republic of Zaire) when sectional warfare in that newly independent nation (formerly the Belgian Congo) threatened to destroy the country. With UN aid, the central Congolese government began to achieve its goal of unifying the country (1960–1964).

9. Cyprus. Aiming to prevent the outbreak of a full-scale civil war between the Greek and Turkish inhabitants of Cyprus, the UN sent a force to the island to halt the fighting and restore peace (1964–1965). Violence erupted once again in 1974 when Greek Cypriots seeking union with Greece seized control of the island's government and Turkey rushed in troops to protect the Turkish Cypriots. The invading force occupied the northern section of Cyprus, drove out the Greek residents, and made the area a Turkish enclave. UN resolutions calling for withdrawal of Turkish troops and the return of Greek Cypriot refugees to their homes were ignored. To prevent further outbreaks of violence, the UN continued to maintain a peacekeeping force on Cyprus.

Abandoning all efforts to settle their differences with the Greek occupants of the island, the Turkish Cypriots in 1983 declared their independence. The new Turkish Republic of Northern Cyprus has not been recognized by other nations or by the UN.

10. Namibia (South-West Africa). Once a German possession, this territory had been administered by South Africa as a League of Nations mandate since World War I. After World War II South Africa refused to relinquish control. In 1968 the General Assembly appointed a multinational council to take over the administration of South-West Africa (renamed *Namibia*) and prepare its people for independence. When South Africa refused to cooperate, the Security Council declared that country's occupation of Namibia illegal.

The South-West Africa People's Organization (SWAPO), a local revolutionary group agitating for independence, had been carrying on guerrilla warfare against South African forces since the 1970's. Neighboring Angola had been providing arms to SWAPO and allowing it to maintain bases on Angolan soil. In 1978 the UN proposed a plan that called for (*a*) a cease-fire between SWAPO and South Africa, (*b*) the establishment of a UN-patrolled demilitarized zone between Angola and Namibia, and (*c*) UN-supervised elections to form an independent Namibian government. South Africa demanded that Soviet-supported Cuban troops be withdrawn from Angola before it would agree to give up control of Namibia. In 1988 Angola, Cuba, and South Africa finally signed agreements providing for Namibian independence and the withdrawal of Cuban troops from Angola.

11. Middle East. (*a*) In 1967 war broke out between Israel and three of its Arab neighbors—Egypt, Syria, and Jordan. Once again the UN arranged a cease-fire. In 1973 these countries became involved in still another conflict. After several weeks of bitter fighting, the two sides accepted a Security Council resolution calling for a cease-fire. UN emergency forces were sent to serve as a buffer between the Israeli and Arab armies on the Golan Heights and in the Sinai Peninsula. (*b*) To end guerrilla attacks on Israel by members of the Palestine Liberation Organization (PLO) based in Lebanon, Israeli forces in 1978 invaded Lebanon, attacked the Palestinian enclaves, and ocupied a broad strip of territory along Israel's northern border. The UN negotiated an Israeli withdrawal by agreeing to send a peacekeeping force into southern Lebanon to police the area.

Despite the presence of UN patrols, the PLO continued its campaign of harassing Israel. In 1982 the Israelis invaded Lebanon for the purpose of driving PLO military units from that country. Ignoring a Security Council demand that they withdraw, the Israelis proceeded to carry out their plan. They overran the PLO bases in southern Lebanon, advanced northward to Beirut—where the PLO maintained its headquarters—and forced the Palestinian militants to evacuate Lebanon by sea.

The Israelis withdrew their troops from Lebanon during the first half of 1985. But they left military advisers and agents to watch over a 10-mile "security zone" in southern Lebanon. A UN Interim Force (UNIFIL) also remained to patrol the border between the two countries.

12. Iran-Iraq War. Part of the boundary between Iran and Iraq, the Shatt-al-Arab is a waterway that provides Iraq its only outlet to the sea (the Persian Gulf). A dispute over control and use of this waterway triggered an Iraqi attack on Iran in 1980. Ignoring repeated UN calls for a cease-fire, the antagonists went all-out to destroy one another. Iran attempted to overrun its enemy's territory by launching periodic mass invasions. Iraq resorted to aerial bombings of Iranian urban centers, intermediate-range missle strikes, and the use of poison gas and chemical weapons. Casualties on both sides were enormous. Despite all their efforts, neither side proved able to defeat the other. Therefore, in 1988 Iran and Iraq finally agreed to accept the UN cease-fire proposal.

13. Kuwait. In August, 1990, Iraq invaded and occupied Kuwait, its oil-rich Arab neighbor on the Persian Gulf. The UN condemned the attack and demanded Iraq's withdrawal. When Saddam Hussein, Iraq's leader, failed to comply, the Security Council (*a*) banned all trade and financial dealings with Iraq, (*b*) urged member nations to employ naval power, if necessary, to prevent violations of the embargo by ships at sea, and (*c*) authorized a multinational effort to liberate Kuwait by force if Hussein did not pull out his troops by January 15, 1991.

When that deadline passed, a U.S.-led coalition of 28 nations launched a series of massive air strikes against Iraqi targets. After weeks of continuous aerial bombings, the coalition partners sent ground forces into Kuwait from bases in Saudi Arabia. They quickly routed the Iraqis, drove them from Kuwait, and pursued them into southern Iraq.

In exchange for a formal cease-fire, the UN compelled Iraq to accept the following conditions: (*a*) to destroy or render harmless its chemical and biological weapons (and related manufacturing facilities) as well as its ballistic missiles and nuclear weapons material, (*b*) to pay reparations to Kuwait for the immense damage Iraq had caused, and (*c*) to permit a UN observer force to monitor a demilitarized zone along the Iraq-Kuwait border. The UN also indicated that its economic embargo would not be lifted until Iraq fulfilled all the terms of the cease-fire.

14. Somalia. With more than 1.5 million Somalis facing starvation because of drought and clan warfare, the UN organized a relief effort in 1992 and authorized the dispatch of a multinational force (including 30,000 U.S. soldiers) to handle the distribution of food and supplies to the needy. Opposition by local warlords to the UN presence touched off violent clashes that caused casualties on both sides. The United States withdrew its troops in 1994, and the Security Council recalled the remaining peacekeepers in 1995. Although the UN operation helped ease the famine, it failed to end interclan violence and restore peace to the embattled nation.

15. Former Yugoslavia. The collapse of communism in Eastern Europe led to the partial disintegration of Yugoslavia as four of its six component states set up independent republics. In Croatia, fighting between Croats and Serbs caused such devastation that the Security Council in 1992 sent in a UN Protection Force to separate the two sides and enforce a cease-fire.

In Bosnia and Herzegovina—populated by Muslims (44%), Serbs (33%), and Croats (18%)—Serbs, assisted by neighboring Serbia, launched a campaign to evict Muslims living in their midst (a policy called "ethnic cleansing"). They massacred thousands of Muslims and laid siege to Sarajevo, the Bosnian capital.

The Security Council (*a*) called for airlifts of food, medicine, and other necessities to Bosnia, (*b*) sent in UN peacekeepers to supervise the distribution of aid, (*c*) authorized UN members to use military force, if necessary, to keep supply lines open, and (*d*) imposed economic sanctions and a blockade on Serbia and Montenegro (the remaining parts of Yugoslavia) to prevent the entry of weapons and supplies that could be used to help the Bosnian Serbs.

Massive NATO air strikes at Bosnian Serb targets in 1995 persuaded the Serbs to enter into peace talks with Croats and Muslims in Bosnia. In late 1995 the three sides signed an agreement calling for the creation of three autonomous regions and for the election of a three-person collective presidency and a federal parliament. About 60,000 NATO troops were sent to Bosnia to supervise the agreement and oversee the elections (held in September 1996).

16. Haiti. When the Haitian military arrested and expelled elected president Jean-Bertrand Aristide and seized control of the country in 1991, the UN imposed an oil, arms, and financial embargo on Haiti. Repeated attempts to negotiate Aristide's return failed. Therefore, the Security Council in 1994 authorized a multinational invasion of Haiti. The imminent arrival of a U.S. attack force convinced the Haitian military leaders to step down and allow the deposed president to resume office. Thousands of U.S. troops landed in September, 1994, helped to restore order, and paved the way for Aristide's return. After other member nations sent peacekeepers to Haiti, the United States, in April, 1995, turned over responsibility for the country's security to the UN.

PROBLEMS OF THE UN

1. Abuse of the Veto. For nearly 45 years, the Soviet Union used its veto power more than 100 times to keep the Security Council from passing resolutions that it opposed. (The other four permanent members exercised this power quite sparingly.) The U.S.S.R's abuse of the veto made the Security Council almost powerless to cope with serious international problems. (With the easing of cold war tensions in the late 1980's, a new spirit of East-West cooperation began to emerge.)

2. Enforcing Decisions. The UN lacks a *permanent* international police force to help it curb agression and maintain peace. It therefore must rely upon member nations to volunteer the military forces it needs to carry out its peace missions. Furthermore, in several instances members who opposed UN intervention have refused to pay their share of the costs of maintaining emergency forces. As a result, the UN is plagued with serious financial problems that threaten to curtail its peacekeeping operations.

3. Loss of Prestige. At times, member nations have boycotted UN meetings to protest consideration of issues that they felt were not the concern of the UN. Some nations have also refused to abide by UN decisions that were contrary to their national interests. Such actions have seriously undermined the prestige of the world organization.

4. Division Into Blocs. Since most countries belong to the UN, its composition tends to reflect the divisions that exist in the world. For more than four decades, nearly all the members associated themselves with one of three major groupings: (*a*) the **Western bloc,** comprising most countries of the Western Hemisphere and Western Europe, and several other nations that generally follow the lead of the United States; (*b*) the **Communist bloc,** made up of the Soviet Union and the countries it dominated; and (*c*) the **Afro-Asian bloc,** often identified as the *Third World,* which includes most of the newly independent countries and is numerically the largest group. Since it holds the balance of power, it generally plays a key role in UN proceedings. Among the Afro-Asian nations are a number of Middle Eastern countries that share a common Islamic heritage and religion. This *Arab bloc* formed a united front of opposition to Israel whenever issues involving that country were taken up in the UN. Bloc voting by these groups created bitterness, rivalry, and dissension within the world organization.

(With the decline of communism in Eastern Europe and the Soviet Union in the late 1980's and early 1990's, bloc voting became less of a problem at the UN.)

5. Political Manipulation of UN Agencies. Member nations often attempt to influence UN agencies to take positions on international issues that will promote their interests and political views at the expense of other members who have less support. Such tactics caused the United States to withdraw from the ILO in 1977 (it later returned) and from UNESCO in 1984.

Multiple-Choice Test

1. The permanent headquarters of the United Nations is in (*a*) Geneva   (*b*) New York City   (*c*) Paris   (*d*) The Hague.
2. The Atlantic Charter was most similar in its provisions to   (*a*) the Platt Amendment   (*b*) the Roosevelt Corollary   (*c*) the Stimson Doctrine   (*d*) the Kellogg-Briand Pact.
3. One similarity of the League of Nations and the United Nations is that both   (*a*) included all major nations as members   (*b*) allowed each member nation an equal vote in the Assembly   (*c*) were dominated by the same "Big Five" powers   (*d*) created an international police force.
4. Which was an achievement of the United Nations?   (*a*) release of Hungary from the control of the Soviet Union   (*b*) awarding of Kashmir to Pakistan   (*c*) withdrawal of French and British troops from the Suez Canal zone   (*d*) establishing a permanent international police force capable of maintaining peace anywhere in the world.
5. Which organ of the United Nations provides a forum for the expression of opinions by all members?   (*a*) Security Council   (*b*) Trusteeship Council   (*c*) General Assembly   (*d*) International Court of Justice.
6. To be chosen Secretary General of the United Nations, a candidate is   (*a*) recommended by the Security Council and elected by the General Assembly   (*b*) recommended by the General Assembly and appointed by the Security Council   (*c*) nominated by the President of Russia and the President of the United States and elected at a joint session of the Council and the Assembly   (*d*) recommended by the Security Council and elected by a majority of the judges of the International Court of Justice.
7. The United Nations was officially established at the   (*a*) San Francisco Conference   (*b*) Washington Conference   (*c*) Bogotá Conference   (*d*) London Conference.

8. All of the following countries were founding members of the United Nations EXCEPT (*a*) France (*b*) Israel (*c*) Canada (*d*) Brazil.

9. The mass slaying of racial, national, or religious groups—a practice outlawed by the United Nations—is known as (*a*) totalitarianism (*b*) regicide (*c*) genocide (*d*) nihilism.

10. All of the following member nations have veto power over actions of the Security Council EXCEPT (*a*) Great Britain (*b*) the United States (*c*) Russia (*d*) India.

11. A UN agency that aids children who are victims of war or poverty is (*a*) UNESCO (*b*) FAO (*c*) UNICEF (*d*) ILO.

12. Noteworthy achievements of the UN include all of the following EXCEPT (*a*) formation of an independent Cyprus (*b*) adoption of the Declaration of Human Rights (*c*) creation of the State of Israel (*d*) establishment of the Republic of Indonesia.

13. Temporary police forces have been organized on various occasions by the UN and sent to all of the following countries EXCEPT (*a*) Cyprus (*b*) Egypt (*c*) Switzerland (*d*) Lebanon.

14. All of the following agencies are associated with the UN EXCEPT (*a*) WHO (*b*) SEC (*c*) IMF (*d*) WTO.

15. Which of the following statements relating to the United Nations is NOT true (*a*) The Afro-Asian bloc is the group of member nations that is numerically the largest in the UN. (*b*) Togo, Cameroon, Somalia, and Western Samoa were trust territories that acquired independence. (*c*) The UN has never requested its members to intervene militarily to help stop an invasion. (*d*) The Soviet Union used its veto power in the Security Council more than 100 times to block measures that it opposed.

Essay Questions

1. a. Discuss reasons that may account for the fact that the United States joined the United Nations although it did not join the League of Nations.
   b. Describe *two* problems that have been brought before the United Nations.

2. (*a*) List *each* of the Four Freedoms upon which President Franklin D. Roosevelt hoped the post-World War II world would be founded. (*b*) Select *two* of the freedoms given in answer to *a* and show how each can help to improve the condition of the world.

3. The General Assembly of the United Nations. has been called the "town meeting of the world." (*a*) Why is this a good name for the General Assembly? (*b*) Name *three* nations that are represented in the General Assembly. (*c*) In what city does the General Assembly meet? (*d*) What is the Uniting for Peace Resolution that the General Assembly adopted in the 1950's? (*e*) Why was this resolution passed?

4. Discuss the organization of the UN, listing *four* organs and *one* function of each.

5. (*a*) Why was the United nations created? (*b*) Name the nations that are the members of the "Big Five." (*c*) Why is the success of the UN important to the United States? (*d*) Name the American whose service as a UN mediator helped to end the Arab-Israeli war of 1948.

Part 2. America Leads the Free World in the Cold War

RUSSIA BECOMES A COMMUNIST STATE

As noted earlier, a revolution took place in Russia during World War I, and the Bolsheviks, or Communists, seized control of the country. They established a Communist dictatorship and took over all sectors of the economy—farms, mines, factories, power plants, stores, banks, and transportation facilities. They began to regulate every phase of the people's lives. Russia became known officially as the *Union of Soviet Socialist Republics* (*U.S.S.R.*). More commonly it was called the Soviet Union, Soviet Russia, or Russia.

The leaders of Soviet Russia advocated the spread of communism throughout the world by revolutionary means. They encouraged the formation of Communist parties in other countries, taught Communist techniques and doctrines to foreign revolutionists, and distributed propaganda urging people in other lands to overthrow their governments. For these reasons, relations between the Soviet Union and the Western democracies before World War II were quite strained.

RUSSIA GAINS CONTROL OF EASTERN EUROPE

During the war, while the U.S.S.R. and the Western democracies were fighting a common enemy, relations improved. After the war, however, Russia vigorously renewed its efforts to spread communism.

While its troops were occupying Eastern Europe, the Soviet Union took steps to consolidate its position in the area and to isolate it from the West. The barrier that the Soviets set up between Eastern and Western Europe became known as the "iron curtain." Behind this protective facade, the U.S.S.R. encouraged and supported the establishment of pro-Soviet, Communist governments in Bulgaria, Czechoslovakia, Hungary, Poland, and Rumania (and later in East Germany). (See map, page 403.) These countries became *satellites* of the Soviet Union, following its lead in foreign and domestic affairs. (Although Yugoslavia and Albania also became Communist nations, they remained independent of Soviet control.) In Hungary and Czechoslovakia, opposition to Soviet domination and efforts to attain a freer society were brutally suppressed by Soviet troops in 1956 and 1968 respectively.

THE COLD WAR BEGINS

Russia's ruthless domination of Eastern Europe and its active support of Communist movements in the rest of the world raised the fear that it was seeking world revolution and conquest. Concern over Soviet intentions was further aroused by Russia's obstructionist tactics in the UN and by its unwillingness to cooperate with Western nations in solving problems and building a peaceful world.

The United States came to the conclusion that (1) communism endangered the existence of every peace-loving and independent nation

Carmack in *The Christian Science Monitor*

Double Emblem

in the world, and (2) most countries could not successfully combat communism or maintain their independence without U.S. help. The United States therefore took the lead in curbing further Communist expansion—a policy described as *containment*. Soviet moves to extend communism and American countermoves to halt its spread became known as the *cold war*—a struggle fought with economic, political, and diplomatic weapons and sometimes with guns in "limited" wars.

UNITED STATES EXTENDS AID TO THE FREE WORLD

TRUMAN DOCTRINE

Greek revolutionaries, supported by men and equipment from neighboring Communist countries, attempted to seize control of Greece (1947). At the same time the Soviet Union demanded that Turkey permit it to share control of the straits between the Black Sea and the Mediterranean. Fearing that both nations would fall under Communist control, President Harry S. Truman declared that "it must be the policy of the United States to support free peoples who are resisting attempted subjugation [conquest] by armed minorities or by outside pressures." This principle became known as the *Truman Doctrine*. The United States rushed military equipment, urgently needed supplies, and military advisers to Greece and Turkey. With this help, Greece was able to put down the rebellion, and Turkey successfully resisted Russia's demands.

The United States also took steps to bolster the defenses of its Western allies, as well as of South Korea, the Philippines, Nationalist China, and other nations threatened by communism. Over the years, many billions of dollars were spent to (1) equip free world nations with weapons and (2) train troops of U.S. allies in the techniques of modern warfare.

EUROPEAN RECOVERY PROGRAM (MARSHALL PLAN)

Secretary of State George C. Marshall offered American financial assistance to the nations of Europe to aid in their recovery from the destruction of war (1947). Stating that "our policy is directed not against any country or doctrine but against hunger, poverty, desperation, and chaos," he called upon Europe to draw up a blueprint of its economic needs.

Acting upon Marshall's proposal, 16 nations met in Paris and adopted a four-year, multibillion-dollar plan to provide participants with food, fuel, raw materials, and machinery. In 1948 Congress approved the *Marshall Plan*, also known as the *European Recovery Program* (*ERP*), and appropriated $5 billion for its first year of operation.

Although they were eligible to participate, Russia and its satellites rejected the plan and did all they could to oppose it. They organized the *Cominform* to spread propaganda against the ERP, to organize strikes in Marshall Plan countries, and to sabotage American foreign aid shipments. Most observers believed that Russia's aim in opposing the ERP was to retard Europe's economic recovery and thereby perpetuate poverty and misery—conditions that enable communism to thrive.

The United States extended more than $15 billion in economic aid during the four-year life of the Marshall Plan. This aid enabled the participating nations to raise their industrial and agricultural production above pre-war levels and greatly stimulated international trade. Furthermore, the Marshall Plan stemmed Communist advances in the participating countries by reducing unemployment, raising living standards, and helping to restore political and economic stability.

Foreign economic aid was originally scheduled to end in 1952. However, the ongoing crisis in East-West relations compelled the United States to continue its program of economic assistance to the free world. Greater emphasis was placed upon aid to underdeveloped countries. To these nations the United States provided raw materials, machinery, and food to help them achieve the economic growth and stability necessary to preserve their independence.

POINT FOUR PROGRAM

The fourth point in President Truman's 1949 Inaugural Address was a proposal that the United States use its scientific and industrial "know-how" to help raise living standards in the underdeveloped areas of the world. Under the Point Four Program, invaluable technical aid has been extended to some 60 countries in Asia, Africa, and Latin America. American experts in various fields—doctors, nurses, educators, engineers, veterinarians, and agricultural specialists—have worked to improve living conditions in these areas by fighting disease, introducing modern educational methods, building power and irrigation projects, and teaching farmers how to care for livestock and increase food production.

PEACE CORPS

President John F. Kennedy in 1961 created the *Peace Corps*. This agency aims to promote world peace and friendship by sending American volunteers to underdeveloped countries to live among the people and show them how to raise their living standards. Thousands of Peace Corps volunteers have been sent abroad to teach in schools, train workers to operate modern machinery, demonstrate modern methods of sanitation, and perform many other useful tasks.

THE COLD WAR IN EUROPE

NORTH ATLANTIC TREATY

In 1949 the United States, Canada, and 10 countries of Western Europe (Belgium, Denmark, France, Iceland, Italy, Luxembourg, the Netherlands, Norway, Portugal, and Great Britain) entered into a pact of mutual defense called the *North Atlantic Treaty*. The purpose of the treaty was to protect the signatories against possible Russian aggression. These nations (1) agreed that an armed attack upon one would be considered an attack upon all, and (2) pledged to take any action necessary to maintain the security of the North Atlantic area. By becoming a member of this pact, the United States abandoned its traditional policy of nonalignment in time of peace.

In 1950 the pact members agreed to create a unified military force for the defense of Western Europe. It was to consist of military units assigned to it by the participating nations. (The United States contributed about 350,000 troops.) Eisenhower was appointed the first head of the *North Atlantic Treaty Organization (NATO)* defense forces. He assumed the title *Supreme Allied Commander in Europe (SACEUR)*. NATO headquarters, established at first in Paris, were later transferred to Brussels, Belgium.

Greece and Turkey became NATO members in 1952, thereby extending the security guarantees of the pact to the eastern Mediterranean. The alliance was further enlarged by the admission of West Germany in 1955 and Spain in 1982.

DEFENSE AGREEMENT WITH SPAIN

The United States entered into a military and economic agreement with Spain in 1953. It provided for the (1) use of Spanish ports as naval

The Cold War Divides Europe

bases by the American Mediterranean fleet, (2) establishment of airfields and supply depots by the U.S. Air Force on Spanish soil, and (3) granting of economic aid and weapons to Spain to strengthen its economy and help modernize its armed forces.

BERLIN BLOCKADE

After World War II Berlin, the pre-war capital of Germany, was divided into four zones. Each was occupied by one of the wartime Allies. Since Berlin was deep inside the Soviet sector of Germany, the Russians controlled the access routes between Berlin and the West.

Fearing that the Western powers would make Berlin a showplace of democracy inside Communist territory, Russia in 1948 tried to force the United States, Britain, and France to leave. It clamped a blockade on the city by refusing to let trucks and trains from the West enter East Germany and travel to Berlin. Two million West Berliners faced starvation.

The Western Allies responded by starting a gigantic *airlift*. For 11 months huge cargo planes flew thousands of tons of food, coal, and other supplies into Berlin. The airlift reached its peak in April, 1949, when in a single day nearly 1,400 planes brought in some 13,000 tons of supplies. The following month Russia lifted the blockade.

WEST GERMANY IS BROUGHT INTO THE WESTERN ALLIANCE

After World War II the Western powers and the Soviet Union could agree neither on a peace treaty for Germany nor on the establishment of a unified government for that country. To end the stalemate, the United States, Britain, and France decided in 1949 to merge their zones of occupation and create a republic in the western part of Germany, with Bonn as its capital. West Germany received Marshall Plan aid from the United States and was slowly brought into the ranks of the Western powers.

In 1955 the Western Allies (1) ended their 10-year occupation of West Germany, (2) granted that country full independence, (3) permitted it to establish an army (not to exceed 500,000 soldiers) and to manufacture military equipment (except atomic weapons, guided missiles, and large warships), and (4) invited it to become the 15th member of NATO. West Germany's newly created army became an important part of the NATO forces.

The Russians responded by proclaiming Soviet-occupied East Germany a sovereign state, with East Berlin as its capital. East Germany became another Soviet satellite.

RUSSIA ORGANIZES AN ANTI-NATO BLOC

One of the main aims of Russia's post-war foreign policy was to keep West Germany disarmed and separated from the Western Allies. When the Western powers granted independence to West Germany and admitted it into NATO, Russia organized an alliance of its own. In 1955 eight Communist countries—the Soviet Union, Poland, Czechoslovakia, Bulgaria, Hungary, Rumania, Albania, and East Germany—signed the *Warsaw Pact*. It provided for an organization somewhat similar to NATO. The armed forces of these nations were placed under a unified military command, with headquarters in Moscow. (Albania withdrew from the pact in 1968.)

GERMANY REMAINS A FOCAL POINT OF THE COLD WAR

Russia persisted in its efforts to stir up trouble in Germany. It conducted a continuing propaganda campaign against West Germany. It repeatedly rejected Western demands for the unification of East and West Germany on the basis of free elections. It periodically attempted to cut off Berlin from the West.

In 1961 the Soviet Union demanded that the Western powers remove their troops from West Berlin and sign a peace treaty confirming the division of Germany. The Allies rejected these demands. President Kennedy assured the people of West Berlin that the United States would not abandon them. He sent reinforcements to the city and ordered a buildup of American military strength. Faced with this display of Allied determination and force, Russia backed down.

Also in 1961, the Communists erected a fortified wall between East and West Berlin, effectively separating the two parts of the city. Thereby, they cut off an escape route by which nearly 3 million East Germans

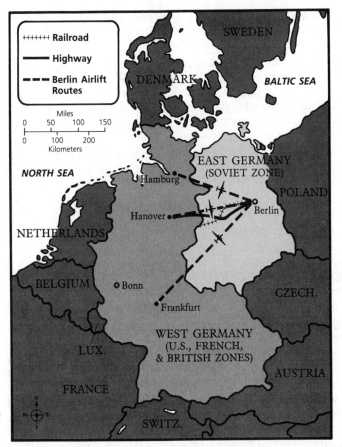

The Cold War Divides Germany

had fled to the West since 1949. The Berlin Wall further increased East-West tensions in the divided city.

WEST GERMAN–EASTERN EUROPEAN RELATIONS IMPROVE

During the 1960's West Germany emerged as one of the world's leading industrial nations and as the strongest economic power in Europe. Under the leadership of Chancellor Willy Brandt, it embarked on a policy of improving relations with Eastern Europe.

1. West Germany negotiated a pact with the Soviet Union (1970) that pledged each to (*a*) refrain from using force against the other, (*b*) settle all disputes peacefully, and (*c*) accept the existing frontiers of all states in Europe (including the western border of Poland and the boundaries of East and West Germany). It also signed a treaty with Poland accepting that country's post-war western boundary. Thereby West Germany renounced title to 40,000 square miles of former German territory.

2. The four occupying powers negotiated an agreement to improve conditions in Berlin (1971). Traffic between West Germany and West

Berlin was allowed to move freely across East German territory; and West Berliners were permitted periodic visits to friends and relatives in East Berlin and East Germany.

3. As a first step toward normalizing East German-West German relations, both countries signed a treaty in 1972 (*a*) mutually recognizing the fact that two German states existed, (*b*) establishing formal relations (but not full diplomatic ties) between the two states, and (*c*) opening new border crossing points to afford greater opportunity for the residents of the two states to visit each other.

These moves decreased political tensions in Europe; opened the door to an expansion of trade between West Germany and the Communist bloc; paved the way for the admission of West Germany and East Germany into the UN; and led to the establishment of diplomatic relations between the Western powers and East Germany.

(For post-Cold War developments in Europe see pages 447–449.)

THE COLD WAR ENGULFS THE FAR EAST

COMMUNISTS GAIN CONTROL OF CHINA

Beginning in the 1920's, the Chinese Communists, led by *Mao Zedong* (Mao Tse-tung), waged a civil war against the Nationalist government of *Chiang Kai-shek*. At the close of World War II, the Chinese Communists acquired huge quantities of captured Japanese weapons from the Russians. Resuming their campaign, they drove the Nationalist armies from Manchuria in 1948, overran the rest of China in 1949, and proclaimed a "People's Republic." Communist China and Russia signed a treaty of "friendship, alliance, and mutual assistance." The United States and the United Nations, however, refused to recognize the People's Republic of China.

The Nationalists withdrew to Taiwan (formerly Formosa), a large island 100 miles off China's coast. In addition, they retained control of the Pescadores, a group of islands near Taiwan, and of several small islands (including Quemoy and Matsu) close to the mainland.

During the 1950's and 1960's, Red China sought to further the spread of communism in Asia by (1) intervening in the Korean War on the side of the North Korean Communists, (2) invading and occupying Tibet, which had been self-governing since 1911, (3) sending military supplies to Communist guerrilla forces in Indochina, (4) menacing Taiwan and the offshore islands held by the Chinese Nationalists, (5) invading and occupying Indian territory along the Chinese border, and (6) aiding the North Vietnamese and Vietcong in their attempt to seize control of South Vietnam.

KOREAN WAR

1. **Background.** Korea, annexed by Japan in 1910, was surrendered to the Allies in 1945. Pending the establishment of self-government, Russia occupied the northern part of the country, the United States the

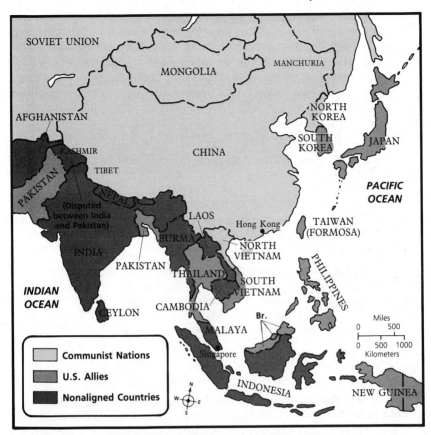

The Cold War Divides the Far East (1960)

southern part. The dividing line was the *38th parallel.* In 1947 the UN sent a commission to Korea to supervise elections and to assist in forming a united government. When North Korea refused to cooperate, elections were held only in the south, where the Republic of Korea was established. The United States and the United Nations recognized the new government. The United States withdrew its occupation forces and gave economic and military aid to the new nation.

In Russian-occupied North Korea, a Communist-sponsored "People's Republic" was set up, patterned after the puppet governments of the other Soviet satellites. The Russians withdrew their troops but maintained close economic and political ties with the North Koreans.

2. War Breaks Out. In June, 1950, the North Korean army invaded South Korea. The UN Security Council ordered the invaders to withdraw their forces. When North Korea refused to obey, the Council called upon all members of the UN to help enforce its demands. The Council was able to act promptly because the Soviet Union was boycotting the UN at the time and could not veto the resolution.

President Truman immediately ordered U.S. armed forces to support the South Koreans. Although other UN members also pledged aid to the invaded nation, the war was fought mainly by South Koreans and Americans. Douglas MacArthur commanded the UN forces in Korea.

Equipped with tanks and other modern weapons supplied by the Soviet Union and Red China, the North Koreans quickly captured the capital city of Seoul. The outnumbered UN forces retreated southward. Soon only a small area around the port of Pusan, in the southeastern corner of South Korea, remained in UN hands.

In September, 1950, MacArthur launched a counterattack. He landed 50,000 American marines and infantry at Inchon, 150 miles north of the enemy lines, while the UN troops in the Pusan area began to drive northward. MacArthur drove the invaders back across the 38th parallel, captured the North Korean capital of Pyongyang, and pushed toward the Yalu River, the boundary between North Korea and the Chinese province of Manchuria.

3. Communist China Intervenes. In November, 1950, more than 200,000 Chinese troops secretly entered North Korea from Manchuria. They attacked the advancing UN armies and threw them back into South Korea. The Chinese crossed the 38th parallel and advanced 70 miles into South Korea before being stopped.

In the spring of 1951, the UN troops resumed the offensive, pushed the Communists back into North Korea, and set up a strong defense line about 25 miles north of the 38th parallel.

4. The War Becomes a Stalemate. By June, 1951, the war had become a "fluid stalemate." Both sides were capable of starting limited offensives, but neither side could achieve a complete victory. The Communists could not hope to win unless Russia intervened, but this would have meant the beginning of World War III. The UN forces could not hope to drive the Chinese from North Korea unless the United States bombed military targets and supply bases in China proper, which might have involved the U.S. in a large-scale war with China and Russia.

5. An Armistice Is Negotiated. In July, 1951, the Communists accepted an American proposal to discuss armistice terms. The two sides were soon deadlocked over the problem of prisoner exchange. The Communists demanded *forced repatriation*, that is, that all prisoners held by the UN be returned to either Red China or North Korea, regardless of the wishes of the prisoners. The UN insisted on *voluntary repatriation*, that is, that only those prisoners who wished to go home would be turned over to the Communists. Two years after the beginning of the armistice talks, the Reds finally accepted the principle of voluntary repatriation, and a cease-fire agreement was signed.

The bitter 37-month Korean War came to an end in July, 1953. Total casualties amounted to 1.5 million for the Communists and 580,000 for the UN forces. The UN losses included 54,000 Americans killed and 103,000 wounded.

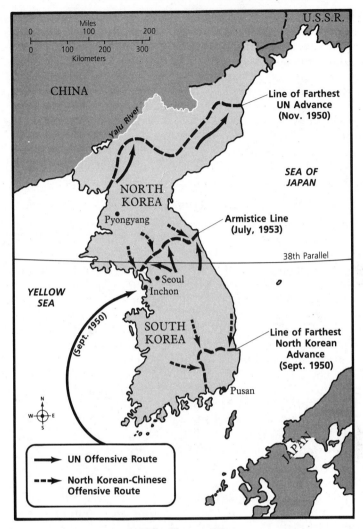

The Korean War

6. Aftermath of the Korean War. Each side withdrew 1.25 miles from the final battle line, thus forming a 2.5-mile neutral zone between the two sides. Those prisoners wishing to return to their homeland were sent back. Anti-Communist North Koreans and Chinese were allowed to remain in South Korea. The United States entered into a pact with the Republic of Korea under which (*a*) U.S. troops remained in South Korea to guard it from further Communist attacks, and (*b*) America provided economic aid to South Korea.

JAPANESE PEACE TREATY

For five years after V-J Day, the Western Allies and the Soviet Union could not agree on a peace treaty for Japan. The United States decided to break the deadlock by preparing a treaty without Russia's cooperation. In San Francisco, in 1951, the United States and 48 other nations signed a peace treaty with Japan. It provided for the withdrawal of Allied occupation troops; the restoration of Japan's status as an independent nation; and the retention by Japan of its four home islands. Japan surrendered all claims to its former possessions, including Korea and Taiwan; and agreed to let the United States continue to administer the Ryukyu Islands, including Okinawa. (These islands were returned to Japan in 1972.)

Japan promised to abide by the principles of the United Nations Charter, becoming a member of the UN in 1956. (In the same year the Soviet Union concluded a separate agreement with Japan.)

DEFENSE PACTS WITH FAR EASTERN NATIONS

During the 1950's, the United States took the following steps to prevent the further spread of communism in the Pacific and to protect the countries of the Far East from aggression:

1. Upon the outbreak of the Korean War, President Truman (*a*) ordered the U.S. Navy to guard Taiwan, (*b*) sent a military advisory group and weapons to help the Chinese Nationalists defend the island, and (*c*) provided economic aid to bolster Taiwan's industry and agriculture. In 1954 the United States entered into a pact with Nationalist China pledging U.S. assistance in the event of an attack on Taiwan. (The United States terminated the pact as of 1980.)

2. The United States entered into a security treaty with Japan (1951) that permitted the United States to maintain bases and armed forces in that country for the purpose of protecting it against attack.

3. The United States signed the *ANZUS Pact* with Australia and New Zealand (1951). This treaty stated that an armed attack upon any of the signatories would be dangerous to the peace and safety of the others. Each nation pledged to take whatever action was needed to meet the common danger.

4. The United States signed a mutual defense treaty with the Republic of the Philippines (1951) guaranteeing that each country would come to the aid of the other in the event of an attack.

5. The United States, Britain, France, Australia, New Zealand, the Philippines, Thailand, and Pakistan organized the *Southeast Asia Treaty Organization* (*SEATO*) in 1954. The agreement provided for collective defense and economic cooperation in Southeast Asia. (In 1975 the members agreed to phase out the alliance.)

THE COLD WAR SHIFTS TO INDOCHINA

1. **Background.** When the French returned to reclaim possession of Indochina after World War II, they found that a native movement for independence had sprung up during their absence. It was led by a revolutionary organization called the *Vietminh*, headed by a Russian-trained Communist, *Ho Chi Minh*. The rebels controlled large sections of eastern Indochina and had established their own government in these areas.

Justus in The Minneapolis Star

The Major Battle

To satisfy the demands of the Indochinese for greater self-rule, France granted partial independence to Indochina in 1949. France divided the colony into three Associated States: Vietnam, Laos, and Cambodia. Although each had its own government, France retained control of their foreign affairs and trade, and French troops continued to occupy the area.

2. The French Withdraw From Indochina. Aided by weapons and advisers sent by Red China and Russia, the Vietminh stepped up its attacks. To prevent the fall of Indochina to the Reds, the United States extended economic and military assistance to the Associated States and shouldered an ever-increasing share of France's war costs.

Despite American aid, the French were unable to put down the rebellion. By the spring of 1954, nearly all of northern Vietnam was in Communist hands. The French at home, weary of supporting the seemingly endless war so costly in lives and money, were clamoring for peace at any cost.

At the request of France, a conference of all interested parties was convened in 1954 in Geneva, Switzerland, to end the war in Indochina. The French and the Vietminh signed an armistice providing that (*a*) Vietnam be divided at the 17th parallel, the northern portion to go to the Vietminh, (*b*) the Vietminh evacuate the areas it held in other parts of Indochina, and (*c*) Vietnam be reunified by an election to be held in 1956.

General elections did not take place in Vietnam, and the country remained divided. North Vietnam became a highly centralized Communist state, and South Vietnam an independent, pro-Western country.

France also granted independence to Laos and Cambodia and withdrew from Indochina.

3. The Reds Threaten Laos. The *Pathet Lao*, pro-Communist guerrilla forces, were entrenched in the northern provinces of Laos, near Red China and North Vietnam. They launched a determined drive in 1960 to take over all of Laos. The Pathet Lao were equipped with modern weapons supplied by Russia and Red China, and were reinforced by North Vietnamese technicians and troops. The Western-backed Laotian government received large-scale American military aid. Nevertheless, the guerrillas quickly extended their control southward.

The West became alarmed at the prospect of a Communist takeover in Laos. President Kennedy informed the Russians that a peaceful settlement in Laos was an essential first step for an improvement in Soviet-American relations. Prime Minister Macmillan of England proposed that Britain and Russia jointly appeal to both sides in Laos for a cease-fire and urged that a conference be held to settle the dispute.

Heeding a joint request by Russia and Britain, as well as pressure from the United States, the Laotians halted their fighting. In 1961, at a conference attended by 14 nations in Geneva, (*a*) the Laotian factions agreed to form a unified, neutralist government, and (*b*) the participating nations pledged to guarantee Laos' neutrality and independence.

VIETNAM WAR

1. Background. In the late 1950's pro-Communist guerrillas in South Vietnam, called the *Vietcong*, began a campaign to seize power. They attacked outlying military posts, murdered public officials, terrorized farming villages, and gained control of large sections of the country. In the early 1960's, in anticipation of ultimate victory, they formed a political organization called the National Liberation Front (NLF). They also stepped up their acts of terrorism and guerrilla attacks.

2. The United States Extends Aid to South Vietnam. To save South Vietnam from the Communists, the United States increased its economic assistance to that country and stepped up shipments of weapons and other military equipment. It also sent over technicians and military personnel to advise, reorganize, and train the South Vietnamese army.

Despite this aid, the South Vietnamese government proved unable to cope with the Vietcong. As a result, the role of the United States began to change from adviser to participant. (*a*) American-piloted helicopters began to fly Vietnamese troops into battle. (*b*) Americans took an increasingly larger part in ground and air operations. (*c*) Nearly 30,000 troops were sent to American military installations there. (*d*) U.S. planes bombed North Vietnam in retaliation for attacks by the North Vietnamese on American warships in the Gulf of Tonkin.

3. The United States Becomes Deeply Involved in Vietnam. In 1965 the struggle entered a new phase when President Lyndon Johnson

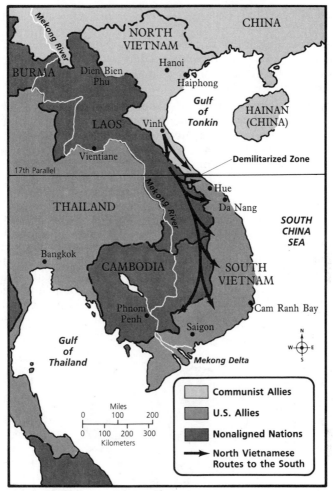

War in Southeast Asia

charged that North Vietnam was waging open aggression against South Vietnam by sending supplies and troops to the Vietcong. Johnson warned that such aggression must stop. To stem the flow of North Vietnamese aid to the Vietcong, the President ordered U.S. planes to bomb munition dumps, military posts, supply routes, and other strategic targets in North Vietnam. He also authorized the commander of the American forces in South Vietnam to send U.S. troops into combat against the Vietcong and the North Vietnamese military units that had infiltrated southward. Johnson announced that U.S. fighting strength in South Vietnam would be increased.

During the next few years, American involvement in the war in Vietnam expanded considerably. More and more troops were sent to the area. By early 1969 there were nearly 550,000 Americans in South Vietnam, plus thousands more aboard U.S. naval vessels offshore and stationed at bases in Thailand, the Philippines, Okinawa, and Guam. U.S. ground forces fought hundreds of bloody engagements with the enemy in the highlands, jungles, and rice paddies of South Vietnam. In the air, U.S. bombers and fighters continued to strike at the infiltration routes used by the North Vietnamese, and to bomb military and industrial targets in North Vietnam.

U.S. war costs also rose sharply—from $6 billion in 1966 to $22 billion in 1969. Enormous sums were spent to build airfields, deep-water ports, highways, communication facilities, military bases, and supply depots in South Vietnam; and to provide South Vietnamese and American forces with the latest military equipment.

4. Steps Are Taken to Negotiate a Settlement. Although the "search and destroy" operations of the South Vietnamese and Americans succeeded in routing the guerrillas from many of their strongholds, the Vietcong still retained their hold on large sections of rural South Vietnam. In addition, they continued to terrorize Saigon, Hue, Da Nang, and other cities by armed raids and rocket bombardments. They also launched repeated attacks on military bases and airfields throughout the country. The Vietcong suffered heavy casualties, but their ranks were constantly replenished by North Vietnamese reinforcements. They also received a steady supply of Russian and Chinese military equipment via North Vietnam.

Canfield in The Newark Evening News

"When I started, he was just about so big."

Early in 1968, during the time of the Lunar New Year (known as *Tet*), the Vietcong and North Vietnamese launched a savage attack against Saigon, Hue, and other urban centers; besieged U.S. forces at Khe Sanh; and raided military outposts throughout the country. Although the attackers were eventually driven off, the *Tet Offensive* demonstrated that the war was far from over, and that U.S. troops would have to remain in Vietnam indefinitely if total victory continued to be the U.S. objective.

In the spring of 1968 President Johnson announced that the United States would end the bombing of most of North Vietnam as a first step toward de-escalating the war. He also offered to meet with the North Vietnamese to discuss further steps toward peace. Hanoi accepted the offer. Representatives of the two countries began a series of meetings in Paris shortly thereafter.

In the fall of 1968 Johnson ordered a complete halt to all bombardment of North Vietnam. That country then agreed to allow South Vietnam to participate in the negotiations, and the United States in turn agreed to let the Vietcong take part. The expanded peace talks began early in 1969 but had little effect on the fighting during the next few years.

5. The War Extends Into Cambodia and Laos. Prince Norodom Sihanouk, Cambodia's long-time leader, declared his country's neutrality in the East-West struggle in Southeast Asia. Nevertheless, he was unwilling or unable to prevent the Vietcong and North Vietnamese from setting up supply depots and bases on the Cambodian side of the Vietnam border. When pursued by the Americans and South Vietnamese, the Vietcong and North Vietnamese frequently escaped to these sanctuaries. They also used the bases to launch surprise raids against South Vietnam.

In 1970 a pro-Western Cambodian group headed by Lon Nol ousted Prince Sihanouk and gained control of the government. President Nixon thereupon authorized U.S. forces in Vietnam to enter Cambodia and destroy the enemy supply depots in that country. He restricted the operation to the enemy bases along the border and withdrew the troops after two months.

Driven from their border sanctuaries, the North Vietnamese and Vietcong seized control of the northeastern section of Cambodia. Linking up with local Cambodian guerrillas, the *Khmer Rouge*, they fanned out westward and southward, occupying the site of the famed *Angkor Wat* temples and moving toward the outskirts of *Phnom Penh*, the capital. To prevent the complete collapse of the Cambodian government, the United States sent in large quantities of military supplies, and U.S. bombers provided massive air support to the Cambodian army during the next three years.

Laos also became a battleground of the war. Over the years the North Vietnamese had secretly developed a network of supply routes through the jungles and mountains of southern Laos. Along this *Ho Chi Minh Trail* they transported troops and equipment to the guerrillas in South Vietnam and Cambodia. Early in 1971 the South Vietnamese army, supported by American air power, crossed into Laos to disrupt the enemy supply lines. The joint effort was fiercely resisted by the Communists, and the South Vietnamese retreated.

6. The United States Withdraws Most of Its Ground Forces. A short time after President Nixon assumed office in 1969, he announced that American combat troops would be gradually withdrawn from Vietnam and replaced in the field by South Vietnamese. (The effort to turn over a growing share of the combat burden to South Vietnamese forces was known as *Vietnamization*.) Between 1969 and 1972 more than 500,000 U.S. soldiers were pulled out of Vietnam, reducing U.S. military strength in that country to 25,000. This residual force was kept to help the South Vietnamese with supply and logistical operations and to provide combat support with helicopters.

7. The War Flares Up Anew. In the spring of 1972 the Communists launched an all-out drive, supported by tanks and rockets, against key South Vietnamese strongholds in various sections of the country. Declaring that "we will never surrender our friends to Communist aggression," Nixon (*a*) increased American air and naval strength in the area, (*b*) stepped up air support of the hard-pressed South Vietnamese troops, and (*c*) ordered the resumption of bombing of strategic targets in North Vietnam. In addition, to cut off Hanoi's supply of war materials, he authorized the mining of North Vietnamese ports and the bombing of rail and highway links with China. The massive use of American air and sea power blunted the Red offensive and enabled the South Vietnamese to withstand the attackers.

The heaviest American bombings of the war occurred in December, 1972, when Nixon ordered a renewal of air attacks above the 20th parallel in North Vietnam, including targets in the densely populated Hanoi-Haiphong area. Round-the-clock raids were carried out for 12 days before the bombings were halted.

8. A Cease-Fire Agreement Is Negotiated. The formal peace talks in Paris dragged on for more than four years without making any significant progress. To break the deadlock, *Henry A. Kissinger*, President Nixon's foreign policy adviser, and *Le Duc Tho*, North Vietnam's chief negotiator, held a series of secret meetings and finally hammered out a compromise agreement that was acceptable to both sides.

Signed in January, 1973, the Paris Agreement provided for the following: (*a*) an immediate cease-fire, with both sides retaining control of the areas that they then occupied in South Vietnam; (*b*) withdrawal of all American military personnel from Vietnam within 60 days; (*c*) acceptance of the presence of North Vietnamese troops already in the South but a prohibition on the admission of reinforcements; (*d*) release of U.S. prisoners of war (POW's) and the exchange of all captured military and civilian personnel held by both sides; and (*e*) withdrawal of all Vietnamese and other foreign troops from Laos and Cambodia.

The United States and North Vietnam agreed to respect "the South Vietnamese people's right to self-determination." The existing government of South Vietnam was to remain in power pending an election.

The United States accepted the principle that "Vietnam is one country temporarily divided into two zones" and approved the eventual reunification of Vietnam "through peaceful means on the basis of discussions and agreements between North and South Vietnam." For the present, both sides agreed to accept the 17th parallel as the line of demarcation between the two sections and to respect the demilitarized zone (DMZ) along that line.

9. Costs of the War. During America's 12-year involvement in Vietnam—the longest war in U.S. history and the most divisive conflict since the Civil War—some 58,000 Americans lost their lives and more than 150,000 were wounded. U.S. war costs amounted to nearly $150 billion. More than 1 million North and South Vietnamese died as a result of the war; countless others were wounded or made homeless.

10. Aftermath of the War

a. *Vietnam.* The United States withdrew its troops from South Vietnam on schedule, and North Vietnam released its U.S. prisoners. Other parts of the agreement, however, were not carried out. Despite the cease-fire, fighting erupted daily, each side blaming the other for the outbreaks. Before long, full-scale warfare resumed. Heavy fighting continued for the next two years. Early in 1975, the North Vietnamese launched an all-out offensive against government outposts in the Central Highlands. The demoralized South Vietnamese beat a hasty retreat, which soon turned into a rout. Panic swept the country, resistance collapsed, and the Saigon government surrendered. (Large numbers of South Vietnamese, fearing Communist control, fled the country. The United States granted asylum to many of these refugees.)

After the surrender, the North Vietnamese consolidated their hold on South Vietnam. In 1976 North and South Vietnam were reunited as the Socialist Republic of Vietnam, with Hanoi as its capital. Saigon, the former capital of South Vietnam, was renamed *Ho Chi Minh City.*

A U.S. ban on trade with Vietnam, imposed in 1975, was lifted by President Clinton in 1994. Then in 1995 he officially recognized the government of Vietnam, and the two countries exchanged ambassadors.

b. *Cambodia.* The Paris Agreement did not end the war in Cambodia. The Khmer Rouge continued their campaign to overthrow the Lon Nol government, finally succeeding in 1975. They established a Communist regime, expelled all foreigners, and proceeded to carry out a harsh program of political, social, and economic reorganization. Political observers estimate that between 1 and 2 million Cambodians died from hunger and disease or in political purges after the takeover.

Border disputes, coupled with traditional Cambodian-Vietnamese hostility, led to an outbreak of war between the two countries in 1977. Vietnam invaded Cambodia, overthrew the existing government, and installed a pro-Vietnamese regime in Phnom Penh (1979). For the next 10 years, the United States and the UN refused to recognize the new government, and native resistance groups carried on guerrilla warfare against the occupying Vietnamese.

In 1989 Vietnam withdrew its troops. UN-sponsored elections led to the adoption of a new Cambodian constitution and the establishment of a monarchy in 1993. The Khmer Rouge, which had boycotted the elections, violently opposed the new regime.

c. Laos. Following the signing of the Paris Agreement, warring factions in Laos agreed to a cease-fire, the withdrawal of foreign troops, and the formation of a coalition government. However, the Pathet Lao soon resumed their drive to take over the country, finally succeeding in 1975.

THE COLD WAR SPREADS TO THE MIDDLE EAST

BACKGROUND

The Middle East, a region that includes northeastern Africa and southwestern Asia, is often called "the crossroads of the world." Here is located the Suez Canal, the main artery of sea commerce between Europe and the Far East. Here, too, lie the world's richest oil fields, containing two-thirds of the earth's petroleum resources.

Before World War II many of the countries of the Middle East were ruled by England and France, but since the war almost all of them have achieved independence. Most of the inhabitants of the area are Arabs, and nearly all are *Muslims* (adherents of the Islamic religion). Poverty and illiteracy are widespread, and democracy is virtually unknown.

CENTRAL TREATY ORGANIZATION (CENTO)

In 1955 the United States recommended that the nations of the Middle East join together in a defensive alliance to prevent the Soviet Union from extending its influence into the area. Turkey, Iraq, and Iran, the Middle Eastern countries closest to Russia and therefore most concerned with the possibility of a Soviet attack, approved the American idea. So did Pakistan (a central Asian nation situated near both Russia and the Middle East) and Great Britain (whose economy depended upon Middle Eastern oil). In the Baghdad Pact, these five countries agreed to establish a Middle East Treaty Organization patterned after NATO and SEATO.

Although the United States did not join the organization, it provided military and economic aid to the pact members, shared the cost of maintaining a permanent secretariat, and participated in the work of many of the organization's committees.

In 1958 Iraq's pro-Western ruler was assassinated and pro-Soviet leftists gained control of the government. The following year Iraq withdrew from the treaty organization. The remaining members reorganized the alliance under the name *Central Treaty Organization (CENTO)*.

Twenty years later, after the Shah of Iran had been overthrown, that country withdrew from CENTO. Pakistan, too, resigned its membership. As a result, the Secretary General of CENTO announced that the organization would be dissolved (1979).

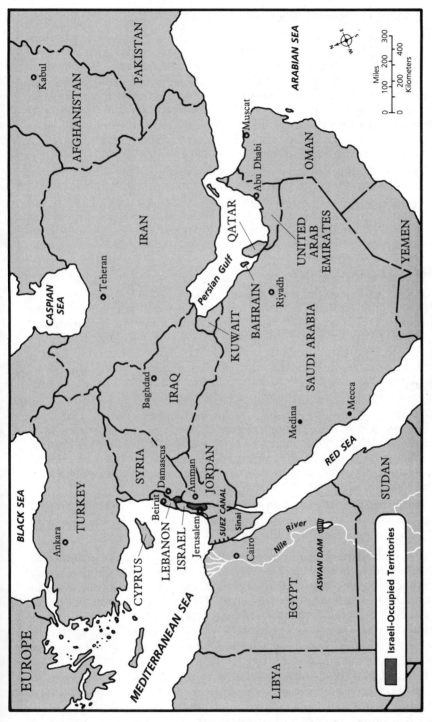

The Middle East Today

THE SOVIETS CHANGE THEIR COLD WAR TACTICS

In the mid-1950's the Russians embarked on a campaign to win over the underdeveloped nations of Africa and Asia. Although their basic objective of worldwide domination did not change, they altered their tactics toward achieving that end. The Soviets sent goodwill missions to various countries in an attempt to win their friendship. They set themselves up as the champions of the underprivileged and denounced the Western powers as imperialists whose aim it is to exploit the weak nations of the world. They also offered technical and economic aid to countries needing such assistance.

Specifically, the Russians (1) agreed to supply Egypt with jet planes, tanks, heavy artillery, and naval craft in exchange for Egyptian cotton, (2) offered financial aid and favorable trade agreements to Syria, Lebanon, Turkey, and Pakistan, (3) promised arms to Saudi Arabia and Iraq, and (4) conducted a vigorous propaganda campaign to stir up anti-Western sentiment among the Arabs.

THE SUEZ CANAL CRISIS

1. Nasser Seizes the Suez Canal. *Gamal Abdel Nasser*, President of Egypt, requested financial help from the United States and Britain to build a huge dam at Aswan, on the upper Nile River, for irrigation and hydroelectric power. After receiving a favorable response, Nasser attempted to get better terms from Russia. The United States and Britain were angered by (*a*) Nasser's effort to play one side against the other, (*b*) his anti-Western policies, and (*c*) his arms and trade agreements with the Soviets. In 1956 they therefore withdrew their offer of aid.

Nasser retaliated by seizing control of the Suez Canal. This vital waterway, which runs through Egypt, was owned and operated by a private company whose shareholders were mostly British and French. The status of the canal as an international waterway—open to ships of all nations in peace and in war—had been guaranteed since 1888 by a treaty signed by the world's maritime nations.

Declaring that the Suez Canal belonged to Egypt, Nasser announced that his country would operate the waterway and use the toll money to pay for the construction of the Aswan Dam.

2. Israel, Britain, and France Invade Egypt. Despite the armistice of 1949, frequent border clashes took place between Israel and its Arab neighbors in the years that followed. With Nasser's rise to power in 1954, Arab-Israeli relations worsened. He stirred up Arab sentiment for Israel's downfall; strengthened the Egyptian army with Communist-supplied arms; trained an organization of terrorists, or *fedayeen,* to carry out surprise attacks on Israeli farm settlements; and, after assuming control of the Suez Canal, barred Israel-bound ships from using it.

In the fall of 1956, Israel retaliated by invading Egypt. It aimed to wipe out the fedayeen bases located there, destroy the powerful new weapons that Egypt had acquired, and bring about Nasser's downfall. Israeli armored columns and paratroopers quickly gained possession of Egypt's Sinai Peninsula. They advanced to a distance 13 miles from the

Fischetti, *Reprinted by permission of NEA*

Foreign Aid

Suez Canal, captured or routed the Egyptian army east of the canal, and seized about $50 million worth of Communist-built military equipment.

While the Israeli campaign was in progress, Britain and France took steps to regain control of the canal and safeguard its operation. A combined Anglo-French force of paratroopers invaded Egypt, seized the northern part of the canal, and occupied key positions along the waterway. The Egyptians responded by sinking 50 of their own ships in the canal, thus making it unusable.

3. The Crisis Subsides. The United States and the UN severely criticized the action taken by Israel, Britain, and France. By an overwhelming majority, the General Assembly passed a resolution demanding that (*a*) all parties involved in the hostilities agree to an immediate cease-fire, (*b*) the invaders withdraw their forces from Egypt, and (*c*) Israel and Egypt stop raiding each other's territory and observe the armistice of 1949.

The pressure of world opinion, the disapproval of the United States, and threats by Russia to send an army of "volunteers" to aid Egypt forced Britain, France, and Israel to back down. Eight days after the fighting began, they agreed to a cease-fire. Shortly thereafter the UN dispatched a *United Nations Emergency Force (UNEF)* to Egypt to supervise the truce. Anglo-French troops were withdrawn from Egyptian soil by the end of 1956, and the last contingent of Israelis left several months later. UN salvage teams undertook the task of clearing the Suez Canal, and in the spring of 1957 it was reopened to shipping. The following year Nasser agreed to reimburse the Suez Canal Company for the loss of its property.

THE EISENHOWER DOCTRINE

In 1957 President Eisenhower said, "If power-hungry Communists should either falsely or correctly estimate that the Middle East is inadequately defended, they might be tempted to use open measures of armed attack." Therefore, he asked Congress (1) to approve economic and military assistance for the Middle East, and (2) to authorize him to send troops to any Middle Eastern nation requesting help against Communist aggression.

This policy of using U.S. economic and military power to prevent Communists from gaining control of the Middle East became known as the *Eisenhower Doctrine*.

U.S. AND BRITAIN SEND TROOPS TO THE MIDDLE EAST

In 1958 a revolution broke out in Iraq. The insurgents, led by a group of army officers, included Iraqi pro-Nasserites and Communists. They assassinated pro-Western King Faisal II and seized control of the Iraqi government. Alarmed at the prospect of similar upheavals in their own countries, the president of Lebanon appealed to the United States for help, and the king of Jordan appealed to Britain.

The two Western powers immediately responded to these appeals. President Eisenhower dispatched a force of marines, supported by sea and air power, to Lebanon. Britain sent troops into Jordan. Under the watchful eye of the American troops, the political turmoil in Lebanon subsided. After order had been restored, all U.S. forces were withdrawn from Lebanon. Shortly thereafter, England removed its troops from Jordan.

THE MIDDLE EAST ERUPTS ONCE AGAIN

1. Nasser Provokes Another Crisis. For 10 years after the Suez crisis of 1956, an uneasy peace reigned in the Middle East. Russia provided technical and economic aid to the Arab states (including the financing of Egypt's Aswan Dam), and bolstered their armed forces with large quantities of Soviet weapons. Seeking to counter Russia's influence, the Western powers also supplied economic assistance and limited quantities of weapons to the Arabs. The West likewise furnished arms and aid to Israel.

During this time the UNEF supervised the observance of the Egyptian-Israeli truce. It patrolled the border between the two countries and kept a watchful eye on the Strait of Tiran at the southern tip of the Sinai Peninsula. This strait, an international waterway connecting the Gulf of 'Aqaba with the Red Sea, provides the only access to Israel's southern port of Eilat.

In 1967 Nasser suddenly demanded the withdrawal of the UNEF from Egypt. He then massed his troops along Israel's western border; reactivated the fortress of Sharm al-Sheikh, whose coastal batteries control the Strait of Tiran; and announced the closing of the Gulf of 'Aqaba to shipping bound for Israel. At the same time, Jordan and Syria stationed their armies along Israel's eastern border. The other Arab states pledged their support for a war against Israel.

2. Israel Defeats the Arabs in the Six-Day War. With its southern sea route cut off by the Egyptian blockade and its existence threatened by a ring of armies encircling its borders, Israel prepared to meet the Arab challenge. For two weeks, the United States and other powers attempted to convince Nasser to open the Strait of Tiran and thereby ease the crisis, but their efforts failed. Early in June, 1967, war broke out.

Within a few hours, the Israelis won control of the skies by destroying the air power of their opponents. Although heavily outnumbered, the Israeli ground forces then proceeded to crush the Egyptian armies, seize the Gaza Strip, and overrun the Sinai Peninsula. Before long they were in possession of Sharm al-Sheikh, thus breaking Egypt's blockade, and were encamped on the eastern bank of the Suez Canal. On the Jordanian front, the Israelis defeated King Hussein's Arab Legion, captured the Old City section of Jerusalem, as well as the historic towns of Bethlehem, Hebron, and Jericho, and occupied all of Jordan west of the Jordan River. In the north, Israeli troops crossed into Syria and took possession of the Golan Heights, which overlook Israeli settlements in eastern Galilee.

Shortly after hostilities began, the UN Security Council ordered the nations involved to stop fighting. One by one, each of the warring countries agreed to accept the cease-fire order. Six days after it started, the war ended.

The Security Council then passed a resolution calling for (*a*) Israeli withdrawal from occupied Arab territories, (*b*) the right of all Middle Eastern countries to have safe and recognized boundaries, (*c*) freedom of navigation through international waterways in the area, and (*d*) a just settlement of the problem of Palestinian Arab refugees.

(The Palestinian Arab refugee problem arose in 1948 when Egypt, Syria, and Jordan attacked the newly proclaimed state of Israel. To escape the fighting, about 75% of the Arab inhabitants of the area abandoned their homes and fled to neighboring countries. They expected to return after Israel was defeated, but such an outcome did not materialize. Although the host countries permitted the Palestinians to remain, they kept them apart from their own people—settling them in refugee camps and affording them little opportunity to obtain jobs, provide for their families, or lead normal lives. For their survival, the Palestinian refugees had to depend on aid provided by international agencies and charities.)

3. Arab-Israeli Hostilities Persist. Israel's victory ended the immediate threat to its security but did not solve the Arab-Israeli problem or bring peace to the Middle East. The Arab states rebuilt their military strength with Soviet arms, and continued to call for Israel's destruction. Israel, in turn, obtained additional aircraft and other weapons from the United States. It refused to return any of the territory it had seized until the Arab governments agreed to negotiate a settlement guaranteeing its security as well as its shipping rights through the Suez Canal and the Strait of Tiran.

Along the cease-fire lines, clashes between the two sides broke out almost daily. In 1970, at the urging of the United States and Russia, the warring states agreed to restore the cease-fire and start negotiating a settlement through the UN. However, little progress was made in reconciling Arab-Israeli differences.

In the fall of 1970, President Nasser of Egypt suffered a fatal heart attack. His successor, *Anwar el-Sadat*, vowed to follow in Nasser's footsteps and continue the struggle against Israel.

4. Another Arab-Israeli War Is Fought in 1973. A fourth war broke out in October, 1973, when Egyptian troops crossed the Suez Canal into the Israeli-occupied Sinai Peninsula and Syrian armored columns moved into the Israeli-held Golan Heights. The attack occurred on the holiest day of the Jewish year, *Yom Kippur*, when most Israelis were attending religious services. Caught by surprise, the Israelis were thrown back on both fronts. Mobilizing their forces, they soon halted the Syrians, drove them from the Golan Heights, and advanced to within 21 miles of the Syrian capital of Damascus.

On the Sinai front the Egyptians dislodged the Israelis from their positions along the Suez Canal and forced them to withdraw into the desert. After stopping the Syrians, the Israelis shifted their attention southward, halted the Egyptian advance, and launched a counterattack. They drove a wedge between the two Egyptian armies in Sinai, crossed the canal, established a beachhead on the west bank, and seized control of the southern half of the waterway. They destroyed the Russian-supplied network of surface-to-air missiles (SAM's) that had provided a protective umbrella for the Egyptian crossing of the canal; advanced to within 50 miles of the Egyptian capital; and cut the main supply routes from Cairo to Suez, thus threatening the total destruction of Egypt's forces in Sinai.

At the outbreak of the war, the Russians had pledged to assist Syria and Egypt in every way. To replace the losses suffered by their Arab allies, they shipped in huge quantities of tanks, missiles, and ammunition. The United States countered the Soviet action by airlifting tanks, planes, and electronic equipment to Israel. When the tide of battle turned in Israel's favor, the Soviet Union accepted an American proposal to jointly sponsor a cease-fire resolution. Hastily rushed through the Security Council, it provided for an immediate end to the fighting and called on all parties to start peace negotiations.

The warring states accepted the cease-fire. Fighting on the Sinai front continued for several days, however, as the Egyptian Third Army, trapped behind Israeli lines, tried to break out, and the Israelis cut off their last escape route. When reports were received that Russia was planning to send in troops to assist the entrapped Egyptians, President Nixon ordered all U.S. forces around the world on a "precautionary alert." The threat of a major Soviet-American confrontation in the Middle East ended when the two countries agreed that a UN emergency force from among the smaller nations should be sent to the combat zones to serve as a buffer between the Arabs and the Israelis.

5. Aftermath of the Yom Kippur War

a. Egypt and Israel signed a disengagement pact (1974) that provided for (1) Israeli withdrawal from both banks of the Suez Canal, (2) Egyptian retention of a seven-mile-wide strip of land along the canal's east bank, and (3) creation of a neutral zone, patrolled by UN troops, between the two sides in Sinai. Egypt also took steps to clear and reopen the Suez Canal, which had been closed to shipping since 1967.

b. Syria and Israel negotiated an agreement (1974) providing for Israeli withdrawal from all Syrian territory occupied in 1973 and from a small area captured in 1967. A buffer zone, patrolled by UN troops, was set up between the two sides.

c. A second agreement (1975) between Israel and Egypt (1) restored an additional section of Sinai to Egypt, including the Abu Rudeis oilfields and the strategic Mitla and Gidi passes, (2) authorized the United States to set up electronic monitoring stations in the area to check on agreement violations by either side, and (3) allowed passage through the Suez Canal of nonmilitary cargoes to and from Israel.

6. The Arab States Use Oil as a Political Weapon.
During the Yom Kippur War, Saudi Arabia, Libya, Kuwait, and other Arab states that control most of the region's oil resources, halted all oil shipments to the United States. They threatened to continue the embargo until American aid to Israel was stopped. They also reduced the flow of oil to Western Europe and Japan and increased the price of oil sharply. Their aim was to punish Israel's friends and to force America's allies to exert pressure on the United States to change its Middle Eastern policy. The resulting energy shortage caused serious economic dislocation in the affected countries. In the spring of 1974, the Arabs lifted the embargo and restored oil deliveries to normal levels. But they retained the fourfold increase in oil prices. Although the Arab states failed to achieve their main political objective, they succeeded in increasing their oil revenues

enormously and made the industrial nations keenly aware of their dependence on Middle Eastern oil.

7. Egypt and Israel Sign a Formal Peace Treaty. Late in 1977, President Sadat of Egypt startled the world by declaring his willingness to negotiate a full settlement with Israel. His dramatic announcement led to an exchange of visits and to the start of discussions on peace terms. In 1978, at the invitation of U.S. President Carter, the heads of Israel and Egypt met at Camp David, Maryland, and tentatively agreed upon a framework for peace. It took six more difficult months of negotiations before a final agreement was reached. The 30-year state of war between Egypt and Israel ended in March, 1979, when a formal peace treaty was signed in Washington, D.C.

The treaty called for the (*a*) evacuation of Israel's military forces and civilians from the Sinai Peninsula in a series of phased withdrawals over a three-year period; (*b*) establishment of normal and friendly relations between the two countries; and (*c*) participation of both parties in efforts to resolve the Palestinian problem. The United States agreed to provide substantial economic and military assistance to both Egypt and Israel, and to play an active role in negotiating an agreement on Palestinian self-rule.

8. Arab Reaction to the Egyptian-Israeli Pact. The Arab states denounced Egypt for shattering their united front of opposition to Israel. They broke off diplomatic relations and took other steps to isolate Egypt from the Arab world. Unable to depend on Egypt for military support in the event of another conflict with Israel, Syria strengthened its ties with the U.S.S.R. In 1980 it signed a treaty with the Soviet Union that provided for military, economic, and technological aid.

9. Israel and the PLO Agree to Negotiate. Over the years, U.S. diplomats and others have made numerous attempts to bring the Israelis and Palestinians together to work out a solution to the Palestinian problem. A major obstacle was disagreement over the role of the *Palestine Liberation Organization* (*PLO*), headed by Yasir Arafat. A combination of several militant guerrilla groups, the PLO had been designated by the Arab countries as "the sole legitimate representative of all the Palestinian people." The Palestinians declined to participate in any discussions with Israel unless the PLO was a party to the negotiations. This demand was unacceptable to the Israelis because the PLO refused to acknowledge Israel's existence and was responsible for carrying out many terrorist acts.

Violent clashes between Palestinian protesters and Israeli soldiers and police occurred almost daily in the occupied territories. When the Labor Party rose to power in Israel in 1992, its leaders issued a call for peace and reconciliation with the country's Arab neighbors. Prime Minister Yitzhak Rabin and Foreign Minister Shimon Peres initiated secret talks with the PLO that led to a historic breakthrough. Arafat declared that "the PLO recognizes the right of the State of Israel to live in peace and security." Rabin, in turn, stated that Israel recognizes the PLO as the representative of the Palestinian people.

In September, 1993, a dramatic ceremony was held at the White House in Washington, D.C. With President Clinton officiating, Rabin and Arafat signed a declaration of principles for interim Palestinian self-rule. Despite efforts by Israeli and Arab extremists to derail the peace process, agreements were later worked out for Israeli withdrawal from the Gaza Strip, Jericho, and seven other West Bank cities (including Bethlehem and Hebron). Between 1994 and 1997 the new Palestinian Authority assumed control of these areas. Still to be resolved were such issues as the status of Jerusalem, Jewish settlements on the West Bank, final borders, and Palestinian refugees.

As an outgrowth of the Israeli-Palestinian accord, Jordan ended its 46-year state of war and signed a peace treaty with Israel in October, 1994. Other Arab and Third World countries also announced their readiness to establish normal relations with the Jewish state.

THE COLD WAR REACHES LATIN AMERICA

CASTRO RISES TO POWER IN CUBA

In 1956 a young revolutionary named *Fidel Castro* began a revolt against Cuba's military dictator, Fulgencio Batista. Castro gained many followers by promising to restore political democracy and introduce a program of social and economic reform. After several years of guerrilla warfare, his rebel band finally overcame Batista's forces, entered the capital city of Havana, and seized control (1959). Castro became head of the new government, serving first as prime minister and then as president.

At first, Americans were generally sympathetic to Castro and his aims. But public opinion in the United States soon became sharply critical of Castro. (1) He ruthlessly executed nearly 1,000 Cubans whom his military courts had hastily tried and condemned for their opposition to his movement. (2) He broke his often-repeated promise to hold "immediate and honest elections." (3) He elevated Communist sympathizers to positions of power in the government. (4) He curtailed freedom of speech, press, and religion. (5) He deported many Catholic priests and nuns. (6) He denounced Americans as "Yankee imperialists" who were seeking to hold his country in "economic slavery." (7) He took over American-owned sugar plantations and other agricultural property.

CUBA TURNS TOWARD THE COMMUNIST BLOC

To reduce Cuba's economic dependence on the United States, Castro negotiated a trade agreement with Russia. In exchange for Cuban sugar, the Soviet Union agreed to provide Cuba with oil, machinery, and other manufactured products. The U.S.S.R. and other Communist countries also began to supply Castro with large shipments of arms and to send military experts to train the Cuban army.

When several American-owned oil refineries in Cuba refused to process Russian oil, Castro ordered their seizure. In retaliation President Eisenhower halted the importation of Cuban sugar. Castro thereupon seized all remaining American assets in Cuba and threatened to take over the American naval base at Guantánamo Bay.

The fears of many American observers that Cuba was becoming a Communist beachhead in the Western Hemisphere were further confirmed when (1) Russia pledged military support to Castro if the United States intervened in Cuba, and (2) Castro announced his determination to communize Cuba.

THE UNITED STATES AND THE OAS ATTEMPT TO CURB CASTRO

Growing increasingly concerned over the rise of a Communist state in the Western Hemisphere, the United States and the Organization of American States took the following measures to curb Castro:

1. The OAS (*a*) at the *San José Conference* (1960) passed a resolution condemning intervention by outside powers in the Western Hemisphere, and (*b*) at the *Punta del Este Conference* (1962) voted by a two-thirds majority to exclude Cuba from participation in its affairs.

Central America and the Caribbean Today

2. The United States (*a*) placed an embargo on the export of American goods (except food and medicine) to Cuba and halted all imports from Cuba, (*b*) ordered American naval units to patrol the coasts of Guatemala and Nicaragua to prevent an invasion of these countries by Castro's followers, (*c*) broke off diplomatic relations with Cuba (1961), and (*d*) encouraged anti-Castro Cuban exiles to invade their homeland.

BAY OF PIGS INVASION

More than 500,000 Cubans, including former supporters of Castro, had fled to the United States to escape his oppressive rule. In 1961 several thousand of these exiles, armed and trained by the United States government, launched an invasion of Cuba at the Bay of Pigs. This ill-advised and poorly planned invasion attempt failed, and the hopelessly outnumbered invaders were quickly crushed by Castro's army.

A MISSILE CRISIS ERUPTS IN CUBA

In the fall of 1962 the United States discovered that Russia was converting Cuba into an offensive military base. Photographs taken by American planes showed that Soviet technicians in Cuba were building missile-launching sites and airfields for long-range jet bombers. The missiles that the Russians were installing were capable of carrying nuclear warheads to targets anywhere in the Western Hemisphere.

President Kennedy acted quickly and daringly to counter the Soviet threat. (1) He clamped a blockade on Cuba and ordered U.S. forces to turn back any ship carrying offensive military equipment to the island. (2) He demanded the immediate dismantling and removal of existing missiles and bombers. (3) He warned that the United States would take

Eric in The Atlanta Journal

Clampdown on a Holdup

further action if offensive military preparations continued. (4) He declared that the United States would retaliate against Russia with the full force of its nuclear might if any missiles were launched from Cuba against any nation in the Western Hemisphere.

America's armed forces prepared for combat. Its naval vessels took up blockade positions around Cuba and its patrol planes searched the seas for Cuba-bound freighters from Communist countries. Reconnaissance planes flew over Cuba to obtain up-to-date photographs of the Russian military buildup.

Kennedy's bold moves caught Moscow off guard, and the Soviet leaders backed away from a showdown. They called back Soviet ships carrying offensive weapons to Cuba. They agreed to halt construction of the missile bases, to destroy the installations already erected, and to dismantle and remove their missiles and bombers. Kennedy, in turn, promised to lift the Cuban blockade upon the completion of the Soviet withdrawal. He also assured the Russians that the United States would not invade Cuba if all the conditions agreed upon were fulfilled.

The Russians carried out their part of the agreement, and the Cuban missile crisis subsided. Cuba, however, remained a Communist beachhead in the Western Hemisphere.

LATER CUBAN-AMERICAN DEVELOPMENTS

Starting in the 1970's, U.S.-Cuban relations improved somewhat. In 1973 the two countries negotiated an antihijacking agreement requiring each side to either prosecute or return for trial anyone who hijacked a boat or plane and brought it to the other's territory. Two years later the U.S. eased its boycott of Cuba by permitting foreign subsidiaries of U.S. companies to trade with that country. In 1977 the two countries agreed to regulate fishing in waters between the two countries and to set up a diplomatic office in each other's capital (but not to restore full diplomatic ties). In 1980 Castro allowed more than 100,000 Cubans who wished to join their families abroad to emigrate to the U.S. And in 1984 Reagan granted up to 20,000 immigrant visas a year to Cubans.

A complete restoration of normal relations did not materialize, however. One obstacle was the U.S. demand for compensation of U.S. citizens whose property had been seized by Castro. The United States also objected to Cuban intervention in African countries on the side of Marxist governments and rebel groups, and to Cuban backing of leftist regimes and revolutionists in Latin America. (Such efforts to further the spread of communism abroad ended when the cold war subsided in the early 1990's.)

Having enjoyed a preferential trading status with Eastern Europe and the Soviet Union, Cuba suffered a severe economic setback after the Communist bloc collapsed. As a replacement, Cuba sought to win support among Americans for the lifting of the U.S. trade embargo.

TURMOIL IN CENTRAL AMERICA

1. A Revolution Occurs in Nicaragua. Ever since 1936, Nicaragua, the largest country in Central America, had been ruled by members of the Somoza family. For more than 40 years the Somozas had retained control of the government by ruthlessly suppressing all political opposition. In the late 1970's dissatisfaction with their dictatorial and oppressive rule touched off a popular uprising that was supported by a broad cross section of Nicaraguan society. In the forefront of the revolt was the *Sandinista National Liberation Front,* an anti-Somoza organization that included moderate elements, but was dominated by radical Marxists—many of them trained and armed by Cuba.

Unable to quell the rebellion, Anastasio Somoza resigned as President and fled the country in 1979. The Sandinistas quickly took control, confiscated the Somoza family's property and business assets, and appointed a *junta* (political committee) to govern the nation. This group promised to introduce needed social and economic reforms and to hold elections for the purpose of establishing a democratic government. Once in power, however, the junta proceeded to consolidate its position by postponing elections, imposing press censorship, and strengthening its armed forces with Soviet and Cuban weapons and equipment.

2. The United States Becomes Involved in Nicaragua. Reacting favorably to the moderate program of reform first proposed by the Sandinistas, President Carter agreed to provide economic aid to the new regime. During the early months of the Reagan administration, however, events in Nicaragua caused the United States to change its policy toward the Sandinista government. Fearing that the junta was aiming to establish a Cuban-style Marxist state, and accusing it of supplying arms to leftist guerrillas seeking to overthrow the government of El Salvador, President Reagan suspended U.S. aid to Nicaragua. He also authorized the Central Intelligence Agency (CIA) to provide covert (secret) assistance to anti-Sandinista guerrilla groups (called *contras*) based in Honduras and Costa Rica. The contras comprised (*a*) former Sandinista supporters who had broken away because they opposed the leftist policies of the new regime, and (*b*) members of Somoza's National Guard who had fled Nicaragua after the revolution. Contra raids into Nicaragua and Sandinista troop counterattacks on contra bases in Honduras and Costa Rica resulted in much bloodshed and destruction.

The junta accused the United States of launching an undeclared war against Nicaragua and attempting to destroy the Sandinista revolution. The Reagan administration, in turn, justified its support of the contras on the grounds that it would halt the export of the Sandinista revolution to other parts of Central America. A report issued in 1984 by a presidential commission headed by former Secretary of State Henry Kissinger (*a*) warned that Soviet and Cuban backing of the Nicaraguan government posed a threat to the security of the region, (*b*) supported continued aid to anti-Sandinista elements in Nicaragua, (*c*) proposed that the United States provide an $8 billion program of economic aid to Central America, and (*d*) recommended a sizable increase in U.S. military assistance to El Salvador, where the government had been waging a civil war against left-wing rebels since 1979.

3. Nicaraguan Problem Persists. After numerous postponements, elections were finally held in Nicaragua in late 1984. Daniel Ortega, who had served as coordinator of the junta, was elected President. Declaring the elections a "sham," Reagan asked Congress to provide funds for additional American aid to the contras. His request encountered opposition. Some members of Congress argued that Reagan's policy would be viewed by Latin America as a replay of "Yankee imperialism"; others criticized his use of the CIA to direct the mining of Nicaraguan ports; and still others warned that the administration was embarking on a course that could lead to ever-increasing expenditures, the introduction of American troops, and U.S. involvement in "another Vietnam."

Failing to win congressional support, in the spring of 1985 Reagan imposed a total embargo on American trade with Nicaragua. Cut off from the source of 30% of its imports and the market for nearly 50% of its exports, Nicaragua turned to the Soviet bloc for financial help and replacement of its lost markets. Congress responded by reversing its previous stand and voting to extend $27 million in nonmilitary aid to the contras (June, 1985). The following year it approved an additional $100 million for the Nicaraguan rebels, including $70 million in military aid. With this money, the contras acquired more arms and equipment and intensified their campaign against the Sandinista government. When Reagan sought to extend U.S. military assistance to the contras into 1988 and beyond, Congress rejected his request. It did, however, agree to provide $48 million more for food, clothing, medical services, and other "humanitarian aid" to the rebels.

4. Steps Are Taken to Restore Peace. As the war continued, with no end in sight, Mexico, Venezuela, Colombia, and Panama (the "Contadora Group") made several unsuccessful attempts to negotiate a settlement between the two sides. Early in 1987, a more promising effort was launched by President Oscar Arias of Costa Rica. To end the conflict in Nicaragua and to restore peace and stability to Central America, he proposed the following program:

 a. discussions to resolve disputes between governments and unarmed opposition groups in every country;

 b. cease-fires in countries where guerrilla forces were warring against existing governments;

 c. restoration of freedom of the press and other civil liberties wherever such rights had been set aside;

 d. discontinuance of military aid to insurgent forces in Central America by outside powers.

The *Arias Plan* (for which Arias received a Nobel Peace Prize) was approved by the heads of state of the various Central American countries, including Nicaragua. The Sandinista government took steps to comply with the plan by (*a*) permitting the banned opposition newspaper *La Prensa* to resume publication, (*b*) freeing a number of political prisoners, and (*c*) agreeing to start a dialogue with the contras.

In March, 1988, the Sandinistas and contras negotiated a preliminary cease-fire agreement. It called for a temporary halt to all military operations to allow the two sides time to arrange an end to the war. When their talks broke down, the heads of the other Central American states met with the antagonists in early 1989 and helped them reach an accord. The contras agreed to disband their forces and dismantle their bases in Honduras and Costa Rica in return for (*a*) the right to return home without fear of punishment, (*b*) the release of anti-Sandinistas jailed by the Ortega government, (*c*) the enactment of laws guaranteeing freedom of the press and electoral reforms, and (*d*) advancing the date of new elections to February, 1990.

Assured that free elections would be held, a number of anti-Sandinista groups formed a political coalition called the National Opposition Union. They chose Violeta Barrios de Chamorro, owner of the newspaper *La Prensa,* as their presidential candidate. Opposing her was the incumbent president, Daniel Ortega. Although the Sandinistas expected to sweep the election, they were decisively defeated. The new opposition group assumed office and the Sandinistas lost control of Nicaragua.

AMERICAN TROOPS INTERVENE IN GRENADA

The Caribbean island of Grenada, formerly a British possession, became an independent nation in 1974. Five years later, Grenadian leftists seized control of the government in a bloodless coup. Under the leadership of Prime Minister Maurice Bishop, a Marxist with close ties to Fidel Castro, the new regime undertook a number of development projects with Soviet-bloc assistance. Included was the construction of a large international airport, utilizing Cuban money, workers, and technical advisers. Many U.S. and Caribbean officials suspected that the airport was being built for military use by Cuban and Soviet aircraft rather than for commercial purposes.

In October, 1983, a power struggle broke out between rival factions in the Grenadian government. Hard-line Marxists, believing the Prime Minister to be too moderate, overthrew him in a military coup. Bishop and several members of his cabinet were executed by Grenadian troops. A new Revolutionary Military Council assumed control of the government and severely restricted the freedom of the people.

Other Caribbean countries, concerned with the region's stability, asked the United States to help them restore order and democracy to Grenada. President Reagan quickly agreed. He wanted not only to forestall the establishment of another Soviet satellite in the Western Hemisphere, he also wished to guarantee the safety of the 1,000 American students enrolled in a medical school on the island.

A few days after the coup, U.S. troops, supported by soldiers and police from six Caribbean nations, invaded Grenada. Despite fierce resistance from the Grenadian Army, aided by Cuban soldiers and construction workers, the attackers soon gained control of the island. Most of the population welcomed them as liberators.

In the aftermath of the invasion, the revolutionary government was disbanded and its leaders arrested on charges of murder. A temporary council was appointed to govern Grenada until new elections could be held. The Cubans were allowed to return home. The United States withdrew the bulk of its forces before the end of 1983, leaving about 300 American troops and 450 members of the Caribbean peacekeeping force to maintain security until a new government could be elected. General elections took place in December, 1984, and a coalition of conservative groups called the New National party won an overwhelming victory. In June, 1985, after the new regime had been firmly established, the remaining peacekeeping troops left Grenada.

The United States extended financial aid to strengthen the island's economy and to enable the Grenadian government to complete the construction of the airport. This facility, it was hoped, would contribute to the island's prosperity by stimulating the growth of tourism.

THE COLD WAR EXTENDS INTO SPACE

RUSSIA LAUNCHES THE FIRST SPACE SATELLITES

In October, 1957, the Soviet Union launched the world's first artificial satellite, *Sputnik I*, and placed it into orbit around the earth. The following month the Soviets orbited *Sputnik II*—a fully instrumented space vehicle carrying a dog. To enable the dog to survive in space, the satellite was equipped with oxygen, food, and a heating system.

AMERICAN REACTION TO THE SOVIET FEAT

Although the United States was planning a similar project, Americans were startled by the ability of the Russians to (*a*) beat them into space and (*b*) launch satellites that were substantially larger than the ones the United States intended to send aloft. The Soviet achievements raised serious military problems for the United States.

1. Since Russia had developed rocket engines powerful enough to boost large satellites into orbit, it was clearly ahead of the United States in missile development. Russia had already successfully tested an *intercontinental ballistic missile (ICBM)* capable of traveling over 5,000 miles to its target. Cities, industrial plants, and military installations throughout the United States were now within the reach of Russian ICBM's armed with nuclear warheads. The United States, meanwhile, was still seeking to perfect an ICBM of its own.

2. The Russians could dominate the entire earth by arming future satellites with nuclear bombs. These bombs, controlled from Soviet bases by electronic mechanisms, could be dropped upon any country as the satellites circled the globe.

3. The satellites pointed the way to space travel and raised the possibility of the establishment of Russian military bases on the moon.

Senator (later President) Lyndon Johnson of Texas declared: "The exploration of outer space will dominate the [future] affairs of mankind just as the exploration of the Western Hemisphere dominated the affairs of mankind in the 16th and 17th centuries. It is urgent that we lay our plans now."

To meet the challenge of Soviet scientific advances, the United States increased its expenditures for missile and space projects and stepped up its program of scientific education and research.

THE UNITED STATES ENTERS THE SPACE RACE

In January, 1958, the United States successfully launched its first satellite, *Explorer 1*, from Cape Canaveral, Florida. Within the next five months, three more instrument-laden vehicles were placed into orbit around the earth. Although the U.S. satellites were considerably smaller than the Russian ones, these launchings marked America's entry into the space race.

In the years that followed, the United States made substantial progress in space technology. Hundreds of earth-orbiting vehicles were launched. Some were equipped with scientific instruments to increase knowledge of outer space, to improve the science of forecasting the weather, to serve as navigational aids for ships and planes, and to help establish a more efficient system of worldwide communication by radio, telephone, and television. Others were designed to test the possibility of sending people into space in a sealed capsule and bringing them back to earth. Still others were sent aloft to explore the moon, the sun, and the planets.

The United States also developed an operational ICBM, the Atlas, in 1960, and produced several improved ICBM's—the Titan and the Minuteman—shortly thereafter. Nevertheless, America continued to lag behind Russia in rocket power and booster capacity. This inferiority was finally overcome in 1964, when a *Saturn 1* rocket carried a 20,000-pound payload aloft. With the introduction of the *Saturn 5* in 1967, the United States increased its booster capability fivefold. Until it was taken out of service in 1973, the *Saturn 5* played a key role in America's space program: powering the vehicles that transported American astronauts to the moon and launching America's first space station.

THE RUSSIANS JOURNEY INTO SPACE

One of the major goals in the space race was to send people into space and bring them safely back to earth. In 1961 the Soviets achieved a spectacular "first" when they rocketed a manned spaceship, *Vostok I*, into orbit and brought it back to earth after it had completed one circuit of the globe. *Yuri Gagarin*, the pilot of *Vostok I*, thus became the world's first spaceman.

In a second flight that year, Gherman Titov circled the earth 17 times. The following year two astronauts (cosmonauts) were launched into space in separate craft on the same day. They flew 64 and 48 orbits respectively. In 1963 Valentina Tereshkova earned the distinction of becoming the world's first spacewoman. In 1964 a space pilot, a doctor, and a scientist orbited the globe in a three-person vehicle.

During a two-person flight in 1965, one of the Russians, clad in a spacesuit, ventured out of the ship and spent 10 minutes in the void of space. Four years later two manned vehicles joined together while in orbit, and several of the astronauts transferred from one craft to the other. And in 1970 two Soviet cosmonauts set an endurance record of 17.5 days in space.

In 1971 the Russians placed a large, unmanned spacecraft, called *Salyut*, into earth orbit. As roomy as a 40-foot house trailer, it was equipped with research facilities, living quarters, life-support systems, and a docking unit. Three cosmonauts subsequently occupied the orbiting laboratory for 23 days but died on their return to earth because of an accident aboard their spaceship.

In 1977 the U.S.S.R. launched *Salyut 6* into orbit. Successive teams of Soviet astronauts set new endurance records for humans in space by living in the 19-ton space station for 96 days in 1977–1978, 140 days in 1978, and 175 days in 1979. The *Salyut 6* reentered the earth's atmosphere and disintegrated in 1983.

AMERICANS VENTURE INTO SPACE: PROJECT MERCURY

1. Preliminary Steps. In 1958 the *National Aeronautics and Space Administration (NASA)* initiated *Project Mercury*, a program to send Americans into space. Seven astronauts were chosen to begin intensive training for space flight. Scientists conducted experiments to determine the capability of humans to withstand the rigors of space. Engineers designed a Mercury capsule large enough to provide a space traveler with housing and life-support equipment, and devised techniques to bring a capsule safely back to earth.

Flight tests began in late 1960, when the first Mercury capsule was fired into orbit and brought back to earth. After conducting three successful unmanned flight tests, including one in which a chimpanzee was carried 155 miles up and recovered safely, NASA prepared for a flight with a human aboard.

2. Suborbital Flights. *Alan Shepard*, chosen to be the first American astronaut, was propelled into space in a Mercury capsule in 1961. He zoomed upward to a height of 115 miles, radioed back reports on his reactions and the functioning of his instruments, and returned to earth. A second and similar flight was successfully carried out by Virgil Grissom.

3. Americans in Orbit. In 1962 *John Glenn* soared skyward in the *Friendship 7*, and became the first American to orbit the earth. This feat was duplicated several months later by Scott Carpenter in the space capsule *Aurora 7*. In the same year Walter Schirra, in the *Sigma 7*, orbited the earth six times. In 1963 Gordon Cooper, in the *Faith 7*, achieved 22 orbits. These flights marked the attainment of the objectives of Project Mercury.

THE UNITED STATES PLANS A MANNED LUNAR EXPEDITION

Heeding President Kennedy's request that the United States take "a clearly leading role in space achievement," NASA undertook a program to land Americans on the moon by the end of the 1960's. It established a *Manned Spacecraft Center* at Houston, Texas, selected additional test pilots for training as astronauts, and laid plans for two new enterprises:

1. Project Gemini: a program for the design and testing of a two-person spacecraft, and for the development of techniques to enable manned vehicles to meet and dock in space.

2. Project Apollo: a program aimed at achieving a manned moon landing before 1970.

PROJECT GEMINI ATTAINS ITS AIMS

Manned Gemini flights began in the spring of 1965 when Virgil Grissom and John Young soared into space in a two-person space capsule. Grissom put the vehicle through a series of flight maneuvers and brought it back to earth after three orbits.

Nine other pairs of astronauts undertook space journeys in 1965–1966. Edward White became the first American to "walk" in space when he stayed outside his vehicle for 20 minutes. Frank Borman and James Lovell, in *Gemini 7*, made a record-breaking trip of 206 orbits, remaining in space for 14 days. While these men were in flight, Walter Schirra and Thomas Stafford were also shot into orbit and maneuvered their craft, *Gemini 6*, close to *Gemini 7*, thus accomplishing the first rendezvous in space. David Scott and Neil Armstrong achieved the first linkup in space when they docked their ship with an orbiting Agena rocket. Later Charles Conrad and Richard Gordon docked with an Agena, restarted that rocket's engine, and propelled the combined vehicles to a new altitude record for manned spacecraft.

Palmer in The Springfield (Mo.) Leader & Press

What Great Discoveries Lie Ahead?

In the fall of 1966 James Lovell and Edwin Aldrin successfully completed the Gemini series of flights. They practiced rendezvous maneuvers and docking with a target satellite, and spent much time in extravehicular activity (activity outside their spacecraft).

PROJECT APOLLO BEGINS

Project Apollo was initiated in 1966 when an unmanned craft designed for a flight to the moon was lifted into space. Early in 1967 the program suffered a severe setback when a flash fire inside an Apollo spacecraft that was undergoing tests killed the three astronauts who were to be its crew. This tragedy necessitated a number of design changes in the ship to prevent similar accidents in the future. Later that year a giant three-stage rocket, the *Saturn 5*, was successfully tested. Capable of generating 7.5 million pounds of thrust, this booster had sufficient power to carry an Apollo spacecraft and lunar landing vehicle aloft and to speed them on their way to the moon. In 1968 a lunar landing craft, or lunar module (LM—pronounced "lem"), passed its space test; and three astronauts checked out the reliability of the Apollo spacecraft in an 11-day, 163-orbit journey around the earth.

Late in 1968 Frank Borman, James Lovell, and William Anders set forth on the first voyage across space to another celestial body. Launched skyward by a *Saturn 5* rocket, *Apollo 8* orbited the earth several times and then was thrust on its way toward the moon by an additional burst from the still-attached third stage of the Saturn. As the spacecraft approached its destination several days later, the astronauts reduced its speed and placed it in a circular orbit 70 miles above the moon's surface. During the ship's 10 revolutions around the moon, the astronauts photographed the lunar surface, performed various tests of the craft's systems, and transmitted a Christmas Eve telecast to earth. They then fired the ship's main rocket engine to push the Apollo out of lunar orbit and headed for home.

Two more test flights took place early in 1969. The first, in earth orbit, checked out the capabilities of the lunar landing craft. The second, an eight-day moon flight, conducted a final dress rehearsal of a lunar landing.

AMERICAN ASTRONAUTS LAND ON THE MOON

From a launch pad at Cape Canaveral (then called Cape Kennedy), Florida, *Apollo 11* began a voyage to the moon in July, 1969. Aboard the spacecraft were *Neil Armstrong,* commander of the mission, *Edwin Aldrin,* and *Michael Collins.* On the fourth day of their journey, after the spacecraft had entered lunar orbit, Armstrong and Aldrin crawled from the command module into the lunar module, undocked the LM from the mother ship, and started downward toward the moon. They steered their craft to a safe landing on a level, rock-strewn plain in the Sea of Tranquility. Armstrong opened the craft's hatch, climbed slowly down the ladder, and stepped onto the moon. Aldrin followed.

During their 2 hours and 21 minutes on the lunar surface, they planted an American flag, talked by radio to President Nixon, set up scientific equipment to be left on the moon, filled boxes with rocks and soil samples to take back to earth, and snapped many pictures. They also left a plaque containing the following message:

> HERE MEN FROM THE PLANET EARTH
> FIRST SET FOOT UPON THE MOON
> JULY 1969, A.D.
> WE CAME IN PEACE FOR ALL MANKIND

Reentering their vehicle, the astronauts rocketed the ascent stage into lunar orbit and rejoined the mother ship. After casting the LM adrift, the three astronauts headed for earth in the command module. The historic eight-day voyage of *Apollo 11* ended with a safe splashdown in the Pacific.

NASA COMPLETES PROJECT APOLLO

Charles Conrad, Alan Bean, and Richard Gordon in *Apollo 12* participated in a second successful moon flight and lunar landing in 1969. Conrad and Bean landed on a rolling plain called the Ocean of Storms. They set up an array of scientific equipment and collected samples of moon rocks. In 1970 a near disaster occurred during the flight of *Apollo 13* when an explosion wrecked the power supply of the command module. Utilizing the supply system of the attached lunar module, the astronauts succeeded in bringing the crippled craft back to earth. Early in 1971 a third successful moon mission was carried out by the crew of *Apollo 14*—Alan Shepard, Edgar Mitchell, and Stuart Roosa. Shepard and Mitchell spent many hours exploring a hilly, rock-strewn area on the moon, set out packages of experimental equipment, and collected a large quantity of soil and rock samples. Later that year a fourth successful lunar expedition was carried out by David Scott, Alfred Worden, and James Irwin in *Apollo 15*. Their mission was the first to transport a surface vehicle to the moon. Scott and Worden used the Rover to explore the lunar terrain.

In the spring of 1972 John Young, Charles Duke, and Thomas Mattingly, in *Apollo 16,* journeyed to the rugged lunar highlands for the first time. Young and Duke spent 71 hours on the moon. In December, 1972, the sixth and final flight of the series was carried out by *Apollo 17,* manned by Eugene Cernan, Ronald Evans, and Harrison Schmitt. During their record-breaking stay of 75 hours, Schmitt and Cernan explored the Sea of Serenity on foot and in a lunar rover, and brought back a large collection of soil and rock samples.

THE UNITED STATES ORBITS A SPACE STATION

Skylab, America's first manned, orbiting space station, was launched in 1973. Developed at a cost of $2.5 billion, the 85-ton vehicle was equipped with living quarters, life-support systems, and extensive laboratory facilities. Although an accident after lift-off reduced *Skylab's* power supply and caused other damage, three astronauts (Charles Conrad, Joseph Kerwin, and Paul Weitz) soon took up residence in the space station, repaired the damage, and remained aboard for 28 days. A second crew occupied the station for 59 days (1973) and a third for 84 days (1974). *Skylab* plunged back to earth in 1979. It disintegrated during the descent, its fragments falling harmlessly onto uninhabited areas.

AMERICA DEVELOPS A SPACE SHUTTLE

President Nixon in 1972 announced plans for the development of a reusable space shuttle that would (*a*) make flights in and out of orbit a routine, everyday affair, (*b*) reduce the cost of launching a pound of payload by 85%, (*c*) simplify the placement and servicing of unmanned space satellites, and (*d*) facilitate the ferrying of astronauts to and from orbiting space stations.

Nine years later, after an expenditure of $10 billion in development costs, the world's first reusable spacecraft—the space shuttle *Columbia*—was completed. Launched from the Kennedy Space Center at Cape Canaveral, Florida, in April, 1981, it went smoothly into orbit, circled the globe 36 times, and returned to earth two days later, gliding to a perfect landing at Edwards Air Force Base in California. On *Columbia's* historic maiden voyage, John Young served as pilot and Robert Crippen as copilot.

With the addition of the *Challenger, Discovery,* and *Atlantis* to America's space fleet, numerous missions were flown successfully between 1981 and the start of 1986. During these flights, crew members placed communications and other specialized satellites into orbit, performed scientific experiments, repaired nonfunctioning satellites that had been launched earlier, and practiced construction techniques for assembling future space stations. Among the many flight participants were Sally K. Ride, the first American woman in space, and Guion Bluford, the first black American astronaut.

A TRAGIC ACCIDENT DISRUPTS AMERICA'S SPACE EFFORT

By 1986, shuttle flights had become so routine and appeared to be so safe that NASA planned to step up their frequency and to include ordinary citizens as crew members. In late January preparations were completed for the 25th mission of the space fleet—a flight by the space shuttle *Challenger*. Among the crew of seven was a high school teacher from Concord, New Hampshire—Christa McAuliffe.

Shortly after lift-off, when the shuttle was 10 miles above the earth, a violent explosion blew the ship apart, scattering flaming debris over a wide area. All seven astronauts on board perished. The disaster, witnessed by thousands of spectators at Cape Canaveral and by millions of others on TV, was the worst in the history of the American space program.

NASA suspended all shuttle flights indefinitely while it investigated the cause of the accident. When it was determined that fuel escaping from a leaky seal in the booster rocket joint had touched off the explosion, steps were taken to design and install safer seal mechanisms and to effect other improvements in the remaining shuttles.

AMERICAN SHUTTLE FLIGHTS RESUME

In 1988 NASA resumed space shuttle flights with the launching of the redesigned *Discovery.* Then in 1992 a new space shuttle, *Endeavour,* was added to the fleet. On its second flight, in 1993, technical specialists aboard the craft succeeded in repairing the $1.5 billion Hubble Space Telescope. From 1988 to early 1997, more than 55 successful shuttle flights took place.

SOVIET SPACE EXPANSION CONTINUES

Although the Russians lagged behind the Americans in such developments as manned lunar landings and reusable space shuttles, they continued to forge ahead in rocketry and long-duration, manned space flights. In 1983 the Soviets replaced *Salyut 6* with another space station, *Salyut 7.* The following year three cosmonauts occupied this vehicle for 237 days. In 1986 the Soviets placed a second space station into orbit. The *Mir,* 40% larger than the *Salyut,* had separate living quarters for its occupants, a common area for eating and recreation, a control room, six docking ports, and spaces for work areas and laboratories. The Russians achieved a space-age first by ferrying astronauts between their two orbiting stations. (*Salyut 7* fell back to earth in 1991.)

In 1987 the Soviets scored a major breakthrough in heavy-duty booster technology by successfully testing the Energia—a rocket capable of putting a 100-ton payload into orbit. The following year they launched their first space shuttle, *Buran,* a vehicle similar to the U.S. shuttles in shape and size. Also in 1988 two Soviet cosmonauts set a new endurance record for humans in space by remaining aboard the orbiting *Mir* for a full year. And in 1990 the Soviet Union added a materials-processing module to the *Mir,* thereby enlarging its operational capacity by one-third. (In 1994 the United States and Russia agreed to build and operate a new international space station. In 1995 and 1996 the U.S. shuttle *Atlantis* made four trips to the *Mir,* exchanging crew members and delivering U.S. astronauts for lengthy stays aboard the Russian space outpost.)

THE COLD WAR BEGINS TO THAW

TWO HISTORIC SUMMIT MEETINGS ARE HELD

Abandoning the 20-year-old American policy of seeking to isolate the world's most populous country, President Nixon in 1971 announced that (*a*) he would visit Communist China, and (*b*) the United States would vote to seat the People's Republic in the UN. Early in 1972 Nixon spent a week in China, meeting that nation's leaders, exchanging views on mutual problems, and exploring ways of improving cultural and trade relations. Although such difficult issues as mainland China's claim to Taiwan, the presence of U.S. forces on that island, and the formal recognition of the People's Republic of China by the United States remained unsettled, the two nations pledged to adhere to the principle of peaceful coexistence and to work toward the goal of establishing normal relations.

Nixon also journeyed to the Soviet Union in 1972 and concluded a series of agreements that had been under negotiation for some time. In these *Moscow Accords* the world's two superpowers agreed to: (1) curb the nuclear arms race; (2) coordinate research on public health problems; (3) exchange data on new developments in science and technology; (4) explore ways of expanding trade; (5) participate in joint space projects; and (6) establish rules for avoiding confrontations at sea.

RELATIONS WITH CHINA IMPROVE

The United States and Communist China agreed to set up and staff "liaison offices" in Beijing and Washington (1973)—an action that, in effect, represented the establishment of diplomatic relations between the two countries. Talks were begun to settle the claims of U.S. citizens whose property in China had been seized by the Communist government and to resolve the problem of blocked Chinese assets in the United States. Trade and travel restrictions were eased, and a brisk interchange of people and goods began to develop. Then in 1979 the U.S. severed its formal ties with Nationalist China and established full diplomatic relations with the People's Republic of China.

CLOSER TIES ARE ESTABLISHED WITH RUSSIA

1. The trade freeze between the United States and the Soviet Union, in effect since 1949, ended in 1972. Faced with a serious food shortage because of crop failure, Russia purchased $1 billion worth of grain from the United States. Large purchases were also made in subsequent years.

Seeking to modernize its industry and agriculture and to spur the production of consumer goods, the U.S.S.R. (*a*) negotiated a multibillion-dollar deal with American companies for the exchange of chemicals and agricultural fertilizers, (*b*) invited American industrialists to supply equipment for the construction of new manufacturing facilities in the Soviet Union, and (*c*) sought to induce American financial institutions to furnish capital for the development of Russia's natural resources in Siberia.

2. The Arab-Israeli conflict of 1973 nearly triggered a confrontation between the United States and the Soviet Union. Realizing that their conflicting interests in the Middle East could destroy the policy of *détente* (relaxation of tensions) that they were seeking to promote, the United States and Russia agreed to cosponsor an Arab-Israeli peace conference.

3. The two rivals in space exploration agreed to conduct a joint Apollo-Soyuz space effort. A special docking airlock module was developed to enable the two craft to link up while in space and to permit the

American and Russian crews to exchange visits. The mission was successfully completed in 1975.

THE HELSINKI AGREEMENT

After three years of negotiations, representatives of 35 Soviet and Western bloc nations, including the United States and Canada, gathered in Helsinki, Finland, in 1975 to sign a document called the "Final Act of the Conference on Security and Cooperation in Europe." It provided for greater East-West economic cooperation, respect for human rights, the freer movement of people and ideas from one country to another, and acceptance by the signatories of the changes that had taken place in European boundaries since World War II.

Despite the Helsinki Agreement, the U.S.S.R. continued to (1) suppress free speech by exiling or imprisoning Soviet dissidents who publicly criticized the government, (2) deny exit visas to many of the Russian Jews who wished to emigrate to Israel, and (3) harass foreign correspondents whose dispatches displeased the authorities. Such Russian violations of human rights were denounced by the United States and cast a pall on the evolving relationship between the two countries.

STEPS ARE TAKEN TO CURB THE ARMS RACE

1. Restraining Nuclear Expansion. At the end of World War II the United States was the world's only nuclear power. Shortly thereafter the Soviet Union developed an atomic bomb, as did Great Britain, France, and Communist China. Other nations also announced plans to do so. Realizing that the indiscriminate testing of nuclear devices endangered the environment, and that the acquisition of nuclear weapons by more and more nations increased the threat of accidental or deliberate nuclear war, the United States and Russia in the 1960's jointly sponsored treaties, which most countries signed, (a) prohibiting nuclear testing in the atmosphere, in outer space, and under water; (b) banning the use of nuclear weapons in space; (c) forbidding nuclear powers from transferring atomic weapons to other nations; and (d) barring nonnuclear nations from acquiring or developing such weapons.

2. Strategic Arms Limitation Talks (SALT). Over the years the United States and Russia continued to develop more powerful nuclear weapons, including missile systems to transport warheads to distant targets. Since each power already had the capability of completely destroying the other, both began to recognize the futility of expanding their nuclear arsenals. Furthermore, their arms race was enormously costly, absorbing vast sums that were sorely needed for other national purposes. As a result, the two nations agreed in 1969 to begin *Strategic Arms Limitation Talks (SALT)*. The first fruits of these discussions emerged in 1972, when (a) an agreement was reached to freeze their offensive missiles at current levels for a period of five years, and (b) an *Antiballistic Missile Treaty* was signed limiting the deployment of antiballistic missiles (ABM's) to two locations (later reduced to one) in each country. (An antiballistic missile is a defensive weapon designed to intercept and destroy an incoming enemy missile.)

To further slow the arms race, the United States and Russia in 1974 agreed to negotiate a reduction in the total number of offensive nuclear weapons and delivery vehicles that each could deploy. Disagreement over exactly what weapons should be included in these limits delayed a second arms limitation agreement until 1979. The SALT II Treaty was signed by the two countries in that year, but President Carter asked the U.S. Senate to defer action on its ratification after the Soviet Union invaded Afghanistan. Although the treaty was never ratified, both sides unofficially decided to observe the limits it imposed.

During the 1980's Soviet and U.S. representatives sought to reach agreement on further arms reductions. In exchange for the removal of Soviet intermediate-range ballistic missiles (IRBM's) based in Europe (aimed at targets in NATO countries) the United States offered to cancel its plans to furnish its NATO allies a counterforce of modern IRBM's. The Soviets rejected the proposal.

Discussions also took place on reducing the number of intercontinental ballistic missiles (ICBM's) and launchers that each side possessed. But a mutually acceptable plan failed to emerge.

3. Reagan Proposes a Strategic Defense Initiative (SDI). In 1983 President Reagan proposed the construction of a missile defense system that would make nuclear weapons "impotent and obsolete." His program, officially named the Strategic Defense Initiative (SDI), became popularly known as "Star Wars." It called for the development of technologically advanced detection devices and defensive weapons—based on land, at sea, and in space—that would shield the American people from nuclear attack by intercepting and destroying enemy missiles before they reached U.S. shores. Reagan anticipated that perfecting such a system would require five-to-ten years of research and development and an outlay of tens of billions of dollars.

The Soviets denounced Reagan's plan. They asserted that the 1972 ABM Treaty barred the development, testing, and deployment of space-based missile-defense systems; and that SDI therefore violated the agreement that both nations had signed. They also feared that SDI would protect Americans from Soviet missiles but leave the Soviet people vulnerable to a nuclear attack by the United States. To forestall such a possibility, the U.S.S.R. would be forced to develop a similar defense system—a costly undertaking that they wished to avoid. Soviet leaders declared that they would not sign any arms accord with the United States unless Reagan agreed to narrow the scope of his "Star Wars" program.

THE COLD WAR ENDS

THE SOVIET UNION ADOPTS NEW POLICIES

Mikhail Gorbachev assumed leadership of the Soviet Union in 1985, first as General Secretary of the Communist party and later as President of the U.S.S.R. Seeking to strengthen his country's ailing economy and to prevent its total collapse, he initiated a reform program called *perestroika* (restructuring). It (*a*) aimed to minimize economic planning and control by the central government; (*b*) encouraged local plant managers to make their own production decisions, to turn out higher quality consumer goods, and to operate at a profit; and (*c*) legalized the establishment of small, privately owned businesses.

A second element of his program was called *glasnost* (openness), a commitment to freedom of speech and public discussion of political issues and government policies. Gorbachev also promised to promote democracy by allowing rival candidates to compete for political office and permitting multiparty elections.

EASTERN EUROPE ABANDONS COMMUNISM

The policy changes proposed by Gorbachev for the U.S.S.R. encouraged the Soviet satellite countries behind the Iron Curtain to institute major reforms of their own. In June, 1989, a Polish trade union group called *Solidarity* ousted the entrenched Communist party from power in the first free election to be held in that country since 1947. The new government soon took steps to replace the state-controlled economic system with a competitive market economy. When Gorbachev made no attempt to restore the status quo in Poland, other East Europeans also moved to free themselves from Communist control. By the end of 1989, Hungary, Czechoslovakia, Rumania (and later Bulgaria) succeeded in displacing their Communist leaders, adopting multiparty political systems, and introducing free market economies. Not to be outdone, Yugoslavia and Albania—two East European countries that had not been affiliated with the Soviet bloc—also abandoned communism.

EAST AND WEST GERMANY ARE REUNITED

East Germany was the last remaining Soviet satellite in Europe. It was headed by a hard-line German Communist, whose regime was supported by an occupying force of 360,000 Soviet troops. Dissatisfaction with conditions at home, coupled with news of reform in neighboring countries, prompted thousands of East Germans to flee. They headed eastward to Poland, Czechoslovakia, and Hungary and from there made their way westward to West Germany—where they were welcomed as refugees. This mass exodus, along with huge street demonstrations in East Germany's major cities, led to a change in the leadership of the Communist party. Continued pressure for reform forced the government to open the Berlin Wall in November, 1989, thereby providing East Germans direct access to West Germany. It also spurred the holding of free elections in early 1990 and the selection of a new government ready to negotiate reunification with West Germany.

In a series of "two plus four" meetings, the two Germanys pledged to respect the existing border with Poland, and the four World War II allies (the U.S., Britain, France, and the U.S.S.R.) agreed to suspend their rights and responsibilities in both sections of the country. East and West Germany created a monetary union in the summer of 1990, merged politically in October, and restored Berlin as the capital of united Germany in 1991.

NEW ARMS CONTROL AGREEMENTS ARE NEGOTIATED

1. Intermediate Nuclear Force (INF) Treaty. In February, 1987, Gorbachev announced that the Soviet Union was prepared to discuss the elimination of Soviet and American IRBM's from Europe. His offer represented a change in Russia's previous position because it did not include a condition that the United States limit its Strategic Defense Initiative. Reagan responded by directing U.S. arms negotiators in Geneva to draw up an agreement that would be acceptable to both sides.

In December, 1987, at a summit meeting in Washington, D.C., Reagan and Gorbachev signed the missile treaty that their delegates had drawn up. It obligated both countries to eliminate all their shorter-range missiles (having a range of 300 to 600 miles) and intermediate-range missiles (with a range of 700 to 3,300 miles), as well as all launching devices and support equipment for such missiles. The document also spelled out procedures for on-site inspection of each other's missile-operating bases and production facilities. The INF Treaty became effective in May, 1988, upon its ratification by the U.S. Senate.

2. Conventional Forces in Europe (CFE) Treaty. In November, 1990, the United States, the Soviet Union, and 20 other NATO and Warsaw Pact members signed a far-reaching agreement to reduce their conventional (nonnuclear) forces in Europe. It set limits on the number of tanks, armored vehicles, artillery pieces, helicopters, and combat aircraft that each side could maintain in the treaty zone—a region stretching from the Atlantic Ocean to the Ural Mountains. Ceilings imposed by the CFE Treaty required the U.S.S.R. to withdraw thousands of pieces of military equipment from Europe, and to destroy thousands more, so as to bring its forces down to NATO's level. The U.S. Senate ratified the treaty in July, 1991.

3. Strategic Arms Reduction Treaty (START I). At a summit meeting in Moscow in July, 1991, Bush and Gorbachev signed a treaty that required both sides to reduce their arsenals of intercontinental ballistic missiles and delivery systems by 30% over seven years. Although the U.S. Senate approved the treaty in October, 1992, Russia postponed its implementation until Belarus, Kazakhstan, and Ukraine (which had become independent states upon the breakup of the U.S.S.R.) agreed to transfer the nuclear weapons located on their territory and accede to the Nuclear Non-Proliferation Treaty as nonnuclear nations. After they had all accepted these conditions, START I became effective in December, 1994.

4. START II. Negotiated in 1993, this agreement called for both sides to reduce their ICBM stockpiles by about two-thirds over ten years and eliminate all land-based multiple-warhead missiles. Ratification by the Russian legislature is pending.

THE POST-COLD WAR ERA DAWNS

EASTERN EUROPE ASSERTS ITS INDEPENDENCE.

As the former Soviet satellites regained control of their armed forces and negotiated the withdrawal of Russian troops from their soil, each, in turn, opted to withdraw from the Soviet-dominated Warsaw Pact. This military alliance, which had been formed in 1955 as a counterweight to NATO, was formally dissolved in 1991.

Seeking to free themselves from economic domination by the U.S.S.R., the members of *Comecon* (the trading bloc that Moscow had organized in 1949 to bind Eastern Europe economically to the Soviet Union) voted to disband the organization in 1991. The East Europeans turned to the West for technical help to modernize their industries and invited Western companies to form partnerships with local business groups.

THE COMMUNIST PARTY LOSES POWER IN THE U.S.S.R.

Gorbachev's policies of *glasnost* and *perestroika* touched off widespread demands for change in the Soviet Union. Articles criticizing the government and its policies began to appear in newspapers and magazines throughout the country. People demonstrated their resentment of local party bosses and their anger at the lack of basic goods and services by dropping out of the Communist party and joining one of the protest movements that were beginning to spring up. A number of well-known government officials also withdrew from the party and affiliated themselves with the newly formed Democratic Reform Movement. The decline in public support for the once all-powerful Communist party was graphically illustrated early in 1991, when opposition candidates for office in such important cities as Moscow, Leningrad (renamed St. Petersburg), and Kiev—and in the largest Soviet republic (called Russia)—easily defeated the officially sponsored party nominees.

In August, 1991, a group of hard-line officials of the central government launched a coup to overthrow President Gorbachev, seize control of the country, and restore the power of the Communist party. They held Gorbachev captive at his vacation home for three days; dispatched troops and armored vehicles to Moscow and other cities to put down any resistance; and ordered the capture of Boris Yeltsin, an outspoken anti-Communist and the popular president of the Russian republic. As the insurgents approached Yeltsin's headquarters in Moscow, thousands of Muscovites took to the streets, erected barricades, and forced the rebels to withdraw. Opposition to the coup also flared in other cities.

Unable to arouse support for their takeover attempt, the conspirators surrendered and were placed under arrest. Upon his return to Moscow, Gorbachev resigned his position as head of the Communist party, disbanded its leadership and dismissed dozens of high government officials who had not opposed the conspiracy. The aborted coup accelerated the decline of the Communist party and broke its grip on the country.

INTERNAL CONFLICTS DISRUPT THE SOVIET UNION

The population of the Soviet Union comprised more than 120 ethnic groups, each with its own culture, language, traditions, and religious beliefs. For more than 70 years, the central government had made strenuous efforts to weld the various ethnicities into a distinctive Soviet nationality, but to no avail. It was equally unsuccessful in its attempts to suppress religion and promote atheism.

With the rise of *perestroika* and *glasnost* and the loosening of the Communist party's hold on the country, numerous ethnic and religious groups began to clamor for change and reform. Three of the Soviet Union's 15 republics—Lithuania, Latvia, and Estonia—declared their intention to secede. (These Baltic states had been forcibly annexed by the Soviets during World War II.) The central government rejected their demands. It exerted economic pressure to force them to withdraw their declaration of independence and sent in troops to prevent their takeover of public facilities. Violence erupted and many demonstrators were injured or killed. The Balts refused to back down, however, and continued to agitate for freedom. Their efforts bore fruit in the summer of 1991 when 60 countries, including the United States, recognized the independence of the three Baltic states and the U.S.S.R. formally acknowledged their secession from the Soviet Union.

In several Soviet republics, animosity between Christians and Muslims touched off riots and bloody clashes. Harsh intervention by Soviet troops aroused much resentment. Demands arose for the rearrangement of borders between republics and for greater local control over internal affairs. In other republics, regional leaders called for more self-government, and asserted that locally enacted laws should take priority over legislation passed by the central government.

To prevent the breakup of the Soviet Union, Gorbachev proposed the adoption of a new constitution that would reorganize the structure of the U.S.S.R. and grant each republic more political and economic power. Although some of the republics agreed to accept the suggested changes, others called for (*a*) the establishment of a loose political federation, (*b*) a commonwealth of self-governing states, or (*c*) a nonpolitical economic association. Still others came out for complete independence.

COOPERATION REPLACES CONFRONTATION IN EAST-WEST RELATIONS

1. With the Soviet economy near collapse, Gorbachev turned to the capitalist world for help in reforming his country's economic system. Recognizing that progress toward a market economy and private ownership of property would be neither quick nor easy, the United States and six other major industrialized countries offered him large-scale technical assistance and held out hope for substantial financial aid after he introduced the needed economic reforms. They also pledged to help the Soviet Union become a full-fledged member of the world economic community by associating it with the International Monetary Fund (IMF), the World Bank, and other Western financial institutions.

2. The new spirit of East-West cooperation was evident at the UN. When Iraq invaded Kuwait, the Security Council was able to act quickly because the U.S. and the U.S.S.R. both supported economic sanctions against the aggressor and the use of force to liberate the occupied country. (See pages 394–395.)

3. Declaring that "the prospect of a Soviet invasion into Western Europe is no longer a realistic threat," Bush announced, in the fall of 1991, that the United States would remove all tactical nuclear weapons from its land bases in Europe and Asia. (A tactical weapon is a short-range, nuclear-armed artillery shell or missile used in ground warfare.) Similar weapons stored in the U.S. would likewise be destroyed. Recognizing "the major changes in the international military landscape," he also promised to withdraw all tactical nuclear weapons from American surface ships, attack submarines, and land-based naval aircraft.

Although Bush took this step unilaterally, he invited the Soviet Union to respond in kind. Shortly thereafter, Gorbachev matched Bush's arms initiative by announcing the elimination or reduction of a range of Soviet tactical nuclear weapons based on land and at sea. NATO also followed Bush's lead by slashing its nuclear arsenal in Europe.

THE SOVIET REPUBLICS DISSOLVE THE U.S.S.R.

During the fall of 1991, Gorbachev strove to rally support for the continuance of a unified Soviet Union. But the clamor for independence grew ever more persistent. In December, the leaders of three key republics—Russia, Ukraine, and Byelorussia (now called Belarus)—issued a joint declaration that the U.S.S.R. "is ceasing its existence." They also proclaimed the formation of a *Commonwealth of Independent States* and invited all members of the former union to join it.

All but one of the remaining republics accepted the offer. By the end of the year, the 11 participants signed an agreement that guaranteed their separate sovereignties but provided for the creation of several coordinating bodies to oversee the handling of such common concerns as defense, foreign affairs, and economic policies. The new commonwealth pledged to assume all international obligations of the former Soviet Union as well as control over its nuclear arsenal.

The official end of the U.S.S.R. was marked by the resignation of Mikhail Gorbachev as its President and the replacement of the Communist regime's red flag (with its hammer-and-sickle emblem) by the individual flags of the newly independent states.

President Bush quickly recognized the independence of all the former Soviet republics. He agreed to support the Russian republic's assumption of U.S.S.R.'s permanent seat on the Security Council and to sponsor membership in the UN for those states that were not already members.

Highlights of the Cold War:
A Chronological Summary

For 45 years (1945–1990), the United States and the Soviet Union competed for supremacy in every region of the world. Their conflict, known as the cold war, divided the world into two opposing camps. In the Communist camp, leaders of the U.S.S.R. and its satellites ruled dictatorially in the name of the working class. Democratic elections and free enterprise were prohibited. In the Western camp, the United States and its allies emphasized democracy and private ownership of property. Major events in the cold war may be loosely divided into four phases:

First Phase: Communist Advances and U.S. Containment

The first and most intense phase of the cold war spanned a 25-year period from the end of World War II to 1970.

1945 Upon Germany's surrender, the Soviet dictator Joseph Stalin conferred with U.S. President Harry Truman and British Prime Minister Winston Churchill on the division of Germany and its capital, Berlin, into four zones of occupation. The failure of Soviet troops to leave Eastern Europe after the war aroused the distrust of the non-Communist West.

1946–1949 Backed by Soviet forces, Communists in Eastern Europe seized control of the governments of Poland, Hungary, Czechoslovakia, Rumania, Bulgaria, and East Germany. Albania and Yugoslavia also became Communist states. Winston Churchill declared (1946) that the Communists had lowered an "iron curtain" across the continent, thereby cutting off Eastern Europe from the West.

1947 To stop Communist forces from gaining control of Greece and Turkey, President Truman persuaded Congress to provide military aid to these countries. He adopted a policy of *containment*: the application of whatever counterforce was necessary to prevent any more nations from falling under Communist governments.

1948 Soviet forces in East Germany blockaded ground routes between West Berlin and West Germany. Truman ordered a massive airlift to West Berlin, thus preventing this section of the city from falling under Communist control.

To help rebuild a war-torn, weakened Europe, Truman announced a multibillion dollar program of economic aid—the Marshall Plan. The aid effectively checked the growth of Communist parties in Western Europe.

1949 The Soviets tested an atomic bomb, and the nuclear arms race began.

Communists led by Mao Zedong seized control of China's government; their anti-Communist opponents fled to Taiwan.

The United States, Canada, and 10 other Western countries set up the North Atlantic Treaty Organization (NATO), a military alliance for mutual defense against Soviet aggression in Europe.

Berlin Airlift

450

Korean War

1950–1953 Communist North Korea invaded South Korea. The United Nations authorized the use of troops to defend South Korea. UN forces (mainly U.S. and South Korean) fought for three years against both North Koreans and their Chinese allies.

1953–1954 U.S. Senate hearings led by Senator Joseph McCarthy stirred widespread fears of Communist influence within the United States.
The Soviet dictator Joseph Stalin died.

1955 The Soviet Union and its satellites in Eastern Europe formed the Warsaw Pact, a military alliance to counter NATO.

1955–1958 Seeking to extend its influence in the Middle East, the Soviet Union offered technical, economic, and military aid to several Arab states.

1956 Soviet forces brutally suppressed an uprising of anti-Communist "freedom fighters" in Hungary.

1957 The U.S.S.R. launched *Sputnik,* the first artificial satellite in space. The news aroused concern in the United States that the Soviets were gaining a technological edge. The space race began.

1959–1961 Fidel Castro gained power in Cuba (1959) and set up a Communist state. Presidents Eisenhowever and Kennedy approved efforts by the CIA to overthrow Castro. Cuban exiles, trained by the CIA, un-

successfully invaded Cuba at the Bay of Pigs (1961).

1961 In Berlin, the Soviets and East Germans erected a wall to stop East Berliners from migrating to the West.

1962 President Kennedy ordered a naval blockade of Cuba and forced the Soviets to remove their nuclear missiles from the island.

1963–1969 To prevent the takeover of South Vietnam by North Vietnamese-assisted Communist insurgents, the United States under Presidents Kennedy and Johnson sent increasing numbers of troops to the area. Losses on both sides were high. Many Americans began to question whether the war was worth the cost.

1968 Soviet tanks moved into Czechoslovakia to suppress challenges to Communist rule in that country. To counterbalance Soviet moves to expand its influence in the Middle East, the United States increased its program of military and economic aid to Israel.

1969 U.S. astronauts walked on the moon. The dramatic success of this mission established U.S. superiority in the space race.

First landing on the moon

Second Phase: Attempts at Détente

In the early 1970s, U.S. President Richard Nixon and Soviet leader Leonid Brezhnev took steps to reduce cold war tensions. Presidents Ford and Carter continued this policy of détente (relaxation of tensions) by making trade agreements and conducting arms control negotiations with the Soviets.

1972   Nixon traveled to the People's Republic of China and met with Communist leaders there. His trip reversed the 23-year-old cold war policy of hostility toward China's government.

After years of negotiations, the U.S. and the U.S.S.R. agreed to freeze the production of offensive nuclear missiles and to limit the deployment of antiballistic missiles.

1973   Nixon brought U.S. involvement in the Vietnam War to an end.

1975   The Southeast Asian nations of South Vietnam, Laos, and Cambodia fell to Communist forces.

1979   President Carter extended official U.S. recognition to the People's Republic of China.

Nixon in China

Third Phase: Détente in Trouble

U.S.-Soviet relations entered a troubled period as a result of a civil war in Afghanistan.

1979   Soviet troops invaded Afghanistan in an attempt to defend that country's pro-Soviet government against rebel forces. President Carter condemned Soviet aggression and placed an embargo on grain sales to the Soviet Union.

1981   President Reagan called the Soviet Union "an evil empire" and persuaded Congress to enact large increases in U.S. spending on defense. At the same time, he asked for more military aid to anti-Communist forces in Central America.

1981–1986   Congress generally supported Reagan's requests for aid to the contras—rebel forces trying to overthrow a Communist regime in Nicaragua.

1983   U.S. forces invaded Grenada and overthrew its Cuban-backed Communist government.

U.S.-Backed Afghan Rebels

452

Fourth Phase: Gorbachev's Reforms and Soviet Collapse

U.S.-Soviet relations improved dramatically when a new leader, Mikhail Gorbachev, rose to power in the Soviet Union.

1985 In his first year as Soviet leader, Gorbachev began to reform the Soviet economic and political systems.

1986–1988 Hoping to relieve the ailing Soviet economy from the costs of the arms race, Gorbachev met Reagan in a series of summit talks. They agreed to significant reductions in nuclear arms.

Gorbachev and Reagan

1989–1990 Beginning with Poland, reformers in every country of Eastern Europe challenged the Communist system. In one country after another, free elections were held for the first time in 40 years. The Soviet Union permitted its former satellites to establish non-Communist, democratic governments. Germans tore down the Berlin Wall (1989). This event symbolized the breakdown of communism in Eastern Europe. East Germany reunited with West Germany (1990).

Fall of the Berlin Wall

1991 The Soviets approved U.S. actions in the Persian Gulf War (the first war since 1945 in which the two superpowers pursued a common policy).

Despite Gorbachev's reforms, the Soviet economy continued to decline. Republics of the Soviet Union demanded independence. The Communist Party lost all power. The Soviet Union dissolved, as most of the newly independent republics formed a loose confederation. Gorbachev resigned. Russia and other republics sought U.S. assistance in reforming their economies. The cold war was over.

The Republics of the Former Soviet Union

Member of Commonwealth of Independent States

Republic outside the Commonwealth

FINLAND

St. Petersburg

Moscow

ESTONIA

LATVIA

LITHUANIA

BELARUS (Byelorussia)

Minsk

POLAND

SLOVAKIA

HUNGARY

RUMANIA

Kiev

UKRAINE

MOLDOVA

BULGARIA

TURKEY

GEORGIA

ARMENIA

AZERBAIJAN

IRAQ

IRAN

RUSSIA

KAZAKHSTAN

UZBEKISTAN

TURKMENISTAN

TAJIKISTAN

KYRGYZSTAN

AFGHANISTAN

MONGOLIA

CHINA

N. KOREA

S. KOREA

JAPAN

Multiple-Choice Test

1. A purpose of the Marshall Plan was to (*a*) promote political reforms in Latin America (*b*) convert post-war Germany into an agricultural nation (*c*) encourage the economic recovery of Western Europe (*d*) compel the Soviet Union to withdraw its troops from Eastern Europe.

2. At one time or another the United States has been at war with all of the following EXCEPT (*a*) Germany (*b*) Italy (*c*) Sweden (*d*) Spain.

3. The chief reason for the formation of NATO was to (*a*) provide a defense organization for its members (*b*) promote trade relations with Latin America (*c*) check the spread of communism in Asia (*d*) give economic help to European countries.

4. The first countries to receive U.S. military aid under the Truman Doctrine were (*a*) England and France (*b*) Greece and Turkey (*c*) Italy and Portugal (*d*) Korea and Formosa.

5. A missile having a range of 5,000 miles or more is known as (*a*) a Polaris (*b*) a Sputnik (*c*) an Explorer (*d*) an ICBM.

6. Agreements concluded between the Western powers and West Germany in 1955 provided for all of the following EXCEPT that (*a*) West Germany was to become an independent nation (*b*) West Germany was granted limited rearmament rights (*c*) West Germany was to become a member of the UN (*d*) West Germany was to become a member of NATO.

Base your answers to questions 7 and 8 on the passage below and on your knowledge of social studies.

"From Stettin in the Baltic to Trieste in the Adriatic, an iron curtain has descended across the Continent. Behind that line lie all the capitals of the ancient states of central and eastern Europe. . . . all are subject, in one form or another, not only to Soviet influence but to a very high and increasing measure of control from Moscow."

—Winston Churchill

7. When did the situation described in the passage occur? (*a*) toward the close of World War I (*b*) during the Great Depression (*c*) soon after World War II (*d*) during the Vietnam War.

8. This observation by Winston Churchill is often regarded as the symbolic start of (*a*) détente (*b*) the cold war (*c*) balance-of-power politics (*d*) the United States policy of neutrality.

9. To prevent the establishment of another Soviet satellite in the Western Hemisphere, President Reagan in 1983 ordered U.S. troops to invade (*a*) Haiti (*b*) Grenada (*c*) Nicaragua (*d*) the Dominican Republic.

10. The term *Peace Corps* refers to a (*a*) policy of extending economic aid to countries threatened by communism (*b*) proposal for ending nuclear testing (*c*) program for ending political instability in Africa (*d*) policy of providing volunteers to help underdeveloped nations.

11. An important reason for the blockade clamped by President Kennedy on Cuba in 1962 was to (*a*) protect refugees escaping from the Cuban mainland (*b*) protect the national security of the United States (*c*) prevent a Cuban invasion of the Dominican Republic (*d*) prevent Communist China from trading with Cuba.

12. All of the following European countries were Soviet satellites for more than

40 years EXCEPT   (*a*) Czechoslovakia   (*b*) East Germany   (*c*) Luxembourg
(*d*) Hungary.

13. In 1955 eight Communist countries in Europe formed an organization
similar to NATO with the signing of the   (*a*) Locarno Pact   (*b*) Warsaw
Pact   (*c*) Baghdad Pact   (*d*) Leningrad Pact.

14. The Chinese Communist leader who seized control of the mainland of
China in 1949 was   (*a*) Chiang Kai-shek   (*b*) Ho Chi Minh   (*c*) Sun Yat-sen
(*d*) Mao Zedong.

15. A purpose of the Eisenhower Doctrine was to halt Communist aggression
in   (*a*) the Middle East   (*b*) the Caribbean   (*c*) Latin America   (*d*) East Asia.

16. All of the following were policies introduced by Gorbachev into the Soviet
Union EXCEPT   (*a*) democratization   (*b*) *perestroika*   (*c*) *apartheid*   (*d*) *glasnost*.

17. President Carter helped negotiate a peace treaty between   (*a*) Syria and
Libya   (*b*) Israel and Jordan   (*c*) Iraq and Iran   (*d*) Egypt and Israel.

18. All of the following were signs of a cold war thaw EXCEPT   (*a*) Albania's
withdrawal from the Warsaw Pact   (*b*) Nixon's visit to the People's Republic
of China   (*c*) the INF Treaty   (*d*) the SALT agreement.

19. The first astronauts to land on the moon were   (*a*) Frank Borman and
James Lovell   (*b*) Edward White and Walter Schirra   (*c*) Neil Armstrong
and Edwin Aldrin   (*d*) Eugene Cernan and Harrison Schmitt.

20. An American statesman who played an important role in negotiating the
Vietnam cease-fire agreement of 1973 was (*a*) Bernard Baruch   (*b*) Henry
A. Kissinger   (*c*) John Foster Dulles   (*d*) George C. Marshall.

21. Insurgent forces called the *contras* received U.S. aid in their effort to
overthrow the government of (*a*) El Salvador   (*b*) Nicaragua   (*c*) Honduras
(*d*) Costa Rica.

22. Which generalization is best supported by the history of the world from
1950 to 1988?   (*a*) Big powers abandoned their nationalistic policies.   (*b*)
The spirit of nationalism was replaced by a spirit of internationalism.   (*c*)
All nations moved to abandon their imperialistic policies.   (*d*) Crises in
world trouble spots more often ended in deadlocks than in permanent
solutions.

23. All of the following pairs of places are correctly matched EXCEPT   (*a*)
Hanoi—North Vietnam   (*b*) Seoul—South Korea   (*c*) Phnom Penh—Laos
(*d*) Beijing—China.

24. ANZUS is a term that refers to a mutual security pact among the United
States,   (*a*) Great Britain, and France   (*b*) New Zealand, and Australia   (*c*)
Taiwan, and South Korea   (*d*) the Philippines, and Japan.

25. A major obstacle to economic growth in most underdeveloped countries is
a lack of   (*a*) unskilled labor   (*b*) natural resources   (*c*) financial resources
(*d*) convenient domestic markets.

Modified True-False Test

1. The term used to describe the barrier that the Soviet Union imposed
between Eastern Europe and the Western world after World War II is the
great divide.

2. The term that best describes the post-war conflict between the Western
democracies and communism is the *war to end war.*

3. The technique used by the Allies to break the Russian blockade of Berlin in 1948–1949 was the *airlift.*
4. The first commander of the UN forces during the Korean War was *Dwight D. Eisenhower.*
5. The *Welland Canal* is a Middle Eastern waterway that provides a shortcut between the Far East and Europe.
6. The United States sent troops into *Lebanon* in 1958 to help that Middle Eastern country maintain its independence.
7. The American naval base of Guantánamo is located in *Alaska.*
8. *Fulgencio Batista* seized control of Cuba in 1959 and converted his country into a Communist state.
9. The OAS, at the *Punta del Este* Conference, voted to exclude Cuba from participation in its affairs.
10. The name for the space satellite that the Soviet Union launched in 1957 is *Skolnik I.*
11. *Yuri Gagarin*, a Russian, was the world's first spaceman.
12. *Alan B. Shepard* was the first American to orbit the earth.
13. The American program to land people on the moon was designated as Project *Apollo.*
14. The agency responsible for coordinating America's space program is called the *Office of Science and Technology.*
15. America's first space shuttle was named *Salyut.*

Essay Questions

1. (a) State *three* ways in which Americans have helped the people of European countries since World War II. (b) Name *two* European countries that have received help. (c) Give *one* reason why *each* of the countries named was in special need of help.
2. The cold war was waged after the close of World War II, and at times the friction caused enough heat to produce crises. Select *two* of the areas listed below in which a crisis developed. For *each* area chosen discuss (a) an issue that led to a crisis, and (b) an action taken by the United States government to deal with the crisis.

　　　　　Cuba　　　Germany　　　Korea　　　Southeast Asia
3. A study of American foreign policy reveals that the United States has frequently altered its policy toward a country to meet changing conditions. (a) Show how U.S. policy toward Nazi Germany *differed* from its policy toward West Germany after the end of World War II. (b) Show how U.S. policy toward the Soviet Union during World War II *differed* from its policy toward the Soviet Union in the quarter century after the war.
4. (a) Show how the United States attempted to meet the threat of Communist China during the period 1950–1970. (b) List *three* actions taken by the American government since 1970 that indicate a change of policy toward the People's Republic of China.
5. Identify *five* of the following: START, SDI, *perestroika, glasnost,* "two plus four," CFE, INF, SALT, ICBM, IRBM.

UNIT XI. PRESIDENTIAL ADMINISTRATIONS SINCE WORLD WAR II

PRESIDENT TRUMAN'S "FAIR DEAL"

EARLY CAREER

Harry S. Truman was born in Lamar, Missouri, in 1884 and spent most of his childhood in Independence, Missouri. After graduating from high school, he worked for several years as a clerk and bookkeeper in Kansas City, Missouri, and then took over the operation of the family farm in nearby Grandview. During World War I he served in the army as an artillery officer. After the war he opened a men's clothing store in Kansas City. When this venture failed, he decided to seek a career in politics. Elected county judge, he held this position almost continuously from 1922 to 1934.

Truman won election to the U.S. Senate in 1934 and was reelected in 1940. There he gained national prominence as head of a committee investigating government defense contracts. Nominated as Franklin D. Roosevelt's running mate in the campaign of 1944, he became Vice President when the Democrats won.

TRUMAN SUCCEEDS ROOSEVELT AS PRESIDENT

Upon Roosevelt's death in April, 1945, Truman was sworn in as the nation's 33rd President. (Three years later he ran for a second term and won a surprise victory over his Republican opponent, Governor Thomas E. Dewey of New York, whose election had been predicted by most political experts.)

When Truman became President in 1945, the Allied armies were overrunning Germany, and the United States was preparing to invade Japan. During his first month in office, while a conference was being held in San Francisco to organize the United Nations, Germany surrendered. Shortly thereafter Truman went to Germany to meet with the heads of the British and Russian governments. There at the Potsdam Conference the leaders of the Big Three made plans for the occupation of Germany and for the prosecution of the war against Japan. Before the conference ended, Truman received word that America's highly secret atomic bomb project had been successfully completed. On his way home from Potsdam, he authorized the use of the atomic bomb against Japan, thus forcing that nation to surrender and bringing World War II to an end.

THE NATION DEMOBILIZES

With World War II over, millions of Americans were discharged from the armed forces and restored to civilian life. The *Servicemen's Readjustment Act of 1944 (G.I. Bill of Rights)* provided the returning veterans with

458

cash payments; education at government expense; loans for the purchase of homes, farms, and businesses; and unemployment benefits for a period of up to one year.

Industry began to switch over from war production to the manufacture of peacetime goods. The removal of price controls and the great demand for products of all kinds led to a sharp rise in prices. Strikes broke out in major industries as labor demanded higher pay to keep up with the rising cost of living. As production costs mounted, as prices rose, and as labor sought higher wages, inflation became a serious problem. Although the nation enjoyed a post-war boom and prosperity continued almost without interruption for many years, inflation remained a continuing threat to the economy.

TRUMAN'S "FAIR DEAL" PROGRAM ENCOUNTERS OPPOSITION

President Truman urged Congress to enact a comprehensive list of social and economic reforms to give "every segment of our economy and every individual a fair deal." Most of his *Fair Deal* program of domestic legislation received little support. Congress rejected his recommendations for a national health insurance plan, federal aid to education, a new program of aid to farmers (the Brannan Plan), and a civil rights program to eliminate racial discrimination and segregation. (Although Congress failed to accept his civil rights proposals, Truman utilized his executive powers to effect several reforms. He banned discrimination in the hiring of federal employees and ordered military officials to desegregate the armed forces and provide equal treatment and opportunity to all its personnel.)

The only Fair Deal measures passed were (1) several housing acts authorizing the construction, with federal aid, of low-cost public housing and slum clearance projects, (2) an increase in the minimum wage from 40¢ to 75¢ per hour, (3) an expansion of Social Security benefits and coverage, and (4) an increase from $5,000 to $10,000 in the size of bank accounts protected by federal insurance.

OTHER DOMESTIC LEGISLATION IS PASSED

Congress amended the National Labor Relations Act of 1935 by passing the Taft-Hartley Act over Truman's veto (see page 271). It also took steps to curb subversive activities by enacting the *McCarran Act.* This law barred Communists from employment in government jobs and defense plants; required Communist organizations to register with the Department of Justice; and permitted the deportation, and forbade the entry, of any alien who was a member of a totalitarian (Communist, Nazi, Fascist) organization. Congress also approved (1) the Presidential Succession Act of 1947, (2) the National Security Act, consolidating the various branches of the armed forces into a single *Department of Defense;* establishing a National Security Council (NSC) to advise the President; and creating a Central Intelligence Agency (CIA) to coordinate and evaluate information and activities relating to the nation's security, and (3) the Twenty-second Amendment, limiting future Presidents to two terms in office.

TRUMAN MAKES FAR-REACHING FOREIGN POLICY DECISIONS

Few Presidents have made foreign policy decisions as far-reaching in effect as those made by Truman. (1) At the start of his term he made the difficult decision to use the atomic bomb against Japan. (2) To meet the challenge of international communism and to promote economic recovery in war-torn countries, he launched such programs as the Truman Doctrine, the Marshall Plan, the Point Four Program, and the North Atlantic Treaty Organization. (3) To prevent the North Korean Communists from taking over South Korea, he sent U.S. armed forces to aid the South Koreans.

EFFECTS OF THE KOREAN WAR ON THE NATION

At the outbreak of the Korean War in 1950, the Truman administration hoped that the campaign would be a short one. As the fighting dragged on, the President declared a national emergency and mobilized the nation's resources. The Selective Service System drafted men to increase the armed forces from 1.5 to 3.5 million. Reservists were recalled to active duty. Additional billions of dollars were appropriated for defense purposes, and higher income taxes were levied to help defray the nation's military expenses. Under the *Defense Production Act*, temporary agencies were set up to administer price and wage controls, to supervise the allotment of vital raw materials, and to speed up military production.

THE EISENHOWER ADMINISTRATION

EISENHOWER'S EARLY CAREER

Born in Denison, Texas, in 1890 and raised in Abilene, Kansas, Dwight D. Eisenhower entered West Point in 1911 and became an army officer. In World War I he was assigned to a tank-training center in the United States, and after the war he served as a tank commander and troop instructor. Becoming an expert military tactician, "Ike" held various posts in the late Twenties and Thirties including the position of aide to Douglas MacArthur, the Army Chief of Staff.

Soon after the United States entered World War II, Eisenhower, now a general, was placed in command of American forces in Europe. He planned the successful Allied campaigns in French North Africa and Italy in 1942–1943. Appointed Supreme Allied Commander, he organized the invasion of France in 1944 and led the Allies to victory in Western Europe.

After the war Eisenhower served as Army Chief of Staff. He retired from active duty in 1948 and became president of Columbia University. Two years later, when the North Atlantic Treaty signatories agreed to create a unified military force as a defense against Russia, they selected Eisenhower to organize the NATO army. He held the post of Supreme Allied Commander in Europe (SACEUR) until the spring of 1952, when he resigned to enter the presidential race in the United States.

PRESIDENTIAL ELECTION CAMPAIGN OF 1952

In 1952 the Republicans nominated Eisenhower, the nation's most popular hero of World War II, as their candidate for President. Their vice presidential nominee was Senator Richard M. Nixon of California. When Truman declined to run for another term, the Democrats selected Governor Adlai E. Stevenson of Illinois as their candidate for the presidency.

In the spirited campaign that followed, the Republicans argued that it was "time for a change." They claimed that high officials of the Democratic administration had misused their positions for personal gain, that the Democrats had permitted Communist sympathizers to remain in the government, and that the Democrats had no plan for ending the Korean War.

The Democrats asserted that the nation had prospered under their rule and that the best way to insure continued prosperity was to continue the domestic policies of the New Deal and the Fair Deal. They also argued that the foreign policy of the Truman administration had effectively blocked the spread of communism.

EISENHOWER BECOMES THE NATION'S 34TH PRESIDENT

Eisenhower won a landslide victory, receiving nearly 34 million votes to Stevenson's 27.5 million, and winning 442 electoral votes to Stevenson's 89. He cracked the Solid South, carrying four traditionally Democratic states in that region.

During his first term as President, Eisenhower suffered both a heart attack and an abdominal ailment that required surgery. He rallied from these illnesses, however, and agreed to run for another term in 1956. The Democrats nominated Stevenson to oppose Eisenhower a second time.

Once again Eisenhower overwhelmed Stevenson. He received 9.5 million more popular votes than his opponent and won the electoral votes of all but seven states.

THE DEMOCRATS CONTROL CONGRESS

When Eisenhower was swept into office in 1952, the Republicans also gained control of Congress, but by a slim margin. In 1954, however, the Democrats won a majority in both houses. In 1956, despite Eisenhower's landslide vote, the Republicans were unable to win control of either house. The Democrats scored additional gains in 1958, securing the largest majority in Congress since Franklin D. Roosevelt's overwhelming victory in 1936.

The Republican administration and the Democratic leaders of Congress pledged that the nation's welfare would not be sacrificed to party politics. Most of Eisenhower's program of domestic and foreign legislation was enacted with *bipartisan support*, that is, with the support of both political parties in Congress.

THE ST. LAWRENCE SEAWAY IS BUILT

For many years, Americans and Canadians had urged (1) that the St. Lawrence River be deepened and widened to provide ocean-going vessels a seaway from the Atlantic to the interior of North America, and (2) that hydroelectric power resources of the river be harnessed. Every U.S. President since Wilson had requested congressional approval for such a project, but opposition by railroads, seaports, and power and coal interests had prevented favorable action.

President Eisenhower declared that the seaway was vital to the country's national security. In 1953 he allowed New York State to join with the Province of Ontario, Canada, in building a hydroelectric power plant along the International Rapids section of the St. Lawrence. This project did not require congressional approval. In 1954, when Canada seemed determined to build the seaway by itself, if necessary, Congress approved American participation in its construction.

The $1 billion power project and seaway were completed in 1959. The huge Barnhart Island power dam, equipped with 32 generators, provided a vast new supply of electricity to northern New York, Vermont, and parts of Canada. The newly dredged channels and the newly built dams and locks made the entire St. Lawrence navigable for ocean-going vessels. Large ships could now journey from the Atlantic to ports on the Great Lakes as far inland as Duluth, Minnesota—2,450 miles from the ocean.

ATOMIC ENERGY IS PUT TO WORK

A new era in transportation dawned in 1954 when the U.S. Navy launched the world's first atomic-powered submarine. This vessel, named the *Nautilus*, was able to travel around the world without refueling and could remain submerged for several months. The effectiveness of nuclear submarines was dramatically demonstrated in 1958 when the *Nautilus* sailed across the North Pole, traveling for 1,830 miles under the polar icecap. Within the next few years, many more atomic-powered submarines were added to the fleet. Equipped with long-range missiles capable of firing nuclear warheads at targets thousands of miles away, these vessels greatly increased America's sea power.

Atomic energy also began to play an important non-military role. Scientists discovered many important uses for *radioisotopes*. These are radioactive substances employed in medical, agricultural, and industrial research. Nuclear reactors provided a new source of fuel for the production of electricity. The first commercial nuclear power plant was dedicated by Eisenhower in 1958 at Shippingport, Pennsylvania. Many other such plants have been built since then.

In 1953 President Eisenhower announced his "atoms for peace" program. He proposed that the nations of the world share their atomic know-how and atomic material for peaceful purposes. In response to his proposal, the UN sponsored the International Atomic Energy Agency. This body collects and distributes technical information and supplies fissionable material to nations seeking nuclear development for peaceful purposes. To demonstrate to the world a peaceful application of atomic energy, the United States built the nuclear-powered cargo-and-passenger ship *Savannah.*

A VAST ROAD-BUILDING PLAN IS ADOPTED

To keep pace with the ever-increasing traffic on the nation's highways, Congress in 1956 enacted a major bill for highway construction. It provided for the building of a network of superhighways to connect 90% of all cities having a population of 50,000 or more. Nine-tenths of the cost, now estimated at about $100 billion, was to be borne by the federal government. This 42,500-mile National System of Interstate and Defense Highways took some 35 years to complete.

NEW ANTI-COMMUNIST LAWS ARE PASSED

To strengthen existing legislation for the control of communism within the United States, measures were enacted to (1) deprive the Communist party in this country of all legal rights, (2) revoke the citizenship of naturalized citizens who advocate the overthrow of the government by force, (3) further curb the influence of Communists in labor unions, and (4) provide the death penalty for persons convicted of spying in peacetime.

SENATOR McCARTHY SEEKS OUT COMMUNISTS

Senator Joseph McCarthy of Wisconsin attracted national attention when he served as the head of several Senate committees investigating Communist influence in government, education, defense industries, and other fields. The tactics he used in his hunt for Communists gave rise to the term "McCarthyism." McCarthy's supporters praised him for protecting America against Communist subversion. His opponents criticized him for conducting a "witch hunt," for creating an atmosphere of hysteria, and for making irresponsible accusations that harmed the reputations of loyal Americans. "McCarthyism" stirred up much controversy in the early 1950's. His political influence waned when the U.S. Senate in December, 1954, formally "condemned" him for "conduct unbecoming a member" of that body.

STEPS ARE TAKEN TO ASSURE CIVIL RIGHTS FOR BLACKS

1. In *Brown* v. *Board of Education of Topeka, Kansas* (May, 1954) the U.S. Supreme Court unanimously ruled that racial segregation in public schools was a violation of the Fourteenth Amendment and was therefore unconstitutional. Later Court decisions (*a*) reaffirmed the principle of public education without racial discrimination, and (*b*) instructed the federal courts to require a prompt and reasonable start toward desegregation.

The Southern states began to integrate their schools slowly and with great reluctance. In 1957 a school integration crisis occurred in Arkansas when Governor Orval Faubus defied a court order to end segregation in the public schools of Little Rock. He warned that riots would erupt if black students were admitted to Central High School and ordered the Arkansas National Guard to bar their entry. President Eisenhower dispatched federal troops into Little Rock to enforce the law and to prevent rioting. Under the watchful eyes of the troops, black students gained admission to the school, and the crisis subsided.

2. With the passage of the Civil Rights Act of 1957, Congress, for the first time since reconstruction, took steps to protect the voting rights of Southern blacks.

(For a full discussion of civil rights, see pages 301–306.)

OTHER DOMESTIC HIGHLIGHTS

(1) The Department of Health, Education, and Welfare (later renamed the Department of Health and Human Services) was created in 1953 to consolidate the work of various independent agencies. (2) An Air Force Academy was established at Colorado Springs, Colorado. (3) A *soil bank program* was adopted to reduce farm surpluses and assure higher prices to farmers. Cash payments were made to farmers who removed acreage from cultivation and planted soil-conserving crops. (4) Alaska and Hawaii were admitted into the Union as the 49th and 50th states.

THE SPACE AGE BEGINS

In the fall of 1957 Russia placed the first artificial satellite, *Sputnik I*, into orbit, thus ushering in the space age. The U.S. failure to beat the Russians into space aroused demands that America speed up its space projects, improve educational standards, and train more scientists and engineers.

Eisenhower appointed a special assistant to advise him on science and technology. Congress established the National Aeronautics and Space Administration (NASA) to coordinate space programs. It also passed the National Defense Education Act of 1958 (see page 294).

The United States successfully entered the space race when it orbited *Explorer I* early in 1958.

FOREIGN AFFAIRS HIGHLIGHTS

During Eisenhower's administration, (1) a truce was signed ending the Korean War, (2) the Southeast Asia Treaty Organization was formed, (3) the Eisenhower Doctrine was proclaimed, (4) U.S. troops were sent to Lebanon, and (5) the United States broke off diplomatic relations with Cuba.

PRESIDENT KENNEDY'S "NEW FRONTIER"

THE MAJOR PARTIES CHOOSE THEIR CANDIDATES

The two leading contenders for the Democratic presidential nomination in 1960 were Senator John F. Kennedy of Massachusetts and Senator Lyndon B. Johnson of Texas. Kennedy had campaigned throughout the nation for many months and had entered and won seven state primaries. At the convention he gained the nomination easily. Johnson became the Democratic candidate for Vice President.

With President Eisenhower ineligible for a third term because of the Twenty-second Amendment, the Republicans chose Vice President Richard M. Nixon of California as their nominee for President.

KENNEDY WINS THE 1960 ELECTION

A new element was introduced into presidential campaigning when Nixon and Kennedy held a series of televised debates. The entire nation was able to see and hear the opposing candidates discuss the vital issues of the day on television. In the opinion of many political observers, these TV debates played a decisive role in deciding the outcome of the election.

Kennedy charged that during the years of the Eisenhower administration, the United States had lost ground to Russia in the cold war and that the prestige of the United States had declined because of its failure to match Soviet space achievements. He also claimed that the nation's economy had not expanded sufficiently while the Republicans were in power.

Nixon argued that the Eisenhower administration had (1) provided strong and experienced leadership for the free world, (2) terminated the Korean War, (3) curbed Communist expansion, (4) kept the nation at peace, and (5) fostered economic prosperity.

Political observers wondered whether Kennedy, like Alfred E. Smith in 1928, would lose support because he was a Roman Catholic. Kennedy's repeated declarations that he would not be influenced by Church pressures eased the minds of many people and reduced the impact of the religious issue.

In the election, the popular vote was very close. Kennedy received 34,227,000 votes to Nixon's 34,109,000. Kennedy, however, carried most of the larger states. He acquired 303 electoral votes to Nixon's 219, thereby winning the election. The Democrats also retained control of Congress.

THE 35TH PRESIDENT

John Fitzgerald Kennedy was born in 1917 in Brookline, Massachusetts. He was the second oldest of nine children in the family of Joseph P. Kennedy, a wealthy banker who occupied several important positions in the administration of Franklin D. Roosevelt. Young "Jack" Kennedy attended private elementary and prep schools and graduated with honors from Harvard University in 1940.

Enlisting in the U.S. Navy in 1941, he became a combat hero as the commander of a PT boat in the Solomon Islands and was decorated for bravery. In 1945 he was released because of injuries. The following year he entered politics and won election to the House of Representatives, where he served for three terms. He ran for the Senate in 1952. The Republicans carried Massachusetts in the presidential vote, but Kennedy scored a political upset by defeating his Republican opponent, Henry Cabot Lodge.

At the Democratic National Convention in 1956, Kennedy came close to winning the party's nomination for Vice President. In 1958 he was reelected to the Senate, and at the start of 1960 he announced his intention to run for the presidency.

Kennedy was the youngest person ever to be elected President. (Theodore Roosevelt had been younger when he took office in 1901, but he had succeeded to the presidency upon the death of McKinley.) Kennedy was also the first Roman Catholic to become the nation's Chief Executive.

President Kennedy concluded his Inaugural Address with the stirring request: "And so, my fellow Americans: ask not what your country can do for you—ask what you can do for your country."

KENNEDY'S "NEW FRONTIER" PROGRAM

The Kennedy administration's program, labeled the *New Frontier,* received its name from the President's declaration, "We stand today on the edge of a new frontier—the frontier of the Sixties."

Kennedy submitted to Congress an extensive list of recommendations for new legislation. His requests met with a mixed reception.

1. Proposals Enacted Into Law

a. Housing and Other Facilities. Funds were appropriated to expand urban renewal projects; help middle-income families obtain better housing; spur the construction of hospitals, mental health centers, and facilities for higher education; and provide residential, medical, and recreational facilities for senior citizens (elderly people).

b. Poverty. Loans and grants were authorized to speed the economic growth of communities that suffered from persistent unemployment and business distress, and to retrain unemployed workers for jobs in other fields.

c. Trade Expansion Act. The President was granted broad authority to negotiate tariff reductions with foreign countries on a reciprocal basis. Provision was made for federal assistance to domestic industries hurt by the lowering of tariffs.

d. Communications Satellite Act. Congress approved the establishment of a privately owned and privately financed Communications Satellite Corporation (COMSAT) to operate a billion-dollar global communications system. Utilizing earth-orbiting satellites, the new system began relaying TV programs and telephone and telegraph messages throughout the world (1965).

e. Other Laws. The minimum wage was raised from $1.00 to $1.25 an hour. Social Security benefits were improved.

2. Proposals Deferred. The following Kennedy proposals failed to pass while he was President, but were enacted under his successor: (*a*) federal aid to education, (*b*) a broad program of medical care for the aged, (*c*) establishment of a Cabinet-level department of urban affairs and housing, (*d*) tax reduction and reform, and (*e*) legislation to end segregation in the use of public facilities and to strengthen the federal government's power to protect the civil rights of blacks.

FOREIGN AFFAIRS

During the Kennedy administration (1) the United States initiated the *Alliance for Progress*, a program of aid to Latin America, (2) the Cuban missile crisis occurred, (3) American military advisers, troops, and equipment were sent to Southeast Asia when the Communists threatened South Vietnam, Thailand, and Laos, and (4) the United States, Russia, and Britain signed a *Nuclear Test-Ban Treaty* (1963). This agreement banned nuclear testing in the atmosphere, in outer space, and under water. Testing was permitted underground.

JOHN F. KENNEDY IS KILLED BY AN ASSASSIN

On November 22, 1963, while riding in an open car through Dallas, Texas, on his way to address a luncheon gathering, President Kennedy was shot by a sniper and killed. Lee Harvey Oswald was charged with the slaying, but was himself murdered before he could be brought to trial.

Vice President Johnson was immediately sworn in as President. Addressing a joint session of Congress five days later, the new President declared: "No words are strong enough to express [my] determination to continue the forward thrust of America that he [President Kennedy] began. Now the ideas and the ideals which he so nobly represented must and will be translated into action."

The confidence and firmness that Johnson displayed in taking over the reins of government reassured the nation and helped ease the shock of the sudden change in leadership.

PRESIDENT JOHNSON'S "GREAT SOCIETY"

THE 36TH PRESIDENT

Lyndon Baines Johnson was born in 1908 in a farmhouse near Stonewall, Texas. After finishing high school, Johnson held various jobs before enrolling at Southwest Texas State Teachers College. He received his degree at the age of 22 and became a teacher in a Houston high school.

In 1931 he came to Washington as secretary to a member of Congress. In 1935 President Roosevelt appointed him Texas state administrator of the National Youth Administration. In a special election two years later, he won a seat in the House of Representatives.

In 1941 Johnson became the first member of Congress to enter active duty in the armed forces, serving as a lieutenant commander in the navy. Recalled to Washington, Johnson continued his political career, serving in the House until 1949 and in the Senate until 1961.

In 1960 Johnson was Kennedy's strongest rival for the Democratic presidential nomination but lost to the Massachusetts Senator on the first convention ballot. When Kennedy asked him to become his running mate, he accepted, and the Kennedy-Johnson slate went on to win the election.

JOHNSON SCORES AN OVERWHELMING VICTORY IN 1964

At the 1964 Democratic National Convention, President Johnson was nominated by acclamation for Chief Executive. Senator Hubert H. Humphrey of Minnesota was picked as his running mate. The Republicans, dominated by the party's conservative wing, chose Senator Barry M. Goldwater of Arizona to run for President.

Goldwater called for a more aggressive policy toward communism abroad. He argued that the expanding powers of the federal government, especially its growing array of social welfare programs, were destroying American initiative and freedom. He condemned federal action in the field of civil rights as unconstitutional, insisting that segregation was a problem to be handled by the states and local communities.

Johnson, on the other hand, emphasized the need for restraint and flexibility in foreign policy in order to prevent the outbreak of nuclear war. He declared that prosperity and progress at home were founded on the federal programs already in effect, and he pledged to pursue the course that President Kennedy had begun and that he (Johnson) had continued.

In the election Johnson won by a landslide, polling a record-breaking popular vote of 43 million to Goldwater's 27 million and receiving 486 electoral votes to his opponent's 52. Johnson carried every state but six. The Democrats also strengthened their hold on Congress.

JOHNSON'S PROGRAM FOR A "GREAT SOCIETY"

The President described the main goal of his administration as the building of a "Great Society." He outlined objectives ranging from achieving peace and freedom throughout the world to beautifying America, eliminating slums, preventing air and water pollution, checking crime, reducing poverty, encouraging the arts and sciences, and expanding education.

In the first few years of his administration, Johnson maintained a close working relationship with Congress. He succeeded in winning congressional approval for several key Kennedy recommendations and for a number of his own Great Society measures, as follows:

1. **War on Poverty**

   a. The *Economic Opportunity Act* (1964) authorized the federal government to launch a "war on poverty." An *Office of Economic Opportunity* was set up to direct the various phases of the antipoverty campaign. These included (1) a *Job Corps* to provide unemployed young people with work experience and schooling at conservation camps and training centers, (2) part-time jobs for needy students to enable them to continue their education, (3) community work projects, and (4) a domestic version of the Peace Corps, called *VISTA* (*Volunteers in Service to America*, now part of AmeriCorps—the national service initiative that engages thousands of Americans in solving pressing community and national problems, see page 506).

b. The *Appalachian Development Act* (1965) approved a program of aid to *Appalachia*, a region that stretches through 11 states from Pennsylvania to Alabama. It was generally considered to be the country's largest economically depressed section. The money was to be used to build modern highways, sewage-treatment plants, hospitals, and vocational education facilities; to improve timber production; and to restore land scarred by mines.

c. The *Fair Labor Standards Act* of 1938 was amended once again to extend its coverage to more workers, and to increase the minimum wage from $1.25 to $1.40 per hour in 1967 and to $1.60 in 1968.

2. Urban Problems

a. All federal programs of public housing, urban renewal, community planning, mass transportation, and other related activities were consolidated into a *Department of Housing and Urban Development* (1965).

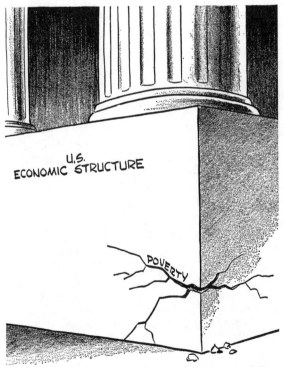

Palmer in The Springfield (Mo.) Leader & Press

Flaw

b. To meet commuting problems in congested urban areas, the *Mass Transit Act* extended federal aid to municipalities for the construction and improvement of subway, bus, and rail systems. In addition, the *High-Speed Ground Transportation Act* allotted federal funds for research on developing better and faster trains.

c. The *Demonstration Cities and Metropolitan Development Act* (1966) extended federal aid to cities for the construction of "demonstration" projects in urban slums. The law also made federal funds available to private builders to encourage the development of entirely new urban centers.

3. Health, Safety, and Consumer Protection

a. Social Security was expanded in 1965 to include a program of medical care for the aged (*Medicare*). (See page 270.)

b. Federal grants were authorized for regional programs of coordinated medical research in heart disease, cancer, stroke, and related diseases.

c. The *Water Quality Act* (1965) and *Clean Waters Restoration Act* (1966) (1) set up a federal Water Pollution Control Administration, (2) authorized federal grants for research on methods to control water pollution, and (3) granted funds to help communities build sewage-treatment plants and undertake other projects to keep their water pure. The *Air Quality Act* (1967) empowered the federal government to assist the states in setting clean air standards and combatting air pollution.

d. The *Traffic Safety Act* (1966) authorized the establishment of federal safety standards for motor vehicles. The *Highway Safety Act* (1966) provided federal grants to the states for traffic safety programs.

e. The *Truth-in-Packaging Act* (1966) required that packaged items be labeled clearly and accurately as to contents and quantity. The *Product Safety Act* (1967) created a national commission empowered to inform the public of dangerous products on the market.

f. The *Meat Inspection Act* (1967) and *Wholesome Poultry Products Act* (1968) allotted funds to the states to help them improve their inspection of meat and poultry processors whose products are marketed intrastate. It authorized the Department of Agriculture to undertake inspection in states that failed to maintain federal standards.

g. The *Consumer Credit Protection Act* (1968), or *Truth-in-Lending Act*, required businesses that extend credit or lend money to state clearly how much consumers must actually pay in interest or other charges.

h. The *Crime Control and Safe Streets Act* (1968) granted funds to the states for the improvement of local law enforcement. It also banned the sale of handguns by mail order, and their over-the-counter sale to persons under 21. The *Gun Control Act* (1968) prohibited mail-order interstate sales of rifles and shotguns, and forbade their sale to anyone under 18.

4. Civil Rights

a. The *Civil Rights Act of 1964* outlawed segregation in hotels, restaurants, theaters, and other public accommodations. (See page 305.)

b. Although the Civil Rights Acts of 1957 and 1960 had given the vote to many Southern blacks, about 2 million blacks in seven states were still prevented from exercising their right to vote by the use of literacy and character tests. The *Voting Rights Act of 1965* suspended such tests and authorized federal registration of voters in states and localities where less than 50% of the voting-age population was registered or had voted in the 1964 election. (See page 303.)

c. The *Civil Rights Act of 1968* prohibited discrimination in the sale or rental of houses and apartments. (See page 305.) It also (1) provided severe penalties for persons convicted of intimidating or injuring civil rights workers, and (2) made it a federal crime to travel across state lines or to use interstate communications for the purpose of inciting a riot.

5. Education. The *Elementary and Secondary Education Act* (1965) established a comprehensive program of federal aid to public schools. ESEA also provided some assistance to parochial and private schools. (See page 295.) The *Higher Education Act* extended additional federal aid to college students and to institutions of higher learning.

6. Immigration. The *Immigration Act of 1965* ended the policy of limiting admission to the United States on the basis of national origin. (See page 280.)

7. Transportation. Some 30 federal agencies dealing with travel by air, rail, highway, and water were grouped into a *Department of Transportation* (1966).

EFFECTS OF THE VIETNAM WAR ON THE NATION

The most serious foreign problem troubling the nation during Johnson's administration was the war in Vietnam. What had begun in 1950 as a minor program of aid to the French in Indochina became after 1965 a major American commitment. It involved half a million troops, billions of dollars in expenditures, and the threat of "total" war with Communist China and the Soviet Union.

· Most Americans supported the view that the United States had an obligation to help South Vietnam preserve its independence. Nevertheless, there was growing concern over the ever-increasing escalation of the war, the assumption by U.S. troops of the main burden of the fighting, and the rising cost in American lives and money. As time passed and the war became stalemated, more and more people came to believe that it had been a mistake to involve U.S. troops in Vietnam. Opponents of the war organized peace demonstrations and signed petitions demanding a halt to the bombing of North Vietnam. In addition, many political leaders of both parties publicly voiced their concern over the administration's war policies. The change in the public's attitude toward the war caused Johnson's popularity to decline sharply.

The war also created a serious split in the Democratic party, as two longtime critics of Johnson's Vietnam policies challenged the President for the party's nomination in 1968. Each of these men, Senator Eugene

McCarthy of Minnesota and Senator Robert F. Kennedy of New York, gained a large and enthusiastic following among anti-Johnson Democrats.

At the end of March, 1968, Johnson ordered a halt to the bombing of most of North Vietnam as a first step toward de-escalating the war. He also stated that he would neither seek nor accept nomination for another term.

THE NIXON ADMINISTRATION

PRESIDENTIAL ELECTION OF 1968

1. The Democrats Nominate Humphrey. Vice President Hubert H. Humphrey, a staunch advocate of the administration's domestic and foreign programs, declared himself a candidate for the Democratic nomination after Johnson withdrew. Humphrey sought support among the party regulars in local political organizations, labor unions, and big-city voting blocs. He and his two rivals, McCarthy and Kennedy, competed for convention delegates in a series of state primaries. Immediately after his victory in the California primary election, Robert F. Kennedy was killed by an assassin.

At the Democratic National Convention, Humphrey's delegates were in control. They endorsed the administration's handling of the Vietnam War, nominated Humphrey for the presidency, and selected Senator Edmund S. Muskie of Maine as his running mate.

2. The Republicans Select Nixon. The leading contender for the Republican presidential nomination was former Vice President Richard M. Nixon. The Republican National Convention chose him as the party's candidate for that office on the first ballot and nominated Governor Spiro T. Agnew of Maryland for the vice presidency.

3. Wallace Runs as a Third-Party Candidate. George C. Wallace, a former Democratic governor of Alabama, entered the race for the presidency as a third-party candidate. He had achieved national prominence by his opposition to the federal government's attempts to speed desegregation in the South.

4. A Three-Way Campaign Ensues. The two issues that dominated the election campaign were Vietnam and "law and order." Although Nixon indicated his support for Johnson's basic policy on Vietnam, he promised to provide "fresh ideas and new men and new leadership" to end the war, and to adopt a foreign policy that would avoid future Vietnams. Blaming the Democrats for the urban crisis, he promised to wage an "all-out" crusade against crime, to curb riots and disorders in the nation's cities, and to institute new programs to help solve the problems of slum dwellers.

Although Humphrey's efforts were hampered by his past defense of administration policies, he promised to seek a quick end to the war. He also pledged a vigorous campaign against lawlessness, combined with an attack on the causes of crime and disorder. He called for a continuation of the Great Society measures that had been designed to solve the problems of slums and poverty.

Many political experts thought that Wallace's appeal would be concentrated in the South. But he also drew large audiences of enthusiastic supporters (as well as hecklers) in Northern industrial centers, where he denounced the breakdown of law and order and the growing disrespect for established institutions. He pledged to quell riots with troops and bayonets, and to work for a change in the federal guidelines on desegregation.

5. Nixon Wins by a Narrow Margin. Early in the campaign, all signs seemed to point to an overwhelming Republican victory. But by election eve, the opinion polls showed Nixon and Humphrey running neck and neck. These predictions were borne out in the actual voting. Of more than 73 million votes cast, Nixon received 31,770,000 to Humphrey's 31,270,000. However, Nixon edged out his opponent in a number of key states (California, Illinois, Indiana, New Jersey, and Ohio), thereby amassing 301 electoral votes to Humphrey's 191. Despite Nixon's victory, the Democrats retained control of Congress.

Wallace polled nearly 10 million votes, the largest total for a third-party candidate up to that time. His strength was concentrated in the Deep South, where he carried five states and won 46 electoral votes.

6. Nixon is Reelected in 1972. Four years later, the Republicans unanimously nominated Nixon and Agnew for a second term. As their presidential candidate, the Democrats chose Senator George McGovern of South Dakota—someone comparatively unknown in national politics. There had been bitter rivalry among the various contenders for the Democratic nomination during the spring primaries and disputes over the seating of delegates at the Democratic National Convention. These factors, as well as opposition to McGovern's liberal views by many middle-of-the-road Democrats, shattered the unity of the party. As a result, Nixon scored an overwhelming victory on election day. Receiving the support of nearly 61% of the voters, he polled 47 million popular votes to his opponent's 29 million and carried every state except Massachusetts. (He also lost the District of Columbia.) Nixon's triumph, while impressive, was personal. Ticket-splitting throughout the country enabled the Democrats to retain control of Congress once again.

THE 37TH PRESIDENT

Richard Milhous Nixon was born in 1913 in Yorba Linda, California, and was raised in nearby Whittier. He enrolled at Whittier College (a Quaker institution), and later studied law at Duke University in Durham, North Carolina. Graduating with honors in 1937, he returned home to practice law.

During World War II Nixon served in the Pacific as a naval officer, rising to the rank of lieutenant commander. While awaiting discharge from the service in 1946, he accepted an invitation from Republican leaders in his home district to run for Congress. He conducted a hard-hitting campaign and scored a surprise victory. Reelected in 1948, Nixon gained national prominence as a member of the House Un-American Activities Committee. In 1950 he was elected to the Senate in a bitter political contest.

Selected as Eisenhower's running mate in 1952 and again in 1956, Nixon served as Vice President for eight years. He became the Republican standard-bearer in the presidential election of 1960 but lost to John F. Kennedy in a close race. In 1962 he tried a political comeback by running for governor of California, but met with defeat. Withdrawing from public life, he moved to New York City and resumed his law career.

Nixon returned to politics to campaign for Republican candidates in 1964 and 1966, and gradually emerged as the leader who could win the support of both the liberal and conservative factions of his party. He declared himself a candidate for the presidency early in 1968, easily gained the Republican nomination, and went on to win the election.

NIXON AND THE VIETNAM WAR

The chief problem facing President Nixon when he assumed office in 1969 was the country's involvement in Vietnam—an issue that had shattered the nation's unity during Johnson's administration. Having made a campaign pledge to seek an end to the war, Nixon's objective now was to find the means to do so. When the formal peace talks in Paris bogged down, he dispatched Henry Kissinger, his national security adviser (later Secretary of State), to work out a settlement in secret talks with Le Duc Tho, a high North Vietnamese official. He also took steps to implement the policy of *Vietnamization* (the replacement of U.S. combat troops by South Vietnamese). Between 1969 and 1972 more than 500,000 American soldiers were withdrawn from Vietnam.

At the same time, however, Nixon widened the scope of America's participation in the war by (1) sending U.S. troops into Cambodia to wipe out Communist bases in that country; (2) authorizing U.S bombers to provide continuing air support to the Cambodian army; (3) committing American air power to a South Vietnamese drive into Laos; and (4) ordering a resumption of the bombing of military targets in North Vietnam and the mining of its ports in an effort to cripple that country's offensive capability.

The war continued to be responsible for many of the nation's internal problems during Nixon's first term. Massive anti-war demonstrations were held in Washington and other cities, and anti-war protests took place on hundreds of college campuses. The country became increasingly polarized (divided) as administration supporters clashed with dissenters. In Congress, too, the war created serious divisions. Resolutions were introduced to curb the President's war powers, and attempts were made to force Nixon to speed U.S. withdrawal from Southeast Asia by curtailing defense appropriations. In addition, the demands of the war on the American economy helped to push inflation to its highest rate since the Korean War.

At the start of Nixon's second term in 1973, a Vietnam cease-fire accord acceptable to both sides was finally reached. All U.S. troops were brought home, and U.S. prisoners of war were released. The drafting of young men under Selective Service was halted; and the government switched from draftees to volunteers to meet the needs of the armed forces. But U.S. involvement in Indochina did not terminate completely. When the Vietnamese Communists continued their offensive operations in Cambodia, Nixon sent in U.S. bombers to support the Cambodian army. Claiming that the President was exceeding his authority, Congress voted to cut off all funds for the bombing of Cambodia. Nixon agreed to end the bombing by August, 1973, and to seek congressional approval for any further military operation in Indochina.

OTHER FOREIGN HIGHLIGHTS

a. The Senate ratified the *Nuclear Non-Proliferation Treaty,* which prohibits nuclear powers from transferring atomic weapons to other nations and bars non-nuclear nations from developing such weapons.

b. President Nixon journeyed to Peking and Moscow (1972). These historic visits appeared to mark the end of a quarter-century of cold war confrontation and the beginning of a new era of peaceful coexistence, or détente, between the United States and the two most powerful Communist nations.

IMPORTANT LEGISLATIVE ENACTMENTS

1. Voting Reforms. In 1970 Congress renewed the life of the Voting Rights Act of 1965 for another five years; extended its application to certain Northern cities and counties; barred the use of literacy tests as a voting qualification; and abolished residency requirements of longer than 30 days for presidential elections. (See page 303.)

Attached to the bill was a rider lowering the voting age from 21 to 18. Upon signing the measure, Nixon urged that its constitutionality be quickly tested in the Supreme Court. The Court upheld the 18-year-old vote provision in federal elections but not in state and local elections. Thereupon Congress proposed the Twenty-sixth Amendment, which stated that the right of citizens 18 years of age or older to vote shall not be denied by the United States or by any state on account of age. The new amendment was ratified by the states in 1971. (See page 290.)

2. Curbing Pollution. To clean up the nation's waterways, Congress appropriated funds to help the states and municipalities plan and build sewage disposal plants. Congress also (*a*) required motor vehicle manufacturers to eliminate the most harmful exhaust emissions from their products by 1977, (*b*) increased penalties for oil spills by ships and by offshore and onshore installations, (*c*) established controls over thermal pollution from atomic power plants, (*d*) set water quality standards, (*e*) barred the dumping of hazardous materials into ocean waters, and (*f*) authorized the government to set noise limits for motor vehicles, trains, jackhammers, and other sources of noise pollution.

An *Environmental Protection Agency (EPA)* was created to coordinate the anti-pollution activities and responsibilities of the federal government.

3. Postal Service Reorganization. Upon Nixon's recommendation, Congress passed the *Postal Reorganization Act* (1970). It provided for replacement of the 200-year-old Post Office Department by a new, independent agency called the *United States Postal Service.* Headed by a Postmaster General and an 11-member board of governors, this government-owned corporation was charged with the responsibility of providing better, faster, and more dependable mail service and of converting the nation's postal system to a self-supporting operation.

4. Strengthening Federal Crime Laws. A major administration-backed bill that Congress enacted was the *Omnibus Crime Control Act* (1970). It prescribed the death penalty for anyone convicted of a fatal bombing; permitted FBI agents to investigate and federal attorneys to prosecute persons accused of bombings and arson on college campuses and at other federally aided institutions; prohibited the investment of money from organized crime in legitimate interstate businesses; and permitted judges to impose additional sentences of up to 25 years on certain "dangerous offenders" convicted of crimes that carry lesser penalties.

5. Revenue Sharing. To reverse the trend of centralizing more and more public spending programs—and all decisions about them—in Washington, Nixon proposed to return to the states, counties, and cities a portion of the tax revenues collected by the federal government. Since the money could be used for ordinary operating expenses—such as the maintenance of police and fire departments, public transportation, garbage collection, and sewage disposal—as well as for new capital improvements, the plan would provide state and local governments desperately needed assistance in maintaining adequate levels of public service. A revenue sharing bill, enacted by Congress in 1972, allotted $30 billion for this purpose over a five-year period.

6. Labor and Consumer Measures
   a. The *Rail Passenger Service Act* of 1970 created a semipublic company, called *AMTRAK,* to operate a nationwide system of passenger trains.

   b. The *Occupational Safety and Health Act (OSHA)* of 1972 empowered federal OSHA inspectors to visit places of employment without any advance notice to check for violations of safety and health standards.

   c. The *Product Safety Act* of 1972 created an independent commission with power to set and enforce safety standards for consumer products and to ban the sale of unsafe items.

   d. A $23-billion highway bill passed in 1973 authorized, for the first time, the use of Highway Trust Fund monies for the improvement of such mass transit facilities as buses, rail systems, and subways.

   e. The *Minimum Wage Act* of 1974 brought more workers under the law's protection and scheduled an increase in the minimum wage from $1.60 to $2.00 in 1974, to $2.10 in 1975, and to $2.30 in 1976.

7. Political Reform. Congress passed a law (effective April, 1972) setting limits on the amounts presidential and congressional candidates may spend on political advertising and requiring public disclosure of all election campaign contributions and expenditures.

8. Women's Rights. Congress approved, and sent to the states for ratification, an amendment to the Constitution prohibiting all forms of discrimination based on sex (see page 300).

THE NATION'S POPULATION IS COUNTED

The census of 1970 revealed that the population of the United States was 203 million, an increase of 24 million since 1960. Once again, as in the census of 1960, the West led in rate of growth, registering a gain of 22.5% compared to 13% for the nation as a whole. California, with a population of almost 20 million, replaced New York as the most populous state. The dramatic shifts in population from one state to another required the reassignment of 11 of the 435 seats in the House of Representatives. California gained five seats; Florida, three; and Arizona, Colorado, and Texas, one each. New York and Pennsylvania lost two each; Alabama, Iowa, North Dakota, Ohio, Tennessee, West Virginia, and Wisconsin lost one each.

A NEW INTERNAL WATERWAY SYSTEM IS COMPLETED

The Arkansas River Navigation System, which took 18 years to build and cost more than a billion dollars, was completed in 1971. A series of locks and dams tamed the turbulent river, making it navigable from Catoosa (near Tulsa), Oklahoma, to the Mississippi. By providing low-cost water transportation, flood control, and hydroelectric power, the project helped to spur the economic development of Oklahoma and Arkansas, as well as of the entire Arkansas River Basin.

THE BATTLE AGAINST INFLATION CONTINUES

Between 1969 and 1971, prices of goods and services soared, and the cost of living rose ever higher. To halt the inflationary spiral, the government imposed mandatory controls on the economy in August, 1971. A Cost of Living Council was established to oversee the stabilization program.

During Phase 1, which lasted for 90 days, all wages and prices were frozen at existing levels. In Phase 2, goods and services were permitted to rise by 2.5% and wages by 5.5%. Seeking to restore a freer economy, the President switched to a Phase 3 program of voluntary controls early in 1973. Under these relaxed regulations, wholesale and consumer prices began to rise so sharply that runaway inflation appeared to be developing. Bowing to public and congressional pressure, Nixon clamped a 60-day freeze on prices in June, 1973. Two months later, a Phase 4 program of modified wage-price restraints was put into effect. It lasted until April, 1974, when wage and price controls were lifted.

The problem was far from solved, however. *Double-digit inflation* (inflation at a rate of 10% or higher) persisted throughout 1974. The situation was aggravated by an energy crisis, caused by the cutoff of oil shipments from the Middle East in the fall of 1973 and by a subsequent fourfold increase in the price of imported oil. The ever-rising cost of living weakened consumer purchasing power to such an extent that production fell, unemployment spread, and the nation experienced an unusual combination of recession and inflation (*stagflation*).

THE NIXON ADMINISTRATION COLLAPSES

1. The Watergate Affair Erupts. In June, 1972, during the presidential election campaign, five men were arrested for breaking into the offices of the Democratic National Committee in the Watergate apartment and office complex in Washington, D.C. The intruders, equipped with cameras and electronic "bugging" equipment, were led by James McCord, the security coordinator of the Republican Committee to Reelect the President (CREEP). The Democrats denounced the raid as "a blatant act of political espionage" and filed suit against Nixon's reelection committee. White House officials dismissed the break-in as a "third-rate burglary attempt," and the incident had little effect on public opinion in the months before the election.

In January, 1973, the five Watergate burglars and two other conspirators who had been indicted by a federal grand jury were tried and convicted for conspiracy, burglary, and wiretapping. But the Watergate affair did not end there. Two months later, the Watergate trial judge, John Sirica, disclosed a letter from McCord charging that (*a*) pressure had been applied to him and the other defendants to plead guilty and remain silent, (*b*) "others" were involved in the spying, and (*c*) government witnesses had committed perjury during the trial.

As speculation arose over the extent of the involvement of Nixon administration personnel in the Watergate conspiracy, a new federal jury was summoned to look into the case; newspaper reporters began to conduct inquiries of their own and to publish startling disclosures about Watergate and other political "dirty tricks"; a Senate committee chaired by Sam Ervin of North Carolina was formed to hold public hearings on the scandal; and a special federal prosecutor, Archibald Cox, was brought in to conduct a thorough investigation of the affair for the Justice Department.

2. A Major Political Scandal Unfolds. Information uncovered in the various investigations revealed that (*a*) members of the White House Staff and officials of Nixon's reelection committee had participated in the planning and cover-up of the Watergate break-in; (*b*) money raised by CREEP for the election campaign had been used to pay for the Watergate operation, for other political and sabotage activities against Democratic candidates, and for "hush money" payments to the Watergate defendants; and (*c*) presidential aides had exerted pressure on CIA and FBI officials to support the Watergate cover-up. As a result of these disclosures a number of high-ranking administration officials were either fired by the President or forced to resign. Many were later brought to trial, found guilty, and sent to jail.

3. The White House Tapes Controversy. During the televised Ervin Committee hearings in the summer of 1973, a witness revealed that the President had secretly tape-recorded his conversations at the White House and at the Executive Office Building. When the various agencies investigating Watergate requested access to certain tapes bearing on the affair, Nixon refused to comply. He claimed executive privilege, and argued that national security, the doctrine of separation of powers, and the integrity of the presidency would be seriously injured by the surrender of such confidential White House material.

In October, 1973, the U.S. Court of Appeals upheld a lower court order requiring the President to turn over some key tapes requested by Archibald Cox, the special Watergate prosecutor. When Cox declined the President's offer of written summaries of the tapes, Nixon ordered his dismissal. Elliot Richardson, the Attorney General, resigned rather than carry out the President's order. The Deputy Attorney General also refused and was fired. This "Saturday Night Massacre" touched off a storm of criticism. Ordinary citizens throughout the country demanded the President's removal from office, and impeachment resolutions were introduced in the House of Representatives. Thereupon, Nixon agreed to surrender the disputed tapes.

The tapes controversy preoccupied the nation for the next nine months. The White House continued to resist the mounting demand for additional tapes, releasing instead huge quantities of heavily censored transcripts. Finally, in July, 1974, the Supreme Court, in a historic decision, ruled that the President must relinquish the sought-for recordings.

4. Nixon Resigns. In February, 1974, the House of Representatives authorized its Judiciary Committee to conduct an impeachment inquiry. For six months the committee examined all the available evidence compiled in the other investigations, conducted inquiries of its own, and then submitted its recommendation that the House vote to impeach the President on the following grounds:

a. Using the powers of his high office, he had engaged personally and through his agents in a course of conduct designed to delay and obstruct the investigation of the Watergate break-in; to cover up and protect those responsible; and to conceal the existence and scope of other unlawful activities.

b. He repeatedly engaged in conduct violating the constitutional rights of citizens and used federal agencies for purposes not authorized by law.

c. He willfully disobeyed the committee's subpoenas for tapes and documents.

Realizing that he had lost the support of the public, the press, and his own party, and that his impeachment by the House and his conviction by the Senate were highly probable, Nixon resigned in August, 1974. He thus became the first President in the nation's history to resign from office.

5. Vice President Agnew's Political Career Ends in Disgrace. While the country was in the throes of the Watergate scandal, it became known that Spiro Agnew was under investigation by the Justice Department for extortion, bribery, and tax fraud. Evidence accumulated that during the 1960's, when he had been a public official in Maryland, he had received kickbacks from contractors and others who sought government business. Faced with indictment and trial, Agnew resigned as Vice President in October, 1973. He pleaded "no contest" to a charge of federal income tax evasion and was sentenced to three years probation and fined $10,000.

6. Ford Becomes Vice President and Then President. Upon Agnew's resignation, Nixon nominated Representative Gerald R. Ford of Michigan to replace him, and the Senate and House confirmed his choice. (This was the first time that the Twenty-fifth Amendment was used to fill a vice presidential vacancy.) When Nixon resigned, Ford assumed office as the country's Chief Executive. In his Inaugural Address, he said: "Our long national nightmare is over. Our Constitution works. Our great republic is a government of laws and not of men. Here, the people rule." He also called upon the nation to "bind up the internal wounds of Watergate."

THE FORD ADMINISTRATION

THE 38TH PRESIDENT

Gerald Ford was born in Omaha, Nebraska, in 1913 and was raised in Grand Rapids, Michigan. After graduating from the University of Michigan, he obtained a law degree from Yale and returned home to practice law. During World War II Ford served in the U.S. Navy. In 1948 he ran for Congress as the Republican candidate of his Grand Rapids district and won. He remained in Congress for the next 25 years. Chosen as minority leader of the House in 1965, he rose to national prominence as a conservative Republican spokesperson and a popular member of Congress. In 1973 he left his congressional post to accept the vice presidency.

FORD PARDONS NIXON

In September, 1974, Ford granted Nixon "a full, free, and absolute pardon" for all federal crimes that he "committed or may have committed or taken part in" while in office. He took this step he said (1) to avoid the "prolonged and divisive debate" that would have resulted from the possible indictment and trial of the former President; and (2) to spare Richard Nixon further punishment and degradation. Reaction to the pardon was strong but divided. Some hailed it as an act of mercy; many contended that it violated the constitutional principle of equal justice for all. Why should the principal in the Watergate affair be exempted from prosecution, they argued, while many of his subordinates faced trial or had already been imprisoned for their participation?

THE DEMOCRATS EXPAND THEIR POLITICAL POWER

The Republican party, tainted by Watergate, suffered a severe setback in the election of 1974. The Democrats increased their representation in the Senate from 58 to 61 and in the House from 248 to 292. They also won control of 36 states, including 8 of the 10 largest—where three-fourths of the population lived.

ROCKEFELLER IS SELECTED AS VICE PRESIDENT

Nelson A. Rockefeller, the former governor of New York, was nominated by President Ford for the vice presidency. After a long and searching inquiry, Congress confirmed him for the position in December, 1974.

PAST PROBLEMS CONTINUE TO PLAGUE FORD

After a decade of foreign wars and domestic turmoil, the Ford administration was a period of comparative peace, both at home and abroad. But many of the problems that had troubled the nation in the recent past persisted. High unemployment, severe inflation, and sluggish recovery from the economic recession of 1974 continued to inflict hardship on millions of Americans. The administration's failure to resolve these problems raised doubts about its ability to manage the nation's economy. Disillusionment with the government, stemming from the Vietnam War and the long ordeal of Watergate, was further heightened by (1) additional disclosures of illegal activities by the CIA and FBI, (2) revelations of scandalous and unethical behavior by some members of Congress, and (3) reports that foreign and domestic officials had taken bribes from large American corporations. These disclosures aroused public resentment against the abuse of power by politicians in general; cast a pall on the Ford administration because of the close association between Ford and his predecessor; and set the stage for the emergence of new candidates in the election of 1976.

NEW LEGISLATION IS ENACTED

Relations between the Democratic-controlled Congress and the Republican President were quite strained during Ford's tenure in office. His efforts to cut back on federal spending and impose limits on social legislation clashed with congressional attempts to expand government services and led to a "battle of the vetoes" between Ford and Congress. The President vetoed a total of 84 bills passed by the 93rd and 94th Congresses; the House and Senate overrode 16 of his vetoes. Major bills enacted into law included the following:

1. **Political Reforms**
    a. The *Campaign Finance Act* (1974) was passed as a result of campaign-spending violations that came to light during the Watergate investigations. It sought to reduce the political influence on presidential candidates of special-interest groups and wealthy individuals by (1) financing presidential campaigns with federal funds, (2) setting limits

on candidate contributions and expenditures, and (3) creating a strong, independent *Federal Election Commission* to enforce the law.

b. The Voting Rights Act of 1965 was renewed in 1975 for another seven years. Its application was also extended to cover Spanish-speaking and Asian Americans, as well as Indians and Alaskan natives.

c. To promote confidence in the fairness of decisions made by federal agencies, Congress passed the *Government in the Sunshine Act* (1976). It required about 50 executive agencies and regulatory commissions to open their meetings to the press and the public except when topics of a confidential nature were being considered. If closed sessions were held, official records of the proceedings were to be kept.

d. To curtail a President's power to prolong a state of national emergency indefinitely, Congress passed the *National Emergencies Act* (1976). It provided for periodic review by Congress of states of national emergency ordered by a President; and authorized Congress to terminate such a decree if, in its judgment, it was no longer warranted.

2. Labor and Consumer Measures
a. To give workers in private industry some basic protection against the loss of retirement benefits, Congress in 1974 passed the *Employee Retirement Income Security Act (ERISA)*. (See page 271.)

b. With 8.5% of the labor force out of work, Congress approved a bill extending unemployment benefits from 52 weeks to 65 weeks (1975). In addition, the federally subsidized *Food Stamp Program,* which enables low-income families to purchase food at a fraction of its actual cost, was expanded (1976); and a $3.95 billion public works jobs bill was approved (over the President's veto). It provided funds to state and local governments for such projects as parks and waterways and for the maintenance of fire and police protection (1976).

c. To protect leasers of cars and appliances from misleading advertising and unfair charges, a *Consumer Leasing Protection Act* was passed (1976). Another law prohibited companies providing credit to consumers from withholding their services because of an applicant's age, color, religion, race, or national origin (1976). It was an extension of the previously enacted *Equal Credit Opportunity Act,* which barred discrimination against credit applicants on the basis of sex or marital status.

3. Foreign Trade. The *Trade Reform Act* of 1974 granted the President broad authority to (*a*) negotiate trade agreements with foreign countries, (*b*) grant or withhold special trading arrangements with various nations, (*c*) reduce or suspend duties on foreign imports in order to combat rising prices of domestic goods, (*d*) raise tariffs to protect American industries injured by competition from foreign imports, and (*e*) allow imports from less-developed nations to enter the United States duty-free. (Senate action on the bill had been delayed for a year by a controversy over the extension of trade concessions and credits to Russia while that country restricted emigration of its citizens, especially Jews wishing to go to Israel. As passed, the bill provided for trade concessions to Communist countries that did not restrict emigration.)

4. Copyright Protection. For the first time since 1909 the copyright law was revised (1976). From the previous maximum of 56 years, the length of copyright protection was extended to the lifetime of the work's creator plus 50 years. It also set standards for fair use of copyrighted materials by schools and libraries by spelling out guidelines limiting photocopying and other forms of reproduction.

5. Railroad Reorganization. Seven major railroads serving the Northeast and Midwest were bankrupt and in danger of complete collapse. Recognizing the importance of these lines to the nation's transportation system, Congress approved a bill authorizing the creation of a government-sponsored Consolidated Rail Corporation to acquire the properties and to merge them into a single network (1975). Funded by a $2-billion federal loan, *Conrail* began operations in 1976.

AMERICANS CELEBRATE THE NATION'S BICENTENNIAL

The year 1976 marked the 200th anniversary of the Declaration of Independence. The nation celebrated the occasion with a year-long series of exhibitions, parades, concerts, patriotic displays, tours of historic sites, and other commemorative events. The most spectacular was Operation Sail. On July 4, 16 tall-masted sailing vessels and 53 warships from all parts of the world passed in review in New York Harbor and the Hudson River. Some 6 million people along the shore and in small pleasure boats watched and cheered, while millions of others observed the impressive spectacle on TV.

FOREIGN AFFAIRS HIGHLIGHTS UNDER FORD

1. Soviet-American Relations. (*a*) An agreement to limit the number of offensive nuclear weapons in each side's possession was negotiated at Vladivostok, U.S.S.R., in 1974. (*b*) The United States agreed to sell Russia 6 to 8 million tons of grain annually for a period of five years, starting in 1976. (*c*) American and Soviet astronauts participated in a joint space project, the Apollo-Soyuz linkup. (*d*) Ford and Soviet leader Leonid Brezhnev signed a treaty placing limits on the size of underground nuclear explosions for peaceful purposes and providing for American on-site inspection of Soviet tests. (*e*) The United States, Russia, and 33 other nations signed the "Final Act of the Conference on Security and Cooperation in Europe" at Helsinki, Finland.

2. Southeast Asia. (*a*) South Vietnam surrendered to the Vietcong and North Vietnamese in 1975. Before the final collapse, the United States rushed in planes and ships to evacuate American civilians still remaining in the country as well as South Vietnamese seeking to escape from Communist control. The United States granted asylum to 130,000 South Vietnamese, and Congress appropriated more than $400 million to finance their resettlement. (*b*) The Khmer Rouge overran Cambodia and the Pathet Lao assumed power in Laos, thus completing the Communist takeover of Indochina. (*c*) The members of SEATO agreed to phase out its activities and dissolve the organization. (*d*) The last American forces in Southeast Asia were withdrawn when Thailand ordered the United States to close its military bases in that country and to remove its troops.

THE CARTER ADMINISTRATION

PRESIDENTIAL ELECTION OF 1976

1. The Democrats Nominate Carter. More than a dozen Democrats entered the race for their party's presidential nomination in the election of 1976. Most were well-known political figures. Also announcing his candidacy was a little-known Southerner, Governor Jimmy Carter of Georgia.

In previous election campaigns, only a small fraction of the delegates to the Democratic Party's National Convention were chosen in state primaries, thus enabling professional politicians in control of large blocs of votes to serve as "kingmakers." In this election 75% of the delegates were scheduled to be chosen by party members in presidential primaries. In addition, new rules adopted by the party permitted each candidate to win a proportionate share of a state's delegates. (In past primaries a "winner-take-all" rule largely prevailed.)

The candidates with national reputations chose to concentrate their efforts in a limited number of key states. Carter decided to "run everywhere" because he was relatively unknown and needed as much exposure as possible. He entered every state caucus and 30 presidential primaries, traveled the length and breadth of the land seeking support, and stressed such themes as openness, honesty, trust, and morality in his speeches. To a public that had grown cynical toward officials in Washington and weary of politics in general because of Vietnam and Watergate, Carter's promise to restore a high moral tone to the government and to make it "as good and decent as are the American people" struck a responsive chord.

Early victories in the Iowa caucuses and the New Hampshire primary won Carter national attention. In the state primaries that followed, he collected enough delegate support to assure his nomination. When the Democratic National Convention convened in July, Carter was selected as the party's candidate for President on the first ballot. The delegates also supported his choice of Senator Walter Mondale of Minnesota as his running mate and approved a platform that reflected Carter's moderate-to-liberal views on national issues.

2. The Republicans Choose Ford. The two contenders for the Republican nomination were President Ford and Ronald Reagan, the former Governor of California. Each sought support for his candidacy in a series of hotly contested primaries that failed to provide either with a commanding lead. The fierce intraparty struggle was finally resolved at the Republican National Convention, where Ford won a narrow victory over his challenger. Senator Robert Dole of Kansas became the party's nominee for Vice President.

3. The Candidates Campaign for Election. The campaign centered about such issues as the economy, the character of the candidates, and the desirability of change. Carter criticized Ford for his lack of leadership and his inability to deal with inflation, unemployment, and the energy crisis. He called for new federal initiatives to increase employment and revive the lagging economy. Carter promised to (*a*) seek tax and welfare reform, (*b*) reorganize the federal bureaucracy, (*c*) create a Cabinet-level department to coordinate energy policies, (*d*) place greater stress on preserving the environment, (*e*) increase federal aid to public education, and (*f*) support the adoption of a national health insurance system.

Ford, for the most part, ran on his record. He asserted that he had restored trust in the White House; took pride in the fact the the country was at peace; promised to continue his existing foreign policy; and reaffirmed his support of domestic policies that called for "less government, less spending, less inflation." The President portrayed Carter as inexperienced, unknown, indecisive, and deceptive.

A series of three Ford-Carter television debates, viewed by an average audience of 70 million Americans, enabled the electorate to compare the "presidential stature" of the two candidates.

4. Carter Defeats Ford. At the start of the race, opinion polls indicated that Carter had a commanding lead over Ford. His margin narrowed as the campaign progressed, and by election eve the two candidates appeared to be about even.

On election day, Carter won a narrow victory over Ford, polling 40,800,000 popular votes as against his opponent's 39,100,000. He carried only 23 states and the District of Columbia, compared to Ford's 27, but Carter's states were more heavily populated, providing him 297 electoral votes to Ford's 240.

The Democrats not only gained control of the Executive Branch for the first time in eight years, they also retained their overwhelming majorities in the Senate, the House of Representatives, and many of the nation's statehouses.

THE 39TH PRESIDENT

James Earl Carter, Jr., better known as Jimmy Carter, was born on October 1, 1924, in Plains, Georgia, where his family operated a farm and store. After attending Georgia Tech for one year, he entered the U.S. Naval Academy at Annapolis. Graduating in 1946, he served at sea for five years and then entered the Navy's nuclear submarine program. He studied nuclear physics at Union College in Schenectady, New York, and became a specialist in nuclear engineering.

Upon his father's death in 1953, he left the U.S. Navy and returned to Plains to take over the family's agribusinesses—peanut raising, cotton-ginning, and operating storage facilities. He prospered in these endeavors and also became involved in community and church affairs. Entering politics, he was elected to the Georgia State Senate in 1962, ran unsuccessfully for governor in 1966, and then won election to that office in 1970. Near the end of his four-year term, he announced his intention to run for the presidency.

Virtually unknown outside his home state, Carter appeared to have little chance of succeeding. Seeking political support, he spent a grueling two years making 1,500 speeches in a thousand cities and towns in all 50 states. Slowly but surely his persistence was rewarded. He overcame his opponents in the party primaries, gained the Democratic nomination, and went on to beat Ford in the election. By so doing, he became the first candidate from the Deep South to win the presidency since Zachary Taylor's victory in 1848.

DOMESTIC PROBLEMS AND PROGRESS

1. Energy

a. A major problem confronting the new President was the nation's dependence on imported oil. To coordinate federal energy programs and policies, Carter consolidated a number of scattered agencies into a single, Cabinet-level *Department of Energy* (1977). He also proposed a comprehensive energy program to conserve domestic supplies of oil and gas and reduce oil imports. Although Congress rejected several of his key recommendations, it did enact legislation in 1978 that (1) allowed the price of newly discovered natural gas to rise 10% a year until 1985, when all federal controls would be lifted; (2) required new industrial and utility plants to use fuels other than oil or gas; (3) ordered existing utilities to switch from oil and gas to coal or other fuels by 1990; (4) provided funds for the installation of energy-saving equipment and materials in schools and hospitals; and (5) granted tax credits to owners of homes and businesses who installed such devices.

b. In 1979 the nation's energy problem grew ever more troublesome. The cost of oil imports rose another 50% as members of the Organization of Petroleum Exporting Countries (OPEC) continued to increase their charges for this vital commodity. Since imported oil constituted one-half of U.S. supplies, these increases were reflected in sharply higher prices for gasoline, home heating oil, electricity, and other petroleum-based products and services. The situation was aggravated by a political upheaval in Iran, which curtailed U.S. imports from that source. The resulting oil shortage reduced available supplies of gasoline for the nation's motorists and caused prices to skyrocket further. The average price of gasoline rose to $1.00 per gallon in 1979 and to $1.25 in 1980.

To spur the exploration and development of new oil deposits in the United States, Carter announced that domestic oil prices would be decontrolled. Congress placed a "windfall" profits tax on the earnings of the nation's oil companies to limit the benefits they would derive from higher prices. Congress also responded favorably to the President's request that steps be taken to develop alternative energy sources. In 1980 it authorized the expenditure of $20 billion for the construction of facilities to convert coal, oil shale, and tar sands into synthetic fuels (synfuels); and created a new agency, the *Synthetic Fuels Corporation,* to administer the program.

2. Labor. Congress passed a new minimum wage bill, lifting the hourly rate over four years from $2.65 in 1978 to $3.35 in 1981. It also (*a*) raised the minimum mandatory retirement age from 65 to 70, (*b*) created a *Young Adult Conservation Corps* to provide jobs for young people, (*c*) appropriated billions of dollars to fund additional public-service jobs for the unemployed, (*d*) increased social security taxes to keep the system solvent, and (*e*) required the President to set annual goals for employment, production, and inflation with the objective of reducing the national jobless rate to 4% and inflation to 3% by 1983 (*Humphrey-Hawkins Bill*).

3. Environment. (*a*) The first federal measure to regulate strip mining of coal was enacted in 1977. It required mine owners to restore the surface of land defaced by mining operations, replant grass and trees, and prevent pollution of nearby streams. It also imposed a tax on newly mined coal to pay for the reclamation of lands previously damaged by unrestricted strip mining. (*b*) Congress in 1980 established a $1.6 billion "superfund" to pay for the cleanup of toxic wastes dumped by chemical and oil companies at various sites throughout the country. The toxic waste superfund, administered by the Environmental Protection Agency (EPA), was to be financed mainly be fees levied on the polluting industries. The legislation grew out of the discovery that a housing development in the Love Canal area of Niagara Falls, New York, had been built on an abandoned chemical dump, and that the toxic wastes were endangering the lives of the development's residents. Senator Edward Kennedy warned that as many as 1.5 million Americans might be living close to toxic waste dumps. The EPA estimated that there were 30,000 such dumps, of which it had discovered more than 600, including 100 that were extremely dangerous to human health.

4. Inflation. Carter hoped to slow inflation by persuading the public to accept voluntary wage-price guidelines. They included ceilings of 7% on pay increases and 5.75% on price rises. Businesses were required to certify their compliance and were threatened with sanctions, such as ineligibility for government contracts, if they failed to comply. Despite these and other anti-inflation measures, the cost of living spiraled ever higher. Inflation rose from 6.5% in 1977 to 9% in 1978, and to 13% in 1979. It soared to 18% in early 1980 but ended the year at 13.5%.

5. Education. All federal programs relating to education were transferred from the Department of Health, Education, and Welfare (HEW) and from other federal agencies to a new Cabinet-level *Department of Education* (1979). HEW was renamed the *Department of Health and Human Services*.

6. Census. The Census Bureau determined that the population of the United States was 226,500,000 in 1980, an increase of 23 million, or 11%, over the 1970 figure. The West had the highest rate of growth during that decade, its population rising by 24%. The South was the second fastest growing region, with an increase of 20%. The population of the Northeast remained virtually unchanged, and the Midwest increased by only 4%. The three states with the largest numerical population gains were California (+3.7 million), Texas (+3 million), and Florida (+2.9 million).

FOREIGN AFFAIRS

1. In his Inaugural Address, Carter declared that "we can never be indifferent to the fate of freedom elsewhere. Our moral sense dictates a clearcut preference for those societies which share with us an abiding respect for individual human rights." The "human rights" theme became a key element of the administration's foreign policy. The United States (*a*) warned South Africa that it could no longer rely on our support if it continued to deny equal rights to its black majority; (*b*) reduced foreign aid to Argentina, Uruguay, and Ethiopia because of human rights violations in these countries; (c) barred the sale of sophisticated computers and other advanced equipment to the Soviet Union because it suppressed free speech and restricted the right of its citizens to emigrate.

2. Treaties granting Panama control of the canal by the year 2000 were signed by the President and ratified by the Senate.

3. Late in 1978 Carter announced that the United States and the People's Republic of China had agreed to establish full diplomatic relations as of January 1, 1979. He also declared that the United States would sever diplomatic relations with the Republic of China in Taiwan and terminate its defense treaty with that government.

4. When peace talks between Egypt and Israel faltered in 1978, Carter invited the leaders of the two countries to resume negotiations at Camp David, the presidential retreat in Maryland. With his active participation, a framework for peace was agreed upon. Six months later, in March, 1979, the two leaders journeyed to Washington to sign a formal treaty of peace in the White House. Both praised Carter for his role in bringing the two sides together.

The President also promised to (*a*) build several new air bases in Israel as replacements for the installations that Israel was giving up in Sinai, (*b*) take appropriate action to prevent violations of the treaty, and (*c*) provide economic assistance and military equipment to both nations.

5. Carter signed a second arms limitation agreement (SALT II) with the Soviet Union and sent it to the Senate for ratification (1979). When the Russians invaded Afghanistan in early 1980, Carter asked the Senate to postpone consideration of the treaty. As a result, SALT II was never ratified.

A HOSTAGE CRISIS ERUPTS

Unable to quell a revolt by dissident groups opposed to his rule, the pro-Western Shah of Iran, Mohammed Reza Pahlevi, fled the country in 1979. A Muslim religious leader, *Ayatollah Ruhollah Khomeini,* assumed control, established an Islamic republic, and influenced the adoption of a constitution that granted him dictatorial powers.

After Carter permitted the ailing Shah to enter the United States for medical treatment, a mob of Iranian militants occupied the U.S. Embassy in Teheran, the capital of Iran, and took more than 50 Americans hostage (November, 1979). In exchange for the hostages, they demanded that the Shah be sent back to Iran for trial and punishment. Carter rejected the demand, denounced the embassy seizure as a violation of international law, and insisted that the hostages be released unharmed. When the militants, supported by Khomeini, turned down his request, Carter cut off American purchases of Iranian oil, froze all official Iranian assets in the United States (valued at $11 billion), and ordered the deportation of Iranian students found to be in the country illegally.

Although the Shah left the United States in December, 1979 (he died of cancer in July, 1980), the Iranians continued to hold the U.S. hostages captive. In April, 1980, Carter severed diplomatic relations with Iran and imposed an embargo on trade with that country (except for food and medicine). He also authorized the military to send airborne commandos to Iran to rescue the hostages, but called off the operation when three of the eight helicopters involved in the mission broke down en route to their destination.

In the fall of 1980 Iran presented a list of conditions for the release of the hostages. After months of negotiation, with the government of Algeria acting as an intermediary, a settlement was finally reached. The United States agreed to release the frozen Iranian assets—part to be turned over to the Khomeini government; the balance to be used to repay American banks for loans they had made to the former Shah's regime, and to settle claims of private American companies that had done business with Iran. The United States also agreed to lift its trade embargo; to refrain from interfering in Iran's internal affairs; and to track down and freeze the assets of the late Shah that were located in the United States.

In January, 1981, after 444 days of captivity, the 52 hostages were freed. Upon their return home, they were greeted as heroes and welcomed by the entire nation in a spontaneous outburst of emotion.

THE REAGAN ADMINISTRATION

PRESIDENTIAL ELECTION OF 1980

1. The Parties Choose Their Candidates. Among the leading Republican candidates for the presidency were Ronald Reagan, a former governor of California; Representative John Anderson of Illinois; Senator Howard Baker of Tennessee; and George Bush, a former member of Congress, Ambassador to the UN, and Director of the CIA. During the primaries, Reagan quickly became the front-runner, collecting enough delegate support to assure his nomination. When the Republican National Convention met in Detroit, he was chosen as the party's presidential candidate on the first ballot. George Bush became his running mate.

Senator Edward Kennedy of Massachusetts ran against Carter for the Democratic presidential nomination but failed to gain sufficient support during the primaries to be a serious contender. At the Democratic

National Convention in New York City, Carter and Mondale were renominated on the first ballot.

John Anderson, who had lost to Reagan in the Republican primaries, decided to run for the presidency as an independent.

2. Reagan Wins by a Landslide. In the campaign that followed, Carter presented himself as a proponent of peace and a supporter of the liberal traditions of the Democratic party. He called his opponent a "dangerous" extremist who would divide the nation by his policies. Reagan portrayed Carter as an ineffective leader, criticizing him for his failure (*a*) to solve the nation's problems of double-digit inflation, rising unemployment, high interest rates, and declining productivity; (*b*) to obtain the release of the American hostages in Iran; (*c*) to strengthen adequately the nation's military defenses; and (*d*) to recognize the seriousness of the Communist threat abroad.

Although most political observers predicted that the race would be close, Reagan scored an overwhelming victory at the polls. He received 43,900,000 popular votes to Carter's 35,500,000; and won 489 electoral votes from 44 states compared to Carter's 49 from 6 states and the District of Columbia. (Anderson's popular vote totalled 5,700,000.)

Reagan's landslide was broadly based. He had not only the backing of old-line conservatives and members of the "New Right," but also the support of independent voters and some traditional Democrats within the ranks of organized labor and big-city ethnic groups. The Republican tide that swept Reagan into office also enabled that party to capture control of the Senate for the first time since 1954. The Democrats, however, retained their majority in the House.

THE 40TH PRESIDENT

Ronald Wilson Reagan was born in Tampico, Illinois, on February 6, 1911. After graduating from Eureka College in 1932, he worked as a sports announcer for radio stations in Davenport and Des Moines, Iowa. In 1937 he began a long career as a motion picture actor, appearing in more than 50 films including: *Knute Rockne—All American* (1940), *King's Row* (1942), *The Hasty Heart* (1950), *The Winning Team* (1952), and *Hellcats of the Navy* (1957). He also served as president of the Screen Actors Guild (1947–1952; 1959–1960). When his movie career declined, he became a host and performer on TV.

During the presidential campaign of Barry Goldwater in 1964, Reagan gained national recognition as a persuasive spokesperson for the conservative wing of the Republican party. His success as a political speaker encouraged him to run for governor of California in 1966. He defeated his Democratic opponent, won reelection four years later, and served as governor until 1975. Seeking national office, Reagan made two unsuccessful attempts to secure nomination as the Republican presidential candidate, in 1968 and 1976. On his third try, in 1980, he finally succeeded. He won the election and became the nation's 40th President. At age 69, Reagan was the oldest person ever elected to the presidency.

Two months after his inauguration, the new President was shot in the chest in an assassination attempt. After undergoing emergency surgery for removal of a bullet, Reagan made a rapid recovery. He resumed his active presidential schedule shortly after his release from the hospital.

REAGAN IS REELECTED IN 1984

The Republicans nominated Reagan and Bush for a second term in 1984. To oppose them, the Democrats selected former Vice President Walter Mondale as their presidential candidate and Representative Geraldine Ferraro, a three-term member of Congress from New York, as his running mate. This selection marked the first time that a major party chose a woman to be a candidate for the nation's second-highest office.

The outcome of the election was never in doubt. The campaign took place during a period of economic recovery—a factor that worked in the Republicans' favor. In addition, Reagan was a popular President, projecting an image of leadership, patriotism, and optimism. As a result, he won another resounding victory, capturing 59% of the popular vote (54,500,000) to Mondale's 41% (37,500,000); and 525 electoral votes to his opponent's 13. Reagan carried 49 states; Mondale won only his home state of Minnesota and the District of Columbia.

ECONOMIC DEVELOPMENTS

1. Economic Recovery Tax Act (1981). With inflation and interest rates at double-digit levels, unemployment high, the economy stagnant, and the national debt nearing a trillion dollars, Reagan declared that "we're in the worst economic mess since the Great Depression." Promising to "try something different," he proposed a package of budget cuts and tax cuts designed to reduce the size of the federal government, slow the expansion of domestic social programs, and stimulate the growth of the economy.

Congress responded by passing the *Economic Recovery Tax Act*. The measure (*a*) cut personal income taxes by 25% over a three-year period; (*b*) lowered business taxes by liberalizing tax credits for the purchase of new machinery and other equipment and for the write-off of research and development costs; (*c*) cut back federal spending for education, environmental projects, health, housing, urban development, food stamps, and other social and cultural programs; and (*d*) cancelled the previous administration's synthetic fuel projects. (Excluded from the budget cuts were outlays for defense. Congress approved Reagan's request that military appropriations be increased to strengthen the nation's armed forces.)

2. Budget Deficits: A Persistent Problem. Reagan hoped that the tax cuts would encourage people to invest their savings in productive enterprises and provide businesses an incentive to expand. He believed that the resulting economic upsurge would increase federal revenues despite the lower tax rates. He also expected to attain a balanced budget by 1984.

But such an outcome did not materialize. A recession that started in the fall of 1981 forced many corporations to cut back production, close down plants, and lay off workers. Unemployment rose to more than 9.5% in 1982 and 1983—the highest rate since 1940. As a result, federal outlays for unemployment insurance and welfare aid increased sharply. In addition, tax revenues plummeted because of the decline in business profits, high unemployment, and the impact of the reduced tax rates.

In 1981 federal expenditures exceeded income by $79 billion. The *budget deficit* climbed sharply in succeeding years, reaching a peak of $221 billion in 1986.

3. Gramm-Rudman-Hollings Act (1985). The succession of budget deficits more than doubled the national debt between 1980 and 1988— from $900 billion to over $2.6 trillion. Just to meet interest payments on a debt of this magnitude cost the government about $185 billion a year. Alarmed at the prospect of continuing deficits and an ever-growing burden of debt, Congress enacted a balanced budget law in late 1985. It set progressively lower deficit targets each year, beginning in fiscal year 1986, and required a balanced federal budget by fiscal year 1991. It also called for automatic spending cuts if the annual targets were not met. An amendment to the act, passed in 1986, granted the Office of Management and Budget the authority to order the necessary spending cuts.

4. Inflation. A dramatic decline in the inflation rate occurred during Reagan's administration. In 1980, Carter's last year in office, consumer prices had risen 13.5%. The rate of increase dropped to 6% in 1982, 4% in 1984, and 2% in 1986, but climbed back to 3.5% in 1987 and 4.5% in 1988. Contributing to the slowing of the inflationary spiral were the following: (*a*) a sharp drop in oil prices; (*b*) the "tight money" policy of the Federal Reserve Board, which kept interest rates high and restrained overexpansion by limiting the amount of money available for loans; (*c*) the recession of 1981–1983, which decreased the demand for goods and services; (*d*) relatively small wage increases; and (*e*) competition from low-priced imports.

5. Tax Reform Act (1986). Shortly after the start of his second term, Reagan announced his support for sweeping revisions of the nation's tax laws. Calling the existing tax system "unwise, unwanted, and unfair," he proposed to cut the tax burdens of most individual taxpayers and to close "loopholes that benefit a privileged few." Most members of Congress favored the idea of tax reform but each had a different plan for its implementation. After more than a year of discussion, negotiation, and wrangling, Congress finally approved the most comprehensive changes in the federal income tax system since World War II.

Key provisions of the *Tax Reform Act of 1986* were the following:

a. For individual taxpayers, the 14 rate brackets of the old law, ranging from 11% to 50%, were replaced by two new brackets: 15% and 28%.

b. Personal exemptions (for self, spouse, dependents) were raised to $2,000 and standard deductions were increased to $3,000 for single filers and $5,000 for joint filers. As a result of these provisions, millions of low-income Americans were no longer required to pay income taxes.

c. Many personal deductions were abolished or limited. Capital gains, previously taxed at a much lower rate than other income, were now subject to the same rate as wages and salaries. And most tax shelters used by wealthy people to reduce their taxes were disallowed.

d. The top corporate tax rate was lowered from 46% to 34%.

OTHER DOMESTIC ISSUES

1. Immigration. Thousands of foreigners were entering the country illegally each year seeking employment and better living conditions. To curtail the influx of illegal aliens, Congress passed the *Immigration Reform and Control Act of 1986*. It required employers to verify the citizenship status of job applicants; prohibited the hiring of illegal aliens; and offered legal status to several million aliens who had entered the United States illegally before January 1, 1982, and had lived there continuously since that time.

2. The Environment. (*a*) In 1986 Congress approved a fivefold expansion of the program to clean up abandoned hazardous waste dumps. It authorized spending $9 billion for this purpose over a five-year period; required the Environmental Protection Agency to set standards of cleanliness; and imposed a new tax on corporations and on crude oil and motor fuel to help finance the program. The tax money would be placed in a special toxic waste "Superfund." (*b*) The *Clean Water Act*, passed in 1987 over Reagan's veto, provided $18 billion to state and local governments (over a seven-year period) for the construction of sewage treatment plants, and allocated an additional $2 billion for other programs to clean up the nation's water supplies.

3. Water Projects. A $16.3 billion program to conserve and develop the nation's water resources was approved by Congress in 1986. The first major water projects bill in 15 years, it provided federal financing for hundreds of harbor-dredging, flood-control, and other waterway improvement projects throughout the country. It also required local communities to pay part of the costs of these programs.

4. Drugs. Responding to national concerns about drug abuse, Congress passed the *Omnibus Drug Act* (1986). It increased federal penalties for drug crimes and allotted $1.7 billion for anti-drug enforcement, education, and treatment programs.

5. Social Security. With the Social Security System paying out more than it was taking in, Congress took steps to reverse the trend and assure that the system would be able to meet its obligations for years to come. To generate more revenue, the new law passed in 1983 (*a*) imposed higher Social Security payroll taxes on working people, (*b*) required middle-income and upper-income retirees to pay taxes on half of their Social Security benefits, (*c*) extended payroll taxation to employees of the federal government, and (*d*) after the year 2000, raised the age at which retired workers could draw full benefits (from age 65 to age 67).

6. Retirement. To end age discrimination in employment, Congress in 1986 abolished mandatory retirement at age 70 for most workers. Exceptions included police officers, fire fighters, tenured university faculty, and high corporate executives. (People in these categories did not come under the protection of this law until 1994.)

7. Japanese–American Reparations. "To right a grave wrong," the President signed legislation in 1988 extending apologies to the 120,000 Japanese–Americans who had been forcibly removed from their homes on the West Coast during World War II and placed in internment camps. The bill also established a $1.25 billion trust fund to pay $20,000 tax-free to each surviving internee.

8. Other Reagan Proposals. Many key items on Reagan's political agenda failed to win congressional approval. These included the adoption of a plan to allow tuition tax credits to parents who send their children to private schools; and passage of constitutional amendments to (*a*) outlaw abortion, (*b*) allow prayer in public schools, (*c*) require a balanced federal budget, and (*d*) grant a President the power to veto individual items in appropriation bills.

DEMOCRATS REGAIN CONTROL OF THE SENATE

During the first six years of his administration, Reagan enjoyed the support of a Republican-controlled Senate. In the 1986 congressional elections, the Democrats won 20 of the 34 senatorial contests, thereby increasing their representation from 47 to 55 seats and wresting control of the Senate from the Republicans. They also strengthened their hold on the House. When the 100th Congress convened in January, 1987, the Democrats occupied a majority of the seats in both houses.

FOREIGN DEVELOPMENTS

1. Grain Agreement With U.S.S.R. Reagan lifted the embargo on grain shipments to the Soviet Union that Carter had imposed in 1979 after the Russians invaded Afghanistan. He claimed that the embargo had hurt American farmers but had not harmed the Russians, since the latter could obtain all the grain they needed from Canada, Argentina, and other sources. In 1983 Reagan negotiated a new, five-year agreement with the U.S.S.R. for the purchase of American grain. It stipulated that the United States would not embargo grain shipments during the life of the pact.

2. Korean Airline Massacre. When a South Korean passenger plane, en route from Alaska to Seoul, flew off course over Soviet territory, a Russian fighter jet shot it down (1983). All 269 on board, including 61 Americans, died when the airliner plunged into the Sea of Japan. The tragedy aroused a storm of criticism around the world. In a nationally televised speech, Reagan denounced the Soviet Union for what he called "the Korean Airline Massacre." Congress unanimously adopted a resolution condemning "this cold-blooded attack" as "one of the most infamous and reprehensible acts in history."

3. Nuclear Missiles for NATO. To counter the threat of Soviet missiles targeted at NATO allies, Reagan authorized the deployment of U.S. intermediate-range nuclear missiles in Western Europe (1983). Earlier, the United States had offered to cancel its deployment plans if the Soviet Union would agree to dismantle its medium-range missiles in Eastern Europe and Asia. The Russians rejected the offer. In 1987, however, they reversed their stand and negotiated a missile agreement (the *INF Treaty*) with the United States. It obligated both countries to remove and destroy all of their shorter-range and intermediate-range missiles within three years after the treaty was ratified.

4. Strategic Defense Initiative. In 1983 Reagan proposed the Strategic Defense Initiative (SDI)—also known as "Star Wars." (See page 444.)

5. U.S. Marines in Lebanon. Reagan sent a force of U.S. marines to Lebanon to participate in a multinational effort to restore peace to that war-torn country. In October, 1983, suicidal terrorists crashed a truck loaded with powerful explosives into the marine compound at the Beirut airport, demolishing a headquarters building and killing 241 American troops. Reagan blamed fundamentalist Muslims associated with Iran and Syria for this atrocity and for other terrorist attacks on U.S. personnel and installations. As conditions in Lebanon worsened, the President ordered the marines stationed in Beirut to withdraw.

6. Grenada. When hard-line Marxists, supported by Cuba, seized control of Grenada in the fall of 1983, Reagan ordered U.S. troops to invade that Caribbean island. (See pages 433–434.)

7. *Achille Lauro* Hijacking. In October, 1985, Palestinian terrorists hijacked an Italian cruise ship, the *Achille Lauro*, in the Mediterranean Sea off the coast of Egypt. They threatened to blow up the vessel unless Israel released a number of Palestinian prisoners. (The terrorists apparently hoped that the United States and other Western countries would exert pressure on Israel to meet their demands.) After a two-day ordeal, during which an elderly, wheelchair-bound American tourist was murdered and thrown overboard, the hijackers surrendered in Egypt. In exchange, Egyptian authorities promised them safe conduct to an undisclosed location. When an Egyptian plane was flying them out of the country, U.S. Navy fighter jets intercepted the craft and forced it to land at a NATO base in Sicily. The hijackers were arrested and later tried in Italy for kidnapping and murder.

8. Terrorist Attacks in Europe. Palestinian terrorists struck again in December, 1985, this time at airports in Rome and Vienna. Hurling grenades and firing indiscriminately at travelers clustered near an Israeli airline's ticket counter, they killed 20 people and wounded more than 100 others. Five Americans died in the attacks.

Reagan accused the Libyan leader, Muammar al-Qaddafi, of promoting international terrorism and providing support to the group that had carried out the raids. Declaring Qaddafi's actions a threat to U.S. national security, the President cut off trade with Libya, ordered U.S. citizens to leave that country, and froze all Libyan government assets in the United States and in U.S. bank branches overseas.

9. Disputes With Libya. In the spring of 1986 a dispute over the status of the Gulf of Sidra led to a military confrontation between the United States and Libya. Qaddafi asserted that the entire waterway was part of Libya. Americans contended that Libyan jurisdiction did not extend to more than 12 miles offshore from that country's coastline. Declaring Qaddafi's claim a violation of freedom of the seas, Reagan authorized U.S. planes to overfly the gulf. When Libya fired missiles at the aircraft, U.S. Navy planes attacked and sank two Libyan patrol boats and knocked out a missile site on the Libyan coast.

Another clash occurred several weeks later after a bomb explosion in West Berlin destroyed a discotheque frequented by U.S. military personnel. The blast killed two people and injured hundreds of others. Reagan blamed Libya for the bombing, stating that he had "irrefutable" proof of Qaddafi's involvement in its planning and execution. In retaliation, Reagan ordered air strikes on strategic sites in the Libyan cities of Tripoli and Benghazi. Targets included barracks, military airfields, and a port reportedly used as a training camp for terrorists.

10. Apartheid. Seeking to exert pressure on the government of South Africa to change its policies of racial separation (*apartheid*), Congress passed a bill imposing stiff economic sanctions on that country. The legislation banned all new investments by Americans in South African enterprises; prohibited the importation of South African steel, iron, coal, uranium, textiles, and agricultural products; forbade the export of crude oil, oil products, and munitions to South Africa; and cancelled landing rights in the United States for South African airlines.

Reagan vetoed the bill, contending that "punitive sanctions" would weaken that country's economy, increase unemployment, and thereby hurt the blacks—"the very people they are intended to help." By more than a two-thirds vote, both the House and the Senate overrode the President's veto, and the sanctions bill became law (1986).

11. Nicaragua. Fearing the establishment of a Soviet-dominated, Cuban-style Marxist state in Nicaragua, Reagan adopted a tough policy toward the Sandinista-controlled government in that country. (See pages 430–433.)

12. Iran. Reagan had often accused Iran of being a major sponsor of international terrorism. He claimed that Lebanese Arabs loyal to Iran were responsible for (*a*) the 1983 bombings of the U.S. Embassy and U.S. marine barracks in Beirut—terrorist attacks that had caused more than 250 American deaths, and (*b*) the seizure of a number of American hostages in Lebanon. Blaming Iran for complicity in these anti-American acts, Reagan instituted an embargo on the sale of arms to that country and urged America's allies to do likewise.

13. The Iran-Contra Affair. In late 1986 the nation was startled to learn that (*a*) despite the embargo, the Reagan administration had secretly sold arms to Iran and (*b*) certain top government officials had used the profits from the sales to finance the Nicaraguan rebels. Since these transactions had taken place during the period when Congress had banned official U.S. assistance to the contras, the disclosures touched off a major scandal that became known as the "Iran-Contra Affair."

Speculation quickly arose over which administration personnel had been involved in the affair, whether they had engaged in unlawful acts, and whether their activities warranted criminal prosecution. Official inquiries and investigations were carried out by several groups seeking answers to these questions.

a. The Senate Select Committee on Intelligence concluded that the President's Iranian arms initiative was prompted by (1) a desire to gain Iran's support for freeing American hostages held by pro-Iranian Arabs in Lebanon, and (2) an interest in establishing a relationship with "moderate" elements in the Iranian government.

b. The Tower Commission, a special panel appointed by Reagan to look into the matter, found that the National Security Council was largely responsible for organizing the Iran arms sales and transferring the proceeds to the contras. Reporting on the President's role in the affair, the commission (1) accepted his statement that he had no knowledge of the diversion of Iranian arms profits to the contras, but (2) criticized him for failing to control the actions of the NSC.

c. Special committees of both houses of Congress conducted their own investigations. Their combined report asserted that a "cabal of zealots" in the administration had managed to take control of foreign policy in key areas. It declared that President Reagan bore "the ultimate responsibility" for wrongdoing by his aides.

d. An independent counsel, or special prosecutor, was selected to conduct a separate investigation to determine if any criminal indictments were warranted. One Reagan official was tried and found guilty of withholding information from Congress. Another was convicted of obstructing Congress by altering, destroying, concealing, and removing documents relating to the Iran-Contra Affair. Still others were charged with conspiring to defraud the government.

THE BUSH ADMINISTRATION

PRESIDENTIAL ELECTION OF 1988

1. Many Presidential Candidates Enter the Race. In early 1988, the two major parties held a series of statewide primaries and caucuses to select delegates to their respective national conventions. Seeking delegate support for their candidacy were such prominent Republicans as Vice President Bush, Senator Robert Dole of Kansas, Representative Jack Kemp of New York, and the popular TV evangelist Pat Robertson. Among the leading Democratic presidential candidates were former Arizona governor Bruce Babbitt, Senator Joseph Biden of Delaware, Governor Michael Dukakis of Massachusetts, Representative Richard Gephardt of Missouri, Senator Albert Gore of Tennessee, civil rights activist the Reverend Jesse Jackson, and Senator Paul Simon of Illinois.

2. The Democrats Select Dukakis. The large number of contenders for the Democratic nomination began to dwindle as the selection process took its toll. Some candidates withdrew because they failed to attract sufficient delegate support. Others were unable to raise enough money to continue campaigning. Toward the end of April, only Dukakis and Jackson remained in the race. Dukakis took a commanding lead over Jackson in the national delegate count by scoring a sweeping victory in the Pennsylvania primary. He moved farther ahead in May by carrying Ohio and Indiana, and brought his campaign to a successful end in June by winning California and New Jersey.

Jackson, who scored the second-highest delegate count in the Democratic primaries, earned the distinction of becoming the first black American to receive substantial national support in a presidential campaign.

At the Democratic National Convention, held in Atlanta in July, the delegates selected Dukakis as the party's presidential candidate and approved his choice of Senator Lloyd Bentsen of Texas as the vice presidential nominee.

3. The Republicans Nominate Bush. Although Bush got off to a poor start in the primaries, finishing third in the Iowa caucuses, he made a strong comeback in the contests that followed. He outpolled his rivals in New Hampshire, performed well in the numerous state primaries that were held on "Super Tuesday," and scored a clear win over Dole, his chief competitor, in Illinois. Unable to overtake the frontrunner, Bush's opponents withdrew from the race, thereby assuring his nomination. Bush became the official Republican nominee in August at the party's convention in New Orleans.

As his running mate, Bush chose James Danforth (Dan) Quayle, a young and relatively unknown U.S. senator from Indiana.

4. The Candidates Compete for Election. During the fall campaign, Bush asserted that his years of experience in national affairs made him better qualified for the nation's highest office than did Dukakis's service as a governor. Dukakis countered by stressing the importance of competence. He presented his record as governor of Massachusetts as proof of his ability to maintain a balanced budget, to improve economic conditions in his state, and to manage public affairs efficiently. He accused the Reagan administration of mismanagement and incompetence, citing such examples as (a) the ever-growing federal budget deficit, (b) the unethical conduct of many Reagan appointees (the "sleaze factor"), and (c) the failure to stem the flow of illegal drugs into the country, to curb crime, and to reduce environmental pollution.

On national defense and foreign policy issues, Bush favored continuing Reagan's massive military buildup (including the addition of new weapons systems), SDI ("Star Wars") research and testing, and aid to the Nicaraguan contras. Dukakis proposed a leveling-off of defense expenditures, opposed the deployment of SDI weapons in space, and disapproved of further contra aid.

Seeking to widen the gap between himself and his opponent, Bush portrayed Dukakis as a "dangerous liberal" who supported abortion, advocated gun control, and opposed capital punishment. In speeches and TV commercials, Bush charged that Dukakis was soft on crime. Bush questioned Dukakis's patriotism. Although many political observers criticized Bush's campaign tactics as negative and trivial, they proved to be very effective. As the weeks progressed, public opinion polls showed Bush pulling steadily ahead of Dukakis.

5. Bush Defeats Dukakis. On election day, Bush received 54% of the popular vote (49,900,000) compared to Dukakis's 46% (41,900,000). Bush won 426 electoral votes from 40 states as against 112 from 10 states and the District of Columbia for his Democratic opponent. (Dukakis's electoral count later dropped to 111 when an elector from West Virginia chose Bentsen for President and Dukakis for Vice President.)

Although the Republicans succeeded in retaining the presidency, they were unable to gain control of either the Senate or the House. When the first session of the 101st Congress opened in January, 1989, there were 55 Democrats and 45 Republicans in the Senate; and 259 Democrats and 174 Republicans in the House. (Two seats were vacant.)

THE 41ST PRESIDENT

George Herbert Walker Bush was born in Milton, Massachusetts, on June 12, 1924, and grew up in Greenwich, Connecticut. After graduating from Phillips Academy in Andover, Massachusetts, in 1942, 18-year-old George enlisted in the navy. He progressed from enlisted man to officer (becoming the navy's youngest pilot), saw action in the Pacific, and was decorated for bravery. At the end of World War II, Bush enrolled at Yale, where he majored in economics and earned a B.A. in 1948. Turning down an offer to join his father's investment banking firm on Wall Street, Bush headed for Texas. He took a job with a petroleum machinery company there. Then he established his own oil exploration, drilling, and equipment business.

Seeking to represent Texas in the U.S. Congress, Bush ran unsuccessfully for the Senate in 1964; won election to the House of Representatives two years later; and lost a second bid for the Senate in 1970. President Nixon named him Ambassador to the UN in 1970 and later designated him to be chairman of the Republican National Committee. President Ford in 1974 sent him to China to serve as head of the U.S. Liaison office in Beijing and later appointed him Director of the Central Intelligence Agency (CIA).

In 1980 Bush decided to make a run for the presidency, but he lost out to Reagan in the primaries. Selected as Reagan's running mate, he was elected Vice President that year and again in 1984. Four years later, he was chosen to head the Republican ticket, won the election, and became the nation's 41st President.

DOMESTIC HIGHLIGHTS

1. Census. Totals issued by the Census Bureau indicated that the nation's population was 249,500,000 in 1990—an increase of 23 million, or 10%, over the 1980 figures. Most of the growth was in the West and South, with California gaining 6.2 million residents, Florida, 3.3 million, and Texas, 2.8 million. More than 25% of the increase was due to immigration, with nearly 6 million people coming to our shores during the 1980's (largely from Asia and Latin America).

The census data required a shift of 19 seats in the House of Representatives. California gained seven; Florida, four; Texas, three; and five other states, one each. New York lost three seats; Pennsylvania, Ohio, Michigan, and Illinois, two each; and eight other states, one each.

2. Budget. To reduce the federal deficit, Congress passed a bill in 1990 that increased taxes by $140 billion over five years. The measure (*a*) raised the top income tax rate from 28% to 31%, (*b*) phased out exemptions for upper-income taxpayers, (*c*) increased excise taxes on gasoline, cigarettes, and alcohol, and (*d*) imposed a "luxury tax" on expensive cars, yachts, airplanes, and furs. The new law also cut spending on Medicaid, Medicare, federal pensions, and student loans.

3. Minumum Wage. Effective in 1991, the minimum wage was increased from $3.35 to $4.25 an hour.

4. Basic Rights for the Disabled. *The Americans With Disabilities Act* banned discrimination in employment, public accommodations, communications, and transportation against people with a physical or mental condition that substantially limited major life activities (such as seeing, hearing, or walking). The classification of disabled included victims of AIDS, drug addicts, and alcoholics undergoing treatment.

5. Savings and Loan Bailout. Like other banking institutions, savings and loan associations (more commonly called S & L's or "thrifts") take in deposits from the public and lend the money out to borrowers. Unlike banks, however, S & L's traditionally concern themselves with financing home purchases by providing long-term mortgage loans. During the 1980's, the Reagan administration deregulated the S & L's, allowing them to make loans to and investments in a wide range of commercial enterprises. Taking advantage of the new opportunities open to them, many thrifts overextended themselves by making risky and even reckless investments—particularly in real estate. Some also attempted to increase their income by purchasing high-interest "junk bonds."

As the U.S. economy weakened in the late 1980's, numerous S & L-financed ventures defaulted on their loans, driving dozens of thrifts into insolvency. By the time President Bush assumed office, the number of troubled S & L's reached into the hundreds. Since the federal government insures depositors' accounts up to $100,000, it was forced to intervene and rescue the failed institutions. Congress authorized the expenditure of billions of dollars to close or merge insolvent thrifts, and created a Resolution Trust Corporation to administer the program and dispose of the properties held by failed S & L's. The Congressional Budget Office predicted that the bailout would continue until 1995, would involve the closing or merger of 1,500 institutions, and would cost American taxpayers about $200 billion.

Federal investigations of the S & L crisis led to the indictment of hundreds of thrift directors and officers for fraud and other crimes. In addition, investors in failed thrifts filed lawsuits against many S & L officials, contending that they had abused their positions by paying themselves extravagant salaries and spending large sums on travel, entertainment, and other personal, non-business activities.

By permission of Mike Luckovich and Creators Syndicate

FOREIGN AFFAIRS

1. Invasion of Panama. Although nominally the head of Panama's defense forces, General Manuel Noriega was, in fact, that country's dictator. He controlled the legislature, ruthlessly suppressed opposition to his rule, violated the rights of Panamanian citizens, and was believed to be involved in the smuggling of illegal drugs to the United States. In 1988 the Reagan administration became openly involved in supporting local Panamanian efforts to oust Noriega. Two U.S. federal grand juries indicted him on charges of drug trafficking and racketeering. The U.S. government froze Panamanian assets on deposit in U.S. banks and withheld payments due Panama from the operation of the Panama Canal and the pipeline that transports oil across the isthmus.

In the spring of 1989, under the watchful eye of international observers (including former U.S. President Jimmy Carter), Panama held an election to select a new president. When Noriega's hand-picked choice was decisively defeated by an opposition candidate, Guillermo Endara, Noriega influenced the legislature to annul the election, claiming foreign interference. Bush, who had succeeded Reagan as President earlier that year, declared that Endara had won a clear-cut victory and called on Panamanians to overthrow Noriega. A group of army officers attempted to oust Noriega in October but the coup failed. Noriega asserted that U.S. armed forces guarding the Panama Canal had participated in the plot against him. He requested the legislature to appoint him head of government and to declare the U.S. and Panama to be in a state of war.

Following a series of threats and attacks upon Americans in Panama, including the killing of an unarmed U.S. marine by Panamanian soldiers, Bush sent in military forces to protect American lives and to capture Noriega (December, 1989). The invading troops seized the headquarters of the Panama Defense Forces, as well as military and strategic locations in and around Panama City. Noriega surrendered, was taken to Miami, Florida, and held there for trial. Found guilty of drug trafficking, money laundering, and racketeering, he was sentenced to a 40-year prison term. Endara was sworn in as president of Panama; and most United States forces were withdrawn from the embattled country in early 1990.

2. Operation Desert Storm. When Saddam Hussein, Iraq's dictatorial leader, overran Kuwait in August, 1990, Bush denounced the attack as "naked aggression." He quickly banned U.S. trade with Iraq, froze Iraqi and Kuwaiti assets in the United States, and dispatched an aircraft carrier battle group to the Persian Gulf. He also rallied international support for collective action against the aggressor.

With Kuwait in his possession, Hussein was in position to invade neighboring Saudi Arabia—a country with the world's largest petroleum deposits. To forestall such a possibility, Bush sent a strong military force to defend that desert kingdom. Other nations followed America's lead, but on a smaller scale. During the next 10 months, Saudi Arabia and the Persian Gulf region became the focus of one of the largest arms buildups in American military history. Stationed in the area were more than half a million U.S. troops, thousands of tanks and armored vehicles, nearly 2,000 warplanes, half a dozen aircraft carriers, and numerous other naval vessels. In addition, 27 allied nations were represented by soldiers, planes, tanks, and warships of their own.

After repeated efforts to persuade Hussein to withdraw from Kuwait failed, the United States and its allies launched a military campaign to drive him out. The combined forces were led by an American general, H. Norman Schwarzkopf. Code-named "Operation Desert Storm," the Persian Gulf War began in mid-January, 1991, with a series of massive air strikes against strategic targets in Iraq and Kuwait. Allied warplanes quickly drove the Iraqi air force from the skies and carried out thousands of bombing missions against enemy military installations. The air campaign lasted for more than five weeks. In late February, after Hussein ignored a final warning by Bush that the Iraqis withdraw or face destruction, allied ground forces stormed into the occupied country from bases in Saudi Arabia. In lightning-fast fashion, mobile armored units routed the Iraqis, destroyed their weapons and military equipment, took thousands of prisoners, and forced the demoralized survivors to beat a hasty retreat to Iraq. The ground war ended 100 hours after it began. On February 27, 1991, Bush declared that "Kuwait is liberated" and ordered allied forces to suspend offensive operations against Hussein's battered army. A short while later, the United States began to dismantle its bases in the Gulf area and to send its military personnel home. (See pages 394–395.)

THE CLINTON ADMINISTRATION

PRESIDENTIAL ELECTION OF 1992

1. The Democrats Choose Clinton. The chief contenders for the Democratic presidential nomination in 1992 were former Governor Jerry Brown of California, Governor Bill Clinton of Arkansas, Senator Tom Harkin of Iowa, Senator Bob Kerrey of Nebraska, and former Senator Paul Tsongas of Massachusetts. Other prominent Democrats decided not to enter the race because they believed that the Republicans would win the election easily as a result of Bush's successful management of the Persian Gulf War.

Failing to attract sufficient support in the early state primaries and caucuses, and unable to raise enough money to continue campaigning, Harkin, Kerrey, and Tsongas soon dropped out of the contest. Clinton, who had become the front-runner, maintained his lead over his remaining competitor (Brown) in the primaries that followed. Upon winning in California, New Jersey, Ohio, and three other states in June, Clinton succeeded in capturing enough delegates to clinch the nomination.

When the Democratic National Convention convened in New York City in July, the delegates chose Clinton as the party's nominee for president and approved his choice of Senator Albert (Al) Gore, Jr., of Tennessee as the vice presidential candidate.

2. The Republicans Select Bush. The choice of a Republican presidential candidate was marked by a contest between George Bush and Pat Buchanan, a conservative newspaper columnist and TV talk-show personality. Buchanan criticized Bush for spending too much time on foreign affairs, ignoring the U.S. economy, and breaking his "no new taxes" promise to the American people. Although Buchanan drew many votes in the various state primaries, ranging from 37% in New Hampshire to 26% in California, Bush amassed sufficient delegate support to assure his nomination.

At the party's national convention in Houston in early August, the Republicans renominated Bush for President and Dan Quayle for Vice President.

3. Perot Runs as an Independent. H. Ross Perot was a Texas billionaire who had made his fortune as the founder and operator of a highly successful electronic data-processing business. Criticizing the leaders of both major parties for their mismanagement of the nation's economy, he declared in March that he would seek the presidency as an independent if his supporters obtained enough petitions to place his name on the ballots of all 50 states. Volunteers working on his behalf succeeded in reaching this goal by September. To finance their efforts and to gain national recognition, Perot spent about $60 million of his own money, mostly on TV ads.

4. The Candidates Campaign for Election. At the start of the campaign it appeared that Bush would be reelected easily. He enjoyed a high approval rating in public opinion polls for his leadership role in the war against Iraq, and for serving as President during the collapse of communism in eastern Europe and the Soviet Union. But it soon became apparent that the outcome of the election was unpredictable. People were unhappy about the country's persistent economic problems, uneasy about the future, and concerned about the ever-mounting national debt. Many were critical of the administration's inability to restore prosperity, and seemed ready for a change.

With the unemployment rate at an 8-year high and the number of families with incomes below the poverty line at the highest level in 9 years, Clinton focused his campaign on economic issues. He vowed to restore the economy, reduce joblessness, raise the income level of the neediest, and help "the forgotten middle class." He called for an expenditure of $200 billion over 4 years on the nation's cities, public works, education, and the training of workers. He proposed to raise $150 billion in new taxes over 4 years by increasing rates for wealthy Americans and reducing tax breaks for corporations. He also promised to lower annual federal budget deficits by 50% within 4 years.

Bush blamed the nation's economic problems on the failure of the Democratic-controlled Congress to implement his recommendations. He criticized Clinton's proposals as a "tax and spend" program and asserted that his opponent's economic plan was based on "smoke and mirrors." Declaring that the economy was on the road to recovery, Bush came out for "across the board" tax cuts, a lower capital gains tax, and a cap on all entitlement programs except Social Security.

On other issues, Bush stressed his commitment to traditional "family values," and claimed that only he had the experience and character to lead the nation. Referring to controversial reports about Clinton's draft record and activities during the Vietnam War, Bush accused him of failing to "come clean with the American people."

Describing himself as a Washington outsider, Perot promised to operate the government in an efficient and businesslike fashion, to end legislative gridlock, and to eliminate the federal budget deficit in 5 years. Many people responded favorably to his folksy and forthright presentations. He lost much of his momentum by abruptly dropping out of the race in July, but regained a number of his followers when he resumed campaigning in October.

The candidates sought to arouse voter interest by touring the country, addressing mass rallies, appearing on popular TV talk shows, and engaging in three televised presidential debates. (The vice presidential candidates also held one TV debate of their own.)

5. Clinton Emerges the Victor. In the November election, Clinton won 43% of the popular vote (43,700,000), compared to Bush's 38% (38,100,000) and Perot's 19% (19,200,000). Perot's showing was the best for a third party or independent candidate since Theodore Roosevelt's unsuccessful attempt to regain the presidency in 1912. Clinton collected 370 electoral votes from 32 states and the District of Columbia; Bush acquired 168 from 18 states; and Perot received none.

The Democrats also succeeded in retaining control of Congress. But the makeup of both houses was substantially changed. An unusual number of senators and representatives had chosen not to seek reelection. Others had been defeated in the primaries or in the general election. As a result, more newcomers were elected to Congress than in any year since 1948, including a record number of women, blacks, and Hispanics. Noteworthy was the election of the first African American woman, Carol Mosely-Braun of Illinois, to the Senate.

THE 42ND PRESIDENT

William Jefferson Blythe was born in Hope, Arkansas, on August 16, 1946. Several months before his birth, his father was killed in an automobile accident. His mother later married Roger Clinton and, at the age of 15, William Blythe legally changed his name to William Clinton. He attended Georgetown University of Washington, D.C., earning a B.S. degree in international affairs; won a Rhodes scholarship to Oxford University in England; and obtained a law degree from Yale University. Here he met a fellow law student, Hillary Rodham, whom he married in 1975. After graduating, he taught at the University of Arkansas and practiced law.

Clinton ran unsuccessfully for Congress in 1974, won election as attorney general of Arkansas three years later, and became governor of the state in 1978. He lost a 1980 reelection bid, but won again in 1982, retaining the governorship for the next ten years. Named one of the most effective governors in the nation by a national poll of governors, Clinton gained national recognition as chairman of the National Governors Association and as cofounder and head of the moderate Democratic Leadership Council.

In the fall of 1991, Clinton announced his candidacy for the presidency. His campaign faltered at the start because of criticism of his draft record during the Vietnam War, but he gained in strength as he proceeded to outline his program to solve the nation's problems. He then went on to win the election.

At age 46, Clinton became the youngest President since John F. Kennedy. He also was the first member of the post-World War II generation of "baby boomers" to occupy the White House.

DOMESTIC LEGISLATION (1993-1994)

1. Omnibus Budget Reconciliation Act. Clinton submitted an economic program to Congress that aimed to lower the federal deficit by nearly $500 billion over five years. His proposal encountered opposition from Republicans, special interest groups, Perot supporters, and conservative Democrats. They all complained that it relied too heavily on tax increases and not enough on spending cuts. After months of negotiations, a watered-down version was finally passed in August, 1993, by a slim margin of 218 to 216 in the House and a tie-breaking vote by Vice President Gore in the Senate.

Key provisions of the act were the following:

a. Marginal income tax rates were raised from 31% to 36% on taxable incomes above $115,00 for single taxpayers and $140,000 for married couples.

b. An additional surcharge of 10% was imposed on earnings over $250,000, making the effective tax rate 39.6%.

c. The capital gains tax rate was kept at 28%.

d. The portion of Social Security benefits subject to taxation was increased from 50% to 85% for retired couples earning more than $44,000 and single retirees earning more than $34,000.

e. A wage earner's entire salary was made subject to the Medicare payroll tax.

f. The top corporate tax rate was raised from 34% to 35%.

g. The federal tax on gasoline was increased by 4.3¢ a gallon.

Along with the anticipated $250 billion in new revenue that would be obtained from these taxes, the Clinton administration projected that spending cuts over the next five years would reduce the federal deficit by an additional $250 billion. Such savings would be derived from curbing military expenditures, capping Medicare and Medicaid costs, downsizing federal agencies, and curtailing government-funded projects.

2. Family and Medical Leave Act. This bill, passed in 1993, permitted government personnel and employees of companies having 50 or more workers to take up to 12 weeks of unpaid leave a year to deal with the birth or adoption of a child, or with an illness suffered by the employee or a member of his or her family. It obligated the employer to continue health care benefits during the leave and to guarantee the employee's right to return to work.

3. National Voter Registration Act. To facilitate voter registration, Congress approved a bill, popularly named the "motor-voter law," requiring states to allow citizens to register to vote when they apply for or renew their driver's license. The new law also provided citizens the opportunity to register to vote at welfare offices as well as by mail.

4. National Service Program. Sponsored by Clinton and enacted by Congress, it allotted $1.5 billion for a three-year program that would enable 100,000 volunteers to perform community service. The Ameri-Corps participants, mostly young people, would work for up to two years in such public-service areas as education, health and human services, environmental improvement, and public safety. They would receive minimum wages, free health care, and a $4,725 voucher for each year of service. The vouchers could be applied toward educational expenses at a college, university, or technical school.

Part of the program's funds would be granted to schools to encourage them to initiate student projects related to community service.

5. Gun Control (Brady Bill). Named for James Brady, the White House press secretary who was badly wounded during an attempted assassination of President Reagan in 1981, this act required a five-day waiting period for the purchase of a handgun and created a national computer network to enable dealers to check whether a prospective gun buyer is a minor or a drug addict or has a criminal record.

6. Omnibus Violent Crime Control and Prevention Act. This $30 billion crime bill, whose cost would be covered by the elimination of 265,000 federal jobs over six years, (*a*) authorized cities, counties, and towns to hire 100,000 additional police officers, (*b*) allotted funds for the construction of new state prisons, (*c*) expanded the number of federal crimes that are punishable by death, (*d*) banned the manufacture and sale of 19 kinds of semiautomatic assault weapons, and (*e*) provided money for community crime-prevention programs.

The new law also included a "three strikes and you're out" provision that would impose a life sentence upon anyone convicted of a federal crime who had two prior convictions for serious state or federal felonies.

REJECTED PROPOSALS

1. Economic Stimulus Plan. To spur the economy and reduce long-term unemployment, Clinton asked Congress to enact a $16.3 billion economic stimulus bill that would fund public works projects, aid education, and improve social services. Although it passed the House, the bill died in the Senate because the Democrats were unable to garner the 60 votes needed to break a Republican filibuster against it.

2. Health Care Reform. To control soaring medical costs and provide secure medical coverage to all Americans, Clinton proposed a restructuring of the nation's health care system. His plan offered financial incentives to encourage consumers to join low-cost health maintenance organizations (HMO's) and push doctors, hospitals, and insurers to form networks. Large, regional "health alliances," run by the states under federal oversight, would purchase health insurance from insurance companies or from groups of health care providers, collect and distribute premiums, and offer a number of different health plans to consumers in their region.

Although few quarreled with the plan's goals of universal coverage, cost control, and quality care, disagreement over its implementation was widespread. After repeated efforts to negotiate an acceptable compromise failed, the President's ambitious and controversial plan died in Congress.

TRADE PACTS

1. North America Free Trade Agreement (NAFTA). Under negotiation for more than three years (dating back to the Bush administration), NAFTA was ratified in 1993 by the legislatures of Canada and Mexico and approved by the U.S. Congress. The agreement provided for the gradual abolition of tariffs and other trade barriers among the three countries, thereby creating the largest free-trade zone in the world. To address the concerns of certain industries and labor groups over competition from cheap foreign goods and low wages, the Clinton administration negotiated several side agreements and special deals to benefit U.S. agricultural and industrial interests. The three countries also agreed to cooperate in monitoring environmental abuses and to set up a process for investigating labor abuses.

2. World Trade Organization (WTO). A *General Agreement on Tariffs and Trade (GATT)*, negotiated by the United States and other major economic powers in 1948, had been frequently amended over the years. The eighth round of such talks (the Uruguay Round) was completed in 1993. The following year, Congress approved U.S. participation in the new agreement.

Taking effect on July 1, 1995, the agreement (*a*) reduced tariffs on manufactured goods and agricultural products by an average one-third, (*b*) barred countries from using quotas to limit imports, (*c*) protected intellectual property such as patents, copyrights, trade secrets, and trade-marks (to curb piracy of books, movies, compact disks, computer software, and prescription drugs), and (*d*) created a *World Trade Organization (WTO)* with the power to enforce the new trade pact and assess penalties against member nations that violate the accord.

THE REPUBLICANS WIN A SWEEPING VICTORY IN 1994

In the midterm elections of 1994, the Republicans scored a major upset, winning control of both houses of Congress for the first time since 1952. Their margin in the Senate was 53–47 and in the House, 230-204 (with one independent). Their success at the state level was equally dramatic. They made a net gain of 11 governorships, and now controlled three-fifths of the nation's statehouses, including those of seven of the eight largest states.

During the election campaign, many Republican candidates for House seats endorsed a set of proposals for legislative actions that they called their "Contract With America." This program was initiated by Representative Newt Gingrich from Georgia, who became the Speaker of the House when the 104th Congress convened in January, 1995.

THE REPUBLICANS SEEK TO FULFILL THEIR "CONTRACT WITH AMERICA"

Under the leadership of Newt Gingrich, the Republican-dominated House made a determined effort in 1995 to implement the Contract With America. Its legislative roster included such issues as term limits; a balanced budget; a line-item veto; reform of welfare, judicial, and product-liability laws; eliminating numerous federal agencies and programs; and transferring several federal functions to the states. Although the House quickly passed many items on the Contract agenda, the Senate delayed action on some of them, and the President vetoed others after they had been approved by both houses.

Two constitutional amendments that were high on the Republican priority list also failed to pass. One, placing 12-year limits on congressional service, was rejected by the House. The other, requiring a balanced federal budget by the year 2002, passed the House but was narrowly defeated in the Senate.

A budget deadlock between Congress and the Clinton administration led to a partial shutdown of the federal government for six days in November, 1995, and for 21 days in the following two months. The dispute was finally resolved in 1996 when the Republicans agreed to drop some of their demands for large spending cuts, and Clinton agreed to accept a seven-year plan to balance the federal budget.

In 1996 the Republicans began to realize that their "revolution" had lost much of its appeal. A number of people viewed the Republican push to control Medicare and other federal entitlements as threats to their well-being. Many also disapproved the Republican tactics of forcing the government to furlough thousands of employees and shut down some of its operations to compel Clinton to accept huge spending cuts. In addition, the emergence of a bloc of centrist Republicans and Democrats within Congress itself impeded the efforts of the Contract's supporters. As a result, congressional leaders decided to adopt a more moderate legislative agenda to justify themselves to the nation's voters.

DOMESTIC LEGISLATION (1995–1996)

1. Congressional Accountability Act. This law granted congressional employees the same employment and civil rights protection that most U.S. workers already enjoyed.

2. Unfunded Mandate Reform Act. To ease financial burdens, this law barred Congress from imposing new mandates (requirements) on states and cities without providing federal money to pay for them.

3. Abolition of the Interstate Commerce Commission. With the advent of deregulation in the 1980's, the ICC lost most of its powers to set transportation rates. Nevertheless, it continued to exist until 1996, when the agency was dissolved.

4. Minimum Wage. Responding to public opinion polls that revealed overwhelming support for an increase in the minimum wage, Congress raised the rate from $4.25 to $4.75 effective October 1, 1996, and to $5.15 on September 1, 1997.

5. Line-Item Veto. For many years, reformers had sought to give a President the right to eliminate specific items from a spending bill while approving the rest of it. Such a procedure would enable the Chief Executive to veto "pork" or other unacceptable items in the bill without requiring him or her to reject it entirely and return it to Congress for reconsideration. This so-called *line-item veto* was passed by Congress in 1996 and signed by President Clinton. (Exempt from the line-item veto were such entitlement programs as Medicare and Social Security as well as broad-based tax cuts.)

6. Telecommunications Reform Act. With bipartisan support, Congress passed a landmark law that aimed to transform the nation's communications industry. It lifted existing government controls and promoted a free-for-all rivalry for customers among local telephone companies, long-distance carriers, and cable television operators. It was hoped that such competition would benefit consumers by lowering prices, improving service, and introducing innovative new products.

7. Health Insurance Portability and Accountability Act. Jointly sponsored by Democratic Senator Edward Kennedy of Massachusetts and Republican Senator Nancy Kassebaum of Kansas, this law enables workers to transfer their health insurance from job to job and protects insured workers who have pre-existing medical problems from losing their coverage if they change jobs.

8. Freedom to Farm Act. Initiated during the 1930's, the federal farm subsidy program aimed to limit surpluses of agricultural products and thereby prevent prices of these products from falling. In 1996 Congress decided to phase out government controls and allow farmers to decide for themselves which crops to grow and how much land to cultivate. Instead of subsidies, farmers would receive a declining schedule of "transition payments," which would end in seven years.

9. Upgrading Drinking Water. Congress approved a measure to revise federal drinking water standards and help states finance improvements in municipal water systems. It required municipal water suppliers to control harmful pollutants in tap water and extended federal loans to the states for local water projects.

10. Welfare Reform. During the 1992 presidential campaign, Clinton promised to "end welfare as we know it." And in the congressional races of 1994, the Republicans listed welfare reform as a key item in their "Contract With America." Although both Democrats and Republicans recognized the need for change in this area, for a long time they could not reconcile their differences. After rejecting two congressional bills that called for a major overhaul of welfare, the President reluctantly accepted a third, signing it into law in August, 1996, even though he called the measure "flawed."

Affecting most of the nearly 13 million people on welfare and many of the 25 million who receive food stamps, this landmark law effectively ended welfare as a federal entitlement. It reversed 60 years of social policy that dated back to the New Deal. Among its provisions were the following:

a. The federal guarantee of monthly cash benefits to poor families with children would be terminated.

b. Each state would receive a lump sum, or block grant, of federal money to run its own welfare and job programs.

c. The head of every family on welfare would have to find work within two years, or the family would lose its benefits. After receiving welfare for two months, adults would be required to perform community service (popularly known as *workfare*).

d. Lifetime welfare benefits would be limited to five years. (Some hardship exemptions, however, would be available.)

e. A state could provide payments to an unmarried parent under 18 only if she or he stays in school and lives with an adult.

f. To assure a full federal grant, a state would have to maintain a welfare spending level of at least 75% (and sometimes 80%) of its 1994 level.

g. Supplementary Security Income (SSI) and food stamps would end for non-citizens now receiving benefits.

h. Future immigrants who have not become citizens would be ineligible for most federal welfare benefits and social services during their first five years in the United States.

i. The federal guarantee of food stamps for poor people would be retained, but this program would be cut by $24 billion over six years. Also preserved was Medicaid for people who had qualified for welfare under previous laws.

PRESIDENTIAL ELECTION OF 1996

1. The Candidates. Unchallenged in the primaries, Clinton became the Democratic party choice for President for the second time. (Once again his running mate was Al Gore.) Among the Republicans who sought to compete against Clinton were former Senate Majority Leader Robert (Bob) Dole of Kansas; Patrick Buchanan, a conservative columnist and television commentator; and Steve Forbes, a magazine publisher. Strongly supported by most middle-of-the-road Republicans, Dole gained his party's nomination. H. Ross Perot, who had run in 1992 as an independent, entered the race as the nominee of the Reform party (which he had formed).

2. The Campaign. Stressing economic issues, Clinton claimed that 10 million jobs had been created during his first term. He further stressed that the unemployment rate was at its lowest level in many years, inflation had been kept in check, and stock prices had risen to new highs. Dole rebutted by claiming that economic growth was sluggish and that many of the new jobs created recently were low paying. He blamed the slow growth of the economy on Clinton's Budget Reconciliation Act of 1993, which had raised taxes on upper middle class Americans. (This law had been passed by a Democratic-controlled Congress without Republican support.) To lift consumer spending and create more jobs, Dole came out for a 15% cut in federal income taxes. He also promised to shrink the federal budget deficit and aim for a balanced budget.

Clinton and other Democrats called Dole's economic proposals unrealistic. They went on to accuse the Republicans of planning to reduce Medicare benefits and cut education and environmental programs. The Republicans, in turn, sought to make "character" and "integrity" issues in the election. They pointed to the scandals that had appeared in the news media concerning White House personnel, including large campaign contributions that the Democrats had taken from foreigners.

3. The Election. Less than half of the nation's eligible voters went to the polls on Election Day. This was the lowest percentage turnout in a presidential election since 1924. Clinton received 49% of the popular vote (well ahead of the 43% he had scored against Bush in 1992), while Dole won 41% and Perot, 8%. (Other minor party candidates shared the remaining 2%.) Surpassing Dole in all regions of the country except the South and the Great Plains, Clinton acquired 379 electoral votes from 31 states and the District of Columbia; Dole collected 159 electoral votes from 19 states.

Despite Clinton's victory, the Republicans managed to retain control of Congress. They expanded their hold on the Senate by two seats (to 55) and reduced their numbers in the House by three seats (to 227).

FOREIGN HIGHLIGHTS

1. Russia and Ukraine. In January, 1994, at a summit meeting in Moscow between Clinton and Russian President Boris Yeltsin, the United States and Russia reduced the threat of mutual nuclear devastation by agreeing that none of their strategic weapons would be aimed at the territory of any country. Clinton also signed an agreement with President Leonid Kravchuk of Ukraine that called for Ukraine to deactivate and dismantle its nuclear arsenal of ICBM's and warheads (formerly part of the Soviet arsenal) in exchange for $1 billion in U.S. aid and a pledge of assistance in the event of an external attack.

2. Vietnam. President Clinton in 1995 announced the establishment of full diplomatic relations with Vietnam despite opposition to the measure from some veterans' groups and relatives of American service personnel still missing in action from the Vietnam War.

3. Somalia. Mounting casualties and continuing opposition from powerful Somali warlords induced Clinton to order the recall of U.S. military personnel. The last U.S. troops left Somalia in March, 1994 (see page 395).

4. Middle East. Although not directly involved in the negotiations that led to two dramatic breakthroughs in the Middle East, Clinton: (*a*) hosted in 1993 a historic meeting in Washington, D.C., between Yitzhak Rabin, the Prime Minister of Israel, and Yasir Arafat, head of the Palestine Liberation Organization; and (*b*) witnessed the signing of a peace accord at the White House between Israel and Jordan in 1994 (see page 427).

When Iraqi President Saddam Hussein moved 50,000 heavily armed soldiers toward the border with Kuwait in October, 1994, Clinton quickly airlifted thousands of U.S. troops to the region. As a result, the Iraqi dictator pulled his forces back.

5. Cuba. Utilizing rafts, small boats, and anything else that would float, thousands of Cubans sought to escape from conditions at home and reach the United States by water. To stem the flood of immigrants,

Clinton revised the decades-long U.S. policy of accepting such escapees as legitimate seekers of political asylum. He said that refugees would be picked up at sea and placed in holding camps at U.S. bases at Guantánamo Bay (Cuba) and in Panama. U.S.-Cuban negotiations in September, 1994, led to an agreement that provided for the admittance of 20,000 Cubans a year through the regular procedure of applying for visas. Cuba, in turn, promised to make an effort to discourage its citizens from fleeing to the United States.

As a humanitarian gesture, the Clinton administration agreed in May, 1995, to allow most of the detainees at Guantánamo Bay Naval Station to enter the United States. Those with criminal records or other undesirable characteristics, however, would be returned to Communist Cuba.

6. South Africa. With the election in 1994 of Nelson Mandela, head of the once-banned African National Congress, as the first black president of South Africa, the system of enforced racial separation known as apartheid came to an end. As a result, the United States in 1994 lifted economic sanctions that had been in effect since 1986 against that country. Moreover, Clinton offered U.S. assistance to strengthen the economy of South Africa.

7. NATO. The President in 1993 proposed that NATO membership be expanded (at some future time) to include former Soviet-bloc states that had been members of the now defunct Warsaw Pact.

By permission of Chuck Asay and Creators Syndicate

8. Bosnia-Herzegovina. To ease the distress of Bosnian Muslims besieged by the Bosnian Serbs, the United States began parachuting food and medical supplies to Muslim-held areas. Clinton declared that he would tighten the enforcement of economic sanctions and increase political pressure on neighboring Serbia to keep that country from assisting Serbs living in Bosnia. He also indicated his willingness to send U.S. forces to maintain order in Bosnia if the warring factions would settle their differences (see pages 395–396).

9. North Korea. When North Korea refused to allow UN monitors to inspect its nuclear facilities to determine whether a secret nuclear weapons project might be under way, the United States reacted strongly. It threatened to increase its military presence in neighboring South Korea, warned that it might take military action, and asked the UN to impose economic sanctions against North Korea.

In an unofficial visit to North Korea, former President Jimmy Carter succeeded in defusing tensions and arranging a resumption of high-level negotiations between North Korea and the United States. In August, 1994, U.S. and North Korean representatives signed an agreement that allowed UN monitors to inspect a secret nuclear laboratory in that country. In addition, North Korea agreed not to reprocess any more spent fuel rods from its nuclear reactors—a procedure that yields plutonium, a key component of nuclear weapons. The United States, in turn, promised to help North Korea build light-water nuclear reactors (a less accessible source of weapons-grade plutonium) as replacements for its outmoded facilities.

10. Haiti. Meeting Jean-Bertrand Aristide, the ousted president of Haiti, in Washington, D.C., in March, 1993, Clinton declared his intention to restore him to power. Under the pressure of a UN-imposed arms and oil embargo against Haiti and a UN threat to invade that country, Haitian military leader and dictator Raoul Cédras agreed to step down in October. The agreement also called for the UN to lift its embargo and to help police Haiti upon Aristide's arrival.

At the designated time, a contingent of Canadian and U.S. troops were prevented from landing by street demonstrations involving armed thugs. The Haitian military leaders also refused to surrender their positions. The UN thereupon reimposed its embargo and later strengthened it by adding further trade restrictions. The United States sent six warships to assure the blockade's enforcement.

Throughout much of 1994, Clinton hoped that the embargo would force the military regime to accept Aristide's return. As thousands of desperate boat people continued to flee Haiti seeking asylum in the United States, the Clinton administration came to the conclusion that only military intervention would work. In September, the United States assembled a fleet of 23 warships and 20,000 troops and set out for Port-au-Prince, Haiti's capital. Clinton also sent a delegation headed by former President Jimmy Carter to make a final effort to negotiate a transfer of authority. Upon learning that an American invasion force was about to land, the junta agreed to step down. U.S. forces arrived, quickly took control, sent the top military leaders into exile, and reinstalled Aristide as president (see also page 396).

11. Iran. Declaring that "Iran's appetite for acquiring and developing nuclear weapons and the missiles for delivering them" continued to grow, and that "Iran has broadened its role as an inspiration and paymaster for terrorists," Clinton imposed a trade embargo against that country in May, 1995. He cut off all U.S. trade with and investment in Iran, including purchases by American companies (or their foreign branches) of Iranian oil for resale on world markets—transactions that accounted for more than 20% of Iran's oil exports.

12. Nuclear Non-Proliferation Treaty. Signed in 1968 by President Johnson and put into effect by President Nixon in 1970 (after ratification by the U.S. Senate), this treaty aimed to halt the spread of nuclear weapons by limiting their possession to the five countries that already had them—the United States, Great Britain, France, China, and the Soviet Union (now Russia).

In 1995 the agreement came up for renewal at a global conference held in New York City at the UN. After weeks of bitter debate, marked by opposition from a number of countries that lacked such weapons, the Clinton administration succeeded in persuading the delegates to continue to support nuclear arms limitation. As a result, more than 170 nations agreed to extend the Nuclear Non-Proliferation Treaty indefinitely and unconditionally.

Multiple-Choice Test I

1. Inflation usually means that (*a*) prices rise (*b*) all goods are plentiful (*c*) people receive lower wages (*d*) taxes are much lower.

2. The United States is one of the greatest countries in the world for all of the following reasons EXCEPT (*a*) its policy of admitting immigrants (*b*) its use of modern and efficient machines (*c*) its system of free private enterprise (*d*) its uncontrolled use of natural resources.

3. The St. Lawrence Seaway permits large ships to reach the Atlantic Ocean from the (*a*) Hudson River (*b*) Great Lakes (*c*) Delaware River (*d*) Great Salt Lake.

4. During the 1940's, the federal government spent the largest part of its budget for (*a*) education (*b*) internal improvements (*c*) social welfare (*d*) national defense.

5. That it is possible to go under as well as over a polar ice cap was proved by (*a*) army engineers (*b*) Jules Verne (*c*) a U.S. naval vessel (*d*) scientists at a geophysical conference.

6. Which event occurred during the presidency of John F. Kennedy? (*a*) Cuban missile crisis (*b*) Supreme Court school segregation decision (*c*) passage of the Taft-Hartley Act (*d*) formation of NATO.

7. All of the following countries signed the Nuclear Test-Ban Treaty of 1963 EXCEPT (*a*) the Soviet Union (*b*) the United States (*c*) the People's Republic of China (*d*) Great Britain.

8. Which domestic issue in the United States provided the Soviet Union with the best propaganda material during the period of the cold war? (*a*) reciprocal trade (*b*) federal aid to education (*c*) racial segregation (*d*) revision of the Social Security program.

9. Which pairs a President with a term associated with him? (*a*) Lyndon B. Johnson—New Freedom (*b*) Franklin D. Roosevelt—Great Society (*c*) John F. Kennedy—Square Deal (*d*) Harry S. Truman—Fair Deal.

10. The administrations of Grant, Harding, and Truman were similar in that all three Presidents (*a*) faced problems resulting from war (*b*) were Republicans (*c*) led the country back to isolationism (*d*) were succeeded by a President from a different party.

11. All of the following occurred during the administration of President Truman EXCEPT the (*a*) atomic bombing of Hiroshima (*b*) enactment of the Taft-Hartley Act (*c*) establishment of the Department of Defense (*d*) termination of the Korean War.

12. Checks on the policies of Presidents have been exercised on all of the following occasions EXCEPT the (*a*) action of the Senate on the Treaty of Versailles (*b*) action of Congress on the Taft-Hartley Act (*c*) decision of the Supreme Court on the Agricultural Adjustment Act of 1933 (*d*) action of Congress on the Economic Opportunity Act of 1964.

13. Which Cabinet department was created during President Johnson's administration? (*a*) Housing and Urban Development (*b*) Commerce (*c*) Interior (*d*) Health and Human Services.

14. A law passed during the Truman administration to curb subversive activity in the United States was the (*a*) Presidential Succession Act (*b*) Civil Rights Act (*c*) McCarran Act (*d*) Displaced Persons Act.

15. Effective September, 1997, the hourly minimum wage was raised to (*a*) $4.25 (*b*) $4.75 (*c*) $5.15 (*d*) $6.00.

Multiple-Choice Test II

1. The section of the country that experienced the largest population growth during the period 1950–1990 was the   (*a*) Northeast   (*b*) South   (*c*) West   (*d*) Middle West.
2. Jimmy Carter was the   (*a*) 33rd   (*b*) 37th   (*c*) 39th   (*d*) 40th President of the United States.
3. All of the following were Vice Presidents who succeeded to the presidency upon the death of the elected occupant of that office EXCEPT   (*a*) Theodore Roosevelt   (*b*) Franklin D. Roosevelt   (*c*) Harry S. Truman   (*d*) Lyndon B. Johnson.
4. The name of the first American atomic-powered submarine is the   (*a*) *Seawolf*   (*b*) *Nautilus*   (*c*) *Savannah*   (*d*) *Lusitania*.
5. The Space Age began during the administration of President   (*a*) Truman   (*b*) Eisenhower   (*c*) Kennedy   (*d*) Johnson.
6. A law enacted in 1944 to provide educational and other benefits to returning war veterans is known familiarly as the   (*a*) Bounty Act   (*b*) G.I. Bill of Rights   (*c*) Cash and Carry Act   (*d*) Amvets Bonus Act.
7. "Ask not what your country can do for you—ask what you can do for your country" was a statement made by   (*a*) President John F. Kennedy   (*b*) Secretary of State Dean Rusk   (*c*) Senator Robert F. Kennedy   (*d*) Defense Secretary Robert S. McNamara.
8. America's Bicentennial birthday celebration took place during the administration of President   (*a*) Johnson   (*b*) Nixon   (*c*) Carter   (*d*) Ford.
9. During much of the 20th century, immigration to the United States was influenced by laws based on the "national origins" principle. This principle was widely criticized, however, because it   (*a*) permitted unlimited entry to Orientals arriving on the west coast   (*b*) favored migration from Northern and Western Europe   (*c*) gave larger quotas to immigrants from the Western Hemisphere   (*d*) avoided making choices on the basis of country of origin.
10. Those who believe that increasing the purchasing power of the poor is the most effective way of helping them would be most likely to favor   (*a*) an increase in the sales tax   (*b*) lowering corporation taxes   (*c*) a guaranteed minimum income   (*d*) increasing interest rates on savings accounts.
11. According to the official census, the population of the United States in 1990 was about   (*a*) 150 million   (*b*) 200 million   (*c*) 250 million   (*d*) 300 million.
12. Which statement best describes the role of the federal government in education in the United States since World War II?   (*a*) Federal funds for education have greatly increased.   (*b*) Congress has failed to legislate against school segregation.   (*c*) Many states have refused aid from the federal government.   (*d*) Local and state control of education has been replaced by control by the federal government.
13. Which condition must exist in order to establish a bipartisan foreign policy in the United States?   (*a*) A new foreign policy must be created every two years.   (*b*) The Army and the Navy must be under one Defense Department.   (*c*) The executive and legislative branches must be controlled by the same party.   (*d*) Both political parties must be in general agreement as to major foreign policy goals.
14. All of the following occurred during the Nixon administration EXCEPT

the (*a*) "Saturday Night Massacre" (*b*) resignation of Spiro Agnew as Vice President (*c*) enactment of ESEA (*d*) creation of AMTRAK.

15. The following conclusion may be drawn from a study of post-World War II census data: (*a*) New York State is the fastest growing state in the nation. (*b*) Most black Americans live in Alabama and Georgia. (*c*) Florida and California are losing population to the industrial states of the Northeast. (*d*) Most of the nation's population is concentrated in and around large urban centers.

Essay Questions

1. One of the important scientific advances of recent years has been the development of atomic energy. (*a*) Tell one non-military use of atomic energy. (*b*) What use was made of atomic energy in World War II? (*c*) Is it necessary that all countries of the world cooperate in controlling the use of atomic energy? Why or why not?

2. A famous American leader has said that the three great dangers to the American way of life are *communism, intolerance,* and *inflation.* (*a*) Explain what is meant by *each* of the three italicized terms in the statement. (*b*) Choose *one* of these terms and tell why it is a danger to our American way of life and what should be done to fight against it.

3. Conservation, or the wise use of natural resources, is important to the welfare of a nation. One of the most important natural resources of a country is its waterways. (*a*) In what way has the dumping of sewage and waste into waterways affected health and recreation? (*b*) Discuss how rivers can be made to serve people by bringing moisture to dry soil, providing cheap power, and providing transportation.

4. In many sections of the United States during the past 100 years, lumbering and farming have had much the same adverse effect as mining upon the natural resources of the country. (*a*) What is meant by this statement? (*b*) State *three* methods that have been used to correct and change these conditions.

5. Explain how *each* of the following practices can help keep the United States strong: (*a*) thinking of the nation's welfare rather than of one's own selfish interests, (*b*) insisting upon equal rights for all Americans regardless of race, creed, or color, and (*c*) providing better educational opportunities for all young Americans.

6. Show *one* way in which the Eisenhower administration dealt with problems in each of *three* of the following fields: agriculture, conservation, civil rights, labor-management relations, cold war, and transportation.

7. Assume that you are a writer for a newspaper. Write the news story describing the events indicated by each of *two* of the headlines below:

   a. WORLD MOURNS PRESIDENT'S DEATH; NEW CHIEF EXECUTIVE SWORN IN ABOARD PLANE
   b. GREAT SOCIETY PROGRAMS WIN SUPPORT IN CONGRESS
   c. FORD SWORN IN AS PRESIDENT; ASSERTS "NIGHTMARE IS OVER"
   d. IRANIAN MILITANTS ATTACK U.S. EMBASSY: MORE THAN 50 AMERICANS HELD AS HOSTAGES
   e. BUSH LAUNCHES "OPERATION DESERT STORM"

8. An important population shift in the United States during the 20th century has been from rural to urban and suburban areas. (*a*) List *two* reasons for this shift in population. (*b*) Discuss fully *one* major problem facing cities today as a result of this shift in population.

9. Explain why each of *two* of the following presents a more serious problem for America today than 100 years ago: technological development, preservation of the economic system of free enterprise, quality of education, depletion of natural resources, and environmental pollution.

10. The issue of civil rights has played a significant role in United States history since the 1950's. Describe *one* way in which each of the following affected the cause of civil rights: the President, Congress, the Supreme Court, state governments, and organizations of private individuals.

Matching Test

Column A

1. Love Canal
2. Ferraro
3. Contract With America
4. Star Wars
5. S & L's
6. ERISA
7. Gramm-Rudman-Hollings
8. Noriega
9. NAFTA
10. Saddam Hussein

Column B

a. law to protect workers against loss of retirement benefits
b. foreign leader convicted by U.S. court for drug offenses
c. troubled financial institutions
d. toxic waste site
e. law requiring a balanced budget
f. Republican legislative agenda
g. first woman chosen by a major party as candidate for Vice President
h. Strategic Defense Initiative
i. Persian Gulf War
j. trade agreement with Canada and Mexico

UNIT XII. THE FEDERAL GOVERNMENT AND CIVIC RESPONSIBILITY

LEGISLATIVE BRANCH

CONGRESS

Congress is the legislative (lawmaking) branch of the federal government. It consists of the *House of Representatives* and the *Senate*.

1. House of Representatives. The House is composed of 435 members. They are elected for two-year terms. The number of representatives from a state is proportionate to that state's population, based on the latest federal census. Each state, no matter how small its population, is entitled to at least one representative.

The presiding officer, called the *Speaker of the House*, is elected by the representatives from among their own members. The Speaker has the same voting privileges as any other member of the House.

APPORTIONMENT OF HOUSE SEATS BY STATE (1990 CENSUS)

Ala.	7	Hawaii	2	Mass.	10	N.M.	3	S.D.	1
Alaska	1	Idaho	2	Mich.	16	N.Y.	31	Tenn.	9
Ariz.	6	Ill.	20	Minn.	8	N.C.	12	Texas	30
Ark.	4	Ind.	10	Miss.	5	N.D.	1	Utah	3
Calif.	52	Iowa	5	Mo.	9	Ohio	19	Vt.	1
Colo.	6	Kans.	4	Mont.	1	Okla.	6	Va.	11
Conn.	6	Ky.	6	Neb.	3	Ore.	5	Wash.	9
Del.	1	La.	7	Nev.	2	Pa.	21	W.Va.	3
Fla.	23	Me.	2	N.H.	2	R.I.	2	Wis.	9
Ga.	11	Md.	8	N.J.	13	S.C.	6	Wyo.	1

a. Qualifications of Representatives. To qualify for election to the House, a person must be at least 25 years of age, a citizen of the United States for at least seven years, and a resident of the state in which he or she is a candidate.

b. Special Powers of the House. The House of Representatives has the sole power to originate revenue (tax) bills, to *impeach* government officials (charge them with misconduct in office), and to elect a President if no candidate receives a majority of the electoral votes.

2. Senate. Each state, regardless of size or population, is represented by two senators. The Senate is therefore now composed of 100 members. They are elected for six-year terms. The terms of senators are so arranged that every two years one-third of the terms expire.

The presiding officer, called the *President of the Senate*, is the Vice President of the United States. This official casts no vote except when

520

there is a tie. To serve in the Vice President's absence, the senators elect a *President pro tempore* (temporary chairperson) from among their own members.

   a. Qualifications of Senators. To qualify for election to the Senate, a person must be at least 30 years of age, a citizen of the United States for at least nine years, and a resident of the state that he or she seeks to represent.

   b. Special Powers of the Senate. The Senate has the sole power to try impeached officials, to confirm appointments made by the President, to ratify treaties, and to elect a Vice President if no candidate receives a majority of the electoral votes.

COMPENSATION AND PRIVILEGES OF MEMBERS OF CONGRESS

   Both members of the House and senators receive an annual salary of $133,600. Salaries are partially exempt from taxation because most members maintain a home in or near Washington, D.C., as well as in their own states. They are also entitled to (1) offices of their own in the capital and in their home districts; (2) funds for the employment of assistants and clerical help; (3) expense allowances for travel, stationery, telephone service, and telegrams; (4) free postage for official letters (called the *franking privilege*); and (5) government pensions at age 62 if they have served at least six years as members of Congress.

   The Constitution provides that members of Congress may not be arrested while traveling to, attending, or returning from sessions of Congress except in cases of treason, felony, or breach of the peace. They also cannot be held legally liable for any speeches or statements made on the floor of Congress. (This privilege is known as *congressional immunity*.)

SESSIONS OF CONGRESS

   The Constitution states that "The Congress shall assemble at least once in every year." Each Congress holds two regular sessions. The first begins on January 3 following the November election. The second session begins on January 3 of the next year. Each session lasts as long as Congress deems it necessary. In addition, the President may call special sessions of Congress, or of either house.

   Since the First Congress, which began its term on March 4, 1789, Congresses have been numbered consecutively. The term of the 105th Congress began in January, 1997; the 106th will convene in January, 1999.

THE CAPITOL

   The Capitol is the focal point of activities of the legislative branch. The south wing of the huge building is occupied by the House of Representatives, and the north wing by the Senate. In both chambers, members sit in semicircular rows facing the presiding officer's dais, Democrats on one side of the hall and Republicans on the other. A public gallery encircles each chamber. Here visitors may observe Congress in action.

CONGRESSIONAL LEADERS

When a new Congress assembles, the members of each political party, in the House and in the Senate, hold informal conferences, or *caucuses*. These caucuses select the various officials of the two chambers. The caucus of the majority party in the Senate selects a President pro tempore to preside over the Senate in the absence of the Vice President. The caucus of the majority party in the House selects a Speaker to preside over the House.

In addition, each party selects (1) a *floor leader* (known either as the *majority leader* or the *minority leader*) to direct the party's legislative program and to maintain party unity on pending legislation, and (2) a *party whip* to keep track of legislation and to notify members to be on hand when important matters come up for a vote.

CONGRESSIONAL EMPLOYEES

The legislative branch comprises more than the 435 representatives and 100 senators who are elected to represent the people. It also includes 20,000 employees who staff the offices of the individual members, serve as assistants to the various congressional committees, and carry out routine duties necessary to lawmaking.

Among the most important employees of Congress are the following:

1. The **Clerk of the House** serves as the executive secretary of that chamber. He or she presides at the start of a new Congress until a Speaker is elected; maintains the records of the proceedings; and keeps track of the progress of bills and resolutions. The official who carries out similar duties in the Senate is called the **Secretary of the Senate**.

2. The **Parliamentarian** in each house advises the presiding officer on questions of procedure.

3. The **Sergeant at Arms** in the House maintains order, summons witnesses to appear before congressional committees, and disburses the representatives' salaries. In the Senate this official also has charge of the public galleries, supervises the doorkeepers and Capitol police, and is responsible for procuring a quorum if directed to do so. (A *quorum* is the number of members who must be present in order for business to be transacted legally.)

4. The **Doorkeeper** in the House controls admission to the floor of the chamber, has charge of the document room, and supervises the pages.

5. The **Chaplain** in each house opens the daily sessions with prayer.

6. The **Postmaster** in each house handles the large quantity of mail received by members of Congress.

CONGRESSIONAL COMMITTEES

Since thousands of bills are introduced at each session of Congress, it is impossible for the entire Senate and House to give careful consideration to all the proposed legislation. It is also impossible to work out the details of important bills in open debate upon the floor of each chamber. Hence, the House has set up 22 standing committees and the

Senate 16. When a bill is introduced, the Speaker of the House or the President of the Senate refers the bill to the proper committee for consideration.

Among the important committees in the House are *Ways and Means* (which considers all tax legislation), *Rules, Appropriations, International Relations, National Security,* and *Agriculture.* Among the Senate committees are *Finance, Appropriations, Foreign Relations, Energy and Natural Resources, Labor and Human Resources,* and *Commerce, Science, and Transportation.* The committees investigate proposed legislation, discuss it, and amend it. Public hearings may be held at which interested and informed persons appear in order to answer questions and present arguments for or against a bill. If a committee, by a majority vote, approves a bill, it is brought before the House or Senate for a vote. On the other hand, if the committee rejects a bill, it is killed.

In addition to screening proposed legislation, the various congressional committees exercise broad investigative powers. They conduct investigations to determine (1) whether laws already enacted are functioning properly or need to be changed, (2) whether programs authorized by Congress are being administered properly, and (3) what new laws should be passed.

The party in power has majority representation on each committee. Members usually continue on the same committee term after term. The committee member of the majority party who has served longest on the committee is usually made its chairperson. (This system is known as *seniority.*)

HOW A BILL BECOMES A LAW

1. If a bill passes both houses by a majority vote and is signed by the President, it becomes a law.

2. If the President vetoes a bill, it is returned to the house where it originated. If the bill is repassed by a two-thirds vote of both houses, the President's veto is overridden, and the bill becomes a law.

3. If the President takes no action on a bill within 10 days, it becomes a law without the President's signature, provided Congress has not *adjourned* (ended its session) in the meantime. If the President does not sign the bill and Congress adjourns before the 10-day period is up, the bill is automatically vetoed. This is known as a *pocket veto.*

OTHER ACTIVITIES OF CONGRESS

In addition to its national legislative functions, Congress engages in other activities. (1) It governs the District of Columbia, the seat of the nation's capital. (2) It supervises the operations of the Government Printing Office, which handles the government's publications. (3) It maintains the Library of Congress, which houses the world's largest collection of books, manuscripts, papers, and pamphlets. The library's Legislative Reference Service supplies information and special studies to assist members of Congress in their legislative work. (4) It is responsible for the U.S. Botanic Garden, with its collections of agricultural produce.

Also answering to Congress are (5) the General Accounting Office, which audits the government's financial records, (6) the Architect of the Capitol, who maintains the grounds and buildings of the Capitol and the Senate and House office buildings, (7) the Office of Technology Assessment, which provides information on the consequences of uses of technology, and (8) the Congressional Budget Office, which analyzes fiscal policy and the cost of federal programs.

EXECUTIVE BRANCH

THE PRESIDENT

The executive branch of the federal government carries out (executes) the laws of the United States. It is headed by the *President*, who is also known as the *Chief Executive* of the nation. To be eligible for election to this office, a person must be a native-born citizen, at least 35 years of age, and a resident of the United States for at least 14 years.

The President is elected for a term of four years. The Twenty-second Amendment (adopted in 1951) limits a President to two elected terms, or to only one elected term if that individual has served more than two years of another President's term. In case a President dies, resigns, or is removed by impeachment, the Vice President takes over the presidency. If there is no Vice President, the *Presidential Succession Act of 1947* provides that the Speaker of the House and the President pro tempore of the Senate are next in line of succession, followed by the members of the Cabinet in the order of the creation of their departments (see pages 527–529).

The President receives an annual salary of $200,000, an allowance of $50,000 for official expenses, and an additional $120,000 (nontaxable) for travel expenses and official entertainment. The President also receives the use of the White House as a residence and office, the services of a large official staff, and personal transportation facilities. Upon retirement from office, an ex-President is provided a lifetime pension of $143,800 a year, as well as free mailing privileges, free office space, and up to $96,000 a year for office help. Widows of former Presidents are granted lifetime pensions of $20,000 a year.

ELECTING A PRESIDENT

1. The Electoral College System. One of the most perplexing decisions that the Constitutional Convention faced in 1787 was the method of electing the President. Most of the delegates opposed direct election by the people because they feared that it might lead to disorder and mob rule. They also considered election by Congress, but decided against the idea because it might place the President under the control of the legislative branch. After much discussion, the framers of the Constitution finally decided that the President should be elected by a specially chosen group of people called the *electoral college*.

The plan provided that each state would have as many *electors* as it had representatives and senators in Congress. The selection of electors was left to the discretion of the state legislatures. (In eight of the 13 original states, the electors were chosen at first by the state legislatures. By 1860 the electors were chosen by popular election in all the states.) The electors were to assemble in their respective states on a particular day designated by Congress (the first Monday after the second Wednesday in December). According to the Twelfth Amendment, each elector would cast two separate ballots—one for President and one for Vice President. The votes would then be forwarded to the nation's capital. In the presence of both houses of Congress, the President of the Senate would count the votes and announce the winners. If the presidential count ended in a tie, or if no candidate received a majority of the votes, the House would choose the President from among the leading candidates. If a similar conflict arose over the vice presidency, the Senate would settle the matter.

2. Presidential Election Procedure Today. Although the President is still chosen by the electoral college, the system has been so modified that for all practical purposes it can be said that the President is elected directly by the people. The procedure is as follows:

a. At a national convention held during the summer of the presidential election year, each political party nominates its candidates for President and Vice President. Shortly thereafter, in every state, each party selects a slate of electors pledged to the party's candidates for national office.

b. On election day (the first Tuesday after the first Monday in November), the voters in each state go to the polls and choose between the slates of electors. (In most states the names of the candidates for President and Vice President appear on the ballot, but they are used merely to identify the electors pledged to them.) The party that receives the most popular votes for its electors in any state captures *all* the electoral votes of that state.

c. Electors still go through the formal procedure of assembling at their respective state capitals, casting their votes, and forwarding them to the nation's capital for counting. In actuality, however, the electors are merely reaffirming the choice made by the people on election day.

At present, the electoral college consists of 538 members (one for each seat in Congress plus three for the District of Columbia), and 270 electoral votes are needed to elect a President and Vice President.

POWERS OF THE PRESIDENT

The Constitution provides that the President shall have the power to:

1. Supervise the enforcement of federal laws.

2. Appoint (with the consent of the Senate) ambassadors, consuls, Supreme Court judges, and all other federal officials whose appointments are not otherwise provided for by the Constitution or by Congress.

3. Make treaties with foreign countries (with the consent of two-thirds of the Senate).

4. Serve as commander-in-chief of the armed forces.

5. Grant reprieves and pardons for offenses against the United States, except in cases of impeachment.

6. Receive representatives of foreign governments.

7. Recommend legislation to Congress and report to Congress on "the state of the Union."

8. Sign or veto bills passed by Congress.

9. Call special sessions of Congress or of either house.

PRESIDENTIAL OATH OF OFFICE

The President's inauguration takes place on January 20 following the November election. Before assuming office, the President takes the following oath: "I do solemnly swear (or affirm) that I will faithfully execute the office of President of the United States, and will, to the best of my ability, preserve, protect, and defend the Constitution of the United States."

THE VICE PRESIDENT

The qualifications for the office of Vice President are the same as those for the President. The Vice President is elected for a term of four years and receives a salary of $171,500 plus $10,000 for expenses (both taxable). This official's only constitutional duty (unless he or she succeeds to the presidency or serves temporarily as Acting President) is to preside over the Senate.

Since the adoption of the Twenty-fifth Amendment in 1967, the President has had the power to nominate a new Vice President whenever that office becomes vacant. Upon confirmation by a majority vote of both houses of Congress, the nominee assumes office.

PRESIDENTIAL ASSISTANTS

The presidency has often been called "the hardest job in the world." Thus, the Chief Executive utilizes the services of numerous assistants, advisers, and aides. The officials closest to the President are in (1) the *Executive Office of the President,* and (2) the *Cabinet.*

1. Executive Office of the President. The Executive Office employs about 1,600 people in the following agencies:

a. The **White House Office** includes the President's personal staff, administrative assistants, special counsel, press secretary, legislative counsel, military aides, and special assistants. Included too are numerous clerks, stenographers, and other office personnel.

b. The **Office of Management and Budget** draws up the annual budget that the President submits to Congress. It also monitors the programs and performance of the various executive departments and agencies.

c. The **Office of Policy Development** assists the President in the creation of domestic policies and programs.

d. The **National Security Council** advises the President on matters affecting the security of the nation. Under its supervision is the **Central**

Intelligence Agency (CIA), which keeps watch over developments abroad and gathers information relating to national security.

e. The **Council of Economic Advisers** advises the President on problems relating to the nation's economic health.

f. The **Office of Science and Technology Policy** advises the President on scientific, engineering, and technological developments.

g. The **Office of the U.S. Trade Representative** supervises and coordinates the nation's foreign trade agreements.

h. The **Council on Environmental Policy** advises the President on matters relating to air, water, and soil pollution.

i. The **Office of National Drug Control Policy** advises the President on matters relating to illegal drug shipments and drug abuse.

2. The Cabinet. Members of the Cabinet are appointed by the President with consent of the Senate. Their tenure in office is subject to the pleasure of the President. They serve as advisers to the Chief Executive. In addition, they are responsible for the management of the departments over which they preside. (Presidents sometimes invite other key administration personnel to serve on the Cabinet.)

The President's Cabinet includes the following officials: (*a*) Secretary of State, (*b*) Secretary of the Treasury, (*c*) Secretary of Defense, (*d*) Attorney General, (*e*) Secretary of the Interior, (*f*) Secretary of Agriculture, (*g*) Secretary of Commerce, (*h*) Secretary of Labor, (*i*) Secretary of Health and Human Services, (*j*) Secretary of Housing and Urban Development, (*k*) Secretary of Transportation, (*l*) Secretary of Energy, (*m*) Secretary of Education, and (*n*) Secretary of Veterans Affairs.

EXECUTIVE DEPARTMENTS

The departments whose heads are members of the President's Cabinet are known as the *executive departments.* They employ about 2 million civilian employees and conduct a wide range of activities.

1. The **Department of State** handles all matters relating to foreign affairs. It carries on diplomatic correspondence with other nations; maintains the Foreign Service; negotiates treaties; issues passports; and supervises the nation's foreign aid programs through the Agency for International Development.

2. The **Treasury Department** collects federal taxes and other revenue; pays the government's bills; borrows money through the sale of bonds; coins metallic currency and prints paper money; and operates the Secret Service and Internal Revenue Service.

3. The **Department of Defense** directs and coordinates operations of the three branches of the armed forces. The Army, Navy, and Air Force, each headed by a Secretary, exist as equal and separate departments within the Defense Department. Only the Secretary of Defense, however, is a member of the President's Cabinet.

The armed forces are responsible for the defense of the United States, its possessions, and other areas vital to the nation's interests.

4. The **Department of Justice**, whose head is the Attorney General, prosecutes violators of federal laws; administers the federal court system; supervises federal prisons; investigates crimes against the United States through the Federal Bureau of Investigation (FBI); and conducts the Immigration and Naturalization Service.

5. The **Department of the Interior** contains a number of unrelated bureaus which have been placed under the supervision of a single Cabinet officer. It has charge of (*a*) the management and disposition of public lands, (*b*) the development and conservation of natural resources, (*c*) geologic surveys of the United States, (*d*) mines, (*e*) Indian affairs, (*f*) national parks, and (*g*) American overseas possessions.

6. The **Department of Agriculture** conducts research on animal and plant diseases; seeks new crops suitable to American soil; analyzes soil composition; operates experimental stations to improve seeds, develop hardier plants, and increase crop production; and publishes information to aid the farmer. It also supervises meat inspection, manages the national forest reserves, and administers federal farm laws.

7. The **Department of Commerce** promotes foreign and domestic commerce; directs the federal census; regulates weights and measures; grants patents; registers trademarks; promotes travel and tourism; conducts coastal surveys; and operates the National Weather Service.

8. The **Department of Labor** enforces the Fair Labor Standards Act; administers the federal government's share of the unemployment insurance and employment service programs; collects and publishes labor statistics; and seeks to improve the position of women and minority workers.

9. The **Department of Health and Human Services** aims to promote economic security and the health of the nation's citizens. Its chief bureaus are the Public Health Service, the Food and Drug Administration, and the National Institutes of Health.

10. The **Department of Housing and Urban Development** consolidated the functions of the Housing and Home Finance Agency and a variety of other bureaus responsible for such federal programs as public housing, urban renewal, and community planning.

11. The **Department of Transportation** grouped together numerous federal agencies dealing with various aspects of transportation. It includes the Federal Aviation Administration, the Federal Highway Administration, the Coast Guard, the Federal Railroad Administration, the National Highway Traffic Safety Administration, the Urban Mass Transportation Administration, the Maritime Administration, and the St. Lawrence Seaway Development Corporation. It also performs the functions previously assigned to the Interstate Commerce Commission, which Congress abolished in 1996.

12. The **Department of Energy** consolidated such independent agencies as the Federal Energy Administration, the Energy Research and Development Administration, and the Federal Power Commission (renamed the Federal Energy Regulatory Commission); and took over all energy functions previously performed by other executive departments.

13. The **Department of Education** assumed responsibility for the federal Office of Education as well as for the many education programs that had been scattered among various federal agencies and departments.

14. The **Department of Veterans Affairs** supervises the federal programs of hospital and medical care, pensions, insurance, and other benefits provided by law to the nation's war veterans.

INDEPENDENT AGENCIES

In addition to the Executive Office of the President and the executive departments, the executive branch of the government consists of numerous independent agencies. They were created by Congress to regulate, supervise, coordinate, or direct various activities of national importance. Among the important agencies are the following:

1. The **Environmental Protection Agency (EPA)** coordinates the antipollution activities of the federal government.

2. The **Equal Employment Opportunity Commission (EEOC)** seeks to eliminate job discrimination based on sex, religion, race, national origin, or age.

3. The **Export-Import Bank** makes loans to finance trade between the United States and foreign countries.

4. The **Farm Credit Administration** coordinates the various lending organizations established by Congress to aid farmers.

5. The **Federal Communications Commission (FCC)** licenses radio and television stations, as well as professional and amateur operators of such facilities. It also supervises the rates charged for interstate telegraph and telephone service.

6. The **Federal Deposit Insurance Corporation** insures the accounts of depositors in all banks that are members of the FDIC. Its protection has also been extended to depositors in savings and loan institutions.

7. The **Federal Election Commission** regulates campaign spending by candidates for federal office.

8. The **Federal Maritime Commission** regulates U.S. vessels engaged in foreign commerce. It approves fares, freight rates, and mergers.

9. The **Federal Reserve Board (FRB)** controls the nation's money supply and credit, and directs the system of federal reserve banks.

10. The **Federal Trade Commission (FTC)** seeks to prevent unfair trade practices and false or misleading advertising.

11. The **General Services Administration (GSA)** coordinates government purchasing, maintains federal office buildings, and sells U.S. government surplus property.

12. The **National Aeronautics and Space Administration (NASA)** has charge of space research and development.

13. The **National Archives** displays copies of the Declaration of Independence, the U.S. Constitution, and the Bill of Rights; and houses other valuable government records, historic maps, photos, and manuscripts.

14. The **National Labor Relations Board (NLRB)** handles disputes concerning unfair labor practices by employers or unions and conducts elections permitting workers to select a union to represent them.

15. The **National Science Foundation (NSF)** grants funds for scientific research, awards fellowships for science study, and seeks to improve the teaching of science and mathematics in the nation's secondary schools.

16. The **Nuclear Regulatory Commission** regulates the nuclear power industry.

17. The **Office of Personnel Management** administers the operation of the federal merit system. It prepares and conducts examinations for the selection of federal employees.

18. The **Peace Corps** sends U.S. volunteers to poor countries to train people in public health, education, and economic development, thereby promoting peace and international understanding.

19. The **Securities and Exchange Commission (SEC)** regulates the purchase and sale of stocks and bonds, and supervises the operation of stock exchanges to protect investors against fraudulent practices.

20. The **Selective Service System** maintains a national registry of able-bodied young men. It stands ready to supply the armed forces with manpower when called upon to do so.

21. The **Small Business Administration (SBA)** makes loans to small businesses and helps them obtain a fair share of government contracts.

22. The **Smithsonian Institution** operates the National Museum, the National Gallery of Art, the Kennedy Center for the Performing Arts, and other historical, scientific, and cultural establishments.

23. The **Social Security Administration** operates the nation's extensive Social Security system. (This bureau, once part of the Department of Health and Human Services, became an independent agency in 1995.)

24. The **Tennessee Valley Authority (TVA)** operates the Tennessee Valley system of flood control facilities, navigation, and electricity production.

25. The **United States Information Agency (USIA)** acquaints people abroad with the United States and its way of life.

26. The **U.S. Postal Service** operates the nation's far-flung postal system.

LAW ENFORCEMENT AGENCIES

Numerous special agencies have been set up within the various executive departments to combat crime and to enforce the laws of the land. Some of the important law enforcement agencies are the following:

1. The **Secret Service** (Treasury Department) protects the President and Vice President, as well as their families, and tracks down counterfeiters and forgers of the nation's currency.

2. The **Federal Bureau of Investigation** (Department of Justice) investigates violations of federal laws. The FBI collects crime statistics,

maintains a fingerprint file, and operates a crime detection laboratory. In time of war, it seeks out spies, saboteurs, and draft evaders.

3. The **Immigration and Naturalization Service** (Department of Justice) searches for aliens who have entered the country illegally.

4. The **Internal Revenue Service** (Treasury Department) investigates violations of federal tax laws.

5. The **Coast Guard** (Department of Transportation) enforces navigation laws and patrols the nation's coasts to prevent piracy and smuggling.

6. The **Food and Drug Administration** (Department of Health and Human Services) enforces federal laws relating to the purity and quality of foods, drugs, and cosmetics.

7. The **Drug Enforcement Administration** (Department of Justice) enforces federal laws relating to narcotics and controlled substances.

JUDICIAL BRANCH

FEDERAL COURT SYSTEM

The judicial (law interpreting) branch of the federal government consists mainly of three levels of courts: district courts, circuit courts of appeals, and the Supreme Court. In addition, there are special courts that deal with particular types of cases.

Federal judges are appointed by the President with the consent of the Senate. Appointment is for life. Judges cannot be removed except by impeachment.

The Constitution grants the federal courts jurisdiction over the following categories of cases:

1. Cases arising under the Constitution, laws, or treaties of the United States.

2. Cases of admiralty or maritime jurisdiction (legal disputes arising aboard ship or relating to matters connected with shipping).

3. Controversies in which the United States itself is a party.

4. Controversies between two or more states, between citizens of different states, or between a state and a citizen of another state. (Under the Eleventh Amendment, a state may sue a citizen of another state in federal courts, but a state may not itself be sued by such a party.)

5. Cases involving ambassadors or other foreign representatives.

DISTRICT COURTS

The district courts are the lowest courts in the federal judicial system. It is here that most federal cases are first brought to trial. There are 90 judicial districts in the United States, each containing a district court. In addition, Congress has established territorial district courts in Puerto Rico, Guam, and the Virgin Islands. At present each district court has from 2 to 27 judges, depending upon the amount of judicial work within its geographic area.

CIRCUIT COURTS OF APPEALS

The circuit courts of appeals have appellate jurisdiction only. That is, they try only cases that are appealed from the lower district courts or hear appeals from the rulings of such federal agencies as the ICC, NLRB, and SEC. There are 12 judicial circuits in the United States and its territories, each containing a circuit court of appeals. Each of these courts has from 6 to 28 judges, depending upon its case load.

SUPREME COURT

The only court specified by name in the Constitution, the Supreme Court is the highest court in the land. It consists of a Chief Justice and eight associate justices.

The Supreme Court has both original and appellate jurisdiction. That is, some cases are brought directly to the Supreme Court without first being heard in a lower court, and other cases are appealed to it from lower courts—both state and federal.

The Supreme Court has the power of *judicial review*. It may declare acts of Congress or of state governments unconstitutional and therefore invalid. The Court decides cases by a majority vote. Its decisions are final.

SPECIAL COURTS

1. The **Claims Court** hears claims brought against the U.S. government.

2. The **Court of International Trade** handles cases involving tariff disputes and import transactions.

3. The **Court of Appeals for the Federal Circuit**, an appellate court with nationwide jurisdiction, hears appeals from the Claims Court and the Court of International Trade. It also reviews rulings concerning patents and trademarks.

4. The **Tax Court** tries cases involving tax disputes between individuals and the government.

5. The **Court of Military Appeals** reviews court-martial convictions of military personnel.

6. The **Court of Veterans Appeals** reviews decisions on veterans' claims by the Department of Veterans Affairs.

CIVIC RESPONSIBILITY

THE AMERICAN HERITAGE

American heroes and patriots of past generations fought for, gained, and passed on a priceless heritage of freedom, ideals, traditions, and achievements in many fields. Those who enjoy the fruits of their labor are today faced with the task of protecting and strengthening this heritage. Out of the present generation of young Americans must come the heroes, patriots, and enlightened citizens who will preserve the American heritage and pass it on to generations yet unborn.

THE BILL OF RIGHTS

The Bill of Rights, which forms the first 10 amendments to the Constitution, lists and guarantees fundamental rights and freedoms as follows:

1. The right of freedom of religion, speech, and press; the right to assemble peaceably; and the right to petition the government to correct abuses.

2. The right to a fair trial and to trial by jury; protection against unreasonable bail and cruel punishment; protection against unreasonable searches and seizures of persons and property; guarantee of fair compensation for property taken by the government for public use; and the guarantee that no person will be deprived of life, liberty, or property without due process of law.

U.S. GOVERNMENT PROTECTS THE RIGHTS OF THE PEOPLE

The American form of government protects the rights of the people and prevents political abuses in the following ways:

1. Elected representatives are responsible to the people for their actions.

2. Frequent elections enable the people to replace officials who displease the majority.

3. Public opinion exerts a strong influence on legislation and government policies.

4. Checks and balances and the separation of powers prevent any branch of government from abusing its powers.

5. Provision for amending the Constitution makes possible changes desired by the people.

RIGHTS AND DUTIES OF CITIZENSHIP

Those who enjoy the rights and privileges of American citizenship must also assume the duties of citizenship. If these duties are neglected, the whole society is imperiled.

Rights That American Citizens Enjoy in Everyday Life:

1. The right to vote for the candidate of one's choice.

2. The right to worship in one's own way.

3. The right to own property and to be secure in one's own home.

4. The right to choose one's own job and to earn a livelihood.

5. The right to free speech: to speak one's mind freely on all issues.

6. The right to freedom of press: newspapers may criticize the government and comment editorially on all issues; Americans may read any magazine, newspaper, or book that they choose.

7. The right to a free public education.

8. The right to a fair trial and to trial by jury.

9. The right to assemble peaceably with one's neighbors.

10. The right to enjoy and use public facilities, such as museums, parks, and libraries.

Fitzpatrick in The St. Louis Post-Dispatch

Your Vote Makes Your Government

Responsibilities of Good Citizens in Everyday Life:

1. To vote at every election and to investigate the fitness of all candidates for public office.

2. To respect the rights of others who worship in different ways.

3. To respect the property of others.

4. To select the job that one is best suited for; to select a vocation that will enable one to render service to others and to one's community.

5. To respect the rights of others to free speech; to respect the next person's opinion even though it may differ from one's own.

6. To select good books, magazines, and newspapers; to keep informed by reading about current events; to weigh carefully everything that one reads.

7. To take advantage of educational opportunities; to select the proper educational program that will prepare one for a useful life in the future.

8. To serve on a jury willingly.

9. To recognize un-American propaganda; to condemn those who seek to arouse racial and religious prejudice.

10. To take advantage of public facilities; to care for public property.

11. To appreciate the value of good health and to maintain proper health habits.

Engelhardt in The St. Louis Post-Dispatch

First Lesson

12. To obey and respect the laws and institutions of popular government.

13. To be willing to assume leadership in school, community, and nation.

14. To be tolerant of foreigners and help them learn the American way of life.

15. To guard against any attempt to destroy the American way of life.

PATRIOTISM

Patriotism means love for one's country. It means love for the land, the people, and the institutions of America. As Theodore Roosevelt expressed it, "Patriotism should be an integral part of our every feeling at all times, for it is merely another name for those qualities of soul which make a man in peace or in war by day or by night think of his duty to his fellows and of his duty to the nation."

William Tyler Page stated the creed of all patriotic Americans when he wrote:

THE AMERICAN'S CREED

"I believe in the United States of America, as a government of the people, by the people, for the people; whose just powers are derived from the consent of the governed; a democracy in a republic; a sovereign nation of many sovereign states; a perfect union, one and inseparable; established upon those principles of freedom, equality, justice, and humanity for which American patriots sacrificed their lives and fortunes.

"I therefore believe it is my duty to my country to love it, to support its Constitution, to obey its laws, to respect its flag, and to defend it against all enemies."

THE AMERICAN FLAG

The American flag is the symbol of the nation and the ideals in which Americans believe. In their daily lives, Americans can show patriotism by their reverence and respect for their flag.

Description. The flag of the United States has 13 horizontal stripes—seven red and six white, the red and white stripes alternating. The 13 stripes represent the original 13 states. The flag also has a blue field extending to the lower edge of the fourth red stripe, containing 50 five-pointed white stars. There are five rows of six stars staggered with four rows of five stars. Each star has one point upward. The number of stars is the same as the number of states in the Union. The red in the flag symbolizes courage; the white, purity; the blue, loyalty.

Origin. According to tradition, Betsy Ross designed and made the first American flag of stars and stripes. In June, 1777, the Continental Congress adopted the flag of 13 stripes and 13 stars, representing the 13 original states. As new states were admitted to the Union, additional stars were added. The admission of Alaska and Hawaii added the 49th and 50th stars to the flag. The 50-star flag was officially unveiled on July 4, 1960.

The Pledge to the Flag. The pledge of allegiance to the flag is as follows: *I pledge allegiance to the flag of the United States of America and to the Republic for which it stands, one Nation under God, indivisible, with liberty and justice for all.*

Rules for the Display and Use of the Flag:

In 1976, for the first time in 34 years, Congress revised the rules governing the use of the American flag. The amended code states that "the flag represents a living country and is itself considered a living thing." Because of advances made in weather-resistant flag materials and outdoor lighting, the new law lifted the previous display restrictions and permits Old Glory to be flown outdoors around the clock and in any weather as long as an all-weather flag is used and it is properly illuminated.

1. The flag should be displayed on these holidays and special occasions:

    a. New Year's Day, January 1

    b. Martin Luther King Day, third Monday in January

    c. Inauguration Day, January 20

    d. Lincoln's Birthday, February 12

    e. Washington's Birthday, third Monday in February

f. Easter Sunday (the date varies each year)

g. Mother's Day, second Sunday in May

h. Armed Forces Day, third Saturday in May

i. Memorial Day, last Monday in May (half-staff until noon)

j. Flag Day, June 14

k. Independence Day, July 4

l. Labor Day, first Monday in September

m. Citizenship Day, September 17

n. Columbus Day, second Monday in October

o. Veterans Day, November 11

p. Thanksgiving Day, fourth Thursday in November

q. Christmas Day, December 25

r. On state holidays

2. The flag should be displayed during school days on or in front of the schoolhouse.

3. The flag should also be displayed in or near every polling place on election days. The general election is held the first Tuesday after the first Monday in November.

4. When being raised or lowered, the flag may not touch the ground.

5. When the flag is in such condition that it no longer is a fitting emblem for display, it should be destroyed in a dignified manner, preferably by burning.

6. During the ceremony of hoisting or lowering the flag, or when the flag is passing in a parade or in a review, or during the pledge of allegiance, all persons present should face the flag and stand at attention. Those present in uniform should render the military salute. When not in uniform, men should remove their headdress with the right hand and hold it at the left shoulder, the hand being over the heart. Men without hats should place the right hand over the heart. Women also salute by placing the right hand over the heart. (They need not remove their hats.)

7. The flag should be hoisted briskly and lowered slowly and ceremoniously.

8. When used on a speaker's platform, the flag, if displayed flat, should be placed above and behind the speaker with the blue field uppermost and to the observer's left. If flown from a staff, the flag occupies the position of honor and should be placed at the speaker's right as he or she faces the audience.

Multiple-Choice Test I

1. The Constitution of the United States gives the President the power to (*a*) declare war (*b*) regulate commerce (*c*) command the armed forces (*d*) remove Supreme Court justices.

2. The President's "state of the Union" message to Congress is an example of (*a*) a constitutional requirement (*b*) a presidential practice of recent years (*c*) the enforcement of a federal law (*d*) custom and tradition.

3. The Constitution provides that all bills for raising revenue shall (*a*) be submitted by the Director of the Budget (*b*) originate in the House of Representatives (*c*) provide enough money to meet appropriations (*d*) be approved by the Secretary of the Treasury.

4. According to the Constitution, foreign policy is primarily the responsibility of the (*a*) Cabinet (*b*) President (*c*) Congress (*d*) Secretary of State.

5. The Senate differs from the House of Representatives in that (*a*) the Senate is continuously in session (*b*) a two-thirds vote is required to pass bills in the Senate (*c*) senators must be native-born Americans (*d*) one-third of the Senate is elected every two years.

6. A decision of the Supreme Court declaring a law unconstitutional requires a (*a*) majority vote (*b*) two-thirds vote (*c*) three-fourths vote (*d*) unanimous vote.

7. In his oath of inauguration, the President swears (or affirms) to preserve, protect, and defend (*a*) democracy (*b*) the nation (*c*) the states (*d*) the Constitution.

8. Usually, after a bill has been introduced into either house of Congress, it is first (*a*) signed by the presiding officer of that house (*b*) debated by members of that house (*c*) referred to a committee of that house (*d*) considered by a joint committee representing both houses.

9. The number of representatives from New York State was reduced from 34 in 1980 to 31 in 1990 because of (*a*) a change in the total number of members in the House of Representatives (*b*) greater proportionate gains in population in other states (*c*) a shift of population within New York State (*d*) a sharp increase in the population of New York State.

10. Elimination of the electoral college system for selecting the President would require a (*a*) constitutional amendment (*b*) popular referendum (*c*) presidential proclamation (*d*) Supreme Court decision.

11. According to the Constitution, Congress is required to meet (*a*) twice a year (*b*) annually (*c*) once every two years (*d*) only when called into session by the President.

12. Members of the President's Cabinet remain in office (*a*) for a term of four years (*b*) for a term fixed by the House of Representatives (*c*) at the pleasure of the Senate (*d*) at the pleasure of the President.

13. The House of Representatives has the sole power to (*a*) approve presidential appointments (*b*) impeach federal officials (*c*) override presidential vetoes (*d*) hold party caucuses.

14. According to the Presidential Succession Act of 1947, the person next in line of succession after the Vice President is the (*a*) Secretary of State (*b*) Secretary of the Treasury (*c*) Speaker of the House (*d*) President pro tempore of the Senate.

15. Only a simple majority vote is necessary for the   (a) ratification of a treaty by the Senate   (b) proposal of a constitutional amendment by Congress   (c) enactment of a federal law by Congress   (d) overriding of a President's veto by Congress.

Multiple-Choice Test II

1. The Constitution grants the President all of the following EXCEPT the power to   (a) veto a bill passed by Congress   (b) dismiss a senator from office   (c) appoint an ambassador to a foreign country   (d) call a special session of Congress.
2. The framers of the Constitution provided long terms for judges of the Supreme Court in order to   (a) save expenses incurred by frequent changes in office   (b) make it easier for judges to render decisions without political interference   (c) prevent judges from running for political office   (d) reward political followers with secure jobs.
3. A decision of the Supreme Court declaring a law unconstitutional can be nullified by   (a) an amendment to the Constitution   (b) a presidential veto   (c) a vote of the legislatures of three-fourths of the states   (d) a two-thirds vote of Congress.
4. Which is an example of a power belonging only to the U.S. Senate?   (a) the trial of President Andrew Johnson after his impeachment   (b) the selection of a President in the election of 1824 when no candidate received a majority of the electoral votes   (c) the declaration of war against Germany in 1941   (d) the selection of Jim Wright as Speaker after the 1986 election.
5. Which person is an employee of the executive branch of the federal government?   (a) a page in the Senate   (b) a secretary of a member of the House of Representatives   (c) an associate justice of the Supreme Court   (d) a representative of the State Department in a foreign city.
6. The President of the United States is inaugurated on   (a) the first Tuesday after the first Monday in November   (b) January 3   (c) January 20   (d) March 4.
7. The official title of the presiding officer of the House of Representatives is   (a) Chief Executive   (b) Floor Leader   (c) Speaker   (d) Vice President.
8. The number of electoral votes needed to elect a President is   (a) 100   (b) 270   (c) 435   (d) 538.
9. The number of judges on the United States Supreme Court is   (a) three   (b) five   (c) seven   (d) nine.
10. When one state sues another state, the case is tried in   (a) a State Supreme Court   (b) the United States Supreme Court   (c) Congress   (d) the Department of Justice.
11. All of the following courts belong to the federal court system EXCEPT the   (a) circuit court of appeals   (b) district court   (c) magistrate's court   (d) claims court.
12. The Secretary of State in the President's Cabinet is in charge of administering policies concerning   (a) labor-management relations   (b) defense   (c) interstate commerce   (d) relations with foreign countries.
13. All of the following are under the direct supervision of the United States Congress EXCEPT the   (a) Peace Corps   (b) Government Printing Office   (c) Library of Congress   (d) General Accounting Office.

14. All of the following are members of the President's Cabinet EXCEPT the (*a*) Secretary of Housing and Urban Development   (*b*) Secretary of Agriculture   (*c*) Attorney General   (*d*) Secretary of the Army.
15. Each of the following executive departments is correctly paired with one of its functions EXCEPT (*a*) State—issues passports (*b*) Interior—supervises American overseas possessions (*c*) Commerce—operates the National Weather Service (*d*) Health and Human Services—supervises federal meat inspection.

Matching Test

Column A	Column B
1. Export-Import Bank	*a.* Seeks to eliminate job discrimination
2. Federal Deposit Insurance Corporation	*b.* Operates the merit system
3. Environmental Protection Agency	*c.* Coordinates government purchasing
4. Federal Maritime Commission	*d.* Seeks to prevent unfair labor practices
5. Federal Trade Commission	*e.* Extends loans to spur international trade
6. General Services Administration	*f.* Regulates railroads, trucks, and buses operating interstate
7. Equal Employment Opportunity Commission	*g.* Regulates American vessels engaged in foreign trade
8. National Labor Relations Board	*h.* Licenses TV stations
9. Federal Reserve Board	*i.* Coordinates antipollution activities
10. Office of Personnel Management	*j.* Operates historical, scientific, and cultural establishments
11. Department of Transportation	*k.* Insures savings bank accounts
12. Federal Communications Commission	*l.* Administers programs of benefits to ex-soldiers
13. Smithsonian Institution	*m.* Protects investors
14. Department of Veterans Affairs	*n.* Seeks to prevent unfair business practices
15. Securities and Exchange Commission	*o.* Controls money supply and credit

Modified True-False Test

1. The *Secretary of Defense* is the commander-in-chief of the nation's armed forces.
2. The U.S. Supreme Court has *both original and appellate* jurisdiction.
3. The term of the President of the United States is *four* years.
4. The *Department of the Interior* is in charge of Indian affairs.
5. The House of Representatives is composed of *538* members.
6. *California and New York State* are the two states with the largest number of representatives in Congress.
7. Congress holds its sessions in the *White House.*

8. Informal party conferences held by members of Congress to select the various congressional officials are called *nominating conventions.*
9. Washington, D.C., is governed by the *District of Columbia Circuit Court.*
10. The agency within the Justice Department that is responsible for crime prevention and detection interstate is the *Central Intelligence Agency.*

Essay Questions

1. With relation to the office of the President, explain *two* of the following: the necessity for the Twelfth Amendment, the changes brought about by the Twentieth Amendment, and the significance of the Twenty-second Amendment.
2. It has been said that the President of the United States has one of the most difficult jobs in the world. (*a*) Discuss briefly *two* major responsibilities of the President. (*b*) List *three* agencies that are included in the Executive Office of the President and describe how *each* assists the Chief Executive. (*c*) State *one* specific duty or power of the Vice President that is provided for by the Constitution.
3. Individual rights such as *freedom of speech* and *freedom of the press* are a vital part of every American's heritage of freedom. (*a*) List *four* rights other than the two mentioned that are part of this heritage. (*b*) Show by the use of specific examples how any *two* of these rights can be applied to one's everyday life.
4. (*a*) Give *three* qualifications necessary for election to the House of Representatives. (*b*) List *two* special powers granted to the House of Representatives. (*c*) Name *three* powers of Congress. (*d*) List *two* special powers granted to the Senate.
5. The U.S. flag is a symbol of the nation and the ideals in which Americans believe. (*a*) What is the meaning of the stars on the flag? (*b*) What is the meaning of the stripes? (*c*) Give *three* rules in regard to the care of the flag or people's conduct toward it.
6. The inspiring name "Old Glory" was given to the American flag in 1831. (*a*) State the correct method for displaying the flag on a speaker's platform. (*b*) How should a person not in uniform honor the flag when it is being hoisted or lowered, or when it is passing in a procession? (*c*) Write the pledge of allegiance to the flag. (*d*) In a short paragraph, tell how an understanding of the meaning of this pledge can help one become a better citizen.
7. The code of a good American is made up of the rules of self-control, kindness, sportsmanship, self-reliance, truth, and loyalty. (*a*) Select *two* of these rules and tell how each may help one to become a better citizen. (*b*) State *five* things that a person may do to show that he or she is a good citizen.
8. (*a*) Explain the role played by each of *three* of the following in the election of the President of the United States: nominating conventions, party platforms, presidential campaigns, and the electoral college system. (*b*) Give the constitutional qualifications required of a candidate for the office of President.
9. An important duty of a good citizen is the duty of voting for the government officials of one's community, state, and nation. (*a*) Explain fully why it is

important that a citizen take part in all elections. (*b*) Name *one* way by which people can be encouraged to vote in elections. (*c*) Describe *two* ways in which candidates for public office attempt to win votes.

10. Describe *one* function of each of *five* of the following in the operation of Congress: Majority Leader, Party Whip, Secretary of the Senate, Parliamentarian, Sergeant at Arms, Speaker of the House, Chaplain, and Clerk of the House.

Graph Analysis Test

Study the line graph below and answer the questions that follow.

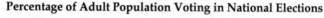

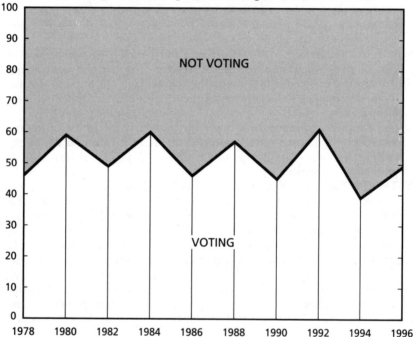

Percentage of Adult Population Voting in National Elections

1. How do you account for the sawtooth pattern of voting displayed in the graph?
2. From the information provided in the graph, could you conclude that a majority of the adult population endorsed the Republican sweep of Congress in 1994? Why or why not?
3. In which year shown did the lowest percentage of the adult population participate in a presidential election? In your opinion, why did so few people vote?

Appendix

THE DECLARATION OF INDEPENDENCE

Note: Capitalization, spelling, punctuation, and paragraphing have been modernized. In addition, the signers' names have been rearranged and grouped alphabetically by state.

In Congress, July 4, 1776

THE UNANIMOUS DECLARATION OF THE THIRTEEN UNITED STATES OF AMERICA

WHEN, IN THE COURSE of human events, it becomes necessary for one people to dissolve the political bands which have connected them with another, and to assume, among the powers of the earth, the separate and equal station to which the laws of nature and of nature's God entitle them, a decent respect to the opinions of mankind requires that they should declare the causes which impel them to the separation.

We hold these truths to be self-evident: that all men are created equal; that they are endowed by their Creator with certain unalienable rights; that among these are life, liberty, and the pursuit of happiness.

That to secure these rights, governments are instituted among men, deriving their just powers from the consent of the governed. That, whenever any form of government becomes destructive of these ends, it is the right of the people to alter or to abolish it, and to institute new government, laying its foundation on such principles, and organizing its powers in such form, as to them shall seem most likely to effect their safety and happiness. Prudence, indeed, will dictate that governments long established should not be changed for light and transient causes; and, accordingly, all experience hath shown that mankind are more disposed to suffer, while evils are sufferable, than to right themselves by abolishing the forms to which they are accustomed. But when a long train of abuses and usurpations, pursuing invariably the same object, evinces a design to reduce them under absolute despotism, it is their right, it is their duty, to throw off such government, and to provide new guards for their future security.

Such has been the patient sufferance of these colonies; and such is now the necessity which constrains them to alter their former systems of government. The history of the present King of Great Britain is a history of repeated injuries and usurpations, all having in direct object the establishment of an absolute tyranny over these states. To prove this, let facts be submitted to a candid world.

-List of grievances by George III showing tyrannical action against the English colonies

He has refused his assent to laws the most wholesome and necessary for the public good.

He has forbidden his governors to pass laws of immediate and pressing importance, unless suspended in their operation till his assent should be obtained; and, when so suspended, he has utterly neglected to attend to them.

He has refused to pass other laws for the accommodation of large districts of people, unless those people would relinquish the right of representation in the legislature—a right inestimable to them and formidable to tyrants only.

He has called together legislative bodies at places unusual, uncomfortable, and distant from the depository of their public records, for the sole purpose of fatiguing them into compliance with his measures.

He has dissolved representative houses repeatedly, for opposing, with manly firmness, his invasions on the rights of the people.

He has refused, for a long time after such dissolutions, to cause others to be elected; whereby the legislative powers, incapable of annihilation, have returned to the people at large for their exercise; the state remaining, in the meantime, exposed to all the dangers of invasion from without and convulsions within.

He has endeavored to prevent the population of these states; for that purpose obstructing the laws for naturalization of foreigners, refusing to pass others to encourage their migration hither, and raising the conditions of new appropriations of lands.

He has obstructed the administration of justice by refusing his assent to laws for establishing judiciary powers.

He has made judges dependent on his will alone for the tenure of their offices and the amount and payment of their salaries.

He has erected a multitude of new offices and sent hither swarms of officers to harass our people and eat out their substance.

He has kept among us, in times of peace, standing armies, without the consent of our legislatures.

He has affected to render the military independent of, and superior to, the civil power.

He has combined with others to subject us to a jurisdiction foreign to our constitution and unacknowledged by our laws, giving his assent to their acts of pretended legislation:

For quartering large bodies of armed troops among us;

For protecting them, by a mock trial, from punishment for any murders which they should commit on the inhabitants of these states;

For cutting off our trade with all parts of the world;

For imposing taxes on us without our consent;

For depriving us, in many cases, of the benefits of trial by jury;

For transporting us beyond seas to be tried for pretended offenses;

For abolishing the free system of English laws in a neighboring province, establishing therein an arbitrary government and enlarging its boundaries, so as to render it at once an example and fit instrument for introducing the same absolute rule into these colonies;

For taking away our charters, abolishing our most valuable laws, and altering fundamentally the forms of our governments;

For suspending our own legislatures, and declaring themselves invested with power to legislate for us in all cases whatsoever.

He has abdicated government here by declaring us out of his protection and waging war against us.

He has plundered our seas, ravaged our coasts, burned our towns, and destroyed the lives of our people.

He is, at this time, transporting large armies of foreign mercenaries to complete the works of death, desolation, and tyranny already begun with circumstances of cruelty and perfidy scarcely paralleled in the most barbarous ages, and totally unworthy the head of a civilized nation.

He has constrained our fellow citizens taken captive on the high seas to bear arms against their country, to become the executioners of their friends and brethren, or to fall themselves by their hands.

He has excited domestic insurrections among us, and has endeavored to bring on the inhabitants of our frontiers the merciless Indian savages, whose known rule of warfare is an undistinguished destruction of all ages, sexes, and conditions.

In every stage of these oppressions we have petitioned for redress in the most humble terms. Our repeated petitions have been answered only by repeated injury. A prince whose character is thus marked by every act which may define a tyrant is unfit to be the ruler of a free people.

Nor have we been wanting in attentions to our British brethren. We have warned them, from time to time, of attempts by their legislature to extend an unwarrantable jurisdiction over us. We have reminded them of the circumstances of our emigration and settlement here. We have appealed to their native justice and magnanimity; and we have conjured them, by the ties of our common kindred, to disavow these usurpations, which would inevitably interrupt our connections and correspondence. They, too, have been deaf to the voice of justice and consanguinity. We must, therefore, acquiesce in the necessity which denounces our separation, and hold them, as we hold the rest of mankind, enemies in war, in peace friends.

We, therefore, the representatives of the United States of America, in General Congress assembled, appealing to the Supreme Judge of the world for the rectitude of our intentions, do, in the name and by authority of the good people of these colonies, solemnly publish and declare: that these united colonies are, and of right ought to be, free and independent states; that they are absolved from all allegiance to the British crown, and that all political connection between them and the state of Great Britain is, and ought to be, totally dissolved; and that, as free and independent states, they have full power to levy war, conclude peace, contract alliances, establish commerce, and to do all other acts and things which independent states may of right do. And for the support of this declaration, with a firm reliance on the protection of Divine Providence, we mutually pledge to each other our lives, our fortunes, and our sacred honor.

Delegates from all 13 Colonies sign the Dec of Ind.

[Signed by]   **John Hancock**
                                   [Massachusetts]

[Connecticut]   **[New Hampshire]**   **[Pennsylvania]**
Samuel Huntington   Josiah Bartlett   George Clymer
Roger Sherman   Matthew Thornton   Benjamin Franklin
William Williams   William Whipple   Robert Morris
Oliver Wolcott   John Morton
                          [New Jersey]   George Ross
[Delaware]   Abraham Clark   Benjamin Rush
Thomas McKean   John Hart   James Smith
George Read   Francis Hopkinson   George Taylor
Caesar Rodney   Richard Stockton   James Wilson
                          John Witherspoon
[Georgia]   **[Rhode Island]**
Button Gwinnett   **[New York]**   William Ellery
Lyman Hall   William Floyd   Stephen Hopkins
George Walton   Francis Lewis
                          Philip Livingston   **[South Carolina]**
[Maryland]   Lewis Morris   Thomas Heyward, Jr.
Charles Carroll   Thomas Lynch, Jr.
  of Carrollton   **[North Carolina]**   Arthur Middleton
Samuel Chase   Joseph Hewes   Edward Rutledge
William Paca   William Hooper
Thomas Stone   John Penn   **[Virginia]**
                                                      Carter Braxton
[Massachusetts]   Benjamin Harrison
John Adams   Thomas Jefferson
Samuel Adams   Francis Lightfoot Lee
Elbridge Gerry   Richard Henry Lee
Robert Treat Paine   Thomas Nelson, Jr.
                                                      George Wythe

THE CONSTITUTION OF THE UNITED STATES OF AMERICA

John Adams political [?] is reflected in the Constitution mostly written by James Madison

Note: Footnotes, headings, and explanations have been added to aid the reader. The explanations within the body of the text are enclosed in brackets []. The parts of the Constitution that are no longer in effect are printed in *italic* type. Capitalization, spelling, and punctuation have been modernized. In addition, the signers' names have been rearranged and grouped alphabetically by state.

PREAMBLE[1]

We the people of the United States, in order to form a more perfect Union, establish justice, insure domestic tranquility,[2] provide for the common defense, promote the general welfare, and secure the blessings of liberty to ourselves and our posterity [descendants], do ordain [issue] and establish this Constitution for the United States of America.

ARTICLE I. Legislative Department

Section 1. Congress

All legislative powers herein granted shall be vested in a Congress of the United States, which shall consist of a Senate and House of Representatives.

---

[1]Introduction.

[2]"Insure domestic tranquility" means *assure peace within the nation.*

Section 2.   House of Representatives

[1] The House of Representatives shall be composed of members chosen every second year by the people of the several states, and the electors [voters] in each state shall have the qualifications requisite [required] for electors of the most numerous branch of the state legislature.

[2] No person shall be a representative who shall not have attained to [reached] the age of twenty-five years and been seven years a citizen of the United States, and who shall not, when elected, be an inhabitant of that state in which he shall be chosen.

[3] Representatives and direct taxes[1] shall be apportioned [divided] among the several states which may be included within this Union according to their respective numbers [population], *which shall be determined by adding to the whole number of free persons, including those bound to service for a term of years* [indentured servants], *and excluding Indians not taxed, three-fifths of all other persons.*[2] The actual enumeration [census] shall be made within three years after the first meeting of the Congress of the United States, and within every subsequent term of ten years, in such manner as they shall by law direct. The number of representatives shall not exceed one for every thirty thousand, but each state shall have at least one representative; *and until such enumeration shall be made, the State of New Hampshire shall be entitled to choose three, Massachusetts eight, Rhode Island and Providence Plantations one, Connecticut five, New York six, New Jersey four, Pennsylvania eight, Delaware one, Maryland six, Virginia ten, North Carolina five, South Carolina five, and Georgia three.*[3]

[4] When vacancies happen in the representation from any state, the executive authority [governor] thereof shall issue writs of election[4] to fill such vacancies.

[5] The House of Representatives shall choose their Speaker and other officers; and shall have the sole power of impeachment.[5]

Section 3.   Senate

[1] The Senate of the United States shall be composed of two senators from each state, *chosen by the legislature thereof,*[6] for six years; and each senator shall have one vote.

---

[1]Modified by Amendment XVI, which granted Congress the power to levy a direct tax on individual incomes rather than on the basis of state populations.

[2]"Other persons" refer to slaves. Amendment XIII abolished slavery; Amendment XIV specifically eliminated the three-fifths formula.

[3]Temporary provision.

[4]"Issue writs of election" means *call a special election.*

[5]"Power of impeachment" means *right to charge federal officials with misconduct.*

[6]Replaced by Amendment XVII, which provided for popular election of senators.

[2] *Immediately after they shall be assembled in consequence of the first election, they shall be divided as equally as may be into three classes. The seats of the senators of the first class shall be vacated at the expiration of the second year, of the second class at the expiration of the fourth year, and of the third class at the expiration of the sixth year,*[1] so that one-third may be chosen every second year; *and if vacancies happen by resignation, or otherwise, during the recess of the legislature of any state, the executive* [governor] *thereof may make temporary appointments until the next meeting of the legislature, which shall then fill such vacancies.*[2]

[3] No person shall be a senator who shall not have attained to the age of thirty years and been nine years a citizen of the United States, and who shall not, when elected, be an inhabitant of that state for which he shall be chosen.

[4] The vice president of the United States shall be president of the Senate, but shall have no vote, unless they be equally divided [tied].

[5] The Senate shall choose their other officers, and also a president pro tempore [temporary presiding officer], in the absence of the vice president, or when he shall exercise the office of president of the United States.

[6] The Senate shall have sole power to try all impeachments.[3] When sitting for that purpose, they shall be on oath or affirmation.[4] When the president of the United States is tried, the chief justice [of the United States] shall preside; and no person shall be convicted without the concurrence [agreement] of two-thirds of the members present.

[7] Judgment in cases of impeachment shall not extend further than to removal from office, and disqualification to hold and enjoy any office of honor, trust, or profit under the United States; but the party convicted shall nevertheless be liable and subject to indictment, trial, judgment, and punishment, according to law.

Section 4.   Elections and Meetings of Congress

[1] The times, places, and manner of holding elections for senators and representatives shall be prescribed [designated] in each state by the legislature thereof; but the Congress may at any time by law make or alter such regulations, except as to the places of choosing senators.

---

[1]Temporary provision, designed to organize the first Senate in such a way that, thereafter, only one-third of its members would be subject to replacement at each successive election.

[2]Modified by Amendment XVII, which permits a governor to select a temporary replacement to fill the vacancy until the next election.

[3]"To try all impeachments" means *to conduct the trials of officials impeached by the House of Representatives.* When trying such cases, the Senate serves as a court.

[4]If taking an oath violates a member's religious principles, that person may "affirm" rather than "swear."

[2] The Congress shall assemble at least once in every year, *and such meeting shall be on the first Monday in December*,[1] unless they shall by law appoint a different day.

Section 5.   Rules and Procedures of the Two Houses

[1] Each house shall be the judge of the elections, returns, and qualifications of its own members,[2] and a majority of each shall constitute a quorum[3] to do business; but a smaller number may adjourn from day to day, and may be authorized to compel the attendance of absent members, in such manner, and under such penalties, as each house may provide.

[2] Each house may determine the rules of its proceedings, punish its members for disorderly behavior, and with the concurrence of two-thirds, expel a member.

[3] Each house shall keep a journal [record] of its proceedings, and from time to time publish the same, excepting such parts as may in their judgment require secrecy; and the yeas [affirmative votes] and nays [negative votes] of the members of either house on any question shall, at the desire of one-fifth of those present, be entered on the journal.

[4] Neither house, during the session of Congress, shall, without the consent of the other, adjourn for more than three days, nor to any other place than that in which the two houses shall be sitting.

Section 6.   Members' Privileges and Restrictions

[1] The senators and representatives shall receive a compensation [salary] for their services, to be ascertained [fixed] by law and paid out of the treasury of the United States. They shall in all cases except treason, felony [serious crime], and breach of the peace [disorderly conduct], be privileged [immune] from arrest during their attendance at the session of their respective houses, and in going to and returning from the same; and for any speech or debate in either house, they shall not be questioned in any other place.[4]

[2] No senator or representative shall, during the time for which he was elected, be appointed to any civil office under the authority of the

---

[1]Amendment XX changed this date to January 3.

[2]This provision empowers either house, by a majority vote, to refuse to seat a newly elected member.

[3]A "quorum" is the *number of members that must be present in order to conduct business.*

[4]"They shall not be questioned in any other place" means that *they may not be sued for slander or libel.* Freedom from arrest during congressional sessions and freedom of speech within the halls of Congress—two privileges granted to members of Congress—are known as *congressional immunity.*

United States, which shall have been created, or the emoluments [salary] whereof shall have been increased, during such time; and no person holding any office under the United States shall be a member of either house during his continuance in office.

Section 7.   Lawmaking Procedures

[1] All bills for raising revenue shall originate [be introduced] in the House of Representatives; but the Senate may propose or concur with [approve] amendments as on other bills.

[2] Every bill which shall have passed the House of Representatives and the Senate shall, before it becomes a law, be presented to the president of the United States; if he approve, he shall sign it, but if not, he shall return it, with his objections, to that house in which it shall have originated, who shall enter the objections at large on their journal, and proceed to reconsider it. If after such reconsideration two-thirds of that house shall agree to pass the bill, it shall be sent, together with the objections, to the other house, by which it shall likewise be reconsidered, and, if approved by two-thirds of that house, it shall become a law. But in all such cases the votes of both houses shall be determined by yeas and nays, and the names of the persons voting for and against the bill shall be entered on the journal of each house respectively. If any bill shall not be returned by the president within ten days (Sundays excepted) after it shall have been presented to him, the same shall be a law, in like manner as if he had signed it, unless the Congress by their adjournment prevent its return, in which case it shall not be a law.[1]

[3] Every order, resolution, or vote to which the concurrence of the Senate and House of Representatives may be necessary (except on a question of adjournment) shall be presented to the president of the United States; and before the same shall take effect, shall be approved by him, or, being disapproved by him, shall be repassed by two-thirds of the Senate and House of Representatives, according to the rules and limitations prescribed in the case of a bill.

Section 8.   Powers of Congress

The Congress shall have power:

[1] To lay and collect taxes, duties, imposts, and excises,[2] to pay the

---

[1]If Congress adjourns before the ten-day period is up, the president can kill a bill by ignoring it ("putting it in his pocket"). Therefore, this type of presidential rejection is called a *pocket veto*.

[2]"Duties, imposts, and excises" are forms of taxation. Duties and imposts are taxes on imports. Excises are taxes on goods produced or services performed within a country.

debts and provide for the common defense and general welfare of the United States; but all duties, imposts, and excises shall be uniform [the same] throughout the United States;

[2] To borrow money on the credit of the United States;

[3] To regulate commerce with foreign nations, and among the several states, and with the Indian tribes;

[4] To establish a uniform rule of naturalization, and uniform laws on the subject of bankruptcies throughout the United States;

[5] To coin money, regulate the value thereof, and of foreign coin, and fix [set] the standard of weights and measures;

[6] To provide for the punishment of counterfeiting[1] the securities and current coin of the United States;

[7] To establish post offices and post roads;

[8] To promote the progress of science and useful arts by securing for limited times to authors and inventors the exclusive right to their respective writings and discoveries;[2]

[9] To constitute tribunals [establish courts] inferior to [lower than] the Supreme Court;

[10] To define and punish piracies and felonies committed on the high seas[3] and offenses against the law of nations [international law];

[11] To declare war, grant letters of marque and reprisal,[4] and make rules concerning captures on land and water;

[12] To raise and support armies, but no appropriation of money to that use shall be for a longer term than two years;

[13] To provide and maintain a navy;

[14] To make rules for the government and regulation of the land and naval forces;

[15] To provide for calling forth the militia[5] to execute [carry out] the laws of the Union, suppress [put down] insurrections [rebellions], and repel [drive back] invasions;

[16] To provide for organizing, arming, and disciplining [training] the militia, and for governing such part of them as may be employed in the service of the United States, reserving to the states respectively the appointment of the officers, and the authority of training the militia according to the discipline [regulations] prescribed by Congress;

---

[1]Making an imitation with the intent of passing it as the genuine article.

[2]Copyright and patent laws, passed by Congress on the basis of this clause, protect the rights of authors and inventors.

[3]Open ocean; waters outside the territorial limits of a country.

[4]Letters of marque and reprisal are government licenses issued to private citizens in time of war authorizing them to fit out armed vessels (called *privateers*) for the purpose of capturing or destroying enemy ships.

[5]Citizen soldiers who are not in the regular armed forces but are subject to military duty in times of emergency; for example, the National Guard.

[17] To exercise exclusive legislation[1] in all cases whatsoever, over such district (not exceeding ten miles square) as may, by cession of particular states, and the acceptance of Congress, become the seat of government of the United States, and to exercise like authority over all places purchased by the consent of the legislature of the state in which the same shall be, for the erection of forts, magazines, arsenals, dockyards, and other needful buildings; and

[18] To make all laws which shall be necessary and proper for carrying into execution the foregoing powers and all other powers vested by this Constitution in the government of the United States, or in any department or officer thereof.[2]

Section 9.   Powers Denied to the Federal Government

[1] *The migration or importation of such persons as any of the states now existing shall think proper to admit shall not be prohibited by the Congress prior to the year 1808; but a tax or duty may be imposed on such importation, not exceeding ten dollars for each person.*[3]

[2] The privilege of the writ of habeas corpus[4] shall not be suspended, unless when in cases of rebellion or invasion the public safety may require it.

[3] No bill of attainder[5] or ex post facto law[6] shall be passed.

[4] No capitation [head] or other direct tax shall be laid, unless in proportion to the census or enumeration herein before directed to be taken.[7]

[5] No tax or duty shall be laid on articles exported from any state.

[6] No preference shall be given by any regulation of commerce or revenue to the ports of one state over those of another; nor shall vessels bound to, or from, one state be obliged to enter, clear, or pay duties in another.

---

[1]"To exercise exclusive legislation . . . over such district" means *to be solely responsible for making the laws for a designated area.*

[2]This is the so-called "elastic clause" of the Constitution, which allows Congress to carry out many actions not specifically listed.

[3]This temporary provision prohibited Congress from interfering with the importation of slaves ("such persons") before 1808.

[4]A "writ of habeas corpus" is a court order obtained by a person taken into custody, demanding to know the reasons for imprisonment. If the court rules that the reasons are insufficient, the prisoner is released.

[5]A law that deprives a person of civil rights without a trial.

[6]A law that punishes a person for a past action that was not unlawful at the time it was committed.

[7]Modified by Amendment XVI.

[7] No money shall be drawn from the treasury, but in consequence of appropriations made by law; and a regular statement and account of the receipts and expenditures of all public money shall be published from time to time.

[8] No title of nobility shall be granted by the United States; and no person holding any office of profit or trust under them shall, without the consent of the Congress, accept of any present, emolument, office, or title, of any kind whatever, from any king, prince, or foreign state.

Section 10. Powers Denied to the States

[1] No state shall enter into any treaty, alliance, or confederation; grant letters of marque and reprisal; coin money; emit bills of credit;[1] make anything but gold and silver coin a tender [legal money] in payment of debts; pass any bill of attainder, ex post facto law, or law impairing the obligation of contracts,[2] or grant any title of nobility.

[2] No state shall, without the consent of the Congress, lay any imposts or duties on imports or exports, except what may be absolutely necessary for executing its inspection laws; and the net produce [income] of all duties and imposts, laid by any state on imports or exports, shall be for the use of the treasury of the United States; and all such laws shall be subject to the revision and control of the Congress.

[3] No state shall, without the consent of Congress, lay any duty of tonnage,[3] keep troops[4] or ships of war in time of peace, enter into any agreement or compact with another state or with a foreign power, or engage in war unless actually invaded or in such imminent [threatening] danger as will not admit of delay.

ARTICLE II. Executive Department

Section 1. President and Vice President

[1] The executive power shall be vested in a president of the United States of America. He shall hold his office during the term of four years,[5] and, together with the vice president, chosen for the same term, be elected as follows:

[2] Each state shall appoint, in such manner as the legislature thereof may direct, a number of electors, equal to the whole number of senators

---

[1]"Emit bills of credit" means *issue paper money.*

[2]"Impairing the obligation of contracts" means *weakening the obligations persons assume when they enter into legal agreements.*

[3]"Duty of tonnage" means a *tax based upon a vessel's cargo-carrying capacity.*

[4]Other than militia.

[5]Amendment XXII limits a president to two terms.

and representatives to which the state may be entitled in the Congress; but no senator or representative, or person holding an office of trust or profit under the United States, shall be appointed an elector.

[3] *The electors shall meet in their respective states, and vote by ballot for two persons, of whom one at least shall not be an inhabitant of the same state with themselves. And they shall make a list of all the persons voted for, and of the number of votes for each; which list they shall sign and certify, and transmit sealed to the seat of the government of the United States, directed to the president of the Senate. The president of the Senate shall, in the presence of the Senate and House of Representatives, open all the certificates, and the votes shall then be counted. The person having the greatest number of votes shall be the president, if such number be a majority of the whole number of electors appointed; and if there be more than one who have such majority, and have an equal number of votes, then the House of Representatives shall immediately choose by ballot one of them for president; and if no person have a majority, then from the five highest on the list the said House shall in like manner choose the president. But in choosing the president, the votes shall be taken by states, the representation from each state having one vote; a quorum for this purpose shall consist of a member or members from two-thirds of the states, and a majority of all the states shall be necessary to a choice. In every case, after the choice of the president, the person having the greatest number of votes of the electors shall be the vice president. But if there should remain two or more who have equal votes, the Senate shall choose from them by ballot the vice president.*[1]

[4] The Congress may determine the time of choosing the electors, and the day on which they shall give their votes; which day shall be the same throughout the United States.

[5] No person except a natural-born citizen, *or a citizen of the United States at the time of the adoption of this Constitution,*[2] shall be eligible to the office of president; neither shall any person be eligible to that office who shall not have attained to the age of thirty-five years and been fourteen years a resident within the United States.

[6] In case of the removal of the president from office, or of his death, resignation, or inability to discharge the powers and duties of the said office, the same shall devolve on the vice president, and the Congress may by law provide for the case of removal, death, resignation, or inability, both of the president and vice president, declaring what officer shall then act as president, and such officer shall act accordingly, until the disability be removed, or a president shall be elected.[3]

---

[1]Replaced by Amendment XII.

[2]Temporary provision.

[3]Modified by Amendments XX and XXV.

[7] The president shall, at stated times, receive for his services a compensation, which shall neither be increased nor diminished [decreased] during the period for which he shall have been elected, and he shall not receive within that period any other emolument from the United States, or any of them.

[8] Before he enter on the execution of his office, he shall take the following oath or affirmation:

"I do solemnly swear (or affirm) that I will faithfully execute the office of President of the United States, and will, to the best of my ability, preserve, protect, and defend the Constitution of the United States."

Section 2.   Powers of the President

[1] The president shall be commander in chief of the army and navy [all the armed forces] of the United States, and of the militia of the several states, when called into the actual service of the United States; he may require the opinion in writing of the principal officer in each of the executive departments upon any subject relating to the duties of their respective offices; and he shall have power to grant reprieves[1] and pardons[2] for offenses against the United States except in cases of impeachment.

[2] He shall have power, by and with the advice and consent of the Senate, to make treaties, provided two-thirds of the senators present concur; and he shall nominate, and, by and with the advice and consent of the Senate, shall appoint ambassadors, other public ministers and consuls, judges of the Supreme Court, and all other officers of the United States whose appointments are not herein otherwise provided for and which shall be established by law; but the Congress may by law vest the appointment of such inferior officers as they think proper in the president alone, in the courts of law, or in the heads of departments.

[3] The president shall have power to fill up all vacancies that may happen during the recess of the Senate, by granting commissions which shall expire at the end of their next session.

Section 3.   Duties and Responsibilities of the President

He shall, from time to time, give to the Congress information of the state of the Union, and recommend to their consideration such measures as he shall judge necessary and expedient [advisable]; he may, on extraordinary [special] occasions, convene both houses, or either of them, and in case of disagreement between them with respect to the time of adjourn-

---

[1]A "reprieve" is a postponement of the execution of a sentence.

[2]A "pardon" is a release from penalty.

ment, he may adjourn them to such time as he shall think proper; he shall receive ambassadors and other public ministers; he shall take care that the laws be faithfully executed, and shall commission [appoint] all the officers of the United States.

Section 4. Impeachment

The president, vice president, and all civil officers[1] of the United States, shall be removed from office on impeachment for, and conviction of, treason, bribery, or other high crimes and misdemeanors [offenses].

ARTICLE III. Judicial Department

Section 1. Federal Courts

The judicial power of the United States shall be vested in one Supreme Court, and in such inferior [lower] courts as the Congress may from time to time ordain and establish. The judges, both of the Supreme and inferior courts, shall hold their offices during good behavior, and shall, at stated times, receive for their services a compensation, which shall not be diminished during their continuance in office.

Section 2. Jurisdiction of Federal Courts

[1] The judicial power shall extend to all cases in law and equity[2] arising under this Constitution, the laws of the United States, and treaties made, or which shall be made, under their authority; to all cases affecting ambassadors, other public ministers, and consuls; to all cases of admiralty and maritime jurisdiction;[3] to controversies [disputes] to which the United States shall be a party; to controversies between two or more states, between a state and citizens of another state,[4] between citizens of different

---

[1]"Civil officers" include executive and judicial officials, but not members of Congress or officers in the armed forces.

[2]"Cases in law" refers mainly to disputes that arise from the violation of, or the interpretation of, federal laws, treaties, or the Constitution. "Equity" is a branch of the law that deals more generally with the prevention of injustice.

[3]Legal disputes involving ships and shipping on the high seas, in territorial waters, and on the navigable waterways within the country.

[4]Modified by Amendment XI, which provides that a state may not be sued in the federal courts by a citizen of another state (or by a citizen of a foreign country). A state, however, retains the right to sue a citizen of another state (or a citizen of a foreign country) in the federal courts.

states, between citizens of the same state claiming lands under grants of different states, and between a state, or the citizens thereof, and foreign states, citizens, or subjects.[1]

[2] In all cases affecting ambassadors, other public ministers, and consuls, and those in which a state shall be a party, the Supreme Court shall have original jurisdiction.[2] In all the other cases before mentioned, the Supreme Court shall have appellate jurisdiction,[3] both as to law and fact, with such exceptions and under such regulations as the Congress shall make.

[3] The trial of all crimes, except in cases of impeachment, shall be by jury; and such trial shall be held in the state where the said crimes shall have been committed; but when not committed within any state, the trial shall be at such place or places as the Congress may by law have directed.

Section 3.   Treason

[1] Treason against the United States shall consist only in levying [carrying on] war against them, or in adhering to [assisting] their enemies, giving them aid and comfort. No person shall be convicted of treason unless on the testimony of two witnesses to the same overt [open; public] act, or on confession in open court.

[2] The Congress shall have power to declare the punishment of treason, but no attainder of treason shall work corruption of blood or forfeiture except during the life of the person attainted.[4]

ARTICLE IV.   Interstate Relations

Section 1.   Official Acts and Records

Full faith and credit shall be given in each state to the public acts, records, and judicial proceedings of every other state.[5] And the Congress

---

[1]Modified by Amendment XI (see footnote 4 on previous page).

[2]"Original jurisdiction" means the authority of a court to hear cases that have not previously been tried by lower courts.

[3]"Appellate jurisdiction" means the authority of a court to review cases that have previously been tried by lower courts.

[4]Punishment imposed on someone for treason may not be extended to that person's children or heirs.

[5]The official acts of each state must be accepted by the other states. The "full faith and credit" clause applies to court judgments, contracts, marriages, corporation charters, etc.

may, by general laws, prescribe the manner in which such acts, records, and proceedings shall be proved, and the effect thereof.

Section 2.   Mutual Obligations of States

[1] The citizens of each state shall be entitled to all privileges and immunities of citizens in the several states.

[2] A person charged in any state with treason, felony, or other crime, who shall flee from justice and be found in another state, shall, on demand of the executive authority of the state from which he fled, be delivered up, to be removed to the state having jurisdiction of the crime.[1]

[3] *No person held to service or labor in one state, under the laws thereof, escaping into another, shall, in consequence of any law or regulation therein, be discharged from such service or labor, but shall be delivered up on claim of the party to whom such service or labor may be due.*[2]

Section 3.   New States and Territories

[1] New states may be admitted by the Congress into this Union; but no new state shall be formed or erected within the jurisdiction of any other state; nor any state be formed by the junction [joining] of two or more states, or parts of states, without the consent of the legislatures of the states concerned as well as of the Congress.

[2] The Congress shall have power to dispose of and make all needful rules and regulations respecting the territory or other property belonging to the United States; and nothing in this Constitution shall be so construed [interpreted] as to prejudice [damage] any claims of the United States, or of any particular state.

Section 4.   Federal Guarantees to the States

The United States shall guarantee to every state in this Union a republican form of government, and shall protect each of them against invasion; and on application of the legislature, or of the executive (when the legislature cannot be convened), against domestic violence [riots].

---

[1]The delivery by one state or government to another of fugitives from justice is called *extradition*.

[2]Since the phrase "person held to service or labor" refers to a slave, this clause was nullified by Amendment XIII.

ARTICLE V. Amending the Constitution

The Congress, whenever two-thirds of both houses shall deem [think] it necessary, shall propose amendments to this Constitution, or, on the application of the legislatures of two-thirds of the several states, shall call a convention for proposing amendments, which, in either case, shall be valid, to all intents and purposes, as part of this Constitution when ratified by the legislatures of three-fourths of the several states, or by conventions in three-fourths thereof, as the one or the other mode [method] of ratification may be proposed by the Congress; provided *that no amendment which may be made prior to the year 1808 shall in any manner affect the first and fourth clauses in the ninth section of the first article; and*[1] that no state, without its consent, shall be deprived of its equal suffrage in the Senate.

ARTICLE VI. Public Debts; Federal Supremacy; Oaths of Office

[1] All debts contracted and engagements [agreements] entered into before the adoption of this Constitution shall be as valid [binding] against the United States under this Constitution as under the Confederation.

[2] This Constitution, and the laws of the United States which shall be made in pursuance thereof, and all treaties made, or which shall be made, under the authority of the United States, shall be the supreme law of the land; and the judges in every state shall be bound thereby, anything in the constitution or laws of any state to the contrary notwithstanding.[2]

[3] The senators and representatives before mentioned, and the members of the several state legislatures, and all executive and judicial officers, both of the United States and of the several states, shall be bound by oath or affirmation to support this Constitution; but no religious test shall ever be required as a qualification to any office or public trust under the United States.

ARTICLE VII. Ratification

The ratification of the conventions of nine states shall be sufficient for the establishment of this Constitution between the states so ratifying the same.

---

[1]Temporary provision.

[2]This "supremacy clause" means that federal laws always override state legislation in cases of conflict.

Done in convention, by the unanimous consent of the states present, the 17th day of September, in the year of our Lord 1787, and of the independence of the United States of America the twelfth. In witness whereof we have hereunto subscribed our names.

[Signed by]   **George Washington**
[President and Deputy
from Virginia]

[Connecticut]
William Samuel Johnson
Roger Sherman

[Delaware]
George Read
Gunning Bedford, Jr.
John Dickinson
Richard Bassett
Jacob Broom

[Georgia]
William Few
Abraham Baldwin

[Maryland]
James McHenry
Dan of St. Thomas
  Jenifer
Daniel Carroll

[Massachusetts]
Nathaniel Gorham
Rufus King

[New Hampshire]
John Langdon
Nicholas Gilman

[New Jersey]
William Livingston
David Brearley
William Paterson
Jonathan Dayton

[New York]
Alexander Hamilton

[North Carolina]
William Blount
Richard Dobbs Spaight
Hugh Williamson

[Pennsylvania]
Benjamin Franklin
Thomas Mifflin
Robert Morris
George Clymer
Thomas Fitzsimons
Jared Ingersoll
James Wilson
Gouverneur Morris

[South Carolina]
John Rutledge
Charles Cotesworth
  Pinckney
Charles Pinckney
Pierce Butler

[Virginia]
John Blair
James Madison, Jr.

AMENDMENTS TO THE CONSTITUTION

Note: The first ten amendments to the Constitution make up the Bill of Rights. The date in parentheses after each amendment is the year in which it was adopted.

AMENDMENT I. Freedom of Religion, Speech, Press, Assembly, and Petition (1791)

Congress shall make no law respecting an establishment of religion, or prohibiting the free exercise thereof;[1] or abridging [reducing] the freedom of speech or of the press; or the right of the people peaceably to assemble, and to petition the government for a redress [correction] of grievances.

AMENDMENT II. Right to Bear Arms (1791)

A well-regulated militia being necessary to the security of a free state, the right of the people to keep and bear arms shall not be infringed [weakened].

AMENDMENT III. Quartering of Troops (1791)

No soldier shall, in time of peace, be quartered [assigned to live] in any house without the consent of the owner, nor in time of war, but in a manner to be prescribed by law.

---

[1]"The free exercise thereof" refers to freedom of worship.

AMENDMENT IV. Searches and Seizures (1791)

The right of the people to be secure [safe] in their persons, houses, papers, and effects [belongings] against unreasonable searches and seizures shall not be violated; and no [search] warrants shall issue but upon probable cause,[1] supported by oath or affirmation, and particularly describing the place to be searched, and the persons or things to be seized.

AMENDMENT V. Rights of the Accused; Property Rights (1791)

No person shall be held to answer for a capital or otherwise infamous crime unless on a presentment or indictment of a grand jury,[2] except in cases arising in the land or naval forces, or in the militia, when in actual service in time of war or public danger; nor shall any person be subject for the same offense to be twice put in jeopardy of life or limb;[3] nor shall be compelled in any criminal case to be a witness against himself; nor be deprived of life, liberty, or property without due process of law;[4] nor shall private property be taken for public use without just compensation.[5]

AMENDMENT VI. Additional Rights of the Accused (1791)

In all criminal prosecutions [trials], the accused shall enjoy the right to a speedy and public trial by an impartial [fair] jury of the state and district wherein the crime shall have been committed, which district shall have been previously ascertained by law; and to be informed of the nature and cause of the accusation; to be confronted with the witnesses against him; to have compulsory process for obtaining witnesses in his favor;[6] and to have the assistance of counsel for his defense.

---

[1]"Probable cause" means *a reasonable ground of suspicion.*

[2]"A capital or otherwise infamous crime" refers to serious offenses punishable by death or by imprisonment. Before someone may be tried for such a crime, a grand jury must decide that sufficient evidence exists to bring that person to trial.

[3]A person may not be tried twice for the same offense (double jeopardy).

[4]"Due process of law" means *proper legal procedure.*

[5]The government has the power of *eminent domain*, or the right to take private property for public use. This provision requires the government to pay the owner a fair price for such property.

[6]The accused person has the right to request the court to issue an order, or subpoena, compelling a witness to appear in court.

AMENDMENT VII.   Civil Suits (1791)

In suits at common law[1] where the value in controversy shall exceed twenty dollars, the right of trial by jury shall be preserved, and no fact tried by a jury shall be otherwise re-examined in any court of the United States, than according to the rules of the common law.

AMENDMENT VIII.   Bails, Fines, and Punishments (1791)

Excessive bail shall not be required, nor excessive fines imposed, nor cruel and unusual punishments inflicted.

AMENDMENT IX.   Rights Not Listed (1791)

The enumeration [listing] in the Constitution of certain rights shall not be construed to deny or disparage [weaken] others retained by the people.

AMENDMENT X.   Powers Reserved to the States and People (1791)

The powers not delegated to the United States by the Constitution, nor prohibited by it to the states, are reserved to the states respectively, or to the people.

AMENDMENT XI.   Suits Against States (1798)

The judicial power of the United States shall not be construed to extend to any suit in law or equity, commenced or prosecuted against one of the United States by citizens of another state, or by citizens or subjects of any foreign state.

AMENDMENT XII.   Election of President and Vice President (1804)

[1] The electors shall meet in their respective states, and vote by ballot for president and vice president, one of whom at least shall not be an

---

[1]"Common law" is law based on custom and precedent (past decisions made in similar cases). Originating in England, it was brought to the English colonies by the early settlers and became the foundation of the American legal system.

inhabitant of the same state with themselves; they shall name in their ballots the person voted for as president, and in distinct [separate] ballots the person voted for as vice president; and they shall make distinct lists of all persons voted for as president, and of all persons voted for as vice president, and of the number of votes for each, which lists they shall sign and certify, and transmit sealed to the seat of the government of the United States, directed to the president of the Senate.

[2] The president of the Senate shall, in the presence of the Senate and House of Representatives, open all the certificates, and the votes shall then be counted; the person having the greatest number of votes for president shall be the president, if such number be a majority of the whole number of electors appointed; and if no person have such majority, then from the persons having the highest numbers not exceeding three on the list of those voted for as president, the House of Representatives shall choose immediately, by ballot, the president. But in choosing the president, the votes shall be taken by states, the representation from each state having one vote; a quorum for this purpose shall consist of a member or members from two-thirds of the states, and a majority of all the states shall be necessary to a choice. And if the House of Representatives shall not choose a president whenever the right of choice shall devolve upon them, *before the fourth day of March next following,*[1] then the vice president shall act as president, as in the case of the death or other constitutional disability of the president.

[3] The person having the greatest number of votes as vice president shall be the vice president, if such number be a majority of the whole number of electors appointed; and if no person have a majority, then, from the two highest numbers on the list, the Senate shall choose the vice president; a quorum for the purpose shall consist of two-thirds of the whole number of senators, and a majority of the whole number shall be necessary to a choice. But no person constitutionally ineligible to the office of president shall be eligible to that of vice president of the United States.

AMENDMENT XIII. Abolition of Slavery (1865)

Section 1. Slavery Forbidden

Neither slavery nor involuntary servitude [compulsory service], except as a punishment for crime whereof the party shall have been duly convicted, shall exist within the United States, or any place subject to their jurisdiction.

---

[1]Changed to January 20 by Amendment XX.

Section 2.   Enforcement Power

Congress shall have power to enforce this article [amendment] by appropriate [suitable] legislation.

AMENDMENT XIV.   Citizenship and Civil Rights (1868)

Section 1.   Rights of Citizens

All persons born or naturalized in the United States, and subject to the jurisdiction thereof, are citizens of the United States and of the state wherein they reside.[1] No state shall make or enforce any law which shall abridge the privileges or immunities of citizens of the United States; nor shall any state deprive any person of life, liberty, or property, without due process of law;[2] nor deny to any person within its jurisdiction the equal protection of the laws.[3]

Section 2.   Apportionment of Representatives in Congress

Representatives shall be apportioned among the several states according to their respective numbers, counting the whole number of persons in each state, excluding Indians not taxed.[4] But when the right to vote at any election for the choice of electors for president and vice president of the United States, representatives in Congress, the executive and judicial officers of a state, or the members of the legislature thereof, is denied to any of the *male* inhabitants of such state, being *twenty-one* years of age and citizens of the United States, or in any way abridged, except for participation in rebellion or other crime, the basis of representation therein shall be reduced in the proportion which the number of such *male* citizens shall bear to the whole number of *male* citizens *twenty-one* years of age in such state.[5]

---

[1] This clause made the former slaves citizens.

[2] The primary purpose of this clause was to protect the civil rights of the former slaves. However, after the Supreme Court broadened the meaning of the word "person" to include "corporation," the clause began to be used to protect business interests as well.

[3] The "equal protection" clause has served as the legal basis for many civil rights cases.

[4] This clause nullifies the three-fifths formula of Article I, Section 2.

[5] Italicized words in this section were invalidated by Amendments XIX and XXVI.

Section 3.   Persons Disqualified From Public Office

No person shall be a senator or representative in Congress, or elector of president and vice president, or hold any office, civil or military, under the United States, or under any state, who, having previously taken an oath, as a member of Congress, or as an officer of the United States, or as a member of any state legislature, or as an executive or judicial officer of any state, to support the Constitution of the United States, shall have engaged in insurrection or rebellion against the same, or given aid or comfort to the enemies thereof. But Congress may, by a vote of two-thirds of each house, remove such disability.

Section 4.   Valid Public Debt Defined

The validity [legality] of the public debt of the United States, authorized by law, including debts incurred for payment of pensions and bounties [extra allowances] for services in suppressing insurrection or rebellion, shall not be questioned. But neither the United States nor any state shall assume or pay any debt or obligation incurred in aid of insurrection or rebellion against the United States, or any claim for the loss or emancipation [liberation] of any slave; but all such debts, obligations, and claims shall be held illegal and void.

Section 5.   Enforcement Power

The Congress shall have power to enforce, by appropriate legislation, the provisions of this article.

AMENDMENT XV.   Right of Suffrage (1870)

Section 1.   Blacks Guaranteed the Vote

The right of citizens of the United States to vote shall not be denied or abridged by the United States or by any state on account of race, color, or previous condition of servitude [slavery].

Section 2.   Enforcement Power

The Congress shall have power to enforce this article by appropriate legislation.

AMENDMENT XVI.   Income Taxes (1913)

The Congress shall have power to lay and collect taxes on incomes, from whatever source derived, without apportionment among the several states, and without regard to any census or enumeration.

AMENDMENT XVII.   Popular Election of Senators (1913)

[1] The Senate of the United States shall be composed of two senators from each state, elected by the people thereof, for six years; and each senator shall have one vote. The electors [voters] in each state shall have the qualifications requisite for electors of the most numerous branch of the state legislatures.[1]

[2] When vacancies happen in the representation of any state in the Senate, the executive authority of such state shall issue writs of election to fill such vacancies: Provided, that the legislature of any state may empower [authorize] the executive thereof to make temporary appointments until the people fill the vacancies by election as the legislature may direct.

[3] *This amendment shall not be so construed as to affect the election or term of any senator chosen before it becomes valid as part of the Constitution.*[2]

AMENDMENT XVIII.   Prohibition (1919)[3]

Section 1.   Intoxicating Liquors Prohibited

After one year from the ratification of this article, the manufacture, sale, or transportation of intoxicating liquors within, the importation thereof into, or the exportation thereof from the United States and all territory subject to the jurisdiction thereof, for beverage purposes, is hereby prohibited.

---

[1]This amendment changed the method of electing senators as given in Article I, Section 3.

[2]Temporary provision designed to protect those elected under the system previously in effect.

[3]This entire amendment was repealed in 1933 by Amendent XXI.

Section 2.   Enforcement Power

The Congress and the several states shall have concurrent power to enforce this article by appropriate legislation.

Section 3.   Conditions of Ratification

This article shall be inoperative unless it shall have been ratified as an amendment to the Constitution by the legislatures of the several states, as provided in the Constitution, within seven years from the date of the submission hereof to the states by the Congress.

AMENDMENT XIX.   Women's Suffrage (1920)

[1] The right of citizens of the United States to vote shall not be denied or abridged by the United States or by any state on account of sex.

[2] Congress shall have power to enforce this article by appropriate legislation.

AMENDMENT XX.   Presidential and Congressional Terms[1] (1933)

Section 1.   Terms of Office

The terms of the president and vice president shall end at noon on the 20th day of January, and the terms of senators and representatives at noon on the 3d day of January, of the years in which such terms would have ended if this article had not been ratified; and the terms of their successors[2] shall then begin.

Section 2.   Convening Congress

The Congress shall assemble at least once in every year, and such meeting shall begin at noon on the 3d day of January, unless they shall by law appoint a different day.[3]

---

[1]This amendment is often called the "Lame Duck" Amendment because it shortened the period (from four months to two) between the elections in November and the time when defeated officeholders or officeholders who do not run again (known as "lame ducks") leave office.

[2]A "successor" is a person who is elected or appointed to replace another in a public office.

[3]This section changed the date given in Article I, Section 4.

Section 3.   Presidential Succession

If, at the time fixed for the beginning of the term of the president, the president-elect[1] shall have died, the vice president-elect shall become president. If a president shall not have been chosen before the time fixed for the beginning of his term, or if the president-elect shall have failed to qualify, then the vice president-elect shall act as president until a president shall have qualified; and the Congress may by law provide for the case wherein neither a president-elect nor a vice president-elect shall have qualified, declaring who shall then act as president, or the manner in which one who is to act shall be selected, and such person shall act accordingly until a president or vice president shall have qualified.

Section 4.   Selection of President and Vice President

The Congress may by law provide for the case of the death of any of the persons from whom the House of Representatives may choose a president whenever the right of choice shall have devolved upon them, and for the case of the death of any of the persons from whom the Senate may choose a vice president whenever the right of choice shall have devolved upon them.

Section 5.   Effective Date

Sections 1 and 2 shall take effect on the 15th day of October following the ratification of this article.[2]

Section 6.   Conditions of Ratification

This article shall be inoperative unless it shall have been ratified as an amendment to the Constitution by the legislatures of three-fourths of the several states within seven years from the date of its submission.[3]

AMENDMENT XXI.   Repeal of Prohibition (1933)

Section 1.   Amendment XVIII Repealed

The Eighteenth Article of amendment to the Constitution of the United States is hereby repealed.

---

[1]A "president-elect" is a person who has been elected to the presidency but has not yet assumed office.

[2]Temporary provision.

[3]Temporary provision.

Section 2. Shipment of Liquor Into "Dry" Areas

The transportation or importation into any state, territory, or possession of the United States for delivery or use therein of intoxicating liquors in violation of the laws thereof is hereby prohibited.[1]

Section 3. Conditions of Ratification

This article shall be inoperative unless it shall have been ratified as an amendment to the Constitution by conventions in the several states,[2] *as provided in the Constitution, within seven years from the date of the submission hereof to the states by the Congress.*[3]

AMENDMENT XXII. Limiting Presidential Terms (1951)

Section 1. Limit Placed on Tenure

No person shall be elected to the office of the president more than twice, and no person who has held the office of president, or acted as president, for more than two years of a term to which some other person was elected president shall be elected to the office of the president more than once. *But this article shall not apply to any person holding the office of president when this article was proposed by the Congress, and shall not prevent any person who may be holding the office of president, or acting as president, during the term within which this article becomes operative from holding the office of president or acting as president during the remainder of such term.*[4]

Section 2. Conditions of Ratification

This article shall be inoperative unless it shall have been ratified as an amendment to the Constitution by the legislatures of three-fourths of the several states within seven years from the date of its submission to the states by the Congress.[5]

---

[1]This section allowed individual states to prohibit the use of intoxicating liquors if they wished to.

[2]This was the first amendment to be submitted by Congress for ratification by state conventions rather than state legislatures.

[3]Temporary provision.

[4]Temporary provision.

[5]Temporary provision.

AMENDMENT XXIII. Suffrage for Washington, D.C. (1961)

Section 1.   D.C. Presidential Electors

The district constituting [making up] the seat of government of the United States shall appoint in such manner as the Congress may direct:

A number of electors of president and vice president equal to the whole number of senators and representatives in Congress to which the district would be entitled if it were a state, but in no event more than the least populous state;[1] they shall be in addition to those appointed by the states, but they shall be considered, for the purposes of the election of president and vice president, to be electors appointed by a state; and they shall meet in the district and perform such duties as provided by the Twelfth Article of amendent.[2]

Section 2.   Enforcement Power

The Congress shall have power to enforce this article by appropriate legislation.

AMENDMENT XXIV.   Poll Taxes (1964)

Section 1.   Poll Tax Barred

The right of citizens of the United States to vote in any primary or other election for president or vice president, for electors for president or vice president, or for senator or representative in Congress, shall not be denied or abridged by the United States or any state by reason of failure to pay any poll tax or other tax.

Section 2.   Enforcement Power

The Congress shall have the power to enforce this article by appropriate legislation.

---

[1] At the present time, the District of Columbia is entitled to three electors.

[2] By providing for electors, this amendment gave residents of Washington, D.C., the right to vote for president and vice president.

AMENDMENT XXV. Presidential Succession and Disability (1967)

Section 1. Elevation of Vice President

In case of the removal of the president from office or his death or resignation, the vice president shall become president.

Section 2. Vice Presidential Vacancy

Whenever there is a vacancy in the office of the vice president, the president shall nominate a vice president who shall take the office upon confirmation by a majority vote of both houses of Congress.

Section 3. Temporary Disability

Whenever the president transmits to the president pro tempore of the Senate and the Speaker of the House of Representatives his written declaration that he is unable to discharge the powers and duties of his office, and until he transmits to them a written declaration to the contrary, such powers and duties shall be discharged by the vice president as acting president.

Section 4. Other Provisions for Presidential Disability

[1] Whenever the vice president and a majority of either the principal officers of the executive departments, or of such other body as Congress may by law provide, transmit to the president pro tempore of the Senate and the Speaker of the House of Representatives their written declaration that the president is unable to discharge the powers and duties of his office, the vice president shall immediately assume the powers and duties of the office as acting president.

[2] Thereafter, when the president transmits to the president pro tempore of the Senate and the Speaker of the House of Representatives his written declaration that no inability exists, he shall resume the powers and duties of his office unless the vice president and a majority of either the principal officers of the executive department, or of such other body as Congress may by law provide, transmit within four days to the president pro tempore of the Senate and the Speaker of the House of Representatives their written declaration that the president is unable to discharge the powers and duties of his office. Thereupon Congress shall decide the issue, assembling within 48 hours for that purpose if not in session. If the Congress, within 21 days after receipt of the latter written declaration, or, if

Congress is not in session, within 21 days after Congress is required to assemble, determines by two-thirds vote of both houses that the president is unable to discharge the powers and duties of his office, the vice president shall continue to discharge the same as acting president; otherwise, the president shall resume the powers and duties of his office.

AMENDMENT XXVI.   The Vote for 18-Year-Olds (1971)

Section 1.   Lowering the Voting Age

The right of citizens of the United States, who are 18 years of age or older, to vote shall not be denied or abridged by the United States or by any state on account of age.

Section 2.   Enforcement Power

The Congress shall have power to enforce this article by appropriate legislation.

AMENDMENT XXVII.   Congressional Pay Raises (1992)

No law varying the compensation for the services of the senators and representatives shall take effect until an election of representatives shall have intervened.[1]

---

[1]This amendment bars Congress from voting itself immediate pay raises. Although it went into effect in 1992, it was first proposed by James Madison in 1789. The ratification process took over 200 years. Not until the 38th state (Michigan) ratified it in 1992 did the amendment become part of the Constitution. Most amendments are ratified more quickly. In recent years, Congress has put a seven-year time limit for ratification. If the necessary three-fourths (38) of the states have not ratified a proposed amendment by then, the amendment becomes invalid.

Reference Tables

U.S. Presidents and Vice Presidents

No.	President	Years in Office	Political Party	State (when elected)	Vice President	State (when elected)
1	George Washington (b. 1732–d. 1799)	1789–1797	None	Virginia	John Adams	Massachusetts
2	John Adams (b. 1735–d. 1826)	1797–1801	Federalist	Massachusetts	Thomas Jefferson	Virginia
3	Thomas Jefferson (b. 1743–d. 1826)	1801–1809	Democratic-Republican	Virginia	Aaron Burr George Clinton	New York New York
4	James Madison (b. 1751–d. 1836)	1809–1817	Democratic-Republican	Virginia	George Clinton Elbridge Gerry	New York Massachusetts
5	James Monroe (b. 1758–d. 1831)	1817–1825	Democratic-Republican	Virginia	Daniel D. Tompkins	New York
6	John Quincy Adams (b. 1767–d. 1848)	1825–1829	National Republican	Massachusetts	John C. Calhoun	South Carolina
7	Andrew Jackson (b. 1767–d. 1845)	1829–1837	Democratic	Tennessee	John C. Calhoun Martin Van Buren	South Carolina New York
8	Martin Van Buren (b. 1782–d. 1862)	1837–1841	Democratic	New York	Richard M. Johnson	Kentucky
9	William H. Harrison (b. 1773–d. 1841)	1841 (died in office)	Whig	Ohio	John Tyler	Virginia
10	John Tyler (b. 1790–d. 1862)	1841–1845	Whig	Virginia	*vacant*	
11	James K. Polk (b. 1795–d. 1849)	1845–1849	Democratic	Tennessee	George M. Dallas	Pennsylvania

	President	Term	Party	State	Vice President	State
12	Zachary Taylor (b. 1784–d. 1850)	1849–1850 (*died in office*)	Whig	Louisiana	Millard Fillmore	New York
13	Millard Fillmore (b. 1800–d. 1874)	1850–1853	Whig	New York	*vacant*	
14	Franklin Pierce (b. 1804–d. 1869)	1853–1857	Democratic	New Hampshire	William R. King	Alabama
15	James Buchanan (b. 1791–d. 1868)	1857–1861	Democratic	Pennsylvania	John C. Breckinridge	Kentucky
16	Abraham Lincoln (b. 1809–d. 1865)	1861–1865 (*died in office*)	Republican	Illinois	Hannibal Hamlin / Andrew Johnson	Maine / Tennessee
17	Andrew Johnson (b. 1808–d. 1875)	1865–1869	Republican	Tennessee	*vacant*	
18	Ulysses S. Grant (b. 1822–d. 1885)	1869–1877	Republican	Illinois	Schuyler Colfax / Henry Wilson	Indiana / Massachusetts
19	Rutherford B. Hayes (b. 1822–d. 1893)	1877–1881	Republican	Ohio	William A. Wheeler	New York
20	James A. Garfield (b. 1831–d. 1881)	1881 (*died in office*)	Republican	Ohio	Chester A. Arthur	New York
21	Chester A. Arthur (b. 1829–d. 1886)	1881–1885	Republican	New York	*vacant*	
22	Grover Cleveland (b. 1837–d. 1908)	1885–1889	Democratic	New York	Thomas A. Hendricks	Indiana
23	Benjamin Harrison (b. 1833–d. 1901)	1889–1893	Republican	Indiana	Levi P. Morton	New York
24	Grover Cleveland (b. 1837–d. 1908)	1893–1897	Democratic	New York	Adlai E. Stevenson	Illinois

U.S. Presidents and Vice Presidents (continued)

No.	President	Years in Office	Political Party	State (when elected)	Vice President	State (when elected)
25	William McKinley (b. 1843-d. 1901)	1897-1901 (died in office)	Republican	Ohio	Garret A. Hobart Theodore Roosevelt	New Jersey New York
26	Theodore Roosevelt (b. 1858-d. 1919)	1901-1909	Republican	New York	vacant (1901-1905) Charles W. Fairbanks	Indiana
27	William H. Taft (b. 1857-d. 1930)	1909-1913	Republican	Ohio	James S. Sherman	New York
28	Woodrow Wilson (b. 1856-d. 1924)	1913-1921	Democratic	New Jersey	Thomas R. Marshall	Indiana
29	Warren G. Harding (b. 1865-d. 1923)	1921-1923 (died in office)	Republican	Ohio	Calvin Coolidge	Massachusetts
30	Calvin Coolidge (b. 1872-d. 1933)	1923-1929	Republican	Massachusetts	vacant (1923-1925) Charles G. Dawes	Illinois
31	Herbert C. Hoover (b. 1874-d. 1964)	1929-1933	Republican	California	Charles Curtis	Kansas
32	Franklin D. Roosevelt (b. 1882-d. 1945)	1933-1945 (died in office)	Democratic	New York	John N. Garner Henry A. Wallace Harry S. Truman	Texas Iowa Missouri
33	Harry S. Truman (b. 1884-d. 1972)	1945-1953	Democratic	Missouri	vacant (1945-1949) Alben W. Barkley	Kentucky
34	Dwight D. Eisenhower (b. 1890-d. 1969)	1953-1961	Republican	New York	Richard M. Nixon	California

	President	Term	Party	State	Vice President	State
35	John F. Kennedy (b. 1917-d. 1963)	1961–1963 (died in office)	Democratic	Massachusetts	Lyndon B. Johnson	Texas
36	Lyndon B. Johnson (b. 1908-d. 1973)	1963–1969	Democratic	Texas	vacant (1963–1965) Hubert H. Humphrey	Minnesota
37	Richard M. Nixon (b. 1913-d. 1994)	1969–1974 (resigned)	Republican	New York	Spiro T. Agnew Gerald R. Ford	Maryland Michigan
38	Gerald R. Ford (b. 1913–)	1974–1977	Republican	Michigan	Nelson A. Rockefeller	New York
39	Jimmy Carter (b. 1924–)	1977–1981	Democratic	Georgia	Walter F. Mondale	Minnesota
40	Ronald W. Reagan (b. 1911–)	1981–1989	Republican	California	George H.W. Bush	Texas
41	George H.W. Bush (b. 1924–)	1989–1993	Republican	Texas	J. Danforth Quayle	Indiana
42	Bill Clinton (b. 1946–)	1993–	Democratic	Arkansas	Albert Gore, Jr.	Tennessee

Profile of the States

State	Date of Admission	Population (1990)	Rank in Population	Area (Sq. Mi.)	Rank in Size	Capital
Alabama	1819	4,041,000	22	52,423	30	Montgomery
Alaska	1959	550,000	50	656,424	1	Juneau
Arizona	1912	3,665,000	29	114,006	6	Phoenix
Arkansas	1836	2,351,000	33	53,182	29	Little Rock
California	1850	29,760,000	1	163,707	3	Sacramento
Colorado	1876	3,294,000	28	104,100	8	Denver
Connecticut	1788*	3,287,000	25	5,544	48	Hartford
Delaware	1787*	666,000	47	2,489	49	Dover
Dist. of Columbia†	—	607,000	—	—	—	Washington
Florida	1845	12,938,000	7	65,758	22	Tallahassee
Georgia	1788*	6,478,000	13	59,441	24	Atlanta
Hawaii	1959	1,108,000	39	10,932	43	Honolulu
Idaho	1890	1,007,000	41	83,574	14	Boise
Illinois	1818	11,431,000	5	57,918	25	Springfield
Indiana	1816	5,544,000	12	36,420	38	Indianapolis
Iowa	1846	2,777,000	27	56,276	26	Des Moines
Kansas	1861	2,478,000	32	82,282	15	Topeka
Kentucky	1792	3,685,000	23	40,411	37	Frankfort
Louisiana	1812	4,220,000	19	51,843	31	Baton Rouge
Maine	1820	1,228,000	38	35,387	39	Augusta
Maryland	1788*	4,781,000	18	12,407	42	Annapolis
Massachusetts	1788*	6,016,000	11	10,555	44	Boston
Michigan	1837	9,295,000	8	96,810	11	Lansing
Minnesota	1858	4,375,000	21	86,943	12	St. Paul
Mississippi	1817	2,573,000	31	48,434	32	Jackson

582

State	Date		Population		Capital
Missouri	1821	15	5,117,000	21	Jefferson City
Montana	1889	44	799,000	4	Helena
Nebraska	1867	35	1,578,000	16	Lincoln
Nevada	1864	43	1,202,000	7	Carson City
New Hampshire	1788*	42	1,109,000	46	Concord
New Jersey	1787*	9	7,730,000	47	Trenton
New Mexico	1912	37	1,515,000	5	Santa Fe
New York	1788*	2	17,990,000	27	Albany
North Carolina	1789*	10	6,629,000	28	Raleigh
North Dakota	1889	46	639,000	19	Bismarck
Ohio	1803	6	10,847,000	34	Columbus
Oklahoma	1907	26	3,146,000	20	Oklahoma City
Oregon	1859	30	2,842,000	9	Salem
Pennsylvania	1787*	4	11,882,000	33	Harrisburg
Rhode Island	1790*	40	1,003,000	50	Providence
South Carolina	1788*	24	3,487,000	40	Columbia
South Dakota	1889	45	696,000	17	Pierre
Tennessee	1796	17	4,877,000	36	Nashville
Texas	1845	3	16,987,000	2	Austin
Utah	1896	36	1,723,000	13	Salt Lake City
Vermont	1791	48	563,000	45	Montpelier
Virginia	1788*	14	6,187,000	35	Richmond
Washington	1889	20	4,867,000	18	Olympia
West Virginia	1863	34	1,793,000	41	Charleston
Wisconsin	1848	16	4,892,000	23	Madison
Wyoming	1890	49	454,000	10	Cheyenne

* One of the original 13 states. Date is that of ratification of the Constitution.
† For the purposes of this table, Washington, D.C., is listed as a state.

Index